ORGANIZATIONAL BEHAVIOR

Third Edition

ROBERT KREITNER
ANGELO KINICKI
Both of
Arizona State University

Chicago • Bogota • Boston • Buenos Aires • Caracas
London • Madrid • Mexico City • Sydney • Toronto

Senior sponsoring editor: Craig Beytien
Senior developmental editor: Libby Rubenstein
Senior marketing manager: Kurt Messersmith
Project editor: Beth Yates
Production manager: Bob Lange
Cover designer: Heidi J. Baughman
Interior designer: Heidi J. Baughman/Kay Fulton
Art coordinator: Heather Burbridge
Cover photograph: Jim Brandenburg/Minden Pictures
Part opener photography: Daniel Cox/Natural Selection
Compositor: Better Graphics, Inc.
Typeface: 10/12 Times Roman
Printer: Von Hoffmann Press, Inc.

Library of Congress Cataloging-in-Publication Data

Kreitner, Robert.
    Organizational behavior / Robert Kreitner, Angelo Kinicki. — 3rd
ed.
        p. cm.
    Includes bibliographical references and index.
    ISBN 0-256-14056-1. — ISBN 0-256-17505-5 (annotated instructor's
ed.)
    1. Organizational behavior.   I. Kinicki, Angelo.   II. Title.
HD58.7.K75   1995
    658.3—dc20   94–19883

Printed in the United States of America
1 2 3 4 5 6 7 8 9 0 VH 1 0 9 8 7 6 5 4

To the joys of life: Margaret's love and laughter, purring cats, mountain hikes, desert rain, and peanut butter.
—R. K.

Dedicated with love to my parents, Madeline Kinicki and Henry Kinicki, and my wife and best friend Joyce Kinicki. Mom and dad, thanks for encouraging me to learn and excel. Joyce, you are the best! Your love, support, encouragement, and advice helped me to grow and develop more than you will ever know. Thanks!
—A.K.

Preface

In today's competitive global economy, managing people effectively and ethically is more important than ever. *People* are the common denominator of organized endeavor, regardless of the organization's size or purpose. No matter how sophisticated an organization's strategy and technology, the *human factor* inevitably is the key to success. The purpose of this textbook is to help present and future managers better understand and manage people at work. This third edition of *Organizational Behavior* is intended for similarly named courses at the undergraduate level. It is the culmination of our 36 years of teaching and researching organizational behavior in the United States and other countries. Thanks to detailed feedback from students, professors, and practicing managers, this edition is slimmer, more disciplined, and more tightly organized. Lots of changes have been made in this edition reflecting new research evidence, new management techniques, and the fruits of our own learning process.

Organizational Behavior, 3rd edition, is a product of the *total quality management* (TQM) process described in Chapter 1. Specifically, it is *user driven* (as a result of carefully listening to our readers), developed through close *teamwork* between the authors and the publisher, and the product of *continuous improvement.* Our TQM approach has helped us achieve a difficult combination of balances. Among them are balances between theory and practice, solid content and interesting coverage, and instructive detail and readability. Students and instructors say they want an up-to-date, relevant, and interesting textbook that actively involves the reader in the learning process. Our efforts toward this end are evidenced by many new topics and real-life examples, a stimulating art program, timely new cases and boxed inserts, end-of-chapter experiential exercises, and over two dozen exercises integrated into the text. We realize that reading a comprehensive textbook is hard work, but we also firmly believe the process should be interesting (and sometimes fun).

STRUCTURAL CHANGES IN THE THIRD EDITION

Like the first two editions, this edition flows from micro (individuals) to macro (groups and organizations) topics. Once again, we have tried to achieve a workable balance between micro and macro topics. As a guide for users of the second edition, these structural changes need to be noted:

- International organizational behavior has been expanded to a full chapter and moved foward (now Chapter 2).
- Our coverage of managing diversity has been moved from Chapter 2 to Chapter 3.
- Discussion of roles and norms has been moved to a more conventional location in Chapter 9, "Group Dynamics."
- Individual and group decision making has been moved forward from Part IV to Part III (now Chapter 11).

- Organizational communication processes has been moved to Part IV (now Chapter 13).
- The chapter numbers in Parts II, III, and IV have been changed to reflect these named realignments.
- Our coverage of organizational culture has been expanded to a full chapter (still Chapter 19).
- Discussion of personality testing has been moved from Advanced Learning Module B to Chapter 4, under the heading of Individual Differences.
- To help shorten the text for more efficient coverage, only two types of boxed inserts (exercises and international) are included in this third edition.

NEW TOPICAL COVERAGE

In keeping with the AACSB's call for greater attention to managing in a *global economy,* managing *cultural diversity,* improving product/service *quality,* and making *ethical* decisions, we have made the following changes in this edition:

- A full chapter on international organizational behavior and cross-cultural management receives up-front attention in Part I (Chapter 2). To ensure integrated coverage of international topics, 25 boxed features entitled ''International OB'' can be found throughout the text.
- Chapter 3 has been completely rewritten to reflect the latest models and techniques for managing cultural diversity. Moreover, we have taken great care to select a culturally diverse array of people in our examples, photos, and cases to make the point that management is for *everyone.*
- Principles of total quality management (TQM) and the contributions of W Edwards Deming are discussed in Chapter 1 to establish a quality-improvement context for the entire textbook. Quality logos, located in the margin adjacent to discussions and examples of quality improvement, can be found throughout the text for integrated coverage.
- Our coverage of ethics has been expanded (now in Chapter 4) to include ethical criteria and moral principles for today's global managers. Ethics logos, located in the margin adjacent to discussions of ethical issues, can be found throughout the text as a reminder of the importance of ethical management.

Supplementing our comprehensive coverage of international, diversity, quality, and ethics topics are the following timely thrusts:

- Because *teams* have become the organizational unit of choice in recent years, we broke with tradition in our previous edition and devoted a complete chapter to managing teams and teamwork. Our readers told us we were on the right track; and so we have updated our coverage of team effectiveness, trust, quality circles, self-managed teams, and cross-functional teams (now Chapter 12).
- One of the most compelling concepts of organizations today is that of the ''learning organization.'' Thus, we have completely reworked Chapter 20 around that valuable concept. Beginning in Chapter 1, extending throughout the text, and culminating in Chapter 20, we repeatedly revisit the notion of *learning organizations.*

Our readers kindly tell us how much they appreciate our efforts to keep this textbook up-to-date. Toward that end, you will find new or significantly improved coverage of the following topics: the downside of downsizing, profile of the 21st-century manager, principles of total quality management (TQM), the Deming legacy, global skills for global managers, managing the foreign assignment cycle, managing cultural diversity, the Big Five personality dimensions, three ethical criteria for managers, general moral principles for global managers, trait/genetic components of job satisfaction, goal commitment, Covey's seven habits of highly effective people as an agenda for self-improvement, stepladder technique for avoiding social loafing, women politicians and socialized power, computer-aided decision making, collaborative computing, evolution of a team, research evidence of what self-managed teams actually do, videoconferencing and communication, common trouble signs for feedback systems, 360-degree performance reviews, managerial credibility, gender and leadership, charismatic leadership, organizational reengineering, new-style versus old-style organizations, the shape of tomorrow's organizations (hourglass, cluster, network), adaptive cultures, corporate vision and values, developing high-performance cultures, readiness for change, and learning organizations.

PEDAGOGICAL FEATURES

The third edition of *Organizational Behavior* is designed to be a complete teaching/learning tool that captures the reader's interest and imparts useful knowledge. Some of the most significant pedagogical features of this text are:

- Classic and modern topics are given balanced treatment in terms of the latest and best available theoretical models, research evidence, and practical applications.
- Several concise learning objectives open each chapter to: (1) focus the reader's attention; and (2) serve as a comprehension check.
- Every chapter begins with a real-name, real-world case study to provide a context for the material at hand. Seventeen of the 20 cases are new to this edition. Each case is immediately followed by a warm-up question to promote learning readiness. A ''Back to the Opening Case'' feature following each chapter offers questions to underscore the practical implications of what was just read.
- A colorful and lively art program includes captioned photographs and 109 figures.
- Hundreds of real-world examples involving large and small, public and private organizations have been incorporated into the textual material to make this edition up-to-date, interesting, and relevant.
- Women play a prominent role throughout this text, as befitting their large and growing presence in the workplace. Lots of female role models are included. Special effort has been devoted to uncovering research insights about relevant and important gender-related differences.
- Key terms are emphasized in bold print where they are first defined and featured in the adjacent margins for review purposes.
- A ''Summary of Key Concepts'' feature at the end of each chapter restates the chapter learning objectives and concisely answers them.
- Twenty-five ''OB Exercise'' boxes are distributed throughout the text to foster personal involvement and greater self-awareness. Readers will gain experiential insights about their motivation to manage, cultural orientation toward time, self-esteem, personal values, perception, motives, sense of fairness, roles, power,

tendency toward office politics, conflict handling style, interpersonal trust, work group autonomy, decision-making style, and stress.

- Ten discussion questions at the end of every chapter challenge the reader to explore the personal and practical implications of what has just been covered. These questions are also useful for class discussion.
- Logos in the margin remind the reader of the importance of quality improvement and ethics.
- Hands-on exercises at the end of each chapter foster experiential learning. Although some of the exercises are best done in classroom groups, facilitated by the instructor, the vast majority can be completed by readers studying alone. Discussion questions for each exercise facilitate students' learning.

Also available with this edition is a computerized version of the test bank, teletest, and instructional videos to accompany the text. These videos are keyed by topic area, such as motivation and leadership. Additionally, there are 60 color acetates for instructors.

WORDS OF APPRECIATION

This textbook is the fruit of many people's labor. Our colleagues at Arizona State University have been supportive from the start. Our ASU students have been enthusiastic and candid academic "customers." We are grateful for their feedback and we hope we have done it justice in this new edition. Sincere appreciation goes to Kim Wade, Arizona State University, and Professor Arnon Reichers, The Ohio State University, for their dedicated, skillful, and timely work on the Instructor's Manual/Test Bank and Lecture Supplement Manual, respectively. Our thanks for a job well done go to Jill Winkelman for her excellent work on the permissions. Both of us appreciate valuable managerial insights from Ed Hargroves, former chief executive officer of CCS Technology Group, Inc and Clint Kreitner, president, Reading Rehabilitation Hospital. The always wise counsel of our friend and colleague Keith Davis is sincerely appreciated.

To the following reviewers of all or portions of the first three edition manuscripts go our gratitude and thanks. Their feedback was thoughtful, rigorous, constructive, and above all, essential to our goal of *kaizen* (continuous improvement):

D Neal Ashworth, University of Richmond; Rebecca Bennett, University of Toledo; Allen Bluedorn, University of Missouri; Gene Bocialetti, University of New Hampshire; Gene Burton, California State University; Noel Byrne, Sonoma State University; Edward Conlon, University of Iowa; Bruce Drake, University of Portland; John Drexler, Jr, Oregon State University; Jon English, George Mason University; Joseph Foerst, Georgia State University; Ronald Gorman, American University; LaVerne Higgins, University of Oregon; Peter Hom, Arizona State University; Avis Johnson, University of Akron; Eileen Kaplan, Montclair State College; David Kuhn, Florida State University; Daniel McAllister, University of Nevada-Las Vegas; Steven Meisel, La Salle University; Tony Mento, Loyola College, Maryland; Sandra Morgan, University of Hartford; Paula Morrow, Iowa State University; Gene Murkison, Georgia Southern College; Margaret Neale, Northwestern University; Philip L Roth, Clemson University; Robert Roth, City University, Bellevue, Washington; Christine Scheck, Northern Illinois University; Chester Schriesheim, University of Miami; Pamela Skyrme, Eckerd College; Lewis

Taylor III, University of Miami, Linda Travino, Penn State University; Don Warrick, University of Colorado; and Pamela Wolfmeyer, Winona State University.

Finally, we would like to thank our wives, Margaret and Joyce, for being thoughtful and patient ''first customers'' of our work. This book has been greatly enhanced by their common sense, reality testing, and managerial experience. Thanks in large measure to their love and moral support, this project was completed on time and it strengthened rather than strained a treasured possession—our friendship.

We hope you enjoy this textbook. Best wishes for success and happiness!

Robert Kreitner
Angelo Kinicki

Contents in Brief

Contents

PART I

THE WORLD OF ORGANIZATIONAL BEHAVIOR

PART
II
INDIVIDUAL BEHAVIOR

PART

III

GROUP AND SOCIAL PROCESSES

P A R T

ORGANIZATIONAL PROCESSES

PART

V

THE EVOLVING ORGANIZATION

ORGANIZATIONAL
BEHAVIOR

THE WORLD OF ORGANIZATIONAL BEHAVIOR

P
A
R
T

I

MANAGING ORGANIZATIONAL BEHAVIOR FOR QUALITY AND RESULTS

Learning OBJECTIVES

When you finish studying the material in this chapter, you should be able to:

1. Define the term *management* and explain what managers do.

2. Explain the concept of motivation to manage and summarize the related cross-cultural research evidence.

3. Characterize 21st-century managers.

4. Define the term *organizational behavior* and explain why OB is a horizontal discipline.

5. Contrast McGregor's Theory X and Theory Y assumptions about employees.

6. Explain the managerial significance of Deming's 85–15 rule.

7. Identify the four principles of total quality management (TQM).

8. Describe the sources of organizational behavior research evidence.

Theory Q Builds People at Quad/Graphics

Sharon Hoogstraten

You could call Harry Quadracci iconoclastic. After all, the founder and president of $600 million printing giant Quad/Graphics, in Peewaukee, Wisconsin, refuses to use organizational charts, or strategic plans, or even budgets. You could call him revolutionary, for his desire to help his co-workers —mostly high school graduates with few aspirations— "become something more than what they ever hoped to be."

But to hear the fifty-seven-year-old former corporate attorney tell it, all the innovations that have distinguished him and his wildly successful company—a camp to teach customers about the printing process, indoctrination classes for new employees, celebrations for "perfect failures"—came about because he was, more than anything else, pragmatic. Twenty years ago, when he launched his company, doing things differently was the only way to survive, he says. "It wasn't any great thesis that I had."

Nowadays, "Harry's Way" or "Theory Q," as Quadracci's management philosophy has come to be known, is widely celebrated as a pathway toward liberating labor-management relationships and encouraging the type of "active risk-taking" required to compete successfully in an increasingly nasty marketplace. You can't argue with success, after all. In an industry that is struggling to maintain double-digit growth, Quadracci's printing company, now the largest privately owned printer in North America, has been boasting average annual growth rates near 40 percent for more than a decade.

To learn more about "Harry's Way," *Business Ethics* managing editor Craig Cox spoke by phone with Quadracci at Quad/Graphics headquarters outside of Milwaukee.

You once called Quad/Graphics a social experiment. What did you mean by that?

What I meant was that all business is an experiment. You try something and if it works, it works. If it doesn't work, you try something else. Quad/Graphics is a social experiment because we've thrown away conventional professional concepts in personnel and business management, and just tried to experiment with the way we can interact in the workplace as individuals and as responsible citizens.

What does that require of you as a leader?

You have to be very, very interactive with everybody. In fact, if you start talking about what I call a value-managed company, if you run your company with a minimum of rules and

---

Someone once said the best place to begin is at the end. This approach is appropriate for the topic of managing people because management is a goal-oriented, or ends-oriented, endeavor. As we will see in the content of this book, a worthy goal for present and future managers is to develop a progressive philosophy for managing our most important resource, *people.* Jack Welch, the respected head of the 268,000-employee[1] General Electric Corporation, recently offered this blunt assessment about succeeding in today's highly competitive global economy:

> If you're not thinking all the time about making every person more valuable, you don't have a chance. What's the alternative? Wasted minds? Uninvolved people? A labor force that's angry or bored? That doesn't make sense![2]

Aside from being an inspiring challenge for all managers, Welch's management philosophy pinpoints two key thrusts of this book. They are described in the following paragraphs.

OPENING CASE

(continued)

a maximum of indoctrination with values, then the most important characteristic of the leader is visibility . . .

And, from what I understand, being nonhierarchical.

There is no term in our company that would equate to "labor–management," because we don't have that division.

You have partners, sponsors, and mentors?

But not labor–management. Our managers who are the bosses wear the same uniforms as their charges. They do the same work: They lead their troops to the beaches of the new technology.

Is that hard for people coming from the outside to understand?

Oh, yes it is. It's a culture gap. It takes about eighteen months before they become adjusted to it. It's more emotional, I think, than an educational thing.

You mean, it has more to do with attitude than ability?

First of all, the one physical handicap that cannot be corrected by education, or by any other means, is attitude. If they've got a bad attitude, I'm sorry, there's nothing you can do with them. But if a person has a reasonably good attitude, they will succeed. You see, we're all more or less equal. The major difference between people is not the ability to learn, it's the rate of learning process. Some people learn things faster than others. So you have to put them in the right learning environment and they will learn, and they will perform.

A lot of what you've done there is turn low-skilled workers into technicians. How do you do it?

Get the employees to stop looking at their shoes. We've got 6,500 employees, and I think we've got less than 500 who are college graduates. Most of them are high school graduates. And when they come into the employment office, they're not looking to the stars, they're looking at their shoes.

They weren't necessarily the aca-demic achievers in high school. They were capable, but for whatever reason —their own expectations, their family's expectations, or maybe matura-tion—the other kids went on to college.

So, in order to make these people become something more than they ever hoped to be, you have to start raising their self-esteem. It's the Pyg-malion effect: Treat them as winners and they become winners.

When they walk in they get a fresh uniform. Daily, they're brought into class and told exactly what's expected of them, and put into an environment of excellence—good surroundings and so forth—good teachers, and no prodding to progress, letting everyone develop at their own speed. Don't do anything fast, just do it right, do it better than anyone else could do it. Then we'll tell you when you're going too slow . . .

Plenty of printing companies survive perfectly well using conventional business practices. Why did you do it differently?

1. *A human resource development thrust.* Are employees a commodity to be hired and discarded depending on the short-run whims of the organization? Or are they a valuable resource to be nurtured and developed? Sadly, as the massive layoffs from corporate downsizings, reorganizations, and mergers in recent years indicate, the first assumption tends to be the rule.

   The raw numbers are stunning: From 1982 to 1991, US industrial giants in the *Fortune* 500 eliminated 3.4 million jobs.[3] In 1993, alone, the more-encompassing list of *Fortune* 1000 companies cut another 4 million jobs.[4] Why? Management desired to reduce costs, boost profits, and improve productivity. But recent research points to disappointing results:

   > . . . of 450 large companies that downsized in 1991 and 1992, only 60% have seen their costs shrink and fewer than half have improved their profits. Among firms that were gunning for increased productivity only a third have actually achieved it.[5]

OPENING CASE

(continued)

Who would come to work for me? I had to start out with people who were unskilled and whom my competitors would not employ. I had to teach them.

Because you couldn't pay the same wages?

Exactly. It's the whole thing that happens with small, start-up companies. And that's where we learned employees are very, very important. We started treating them like winners early on and they became winners. We promoted from within and gave everyone the opportunity. For instance, you read about our parties. That is an educational experience.

I read a lot about your parties. Thousands of Italian sausages, a quarter-ton of baked beans, and hundreds of gallons of beer, wine, and soda. It seems to be a very big part of your company's way of life.

It is a huge deal. Every other year it's black tie, and so when we come to the party, you can't tell who's on what level.

We put on a musical every year, and performing in the musical are myself, the world-famous singing vice-president, and all the new managers. Now, what does this mean? This means a couple things: We've brought everyone else up by having them wear black tie, and all the leaders of the company are brought down by having to make asses of themselves on stage. And in the same manner, we have all these managers—these guys are probably twenty-four, twenty-five, twenty-six years old—and they're taking over significant operating responsibility of the company. And what's the difference between a good manager and a mediocre manager? Only self-confidence. So, consequently, once you get up and make an ass out of yourself in front of three thousand people on stage, what else is left?

You see these kids get up there, and we teach them how to tap dance. They all get together, and they see we can't do our steps, either, and you see them just grow up in front of your eyes. A real flowering.

A lot has been written about your reliance on "active risk-taking." Why can't

most businesses do this? Why can't most businesses thrive on change? What do you do that's so different?

First of all, most businesses wouldn't have their managers singing and dancing with the employees. It's too corny. Business sophistication is the biggest enemy of employee involvement and, therefore, change. Number two is structure.

Too much structure?

Yeah, too much structure. It can't be interactive. There are too many layers.

And that's the reason you don't use budgets?

Exactly. Let's look simply at the organizational chart. When you define a person's responsibility what do you do? You also limit his responsibility. So don't put him in a box. Use the doctrine of assumed responsibility. You see something that has to be done, assume you have the responsibility to do it.

It takes a lot of trust in your employees, though.

Yeah, it takes a lot of trust, but if

Too often, large, mismanaged companies that had engaged in undisciplined hiring during more prosperous times simply became smaller, mismanaged companies. While a layoff can be a necessary part of a comprehensive corporate transformation, as in the case of Welch's 1980s turnaround of General Electric, habitual layoffs are a dead end.[6]

More progressive and far-sighted companies treat their employees as a valuable resource, making layoffs the *last* rather than the first option. They develop "human recycling" programs through retraining and redeployment.[7]

When business lags at one of Minnesota Mining & Manufacturing Co.'s 49 divisions, for example, excess workers are found similar work at another division. Over the past decade, 3M has reassigned about 3,500 workers this way, failing to place only a "handful," says Richard A. Lidstad, vice-president of human resources. "Our employees are *corporate* assets, not assets of a given business. It's like production machinery. In a downturn, you don't just throw it out."[8]

OPENING CASE

(concluded)

you trust your employees, they'll trust you, and they'll rise to your level of belief in them.

But they'll also make mistakes, or in some cases create what you call "perfect failure." Two of your technicians spent a year and almost $800,000 developing a paper folding machine that didn't work. And you celebrated afterward, even gave them a bonus, as I recall. It was like there was a certain nobility attached to that effort.

We have to explore an alternative. If you're right all the time, boy are you going to be out of business in a hurry. It's like the credit manager who comes to the owner and says, "Last year, we had absolutely no bad debt experience. Everybody paid everything." Well, wait a minute. In this economy, not everybody has the money. There must have been a lot of people who were passing us by.

If you give people the freedom to do, then you have to accept the consequences, which are failures and mistakes. But remember: Mistakes are the tuition for learning management. You

only learn management by doing, by making mistakes. If you don't make any mistakes, how are you going to learn what was wrong? If people are afraid of making mistakes then nothing new will happen. . . .

Today you're a certifiable success. The company is racing ahead of its competitors, and your ideas are being copied by businesses all over the country. In other words, you've come a long way. How has all this success affected your life?

I remember when I had six hundred employees working for me, and I don't remember when the point was reached where now I am working for 6,500. The real shift here, is: Why does anyone work in the first place, if your own needs are satisfied? I feel a real responsibility for the employees. I have to give them a full paycheck, a good standard of living for their family, and the opportunities to continue to become something more than what they ever hoped to be.

I would say that concern for their well-being and their futures is much heavier than any other worry I had in

earlier years. To a large extent, it's easier. We have a lot more resources right now, but now I have more people to become concerned with.

Is that your mission now, to make sure these people are taken care of and the company continues to grow and prosper?

I don't like the term "taken care of," but, you know, that they continue to have the opportunity to grow financially and personally.

For Discussion

Do you agree or disagree with the Theory Q way of managing? Explain.

- Additional discussion questions linking this case with the following material appear at the end of this chapter.

Source: C Cox, "Harry V. Quadracci: Business as Social Experiment," *Business Ethics,* May–June 1993, pp 19–21. Excerpted by permission of *Business Ethics* Magazine, Minneapolis, MN.

By putting its people first, 3M enjoys steady profit growth and a reputation for ethical management. Accordingly, this book firmly embraces the idea that people are valuable human resources requiring systematic nurturing and development.

2. *A results-oriented managerial thrust.* Few would argue with the claim that we all should know more about why people behave as they do. After all, by better understanding others, we gain greater understanding of ourselves. But from a managerial standpoint, simply acquiring knowledge about organizational behavior is not enough. That knowledge needs to be put to work to get something accomplished. Managers in all types and sizes of organizations are responsible for getting *results.* The 4-P model of strategic results in Figure 1–1—focusing on *people, products, processes,* and *productivity*—represents management's agenda for *continuous improvement* in the 1990s and beyond. This book strives to help today's and tomorrow's managers achieve these challenging and sometimes conflicting results.

FIGURE 1~1
Strategic Results: The 4-P
Cycle of Continuous
Improvement

People
- Skill development
- Motivation
- Teamwork
- Personal development and learning
- Readiness to change and adapt
- Increased personal responsibility
  for organizational outcomes
- Greater self-management
- Decreased stress

Productivity
- Reduced waste
- Reduced rework
- More efficient use of material,
  human, financial, and informational
  resources

Products
- Greater customer satisfaction
- Better quality goods and services

Processes
- Technological advancement
- Faster product development and
  production cycle times
- System flexibility
- Leaner and more effective administration
- Improved communication and
  information flow
- Organizational learning
- Participative and ethical decision making

The purpose of this chapter is to explore the manager's job, define and examine organizational behavior and its evolution, and consider how we can learn more about organizational behavior. A topical model for the balance of the book also is introduced.

THE MANAGER'S JOB: GETTING THINGS DONE THROUGH OTHERS

management Process of working with and through others to achieve organizational objectives in an efficient manner.

For better or for worse, managers touch our lives in many ways. Schools, hospitals, government agencies, and large and small businesses all require systematic management. Formally defined, **management** is the process of working with and through others to achieve organizational objectives in an efficient manner. From the standpoint of organizational behavior, the central feature of this definition is ''working with and through others.'' Managers play a constantly evolving role. Today's successful managers are no longer the I've-got-everything-under-control order givers of yesteryear. Rather, they need to creatively envision and actively sell bold new directions in an ethical and sensitive manner. Effective managers are team players empowered by the willing and active support of others who are driven by conflicting self-interests. Each of us has a huge stake in how well managers carry out their evolving role. Henry Mintzberg, a respected management scholar, observed: ''No job is more vital to our society than that of the manager. It is the

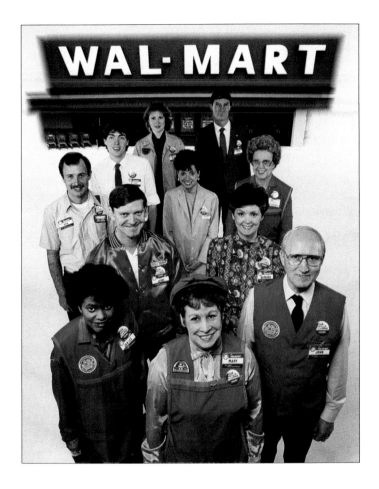

manager who determines whether our social institutions serve us well or whether they squander our talents and resources.''[9]

Extending our managerial thrust, let us take a closer look at the tasks managers perform, the psychological orientation that compels some people to become managers, and the future direction of management.

What Do Managers Do?

Observational studies by Mintzberg and others have found the typical manager's day to be a fragmented collection of brief episodes.[10] Interruptions are commonplace, while large blocks of time for planning and reflective thinking are not. In one particular study, four top-level managers spent 63 percent of their time on activities lasting less than nine minutes each. Only 5 percent of the managers' time was devoted to activities lasting more than a hour.[11] But what specific tasks do managers perform during their hectic and fragmented workdays? More recent research evidence gives us some instructive and interesting answers.

In a survey, researchers asked 1,412 managers (658 first-line supervisors; 553 middle managers; 201 executives) to rank the relative importance of 57 different managerial duties. Statistical analysis of the results revealed seven basic managerial tasks:

1. Managing individual performance.
2. Instructing subordinates.
3. Representing one's staff.
4. Managing group performance.
5. Planning and allocating resources.
6. Coordinating interdependent groups.
7. Monitoring the business environment.[12]

The second phase of the analysis produced task profiles for the three different levels of management (see Figure 1–2). Significantly, this level-by-level comparison overcame a limitation of Mintzberg's observational study that included only five chief executive officers.

Careful examination of the data in Figure 1–2 leads us to the following conclusions:

■ There are basic managerial tasks common to all levels of management.

■ The perceived importance of those tasks changes as one moves up the managerial ladder. As depicted by the percentages shown in Figure 1–2, tasks 1 and 2

● **FIGURE 1–2**   Different Levels of Management Have Different Task Profiles*

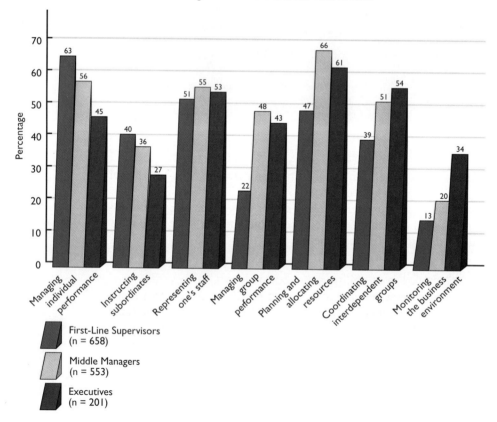

First-Line Supervisors (n = 658)
Middle Managers (n = 553)
Executives (n = 201)

* Numbers refer to the percentage of managers who said the task was of "the utmost" or "considerable" importance.
Source: Data adapted from A I Kraut, P R Pedigo, D D McKenna, and M D Dunnette, "The Role of the Manager: What's Really Important in Different Management Jobs," *Academy of Management Executive*, November 1989, pp 286–93.

are paramount for first-line supervisors; tasks 3, 4, and 5 for middle managers; and tasks 6 and 7 for executives.

■ People-oriented tasks (numbers 1, 2, 3, 4, and 6) comprise the vast bulk of the manager's job.

Summarizing, managers at different levels perform the same basic tasks but with different emphasis. The common denominator of management, however, remains the management of people. This research conclusion is firmly supported by practicing managers. For instance, Andrew J Jones, manager of Honda's engine factory in Britain, recently observed: "The critical thing in the '90s is people."[13] A solid background in organizational behavior can help managers efficiently get things done with and through others.[14]

Motivation to Manage

Is there a formula for managerial success? Experience tells us it takes a combination of ability, desire, and opportunity. Of course, to some degree, luck—such as being in the right place at the right time—plays a role in managerial success. Desire deserves special attention here because it often enables aspiring managers to translate ability, opportunities, and luck into success. Take Frederick W Smith, founder of Federal Express, for example. He built his successful multibillion-dollar airfreight company from an idea he formulated in an economics term paper while studying at Yale University. Ironically, Smith's professor told him it was an ill-conceived idea and gave him a C.[15] Someone with less desire than Smith might have become discouraged and given up. But Smith, like many successful managers, forged ahead despite setbacks. Research on motivation to manage during the last couple of decades has advanced our understanding of desire and other contributors to managerial success.

By identifying personal traits positively correlated with both rapid movement up the career ladder and managerial effectiveness, John B Miner developed a psychometric test for measuring **motivation to manage.** The questionnaire assesses the strength of seven factors (see the OB Exercise). Although the complete questionnaire is not presented in the exercise, we have added scales so you can gauge the strength of your motivation to manage. (Arbitrary norms for comparison purposes are: Total score of: 7–21 = Relatively low motivation to manage; 22–34 = Moderate; 35–49 = Relatively high.) How do you measure up? Remember, though, high motivation to manage is only part of the formula for managerial success. The right combination of ability and opportunity is also necessary.

motivation to manage
Seven personal characteristics involving competitiveness and assertiveness, as measured by Miner's instrument.

Years of motivation-to-manage research by Miner and others has serious implications for America's future global competitiveness. Generally, in recent years, college students in the United States have not scored highly on motivation to manage.[16] Indeed, compared with samples of US college students, samples of students from Japan, China, Mexico, Korea, and Taiwan consistently scored higher on motivation to manage.[17] Miner believes the United States may consequently lag in developing sufficient managerial talent for a tough global marketplace.

In a study by other researchers, MBA students with higher motivation-to-manage scores tended to earn more money after graduation. But students with a higher motivation to manage did not earn better grades or complete their degree program any sooner than those with a lower motivation to manage.[18]

How Strong Is Your Motivation to Manage?
(Circle one number for each factor)

Factor	Description	Scale
1. Authority figures	A desire to meet managerial role requirements in terms of positive relationships with superiors.	Weak 1–2–3–4–5–6–7 Strong
2. Competitive games	A desire to engage in competition with peers involving games or sports and thus meet managerial role requirements in this regard.	Weak 1–2–3–4–5–6–7 Strong
3. Competitive situations	A desire to engage in competition with peers involving occupational or work-related activities and thus meet managerial role requirements in this regard.	Weak 1–2–3–4–5–6–7 Strong
4. Assertive role	A desire to behave in an active and assertive manner involving activities that in this society are often viewed as predominantly masculine and thus to meet managerial role requirements.	Weak 1–2–3–4–5–6–7 Strong
5. Imposing wishes	A desire to tell others what to do and to utilize sanctions in influencing others, thus indicating a capacity to fulfill managerial role requirements in relationships with subordinates.	Weak 1–2–3–4–5–6–7 Strong
6. Standing out from group	A desire to assume a distinctive position of a unique and highly visible nature in a manner that is role-congruent for managerial jobs.	Weak 1–2–3–4–5–6–7 Strong
7. Routine administrative functions	A desire to meet managerial role requirements regarding activities often associated with managerial work that are of a day-to-day administrative nature.	Weak 1–2–3–4–5–6–7 Strong Total =

Source: Adapted from J B Miner and N R Smith, "Decline and Stabilization of Managerial Motivation Over a 20-Year Period," *Journal of Applied Psychology,* June 1982, p 298.

21st-Century Managers

Today's workplace is undergoing immense and permanent changes.[19] Organizations are being "reengineered" for greater speed, efficiency, and flexibility.[20] Teams are pushing aside the individual as the primary building block of organizations. Command-and-control management is giving way to participative management and empowerment. Ego-centered leaders are being replaced by customer-centered leaders. Employees increasingly are being viewed as internal customers. All this creates a mandate for a new kind of manager in the 21st century. Table 1–1 contrasts the characteristics of past and future managers. As the balance of this book will demonstrate, the managerial shift in Table 1–1 is not just a good idea, it is an absolute necessity in the new workplace.

	Past Managers	Future Managers
Primary Role	Order giver, privileged elite, manipulator, controller	Facilitator, team member, teacher, advocate, sponsor
Learning and Knowledge	Periodic learning, narrow specialist	Continuous life-long learning, generalist with multiple specialties
Compensation Criteria	Time, effort, rank	Skills, results
Cultural Orientation	Monocultural, monolingual	Multicultural, multilingual
Primary Source of Influence	Formal authority	Knowledge (technical and interpersonal)
View of People	Potential problem	Primary resource
Primary Communication Pattern	Vertical	Multidirectional
Decision-Making Style	Limited input for individual decisions	Broad-based input for joint decisions
Ethical Considerations	Afterthought	Forethought
Nature of Interpersonal Relationships	Competitive (win–lose)	Cooperative (win–win)
Handling of Power and Key Information	Hoard	Share
Approach to Change	Resist	Facilitate

TABLE 1~1
Evolution of the 21st-Century Manager

V. for

THE FIELD OF ORGANIZATIONAL BEHAVIOR: PAST AND PRESENT

Organizational behavior, commonly referred to as OB, is an interdisciplinary field dedicated to better understanding and managing people at work. By definition, organizational behavior is both research and application oriented. Three basic levels of analysis in OB are individual, group, and organizational. OB draws upon a diverse array of disciplines, including psychology, management, sociology, organization theory, social psychology, statistics, anthropology, general systems theory, economics, information technology, political science, vocational counseling, human stress management, psychometrics, ergonomics, decision theory, and ethics. This rich heritage has spawned many competing perspectives and theories about human work behavior. By the mid-1980s, one researcher had identified 110 distinct theories about behavior within the field of OB.[21]

Organizational behavior is an academic designation. With the exception of teaching/research positions, OB is not an everyday job category such as accounting, marketing, or finance. Students of OB typically do not get jobs in organizational behavior, per se. This reality in no way demeans OB or lessens its importance in effective organizational management. OB is a *horizontal* discipline that cuts across virtually every job category, business function, and professional specialty. Anyone who plans to make a living in a large or small, public or private, organization needs to study organizational behavior.

A historical perspective of the study of people at work helps in studying organizational behavior. According to a management history expert, this is important because

> Historical perspective is the study of a subject in light of its earliest phases and subsequent evolution. Historical perspective differs from history in that the object of historical perspective is to sharpen one's vision of the present, not the past.[22]

organizational behavior
Interdisciplinary field dedicated to better understanding and managing people at work.

In other words, we can better understand where the field of OB is today and where it appears to be headed by appreciating where it has been. Let us examine three significant landmarks in the evolution of understanding and managing people:

1. The human relations movement.
2. The total quality management movement.
3. The contingency approach to management.

The Human Relations Movement

A unique combination of factors during the 1930s fostered the human relations movement. First, following legalization of union–management collective bargaining in the United States in 1935, management began looking for new ways of handling employees. Second, behavioral scientists conducting on-the-job research started calling for more attention to the ''human'' factor. Managers who had lost the battle to keep unions out of their factories heeded the call for better human relations and improved working conditions. One such study, conducted at Western Electric's Chicago-area Hawthorne plant, was a prime stimulus for the human relations movement. Ironically, many of the Hawthorne findings have turned out to be more myth than fact.

The Hawthorne Legacy   Interviews conducted decades later with three subjects of the Hawthorne studies and re-analysis of the original data with modern statistical techniques do not support initial conclusions about the positive effect of supportive supervision. Specifically, money, fear of unemployment during the Great Depression, managerial discipline, and high-quality raw materials—not supportive supervision—turned out to be responsible for high output in the relay assembly test room experiments.[23] Nonetheless, the human relations movement gathered momentum through the 1950s, as academics and managers alike made stirring claims about the powerful impact that individual needs, supportive supervision, and group dynamics apparently had on job performance.

The Writings of Mayo and Follett   Essential to the human relations movement were the writings of Elton Mayo and Mary Parker Follett. Australian-born Mayo, who headed the Harvard researchers at Hawthorne, advised managers to attend to employees' emotional needs in his 1933 classic, *The Human Problems of an Industrial Civilization.* Follett was a true pioneer, not only as a woman management consultant in the male-dominated industrial world of the 1920s, but also as a writer who saw employees as complex combinations of attitudes, beliefs, and needs. Mary Parker Follett was way ahead of her time in telling managers to motivate job performance instead of merely demanding it, a ''pull'' rather than ''push'' strategy. She also built a logical bridge between political democracy and a cooperative spirit in the workplace.[24]

Theory Y   McGregor's modern and positive assumptions about employees being responsible and creative.

McGregor's Theory Y   In 1960, Douglas McGregor wrote a book entitled *The Human Side of Enterprise,* which has become an important philosophical base for the modern view of people at work.[25] Drawing upon his experience as a management consultant, McGregor formulated two sharply contrasting sets of assumptions about human nature (see Table 1–2). His Theory X assumptions were pessimistic

◥ • TABLE 1~2   McGregor's Theory X and Theory Y

Outdated (Theory X) Assumptions about People at Work	Modern (Theory Y) Assumptions about People at Work
1. Most people dislike work; they avoid it when they can.	1. Work is a natural activity, like play or rest.
2. Most people must be coerced and threatened with punishment before they will work. People require close direction when they are working.	2. People are capable of self-direction and self-control if they are committed to objectives.
3. Most people actually prefer to be directed. They tend to avoid responsibility and exhibit little ambition. They are interested only in security.	3. People generally become committed to organizational objectives if they are rewarded for doing so.
	4. The typical employee can learn to accept and seek responsibility.
	5. The typical member of the general population has imagination, ingenuity, and creativity.

Source: Adapted from D McGregor, *The Human Side of Enterprise* (New York: McGraw-Hill, 1960), chap. 4.

and negative and, according to McGregor's interpretation, typical of how managers traditionally perceived employees. To help managers break with this negative tradition, McGregor formulated his **Theory Y,** a modern and positive set of assumptions about people. McGregor believed managers could accomplish more through others by viewing them as self-energized, committed, responsible, and creative beings.

McGregor's Theory Y challenges theorists and practicing managers to adopt a *developmental* approach to employees. Many modern managers endorse McGregor's progressive Theory Y philosophy. Linda Honold, Director of Member Development at Johnsonville Foods in Wisconsin, put it this way: "US companies need to change their beliefs about the ability of average employees. We must expect them to be involved in every aspect of their job. When we do, we will start realizing a dramatic increase in productivity and quality."[26]

New Assumptions about Human Nature   Unfortunately, unsophisticated behavioral research methods caused the human relationists to embrace some naive and misleading conclusions. For example, human relationists believed in the axiom, "A satisfied employee is a hardworking employee." Subsequent research, as discussed later in this book, shows the satisfaction–performance linkage to be more complex than originally thought.

Despite its shortcomings, the human relations movement opened the door to more progressive thinking about human nature. Rather than continuing to view employees as passive economic beings, managers began to see them as active social beings and took steps to create more humane work environments.

The Total Quality Management Movement

A great deal has been written and said about quality in recent years. So much, in fact, that *total quality management* (TQM) has been dismissed by some as just another fad.[27] But disregarding the underlying principles of TQM because the term has become so widespread would be as unwise as ignoring sound nutrition and exercise because of endless discussions about dieting. TQM principles have profound practical implications for managing people today.[28]

total quality management
An organizational culture dedicated to training, continuous improvement, and customer satisfaction.

What Is TQM?   Experts on the subject recently offered this definition of **total quality management:**

> TQM means that the organization's culture is defined by and supports the constant attainment of customer satisfaction through an integrated system of tools, techniques, and training. This involves the continuous improvement of organizational processes, resulting in high quality products and services.[29]

Quality consultant Richard J Schonberger sums up TQM as ''continuous, customer-centered, employee-driven improvement.''[30] TQM is necessarily employee driven because product/service quality cannot be continuously improved without the active learning and participation of *every* employee. Thus, in successful quality improvement programs, TQM principles are embedded in the organization's culture.

The Deming Legacy   TQM is firmly established today thanks in large part to the pioneering work of W Edwards Deming.[31] Ironically, the mathematician credited with Japan's post–World War II quality revolution rarely talked in terms of quality. He instead preferred to discuss ''good management'' during the hard-hitting seminars he delivered right up until his death at age 93 in 1993.[32] Although Deming's passion was the statistical measurement and elimination of variations in industrial processes, he had much to say about how employees should be treated. Among his famous 14 points were calls for the following:

- Formal training in statistical process control techniques and teamwork.
- Helpful leadership, rather than order giving and punishment.
- Elimination of fear so employees will feel free to ask questions.
- Emphasis on continuous process improvements rather than on numerical quotas.
- Teamwork.
- Elimination of barriers to good workmanship.[33]

One of Deming's most enduring lessons for managers is his 85–15 rule.[34] Specifically, when things go wrong, there is roughly an 85 percent chance the *system* (including management, machinery, and rules) is at fault. Only about 15 percent of the time is the individual employee at fault. Unfortunately, as Deming observed, the typical manager spends most of his or her time wrongly blaming and

W Edwards Deming (1900–1993) was an inspiring visionary in the "quality revolution" because of his belief that employee involvement is at the heart of continuous improvement.

Kip Brundage/Woodfin Camp & Associates

punishing individuals for system failures. Statistical analysis is required to uncover system failures.

Principles of TQM   Despite variations in the language and scope of TQM programs, it is possible to identify four common TQM principles:

1. Do it right the first time to eliminate costly rework.
2. Listen to and learn from customers and employees.
3. Make continuous improvement an everyday matter.
4. Build teamwork, trust, and mutual respect.[35]

Deming's influence is clearly evident in this list.[36] Once again, as with the human relations movement, we see people as the key factor in organizational success.

In summary, TQM advocates have made a valuable contribution to the field of OB by providing a *practical* context for managing people. When people are managed according to TQM principles, everyone is more likely to get the employment opportunities and high-quality goods and services they demand. As you will see many times in later chapters, this book is anchored to Deming's philosophy and TQM principles.

The Contingency Approach

Scholars have wrestled for many years with the problem of how best to apply the diverse and growing collection of management tools and techniques. Their answer is the contingency approach. The **contingency approach** calls for using management techniques in a situationally appropriate manner, instead of trying to rely on "one best way." According to a pair of contingency theorists:

> [Contingency theories] developed and their acceptance grew largely because they responded to criticisms that the classical theories advocated "one best way" of organizing and managing. Contingency theories, on the other hand, proposed that the appropriate organizational structure and management style were dependent upon a set of "contingency" factors, usually the uncertainty and instability of the environment.[37]

contingency approach
Using management tools and techniques in a situationally appropriate manner; avoiding the one-best-way mentality.

The contingency approach encourages managers to view organizational behavior within a situational context. According to this modern perspective, evolving situations, not hard-and-fast rules, determine when and where various management techniques are appropriate. For example, as discussed in Chapter 15, contingency researchers have determined that there is no single best style of leadership. Organizational behavior specialists embrace the contingency approach because it helps them realistically interrelate individuals, groups, and organizations. Moreover, the contingency approach sends a clear message to managers: Carefully read the situation and then be flexible enough to adapt (see the International OB on page 18).

Now that we have reviewed OB's historical evolution, we need to address how we learn about OB through a combination of theory, research and practice.

As a human being, with years of interpersonal experience to draw upon, you already know a good deal about people at work. But more systematic and comprehensive understanding is possible and desirable. A working knowledge of current OB theory, research, and practice can help you develop a tightly integrated

LEARNING ABOUT OB FROM THEORY, RESEARCH, AND PRACTICE

INTERNATIONAL OB

A Contingency Approach: Dell Computer Plays It by Ear in Mexico

When Mexico removed import barriers on computers a few years ago, pent-up demand washed over the Mexican border like flood waters bursting a dam. The deluge was so great that telemarketers at Dell Computer Corp. in Texas were having a hard time keeping up with the needs of Mexican businesses and individuals. In a bold move, company executives in May 1992 decided to pack up their direct-marketing strategy and a few sales representatives and try their luck south of the border. They opened an office, set up phone banks and waited for the orders to flood in—and they did, to a certain extent. In the first eight months, Dell managed to grab 5 percent of the market, selling some 10,000 machines. Still, sales were not coming in as fast as the company had anticipated.

Dell executives quickly found out that the problem was cultural: Unlike most Americans, the average Mexican is apprehensive about making a large purchase sight-unseen over the telephone. "People here think that a company that sends you a catalog and tries to sell to you by phone isn't serious," says Vivian Kobeh, Dell Computer de Mexico's marketing and communications manager. "They are not confident that the equipment will arrive and that they will receive the support and maintenance they need after the sale is closed."

Faced with a cultural problem, Dell found a cultural solution by creating a hybrid sales style that's part Mexican, part American. It also has helped transform Dell de Mexico into one of the fastest-growing start-up operations in the history of the Austin, Texas-based multinational. Only the company's Japan subsidiary got off the ground quicker.

Determined to allay fears and wipe out suspicion about buying via telephone, Dell plugged in to Mexico's consumer market with a three-pronged approach:

- To give its computers a visual market presence, it started stocking its PCs in local discount stores like Price Club and Sam's, a subsidiary of Wal-Mart. The company also established an in-house showroom similar to ones at Dell operations around the world. . . .

- Following a strategy first undertaken by the multinational's Austin headquarters last year, Dell de Mexico has expanded its corporate sales staff to seven people from just one. This allowed the company to pick up additional sales through a more traditional way of doing business in Mexico: the time-honored corporate presentation.

- Dell also tripled its Mexico City "Dell Direct" sales staff to 15 people. With the extra telemarketers in place, salespeople not only can reach more potential customers, but they also can spend more time with each one in an attempt to hammer away at the cultural bias against telephone sales.

In what might be a subliminal message to consumers, nearly all of the local staff is Mexican. Kobeh and two salespeople, all of whom speak Spanish, are the only Americans.

The company already has seen some success. About half of Dell's sales currently are made on the telephone. Eventually, it would like to see Mexico's direct sales come closer in line with the U.S. operation, where three-quarters of PC sales are made on the phone. . . .

"The key is Dell's training," says Kobeh. "We train our sales staff to be able to advise customers on what machine will best fit their needs."

It's a concept the company takes seriously. Dell even calls its salespeople "advisers." Training consists of a week-long initial program, followed every two months with a refresher course.

Source: Excerpted from C MacDonald, "The Telemarketing Touch," *America West Airlines Magazine*, January 1994, pp 52, 54.

understanding of why organizational contributors think and act as they do. In order for this to happen, however, prepare yourself for some intellectual surprises from theoretical models, research results, or techniques that may run counter to your current thinking. For instance, conventional wisdom says that physically active employees perform better than their out-of-shape co-workers. But in a study of 522 factory employees (half of whom exercised each workday for 15 minutes before lunch and half of whom did not), both groups did the same amount of work despite the perception among the exercisers that they had accomplished more with less fatigue. So regular exercise, while still a good idea for general health and lifestyle purposes, is not a quick fix for productivity improvement.[38] Recognizing that surprises are what makes learning fun, let us examine the dynamic relationship between OB theory, research, and practice and the value of each.

Figure 1–3 illustrates how theory, research, and practice are related. Throughout the balance of this book, we focus primarily on the central portion, where all three areas overlap. Knowledge of why people behave as they do and what managers can do to improve performance is greatest within this area of maximum overlap. For each major topic, we build a foundation for understanding with generally accepted theory. This theoretical foundation is then tested and expanded by reviewing the latest relevant research findings. After interpreting the research, we discuss the nature and effectiveness of related practical applications.

Sometimes, depending on the subject matter, it is necessary to venture into the large areas outside the central portion of Figure 1–3. For example, an insightful theory supported by convincing research evidence might suggest an untried or different way of managing. In other instances, an innovative management technique might call for an explanatory theoretical model and exploratory research. Each area—theory, research, and practice—supports and in turn is supported by the other two. Each area makes a valuable contribution to our understanding of, and ability to, manage organizational behavior.

Learning from Theory

A respected behavioral scientist, Kurt Lewin, once said there is nothing as practical as a good theory. According to one management researcher, a **theory** is a story that explains "why."[39] Another calls well-constructed theories "disciplined imagination."[40] A good OB theory, then, is a story that effectively explains why individuals and groups behave as they do. Moreover, a good theoretical model

theory   A story defining key terms, providing a conceptual framework, and explaining why something occurs.

1. *Defines* key terms.
2. Constructs a *conceptual framework* that explains how important factors are interrelated. (Graphic models are often used to achieve this end.)
3. Provides a *departure point* for research and practical application.

Indeed, good theories are a fundamental contributor to improved understanding and management of organizational behavior.[41]

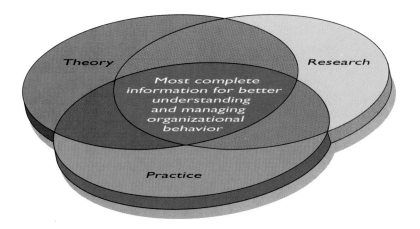

• ↗ FIGURE 1–3

Learning about OB through a Combination of Theory, Research, and Practice

Learning from Research

Because of unfamiliar jargon and complicated statistical procedures, many present and future managers are put off by behavioral research. This is unfortunate because practical lessons can be learned as OB researchers steadily push back the frontier of knowledge. Let us examine the various sources and uses of OB research evidence.

Five Sources of OB Research Insights   To enhance the instructional value of our coverage of major topics, we systematically cite ''hard'' evidence from five different categories. Worthwhile evidence was obtained by drawing upon the following *priority* of research methodologies:

meta-analysis   Pools the results of many studies through statistical procedure.

- *Meta-analyses.*   A **meta-analysis** is a statistical pooling technique that permits behavioral scientists to draw general conclusions about certain variables from many different studies.[42] It typically encompasses a vast number of subjects, often reaching the thousands. Meta-analyses are instructive because they focus on general patterns of research evidence, not fragmented bits and pieces or isolated studies.

field study   Examination of variables in real-life settings.

- *Field studies.*   In OB, a **field study** probes individual or group processes in an organizational setting. Because field studies involve real-life situations, their results often have immediate and practical relevance for managers.

laboratory study   Manipulation and measurement of variables in contrived situations.

- *Laboratory studies.*   In a **laboratory study,** variables are manipulated and measured in contrived situations. College students are commonly used as subjects. The highly controlled nature of laboratory studies enhances research precision. But generalizing the results to organizational management requires caution.[43]

sample survey   Questionnaire responses from a sample of people.

- *Sample surveys.*   In a **sample survey,** samples of people from specified populations respond to questionnaires. The researchers then draw conclusions about the relevant population. Generalizability of the results depends on the quality of the sampling and questioning techniques.

case study   In-depth study of a single person, group, or organization.

- *Case studies.*   A **case study** is an in-depth analysis of a single individual, group, or organization. Because of their limited scope, case studies yield realistic but not very generalizable results.[44]

Three Uses of OB Research Findings   Organizational scholars point out that managers can put relevant research findings to use in three different ways:[45]

1. *Instrumental use.*   This involves directly applying research findings to practical problems. For example, a manager experiencing high stress tries a relaxation technique after reading a research report about its effectiveness.

2. *Conceptual use.*   Research is put to conceptual use when managers derive general enlightenment from its findings. The impact here is less specific and more indirect than with instrumental use. For example, after reading a meta-analysis showing a negative correlation between absenteeism and age,[46] a manager might develop a more positive attitude toward hiring older people.

3. *Symbolic use.*   Symbolic use occurs when research results are relied on to verify or legitimize already held positions. Negative forms of symbolic use involve self-serving bias, prejudice, selective perception, and distortion. For example, tobacco industry spokespersons routinely deny any link between smoking and lung cancer because researchers are largely, but not 100 percent, in agreement about the negative effects of smoking. A positive

example would be managers maintaining their confidence in setting perform-ance goals after reading a research report about the favorable impact of goal setting on job performance.

By systematically reviewing and interpreting research relevant to key topics, this book provides instructive insights about OB. (The mechanics of the scientific method and OB research are discussed in detail in The Advanced Learning Module at the end of this text.)

Learning from Practice

Relative to learning more about how to effectively manage people at work, one might be tempted to ask, "Why bother with theory and research; let's get right down to *how to do it.*" Our answer lies in the contingency approach, discussed earlier. The effectiveness of specific theoretical models or management techniques is contingent on the situations in which they are applied. For example, one cross-cultural study of a large multinational corporation's employees working in 50 countries led the researcher to conclude that most made-in-America management theories and techniques are inappropriate in other cultures.[47] Many otherwise well-intentioned performance-improvement programs based on American cultural values have failed in other cultures because of naive assumptions about trans-ferability. (International cultures are discussed in Chapter 2.) Fortunately, systema-tic research is available that tests our "common sense" assumptions about what works where. Management "cookbooks" that provide only how-to-do-it advice with no underlying theoretical models or supporting research practically guarantee misapplication. As mentioned earlier, theory, research, and practice mutually reinforce one another.

The theory→research→practice sequence discussed in this section will help you better understand each major topic addressed later in this book. Attention now turns to a topical model that sets the stage for what lies ahead.

Figure 1–4 is a topical road map for our journey through this book. Our destination is organizational effectiveness through continuous improvement. Four different criteria for determining whether or not an organization is effective are discussed in Chapter 17. The study of OB can be a wandering and pointless trip if we overlook the need to translate OB lessons into effective and efficient organized endeavor.

At the far left side of our topical road map are managers, those who are responsible for accomplishing organizational results with and through others. The three boxes at the center of our road map correspond to Parts II, III, and IV of this text. Logically, the flow of topical coverage in this book goes from individuals, to group processes, to organizational processes and problems, to organizations. Around the core of our topical road map in Figure 1–4 is the organization. Accordingly, we end our journey with organization-related material in Part V. Organizational structure and design are covered there in Chapters 17 and 18 to establish and develop the *organizational* context of organizational behavior. Rounding out our organizational context are discussions of organizational cultures in Chapter 19 and organizational change in Chapter 20.

The broken line represents a permeable boundary between the organization and its environment. Energy and influence flow both ways across this permeable boundary. Truly, no organization is an island in today's highly interactive and

A TOPICAL MODEL FOR UNDERSTANDING AND MANAGING OB

• FIGURE 1~4   A Topical Model for What Lies Ahead

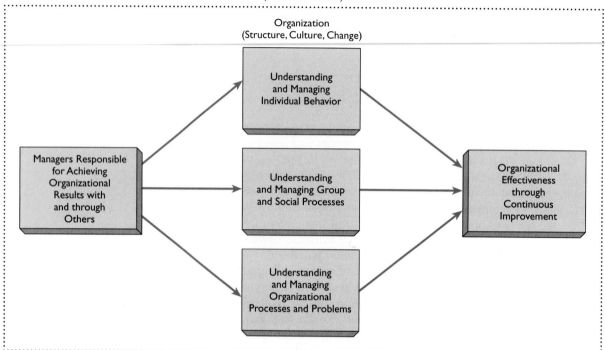

interdependent world. Relative to the *external* environment, international cultures are explored in Chapter 2. Organization–environment contingencies are examined in Chapter 18.

Chapter 3 examines the OB implications of significant demographic and social trends, and Chapter 4 explores important ethical considerations. These discussions provide a realistic context for studying and managing people at work.

Bon voyage! Enjoy your trip through the challenging, interesting, and often surprising world of OB.

BACK TO THE OPENING CASE

Now that you have read Chapter 1, you should be able to answer the following questions about the Quad/Graphics case:

1. What is the key to Harry Quadracci's success at Quad/Graphics?

2. Is Harry Quadracci a 21st-century manager? Explain, using Table 1–1 as a guide.

3. How does Quadracci's Theory Q compare with McGregor's Theories X and Y?

4. What evidence of the four principles of total quality management (TQM) do you detect at Quad/Graphics?

5. Would Harry Quadracci's philosophy of management apply equally well in other cultures around the world? Explain. (Feel free to draw upon your firsthand knowledge of various cultures.)

SUMMARY OF KEY CONCEPTS

1. *Define the term* management, *and explain what managers do.* Management is defined as the process of working with and through others to achieve organizational objectives in an efficient manner. Observational studies by Mintzberg and others found the typical manager's day to be a hectic stream of fragmented activities with lots of interruptions. Other research found most managerial tasks to be people oriented.

2. *Explain the concept of motivation to manage, and summarize the related cross-cultural research evidence.* Miner's motivation-to-manage questionnaire measures seven personal characteristics, including competitive and assertive desires, that predict both career success and managerial effectiveness. International research shows that US students exhibit a comparatively low motivation to manage. Miner thinks this could hurt America's global competitiveness.

3. *Characterize 21st-century managers.* They will be team players who will get things done cooperatively by relying on joint decision making, their knowledge instead of formal authority, and their multicultural skills. They will engage in life-long learning and be compensated on the basis of their skills and results. They will facilitate rather than resist change, share rather than hoard power and key information, and be multidirectional communicators. Ethics will be a forethought instead of an afterthought. They will be generalists with multiple specialties.

4. *Define the term* organizational behavior *and explain why OB is a horizontal discipline.* Organizational behavior (OB) is an interdisciplinary field dedicated to better understanding and managing people at work. It is both research and application oriented. Except for teaching/research positions, one does not normally get a job in OB. Rather, because OB is a horizontal discipline, OB concepts and lessons are applicable to virtually every job category, business function, and professional specialty.

5. *Contrast McGregor's Theory X and Theory Y assumptions about employees.* Theory X employees, according to traditional thinking, dislike work, require close supervision, and are primarily interested in security. According to the modern Theory Y view, employees are capable of self-direction, of seeking responsibility, and of being creative.

6. *Explain the managerial significance of Deming's 85–15 rule.* Deming claimed that about 85 percent of organizational failures are due to system breakdowns involving factors such as management, machinery, or work rules. He believed the workers themselves are responsible for failures only about 15 percent of the time. Consequently, Deming criticized the standard practice of blaming and punishing individuals for what are typically *system* failures beyond their immediate control.

7. *Identify the four principles of total quality management (TQM).* (1) Do it right the first time to eliminate costly rework. (2) Listen to and learn from customers and employees. (3) Make continuous improvement an everyday matter. (4) Build teamwork, trust, and mutual respect.

8. *Describe the sources of organizational behavior research evidence.* Five sources of OB research evidence are meta-analyses (statistically pooled evidence from several studies), field studies (evidence from real-life situations), laboratory studies (evidence from contrived situations), sample surveys (questionnaire data), and case studies (observation of a single person, group, or organization).

DISCUSSION QUESTIONS

1. Why view the typical employee as a human resource?

2. In your opinion, what are the three or four most important strategic results in Figure 1–1? Why?

3. How would you respond to a fellow student who says, "I have a hard time getting along with other people, but I think I could be a good manager"?

4. Based on either personal experience as a manager or on your observation of managers at work, are the seven managerial tasks in Figure 1–2 a realistic portrayal of what managers do?

5. Examining Figure 1–2, which of the three levels of management has the most difficult job? Why?

6. Referring to the OB Exercise, what is your motivation to manage? Do you believe our adaptation of Miner's scale accurately assessed your potential as a manager? Explain.

7. How would you respond to a new manager who

made this statement? "TQM is about statistical process control, not about people."

8. Do you use the contingency approach in your daily affairs? Explain the circumstances.

9. What "practical" theories have you formulated to achieve the things you want in life (e.g., graduating, keeping fit, getting a good job, meeting that special someone)?

10. From a manager's standpoint, which use of research is better: instrumental or conceptual? Explain your rationale.

EXERCISE

Objectives

1. To get to know some of your fellow students.
2. To put the management of people into a lively and interesting historical context.
3. To begin to develop your teamwork skills.

Introduction

This exercise is titled "Timeless Advice." Your creative energy, willingness to see familiar things in unfamiliar ways, and ability to have fun while learning are keys to the success of this warm-up exercise. A 20-minute, small group session will be followed by brief oral presentations and a general class discussion. Total time required is approximately 40 to 45 minutes.

Instructions

Your instructor will divide your class randomly into groups of four to six people each. Acting as a team, with everyone offering ideas and one person serving as official recorder, each group will be responsible for writing a one-page memo to your present class. Subject matter of your group's memo will be "My advice for managing people today is . . ." The fun part of this exercise (and its creative element) involves writing the memo from the viewpoint of the person assigned to your group by your instructor.

Among the memo viewpoints your instructor may assign are the following:

- Harry Quadracci (opening case).
- An ancient Egyptian slave master (building the great pyramids).
- Mary Parker Follett.
- Douglas McGregor.
- A Theory X supervisor of a construction crew (see McGregor's Theories X and Y in Table 1–2).
- W Edwards Deming.

- A TQM coordinator at 3M Company.
- A contingency management theorist.
- A Japanese auto company executive.
- The chief executive officer of IBM in the year 2030.
- Commander of the Starship Enterprise II in the year 3001.
- Others, as assigned by your instructor.

Use your imagination, make sure everyone participates, and try to be true to any historical facts you've encountered. Attempt to be as specific and realistic as possible. Remember, the idea is to provide advice about managing people from another point in time (or from a particular point of view at the present time).

Make sure you manage your 20-minute time limit carefully. A recommended approach is to spend 2 to 3 minutes putting the exercise into proper perspective. Next, take about 10 to 12 minutes brainstorming ideas for your memo, with your recorder jotting down key ideas and phrases. Have your recorder use the remaining time to write your group's one-page memo, with constructive comments and help from the others. Pick a spokesperson to read your group's memo to the class.

Questions for Consideration/ Class Discussion

1. What valuable lessons about managing people have you heard?
2. What have you learned about how NOT to manage people?
3. From the distant past to today, what significant shifts in the management of people seem to have taken place?
4. Where does the management of people appear to be headed?
5. All things considered, what mistakes are today's managers typically making when managing people?
6. How well did your group function as a "team"?

NOTES

[1] Data from "The *Fortune* 500," *Fortune,* April 19, 1993, p 232.

[2] N M Tichy and S Sherman, *Control Your Destiny or Someone Else Will: How Jack Welch Is Making General Electric the World's Most Competitive Corporation* (New York: Doubleday, 1993), p 251.

[3] A B Fisher, "Morale Crisis," *Fortune,* November 18, 1991, p 71.

[4] Data from J Schmit, "AMR Quarterly Loss Totals $253 Million," *USA Today,* January 20, 1994, p 2B.

[5] M D Fefer, "How Layoffs Pay Off," *Fortune,* January 24, 1994, p 12.

[6] See W F Cascio, "Downsizing: What Do We Know? What Have We Learned?" *Academy of Management Executive,* February 1993, pp 95–104; and B Baumohl, "When Downsizing Becomes 'Dumbsizing,'" *Time,* March 15, 1993, p 55.

[7] For more, see J Stuller, "Why Not 'Inplacement'?" *Training,* June 1993, pp 37–41; and R Henkoff, "Getting Beyond Downsizing," *Fortune,* January 10, 1994, pp 58–64.

[8] E Lesly and L Light, "When Layoffs Alone Don't Turn the Tide," *Business Week,* December 7, 1992, p 101. (Emphasis added.)

[9] H Mintzberg, "The Manager's Job: Folklore and Fact," *Harvard Business Review,* July–August 1975, p 61.

[10] See, for example, H Mintzberg, "Managerial Work: Analysis from Observation," *Management Science,* October 1971, pp B97–B110; and F Luthans, "Successful vs. Effective Real Managers," *Academy of Management Executive,* May 1988, pp 127–32. For an instructive critique of the structured observation method, see M J Martinko and W L Gardner, "Beyond Structured Observation: Methodological Issues and New Directions," *Academy of Management Review,* October 1985, pp 676–95. Also see N Fondas, "A Behavioral Job Description for Managers," *Organizational Dynamics,* Summer 1992, pp 47–58.

[11] See L B Kurke and H E Aldrich, "Mintzberg Was Right!: A Replication and Extension of *The Nature of Managerial Work,*" *Management Science,* August 1983, pp 975–84.

[12] Adapted from A I Kraut, P R Pedigo, D D McKenna, and M D Dunnette, "The Role of the Manager: What's Really Important in Different Management Jobs," *Academy of Management Executive,* November 1989, pp 286–93.

[13] R A Melcher, "On Guard, Europe," *Business Week,* December 14, 1992, p 55.

[14] Research support for this contention can be found in S C Harper, "The Challenges Facing CEOs: Past, Present, and Future," *Academy of Management Executive,* August 1992, pp 7–25.

[15] See E Linden, "Frederick W. Smith of Federal Express: He Didn't Get There Overnight." *Inc.,* April 1984, p 89.

[16] These research results are discussed in detail in J B Miner and N R Smith, "Decline and Stabilization of Managerial Motivation Over a 20-Year Period," *Journal of Applied Psychology,* June 1982, pp 297–305.

[17] See J B Miner, J M Wachtel, and B Ebrahimi, "The Managerial Motivation of Potential Managers in the United States and Other Countries of the World: Implications for National Competitiveness and the Productivity Problem," in *Advances in International Comparative Management,* vol. 4, ed S B Prasad (Greenwich, CT: JAI Press, 1989), pp 147–170; and J B Miner, C C Chen, and K C Yu, "Theory Testing Under Adverse Conditions: Motivation to Manage in the People's Republic of China," *Journal of Applied Psychology,* June 1991, pp 343–49.

[18] Based on K M Bartol and D C Martin, "Managerial Motivation among MBA Students: A Longitudinal Assessment," *Journal of Occupational Psychology,* March 1987, pp 1–12.

[19] Interesting discussions can be found in W Kiechel III, "How We Will Work in the Year 2000," *Fortune,* May 17, 1993, pp 38–52; and A B Shostak, "The Nature of Work in the Twenty-First Century: Certain Uncertainties," *Business Horizons,* November–December 1993, pp 30–34.

[20] See, for example, G Hall, J Rosenthal, and J Wade, "How to Make Reengineering *Really* Work," *Harvard Business Review,* November–December 1993, pp 119–31.

[21] See J B Miner, "The Validity and Usefulness of Theories in an Emerging Organizational Science," *Academy of Management Review,* April 1984, pp 296–306.

[22] B S Lawrence, "Historical Perspective: Using the Past to Study the Present," *Academy of Management Review,* April 1984, p 307.

[23] Evidence indicating that the original conclusions of the famous Hawthorne studies were unjustified may be found in R G Greenwood, A A Bolton, and R A Greenwood, "Hawthorne a Half Century Later: Relay Assembly Par-

Participants Remember,'' *Journal of Management,* Fall–Winter 1983, pp 217–31; and R H Franke and J D Kaul, ''The Hawthorne Experiments: First Statistical Interpretation,'' *American Sociological Review,* October 1978, pp 623–43. For a positive interpretation of the Hawthorne studies, see J A Sonnenfeld, ''Shedding Light on the Hawthorne Studies,'' *Journal of Occupational Behaviour,* April 1985, pp 111–30.

[24] See M Parker Follett, *Freedom and Coordination* (London: Management Publications Trust, 1949).

[25] See D McGregor, *The Human Side of Enterprise* (New York: McGraw-Hill, 1960).

[26] L Honold, ''Letters to Fortune,'' *Fortune,* June 4, 1990, p 290.

[27] See, for example, R Zemke, ''TQM: Fatally Flawed or Simply Unfocused?'' *Training,* October 1992, p 8.

[28] Instructive background articles on TQM are R Zemke, ''A Bluffer's Guide to TQM,'' *Training,* April 1993, pp 48–55; R R Gehani, ''Quality Value-Chain: A Meta-Synthesis of Frontiers of Quality Movement,'' *Academy of Management Executive,* May 1993, pp 29–42; and P Mears, ''How to Stop Talking About, and Begin Progress Toward, Total Quality Management,'' *Business Horizons,* May–June 1993, pp 11–14.

[29] M Sashkin and K J Kiser, *Putting Total Quality Management to Work* (San Francisco: Berrett-Koehler, 1993), p 39.

[30] R J Schonberger, ''Total Quality Management Cuts a Broad Swath—Through Manufacturing and Beyond,'' *Organizational Dynamics,* Spring 1992, p 18.

[31] Deming's landmark work is W E Deming, *Out of the Crisis* (Cambridge, MA: MIT, 1986).

[32] See M Trumbull, ''What Is Total Quality Management?'' *The Christian Science Monitor,* May 3, 1993, p 12; and J Hillkirk, ''World-Famous Quality Expert Dead at 93,'' *USA Today,* December 21, 1993, pp 1B–2B.

[33] Based on discussion in M Walton, *Deming Management at Work* (New York: Putnam/Perigee, 1990).

[34] *Ibid.,* p 20.

[35] Adapted from D E Bowen and E E Lawler III ''Total Quality-Oriented Human Resources Management,'' *Organizational Dynamics,* Spring 1992, pp 29–41.

[36] See T F Rienzo, ''Planning Deming Management for Service Organizations,'' *Business Horizons,* May–June 1993, pp 19–29.

[37] H L Tosi, Jr., and J W Slocum, Jr., ''Contingency Theory: Some Suggested Directions,'' *Journal of Management,* Spring 1984, p 9.

[38] Data from O Rosenfeld, G Tenenbaum, H Ruskin, and S T Halfon, ''The Effect of Physical Training on Objective and Subjective Measures of Productivity and Efficiency,'' *Ergonomics,* August 1989, pp 1019–28.

[39] See R L Daft, ''Learning the Craft of Organizational Research,'' *Academy of Management Review,* October 1983, pp 539–46.

[40] See K E Weick, ''Theory Construction as Disciplined Imagination,'' *Academy of Management Review,* October 1989, pp 516–31. Also see D A Whetten's article in the same issue, pp 490–95.

[41] Theory-focused versus problem-focused research is discussed in K E Weick, ''Agenda Setting in Organizational Behavior: A Theory-Focused Approach,'' *Journal of Management Inquiry,* September 1992, pp 171–82.

[42] Complete discussion of this technique can be found in J E Hunter, F L Schmidt, and G B Jackson, *Meta-Analysis. Cumulating Research Findings across Studies* (Beverly Hills, CA: Sage Publications, 1982); and J E Hunter and F L Schmidt, *Methods of Meta-Analysis: Correcting Error and Bias In Research Findings* (Newbury Park, CA: Sage Publications, 1990).

[43] For an interesting debate about the use of students as subjects, see J Greenberg, ''The College Sophomore as Guinea Pig: Setting the Record Straight,'' *Academy of Management Review,* January 1987, pp 157–59; and M E Gordon, L A Slade, and N Schmitt, ''Student Guinea Pigs: Porcine Predictors and Particularistic Phenomena,'' *Academy of Management Review,* January 1987, pp 160–63.

[44] Good discussions of case studies can be found in A S Lee, ''Case Studies as Natural Experiments,'' *Human Relations,* February 1989, pp 117–37; and K M Eisenhardt, ''Building Theories from Case Study Research,'' *Academy of Management Review,* October 1989, pp. 532–50. The case survey technique is discussed in R Larsson, ''Case Survey Methodology: Analysis of Patterns Across Case Studies,'' *Academy of Management Journal,* December 1993, pp 1515–46.

[45] Based on discussion found in J M Beyer and H M Trice, ''The Utilization Process: A Conceptual Framework and Synthesis of Empirical Findings,'' *Administrative Science Quarterly,* December 1982, pp 591–622.

[46] See J J Martocchio, ''Age-Related Differences in Employee Absenteeism: A Meta-Analysis,'' *Psychology & Aging,* December 1989, pp 409–14.

[47] For complete details, see G Hofstede, ''The Cultural Relativity of Organizational Practices and Theories,'' *Journal of International Business Studies,* Fall 1983, pp 75–89. For related discussion, see G Hofstede, ''Cultural Constraints in Management Theories,'' *Academy of Management Executive,* February 1993, pp 81–94.

2

INTERNATIONAL OB: MANAGING ACROSS CULTURES

Learning OBJECTIVES

When you finish studying the material in this chapter, you should be able to:

1. Explain how societal culture and organizational culture combine to influence on-the-job behavior.

2. Distinguish between high-context and low-context cultures.

3. Explain the difference between monochronic and polychronic cultures.

4. Discuss the cultural implications of interpersonal space, language, and religion.

5. Describe the practical lessons from the Hofstede–Bond cross-cultural studies.

6. Explain what cross-cultural studies have found about leadership and conflict-handling styles.

7. Specify why US managers have a comparatively high failure rate in foreign assignments and identify skills needed by today's global managers.

8. Discuss the importance of cross-cultural training relative to the foreign assignment cycle.

OPENING CASE

Pack Your Bags, You've Been Transferred to Kenya

Sharon Hoogstraten

Dale Pilger, General Motors Corp.'s new managing director for Kenya, wonders if he can keep his Kenyan employees from interrupting his paperwork by raising his index finger.

"The finger itself will offend," warns Noah Midamba, a Kenyan. He urges that Mr. Pilger instead greet a worker with an effusive welcome, offer a chair, and request that he wait. It can be even trickier to fire a Kenyan, Mr. Midamba says. The government asked one German auto executive to leave Kenya after he dismissed a man—whose brother was the East African country's vice president.

Mr. Pilger, his adventurous wife, and their two teen-agers, miserable about moving, have come to this Rocky Mountain college town [Boulder, Colorado] for three days of cross-cultural training. The Cortland,

Ohio, family learns to cope with being strangers in a strange land as consultants Moran, Stahl & Boyer International give them a crash immersion in African political history, business practices, social customs, and nonverbal gestures. The training enables managers to grasp cultural differences and handle culture-shock symptoms such as self-pity.

Cross-cultural training is on the rise everywhere because more global-minded corporations moving fast-track executives overseas want to curb the cost of failed expatriate stints. . . .

But as cross-cultural training gains popularity, it attracts growing criticism. A lot of the training is garbage, argues Robert Bontempo, assistant professor of international business at Columbia University. Even customized family training offered by companies like Prudential Insurance Co. of America's Moran Stahl—which typically costs $6,000 for three days—hasn't been scientifically tested. "They charge a huge amount of money, and there's no evidence that these firms do any good" in lowering foreign-transfer flops, Prof. Bontempo contends.

"You don't need research" to prove that cross-cultural training works because so much money has been wasted on failed overseas assign-

ments, counters Gary Wederspahn, director of design and development at Moran Stahl.

General Motors agrees. Despite massive cost cutting lately, the auto giant still spends nearly $500,000 a year on cross-cultural training for about 150 Americans and their families headed abroad. "We think this substantially contributes to the low [premature] return rate" of less than 1% among GM expatriates, says Richard Rachner, GM general director of international personnel. That compares with a 25% rate at concerns that don't properly select and coach expatriates, he adds.

The Pilgers' experience reveals the benefits and drawbacks of such training. Mr. Pilger, a 38-year-old engineer employed by GM for 20 years, sought an overseas post but never lived abroad before. He finds the sessions "worthwhile" in readying him to run a vehicle-assembly plant that is 51% owned by Kenya's government. But he finds the training "horribly empty . . . in helping us prepare for the personal side of the move."

Dale and Nancy Pilger have just spent a week in Nairobi. But the executive's scant knowledge of Africa becomes clear when trainer Jackson Wolfe, a former Peace Corps official, mentions Nigeria. "Is that where Idi

G
lobalization of the economy challenges virtually all employees to become more internationally aware and adept. Those adventurous enough to accept a foreign assignment will experience the cross-cultural arena firsthand. Even employees who stay behind will find it hard to escape today's global economy. Many will be thrust into international relations by working for foreign-owned companies or by dealing with foreign suppliers, customers, and co-workers.

A case in point is the Japanese-owned Honda factory in Marysville, Ohio, that turns out Accord automobiles for sale in the United States and for export to 20 other countries.[1] To increase coordination between Honda's factory in Sayama, Japan, and the Ohio plant, Honda took the following unusual steps:

OPENING CASE

(concluded)

Amin was from?" Mr. Pilger asks The dictator ruled Uganda. With a sheepish smile, Mr. Pilger admits: "We don't know a lot about the world."

The couple's instructors don't always know everything about preparing expatriates for Kenyan culture, either. Mr. Midamba, an adjunct international-relations professor at Kent State University and son of a Kenyan political leader, concedes that he neglected to caution Mr. Pilger's predecessor against holding business dinners at Nairobi restaurants.

As a result, the American manager "got his key people to the restaurant and expected their wives to be there," Mr. Midamba recalls. But "the wives didn't show up." Married women in Kenya view restaurants "as places where you find prostitutes and loose morals," notes Mungai Kimani, another Kenyan trainer.

The blunder partly explains why Mr. Midamba goes to great lengths to teach the Pilgers the art of entertaining at home. Among his tips: Don't be surprised if guests arrive an hour early, an hour late or announce their departure four times.

The Moran Stahl program also zeros in on the family's adjustment (though not to Mr. Pilger's satisfaction). A family's poor adjustment causes more foreign-transfer failures than a manager's work performance. That is the Pilger's greatest fear because 14-year-old Christy and 16-year-old Eric bitterly oppose the move. The lanky, boyish-looking Mr. Pilger remembers Eric's tearful reaction as: " 'You'll have to arrest me if you think you're going to take me to Africa.' "

While distressed by his children's hostility, Mr. Pilger still believes living abroad will be a great growth experience for them. But he says he promised Eric that if "he's miserable" in Kenya, he can return to Ohio for his last year of high school next year.

To ease their adjustment, Christy and Eric receive separate training from their parents. The teens' activities include sampling Indian food (popular in Kenya) as well as learning how to ride Nairobi public buses, speak a little Swahili, and juggle, of all things.

By the training's last day, both youngsters grudgingly accept being uprooted from friends, her swim team, and his brand-new car. Going to Kenya "no longer seems like a death sentence," Christy says. Eric mumbles that he may volunteer at a wild-game reserve.

But their usually upbeat mother has become increasingly upset as she hears more about a country troubled by drought, poverty, and political unrest—where foreigners live behind walled fortresses. Now, at an international parenting session, she clashes with youth trainer Amy Kaplan over whether her offspring can safely ride Nairobi's public buses, even with Mrs. Pilger initially accompanying them.

"All the advice we've gotten is that it's deadly" to ride buses there, Mrs. Pilger frets. Ms. Kaplan retorts: "It's going to be hard" to let teen-agers do their own thing in Kenya, but then they'll be less likely to rebel. The remark fails to quell Mrs. Pilger's fears that she can't handle life abroad. "I'm going to let a lot of people down if I blow this," she adds, her voice quavering with emotion.

For Discussion

Did General Motors adequately prepare the Pilger family for the transfer to Kenya? Explain.

■ Additional discussion questions linking this case with the following material appear at the end of this chapter.

Source: J S Lublin, "Companies Use Cross-Cultural Training to Help Their Employees Adjust Abroad," *The Wall Street Journal*, August 4, 1992, pp B1, B6. Excerpted by permission of *The Wall Street Journal*, © 1992 Dow Jones & Company, Inc. All Rights Reserved Worldwide.

The North American Task Group—a core of about 50 Ohio workers and their families—lived in Japan for two to three years, working cheek-by-jowl with Accord designers. Before, engineers went to Japan for a few weeks, not enough time to build trust and improve communication with the Japanese.

''A lot can be lost in phone calls and faxes. But not if you're right there with the designers,'' paint engineer Terry Hegenderfer says.

Having the Ohio team in Japan also gave the stateside engineers familiar, English-speaking contacts when they had ideas or concerns. Less was lost in translation.

And having a Marysville crew in Japan helped make sure the new car could be built as easily in Ohio as in Sayama, Japan.[2]

Most members of the North American Task Group probably never imagined they and their families would live in Japan for two to three years when they were hired by Honda. By taking full advantage of an unexpected international opportunity, these Honda employees helped their company remain a respected global competitor.

The global economy is a rich mix of cultures, and the time to prepare to work in it is now. Accordingly, the purpose of this chapter is to help you take a step in that direction by exploring the impacts of culture in today's increasingly internationalized organization. This chapter draws upon the area of cultural anthropology. We begin with a model that shows how societal culture and organizational culture (covered in Chapter 19) combine to influence work behavior, followed by a fundamental cultural distinction. Next, we examine key dimensions of international OB with the goal of enhancing cross-cultural awareness. Practical lessons from cross-cultural management research are then reviewed. The chapter concludes by exploring the challenge of accepting a foreign assignment.

CULTURE AND ORGANIZATIONAL BEHAVIOR

How would you, as a manager, interpret the following situations?

An Asian executive for a multinational company, transferred from Taiwan to the Midwest, appears aloof and autocratic to his peers.

A West Coast bank embarks on a ''friendly teller'' campaign, but its Filipino female tellers won't cooperate.

A white manager criticizes a black male employee's work. Instead of getting an explanation, the manager is met with silence and a firm stare.[3]

If you attribute the behavior in these situations to personalities, three descriptions come to mind: arrogant, unfriendly, and hostile. These are reasonable conclusions. Unfortunately, they are probably wrong, being based more on prejudice and stereotypes than on actual fact. However, if you attribute the behavioral outcomes to *cultural* differences, you stand a better chance of making the following more valid interpretations: "As it turns out, Asian culture encourages a more distant managing style, Filipinos associate overly friendly behavior in women with prostitution, and blacks as a group act more deliberately, studying visual cues, than most white men."[4] One cannot afford to overlook relevant cultural contexts when trying to understand and manage organizational behavior.

Culture Defined

While noting that cultures exist in social units of all sizes (from civilizations to countries to ethnic groups to organizations to work groups), Edgar Schein defined **culture** as:

> A pattern of basic assumptions—invented, discovered, or developed by a given group as it learns to cope with its problems of external adaptation and internal integration—that has worked well enough to be considered valid and, therefore, to be taught to new members as the correct way to perceive, think, and feel in relation to those problems.[5]

culture Socially-derived, taken-for-granted assumptions about how to think and act.

The word *taught* needs to be interpreted carefully because it implies formal education or training. While cultural lessons may indeed be taught in schools, religious settings, and on the job, formal inculcation is secondary. Most cultural lessons are learned by observing and imitating role models as they go about their daily affairs or as observed in the media.[6]

Culture Is a Subtle but Pervasive Force

Culture generally remains below the threshold of conscious awareness because it involves *taken-for-granted assumptions* about how one should perceive, think, act, and feel. Cultural anthropologist Edward T Hall put it this way:

> Since much of culture operates outside our awareness, frequently we don't even know what we know. We pick . . . [expectations and assumptions] up in the cradle. We unconsciously learn what to notice and what not to notice, how to divide time and space, how to walk and talk and use our bodies, how to behave as men or women, how to relate to other people, how to handle responsibility, whether experience is seen as whole or fragmented. This applies to all people. The Chinese or the Japanese or the Arabs are as unaware of their assumptions as we are of our own. We each assume that they're part of human nature. What we think of as "mind" is really internalized culture.[7]

In sum, it has been said: "you are your culture, and your culture is you."

A Model of Societal and Organizational Cultures

As illustrated in Figure 2–1, culture influences organizational behavior in two ways. Employees bring their societal culture to work with them in the form of customs and language. Organizational culture, a by-product of societal culture, in turn affects the individual's values/ethics, attitudes, assumptions, and expectations.[8] The term *societal* culture is used here instead of national culture because the boundaries of many modern nation-states were not drawn along cultural lines. The former Soviet Union, for example, included 15 republics and more than 100 ethnic nationalities, many with their own distinct language.[9] Meanwhile, English-speaking Canadians in Vancouver are culturally closer to Americans in Seattle than to their French-speaking countrymen in Quebec. Societal culture is shaped by the various environmental factors listed in the left-hand side of Figure 2–1.

• FIGURE 2~1   Cultural Influences on Organizational Behavior

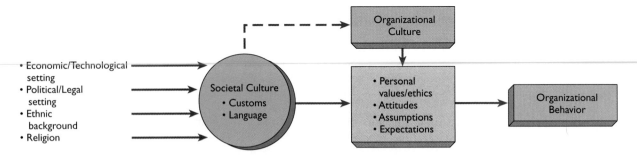

Source: Adapted in part from B J Punnett and S Withane, "Hofstede's Value Survey Module: To Embrace or Abandon?" in *Advances in International Comparative Management*, Vol 5, ed S B Prasad (Greenwich, CT: JAI Press, 1990), pp 69–89.

Once inside the organization's sphere of influence, the individual is further affected by the *organization's* culture. Mixing of societal and organizational cultures can produce interesting dynamics in multinational companies. For example, with French and American employees working side by side at General Electric's medical imaging production facility in Waukesha, Wisconsin, unit head Claude Benchimol has witnessed some culture shock:

> The French are surprised the American parking lots empty out as early as 5 PM; the Americans are surprised the French don't start work at 8 AM. Benchimol feels the French are more talkative and candid. Americans have more of a sense of hierarchy and are less likely to criticize. But they may be growing closer to the French. Says Benchimol: "It's taken a year to get across the idea that we are all entitled to say what we don't like to become more productive and work better."[10]

Same company, same company culture, yet GE's French and American co-workers have different attitudes about time, hierarchy, and communication. They are the products of different societal cultures.

When managing people at work, the individual's societal culture, the organizational culture, and any interaction between the two need to be taken into consideration. Otherwise, mistaken performance attributions will be a serious problem. For example, as detailed in the International OB, American workers' cultural orientation toward quality improvement differs significantly from the Japanese cultural pattern.

High-Context and Low-Context Societal Cultures

Cultural anthropologists believe interesting and valuable lessons can be learned by comparing one culture with another. Many models have been proposed for distinguishing among the world's rich variety of cultures. One general distinction contrasts high-context and low-context cultures[11] (see Figure 2–2). Managers in multicultural settings need to know the difference if they are to communicate and interact effectively.

high-context cultures
Primary meaning derived from nonverbal situational cues.

Reading between the Lines in High-Context Cultures   People from **high-context cultures** rely heavily on situational cues for meaning when perceiving and communicating with another person. Nonverbal cues such as one's official position or status convey messages more powerfully than do spoken words. Thus, we come

INTERNATIONAL OB

Quality: What Motivates American Workers?

As many companies have learned, managing for quality isn't easy. Now, the American Quality Foundation in New York City is kicking off a program to help industry. The program, dubbed "The Stuff Americans Are Made Of," is based on a new study of worker attitudes and behavior headed by psychologist G Clotaire Rapaille. Among the key findings:

- Unlike Japanese workers, Americans aren't interested in making small step-by-step improvements to increase quality. They want to achieve the breakthrough, the impossible dream. The way to motivate them: Ask for the big leap, rather than for tiny steps.
- Change is a threat to Americans when imposed from above but can be positive if workers feel they can

control it. Therefore, managers should talk to employees about the general goal and get them to suggest the changes necessary to achieve it.

- Whereas the Japanese tend to be methodical and rational in their relentless drive to improve things, Americans are more emotional. To improve quality, it's necessary to get US workers to feel they have a personal stake or are achieving things individually.

The right rewards are important, too. Instead of presenting tombstone-like plaques that imply the work is over, Rapaille concludes, companies should reward employees with a new tool that will help them do their jobs better—a laptop computer, for example. Although workers say they would

prefer bonuses, rewarding them with a new tool results in better performance, the study says.

- Americans learn by making mistakes. So it doesn't work when managers demand that workers get it right the first time. The other problem with perfection is that Americans view it as a dead end. Consequently, "zero-defects" carries a negative connotation. Instead, there has to be a mechanism for spreading news of mistakes and the lessons learned from them, so that everyone benefits.

Source: W D Marbach, "Quality: What Motivates American Workers?" *Business Week*, April 12, 1993, p 93. Reprinted from April 12, 1993 issue of *Business Week* by special permission, copyright © 1993 by McGraw-Hill, Inc.

• FIGURE 2-2   Contrasting High-Context and Low-Context Cultures

High-Context
- Establish social trust first
- Value personal relations and goodwill
- Agreement by general trust
- Negotiations slow and ritualistic

Low-Context
- Get down to business first
- Value expertise and performance
- Agreement by specific, legalistic contract
- Negotiations as efficient as possible

Source: M Munter, "Cross-Cultural Communication for Managers," *Business Horizons*, May–June 1993, Figure 3, p 72.

to better understand the ritual of exchanging *and reading* business cards in Japan. Japanese culture is relatively high-context. One's business card, listing employer and official position, conveys vital silent messages to members of Japan's homogeneous society. An intercultural communications authority explains:

> Nearly all communication in Japan takes place within an elaborate and vertically organized social structure. Everyone has a distinct place within this framework. Rarely do people converse without knowing, or determining, who is above and who is below them. Associates are always older or younger, male or female, subordinate or superior. And these distinctions all carry implications for the form of address, choice of words, physical distance, and demeanor. As a result, conversation tends to reflect this formal hierarchy.[12]

Verbal and written communication in high-context cultures such as China, Korea, and Japan are secondary to taken-for-granted cultural assumptions about other people.

low-context cultures
Primary meaning derived from written and spoken words.

Reading the Fine Print in Low-Context Cultures   In **low-context cultures,** written and spoken words carry the burden of shared meaning. True, people in low-context cultures read nonverbal messages from body language, dress, status, and belongings. However, they tend to double-check their perceptions and assumptions verbally. To do so in China or Japan would be to gravely insult the other person, thus causing them to *lose face.* Their positions on the continuum in Figure 2–2 indicate the German preoccupation with written rules for even the finest details of behavior and the American preoccupation with precise legal documents. In high-context cultures, agreements tend to be made on the basis of someone's word or a handshake, after a rather prolonged trust-building period. European-Americans, who have been taught from birth not to take anything for granted, see the handshake as a prelude to demanding a signature on a detailed, lawyer-approved, iron-clad contract.

Implications for a Diverse Work Force   High- and low-context cultural differences can be found in countries with heterogeneous populations such as the United States, Australia, and Canada. African-Americans, Asian-Americans, and Native Americans tend to be higher-context than Americans of European descent. This helps explain our earlier example of the white manager's frustration with the black employee's nonverbal response. Culture dictates how people communicate. The white manager's ignorance of (or insensitivity to) the black employee's cultural context blocked effective communication. (Managing diversity is discussed in detail in the next chapter.)

TOWARD GREATER CROSS-CULTURAL AWARENESS

Aside from being high- or low-context, cultures stand apart in other ways as well. Let us briefly review the following basic factors that vary from culture to culture: time, interpersonal space, language, and religion.[13] This list is intended to be indicative rather than exhaustive. Separately or together these factors can foster huge cross-cultural gaps. Effective multicultural management often depends on whether or not these gaps can be bridged.

A qualification needs to be offered at this juncture. It is important to view all of the cultural differences in this chapter and elsewhere as *tendencies* and *patterns,* rather than as absolutes. As soon as one falls into the trap of assuming *all* Germans are this, *all* British are that, and so on, potentially instructive generalizations become mindless stereotypes.[14] Well-founded cultural generalizations are fundamental to successfully doing business in other cultures. But one needs to be constantly alert to *individuals* who are exceptions to the local cultural rule. For instance, it is possible to encounter talkative and aggressive Japanese and quiet and deferential Americans who simply do not fit their respective cultural molds. Also, tipping the scale against clear cultural differences are space age transportation; global telecommunications, television, and computer networks; tourism; global marketing; and entertainment. These areas are homogenizing the peoples of the world. The result, according to experts on the subject, is an emerging "world culture" in which, someday, people may be more alike than different.[15]

In monochronic cultures such as Germany, the United States, and Canada, time is treated like money. It is *spent, saved,* or *wasted*—terms commonly used when discussing money.

Richard Schneider/The Image Bank

Cultural Perceptions of Time

In North American and Northern European cultures, time seems to be a simple matter. It is linear, relentlessly marching forward, never backward, in standardized chunks. To the American who received a watch for his or her third birthday, time is like money. It is spent, saved, or wasted.[16] Americans are taught to show up 10 minutes early for appointments. When working across cultures, however, time becomes a very complex matter.[17] Imagine a New Yorker's chagrin when left in a waiting room for 45 minutes, only to find a Latin American government official dealing with three other people at once. The North American resents the lack of prompt and undivided attention. The Latin American official resents the North American's impatience and apparent self-centeredness. This vicious cycle of resentment can be explained by the distinction between **monochronic time** and **polychronic time.**

> The former is revealed in the ordered, precise, schedule-driven, use of public time that typifies and even caricatures efficient Northern Europeans and North Americans. The latter is seen in the multiple and cyclical activities and concurrent involvement with different people in Mediterranean, Latin American, and especially Arab cultures.[18]

Monochronic and polychronic are relative rather than absolute concepts. Generally, the more things a person tends to do at once, the more polychronic they are.[19] Monochronic people prefer to do one thing at a time. What is your attitude toward time? (You can find out by completing the Polychronic Attitude Index in the OB Exercise.)

Low-context cultures, such as that of the United States, tend to run on monochronic time while high-context cultures, such as that of Mexico, tend to run on polychronic time. People in polychronic cultures view time as flexible, fluid, and multidimensional. The Germans and Swiss have made an exact science of monochronic time. In fact, a new radio-controlled watch made by a German company, Junghans, is "guaranteed to lose no more than one second in 1 million years."[20] Many a visitor has been a minute late for a Swiss train, only to see its taillights leaving the station. Time is more elastic in polychronic cultures. During the Islamic holy month of Ramadan in Middle Eastern nations, for example, the faithful fast

monochronic time
Preference for doing one thing at a time because time is limited, precisely segmented, and schedule driven.

polychronic time
Preference for doing more than one thing at a time because time is flexible and multidimensional.

OB EXERCISE

The Polychronic Attitude Index

Please consider how you feel about the following statements. Circle your choice on the scale provided: strongly agree, agree, neutral, disagree, or strongly disagree.

	Strongly Disagree	Disagree	Neutral	Agree	Strongly Agree
I do not like to juggle several activities at the same time.	5 points	4 pts	3 pts	2 pts	1 pt
People should not try to do many things at once.	5 pts	4 pts	3 pts	2 pts	1 pt
When I sit down at my desk, I work on one project at a time.	5 pts	4 pts	3 pts	2 pts	1 pt
I am comfortable doing several things at the same time.	1 pt	2 pts	3 pts	4 pts	5 pts

Add up your points, and divide the total by 4. Then plot your score on the scale below.

1.0	1.5	2.0	2.5	3.0	3.5	4.0	4.5	5.0
Monochronic								Polychronic

The lower your score (below 3.0), the more monochronic your orientation; and the higher your score (above 3.0), the more polychronic.

Source: A C Bluedorn, C F Kaufman, and P M Lane, "How Many Things Do You Like to Do at Once? An Introduction to Monochronic and Polychronic Time," *Academy of Management Executive,* November 1992, exhibit two, p 20.

during daylight hours, and the general pace of things markedly slows. Managers need to reset their mental clocks when doing business across cultures.

Interpersonal Space

Anthropologist Edward T Hall noticed a connection between culture and preferred interpersonal distance. People from high-context cultures were observed standing close when talking to someone. Low-context cultures appeared to dictate a greater amount of interpersonal space. Hall applied the term **proxemics** to the study of cultural expectations about interpersonal space.[21] He specified four interpersonal distance zones. Some call them space bubbles. They are *intimate* distance, *personal* distance, *social* distance, and *public* distance. Ranges for the four interpersonal distance zones are illustrated in Figure 2–3, along with selected cultural differences.

North American business conversations normally are conducted at about a 3- to 4-foot range, within the personal zone in Figure 2–3. A range of approximately one foot is common in Latin American and Asian cultures, uncomfortably close for Northern Europeans and North Americans. Arabs like to get even closer. Mis-

proxemics Hall's term for the study of cultural expectations about interpersonal space.

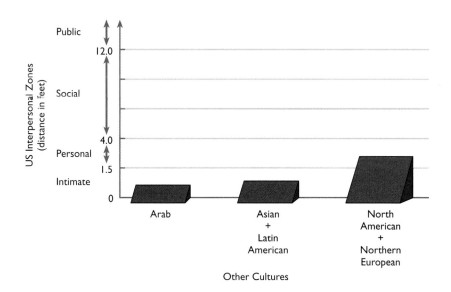

• ⟶ FIGURE 2~3
Interpersonal Distance
Zones for Business
Conversations Vary from
Culture to Culture

matches in culturally dictated interpersonal space zones can prove very distracting for the unprepared. Hall explains:

> Arabs tend to get very close and breathe on you. It's part of the high sensory involvement of a high-context culture. . . .
>
> The American on the receiving end can't identify all the sources of his discomfort but feels that the Arab is pushy. The Arab comes close, the American backs up. The Arab follows, because he can only interact at certain distances. Once the American learns that Arabs handle space differently and that breathing on people is a form of communication, the situation can sometimes be redefined so the American relaxes.[22]

Asian and Middle-Eastern hosts grow weary of having to seemingly chase their low-context guests around at social gatherings to maintain what they feel is proper conversational range. Backing up all evening to keep conversational partners at a proper distance is an awkward experience as well. Awareness of cultural differences, along with skillful accommodation, are essential to productive intercultural business dealings.

Language

More than 3,000 different languages are spoken worldwide. What is the connection between these languages and information processing and behavior? There is an ongoing debate among anthropologists concerning the extent to which language influences perception and behavior. On one side of the argument, the *relativists* claim each language fosters unique perceptions. On the other side, *universalists* state that all languages share common elements and thus foster common thought processes and perceptions. A study involving subjects from eight countries attempted to resolve this debate. Subjects from the United States, Britain, Italy, Greece, former Yugoslavia, Pakistan, Hong Kong, and Vietnam were shown 15 flash cards, each printed with three pairs of words. Language experts certified the various translations as accurate. The idea was to see if adults from different cultures, speaking different languages, would perceive the same semantic elements in the paired words. Illustrative semantic elements, or basic language building blocks, are: opposite = alive/dead; similar = furniture/bed. The researchers found ''considerable cross-cultural agreement on the meaning and use of semantic relations.''[23] Greatest agreement was found for semantic opposites (e.g., alive/dead). These findings tip the scale in favor of the universalists. We await additional research evidence for a definitive answer.

Meanwhile, international managers say there is no substitute for knowing the local language. Scott Latham, president of a US–Japan trade consulting firm, offered this assessment:

> Mutual cultural understanding between the United States and Japan is crucial to better business and improved relations between the two countries. Unfortunately, the Japanese for the most part are miles ahead of us Americans in this department, a factor that accounts for much of the current economic and political tension between us.
>
> Historically, Japanese businessmen had to learn English in order to develop markets in this country, and the Japanese have spent years living in the United States and learning our customs, business regulations, and way of life. We Americans, however, have been slow to make the same effort to learn about Japan.[24]

An American friend of the authors recently stunned and pleased his Motorola co-workers by doing his quarterly report in Japanese, after less than a year in Japan. There reportedly wasn't a dry eye in the room.

For those Americans who claim English has become the universal language of business, there is still no getting around the need for cross-cultural familiarity (see the International OB).

Religion

Religious beliefs and practices can have a profound effect on cross-cultural relations. A comprehensive treatment of different religions is beyond the scope of our present discussion. However, we can examine the relationship between religious affiliation and work-related values. A study of 484 international students at a Midwestern US university uncovered wide variability. The following list gives the most important work-related value for each of five religious affiliations:

Catholic—Consideration (''Concern that employees be taken seriously, be kept informed, and that their judgments be used.'')
Protestant—Employer effectiveness (''Desire to work for a company that is efficient, successful, and a technological leader.'')
Buddhist—Social responsibility (''Concern that the employer be a responsible part of society.'')
Muslim—Continuity (''Desire for stable environment, job longevity, reduction of uncertainty.'')
No religious preference—Professional challenge (''Concern with having a job that provides learning opportunities and opportunities to use skills well.'')[25]

Thus, there was virtually *no agreement* across religions about the primary work value. This led the researchers to conclude: ''Employers might be wise to consider the impact that religious differences (and more broadly, cultural factors) appear to have on the values of employee groups.''[26] Of course, in the United States and other selected countries, equal employment opportunity laws forbid managers from basing employment-related decisions on an applicant's religious preference.

INTERNATIONAL OB

Watch Your Language in the Caribbean

Among the first words a foreigner is apt to hear on a visit to Haiti are: *"Blan, sa k' pase? Ki sa ou ap fe an Ayiti?"* Or a visitor in Jamaica might overhear this exchange: *"Me a gaa a tung." "Wa mek?" "Mi a gaa one flim."*

In the first instance, the Haitian is asking: "Stranger, what's happening? What are you doing in Haiti?"

In the Jamaican exchange, the first speaker says, "I am going to town." He is asked "Why?" The answer: "I'm going to a movie."

The languages being used are Haitian Creole and Jamaican Patois, the two most extensive and organized of the several tongues of the Caribbean region.

Formally, those Caribbean countries, such as Jamaica, that were once ruled as British colonies use English as their official language; Martinique and Guadeloupe use the language of their former French masters. Haiti, also a onetime French colony, uses both French and Creole as official languages. In addition, Spanish is the language of Cuba and the Dominican Republic, while Dutch is spoken on a few islands.

But what marks of all these places—with the exception of the largely monolingual Dominican Repub-lic and Cuba—is the presence of a second, local tongue that overwhelms the official language in everyday use, even among the elite of the different societies.

The disparity forms the basis of an increasingly important regional dispute involving political and economic power, race and class divisions, and national esteem. There is a growing movement to give the local tongues official status and equality with European languages.

On the one side, some speakers of what are considered the more established, traditional languages think that what they hear in Creole or Patois are quaint variations, essentially corruptions of French and English.

These people share the view of Sir Harry Johnston, an English anthropologist who wrote in a 1910 study of black life in the Caribbean that Patois "is a barbarous and clumsy jargon."

To others, particularly the residents of the Caribbean, Creole and Patois are independent languages with their own characters and values—systems of communication just as sophisticated as standard English or French and far more appropriate to the lives, experiences, and images of the region.

In Haiti, for instance, close to 100% of the country's 6 million people speak Creole, with at least 85% using it as their only language and only 2% monolingual in French.

And with its development over the centuries into a written language, Creole increasingly is the vehicle for literature and the broadcast media in spite of pressure by some of the nation's elite to maintain social and economic control by restricting education, politics and high-level business to French.

In Jamaica, where 90% of the people speak Patois, and in the other so-called English-speaking Caribbean nations, Patois is heard more and more on the radio, in songs, and even used in newspapers previously noted for their proper, even old-fashioned Standard English.

As a result, pressure is increasing to declare Patois an official language, to use it as the basis of education and give it equality in business and politics.

Source: Excerpted from K Freed, "Carib-bean*speak*," *Los Angeles Times,* May 11, 1993, pp H1, H5. Copyright, 1993, *Los Angeles Times.* Reprinted by permission.

Nancy Adler, an international OB specialist at Canada's McGill University, has offered the following introductory definition. "**Cross-cultural management**" studies the behavior of people in organizations around the world and trains people to work in organizations with employee and client populations from several cultures."[27] Inherent in this definition are three steps: (1) understand cultural differences, (2) identify culturally appropriate management practices, and (3) teach cross-cultural management lessons. The cross-cultural studies discussed in this section contribute to all three.

The Hofstede~Bond Stream of Research

Instructive insights surfaced in the mid-1980s when the results of two very different cross-cultural management studies were merged. The first study was conducted

PRACTICAL INSIGHTS FROM CROSS-CULTURAL MANAGEMENT RESEARCH

cross-cultural management Understanding and teaching behavioral patterns in different cultures.

under the guidance of Dutch researcher Geert Hofstede. Canadian Michael Harris Bond, at the Chinese University of Hong Kong, was a key researcher in the second study. What follows is a brief overview of each study, a discussion of the combined results, and a summary of important practical implications.

The Two Studies   Hofstede's study is a classic in the annals of cross-cultural management research.[28] He drew his data for that study from a collection of 116,000 attitude surveys administered to IBM employees worldwide between 1967 and 1973. Respondents to the attitude survey, that also asked questions on cultural values and beliefs, included IBM employees from 72 countries. Fifty-three cultures eventually were analyzed and contrasted according to four cultural dimensions. Hofstede's database was unique, not only because of its large size, but also because it allowed him to isolate cultural effects. If his subjects had not performed *similar jobs* in *different countries* for the *same company,* no such control would have been possible. Cross-cultural comparisons were made along the first four dimensions listed in Table 2–1, power distance, individualism–collectivism,[29] masculinity–femininity, and uncertainty avoidance.

Bond's study was much smaller, involving a survey of 100 (50 percent women) students from 22 countries and 5 continents. The survey instrument was the Chinese Value Survey (CVS), based on the Rokeach Value Survey discussed in Chapter 4.[30] The CVS also tapped four cultural dimensions. Three corresponded to Hofstede's first three in Table 2–1. Hofstede's fourth cultural dimension, uncertainty avoidance, was not measured by the CVS. Instead, Bond's study isolated the fifth cultural dimension in Table 2–1. It eventually was renamed *long-term versus short-term orientation* to reflect how strongly a person believes in the long-term thinking promoted by the teachings of the Chinese philosopher Confucius (551–479 BC). According to a recent update by Hofstede: ''On the long-term side one finds values oriented towards the future, like thrift (saving) and persistence. On the short-term side one finds values rather oriented towards the past and present, like respect for tradition and fulfilling social obligations.''[31] Importantly, one may embrace Confucian long-term values without knowing a thing about Confucius.

East Meets West   By merging the two studies, a serious flaw in each was corrected. Namely, Hofstede's study had an inherent Anglo-European bias and Bond's study had a built-in Asian bias. How would cultures compare if viewed through the overlapping lenses of the two studies? Hofstede and Bond were able to answer that question because 18 countries in Bond's study overlapped the 53

◣ • TABLE 2–1
Key Cultural Dimensions in the Hofstede–Bond Studies

Power distance: How much do people expect inequality in social institutions (e.g., family, work organizations, government)?

Individualism–collectivism: How loose or tight is the bond between individuals and societal groups?

Masculinity–femininity: To what extent do people embrace competitive masculine traits (e.g., success, assertiveness and performance) or nurturing feminine traits (e.g., solidarity, personal relationships, service, quality of life)?

Uncertainty avoidance: To what extent do people prefer structured versus unstructured situations?

Long-term versus short-term orientation (Confucian values): To what extent are people oriented toward the future by saving and being persistent versus being oriented toward the present and past by respecting tradition and meeting social obligations?

Source: Adapted from discussion in G Hofstede, "Cultural Constraints in Management Theories," *Academy of Management Executive,* February 1993, pp 81–94.

countries in Hofstede's sample.[32] Table 2–2 lists the countries scoring highest on each of the five cultural dimensions. (Countries earning between 67 and 100 points on a 0–100 relative ranking scale qualified as ''high'' for Table 2–2.) The United States scored the highest in individualism, moderate in power distance, masculinity, and uncertainty avoidance, and low in long-term orientation.

Practical Lessons Individually, and together, the Hofstede and Bond studies yielded the following useful lessons for international managers:

1. Due to varying cultural values, management theories and practices need to be adapted to the local culture. This is particularly true for made-in-America management theories (e.g., Maslow's need hierarchy theory) and Japanese management practices.

2. High long-term orientation was the only one of the five cultural dimensions to correlate positively with national economic growth. (Notice how the four Asian countries listed under high long-term orientation in Table 2–2 have been the world's economic growth leaders over the last 25 years.) This correlation does not bode well for countries scoring lowest on this dimension: Pakistan, Philippines, Canada, Great Britain, and the United States.

3. Industrious cultural values are a necessary but insufficient condition for economic growth. Markets and a supportive political climate also are required to create the right mix. (Thus, Hong Kong's economic success may be at risk because of the pending 1997 takeover by China.)

4. Cultural arrogance is a luxury individuals and nations can no longer afford in a global economy.

A Contingency Model for Cross-Cultural Leadership

If a manager has a favorite leadership style in his or her own culture, will that style be equally appropriate in another culture? According to a recently proposed model that built upon Hofstede's work, the answer is ''not necessarily.''[33] Four leadership styles—directive, supportive, participative, and achievement—were matched with variations of three of Hofstede's cultural dimensions. The dimensions used were power distance, individualism–collectivism, and uncertainty avoidance.

• ↙ **TABLE 2–2**
Countries Scoring the Highest in the Hofstede–Bond Studies

High Power Distance	High Individualism	High Masculinity	High Uncertainty Avoidance	High Long-term Orientation**
Philippines	United States	Japan	Japan	Hong Kong
India	Australia		Korea	Taiwan
Singapore	Great Britain		Brazil	Japan
Brazil	Netherlands		Pakistan	Korea
Hong Kong	Canada		Taiwan	
	New Zealand			
	Sweden			
	Germany*			

* Former West Germany
** Originally called Confucian Dynamism.

Source: Adapted from Exhibit 2 in G Hofstede and M H Bond, ''The Confucius Connection: From Cultural Roots to Economic Growth,'' *Organizational Dynamics*, Spring 1988, pp 12–13.

By combining this model with Hofstede's and Bond's findings, we derived the useful contingency model for cross-cultural leadership in Table 2–3. Participative leadership turned out to be culturally appropriate for all 18 countries. Importantly, this does *not* mean that the participative style is necessarily the *best* style of leadership in cross-cultural management. It simply has broad applicability. One exception surfaced in a recent study in Russia's largest textile mill. The researchers found that both rewarding good performance with American-made goods and motivating performance with feedback and positive reinforcement improved output. But an employee participation program actually made performance *worse*. This may have been due to the Russians' lack of faith in participative schemes, which were found to be untrustworthy in the past.[34]

Also of note, with the exception of France, the directive style appears to be culturally *inappropriate* in North America, Northern Europe, Australia, and New Zealand. Some locations, such as Hong Kong and the Philippines, require great leadership versatility. Leadership needs to be matched to the prevailing cultural climate. (We will discuss leadership further in Chapter 15.)

Interpersonal Conflict-Handling Styles

In a cross-cultural study of Jordanian, Turkish, and US managers, the collaborative (problem-solving) style of handling interpersonal *conflict* emerged as the preferred option in all three cultures. Beyond that there was general disagreement about which backup styles were most appropriate.[35] One practical lesson from this study is that even when we find commonalities across cultures, care needs to be taken not to gloss over underlying differences. (Conflict management is covered in detail in Chapter 10.)

▪ TABLE 2–3
A Contingency Model for Cross-Cultural Leadership

Country	Most Culturally Appropriate Leadership Behaviors			
	Directive	**Supportive**	**Participative**	**Achievement**
Australia		X	X	X
Brazil	X		X	
Canada		X	X	X
France	X		X	
Germany*		X	X	X
Great Britain		X	X	X
Hong Kong	X	X	X	X
India	X		X	X
Italy	X	X	X	
Japan	X	X	X	
Korea	X	X	X	
Netherlands		X	X	X
New Zealand			X	X
Pakistan	X	X	X	
Philippines	X	X	X	X
Sweden			X	X
Taiwan	X	X	X	
United States		X	X	X

* Former West Germany.

Sources: Adapted in part from C A Rodrigues, "The Situation and National Culture as Contingencies for Leadership Behavior: Two Conceptual Models," in *Advances in International Comparative Management* vol. 5, ed S B Prasad (Greenwich, CT: JAI Press, 1990), pp 51–68; and G Hofstede and M H Bond, "The Confucius Connection: From Cultural Roots to Economic Growth," *Organizational Dynamics*, Spring 1988, pp 4–21.

Increasingly, the career path to the executive suite requires one or more successful foreign assignments. All three chief executive officers of America's Big Three auto makers—General Motors, Ford, and Chrysler—spent time managing operations in Europe. As the reach of global companies continues to grow, many opportunities for living and working in foreign countries will arise. Imagine, for example, the opportunities for foreign duty and cross-cultural experiences at Coca-Cola. Sixty-five percent of the Atlanta-based company's sales come from doing business in 195 countries outside the United States.[36] Thus, the purpose of this final section is to help you prepare yourself and others to work successfully in foreign countries.

PREPARING EMPLOYEES FOR SUCCESSFUL FOREIGN ASSIGNMENTS

Why Do US Expatriates Fail in Foreign Assignments?

As we use the term here, **expatriate** refers to anyone living and/or working outside their home country. Hence, they are said to be *expatriated* when transferred to another country and *repatriated* when transferred back home. Cross-cultural expert Rosalie L Tung, drawing upon her own and others' research, concluded that 30 percent of the foreign transfers by US multinational companies turn out to be mistakes. The figures for European and Japanese companies are generally below 5 percent.[37] A "mistake," in this context, means the employee does not perform adequately for the *full* term of his or her foreign assignment. The cost of these failed foreign assignments, estimated at $2 to $2.5 billion annually, is a huge competitive disadvantage for US companies.[38]

expatriate Anyone living or working in a foreign country.

Research has uncovered specific reasons for the failure of US expatriate managers. Listed in decreasing order of frequency, the seven most common reasons are

1. The manager's spouse cannot adjust to new physical or cultural surroundings.
2. The manager cannot adapt to new physical or cultural surroundings.
3. Family problems.
4. The manager is emotionally immature.
5. The manager cannot cope with foreign duties.
6. The manager is not technically competent.
7. The manager lacks the proper motivation for a foreign assignment.[39]

Collectively, *family and personal adjustment problems,* not technical competence, are the main stumbling block for American managers working in foreign countries. US multinational companies clearly need to do a better job of preparing employees and their families for foreign assignments. Unfortunately, as recently as 1992, 57 percent of US companies surveyed had no formal program for preparing expatriates.[40]

The Global Manager

On any given day in today's global economy, a manager can interact with colleagues from several different countries or cultures. For instance, at PolyGram, the British music company, the top 33 managers are from 15 different countries.[41] If they are to be effective, managers in such multicultural situations need to develop *global* skills (see Table 2–4).

Importantly, these global skills will help managers in culturally diverse countries such as the United States and Canada do a more effective job on a day-to-day basis. (We will discuss managing diversity in more detail in the next chapter.)

• TABLE 2–4
Global Skills for Global
Managers

Skill	Description
Global perspective	Broaden focus from one or two countries to a global business perspective.
Cultural responsiveness	Become familiar with many cultures.
Appreciate cultural synergies	Learn the dynamics of multicultural situations.
Cultural adaptability	Be able to live and work effectively in many different cultures.
Cross-cultural communication	Engage in cross-cultural interaction every day, whether at home or in a foreign country.
Cross-cultural collaboration	Work effectively in multicultural teams where everyone is equal.
Acquire broad foreign experience	Move up the career ladder by going from one foreign country to another, instead of taking frequent home-country assignments.

Source: Adapted from N J Adler and S Bartholomew, "Managing Globally Competent People," *Academy of Management Executive*, August 1992, table I, pp 52–65.

Avoiding OB Trouble Spots in Foreign Assignments

Finding the right person (often along with a supportive and adventurous family) for a foreign position is a complex, time consuming, and costly process.[42] For our purposes, it is sufficient to narrow the focus to common OB trouble spots in the foreign assignment cycle. As illustrated in Figure 2–4, the first and last stages of the cycle occur at home. The middle two stages occur in the foreign or host country. Each stage hides an OB-related trouble spot that needs to be anticipated and neutralized. Otherwise, the bill for another failed foreign assignment will grow.

Avoiding Unrealistic Expectations with Cross-Cultural Training   Realistic job previews (RJPs) have proven effective at bringing people's unrealistic expectations about a pending job assignment down to earth by providing a realistic balance of good and bad news. People with realistic expectations tend to quit less often and be more satisfied than those with unrealistic expectations. RJPs are a must for future expatriates. In addition, cross-cultural training is required.

cross-cultural training
Structured experiences to help people adjust to a new culture/country.

   Cross-cultural training is any type of structured experience designed to help departing employees adjust to a foreign culture. As documented in the opening case at the beginning of the chapter, the trend is toward more such training. Although costly, companies believe cross-cultural training is less expensive than failed foreign assignments. Programs vary widely in type and also in rigor.[43] Of course, the greater the difficulty, the greater the time and expense.

- *Easiest.* Predeparture training is limited to informational materials, including books, lectures, films, and videos.
- *Moderately difficult.* Experiential training is conducted through case studies, role playing, assimilators (simulated intercultural incidents), and introductory language instruction.
- *Most difficult.* Departing employees are given some combination of the preceding methods plus comprehensive language instruction and field experience in the target culture. As an example of the latter, PepsiCo Inc. transfers "about 25 young foreign managers a year to the US for one-year assignments in bottling plants"[44]

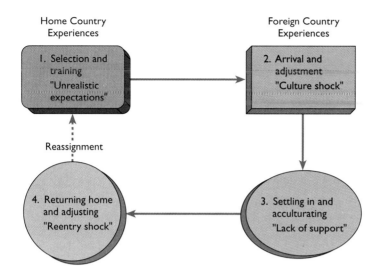

E 2~4The Foreign Assignment Cycle (with OB Trouble Spots)

Which approach is the best? Research to date does not offer a final answer. One study involving US employees in South Korea led the researcher to recommend a *combination* of informational and experiential predeparture training.[45] As a general rule of thumb, the more rigorous the cross-cultural training, the better. Our personal experience with teaching OB to foreign students both in the United States and abroad reminds us that there really is no substitute for an intimate knowledge of the local language and culture.

Avoiding Culture Shock   Have you ever been in a totally unfamiliar situation and felt disoriented and perhaps a bit frightened? If so, you already know something about culture shock. According to anthropologists, **culture shock** involves anxiety and doubt caused by an overload of unfamiliar expectations and social cues.[46] College freshmen often experience a variation of culture shock. An expatriate manager, or family member, may be thrown off balance by an avalanche of strange sights, sounds, and behaviors. Among them may be unreadable road signs, strange-tasting food, inability to use your left hand for social activities (in Islamic countries, the left hand is the toilet hand), or failure to get a laugh with your sure-fire joke. For the expatriate manager trying to concentrate on the fine details of a business negotiation, culture shock is more than an embarrassing inconvenience. It is a disaster! Like the confused college freshman who quits and goes home, culture-shocked employees often panic and go home early.

culture shock Anxiety and doubt caused by an overload of new expectations and cues.

The best defense against culture shock is comprehensive cross-cultural training, including intensive language study. Once again, the only way to pick up subtle—yet important—social cues is via the local language. Quantum, the Milpitas, California, maker of computer hard-disk drives has close ties to its manufacturing partner in Japan, Matsushita-Kotobuki Electronics (MKE).

MKE is constantly proposing changes in design that make new disk drives easier to manufacture. When the product is ready for production, 8 to 10 Quantum engineers descend on MKE's plant in western Japan for at least a month. To smooth teamwork, Quantum is offering courses in Japanese language and culture, down to mastering etiquette at a tea ceremony.[47]

This type of program reduces culture shock by taking the anxiety-producing mystery out of an unfamiliar culture.

Support During the Foreign Assignment   Especially during the first six months, when everything is so new to the expatriate, a support system needs to be in place. *Host-country sponsors,* assigned to individual managers or families, are recommended because they serve as ''cultural seeing-eye dogs.'' In a foreign country, where even the smallest errand can turn into an utterly exhausting production, sponsors can get things done quickly because they know the cultural and geographical territory. Honda's Ohio employees, mentioned at the opening of the chapter, enjoyed the help of family sponsors in Japan:

> Honda smoothed the way with Japanese wives who once lived in the US. They handled emergencies such as when Diana Jett's daughter Ashley needed stitches in her chin. When Task Force Senior Manager Kim Smalley's daughter, desperate to fit in at elementary school, had to have a precisely shaped bag for her harmonica, a Japanese volunteer stayed up late to make it.[48]

Avoiding Reentry Shock   Strange as it may seem, many otherwise successful expatriate managers encounter their first major difficulty only after their foreign assignment is over. Why? Returning to one's native culture is taken for granted because it seems so routine and ordinary. But having adjusted to another country's way of doing things for an extended period of time can put one's own culture and surroundings in a strange new light. Three areas for potential reentry shock are work, social activities, and general environment (e.g., politics, climate, transportation, food).

Work-related adjustments were found to be a major problem for samples of repatriated Finnish, Japanese, and American employees.[49] Upon being repatriated, a 12-year veteran of one US company said: ''Our organizational culture was turned upside down. We now have a different strategic focus, different 'tools' to get the job done, and different buzz words to make it happen. I had to learn a whole new corporate 'language.' ''[50] Reentry shock can be reduced through employee career counseling and home-country sponsors. Simply being aware of the problem of reentry shock is a big step toward effectively dealing with it.

Overall, the key to a successful foreign assignment is making it a well-integrated link in a career chain rather than treating it as an isolated adventure.

BACK TO THE OPENING CASE

Now that you have read Chapter 2, you should be able to answer the following questions about the General Motors/Kenya case:

1. What would you like to tell General Motors' employees in Kenya about working effectively with Americans?
2. Has General Motors done a good job of preparing the Pilger family for an assignment in Kenya? Explain.
3. If you were a cross-cultural consultant, what advice would you give General Motors about preparing employees and their families for foreign assignments?
4. Putting yourself in Dale Pilger's place, would you accept the transfer to Kenya? Explain. Putting yourself in Nancy Pilger's place, would you agree to moving the family to Kenya? Explain.

SUMMARY OF KEY CONCEPTS

1. *Explain how societal culture and organizational culture combine to influence on-the-job behavior.* Culture involves the taken-for-granted assumptions collections of people have about how they should think, act, and feel. Key aspects of societal culture, such as customs and language, are brought to work by the individual. Working together, societal and organizational culture influence the person's values, ethics, attitudes, and expectations.

2. *Distinguish between high-context and low-context cultures.* People from high-context cultures place heavy emphasis on nonverbal cues when communicating. People from low-context cultures infer relatively less from situational cues and extract more meaning from spoken and written words. In high-context cultures such as China and Japan, managers prefer slow negotiations and trust-building meetings, which tends to frustrate low-context Northern Europeans and North Americans who prefer to get right down to business.

3. *Explain the difference between monochronic and polychronic cultures.* People in monochronic cultures are schedule driven and prefer to do one thing at a time. To them, time is like money; it is spent wisely or wasted. In polychronic cultures, there is a tendency to do many things at once and to perceive time as flexible and multidimensional. Polychronic people view monochronic people as being too preoccupied with time.

4. *Discuss the cultural implications of interpersonal space, language, and religion.* Anthropologist Edward Hall coined the term *proxemics* to refer to the study of cultural expectations about interpersonal space. Asians and Latin Americans like to stand close (6 inches to 1 foot) during business conversations, while North Americans and Northern Europeans prefer a larger interpersonal distance (3 to 4 feet). Conflicting expectations about proper interpersonal distance can create awkward cross-cultural situations. Research uncovered a high degree of agreement about semantic elements across eight cultures. Another study found no agreement about the primary work value across five different religious preference groups.

5. *Describe the practical lessons from the Hofstede–Bond cross-cultural studies.* According to the Hofstede–Bond cross-cultural management studies, caution needs to be exercised when transplanting management theories and practices from one culture to another. Also, long-term orientation was the only one of five cultural dimensions in the Hofstede–Bond studies to correlate positively with national economic growth.

6. *Explain what cross-cultural studies have found about leadership and conflict-handling styles.* One cross-cultural management study suggests the need to vary leadership styles from one culture to another. The participative style turned out to be the only leadership style applicable in all 18 countries studied. Another cross-cultural management study of Jordanian, Turkish, and US managers found a common preference for the collaborative problem-solving conflict-handling style. But backup styles varied.

7. *Specify why US managers have a comparatively high failure rate in foreign assignments, and identify skills needed by today's global managers.* American expatriates are troubled by family and personal adjustment problems. Experts say global managers need the following skills: global perspective, cultural responsiveness, appreciation of cultural synergies, cultural adaptability, cross-cultural communication, cross-cultural collaboration, and broad foreign experience.

8. *Discuss the importance of cross-cultural training relative to the foreign assignment cycle.* The foreign assignment cycle has four stages: selection and training, arrival and adjustment, settling in and acculturating, and returning home and adjusting. Cross-cultural training, preferably combining informational and experiential predeparture sessions, can help expatriates avoid two OB trouble spots: unrealistic expectations and culture shock. There are no adequate substitutes for knowing the local language and culture.

DISCUSSION QUESTIONS

1. What are your expectations about being affected by the global economy?

2. Regarding your cultural awareness, how would you describe the prevailing culture in your country to a stranger from another land?

3. What is your personal experience with cross-cultural dealings? What lessons have you learned?

4. Why are people from high-context cultures such as China and Japan likely to be misunderstood by low-context Westerners?

5. Based on your score on the Polychronic Attitude Index, are you relatively monochronic or polychronic? What difficulties do you encounter because of this cultural tendency?

6. In your view, what is the most important lesson for global managers from the Hofstede–Bond studies? Explain.

7. Based on your personal experience with one or more of the countries listed in Table 2–3, do you agree or disagree with the leadership profiles? Explain.

8. What needs to be done to improve the success rate of US managers in foreign assignments?

9. Which of the global manager skills in Table 2–4 do you need to develop? Explain.

10. What is your personal experience with culture shock? Which of the OB trouble spots in Figure 2–4 do you believe is the greatest threat to expatriate employee success? Explain.

EXERCISE

Objectives

1. To increase your cross-cultural awareness.
2. To see how your own work goals compare internationally.

Introduction

In today's multicultural global economy, it is a mistake to assume everyone wants the same things from the job as you do. This exercise provides a ''window'' on the world of work goals.

Instructions

Below is a list of 11 goals potentially attainable in the workplace. In terms of your own personal preferences, rank the goals from 1 to 11 (1 = Most important; 11 = Least important). After you have ranked all 11 work goals, compare your list with the national samples under the heading *Survey Results*. These national samples represent cross sections of employees from all levels and all major occupational groups. (Please complete your ranking now, before looking at the national samples.)

How important are the following in your work life?

Rank	Work Goals
_____	A lot of opportunity to *learn* new things
_____	Good *interpersonal relations* (supervisors, co-workers)
_____	Good opportunity for upgrading or *promotion*
_____	*Convenient work hours*
_____	A lot of *variety*
_____	*Interesting* work (work that you really like)
_____	Good *job security*
_____	A good *match* between your job requirements and your abilities and experience
_____	Good *pay*
_____	Good physical working *conditions* (such as light, temperature, cleanliness, low noise level)
_____	A lot of *autonomy* (you decide how to do your work)[51]

Questions for Consideration/ Class Discussion

1. Which national profile of work goals most closely matches your own? Is this what you expected, or not?

2. Are you surprised by any of the rankings in the four national samples? Explain.

3. What sorts of motivational/leadership adjustments would a manager have to make when moving among the four countries?

Survey Results[52]

Ranking of Work Goals by Country
(I = Most important; 11 = Least important)

Work Goals	United States	Britain	Germany*	Japan
Interesting work	I	I	3	2
Pay	2	2	I	5
Job security	3	3	2	4
Match between person and job	4	6	5	I
Opportunity to learn	5	8	9	7
Variety	6	7	6†	9
Interpersonal relations	7	4	4	6
Autonomy	8	10	8	3
Convenient work hours	9	5	6†	8
Opportunity for promotion	10	11	10	11
Working conditions	11	9	11	10

* Former West Germany.

† Tie.

NOTES

[1] Data from J R Healey and M Clements, ''Restyled Honda 'Must Succeed,' '' *USA Today,* September 2, 1993, pp 1B–2B.

[2] J R Healey, ''Teamwork from the Get-Go,'' *USA Today,* September 2, 1993, p 2B.

[3] M Mabry, ''Pin a Label on a Manager—and Watch What Happens,'' *Newsweek,* May 14, 1990, p 43.

[4] Ibid.

[5] E H Schein, *Organizational Culture and Leadership* (San Francisco: Jossey-Bass, 1985), p 9.

[6] For instructive discussion, see J S Black, H B Gregersen, and M E Mendenhall, *Global Assignments: Successfully Expatriating and Repatriating International Managers* (San Francisco: Jossey-Bass, 1992), Chapter 2.

[7] ''How Cultures Collide,'' *Psychology Today,* July 1976, p 69.

[8] See M Mendenhall, ''A Painless Approach to Integrating 'International' into OB, HRM, and Management Courses,'' *Organizational Behavior Teaching Review,* no. 3 (1988–89), pp 23–27.

[9] See C L Sharma, ''Ethnicity, National Integration, and Education in the Union of Soviet Socialist Republics,'' *The Journal of East and West Studies,* October 1989, pp 75–93; and Rose Brady and Peter Galuszka, ''Shattered Dreams,'' *Business Week,* February 11, 1991, pp 38–42.

[10] Jeremy Main, ''How to Go Global—and Why,'' *Fortune,* August 28, 1989, p 73.

[11] See ''How Cultures Collide,'' pp 66–74, 97; and M Munter, ''Cross-Cultural Communication for Managers,'' *Business Horizons,* May–June 1993, pp 69–78.

[12] D C Barnlund, ''Public and Private Self in Communicating with Japan,'' *Business Horizons,* March–April 1989, p 38.

[13] This list is based on E T Hall, ''The Silent Language in Overseas Business,'' *Harvard Business Review,* May–June 1960, pp 87–96; and R Knotts, ''Cross-Cultural Management: Transformations and Adaptations,'' *Business Horizons,* January–February 1989, pp 29–33.

[14] A discussion of Japanese stereotypes in America can be found in L Smith, ''Fear and Loathing of Japan,'' *Fortune,* February 26, 1990, pp 50–57.

[15] Based on discussion in P R Harris and R T Moran, *Managing Cultural Differences,* 3rd ed (Houston: Gulf Publishing, 1991) p 12.

[16] See, for example, N R Mack, ''Taking Apart the Ticking of Time,'' *The Christian Science Monitor,* August 29, 1991, p 17.

[17] For a comprehensive treatment of time, see J E McGrath and J R Kelly, *Time and Human Interaction: Toward a Social Psychology of Time* (New York: The Guilford Press, 1986).

[18] R W Moore, ''Time, Culture, and Comparative Management: A Review and Future Direction,'' in *Advances in International Comparative Management,* vol. 5, ed S B Prasad (Greenwich, CT.: JAI Press, 1990), pp 7–8.

[19] See A C Bluedorn, C F Kaufman, and P M Lane, ''How Many Things Do You Like to Do at Once? An Introduction to Monochronic and Polychronic Time,'' *Academy of Management Executive,* November 1992, pp 17–26.

[20] O Port, ''You May Have To Reset This Watch—In a Million Years,'' *Business Week,* August 30, 1993, p 65.

[21] See E T Hall, *The Hidden Dimension* (Garden City, NY: Doubleday, 1966).

[22] ''How Cultures Collide,'' p 72.

[23] D Raybeck and D Herrmann, ''A Cross-Cultural Examination of Semantic Relations,'' *Journal of Cross-Cultural Psychology,* December 1990, p 470.

[24] ''Do Cultural Differences Affect US–Japan Business Relations?'' *Economic World,* June 1990, p 11.

[25] Results adapted from and value definitions quoted from S R Safranski and I-W Kwon, ''Religious Groups and Management Value Systems,'' in *Advances in International Comparative Management,* Vol. 3, eds R N Farner and E G McGoun (Greenwich, CT: JAI Press, 1988), pp 171–83.

[26] Ibid., p 180.

[27] N J Adler, *International Dimensions of Organizational Behavior,* 2nd ed (Boston: PWS–Kent, 1991), p 10.

[28] For complete details, see G Hofstede, *Culture's Consequences: International Differences in Work-Related Values,* abridged ed (Newbury Park, CA: Sage Publications, 1984); and G Hofstede, ''The Interaction between National and Organizational Value Systems,'' *Journal of Management Studies,* July 1985, pp 347–57. Also see V J Shackleton and A H Ali, ''Work-Related Values of Managers: A Test of the Hofstede Model,'' *Journal of Cross-Cultural Psychology,* March 1990, pp 109–18; and R Hodgetts, ''A Conversation with Geert Hofstede,'' *Organizational Dynamics,* Spring 1993, 53–61.

[29] For recent research evidence on this key cultural variable, see C H Hui and M J Villareal, ''Individualism–Collectivism and Psychological Needs: Their Relationships in Two Cultures,'' *Journal of Cross-Cultural Psychology,* September 1989, pp 310–23; S H Schwartz, ''Individualism–Collectivism: Critique and Proposed Refinements,'' *Journal of Cross-Cultural Psychology,* June 1990, pp 139–57; and P C Earley, ''East Meets West Meets Mideast: Further Explorations of

Collectivistic and Individualistic Work Groups,'' *Academy of Management Journal,* April 1993, pp 319–48.

[30] See G Hofstede and M H Bond, ''Hofstede's Culture Dimensions: An Independent Validation Using Rokeach's Value Survey,'' *Journal of Cross-Cultural Psychology,* December 1984, pp 417–33. A recent study using the Chinese Value Survey (CVS) is reported in D A Ralston, D J Gustafson, P M Elsass, F Cheung, and R H Terpstra, ''Eastern Values: A Comparison of Managers in the United States, Hong Kong, and the People's Republic of China,'' *Journal of Applied Psychology,* October 1992, pp 664–71.

[31] G Hofstede, ''Cultural Constraints in Management Theories,'' *Academy of Management Executive,* February 1993, p 90.

[32] For complete details, see G Hofstede and M H Bond, ''The Confucius Connection: From Cultural Roots to Economic Growth,'' *Organizational Dynamics,* Spring 1988, pp 4–21.

[33] See C A Rodrigues, ''The Situation and National Culture as Contingencies for Leadership Behavior: Two Conceptual Models,'' in *Advances in International Comparative Management,* Vol. 5, ed S B Prasad (Greenwich, CT: JAI Press, 1990), pp 51–68.

[34] For details, see D H B Welsh, F Luthans, and S M Sommer, ''Managing Russian Factory Workers: The Impact of US-Based Behavioral and Participative Techniques,'' *Academy of Management Journal,* February 1993, pp 58–79.

[35] See M K Kozan, ''Cultural Influences on Styles of Handling Interpersonal Conflicts: Comparisons among Jordanian, Turkish, and US Managers,'' *Human Relations,* September 1989, pp 787–99.

[36] Data from M T Moore, ''Fountain of Growth Found Abroad,'' *USA Today,* August 16, 1993, pp 1B–2B.

[37] Data from R L Tung, ''Expatriate Assignments: Enhancing Success and Minimizing Failure,'' *Academy of Management Executive,* May 1987, pp 117–26.

[38] Data from J S Lublin, ''Companies Use Cross-Cultural Training to Help Their Employees Adjust Abroad,'' *The Wall Street Journal,* August 4, 1992, pp B1, B6.

[39] Adapted from Tung, ''Expatriate Assignments: Enhancing Success and Minimizing Failure,'' p 117. For a study reporting a strong positive correlation between spousal adjustment and expatriate manager adjustment, see J S Black, ''Antecedents to Cross-Cultural Adjustments for Expatriates in Pacific Rim Assignments,'' *Human Relations,* May 1991, p 497–515.

[40] Data from Lublin, ''Companies Use Cross-Cultural Training to Help Their Employees Adjust Abroad.''

[41] Data from B Hagerty, ''Trainers Help Expatriate Employees Build Bridges to Different Cultures,'' *The Wall Street Journal,* June 14, 1993, pp B1, B3. Also see C A Bartlett and S Ghoshal, ''What Is a Global Manager?'' *Harvard Business Review,* September–October 1992, pp 124–32.

[42] An excellent reference book in this area is Black, Gregersen, and Mendenhall, *Global Assignments: Successfully Expatriating and Repatriating International Managers.*

[43] *Ibid.,* p 97.

[44] J S Lublin, ''Younger Managers Learn Global Skills,'' *The Wall Street Journal,* March 31, 1992, p B1.

[45] See P C Earley, ''Intercultural Training for Managers: A Comparison of Documentary and Interpersonal Methods,'' *Academy of Management Journal,* December 1987, pp 685–98; and J S Black and M Mendenhall, ''Cross-Cultural Training Effectiveness: A Review and a Theoretical Framework for Future Research,'' *Academy of Management Review,* January 1990, pp 113–36. Also see M R Hammer and J N Martin, ''The Effects of Cross-Cultural Training on American Managers in a Japanese-American Joint Venture,'' *Journal of Applied Communication Research,* May 1992, pp 161–81; and J K Harrison, ''Individual and Combined Effects of Behavior Modeling and the Cultural Assimilator in Cross-Cultural Management Training,'' *Journal of Applied Psychology,* December 1992, pp 952–62.

[46] See Harris and Moran, *Managing Cultural Differences,* pp 223–28; and M Shilling, ''Avoid Expatriate Culture Shock,'' *HR Magazine,* July 1993, pp 58–63.

[47] S Tully, ''The Modular Corporation,'' *Fortune,* February 8, 1993, pp 108, 112.

[48] K L Miller, ''How a Team of Buckeyes Helped Honda Save a Bundle,'' *Business Week,* September 13, 1993, p 68.

[49] See Black, Gregersen, and Mendenhall, *Global Assignments: Successfully Expatriating and Repatriating International Managers,* p 227. Also see H B Gregersen, ''Commitments to a Parent Company and a Local Work Unit During Repatriation,'' *Personnel Psychology,* Spring 1992, pp 29–54.

[50] Ibid., pp 226–27.

[51] This list of work goals is quoted from I Harpaz, ''The Importance of Work Goals: An International Perspective,'' *Journal of International Business Studies,* First Quarter 1990, p 79.

[52] Adapted from a seven-country summary in Ibid., table 2, p 81.

MANAGING DIVERSITY: RELEASING EVERY EMPLOYEE'S POTENTIAL

Learning OBJECTIVES

When you finish studying the material in this chapter, you should be able to:

1. Define diversity.

2. Discuss the primary and secondary dimensions of diversity.

3. Explain the differences among affirmative action, valuing diversity, and managing diversity.

4. Demonstrate your familiarity with the demographic trends that are creating an increasingly diverse workforce.

5. Highlight the managerial implications of increasing diversity in the workforce.

6. Review the five reasons managing diversity is a competitive advantage.

7. Discuss the organizational practices used to effectively manage diversity.

8. Identify the barriers and challenges to managing diversity.

OPENING CASE

U S WEST Wins an Award for Managing Diversity

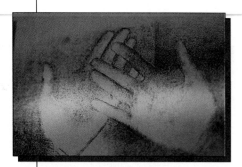

Sharon Hoogstraten

Recently, a vendor was giving a presentation to managers at U S WEST, the Denver-based telecommunications company. Attempting to create camaraderie among participants, he opened the meeting with a joke that made fun of a particular ethnic group. His effort backfired. No one laughed at the joke because U S WEST has spent considerably more than a decade helping employees to respect all people, regardless of any real or perceived differences.

Fifteen years ago everyone would have laughed at his joke and someone would have come up with a better one, explains Darlene Siedschlaw, director of equal employment opportunity and affirmative action compliance. Today, thanks to the company's pluralism efforts, U S \ /EST employees recognize that diversity is strength and that, to survive in a changing society, the company must capitalize on these differences, not ridicule them.

Siedschlaw attributes this shift in attitude to the company's pluralistic philosophy. "Here, pluralism isn't a program with a start and a finish," she says. It's an ongoing process of changing the makeup of U S WEST to reflect the melting pot of American society.

Although many companies are just beginning to grapple with work force diversity, U S WEST already demonstrates significant progress. The company selects women for management jobs 52% of the time, for example. People of color constitute 13% of the managers, and an accelerated development program for women of color is moving more of these women into management positions than ever before.

Furthermore, the company is learning how to respond better to customers who are just as diverse as employees. As Siedschlaw explains, "Pluralism is a sound business strategy."

For its efforts, U S WEST has been recognized as one of PERSONNEL JOURNAL's 1992 Optimas Award winners. The award is given annually to companies that display excellence in human resources management in any one of 10 categories, ranging from quality of life to global outlook. U S WEST is the winner in the managing change category.

The company's pluralism efforts have their roots in sexism and racism workshops developed in the mid-1970s at Northwestern Bell under the direction of President Jack MacAllister. When MacAllister took charge upon divestiture as CEO of U S WEST, his pluralism efforts followed, gradually evolving into the comprehensive set of programs that have an impact on hiring, promotion and the day-to-day activities of every employee. "The key to our success has been the support of top management," Siedschlaw says. "Jack was truly a visionary before his time."

The most far-reaching pluralism effort to date is a training program that all 65,000 U S WEST employees will have attended by April 1993. The company's business leaders—including union stewards who might be occupational employees—are required to attend a three-day program called *Managing a Diverse Workforce.* All other employees will attend a one-day version called *The Value of Human Diversity. . . .*

To ensure that managers embrace this notion fully, the company has developed a *Pluralism Performance Menu,* a vehicle for appraising the top 125 corporate officers based on how well they meet pluralism-related criteria. "For the first time," Siedschlaw says, "Instead of asking the officers 'do you support pluralism,' we'll ask them to demonstrate what they've actually done to support it."

For example, officers will be assessed based on the profiles of employees who are hired or promoted within their function, and whether or not they and their direct reports have attended diversity training.

They also will be evaluated based on the overall profile of their organizations, and whether it's representative of the labor force in that geographic area. In New Mexico, for instance, 50% of U S WEST employees are Hispanic, in keeping with the state's demographics. Having operations in 14 states, the company strives to have the employee make-up at all its locations mirror the regional work force.

(concluded)

If a manager continues to hire and promote only white males from a diverse population base, or otherwise fails to show support for the company's pluralism efforts, he or she could see a salary reduction or lose the annual bonus. "The process had to have teeth in it to get their attention," Siedschlaw explains. . . .

To make sure the concerns of existing employees are addressed, however, the company turns to its eight employee resource groups (ERGs). The groups are organized by employees who have similar interests and concerns, such as Native Americans, veterans, people who have disabilities, and gays and lesbians. The ERGs provide support, offer a collective voice to members, and are a means for them to come forward with their differences.

All the groups, for example, participate in the company's *Pluralism Calendar of Events* by sponsoring employee awareness and education programs. Last February, the company celebrated Black History Month with presentations by members of the Alliance of Black Telecommunications Professionals. In March, U S WEST Women presented topics on women's history, and in September, SOMOS, the Hispanic Resource Network, developed programs on Hispanic Heritage. . . .

The ERGs help the company make better business decisions as well. "When a SOMOS chapter started in Arizona," Siedschlaw says, "members helped the company learn how to communicate better with the Hispanic market there. By developing bilingual printed materials and hiring bilingual

service representatives, we now provide better service to our customers."

The ERGs also help U S WEST with succession planning by providing lists of candidates who they think are ready for advancement. The human resources staff compares this information with similar lists for managers to ensure that the right people are groomed for upper-level positions. "The intent is to develop a pluralistic mix from the bottom up," Siedschlaw points out. . . .

Recognizing that the attention paid to diverse employee groups could leave white males feeling a little left out, U S WEST has developed a workshop to help them adjust to the changes they face. "The role of white men is changing," Siedschlaw says, "not just at work but in their personal lives as well. We're trying to help them adjust to those changing roles and expectations."

With all the efforts underway to sensitize employees to differences in others—not only in terms of ethnicity and age, but in experience, education, physical abilities, religious beliefs and sexual orientation—doesn't the company risk employees' becoming too sensitive?

"Although a few people have told me they're afraid to open their mouths, I don't see it as a significant problem," Siedschlaw says. "Besides, I'm not so naive as to think we've eliminated prejudice altogether. You certainly don't hear blatant words such as 'nigger' or 'queer' any longer, because the work force has become self-policing, but I've learned that, unless people truly embrace pluralism

and it becomes a part of them, the best anyone can be is a 'recovering sexist' [sic] or a 'recovering racist.' "

"There have been a couple of cases in which people couldn't buy into our commitment to a pluralistic work force. It was suggested very strongly that maybe they would like to work for another company," Siedschlaw says.

Although U S WEST has made significant progress in advancing the careers of women and people of color, the company claims it never will be truly pluralistic, because that denotes a finite process. "We'll become *more* pluralistic, however," explains Siedschlaw. "As the demographics of our society continue to change, so will U S WEST."

She adds that glass ceilings at U S WEST are far from being broken. "At every level in the organization there are glass ceilings for women and minorities. We've cracked them all, but to be successful, we must shatter them from the bottom up."

For Discussion

Would you like to work in the type of environment being created at U S WEST? Explain.

- Additional discussion questions linking this case with the following material appear at the end of this chapter.

Source: Excerpted by permission from Shari Caudron, "U S WEST Finds Strength in Diversity," *Personnel Journal*, March 1992, pp 40–43.

I f you had your choice to work with someone who was similar or different from yourself who would you choose? A recent national study of 2,958 employees indicated that the majority of workers of all ages preferred working with people of the same race, sex, gender, and education.[1] We are simply more comfortable interacting with others who share compara-ble attitudes, values, and preferred work behaviors. Similarity reduces conflict and increases understanding among individuals. Fortunately, or unfortunately, man-agers no longer have the choice of managing a homogeneous workforce.

As you will learn in this chapter, the workforce has dramatically changed over the past 15 years. Similarity or homogeneity has been replaced with differences or heterogeneity. In turn, managerial styles and behaviors that worked in the past are no longer appropriate. For example, unlike the ''obedient man'' of the 1950s who strived to blend in and responded positively to a command and control style of leadership, today's employees are being asked to be risk takers that challenge managerial edicts. Successful managers and organizations will be those that effec-tively integrate diverse people into the lifeblood of the organization.

This is a difficult challenge because it forces all of us to confront and deal with our values, stereotypes, prejudices, and beliefs. Consider the following three actual cases:

> An African-American employee at an East Coast company took the day off to celebrate Martin Luther King Jr. Day. Upon returning to work, he discovered a note that had been scribbled on his desk calendar. It read: ''Kill four more, get four more days off.'' An elderly Jewish employee in an East Coast electronics firm was told face-to-face by another employee that the new boss was about to design microwave ovens large enough for people to walk into. A group of 15 employees from a West Coast public utilities corporation marched in a gay pride parade with the company's logo. When they returned to work on Monday, they were greeted by hundreds of letters on their E-mail, one of which read, ''If I had been anywhere near the gay pride march and had had an axe, I would have axed those people.''[2]

These examples reinforce the fact that some people do not leave their values, stereotypes, prejudice, and hate at the building entrance. As repugnant as these examples may be, managers nonetheless have to deal with them. What would you have done if you were a manager in one of these situations?

Managing diversity is a sensitive, potentially volatile, and sometimes uncom-fortable issue. Yet managers are required to deal with it in the name of organiza-tional survival. Accordingly, the purpose of this chapter is to help you get a better understanding of this important context for organizational behavior. It is a natural extension of how to manage across cultures, which was discussed in Chapter 2. We begin by defining diversity. Next, we build the business case for diversity and then describe the organizational practices used to effectively manage diversity. The chapter concludes by examining the barriers and challenges associated with manag-ing diversity.

DEFINING DIVERSITY

diversity   The host of indi-vidual differences that make people different from each other.

Diversity represents the multitude of individual differences that exist among people. This definition underscores an important issue about managing diversity; that is, managing diversity pertains to everybody. It is not an issue of age, race, or gender. It is not an issue of being heterosexual or gay or lesbian, or being Catholic, Jewish, Protestant, or Muslim. Diversity also does not pit white males against all other groups of people. Diversity pertains to the host of individual differences that make all of us unique and different from others.

This section begins our journey into managing diversity by first reviewing the key dimensions of diversity. Because many people associate diversity with affirmative action, this section compares affirmative action, valuing diversity, and managing diversity. They are not the same.[3]

Dimensions of Diversity

Like sea shells on a beach, people come in a variety of shapes, sizes, and colors. This variety represents the essence of diversity. A team of diversity experts identified a set of primary and secondary dimensions of diversity to help distinguish the important ways in which people differ (see Figure 3–1). Taken together, the primary and secondary dimensions of diversity constitute one's personal identity.

Primary Dimensions of Diversity   **Primary dimensions of diversity** are those ''human differences that are inborn and/or that exert an important impact on our early socialization and an ongoing impact throughout our lives.''[4] They represent the core of who we are. Figure 3–1 shows that the primary dimensions include age, race, ethnicity, gender, physical abilities/qualities, and sexual/affectional orientation. There are two additional things to keep in mind about the primary dimensions

primary dimensions of diversity   Personal characteristics that are inborn.

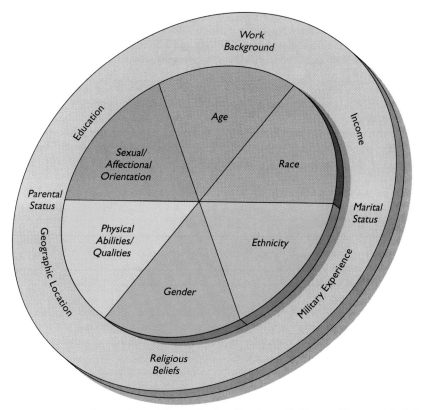

M Loden and J B Rosener, *Workforce America! Managing Employee Diversity as a Vital Resource* (Homewood, IL: Business One Irwin, 1991), p 20.

• FIGURE 3–1
Primary and Secondary
Dimensions of Diversity

of diversity: First, they are salient to other people; that is, we tend to notice them about each other. Second, people tend to develop stereotypes about the primary dimensions of diversity.

Secondary Dimensions of Diversity   **Secondary dimensions of diversity** are personal characteristics that can be changed. They are individual differences that we acquire, discard, and/or modify throughout our lives. Figure 3–1 lists eight key secondary dimensions of diversity. These dimensions add breadth to one's core identity, and they particularly affect one's self-esteem.[5]

The Effect of Diversity on Perceptions and Expectations

The primary and secondary dimensions of diversity play a big role in shaping our values, needs, priorities, aspirations, and perceptions. They also influence the way in which we perceive and interpret our environment. As an example, read the two scenarios in the OB Exercise, and answer the diagnostic questions before reading on.

OB EXERCISE

Dimensions of Diversity Affect Perceptions and Expectations

Consider the following descriptions of two employees working in the same organization:

Stan is 55 years old. He is a college graduate and is a vice president. He is a second-generation Polish-American and a practicing Roman Catholic. His two children are married, and they have children of their own. His wife does volunteer work and is very active in the church. He is in excellent physical health and likes to golf and play racquetball.

Maria is a 30-year-old Mexican-American clerical worker. She is active in Chicanos por la Causa and is a single parent. She has two children under the age of 10. She completed high school after moving to the United States and has just begun to attend evening classes at Mesa Community College. Maria is a practicing Roman Catholic. Although her health is excellent, one of her children is developmentally disabled.

Based on this information, answer the following questions:

1. To what extent are Stan and Maria's goals, needs, and priorities similar and dissimilar?
   _____
   _____
   _____

2. Which employee would prefer the following benefits?
   a. On-site day care _____
   b. A fitness center _____
   c. Tuition reimbursement _____
   d. An executive bonus plan _____
   e. A rigorous affirmative action plan _____
   f. Enhanced retirement benefits _____
   g. Supervisory training _____
   h. Financial aid for special education _____
   i. Corporate membership in a golf club _____

Source: This exercise was taken from A J Kinicki, *Valuing Diversity* (Chandler, AZ: Angelo Kinicki), pp. 1–5.

Based on this limited information, one can speculate that Stan and Maria have different needs and priorities. Although precise answers to the diagnostic questions depend on additional unknown information, you can see that the primary and secondary dimensions of diversity do matter. (You will find it instructive to compare your interpretations with those of your classmates.) Not only do they influence our self identity, but they affect how we are treated at work. Consider the case of police detective Marc Clay:

> A Catholic police detective in the Georgia town of LaGrange was suspended without pay for one day on Ash Wednesday for refusing to remove ashes from his fore-head. . . . When he arrived at work, several officers good-naturedly ''ribbed'' him about the ashes, he said. He explained the Lenten tradition of ashes and his intention to wear them that day until they wore off. However, Police Chief George Yates approached him, asked him what was on his forehead, and then told him to wipe it off. When he declined, he was approached a few moments later by his immediate supervisor, Lt. Barbara Price, who ordered him to remove the ashes or face suspension, he said. When Clay said he knew of no regulation regarding ashes, Price replied, ''I'm giving you a direct order to remove the ashes or go home,'' he said.[6]

Religious beliefs are one of the secondary dimensions of diversity, and they clearly affected detective Clay's suspension.

Affirmative Action and Valuing Diversity

Valuing diversity and managing diversity require organizations to adopt a new way of thinking about differences among people. Rather than pitting one group against another, valuing diversity and managing diversity strive to recognize the unique contribution every employee can make. This philosophy is much different from that of affirmative action. This section highlights the differences among affirmative action, valuing diversity, and managing diversity. Table 3–1 compares these three approaches to managing employee differences.

Affirmative Action   As shown in Table 3–1, **affirmative action** focuses on achieving equality of opportunity in an organization and is legally mandated by Equal Employment Opportunity laws. Affirmative action is an artificial intervention aimed at giving management a chance to correct an imbalance, an injustice, a mistake, and/or outright discrimination.[7] Although affirmative action created tremendous opportunities for women and minorities, it does not foster the type of thinking that is needed to effectively manage diversity.[8] For example, affirmative action is commonly viewed as involving preferential hiring and treatment based on group membership. This view creates tremendous resistance due to perceived injustice, particularly from white males. Consider how Doug Tennant felt after being laid off by Pacific Gas & Electric Company in Tracy, California:

affirmative action   Focuses on achieving equality of opportunity in an organization.

> He says he was the first one in his three-person unit to be laid off. He claims the others— a black woman and a man of Indian descent—were kept on even though he was more qualified. Tennant, who is white, blames PG&E's push for a more diverse workplace. ''I feel like I'm losing out,'' he says. PG&E says his race and sex had nothing to do with his departure.[9]

Affirmative action programs were also found to negatively affect the women and minorities who supposedly benefited from them. Research demonstrated that women and minorities, supposedly hired on the basis of affirmative action, felt negatively stigmatized as unqualified or incompetent. They also experienced lower

Affirmative Action	Valuing Diversity	Managing Diversity
Quantitative. Emphasizes achieving equality of opportunity in the work environment through the changing of organizational demographics. Monitored by statistical reports and analysis.	*Qualitative.* Emphasizes the appreciation of differences and creating an environment in which everyone feels valued and accepted. Monitored by organizational surveys focused on attitudes and perceptions.	*Behavioral.* Emphasizes the building of specific skills and creating policies which get the best from every employee. Monitored by progress toward achieving goals and objectives.
Legally driven. Written plans and statistical goals for specific groups are utilized. Reports are mandated by EEO laws and consent decrees.	*Ethically driven.* Moral and ethical imperatives drive this culture change.	*Strategically driven.* Behaviors and policies are seen as contributing to organizational goals and objectives such as profit and productivity and are tied to reward and results.
Remedial. Specific target groups benefit as past wrongs are remedied. Previously excluded groups have an advantage.	*Idealistic.* Everyone benefits. Everyone feels valued and accepted in an inclusive environment.	*Pragmatic.* The organization benefits; morale, profit, and productivity increase.
Assimilation model. Assumes that groups brought into system will adapt to existing organizational norms.	*Diversity model.* Assumes that groups will retain their own characteristics and shape the organization as well as be shaped by it, creating a common set of values.	*Synergy model.* Assumes that diverse groups will create new ways of working together effectively in a pluralistic environment.
Opens doors in the organization. Affects hiring and promotion decisions.	*Opens attitudes, minds, and the culture.* Affects attitudes of employees.	*Opens the system.* Affects managerial practices and policies.
Resistance due to perceived limits to autonomy in decision making and perceived fears of reverse discrimination.	*Resistance due to* fear of change, discomfort with differences, and desire for return to "good old days."	*Resistance due to* denial of demographic realities, the need for alternative approaches, and/or benefits associated with change; and the difficulty in learning new skills, altering existing systems, and/or finding time to work toward synergistic solutions.

Source: L Gardenswartz and A Rowe, *Managing Diversity: A Complete Desk Reference and Planning Guide* (Homewood, IL: Business One Irwin, 1993), p 405.

job satisfaction and more stress than employees supposedly selected on the basis of merit.[10] Just the same, without affirmative action's focus on hiring and promoting diverse employees, the true valuing and managing of diversity rarely occurs.

valuing diversity
Emphasizes the awareness, recognition, understanding, and appreciation of human differences.

Valuing Diversity Table 3–1 indicates that **valuing diversity** emphasizes the awareness, recognition, understanding, and appreciation of human differences. It revolves around creating an environment in which everyone feels valued and accepted. In essence, valuing diversity entails a cultural change geared toward viewing employee differences as a valuable resource that can contribute to organizational success.[11] This generally takes place through a series of management education and training programs that attempt to improve interpersonal relationships among diverse employees and to minimize blatant expressions of sexism and racism.[12]

Managing diversity has its roots in the controversial EEO and affirmative action legislation enacted during the turbulent 1960s.
Bettye-Lane

Managing Diversity   **Managing diversity** entails enabling people to perform up to their maximum potential. It focuses on changing an organization's culture and infrastructure such that people provide the highest productivity possible. Ann Morrison, a diversity expert, conducted a study of 16 organizations that successfully managed diversity. Her results uncovered three key strategies for success: education, enforcement, and exposure. She describes them as follows:

> The education component of the strategy has two thrusts; one is to prepare nontraditional managers for increasingly responsible posts, and the other is to help traditional managers overcome their prejudice in thinking about and interacting with people who are of a different sex or ethnicity. The second component of the strategy, enforcement, puts teeth in diversity goals and encourages behavior change. The third component, exposure to people with different backgrounds and characteristics, adds a more personal approach to diversity by helping managers get to know and respect others who are different.[13]

More is said about managing diversity later in this chapter.

managing diversity
Creating organizational changes that enable all people to perform up to their maximum potential.

The rationale for managing diversity goes well beyond legal, social, and moral reasons. Quite simply, the primary reason for managing diversity is the ability to grow and maintain a business in an increasingly competitive marketplace. Organizations cannot accomplish this objective if employees fail to contribute their full talents, abilities, motivation, and commitment. Thus, it is essential for an organization to create an environment or culture that allows all employees to reach their full potential. Managing diversity is a critical component of creating such an organization.

This section explores the business need to manage diversity by first reviewing the demographic trends that are creating an increasingly diverse workforce. We then review the key reasons effective management of diversity creates a competitive advantage.

BUILDING THE BUSINESS CASE FOR MANAGING DIVERSITY

Increasing Diversity in the Workforce

workforce demographics
Statistical profiles of adult workers.

Workforce demographics, which are statistical profiles of the characteristics and composition of the adult working population, are an invaluable human-resource planning aid. They enable managers to anticipate and adjust for surpluses or shortages of appropriately skilled individuals. For example, the US workforce is expected to grow approximately 1 percent between 1988 and 2000.[14] However, the number of new jobs created in the United States is projected to exceed this growth. These demographics reveal that organizations need to devise strategies to manage the mismatch in labor supply and demand.

Moreover, general population demographics give managers a preview of the values and motives of future employees. Demographic changes in the US workforce during the last two or three decades have immense implications for organizational behavior. This section explores four demographic trends that are creating an increasingly diverse workforce: (1) women continue to enter the workforce in increasing numbers, (2) people of color represent a growing share of the labor force, (3) there is a critical mismatch between workers' educational attainment and occupational requirements, and (4) the workforce is aging.

Women Entering the Workforce   Table 3–2 shows that approximately 49.5 percent of the new entrants into the workforce between 1990 and 2005 are expected to be women. It also shows that women will account for 42.7 percent of the leavers. Men account for the largest share of retirement-bound employees.

Historically, female employment was concentrated in relatively lower-level and lower paying occupations. In 1992 women were still underpaid relative to men: Women received 71 percent of the equivalent men's salaries.[15] Nonetheless, there are signs that this trend is changing. Women are beginning to obtain employment in professional and managerial jobs traditionally held by men. For instance, the

◄── • **TABLE 3–2**
Projected Entrants and Leavers in the US Workforce from 1990 to 2005

	Entrants		Leavers*	
	1990–2005	**Percent**	**1990–2005**	**Percent**
Total**	55,798	100.0%	29,851	100.0%
Men	28,197	50.5	17,090	57.3
Women	27,601	49.5	12,761	42.7
White, Non-Hispanic	36,425	65.3	24,423	81.8
Men	17,965	32.2	14,204	47.6
Women	18,460	33.1	10,219	34.2
Black	7,250	13.0	3,144	10.5
Men	3,461	6.2	1,553	5.2
Women	3,789	6.8	1,591	5.3
Hispanic	8,768	15.7	1,556	5.2
Men	5,085	9.1	939	3.1
Women	3,683	6.6	617	2.1
Asian and Other Races	3,354	6.0	728	2.4
Men	1,686	3.0	395	1.3
Women	1,668	3.0	333	1.1

* Labor force entrants and leavers, in thousands, 1990–2005
** All groups add to total.
Note: Numbers may not add up due to rounding.
Source: Data were taken from a table presented in T G Exter, "In and Out of Work," *American Demographics,* June 1992, p 63.

percentage of women managers increased from 27 percent in 1981 to 41 percent in 1991. Despite the increase in women managers, however, women still have not broken into the highest echelon of corporate America to any significant extent. Women hold only about 3 percent of all senior executive positions.[16] Negative stereotypes (discussed in Chapter 4) and the lack of mentors have been identified as two key barriers to women reaching the top.[17]

People of Color in the US Workforce   People of color in the United States are projected to add 34.7 percent of the new entrants in the workforce from 1990 to 2005 (see Table 3–2). Hispanics are predicted to account for the largest share of this increase (15.7 percent). Since fewer people of color will leave the workforce than whites between 1990 and 2005, people of color account for an even greater net percentage increase in new workers.

Unfortunately, three additional trends suggest American businesses are not effectively managing people of color. First, people of color are not achieving great strides in advancing into the managerial and professional ranks. Black men and women, for instance, held 7 percent of all white-collar jobs in 1992.[18] People of color also tend to earn less than whites. For example, black and Hispanic women earned 62 cents and 54 cents, respectively, for every dollar earned by white men.[19] Finally, a national study of 2,958 worker attitudes indicated that more than 20 percent of the people of color reported being discriminated against. In turn, these beliefs were correlated with greater incidence of burnout, reduced willingness to take risks, and increased intention to quit one's job.[20]

Mismatch between Educational Attainment and Occupational Requirements
Approximately 26 percent of the labor force has a college degree.[21] Unfortunately, many of these people are working in jobs for which they are overqualified. This creates underemployment. **Underemployment** exists when a job requires less than a person's full potential as determined by his or her formal education, training or skills. Consider the case of Julie Day:

> Formerly a full-time typesetter who made $32,000 a year, Day is working—when she can—as a temporary receptionist or word processor. She had a part-time job briefly, but it ended when her employer ran out of money. Sometimes she gets freelance typesetting jobs; most of the time she doesn't. Altogether, Day, 38, rarely brings home more than $400 a month, she says. Since she was laid off . . . she has given up her apartment and moved in with her 71-year-old father in Falls Church, Va. Her car has stopped running and she can't afford to have it repaired. She prays she doesn't get sick because she has no insurance.[22]

underemployment   A job requires less education, training, or skills than possessed by a worker.

The Bureau of Labor Statistics estimated that 33 percent of college graduates between 1990 and 2005 will be underemployed for part of their careers. Underemployment is associated with higher arrest rates and the likelihood of becoming an unmarried parent for young adults.[23] As true for Julie Day, it also is correlated with job dissatisfaction and psychosocial stress, depression, frustration, hostility, and insecurity.[24]

There is another important educational mismatch. The national high school dropout rate is approximately 11.2 percent, and an estimated 27 million adult Americans are functionally illiterate. This constituted 15 percent of the total adult population in 1992 and 20 percent of the 1992 working population.[25] In contrast to underemployment, dropouts and illiterate individuals are unlikely to have the skills organizations need to remain competitive.

The Aging Workforce   America's population and workforce are getting older. The median age in the United States climbed from just under 28 in 1970 to 30 at the outset of the 1980s. The median workforce age is projected to reach 39 by the year 2000. By the year 2000, half of the population will be over 45 and 36 million people will be over 65. Life expectancy is increasing as well.[26] The United States is not the only country with an aging population. Japan, Eastern Europe, and the former Soviet republics, for example, are expected to encounter significant economic and political problems due to an aging population (see the International OB).

Managerial Implications of Increasing Diversity   Women will be in high demand given future labor shortages. To attract the best workers, companies need to adopt policies and programs that meet the needs of women. Programs such as day care, elder care, flexible work schedules, cafeteria benefit programs, paternal leaves, and less rigid relocation policies are likely to become more common.

Mismatches between the amount of education needed to perform current jobs and the amount of education possessed by members of the workforce are growing. Underemployment among college graduates threatens to erode job satisfaction and work motivation. As well-educated workers begin to look for jobs commensurate with their qualifications and expectations, absenteeism and turnover likely will increase. This problem underscores the need for job redesign (see the discussion in Chapter 6). In addition, organizations will need to consider interventions, such as realistic job previews and positive reinforcement programs, to reduce absenteeism and turnover. On-the-job remedial skills training will be necessary to help the growing number of dropouts cope with job demands.

INTERNATIONAL OB

Aging Populations Strain Eastern Europe and the Former Soviet Republics

Aging populations add to the troubles of Eastern Europe and the former Soviet republics.

The US Census Bureau reports that one in 10 people in these 22 countries—Czechoslovakia and Yugoslavia still counting as one each—was 65 or over in 1990 and that by 2025, the proportion would be one in five. Aging populations characterize all industrialized nations—in the US, for example, one in eight is elderly—but Census suggests that the aging trend is more of a problem for the former Communist nations.

One reason is that most have very liberal pension policies, which will strain scarce economic resources. Efforts to reduce pensions or inability to meet pension obligations could add to political instability.

Another factor is that women greatly outnumber men among the elderly in these countries, and aged women usually require more medical and other care. Elderly women outnumber elderly men practically all over the world, but the disproportion is particularly great in the former Communist countries due to male deaths in World War II. In Russia, for example, elderly women are almost three times as numerous as elderly men.

Source: A L Otten, "People Patterns: Aging Populations Strain Ex-Communist Nations," *The Wall Street Journal*, February 14, 1994, p B1. Reprinted by permission of *The Wall Street Journal*, © 1994 Dow Jones & Company, Inc. All Rights Reserved Worldwide.

Moreover, organizations will continue to be asked to help resolve the educational problems in the United States. Supporting education is good for business and society at large. A better education system not only contributes to the United States's ability to compete internationally, but it facilitates a better quality of life for all its population. RJR Nabisco is an example of an organization that includes education as a corporate priority. Nabisco implemented a series of education initiatives that addressed education issues that concern its employees. The goals of the various initiatives were as follows:

1. Availability of financial assistance to help employees pay for their children's education beyond high school.
2. Time off to allow employees to accompany their children on the first day of school and to attend parent-teacher conferences.
3. Training and incentives for employees who take leadership roles in education.
4. Expanded work-skills training for employees, so that no one is denied promotion or transfer capability because of a lack of basic skills.[27]

With labor force size not expected to increase significantly during the 1990s, a shortage of qualified entry-level workers and late-career managers is predicted. However, as the baby-boom generation reaches retirement age after the turn of the century, the workforce will be top-heavy with older employees, creating the problem of career plateauing for younger workers. **Career plateauing** is defined "as that point in a career [at] which future hierarchical mobility seems unlikely."[28] Because employees frequently view career plateauing as career failure, career plateauing is associated with stress and dissatisfaction.[29] Managers will thus need to find alternatives besides promotions to help employees satisfy their needs and to feel successful.[30] In addition, organizations may need to devise more flexible and creative retirement plans. If managers are to be more responsive to older workers, they also need to be aware of how aging affects one's values and attitudes. Employee values and attitudes are discussed in Chapter 4.

career plateauing The probability of being promoted is very small.

Managing Diversity—A Competitive Advantage

Consultants, academics, and business leaders believe that effectively managing diversity is a competitive advantage. This advantage stems from the process in which the management of diversity affects organizational behavior and effectiveness. Effectively managing diversity can influence an organization's costs and employee attitudes, recruitment of human resources, sales and market share, creativity and innovation, and group problem solving and productivity. This section explores the relationship between managing diversity and each of these outcomes.[31]

Lower Costs and Improved Employee Attitudes   Turnover and absenteeism were found to be higher for women and people of color than for whites. For example, Monsanto learned that people of color quit more frequently than whites because of poor relationships with their managers, lack of timely promotions, feeling they were not appreciated and being given work that did not improve their skills.[32] Corning Glass also reported that turnover among professional women was double that of men between 1980 and 1987 and that the rate for blacks was 2.5 times that for whites.[33] Diversity also was related to employee attitudes.

A study of 814 blacks and 814 whites revealed that blacks, compared with whites, felt less accepted by their peers, perceived lower managerial discretion on their jobs, reached career plateaus more frequently, noted lower levels of career satisfaction, and received lower performance ratings.[34] Organizational surveys further revealed that the majority of respondents witnessed some type of hostility and discrimination toward gay and lesbian employees. Gay and lesbian employees also reported higher levels of stress than heterosexual employees. How important is the issue of sexual preference? Estimates about the percentage of gay and lesbians in the US population range from 3 to 10 percent.[35] Can any organization afford to squelch the motivation and productivity of 3 to 10 percent of its workforce?

Employees' physical abilities/qualities is another dimension of diversity that needs to be effectively managed. Forty-three million Americans have a disability, and only one third of them are working. Seventy percent of those who are not working desire employment. Although these statistics prompted the passage of the **Americans with Disabilities Act** in 1992, which bans discrimination against the disabled in the United States, disabled workers are still finding it difficult to obtain employment.[36] Do you think this segment of the population is being underutilized?

Americans with Disabilities Act Prohibits discrimination against the disabled.

Improved Recruiting Efforts   Attracting and retaining competent employees is a competitive advantage. This is particularly true given the workforce demographics discussed in the preceding section. Organizations that effectively manage diversity are more likely to meet this challenge because women and people of color are attracted to companies that value diversity. Consider Merck & Company's experience after being named one of the 10 best managed companies in America:

> "Let's face it, Merck is not a household name," a spokesman allows. Being *Fortune*'s most admired for three years, he says, helped draw in "over 100,000 applications for jobs from New Jersey alone."[37]

Increased Sales and Market Share   Workforce diversity is the mirror image of consumer diversity. It is thus important for companies to market their products so that they appeal to a diverse marketplace. Schick, for example, saw a significant sales growth after releasing its latest "multicultural" television commercial promoting its razor blades:

> Schick's latest television commercial stars the typical American man. Only this man has several faces—Asian, Caucasian and African-American—dissolving into each other in front of the shaving mirror. . . . The ad uses a special effect known as "morphing" that seamlessly blends the races on screen. "We saw immediate sales growth when we introduced it," says Mr. McSpaden [the company's account representative].[38]

The ad clearly appealed to a market segment that included others beyond white males. As this example illustrates, it can be a costly business decision to ignore diverse consumers who possess substantial buying power. For example, women's 1992 earnings stood at approximately $931 billion, and 41 percent of all people with assets greater than $500,000 were women.[39] Similarly, the annual income of blacks has grown sixfold over the last two decades, to an estimated $270 billion.[40] Other companies such as Dayton Hudson, Aka Communications, and Classic Options have targeted products to gay and lesbian consumers.[41] This strategy was profitable for several magazine publishers. Bruce Fryer, director of magazines for the Waldenbooks chain, for example, says that "gay publications showed the largest increase in our stores of any category, growing 85% in unit sales,'' during 1993.[42]

Moreover, just as women and people of color prefer to work for companies that value diversity, they also may select to buy from such organizations. Consider the advertising philosophy at Federal Express, Xerox, and USAir:

> The new look in ads is also aimed at another constituency: employees. Companies committed to attracting a diverse work force want to project that image in their advertising. Fedex prescreens each ad for 90,000 employees on its in-house cable-TV system and solicits feedback. And Xerox is running an ad depicting a black woman as an assertive, problem-solving Xerox salesperson. ''It's very important for any service company that employees see their reflection and are proud of the way the company is shown on TV,'' says Michael Kirby, director of world-wide strategic advertising for Xerox. An ad for USAir features a black woman executive on her way to deliver an important speech. While most business passengers are white males, a world-class airline should project American diversity, says Patricia Dewey, USAir senior director for advertising and sales promotion. ''Not only will we perhaps get more minority revenue,'' Ms. Dewey says, ''we'll get more loyalty from the general population because that is what they want to see.''[43]

Increased Creativity and Innovation   Preliminary research supports the idea that workforce diversity promotes creativity and innovation. This occurs through the sharing of diverse ideas and perspectives. Rosabeth Moss-Kanter, a management expert, was one of the first to investigate this relationship. Her results indicated that innovative companies deliberately used heterogeneous teams to solve problems, and they employed more women and people of color than less innovative companies. She also noted that innovative companies did a better job of eliminating racism, sexism, and classism.[44]

Increased Group Problem-Solving and Productivity   Because diverse groups possess a broader base of experience and perspectives from which to analyze a problem, they can potentially improve problem solving and performance. Research findings based on short-term groups that varied in terms of values, attitudes, educational backgrounds, and experience supported this conclusion. Heterogeneous groups produced better quality decisions and demonstrated higher productivity than homogeneous groups.[45] Nevertheless, these results must be interpreted cautiously because the experimental samples, tasks, time frames, and environmental situations bear very little resemblance to actual ongoing organizational settings.[46] Recent research has attempted to control for these problems.

Recent studies do not clearly support the proposed benefits of diversity. A study of culturally homogeneous and diverse groups over a period of 17 weeks showed higher performance among homogeneous groups for the first 9 weeks due to the fact that heterogeneous groups experienced less effective group processes than homogeneous groups. Over weeks 10 through 17, however, homogeneous and heterogeneous groups demonstrated similar performance.[47] Additional studies found that work group diversity was significantly associated with increased absenteeism, turnover, and less psychological commitment and intention to stay in the organization.[48]

In summary, research does not clearly support the premise that diversity leads to enhanced problem solving and productivity. It seems that performance is best when there is neither too much nor too little diversity. There are two additional conditions that must be satisfied before diversity can positively contribute to problem solving and performance.

1. Group members must share common values and norms that promote pursuit of the organization's goals.
2. Group members need to be aware of cultural and attitudinal differences of other group members.[49]

Many companies use training programs to promote this awareness.

ORGANIZATIONAL PRACTICES USED TO EFFECTIVELY MANAGE DIVERSITY

Organizations throughout the United States are unsure of what it takes to effectively manage diversity. This is partly due to the fact that top management only recently became aware of the combined need and importance of this issue. Given this awareness, however, some companies are now beginning to implement practices and programs aimed at both valuing and managing diversity.

As previously mentioned, Ann Morrison conducted a landmark study of the diversity practices used by 16 organizations that successfully managed diversity. Her results uncovered 52 different practices, 20 of which were used by the majority of the companies sampled. She classified the 52 practices into three main types: accountability, development, and recruitment.[50] The top 10 practices associated with each type are shown in Table 3–3. They are discussed next in order of relative importance.

Accountability Practices

Accountability practices relate to managers' responsibility to treat diverse employees fairly. Table 3–3 reveals that companies predominantly accomplish this objective by creating administrative procedures aimed at integrating diverse employees into the management ranks (practices number 3, 4, 5, 6, 8, 9, and 10). In contrast, work and family policies, practice 7, focus on creating an environment that fosters employee commitment and productivity. Consider the work and family practices used by Johnson & Johnson, Mattel Inc., Atlantic Richfield Company, Tenneco Inc., and Amoco Corporation:

accountability practices
Focus on treating diverse employees fairly.

> Johnson & Johnson allows employees to bring children to work to get picked up and dropped off for camp during the summer. Mattel Inc. in Segundo, Calif., closes down every Friday afternoon to give employees more time to spend with children. . . . Closer attention is being paid to elder-care too. Atlantic Richfield Co. has set up a toll-free line, and staffed it with counselors providing nationwide referrals to employees seeking care for older relatives. . . . Tenneco Inc. in Houston reimburses for child-care expenses when employees have to be out of town and their spouses aren't around. . . . Chicago-based Amoco Corp. supplies lightweight, miniaturized breast pumps to nursing mothers who must travel; previously nursing women had to carry around much heavier machines. The company also pays up to $750 a year for child-care and dependent-care services needed when an employee is on the road.[51]

Development Practices

development practices
Focus on preparing diverse employees for greater responsibility and advancement.

The use of development practices to manage diversity is relatively new compared with the historical use of accountability and recruitment practices. **Development practices** focus on preparing diverse employees for greater responsibility and

• ⟶ TABLE 3–3
Common Diversity Practices

Accountability Practices

 1. Top management's personal intervention
 2. Internal advocacy groups
 3. Emphasis on EEO statistics, profiles
 4. Inclusion of diversity in performance evaluation goals, ratings
 5. Inclusion of diversity in promotion decisions, criteria
 6. Inclusion of diversity in management succession planning
 7. Work and family policies
 8. Policies against racism, sexism
 9. Internal audit or attitude survey
10. Active AA/EEO committee, office

Development Practices

 1. Diversity training programs
 2. Networks and support groups
 3. Development programs for all high-potential managers
 4. Informal networking activities
 5. Job rotation
 6. Formal mentoring program
 7. Informal mentoring program
 8. Entry development programs for all high-potential new hires
 9. Internal training (such as personal safety or language)
10. Recognition events, awards

Recruitment Practices

 1. Targeted recruitment of nonmanagers
 2. Key outside hires
 3. Extensive public exposure on diversity (AA)
 4. Corporate image as liberal, progressive, or benevolent
 5. Partnerships with educational institutions
 6. Recruitment incentives such as cash supplements
 7. Internships (such as INROADS)
 8. Publications or PR products that highlight diversity
 9. Targeted recruitment of managers
10. Partnerships with nontraditional groups

Source: Abstracted from Tables A.10, A.11, and A.12 in A M Morrison, *The New Leaders: Guidelines on Leadership Diversity in America* (San Francisco: Jossey-Bass, 1992).

advancement. These activities are needed because most nontraditional employees have not been exposed to the type of activities and job assignments that develop effective leadership.[52] Table 3–3 indicates that diversity training programs and networks and support groups are the most frequently used developmental practices. For example, Levi Strauss & Company spends $5 million a year on its "valuing diversity" educational programs. This includes a 3½ day seminar for senior managers.[53]

Networks and support groups provide employees with guidance, support, and reinforcement. Kodak, for example, has five employee networks: for women, working parents, African-Americans, Hispanics, and gays and lesbians.[54] Because white males often feel threatened or attacked by diversity practices, and because this group's commitment to diversity initiatives is critical toward their success, some organizations also have formed white male support groups:

AT&T and Motorola Inc. are hiring consultants to lead seminars that help white males handle anxieties over their changing status. CoreStates Financial Corp. is forming a white men's support group similar to those in place for people of color as well as gays, lesbians, and bisexuals. For all male employees, DuPont Co. is creating a "Men's Forum."[55]

Diversity training is becoming common in corporate America. By creating and listening to this diversity council, Levi Strauss has become a leader in managing diversity.
Mark Richards/PhotoEdit

Recruitment Practices

recruitment practices
Attempts to attract qualified diverse employees at all levels.

Recruitment practices focus on attracting job applicants at all levels who are willing to accept challenging work assignments. This focus is critical because people learn the leadership skills needed for advancement by successfully accomplishing increasingly challenging and responsible work assignments.[56] As shown in Table 3–3, targeted recruitment of nonmanagers (practice 1) and managers (practice 9) are commonly used to identify and recruit women and people of color.[57] Consider the recruitment efforts pursued by JP Morgan, Ryder System, and AT&T:

> Diversity recruiting is a vital aspect of JP Morgan's recruiting process. The company recently developed an in-house diversity summer intern program to identify college and graduate students to join the firm for one or more summers. At Ryder System, encouraging diversity is more than the right thing to do. Last year [1992], Ryder Commercial Leasing & Services exceeded its goal to hire minorities and women. The company also has intensified its efforts to attract minority vendors and to partner with minority firms. AT&T believes that the only way to stay on top is by creating a richly diverse family of AT&T employees. The company supports a wide-ranging diversity curriculum and strong recruitment efforts.[58]

BARRIERS AND CHALLENGES TO MANAGING DIVERSITY

We introduced this chapter by noting that diversity is a sensitive, potentially volatile, and sometimes uncomfortable issue. It is therefore not surprising that organizations encounter significant barriers when trying to move forward with managing diversity. The following is a list of the most common barriers to implementing successful diversity programs:[59]

1. *Inaccurate stereotypes and prejudice.* This barrier manifests itself in the belief that differences are viewed as weaknesses. In turn, this promotes the view that diversity hiring will mean sacrificing competence and quality.[60]

ethnocentrism Belief that one's culture and norms are superior to others.

2. *Ethnocentrism.* The **ethnocentrism** barrier represents the feeling that one's cultural rules and norms are superior or more appropriate than the rules and norms of another culture.

3. *Poor career planning.* This barrier is associated with the lack of oppor-

tunities for diverse employees to get the type of work assignments that qualify them for senior management positions.

4. *An unsupportive and hostile working environment for diverse employees.* Diverse employees are frequently excluded from social events and the friendly camaraderie that takes place in most offices.

5. *Lack of political savvy on the part of diverse employees.* Diverse employees may not get promoted because they do not know how to "play the game" of getting along and getting ahead in an organization. Research reveals that women and people of color are excluded from organizational networks.[61]

6. *Difficulty in balancing career and family issues.* Women still assume the majority of the responsibilities associated with raising children. This makes it harder for women to work evenings and weekends or to frequently travel once they have children. Even without children in the picture, household chores take more of a woman's time than a man's time.[62]

7. *Fears of reverse discrimination.* Some employees believe that managing diversity is a smoke screen for reverse discrimination. This belief leads to very strong resistance because people feel that one person's gain is another's loss.

8. *Diversity is not seen as an organizational priority.* This leads to subtle resistance that shows up in the form of complaints and negative attitudes. Employees may complain about the time, energy, and resources devoted to diversity that could have been spent doing "real work."

9. *The need to revamp the organization's performance appraisal and reward system.* Performance appraisals and reward systems must reinforce the need to effectively manage diversity. This means that success will be based on a new set of criteria. Employees are likely to resist changes that adversely affect their promotions and financial rewards.

10. *Resistance to change.* Effectively managing diversity entails significant organizational and personal change. As discussed in Chapter 20, people resist change for many different reasons.

In summary, managing diversity is a critical component of organizational success. Case studies and limited research inform us that this effort is doomed to failure unless top management is truly committed to managing diversity.

BACK TO THE OPENING CASE

Now that you have read Chapter 3, you should be able to answer the following questions about the U S WEST case.

1. Which of the primary and secondary dimensions of diversity is U S WEST trying to effectively manage?

2. Use Table 3–1 to describe how U S WEST is using a combination of affirmative action, valuing diversity, and managing diversity to change the organization.

3. Describe how U S WEST is using diversity as a competitive advantage.

4. Using Table 3–3 as a point of reference, review the various accountability, development, and recruitment practices U S WEST is using to manage diversity.

5. How has U S WEST attempted to reduce the barriers and challenges to managing diversity? Provide examples.

SUMMARY OF KEY CONCEPTS

1. *Define diversity.* Diversity represents the multitude of individual differences that exist among people. Diversity pertains to everybody. It is not simply an issue of age, race, and gender.

2. *Discuss the primary and secondary dimensions of diversity.* Primary dimensions of diversity represent personal characteristics that are inborn. They significantly affect an individual's early socialization and include age, race, ethnicity, gender, physical abilities/qualities, and sexual/affectional orientation. Secondary dimensions are personal characteristics that can be changed. They are acquired, discarded, and/or modified throughout our lives.

3. *Explain the differences among affirmative action, valuing diversity, and managing diversity.* Affirmative action focuses on achieving equality of opportunity in an organization. It represents an artificial intervention aimed at giving management a chance to correct an imbalance, an injustice, and/or outright discrimination. Valuing diversity emphasizes the awareness, recognition, understanding, and appreciation of human differences. Training programs are the dominant method used to accomplish this objective. Managing diversity entails creating a host of organizational changes that enable all people to perform up to their maximum potential.

4. *Demonstrate your familiarity with the demographic trends that are creating an increasingly diverse workforce.* There are four key demographic trends: (1) half of the new entrants into the workforce between 1990 and 2005 will be women, (2) people of color will account for more than a third of the new entrants into the workforce between 1990 and 2005, (3) a mismatch exists between worker's educational attainment and occupational requirements, and (4) the workforce is aging.

5. *Highlight the managerial implications of increasing diversity in the workforce.* There are five broad managerial implications: (1) To attract the best workers, companies need to adopt policies and programs that particularly meet the needs of women and people of color; (2) techniques such as job redesign,

realistic job previews, and positive reinforcement are needed to reduce the problem of underemployment; (3) remedial skills training will be necessary to help the growing number of dropouts and illiterates cope with job demands; (4) organizations will need to tangibly support education if the United States is to remain globally competitive; and (5) the problem of career plateauing needs to be managed.

6. *Review the five reasons managing diversity is a competitive advantage.* (1) Managing diversity can lower costs and improve employee attitudes. (2) Managing diversity can improve an organization's recruiting efforts. (3) Managing diversity can increase sales and market share. (4) Managing diversity can increase creativity and innovation. (5) Managing diversity can increase group problem solving and productivity.

7. *Discuss the organizational practices used to effectively manage diversity.* There are many different practices organizations can use to manage diversity. Ann Morrison's study of diversity practices identified three main types or categories of activities. Accountability practices relate to a manager's responsibility to treat diverse employees fairly. Development practices focus on preparing diverse employees for greater responsibility and advancement. Recruitment practices emphasize attracting job applicants at all levels who are willing to accept challenging work assignments. Table 3–3 presents a list of activities that are used to accomplish each main type.

8. *Identify the barriers and challenges to managing diversity.* There are 10 barriers to successfully implementing diversity initiatives: (1) inaccurate stereotypes and prejudice, (2) ethnocentrism, (3) poor career planning, (4) an unsupportive and hostile working environment for diverse employees, (5) lack of political savvy on the part of diverse employees, (6) difficulty in balancing career and family issues, (7) fears of reverse discrimination, (8) diversity is not seen as an organizational priority, (9) the need to revamp the organization's performance appraisal and reward system, and (10) resistance to change.

DISCUSSION QUESTIONS

1. Whom do you think would be most resistant to accepting the value or need to manage diversity? Explain.

2. What role does communication play in effectively managing diversity?

3. Does diversity suggest that managers should follow the rule "Do unto others as you would have them do unto you?"

4. Which of the primary and secondary dimensions of diversity is most sensitive or volatile? Discuss your reasoning.

5. Do you think white males are an endangered species? Explain.

6. What is the most critical organizational challenge associated with the increase of people of color in the workforce? What can be done to facilitate the career success of minorities?

7. Why is underemployment a serious human resource management problem? If you have ever been under-employed, what were your feelings about it?

8. How can interpersonal conflict be caused by diversity? Explain your rationale.

9. Have you seen any examples that support the proposition that diversity is a competitive advantage? Describe your experiences.

10. Which of the barriers to managing diversity would be most difficult to reduce? Explain.

EXERCISE

Objectives

1. To improve your ability to manage diversity-related interactions more effectively.
2. To explore different approaches for handling diversity interactions.

Introduction

The interpersonal component of managing diversity can be awkward and uncomfortable. This is partly due to the fact that resolving diversity interactions requires us to deal with situations we may never have encountered before. The purpose of this exercise is to help you manage diversity-related interactions more effectively. To do so, you will be asked to read three scenarios and then decide how you will handle each situation.

Instructions

Presented here are three scenarios depicting diversity-related interactions.[63] Please read the first scenario, and then answer the three questions that follow it. Follow the same procedure for the next two scenarios. Next, divide into groups of three. One at a time, each person should present his or her responses to the three questions for the first scenario. The groups should then discuss the various approaches that were proposed to resolve the diversity interaction and try to arrive at a consensus recom-

mendation. Follow the same procedure for the next two scenarios.

Scenario 1

> Dave, who is one of your direct reports, comes to you and says that he and Scott are having a special commitment ceremony to celebrate the beginning of their lives together. He has invited you to the ceremony. Normally the department has a party and cake for special occasions. Mary, who is one of Dave's peers, has just walked into your office and asks you whether or not you intend to have a party for Dave.
>
> A. How would you respond?
>
> _____
>
> _____
>
> _____
>
> B. What is the potential impact of your response?
>
> _____
>
> _____
>
> _____
>
> C. If you choose not to respond, what is the potential impact of your behavior?
>
> _____
>
> _____
>
> _____

Scenario 2

You have an open position for a supervisor and your top two candidates are a black female and a white female. Both candidates are equally qualified. The position is responsible for five white team leaders. You hire the white female because the work group likes her. The team leaders said that they felt more comfortable with the white female. The vice president of Human Resources has just called you on the phone and asks you to explain why you hired the white female.

A. How would you respond?

_____

_____

_____

B. What is the potential impact of your response?

_____

_____

_____

C. If you choose not to respond, what is the potential impact of your behavior?

_____

_____

_____

Scenario 3

While attending an off-site business meeting, you are waiting in line with a group of team leaders to get your lunch at a buffet. Without any forewarning, one of your peers in the line loudly says, "Thank goodness Terry is at the end of the line. With his size and appetite there wouldn't be any food left for the rest of us." You believe Terry may have heard this comment, and you feel the comment was more of a "weight-related" slur than a joke.

A. How would you respond?

_____

_____

_____

B. What is the potential impact of your response?

_____

_____

_____

C. If you choose not to respond, what is the potential impact of your behavior?

_____

_____

_____

Questions for Consideration/Class Discussion

1. What was the recommended response for each scenario?
2. Which scenario generated the most emotion and disagreement? Explain why this occurred?

3. What is the potential impact of a manager's lack of response to each scenario? Explain.

NOTES

[1] Results are summarized in S Shellenbarger, "Work-Force Study Finds Loyalty Is Weak, Division of Race and Gender Are Deep," *The Wall Street Journal,* September 3, 1993, pp B1, B8.

[2] C Marmer Solomon, "Keeping Hate Out of the Workplace," *Personnel Journal,* July 1992, p 30.

[3] See L Gardenswartz and A Rowe, *Managing Diversity: A Complete Desk Reference and Planning Guide* (Homewood, IL: Business One Irwin, 1993); and C Torres and M Bruxelles, "Capitalizing on Global Diversity," *HRMagazine,* December 1992, pp 30–33.

[4] M Loden and J B Rosener, *Workforce America! Managing Employee Diversity as a Vital Resource* (Homewood, IL: Business One Irwin, 1991), p 18.

[5] Secondary dimensions of diversity are discussed by Loden and Rosener, *Workforce America! Managing Employee Diversity as a Vital Resource.*

[6] P Day, "Detective Gets Suspension for Keeping Ashes," *The Catholic Sun,* March 3, 1994, p 2.

[7] For a thorough discussion of affirmative action and its role in managing diversity, see J H Coil III, and C M Rice,

"Managing Work-Force Diversity in the Nineties: The Impact of the Civil Rights Act of 1991," *Employee Relations Law Journal,* Spring 1993, pp 547–65.

8 See R R Thomas, Jr., "From Affirmative Action to Affirming Diversity," *Harvard Business Review,* March–April 1990, pp 107–17; and P A Galagan, "Navigating the Differences," *Training & Development,* April 1993, pp 29–33.

9 M Galen and A T Palmer, "White, Male, and Worried," *Business Week,* January 31, 1994, p 50.

10 For a thorough review of relevant research, see M E Heilman, "Affirmative Action: Some Unintended Consequences for Working Women," in *Research in Organizational Behavior,* vol 16, eds B M Staw and L L Cummings (Greenwich, CT: JAI Press, 1994), pp 125–69.

11 Valuing diversity is discussed by R R Thomas, Jr., *Beyond Race and Gender* (New York: American Management Association, 1991).

12 The pros and cons of diversity training are discussed by V C Thomas, "The Downside of Diversity," *Training & Development,* January 1994, pp 60–62.

13 A M Morrison, *The New Leaders: Guidelines on Leadership Diversity in America* (San Francisco: Jossey-Bass, 1992), p 78.

14 See V Elliott and A Orgera, "Competing for and with Workforce 2000," *HR Focus,* June 1993, pp 3–4.

15 Statistics are presented in A L Otten, "Gender Pay Gap Eased Over Last Decade," *The Wall Street Journal,* April 15, 1994, p B1.

16 See D R Dalton and I F Kesner, "Cracks in the Glass: The Silent Competence of Women," *Business Horizons,* March–April 1993, pp 6–10.

17 Barriers to women reaching the top are discussed by C M Daily, "The (R)Evolution of the American Woman," *Business Horizons,* March–April 1993, pp 1–4; and A M Morrison, R P White, E Van Velso, and The Center for Creative Leadership, *Breaking the Glass Ceiling: Can Women Reach the Top of America's Largest Corporations?* (New York: Addison-Wesley, 1987).

18 See D J Gaiter, "The Gender Divide: Black Women's Gains in Corporate America Outstrip Black Men's," *The Wall Street Journal,* March 8, 1994, pp A1, A12.

19 See L E Wynter, "Business & Race: Double Whammy Hinders 'Double Minorities,'" *The Wall Street Journal,* January 19, 1994, p B1; and J E Rigdon, "Three Decades After the Equal Pay Act, Women's Wages Remain Far from Parity," *The Wall Street Journal,* pp B1, B3.

20 See Shellenbarger, "Work-Force Study Finds Loyalty Is Weak, Division of Race and Gender Are Deep," pp B1, B8.

21 Educational statistics can be found in Table no 648, US Bureau of the Census, Statistical Abstract of the United States: 1990 (110th ed), Washington, DC.

22 A Swardson, "The Swelling Ranks of the Underemployed," *The Washington Post National Weekly Edition,* February 17–23, 1992, p 20.

23 See C Duff, "Poor Prospects: In a Portland Hot Tub, Young Grads' Anxiety Bubbles to the Surface," *The Wall Street Journal,* July 28, 1993, pp A1, A6; and L S Richman, "Struggling to Save Our Kids," *Fortune,* August 10, 1992, pp 34–40.

24 Supportive results can be found in G Jones-Johnson and C O Herring, "Underemployment among Black Americans," *The Western Journal of Black Studies,* Fall 1993, pp 126–34; and G Jones-Johnson and W R Johnson, "Subjective Underemployment and Psychosocial Stress: The Role of Perceived Social Support and Supervisor Support," *The Journal of Social Psychology,* February 1992, pp 11–21.

25 These statistics were presented in M Gianturco, "An Apple for the Computer," *Forbes,* August 16, 1993, p 110; and "20% of US Workers Functionally Illiterate," *USA Today,* April 1992, p 13.

26 See R J Paul and J B Townsend, "Managing the Older Worker—Don't Just Rinse Away the Gray," *The Academy of Management Executive,* August 1993, pp 67–74.

27 J E Santora, "Nabisco Tackles Tomorrow's Skills Gap," *Personnel Journal,* September 1992, p 48.

28 P M Elsass and D A Ralston, "Individual Responses to the Stress of Career Plateauing," *Journal of Management,* Spring 1989, p 35.

29 Supportive findings can be found in N Nicholson, "Purgatory or Place of Safety? The Managerial Plateau and Organizational Agegrading," *Human Relations,* December 1993, pp 1369–89; and Elsass and Ralston, "Individual Responses to the Stress of Career Plateauing," pp 35–47.

30 Organizational solutions for managing career plateauing are discussed by D Fenn, "Bottoms Up," *Inc.,* July 1993, pp 58–60; B A DeLon, "Keeping Plateaued Performers Motivated," *Library Administration and Management,* Winter 1993, pp 13–15; and S Sherman, "A Brave New Darwinian Workplace," *Fortune,* January 25, 1993, pp 50–56.

31 This discussion is based on an article by T H Cox and S Blake, "Managing Cultural Diversity: Implications for Organizational Competitiveness," *The Academy of Management Executive,* August 1991, pp 45–56.

32 See P A Galagan, "Trading Places at Monsanto," *Training & Development,* April 1993, pp 45–49.

33 Corning's diversity efforts are discussed in K Kazi-Ferrouillet, ''Cracking Corning's Glass Ceiling,'' *The Black Collegian,* March/April 1992 pp 56–61; and C Hymowitz, ''One Firm's Bid to Keep Blacks, Women,'' *The Wall Street Journal,* February 16, 1989, p B1.

34 Details of this study may be found in J H Greenhaus, S Parasuraman, and W M Wormley, ''Effects of Race on Organizational Experiences, Job Performance Evaluations, and Career Outcomes,'' *Academy of Management Journal,* March 1990, pp 64–86.

35 For a discussion of gay and lesbian issues, see J H Lucas and M G Kaplan, ''Unlocking the Corporate Closet,'' *Training & Development,* January 1994, pp 35–38; A D Williamson, ''Is This the Right Time to Come Out?'' *Harvard Business Review,* July–August 1993, pp 18–28; and T A Stewart, ''Gay in Corporate America,'' *Fortune,* December 16, 1991, pp 42–56.

36 For a discussion of issues surrounding workers' disabilities, see R S Foster, Jr., ''The Disabled as Part of a Diverse Workforce,'' *SAM Advanced Management Journal,* Spring 1993, pp 21–27; C Quintanilla, ''Disabilities Act Helps—But Not Much: Disabled People Aren't Getting More Job Offers,'' *The Wall Street Journal,* July 19, 1993, pp B1, B5; and ''Ten Rules for Communicating with Disabled People,'' *ABA Banking Journal,* April 1992, pp 7–9.

37 ''Labor Letter: A Special News Report on People and Their Jobs in Offices, Fields, and Factories,'' *The Wall Street Journal,* October 10, 1989, p A1.

38 L E Wynter, ''Minorities Play the Hero in More TV Ads as Clients Discover Multicultural Sells,'' *The Wall Street Journal,* November 24, 1993, p B1.

39 See ''What Should Business and Government Do for Women in 1993?'' *Working Woman,* November 1992, pp 56–65.

40 Thorough discussions about black consumers are provided by E Morris, ''The Difference in Black and White,'' *American Demographics,* January 1993, pp 44–49; and J C Simpson, ''Buying Black,'' *Time,* August 31, 1992, pp 52–53.

41 See G Stern, ''Marketing: Lifestyle-Appropriate Greeting Cards,'' *The Wall Street Journal,* February 16, 1994, p B1; and M Hudis, ''Major Advertisers Devise New Products for Gay Consumers,'' *Mediaweek,* January 3, 1994, p 2.

42 M Cox, ''New Magazines Cater to People with HIV,'' *The Wall Street Journal,* March 1, 1994, p B1.

43 Wynter, ''Minorities Play the Hero in More TV Ads as Clients Discover Multicultural Sells,'' p B6.

44 See R Moss-Kanter, *The Change Masters* (New York: Simon and Schuster, 1983).

45 A thorough review of this research is provided by R R Mai-Dalton, ''Managing Cultural Diversity on the Individual, Group, and Organizational Levels,'' in *Leadership Theory and Research: Perspectives and Directions,* eds M M Chemers and R Ayman (New York: Academic Press 1993); and R T Mowday and R I Sutton, ''Organizational Behavior: Linking Individuals and Groups to Organizational Contexts,'' in *Annual Review of Psychology,* vol 44, eds L W Porter and M R Rosenzweig (Palo Alto, CA: Annual Reviews Inc., 1993), pp 195–229.

46 Problems with diversity research are summarized by Ibid.; and W E Watson, K Kumar, and L K Michaelson, ''Cultural Diversity's Impact on Interaction Process and Performance: Comparing Homogeneous and Diverse Task Groups,'' *Academy of Management Journal,* June 1993, pp 590–602.

47 Results can be found in Watson, Kumar, and Michaelson, ''Cultural Diversity's Impact on Interaction Process and Performance: Comparing Homogeneous and Diverse Task Groups,'' pp 590–602.

48 Supportive results can be found in M F Wiersema and A Bird, ''Organizational Demography in Japanese Firms: Group Heterogeneity, Individual Dissimilarity, and Top Management Team Turnover,'' *Academy of Management Journal,* October 1993, pp 996–1025; A S Tsui, T D Egan, and C A O'Reilly III, ''Being Different: Relational Demography and Organizational Attachment,'' *Administrative Science Quarterly,* December 1992, pp 549–79; and S E Jackson, J F Brett, V I Sessa, D M Cooper, J A Julin, and K Peyronnin, ''Some Differences Make a Difference: Individual Dissimilarity and Group Heterogeneity as Correlates of Recruitment, Promotions, and Turnover,'' *Journal of Applied Psychology,* October 1991, pp 675–89.

49 See the related discussion by Cox and Blake, ''Managing Cultural Diversity: Implications for Organizational Competitiveness,'' pp 45–56.

50 For complete details and results from this study, see Morrison, *The New Leaders: Guidelines on Leadership Diversity in America.*

51 Information about Johnson & Johnson, Mattel Inc., and Atlantic Richfield was obtained from L Harper, ''Family Friendly: Many Companies Go Farther than the Law Requires,'' *The Wall Street Journal,* January 11, 1994, p A1. Information on Tenneco Inc. and Amoco Corporation was taken from L Harper, ''Business Travel Can Be Rough on an Employee's Personal Life,'' *The Wall Street Journal,* October 5, 1993, p A1.

52 Empirical support is provided by P J Ohlott, M N Ruderman, and C D McCauley, ''Gender Differences in Managers' Developmental Job Experiences,'' *Academy of Management Journal,* February 1994, pp 46–67.

53 A description of Levi Strauss's training program is contained in A Cuneo, "Diverse by Design: How Good Intentions Make Good Business," *Business Week,* October 23, 1992, p 72.

54 Kodak's support groups are discussed in H Allerton, "Diversity Grows More Diverse," *Training & Development,* April 1993, p 31.

55 Galen and Palmer, "White, Male, and Worried," p 53.

56 See Morrison, *The New Leaders: Guidelines on Leadership Diversity in America.*

57 The pros and cons of targeted recruiting is discussed by J S Lublin, "Firms Designate Some Openings for Women Only," *The Wall Street Journal,* February 7, 1994, pp B1, B4.

58 "Managing Diversity," *Black Enterprise,* July 1993, p 84.

59 These barriers were taken from related discussions in E E Spragins, "Benchmark: The Diverse Work Force," *Inc.,* January 1993, p 33; Morrison, *The New Leaders: Guidelines on Leadership Diversity in America;* Gardenswartz and Rowe, *Managing Diversity: A Complete Desk Reference and Planning Guide;* and T Cox, Jr., "The Multicultural Organization," *The Academy of Management Executive,* May 1991, pp 34–47.

60 The affect of race and racism is discussed by S M Nkomo, "The Emperor Has No Clothes: Rewriting Race in Organizations," *Academy of Management Review,* July 1992, pp 487–513; and J Dovidio, "The Subtlety of Racism," *Training & Development,* April 1993, pp 51–57.

61 For a thorough review of this research, see H Ibarra, "Personal Networks of Women and Minorities in Management: A Conceptual Framework," *Academy of Management Review,* January 1993, pp 56–87.

62 Discussions of work-family issues are provided by K G Salwen, "Women Executives See Gains in Job Promotions—But Pay the Price Socially," *The Wall Street Journal,* March 8, 1994, p A1; J A Schneer and F Reitman, "Effects of Alternative Family Structures on Managerial Career Paths," *Academy of Management Journal,* August 1993, pp 830–43; and S A Lobel and L St. Clair, "Effects of Family Responsibilities, Gender, and Career Identity Salience on Performance Outcomes," *Academy of Management Journal,* December 1992, pp 1057–69.

63 These scenarios were developed by A J Kinicki, *Valuing Diversity* (Chandler, AZ: Angelo Kinicki), pp 4-3, 4-7, 4-10.

INDIVIDUAL BEHAVIOR

P
A
R
T

II

INDIVIDUAL DIFFERENCES, VALUES, AND ETHICS

Learning OBJECTIVES

When you finish studying the material in this chapter, you should be able to:

1. Explain the nature and determinants of organization-based self-esteem.

2. Define self-efficacy and explain its sources.

3. Identify and describe the Big Five personality dimensions and specify which one is correlated most strongly with job performance.

4. Explain the difference between an internal and an external locus of control.

5. Describe Carl Jung's cognitive styles typology.

6. Distinguish between instrumental and terminal values.

7. Describe the three basic ethical criteria: utilitarian, rights, and justice.

8. Specify at least four actions managers can take to improve an organization's ethical climate.

What Makes Bill Clinton Tick?

Sharon Hoogstraten

Recent polls have shown that Americans—whatever they think of his policies and his character—appreciate Clinton's formidable energy and his doughty resilience. And Clinton knows these traits are his biggest advantages. As he told a senior Republican lawmaker last fall, "I'm a lot like Baby Huey. I'm fat. I'm ugly. But if you push me down, I keep coming back. I just keep coming back."

Clinton is a complex, highly intense man who does almost everything at full throttle. He watches several movies each week—the White House refuses to release an exact number—and reads five or six books at once. He relaxes not by watching a basketball game on TV, or reading, or picking up the telephone, or doing crossword puzzles, but doing all four simultaneously, while worrying an unlit cigar. Clinton fights his schedulers for

free time every weekend, but then gets jumpy by midday Sunday and is often working in some fashion by Sunday night. [In August 1993,] as he was preparing to leave Washington for his longest vacation in four years, he suddenly got cold feet. Consultant Paul Begala started throwing fastballs. "Mr. President, if you don't go on vacation, the American people are going to think you're weird." Replied Clinton: "I *am* weird."

But after several attempts at rehabilitation, White House officials realize it isn't easy, or perhaps even wise, to try to change the habits of this driven and eccentrically methodical 47-year-old man. If Clinton's work habits are unorthodox, they are also increasingly successful. "He's inventing a new form of chaos theory that works for him," said an Administration veteran. "People are going to have to get used to the fact that this is a different White House. It may look chaotic from the outside. The people who work there may feel it is chaotic. But if it works one more time, they ought to just lock it in and not fool with it. You've got to just hope that it's only going to blow up once in a while."

It was a measure of Clinton's omnivorous personality that he spent part of [1993] going to meetings alone. For several months he had no single, full-time, substantive minder, someone

who would be with him at all times to keep track of the things people asked him to do. So Clinton did it himself, just as he had as Governor, though the arrangement created a troublesome bottleneck. "No one sat with him on every meeting," said an adviser. "He was the only one who knew when two different people were arguing for the same money."

That helps explain why Clinton had such a difficult start. But the problem was complicated by the fact that Clinton wanted it this way: he liked having 20 people report to him, feeding him volumes of information that he would sit and consider in solitude. He wanted to be his own chief of staff, his own legislative director and his own National Security Adviser. He wanted to be as involved in choosing the dozen presidential scholars coming for lunch as in wrestling with the wording of minor speeches. He was reluctant to let even minor White House proclamations go out without review. He recently barked at an aide who tried to release a statement on ethanol, saying he had to run it by two Midwestern Senators—personally. "It's almost a throwback to the old days when Presidents did everything themselves," said an official. Added another, "He tries to keep all these balls in the air. He could get away with it in Little Rock. He was smart enough to pull it off in that

What makes you *you?* What characteristics do you share with others? Which ones set you apart? Perhaps you have a dynamic personality and dress and act accordingly, while a low-key friend dresses conservatively and avoids crowds. Maybe your values, attitudes, and beliefs vary. Someone is politically active, someone else is not. Another person likes ear-splitting heavy metal music while still another prefers soft classical music. Some computer buffs would rather program than eat; other people suffer from computer phobia. Some

OPENING CASE

(concluded)

town. But here? He's not that smart."

Aides say Clinton is aware of the problem but has trouble taking the steps to correct it. Where once he participated in grueling, two- and three-hour briefings on everything from the budget to the rehiring of fired air-traffic controllers, he has begun to realize that he was having, as he put it, "arguments I didn't need to win." He once insisted on sitting through a briefing on maritime reform only to say afterward, "I shouldn't have spent an hour on that." Observed an official: "He does want to be endlessly involved in the minutiae. He sits down, he smiles, he gets engaged and educates himself. And then he walks out of the room and pitches a fit: 'Why did I have to sit through that?' " Said one who minded him for several months: "He'll complain about the schedule, but he's the one who puts the stuff on the schedule in the first place."

Advisers must also contend with the most creative and chaotic part of Clinton's personality: his desire to constantly roam the mental landscape of the presidency. His 9:15 a.m. meeting with top aides, ostensibly to discuss his schedule, often devolves into a general discussion about whatever is in the news. Clinton holds forth in these sessions, skipping among four or five subjects with as many as 10 officials.

Clinton likes to ask whomever he is with for an opinion about whatever is on his mind, whether that person knows much about it or not. In private Clinton will admit to his weakness, likening it to the habit of a schoolboy who enters a public library to browse the history stacks but then loses himself in mysteries. "He can have a 10-minute meeting in two hours," says an aide. . . .

[Scheduled] afternoon free time has given Clinton a chance to do what White House officials call "processing and synthesizing" the data he is constantly gathering on big decisions. Clinton, they say, needs to "internalize" important decisions, putting together policy proposals, ideas, opinion polls, advice from aides, views of outside experts and comments from everyday people in a kind of cerebral Mixmaster. "Early on, no one understood this," says a veteran of Clinton's campaign. "But a whole lot of things have to happen before it becomes *his* policy. He needs to think that he has been through a thorough analysis. He has to hear the good options, the bad options, the difficult options, the crazy ideas and the traditional ideas, so that by the time he makes his case to the American people, he knows it fully, he's internalized it." . . .

During one discussion with economic advisers [in 1993], Clinton made both the conservative and liberal arguments against his deficit-reduction plan; last fall, when his advisers unanimously agreed to oppose a balanced-budget amendment, Clinton immediately took the opposite view in the meeting. "We took it to him, and he bounced it," said an official. "It proves that he wants to hear both sides." (Later Clinton agreed to oppose it.)

For Clinton, this kind of give-and-take enables him to make his case to the public more effectively, and he has developed a high confidence in his ability to sell his ideas once he has internalized them. "The speech," said an official, "is the place where he does the processing. It is the defining event. And that's why," she added, "no one can write it for him."

For Discussion

Is Clinton's personality a plus or minus in his role as President of the United States?

■ Additional discussion questions linking this case with the following material appear at the end of this chapter.

Source: Excerpted from M Duffy, "The State of Bill Clinton," *Time*, February 7, 1994, pp 24–29. Copyright 1994 Time, Inc. Excerpted by permission.

employees pad their expense accounts without a second thought; others call the practice unethical and refrain. Thanks to a vast array of individual differences such as these, modern organizations have a rich and interesting human texture. On the other hand, individual differences make the manager's job endlessly challenging. In fact, according to recent research, "variability among workers is substantial at all levels but increases dramatically with job complexity. In life insurance sales, for example, variability in performance is around six times as great as in routine clerical jobs."[1]

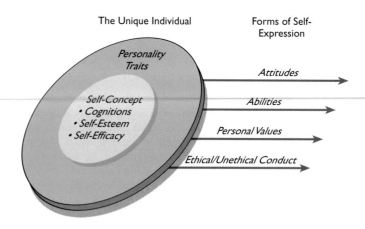

FIGURE 4~1

A Conceptual Model for the Study of Individual Differences in OB

Growing workforce diversity, as discussed in Chapter 3, compels managers to view individual differences in a fresh new way. The case for this new perspective was presented in Britain's *Journal of Managerial Psychology:*

> For many years America's businesses sought homogeneity—a work force that believed in, supported, and presented a particular image. The notion of the company man dressed for success in the banker's blue or corporation's grey flannel suit was *de riguer.* Those able to move into leadership positions succeeded to the extent they behaved and dressed according to a rather narrowly defined standard.
>
> To compete today, and in preparation for the work force of tomorrow, successful businesses and organisations are adapting to both internal and external changes. New operational styles, language, customs, values, and even dress, are a real part of this adaptation. We now hear leaders talking about ''valuing differences,'' and learning to ''manage diversity.''[2]

So rather than limiting diversity, as in the past, today's managers need to better understand and accommodate employee diversity and individual differences.[3]

This chapter explores the following important dimensions of individual differences: (1) self-concept, (2) personality traits, (3) abilities, and (4) personal values and ethics. Figure 4–1 is a conceptual model showing the relationship between self-concept (how you view yourself), personality (how you appear to others), and key forms of self-expression. Considered as an integrated package, these factors provide a foundation for better understanding each organizational contributor as a unique and special individual.

SELF-CONCEPT: THE I AND ME IN OB

self-concept Person's self-perception as a physical, social, spiritual being.

cognitions A person's knowledge, opinions, or beliefs.

Self is the core of one's conscious existence. Awareness of self is referred to as one's self-concept. Sociologist Viktor Gecas defines **self-concept** as ''the concept the individual has of himself as a physical, social, and spiritual or moral being.''[4] In other words, if you have a self-concept, you recognize yourself as a distinct human being. A self-concept would be impossible without the capacity to think. This brings us to the role of cognitions. **Cognitions** represent ''any knowledge, opinion, or belief about the environment, about oneself, or about one's behavior.''[5] Among many different types of cognitions, those involving anticipation, planning, goal setting, evaluating, and setting personal standards are particularly relevant to OB.[6] Several cognition-based topics are discussed in later chapters. Differing cognitive styles are introduced in this chapter. Cognitions play a central role in social perception, as will be discussed in Chapter 5. Also, as we will see in Chapters 6 and 7, modern motivation theories and techniques are powered by cognitions. Successful self-management, covered in Chapter 8, requires cognitive support.

Importantly, ideas of self and self-concept vary from one historical era to another, from one socioeconomic class to another, and from culture to culture.[7] How well one detects and adjusts to different cultural notions of self can spell the difference between success and failure in international dealings. For example, as detailed in the International OB, Japanese–US communication and understanding is often hindered by significantly different degrees of self-disclosure. With a comparatively large public self, Americans pride themselves in being open, honest, candid, and to the point. Meanwhile, Japanese, who culturally discourage self-disclosure, typically view Americans as blunt, prying, and insensitive to formalities. For their part, Americans tend to see Japanese as distant, cold, and evasive.[8]

INTERNATIONAL OB

Culture Dictates the Degree of Self-Disclosure in Japan and the United States

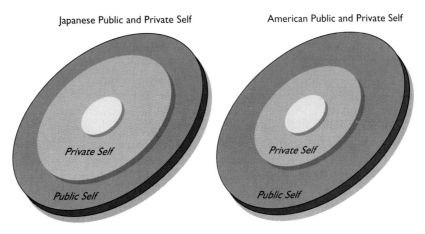

Japanese Public and Private Self   American Public and Private Self

Private Self (the self not revealed to others)
Public Self (the self made accessible to others)

Survey research in Japan and the United States uncovered the following *distinct contrasts* in Japanese versus American self-disclosure:

■ Americans disclosed nearly as much to strangers as the Japanese did to their own fathers.

■ Americans reported two to three times greater physical contact with parents and twice greater contact with friends than the Japanese.

■ The Japanese may be frightened at the prospect of being communicatively invaded (because of the unexpected spontaneity and bluntness of the American); the American is annoyed at the prospect of endless formalities and tangential replies.

■ American emphasis on self-assertion and talkativeness cultivates a communicator who is highly self-oriented and expressive; the Japanese emphasis on "reserve" and "sensitivity" cultivates a communicator who is other-oriented and receptive.

Source: Adapted from D C Barnlund, "Public and Private Self in Communicating with Japan," *Business Horizons*, March–April 1989, pp 32–40.

One culture is not right and the other wrong. They are just different, and a key difference involves culturally rooted conceptions of self and self-disclosure.

Keeping this cultural qualification in mind, let us explore two topics invariably mentioned when behavioral scientists discuss self-concept. They are self-esteem and self-efficacy. Each deserves a closer look by those who want to better understand and effectively manage people at work.

Self-Esteem

self-esteem One's overall self-evaluation.

Self-esteem is a belief about one's own worth based on an overall self-evaluation.[9] Those with low self-esteem tend to view themselves in negative terms. They do not feel good about themselves, tend to have trouble dealing effectively with others, and are hampered by self-doubts. The massive wave of corporate downsizings in recent years has taken its toll on self-esteem. For example, after losing his $50,000-a-year job at CIGNA Corporation, getting divorced, losing his home, and piling up bills and back taxes, Allen Stenhouse said, ''I was determined to find work, but as the months and years wore on, depression set in. You can only be rejected so many times; then you start questioning your own self-worth.''[10]

High self-esteem individuals, in contrast, see themselves as worthwhile, capable, and acceptable.[11] Although high self-esteem generally is considered a good thing because it is associated with better performance and greater satisfaction, recent research uncovered a flaw among those with high self-esteem. Specifically, high self-esteem subjects tended to become egotistical and boastful when faced with pressure situations.[12] So self-esteem, like many other good things in life, appears to be best in moderation.

Feelings of self-esteem are shaped by our circumstances and how others treat us. Researchers who tracked 654 young adults (192 male; 462 female) for eight years found higher self-esteem among those in school or working full-time than among those with part-time jobs or unemployed.[13] In a more recent study, youth-league baseball coaches who were trained in supportive teaching techniques had a positive effect on the self-esteem of young boys. A control group of untrained coaches had no such positive effect.[14] Skillful parental attention during one's developmental years also is critical. Consider, for example, the following bit of advice to busy managers who want to be good parents:

> The most important thing a parent can do for a child is to encourage a high sense of self-esteem. Easier said than done, of course. The tricky part is helping children set appropriate, satisfying goals and then providing an environment that lets them reach the goals on their own. Building your child's self-esteem is an inconvenient, time-consuming, and maddeningly imprecise occupation, and don't be amazed if you mess up. . . . But kids who have a sense of self-worth flourish.[15]

Accordingly, a job-related laboratory study found high self-esteem individuals more willing to accept the challenge of difficult goals than were low self-esteem individuals.[16] Goal setting, as we will see in Chapter 7, is a well-documented motivational technique for improving job performance. Moreover, a study of computer-manufacturing employees found successful work teams to have significantly higher average self-esteem scores than unsuccessful teams.[17] Thus, both individual and group job performance tend to improve as self-esteem increases.[18]

OB EXERCISE

How Strong Is Your Organization-Based Self-Esteem (OBSE)?

Instructions:

Relative to your present (or last) job, how strongly do you agree or disagree with each of the following statements?

		Strongly Disagree				Strongly Agree
1.	I count around here.	1—2—3—4—5				
2.	I am taken seriously around here.	1—2—3—4—5				
3.	I am important around here.	1—2—3—4—5				
4.	I am trusted around here.	1—2—3—4—5				
5.	There is faith in me around here.	1—2—3—4—5				
6.	I can make a difference around here.	1—2—3—4—5				
7.	I am valuable around here.	1—2—3—4—5				
8.	I am helpful around here.	1—2—3—4—5				
9.	I am efficient around here.	1—2—3—4—5				
10.	I am cooperative around here.	1—2—3—4—5				

Total score = ___

Source: Adapted from discussion in J L Pierce, D G Gardner, L L Cummings, and R B Dunham, "Organization-Based Self-Esteem: Construct Definition, Measurement, and Validation," *Academy of Management Journal*, September 1989, pp 622–48.

Organization-Based Self-Esteem   The self-esteem just discussed is a global belief about oneself. But what about self-esteem in organizations, a more restricted context of greater importance to managers? A model of organization-based self-esteem was recently developed and validated with seven studies involving 2,444 teachers, students, managers, and employees. The researchers defined **organization-based self-esteem (OBSE)** as the "self-perceived value that individuals have of themselves as organization members acting within an organizational context."[19] Those scoring high on OBSE tend to view themselves as important, worthwhile, effectual, and meaningful within the context of their employing organization. Take a moment to complete the brief OBSE questionnaire in the OB Exercise. This exercise will help you better understand the concept of organization-based self-esteem, as well as assessing the supportiveness of your work setting. (Arbitrary norms for comparison purposes are: Low OBSE = 10–20; Moderate OBSE = 21–39; High OBSE = 40–50.)

A basic model of OBSE is displayed in Figure 4–2. On the left-hand side of the model are three primary determinants of organization-based self-esteem. OBSE tends to increase when employees believe their supervisors have a genuine concern for employees' welfare. Flexible, organic organization structures generate higher OBSE than do mechanistic (rigid bureaucratic) structures (the organic–mechanistic distinction is discussed in Chapter 18). Complex and challenging jobs foster higher OBSE than do simple, repetitive, and boring jobs. Significantly, these same factors also are associated with greater task motivation.

Factors positively influenced by high OBSE and negatively impacted by low OBSE are listed in the right-hand side of Figure 4–2. Intrinsic motivation refers to

organization-based self-esteem   An organization member's self-perceived value.

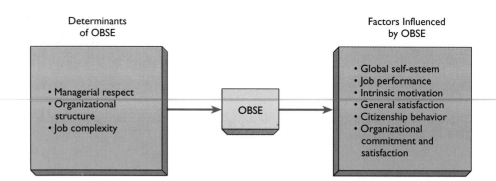

FIGURE 4-2

The Determinants and Consequences of Organization-Based Self-Esteem (OBSE)

personal feelings of accomplishment. Citizenship behavior involves doing things beneficial for the organization itself. The other consequences of OBSE are self-explanatory. In sum, active enhancement of organization-based self-esteem promises to build a very important cognitive bridge to greater productivity and satisfaction.[20]

Practical Tips for Building On-the-Job Self-Esteem   According to a study by the American Society for Personnel Administration (now the Society for Human Resource Management), managers can build employee self-esteem in four ways:

1. Be supportive by showing concern for personal problems, interests, status, and contributions.
2. Offer work involving variety, autonomy, and challenges that suit the individual's values, skills, and abilities.
3. Strive for management–employee cohesiveness and build trust. (Trust, an important teamwork element, is discussed in Chapter 12.)
4. Have faith in each employee's self-management ability (see Chapter 8). Reward successes.[21]

Self-Efficacy

Have you noticed how those who are confident about their ability tend to succeed, while those who are preoccupied with failing tend to fail? Perhaps that explains the comparative golfing performance of your authors! One consistently stays in the fairways and hits the greens. The other spends the day thrashing through the underbrush, wading in water hazards, and blasting out of sand traps. At the heart of this performance mismatch is a specific dimension of self-esteem called self-efficacy. **Self-efficacy** is a person's belief about his or her chances of successfully accomplishing a specific task. According to one OB writer, ''self-efficacy arises from the gradual acquisition of complex cognitive, social, linguistic, and/or physical skills through experience.''[22] Childhood experiences have a powerful effect on a person's self-efficacy. Whoopi Goldberg, for example, attributes much of her success as a performing artist to her mother's guidance. Says Goldberg, who grew up in New York City as Caryn Johnson,

> My mom encouraged me to explore the city, get on the bus and go watch Leonard Bernstein conduct the young people's concerts, go to the museums and planetarium, Central Park and Coney Island. There were always things for me to investigate, and she encouraged me to ask a lot of questions.

self-efficacy Belief in one's ability to do a task.

Thanks, Mom! Whoopi Goldberg attributes much of her success to a strong sense of self-efficacy—a can-do attitude—cultivated by her mother who encouraged her to explore and experience new things.

Reuters/Bettmann

As kids, my mom instilled in both my brother [Clyde] and me an ideal of what life could and should be, and how we could participate in it. It was never intimated to me that I couldn't be exactly what I wanted to be.[23]

Researchers have documented a strong linkage between high self-efficacy expectations and success in widely varied physical and mental tasks, anxiety reduction, addiction control, pain tolerance, and illness recovery.[24] Oppositely, those with low self-efficacy expectations tend to have low success rates. Chronically low self-efficacy is associated with a condition called **learned helplessness,** the severely debilitating belief that one has no control over one's environment.[25] Although self-efficacy sounds like some sort of mental magic, it operates in a very straightforward manner, as a model will show.

learned helplessness
Debilitating lack of faith in one's ability to control the situation.

What Are the Mechanisms of Self-Efficacy?   A basic model of self-efficacy is displayed in Figure 4–3. It draws upon the work of Stanford psychologist Albert Bandura. Let us explore this model with a simple illustrative task. Imagine you have been told to prepare and deliver a 10-minute talk to an OB class of 50 students on the workings of the self-efficacy model in Figure 4–3. Your self-efficacy calculation would involve cognitive appraisal of the interaction between your perceived capability and situational opportunities and obstacles.

As you begin to prepare for your presentation, the four sources of self-efficacy beliefs would come into play. Because prior experience is the most potent source, according to Bandura, it is listed first and connected to self-efficacy beliefs with a solid line.[26] Past success in public speaking would boost your self-efficacy. But bad experiences with delivering speeches would foster low self-efficacy. Regarding behavior models as a source of self-efficacy beliefs, you would be influenced by the success or failure of your classmates in delivering similar talks. Their successes would tend to bolster you (or perhaps their failure would if you were very competitive and had high self-esteem). Likewise, any supportive persuasion from your classmates that you will do a good job would enhance your self-efficacy. Physical and emotional factors also might affect your self-confidence. A sudden case of laryngitis or a bout of stage fright could cause your self-efficacy expecta-

◆ • FIGURE 4-3 A Model of How Self-Efficacy Beliefs Can Pave the Way for Success or Failure

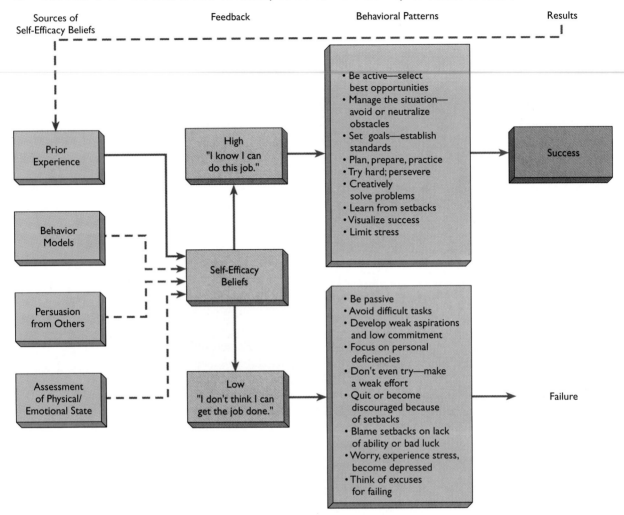

Sources: Adapted from discussion in A Bandura, "Regulation of Cognitive Processes through Perceived Self-Efficacy," *Developmental Psychology*, September 1989, pp 729–35, and R Wood and A Bandura, "Social Cognitive Theory of Organizational Management," *Academy of Management Review*, July 1989, pp 361–84.

tions to plunge. Your cognitive evaluation of the situation then would yield a self-efficacy belief—ranging from high to low expectations for success. Importantly, self-efficacy beliefs are not merely boastful statements based on bravado; they are deep convictions supported by experience.

Moving to the *behavioral patterns* portion of Figure 4–3, we see how self-efficacy beliefs are acted out. In short, if you have high self-efficacy about giving your 10-minute speech you will work harder, more creatively, and longer when preparing for your talk than will your low-self-efficacy classmates. The results would then take shape accordingly. People program themselves for success or failure by enacting their self-efficacy expectations. Positive or negative results subsequently become feedback for one's base of personal experience.

Self-Efficacy Implications for Managers   On-the-job research evidence encourages managers to nurture self-efficacy, both in themselves and in others. In one study, for example, the sales performance of life insurance agents was much better among those with high self-efficacy.[27] Self-efficacy requires constructive action in each of the following managerial areas:

1. *Recruiting/selection/job assignments.* Interview questions can be designed to probe job applicants' general self-efficacy as a basis for determining orientation and training needs. Pencil-and-paper tests for self-efficacy are not in an advanced stage of development and validation. Care needs to be taken not to hire solely on the basis of self-efficacy because studies have detected below-average self-esteem and self-efficacy among women and protected minorities.[28]

2. *Job design.* Complex, challenging, and autonomous jobs tend to enhance perceived self-efficacy. Boring, tedious jobs generally do the opposite.

3. *Training and development.* Employees' self-efficacy expectations for key tasks can be improved through guided experiences, mentoring, and role modeling.[29]

4. *Self-management.* Systematic self-management training, as discussed in Chapter 8, involves enhancement of self-efficacy expectations.

5. *Goal setting and quality improvement.* Goal difficulty needs to match the individual's perceived self-efficacy.[30] As self-efficacy and performance improve, goals and quality standards can be made more challenging.

6. *Coaching.* Those with low self-efficacy and employees victimized by learned helplessness need lots of constructive pointers and positive feedback.

7. *Leadership.* Needed leadership talent surfaces when top management gives high self-efficacy managers a chance to prove themselves under pressure.

8. *Rewards.* Small successes need to be rewarded as stepping-stones to a stronger self-image and greater achievements.

Now that we have a better understanding of self-image, our attention turns to how others see us as unique individuals.

Individuals have their own way of thinking and acting, their own unique style or *personality.* **Personality** is defined as the combination of stable physical and mental characteristics that give the individual his or her identity.[31] These characteristics or traits—including how one looks, thinks, acts, and feels—are the product of interacting genetic and environmental influences. In this section, we explore the nature versus nurture debate, introduce the Big Five personality dimensions, issue some cautions about workplace personality testing, and examine an important personality factor called locus of control.

PERSONALITY AND ORGANIZATIONAL BEHAVIOR

personality Stable physical and mental characteristics responsible for a person's identity.

Nature or Nurture?

Over the years, vigorous debate has surrounded the issue of whether nature (genetic endowment) or nurture (environmental influences) primarily determines personality. For answers, we turn to a novel stream of research involving twins separated at birth. Twins reared in separate homes share a common genetic heritage (nature) but not a common upbringing (nurture). If twins who grew up in different homes end up with similar personality traits, then the scale would tip in favor of genetic endowment (or nature). If they end up with different personalities, then environmental factors (or nurture) would be given the credit. A separated-twin study recently provided instructive OB insights about the influence of genetics on work-related values. Those values included beliefs about achievement, status, and autonomy. The findings are best expressed with this formula: 40 percent genetics + 60 percent environment = Work values.[32] Regarding the full array of personality characteristics, researchers say the nature–nurture balance is roughly 50–50.[33] This evidence thus counters the argument that managers and leaders are born, not made.

Interestingly, the development of mind-altering prescription drugs, such as the widely used antidepressant Prozac, suggests a coming age of personality pills. *Psychopharmacology,* the science of mind-altering drugs, and brain mapping may yet rewrite the nature versus nurture story of personality. *Brain mapping* correlates regions of the brain to specific thoughts and feelings.[34] If Prozac can make healthy people feel happier, is it too far-fetched to envision pills that will boost one's need for achievement and creativity?[35] The ethical implications of using personality-altering drugs in the workplace, both with and without the employee's knowledge, are immense.

The Big Five Personality Dimensions

Long and confusing lists of personality dimensions have been distilled in recent years to the Big Five.[36] They are extraversion, agreeableness, conscientiousness, emotional stability, and openness to experience (see Table 4–1 for descriptions). Standardized personality tests determine how positively or negatively a person scores on each of the Big Five. For example, someone scoring negatively on extraversion would be an introverted person prone to shy and withdrawn behavior.[37] Someone scoring negatively on emotional security would be nervous, tense, angry, and worried. A person's scores on the Big Five reveal a personality profile as unique as his or her fingerprints.

Those interested in OB want to know the connection between the Big Five and job performance. Ideally, Big Five personality dimensions that correlate positively and strongly with job performance would be helpful in the selection, training, and appraisal of employees. A meta-analysis of 117 studies involving 23,994 subjects from many professions offers guidance.[38] Among the Big Five, *conscientiousness* had the strongest positive correlation with job performance and training perfor-

• TABLE 4~1
The Big Five Personality Dimensions

Personality Dimension	Characteristics of a Person Scoring Positively on the Dimension
1. Extraversion	Outgoing, talkative, sociable, assertive
2. Agreeableness	Trusting, good natured, cooperative, soft hearted
3. Conscientiousness	Dependable, responsible, achievement oriented, persistent
4. Emotional stability	Relaxed, secure, unworried
5. Openness to experience	Intellectual, imaginative, curious, broad minded

Source: Adapted from M R Barrick and M K Mount, "Autonomy as a Moderator of the Relationships between the Big Five Personality Dimensions and Job Performance," *Journal of Applied Psychology,* February 1993, pp 111–18.

The extraverted woman in this photo knows "how to make friends and influence people." Networking is critical to career success today.

Edward Caldwell

mance. According to the researchers, "those individuals who exhibit traits associated with a strong sense of purpose, obligation, and persistence generally perform better than those who do not."[39] Another expected finding: Extraversion (an outgoing personality) was associated with success for managers and salespeople. Also, extraversion was a stronger predictor of job performance than agreeableness, across all professions. The researchers concluded, "it appears that being courteous, trusting, straightforward, and soft-hearted has a smaller impact on job performance than being talkative, active, and assertive."[40]

These meta-analysis findings flash a caution light for those using personality tests to screen employees for hiring, training, and promotion. Conscientiousness may have been the best predictor of job performance among the Big Five, but it was *not a strong* predictor. Moreover, the most widely used personality test, the Minnesota Multiphasic Personality Inventory (MMPI), does not directly measure conscientiousness. No surprise that the MMPI and other popular personality tests historically have been poor predictors of job performance.[41]

The practical tips in Table 4–2 can help managers avoid abuses and costly discrimination lawsuits when using personality testing for employment-related decisions.

We now turn our attention to locus of control, an important job-related personality factor.

Locus of Control: Self or Environment?

Individuals vary in terms of how much personal responsibility they take for their behavior and its consequences. Julian Rotter, a personality researcher, identified a dimension of personality he labeled *locus of control* to explain these differences. He proposed that people tend to attribute the causes of their behavior primarily to either themselves or environmental factors.[42] This personality trait produces distinctly different behavior patterns.

People who believe they control the events and consequences that affect their lives are said to possess an **internal locus of control.** For example, such a person tends to attribute positive outcomes, like getting a passing grade on an exam, to his or her own abilities. Similarly, an "internal" tends to blame negative events, like failing an exam, on personal shortcomings—not studying hard enough, perhaps. Many entrepreneurs eventually succeed because their *internal* locus of control

internal locus of control
Attributing outcomes to one's own actions.

TABLE 4~2
Words of Caution about Personality Testing in the Workplace

- Rely on reputable, licensed psychologists for selecting and overseeing the administration, scoring, and interpretation of personality tests.
- Do not make employment-related decisions strictly on the basis of personality test results. Supplement any personality test data with information from reference checks, personal interviews, ability tests, and job performance records.*
- Avoid hiring people on the basis of specified personality profiles. As a case in point, there is no distinct "managerial personality." One study found the combination of mental ability and personality to be responsible for only 21 percent of the variation in managerial success.**
- Regularly assess any possible adverse impact on women and minorities.
- Be wary of slickly packaged gimmicks claiming to accurately assess personalities. A prime example is *graphology,* whereby handwriting "experts" infer personality traits and aptitudes from samples of one's penmanship. This European transplant has enjoyed zealous growth in the United States. But judging from research evidence, graphology is an inappropriate hiring tool and probably an open invitation to discrimination lawsuits. In a meta-analysis of 17 studies, 63 graphologists did a slightly *worse* job of predicting future performance than did a control group of 51 nongraphologists. Indeed, psychologists with no graphology experience consistently outperformed the graphologists.†
- The rapidly growing use of *integrity tests* to screen out dishonest job applicants seems to be justified by recent research evidence. Dishonest people reportedly have a general lack of conscientiousness that is difficult for them to fake, even on a paper-and-pencil test.‡

Sources: *See M P Cronin, "This Is a Test," *Inc.,* August 1993, pp 64–68; **For details, see J S Schippmann and E P Prien, "An Assessment of the Contributions of General Mental Ability and Personality Characteristics to Managerial Success," *Journal of Business and Psychology,* Summer 1989, pp 423–37; †Data from E Neter and G Ben-Shakhar, "The Predictive Validity of Graphological Inferences: A Meta-Analytic Approach," *Personality and Individual Differences,* no. 7, 1989, pp 737–45; and ‡See D S Ones, C Viswesvaran, and F L Schmidt, "Comprehensive Meta-Analysis of Integrity Test Validities: Findings and Implications for Personnel Selection and Theories of Job Performance," *Journal of Applied Psychology,* August 1993, pp 679–703.

helps them overcome setbacks and disappointments. They see themselves as masters of their own fate.[43]

external locus of control
Attributing outcomes to circumstances beyond one's control.

On the other side of this personality dimension are those who believe their performance is the product of circumstances beyond their immediate control. These individuals are said to possess an **external locus of control** and tend to attribute outcomes to environmental causes, such as luck or fate. Unlike someone with an internal locus of control, an "external" would attribute a passing grade on an exam to something external (an easy test or a good day) and attribute a failing grade to an unfair test or problems at home. A shortened version of an instrument Rotter developed to measure one's locus of control is presented in the OB Exercise. (Arbitrary norms for this shortened version are: External locus of control = 1–3; Balanced internal and external locus of control = 4; Internal locus of control = 5–7.) Where is your locus of control: internal, external, or a combination?

Research Findings on Locus of Control   Researchers have found important behavioral differences between internals and externals:

- Internals display greater work motivation.
- Internals have stronger expectations that effort leads to performance.
- Internals exhibit higher performance on tasks involving learning or problem solving, when performance leads to valued rewards.
- There is a stronger relationship between job satisfaction and performance for internals than externals.
- Internals obtain higher salaries and greater salary increases than externals.
- Externals tend to be more anxious than internals.[44]

OB Exercise

Where Is Your Locus of Control?

Circle one letter for each pair of items, in accordance with your beliefs:

1. A. Many of the unhappy things in people's lives are partly due to bad luck.
   B. People's misfortunes result from the mistakes they make.
2. A. Unfortunately, an individual's worth often passes unrecognized no matter how hard he tries.
   B. In the long run, people get the respect they deserve.
3. A. Without the right breaks one cannot be an effective leader.
   B. Capable people who fail to become leaders have not taken advantage of their opportunities.
4. A. I have often found that what is going to happen will happen.
   B. Trusting to fate has never turned out as well for me as making a decision to take a definite course of action.
5. A. Most people don't realize the extent to which their lives are controlled by accidental happenings.
   B. There really is no such thing as "luck."
6. A. In the long run, the bad things that happen to us are balanced by the good ones.
   B. Most misfortunes are the result of lack of ability, ignorance, laziness, or all three.
7. A. Many times I feel I have little influence over the things that happen to me.
   B. It is impossible for me to believe that chance or luck plays an important role in my life.

   Note: In determining your score, A = 0 and B = 1.

Source: Excerpted from J B Rotter, "Generalized Expectancies for Internal versus External Control of Reinforcement," *Psychological Monographs,* vol. 80 (Whole no. 609, 1966), pp 11–12.

Implications of Locus of Control Differences for Managers   The preceding summary of research findings on locus of control has important implications for managing people at work. Let us examine two of them.

First, since internals have a tendency to believe they control the work environment through their behavior, they will attempt to exert control over the work setting. This can be done by trying to influence work procedures, working conditions, task assignments, or relationships with peers and supervisors. As these possibilities imply, internals may resist a manager's attempts to closely supervise their work. Therefore, management may want to place internals in jobs requiring high initiative and low compliance. Externals, on the other hand, might be more amenable to highly structured jobs requiring greater compliance. Direct participation also can bolster the attitudes and performance of externals. This conclusion comes from a field study of 85 computer system users in a wide variety of business and government organizations. Externals who had been significantly involved in designing their organization's computer information system had more favorable attitudes toward the system than their external-locus co-workers who had not participated.[45]

Second, locus of control has implications for reward systems. Given that internals have a greater belief that their effort leads to performance, internals likely would prefer and respond more productively to incentives such as merit pay or sales commissions.[46]

ABILITIES AND PERFORMANCE

ability Stable characteristic responsible for a person's maximum physical or mental performance.

skill Specific capacity to manipulate objects.

Individual differences in abilities and accompanying skills are a central concern for managers because nothing can be accomplished without appropriately skilled personnel. An **ability** represents a broad and stable characteristic responsible for a person's maximum—as opposed to typical—performance on mental and physical tasks. A **skill,** on the other hand, is the specific capacity to physically manipulate objects. Consider this difference as you imagine yourself being the only passenger on a small commuter airplane in which the pilot has just passed out. As the plane nose-dives, your effort and abilities will not be enough to save yourself and the pilot if you do not possess flying skills. As shown in Figure 4–4, successful performance (be it landing an airplane or performing any other job) depends on the right combination of effort, ability, and skill.

Abilities can profoundly affect an organization's bottom line. Selecting employees who have the ability to perform assigned jobs can significantly affect the organization's labor costs. A pair of personnel selection experts noted:

> The use of cognitive ability tests for selection in hiring can produce large labor cost savings, ranging from $18 million per year for small employers such as the Philadelphia police department . . . to $16 billion per year for large employers such as the federal government.[47]

Importantly, the cautions about personality testing and employment-related decisions discussed earlier apply equally to cognitive ability and intelligence testing.

This section explores important cognitive abilities and cognitive styles related to job performance.

Intelligence and Cognitive Abilities

intelligence Capacity for constructive thinking, reasoning, problem solving.

Although experts do not agree on a specific definition, **intelligence** represents an individual's capacity for constructive thinking, reasoning, and problem solving.[48] Historically, intelligence was believed to be an innate capacity, passed genetically from one generation to the next. Research since has shown, however, that intelligence (like personality) also is a function of environmental influences.[49] Organic factors have more recently been added to the formula as a result of mounting evidence of the connection between alcohol and drug abuse by pregnant women and intellectual development problems in their children.[50]

Two Types of Abilities Human intelligence has been studied predominantly through the empirical approach. By examining the relationships between measures

FIGURE 4–4
Performance Depends on the Right Combination of Effort, Ability, and Skill

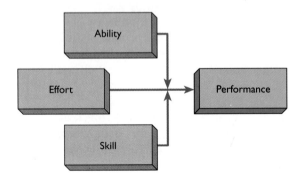

of mental abilities and behavior, researchers have statistically isolated major components of intelligence. Using this empirical procedure, pioneering psychologist Charles Spearman proposed in 1927 that all cognitive performance is determined by two types of abilities. The first can be characterized as a general mental ability needed for *all* cognitive tasks. The second is unique to the task at hand.[51] For example, an individual's ability to complete crossword puzzles is a function of his or her broad mental abilities as well as the specific ability to perceive patterns in partially completed words.

Seven Major Mental Abilities   Through the years, much research has been devoted to developing and expanding Spearman's ideas on the relationship between cognitive abilities and intelligence. One research psychologist listed 120 distinct mental abilities. Table 4–3 contains definitions of the seven most frequently cited mental abilities. Of the seven abilities, personnel selection researchers have found verbal ability, numerical ability, spatial ability, and inductive reasoning to be valid predictors of job performance for both minority and majority applicants.[52]

Jung's Cognitive Styles Typology

Within the context of Jung's theory, the term **cognitive style** refers to mental processes associated with how people perceive and make judgments from information. Although the landmark work on cognitive styles was completed in the 1920s by the noted Swiss psychoanalyst Carl Jung, his ideas did not catch on in the United States until the 1940s. That was when the mother–daughter team of Katharine C Briggs and Isabel Briggs Myers developed the Myers-Briggs Type Indicator (MBTI), an instrument for measuring Jung's cognitive styles. Today, the MBTI is a widely used personal growth and development tool in schools and businesses.[53]

cognitive style   A perceptual and judgmental tendency, according to Jung's typology.

Four Different Cognitive Styles   According to Jung, two dimensions influence perception and two others affect individual judgment. Perception is based on either *sensation,* using one's physical senses to interpret situations, or *intuition,* relying on

Ability	Description
1. Verbal comprehension	The ability to understand what words mean and to readily comprehend what is read.
2. Word fluency	The ability to produce isolated words that fulfill specific symbolic or structural requirements (such as all words that begin with the letter *b* and have two vowels).
3. Numerical	The ability to make quick and accurate arithmetic computations such as adding and subtracting.
4. Spatial	Being able to perceive spatial patterns and to visualize how geometric shapes would look if transformed in shape or position.
5. Memory	Having good rote memory for paired words, symbols, lists of numbers, or other associated items.
6. Perceptual speed	The ability to perceive figures, identify similarities and differences, and carry out tasks involving visual perception.
7. Inductive reasoning	The ability to reason from specifics to general conclusions.

TABLE 4–3
Mental Abilities Underlying Performance

Source: Adapted from M D Dunnette, "Aptitudes, Abilities, and Skills," in *Handbook of Industrial and Organizational Psychology,* ed M D Dunnette (Skokie, IL: Rand McNally, 1976), pp 478–83.

past experience. In turn, judgments are made by either *thinking* or *feeling*. Finally, Jung proposed that an individual's cognitive style is determined by the pairing of one's perception and judgment tendencies. The resulting four cognitive styles are:

- Sensation/thinking (ST).
- Intuition/thinking (NT).
- Sensation/feeling (SF).
- Intuition/feeling (NF).

Characteristics of each style are presented in Figure 4–5.[54] (The exercise at the end of this chapter, patterned after the MBTI, will help you determine your cognitive style.)

An individual with an ST style uses senses for perception and rational thinking for judgment. The ST-style person uses facts and impersonal analysis and develops greater abilities in technical areas involving facts and objects. A successful engineer could be expected to exhibit this cognitive style. In contrast, a person with an NT style focuses on possibilities rather than facts and displays abilities in areas involving theoretical or technical development. This style would enhance the performance of a research scientist. Although an SF person likely is interested in gathering facts, he or she tends to treat others with personal warmth, sympathy, and friendliness. Successful counselors or teachers probably use this style. Finally, an individual with an NF style tends to exhibit artistic flair while relying heavily on personal insights rather than objective facts (see Figure 4–5).

• FIGURE 4–5   People Have Different Cognitive Styles and Corresponding Characteristics

	Decision Style			
	ST Sensation/Thinking	**NT** Intuition/Thinking	**SF** Sensation/Feeling	**NF** Intuition/Feeling
Focus of Attention	Facts	Possibilities	Facts	Possibilities
Method of Handling Things	Impersonal Analysis	Impersonal Analysis	Personal Warmth	Personal Warmth
Tendency to Become	Practical and Matter-of-Fact	Logical and Ingenious	Sympathetic and Friendly	Enthusiastic and Insightful
Expression of Abilities	Technical Skills with Facts and Objects	Theoretical and Technical Developments	Practical Help and Services for People	Understanding and Communicating with People
	Technician	Planner	Teacher	Artist
Representative Occupation		Manager		

Source: W Taggart and D Robey, "Minds and Managers: On the Dual Nature of Human Information Processing and Management," *Academy of Management Review,* April 1981, p 190. Used with permission.

Practical Research Findings   If Jung's cognitive styles typology is valid, then individuals with different cognitive styles should seek different kinds of information when making a decision. A study of 50 MBA students found that those with different cognitive styles did in fact use qualitatively different information while working on a strategic planning problem.[55] Research also has shown that people with different cognitive styles prefer different careers. For example, people who rely on intuition prefer careers in psychology, advertising, teaching, and the arts.

Findings have further shown that individuals who make judgments based on the "thinking" approach have higher work motivation and quality of work life than those who take a "feeling" approach. In addition, individuals with a sensation mode of perception have higher job satisfaction than those relying on intuition.[56] Small business owner/managers with a "thinking" style made more money than their "feeling" counterparts. But no correlation was found between the four Jungian styles and small business owner/manager success.[57] On balance, Jung's cognitive styles typology is useful for training and development purposes but inadequate as a basis for personnel decisions.

Personal Values and Ethics

The 1990s have been called the "three E decade," with the three E's standing for economy, environment, and ethics.[58] Inclusion of ethics in this lofty set of priorities is a clear sign of the times. A growing chorus of calls for greater attention to values and ethics has been heard recently from government, business, and academic leaders alike.[59] They are simply reacting to years of headlines about defense contract scandals, sexual harassment, campaign financing abuses, corporate misconduct, and the jailing of Wall Street's elite. This final section examines personal values and ethics, a pair of intertwined OB topics.

Values Are Enduring Beliefs

According to Milton Rokeach, a leading researcher of values, a **value** is "an enduring belief that a specific mode of conduct or end-state of existence is personally or socially preferable to an opposite or converse mode of conduct or end-state of existence."[60] An individual's **value system** is defined by Rokeach as an "enduring organization of beliefs concerning preferable modes of conduct or end-states of existence along a continuum of relative importance."[61] Extensive research supports Rokeach's contention that different value systems go a long way toward explaining individual differences in behavior. Value→behavior connections have been documented for a wide variety of behaviors, ranging from weight loss, to shopping selections, to political party affiliation, to religious involvement, to choice of college major.[62]

value   Enduring belief in a mode of conduct or end-state.

value system   One's belief system of modes of conduct and end-states, ranked by importance.

Values versus Attitudes

Values are *not* the same as attitudes. An **attitude** is defined as "a learned predisposition to respond in a consistently favorable or unfavorable manner with respect to a given object."[63] Values are broader in scope. In other words, while attitudes relate only to behavior directed toward *specific* objects, persons, or situations, values represent global beliefs that influence behavior across *all* situations.[64] Values and attitudes generally, but not always, are in harmony. A manager

attitude   Consistent learned response to a given object.

who strongly values helpful behavior may have a negative attitude toward helping an unethical co-worker.

What Is Your Value Profile?

Lifelong behavior patterns are dictated by values that are fairly well set by the time an individual is in his or her early teens. For example, consider how early experiences shaped the values of the young founder of Lotus Development Corporation, producer of the highly successful 1–2–3® personal computer spreadsheet program.

> In the 1960s, Mitchell D Kapor revered the Beatles, grew his hair long, and joined protest marches against the Vietnam War. . . .
> While he now describes much of the turmoil of the 1960s as "no more than standard, adolescent growth pains," he says the period imparted a sense of social obligation that he has carried into corporate life. "Many people who came of age in the 60s share a common set of experiences and values," Kapor says. "It's possible to make money and at the same time to have a company where people are proud to work and can be happy."[65]

Although values tend to jell early in life, significant life events—such as having a child, business failure, or surviving a serious accident—can reshape one's value system during adulthood.

In line with Rokeach's distinction between modes of conduct and end-states of existence, he developed a value survey instrument based on what he calls instrumental and terminal values. Take the time now to complete the brief value survey in the OB Exercise. Rokeach contends that his value survey can be used to assess the value systems of individuals or groups.

instrumental values
Valued ways of behaving.

Instrumental Values The instrumental values in Rokeach's value survey involve different categories of behavior. **Instrumental values** are alternative

---

OB EXERCISE

Abbreviated Version of the Rokeach Value Survey*

Instructions:

Rank the five values in each of the two categories from 1 (most important to you) to 5 (least important to you):

Instrumental Values	Terminal Values
Rank	Rank
_____ Ambitious (hardworking, aspiring)	_____ A sense of accomplishment (lasting contribution)
_____ Honest (sincere, truthful)	_____ Happiness (contentedness)
_____ Independent (self-sufficient)	_____ Pleasure (an enjoyable, leisurely life)
_____ Loving (affectionate, tender)	_____ Salvation (saved, eternal life)
_____ Obedient (dutiful, respectful)	_____ Wisdom (a mature understanding of life)

* The complete copyrighted version lists 18 values in each category.

Source: Adapted from M Rokeach, *Beliefs, Attitudes, and Values* (San Francisco: Jossey-Bass, 1968).

behaviors or means by which we achieve desired ends (terminal values). Someone who ranks the instrumental value "honest" high is likely to be honest more often than someone who ranks it low.[66] Thus, instrumental values are a fairly good, but not perfect, predictor of actual behavior. What is your most important instrumental value?[67] In a study of 83 female and 107 male college students, "loving" turned out to be the most highly rated instrumental value.[68]

Terminal Values   Highly ranked **terminal values,** such as wisdom or salvation, are end-states or goals the individual would like to achieve during his or her lifetime. Some would say terminal values are what life is all about. History is full of examples of people who were persecuted or put to death for their passionately held terminal values. Which of the five terminal values in the OB exercise did you rank the highest? In the survey of 190 college students mentioned earlier, "happiness" was the highest-ranked terminal value.[69]

terminal values   Valued end-states or lifetime goals.

Contrary to the impression created by the social turbulence of the 1960s and 1970s, a comparison of national samples conducted in 1968, 1971, 1974, and 1981 revealed relative stability in terminal values among Americans. Six terminal values consistently ranked in the top one-third were family security, a world at peace, freedom, self-respect, happiness, and wisdom.[70]

Ethics and Organizational Behavior

Among the individual differences discussed in this chapter, none is receiving greater attention today than the distinction between ethical and unethical managerial conduct. For instance, fraud is said to have played a role in 60 percent of the savings and loan failures that could eventually cost US taxpayers $500 billion ($5,000 per household).[71] OB is an excellent vantage point for better understanding and improving workplace ethics. If OB can provide insights about managing human work behavior, then it can teach us something about avoiding *misbehavior.*

Ethics involves the study of moral issues and choices. It is concerned with right versus wrong, good versus bad, and the many shades of gray in supposedly black-and-white issues. Relative to the workplace, the terms *business ethics* and *management ethics* are often heard. But, according to James K Baker, chairman of the US Chamber of Commerce and head of a Fortune 500 company, "There is no such thing as business ethics. . . . There's only ethics. What you do over *here* is no different from what you do over *there.*"[72] Moral implications spring from virtually every decision, both on and off the job. Managers are challenged to have moral imagination and the courage to do the right thing. To meet that challenge, present and future managers need a conceptual framework for making ethical decisions.

ethics   Study of moral issues and choices.

A Model of Ethical Behavior   Ethical and unethical conduct is the product of a complex combination of influences (see Figure 4–6). Let us examine key aspects of this model.

At the center of the model in Figure 4–6 is the individual decision maker. He or she has a unique combination of personality characteristics, values, and moral principles, leaning toward or away from ethical behavior. Personal experience with being rewarded or reinforced for certain behaviors and punished for others also shapes the individual's tendency to act ethically or unethically.

Next, we see in Figure 4–6 three major sources of influence on one's role expectations. People play many roles in life, including those of employee or manager. One's expectations for how those roles should be played are shaped by

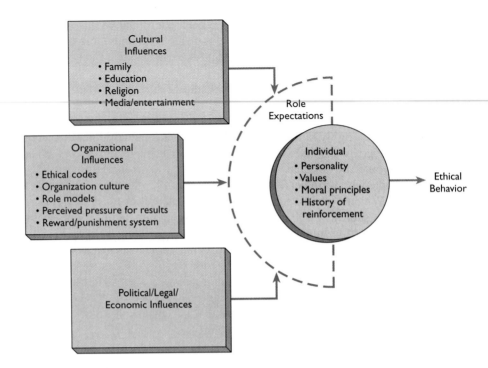

FIGURE 4-6

A Model of Ethical Behavior in the Workplace

cultural, organizational, and general environmental factors. Focusing on one troublesome source of organizational influence, many studies have found a tendency among middle- and lower-level managers to act unethically in the face of perceived pressure for results.[73] By fostering a pressure-cooker atmosphere for results, managers can unwittingly set the stage for unethical shortcuts by employees who seek to please and be loyal to the company.

This was precisely the argument consumer protection officials used in 1992 when charging Sears Tire & Auto Centers with overcharging customers by doing unnecessary vehicle repair work.

> Consumer Affairs officials say Sears pressured employees to sell, setting high quotas. Sales commissions and incentives, such as free trips for top sellers, may have contributed to the high-pressure atmosphere, suggests [California] Bureau of Auto Repair chief James Schoning.[74]

Sears later revised its compensation system. Thus, an organization's reward/punishment system can compound the problem of pressure for results. Worse yet, according to a recent study of 385 managers, supervisors who were considered by their subordinates as being consistently ethical tended to have lower salaries than their less ethical peers.[75]

Because ethical or unethical behavior is the result of person–situation interaction, we need to discuss both the decision maker's moral principles and the organization's ethical climate.

Moral Principles for Global Managers   Today's managers, who increasingly work across cultures in a global economy, need more than lectures about behaving better. They need specific ethical criteria and moral principles to help them gauge the rightness or wrongness of their decisions. According to experts on the subject, history has produced three major ethical criteria:

Utilitarian theory.   Goal: Judge actions by their consequences; achieve the greatest good for the greatest number of people

Theory of rights.   Goal: Basic human rights should be respected.

Theory of justice.   Goal: Rules and rewards should be administered impartially, fairly, and equitably.[76]

Differing value systems and perceptions guarantee competition among these three ethical criteria. Consider, for example, a situation in which the head of a company says a layoff of 10 percent of the payroll is needed to avoid bankruptcy. A utilitarian probably would agree to the layoff because relatively few would suffer while many would benefit. Meanwhile, a rights advocate concerned about the unfortunate layoff victims would object to the layoff. A layoff also would be unacceptable to a justice advocate who believes it would be fairer to cut everyone's pay before resorting to a layoff.

Management consultant and writer Kent Hodgson has helpfully taken managers a step closer to ethical decisions by identifying seven general moral principles (see Table 4–4). Hodgson calls them "the magnificent seven" to emphasize their timeless and worldwide relevance. The three basic ethical criteria just discussed are clearly evident in the magnificent seven, which are more detailed and, hence, more practical. Importantly, according to Hodgson, there are no absolute ethical answers for decision makers. The goal for managers should be to rely on moral principles so their decisions are *principled, appropriate,* and *defensible.*[77] Managers require a supportive organizational climate that translates general moral principles into specific do's and don't's and fosters ethical decisions.

How to Improve the Organization's Ethical Climate   A team of management researchers recommended the following actions for improving on-the-job ethics.[78]

- *Behave ethically yourself.*   Managers are potent role models whose habits and actual behavior send clear signals about the importance of ethical conduct. Ethical behavior is a top-to-bottom proposition.

- *Screen potential employees.*   Surprisingly, employers are generally lax when it comes to checking references, credentials, transcripts, and other information on applicant résumés. More diligent action in this area can screen out those given to fraud and misrepresentation. Integrity testing, covered in Table 4–2, is fairly valid but is no panacea.[79] In the United States, the Employee Polygraph Protection Act of 1988 severely restricted the use of so-called lie detectors in the private business sector.[80] Questionable validity and rampant abuses prompted passage of this legislation.

- *Develop a meaningful code of ethics.*   Codes of ethics can have a positive impact if they satisfy these four criteria:

TABLE 4–4

The Magnificent Seven:
General Moral Principles
for Managers

1. *Dignity of human life: The lives of people are to be respected.* Human beings, by the fact of their existence, have value and dignity. We may not act in ways that directly intend to harm or kill an innocent person. Human beings have a right to live; we have an obligation to respect that right to life. Human life is to be preserved and treated as sacred.

2. *Autonomy: All persons are intrinsically valuable and have the right to self-determination.* We should act in ways that demonstrate each person's worth, dignity, and right to free choice. We have a right to act in ways that assert our own worth and legitimate needs. We should not use others as mere "things," or only as means to an end. Each person has an equal right to basic human liberty, compatible with a similar liberty for others.

3. *Honesty: The truth should be told to those who have a right to know it.* Honesty is also known as integrity, truth telling, and honor. One should speak and act so as to reflect the reality of the situation. Speaking and acting should mirror the way things really are. There are times when others have the right to hear the truth from us; there are times when they do not.

4. *Loyalty: Promises, contracts, and commitments should be honored.* Loyalty includes fidelity, promise keeping, keeping the public trust, good citizenship, excellence in quality of work, reliability, commitment, and honoring just laws, rules, and policies.

5. *Fairness: People should be treated justly.* One has the right to be treated fairly, impartially, and equitably. One has the obligation to treat others fairly and justly. All have the right to the necessities of life—especially those in deep need and the helpless. Justice includes equal, impartial, unbiased treatment. Fairness tolerates diversity and accepts differences in people and their ideas.

6. *Humaneness.* There are two parts: (1) *Our actions ought to accomplish good,* and (2) *we should avoid doing evil.* We should do good to others and to ourselves. We should have concern for the well-being of others; usually, we show this concern in the form of compassion, giving, kindness, serving, and caring.

7. *The common good: Actions should accomplish the "greatest good for the greatest number" of people.* One should act and speak in ways that benefit the welfare of the largest number of people, while trying to protect the rights of individuals.

Source: Reprinted, with permission of the publisher, from *A Rock and a Hard Place: How to Make Ethical Business Decisions When the Choices are Tough* © 1992 Kent Hodgson, pp. 69–73. Published by AMACOM, a division of the American Management Association. All Rights Reserved.

1. They are *distributed* to every employee.
2. They are firmly *supported* by top management.
3. They refer to *specific* practices and ethical dilemmas likely to be encountered by target employees (e.g., salespersons paying kickbacks, purchasing agents receiving payoffs, laboratory scientists doctoring data, or accountants "cooking the books").
4. They are evenly *enforced* with rewards for compliance and strict penalties for noncompliance.

- *Provide ethics training.* Employees can be trained to identify and deal with ethical issues during orientation and through seminar and video training sessions.

- *Reinforce ethical behavior.* As discussed later in Chapter 8, behavior that is reinforced tends to be repeated, whereas behavior that is not reinforced tends to disappear. Ethical conduct too often is punished while unethical behavior is rewarded.

- *Create positions, units, and other structural mechanisms to deal with ethics.* Ethics needs to be an everyday affair, not a one-time announcement of a new ethical code that gets filed away and forgotten. Xerox monitors company ethics with an internal audit committee. General Dynamics has a full-time corporate ethics director and an ethics hot line that logged 3,646 calls in a single year.[81]

BACK TO THE OPENING CASE

Now that you have read Chapter 4, you should be able to answer the following questions about the Bill Clinton case:

1. How would you rate Clinton's self-esteem? Does this help or hinder him as president? Explain.

2. How does Clinton enhance his self-efficacy?

3. Based on the facts of this case, which of the Big Five personality dimensions seems to be Clinton's strongest? Does this help or hinder his effectiveness as president? Explain.

4. What is Clinton's apparent locus of control? How can you tell?

5. Which of Jung's cognitive styles does Clinton exhibit? Does this style help or hinder him as president? Explain.

SUMMARY OF KEY CONCEPTS

1. *Explain the nature and determinants of organization-based self-esteem.* Organization-based self-esteem (OBSE) is an employee's self-perceived value as an organizational member. People high in OBSE see themselves as important and meaningful within the organization. Three primary determinants of high OBSE are managerial respect and concern, flexible organization structure, and complex and challenging jobs.

2. *Define self-efficacy, and explain its sources.* Self-efficacy involves one's belief about his/her ability to accomplish specific tasks. Those extremely low in self-efficacy suffer from learned helplessness. Four sources of self-efficacy beliefs are prior experience, behavior models, persuasion from others, and assessment of one's physical and emotional states. High self-efficacy beliefs foster constructive and goal-oriented action, whereas low self-efficacy fosters passive, failure-prone activities and emotions.

3. *Identify and describe the Big Five personality dimensions, and specify which one is correlated most strongly with job performance.* The Big Five personality dimensions are extraversion (social and talkative), agreeableness (trusting and cooperative), conscientiousness (responsible and persistent), emotional stability (relaxed and unworried), and openness to experience (intellectual and curious). Conscientiousness is the best predictor of job performance.

4. *Explain the difference between an internal and external locus of control.* People with an *internal* locus of control, such as entrepreneurs, believe they are masters of their own fate. Those with an *external* locus of control attribute their behavior and its results to situational forces.

5. *Describe Carl Jung's cognitive styles typology.* By combining two dimensions of perception (sensation and intuition) with two dimensions of judgment (thinking and feeling), Carl Jung identified four cognitive styles. They are sensation/thinking (practical and matter-of-fact), intuition/thinking (logical and ingenious), sensation/feeling (sympathetic and friendly), and intuition/feeling (enthusiastic and insightful).

6. *Distinguish between instrumental and terminal values.* According to Milton Rokeach, instrumental values are personally important ways of behaving (e.g., ambitious, honest). Terminal values are personally important end-states of existence (e.g., happiness, wisdom).

7. *Describe the three basic ethical criteria: utilitarian, rights, and justice.* The utilitarian theory seeks the greatest good for the greatest number of people. The theory of rights strives to respect the basic rights of all people. The theory of justice calls for the impartial, fair, and equitable administration of rules and rewards.

8. *Specify at least four actions managers can take to improve an organization's ethical climate.* They can do so by (1) behaving ethically themselves, (2) screening potential employees, (3) developing a code of ethics, (4) providing ethics training, (5) reinforcing and rewarding ethical behavior, and (6) creating positions and structural mechanisms dealing with ethics.

DISCUSSION QUESTIONS

1. How should the reality of a more diverse workforce affect management's approach to dealing with individual differences?

2. What is your personal experience with organization-based self-esteem?

3. How is someone you know with low self-efficacy, relative to a specified task, "programming themselves for failure?" What could be done to help that individual develop high self-efficacy?

4. What are the ethical implications of managers using personality-altering drugs to enhance employees' job performance, if and when such drugs become available? *Tip:* Use the three ethical criteria and magnificent seven moral principles discussed in this chapter.

5. On scales of Low = 1 to High = 10, how would you rate yourself on the Big Five personality dimensions? Is your personality profile suitable for a managerial position?

6. How would you respond to the following statement? "Whenever possible, managers should hire people with an external locus of control."

7. According to Jung's typology, which cognitive style do you exhibit? How can you tell? Is it an advantage or a disadvantage?

8. Do your top-ranked instrumental and terminal values, according to the Rokeach value survey in the OB Exercise, accurately predict your behavior? Explain pro or con.

9. Which particular source of influence in the left-hand side of Figure 4–6 do you think has had the greatest impact on your ethical behavior? Explain.

10. Which of the magnificent seven in Table 4–4 is the most important moral principle in your life? Explain. Will this help or hinder you as a manager?

EXERCISE

Objectives

1. To identify your cognitive style, according to Carl Jung's typology.[82]
2. To consider the managerial implications of your cognitive style.

Instructions

Please respond to the 16 items below. There are no right or wrong answers. After you have completed all the items, refer to the scoring key, and follow its directions.

Questionnaire

Part I. Circle the response that comes closest to how you usually feel or act.

1. Are you more careful about:
   A. People's feelings
   B. Their rights
2. Do you usually get along better with:
   A. Imaginative people
   B. Realistic people
3. Which of these two is the higher compliment:
   A. A person has real feeling
   B. A person is consistently reasonable

4. In doing something with many other people, does it appeal more to you:
   A. To do it in the accepted way
   B. To invent a way of your own
5. Do you get more annoyed at:
   A. Fancy theories
   B. People who don't like theories
6. It is higher praise to call someone:
   A. A person of vision
   B. A person of common sense
7. Do you more often let:
   A. Your heart rule your head
   B. Your head rule your heart
8. Do you think it is worse:
   A. To show too much warmth
   B. To be unsympathetic
9. If you were a teacher, would you rather teach:
   A. Courses involving theory
   B. Fact courses

Part II. Which word in each of the following pairs appeals to you more? Circle A or B.

10. A. Compassion
    B. Foresight
11. A. Justice
    B. Mercy

12. A. Production
    B. Design
13. A. Gentle
    B. Firm
14. A. Uncritical
    B. Critical
15. A. Literal
    B. Figurative
16. A. Imaginative
    B. Matter of fact

Scoring Key

To categorize your responses to the questionnaire, count one point for each response on the following four scales, and total the number of points recorded in each column. Instructions for classifying your scores are indicated below.

Sensation	Intuition	Thinking	Feeling
2 B ____	2 A ____	1 B ____	1 A ____
4 A ____	4 B ____	3 B ____	3 A ____
5 A ____	5 B ____	7 B ____	7 A ____
6 B ____	6 A ____	8 A ____	8 B ____
9 B ____	9 A ____	10 B ____	10 A ____
12 A ____	12 B ____	11 A ____	11 B ____
15 A ____	15 B ____	13 B ____	13 A ____
16 B ____	16 A ____	14 B ____	14 A ____
Totals = ____	____	____	____

Classifying Total Scores

Write *intuitive* if your intuition score is equal to or greater than your sensation score.

Write *sensation* if sensation is greater than intuition.

Write *feeling* if feeling is greater than thinking.

Write *thinking* if thinking is greater than feeling.

When *thinking* equals feeling, you should write feeling if a male and thinking if a female.

Questions for Consideration/Class Discussion

1. What is your cognitive style?
   Sensation/thinking (ST) ____
   Intuition/thinking (NT) ____
   Sensation/feeling (SF) ____
   Intuition/feeling (NF) ____
2. Do you agree with this assessment? Why or why not?
3. Will your cognitive style, as determined in this exercise, help you achieve your career goal(s)?
4. Would your style be an asset or liability for a managerial position involving getting things done through others?

NOTES

[1] D Seligman, "The Trouble with Buyouts," *Fortune,* November 30, 1992, p 125.

[2] S I Cheldelin and L A Foritano, "Psychometrics: Their Use in Organisation Development," *Journal of Managerial Psychology,* no. 4, 1989, p 21.

[3] See A Rossett and T Bickham, "Diversity Training: Hope, Faith and Cynicism," *Training,* January 1994, pp 40–46.

[4] V Gecas, "The Self-Concept," in *Annual Review of Sociology,* eds R H Turner and J F Short, Jr. (Palo Alto, CA: Annual Reviews Inc., 1982), vol. 8, p 3. Also see A P Brief and R J Aldag, "The 'Self' In Work Organizations: A Conceptual Review," *Academy of Management Review,* January 1981, pp 75–88; and J J Sullivan, "Self Theories and Employee Motivation," *Journal of Management,* June 1989, pp 345–63.

[5] L Festinger, *A Theory of Cognitive Dissonance* (Stanford, CA: Stanford University Press, 1957), p 3.

[6] See J Holt and D M Keats, "Work Cognitions in Multicultural Interaction," *Journal of Cross-Cultural Psychology,* December 1992, pp 421–443.

[7] For contrasting perspectives of self, see P Cushman, "Why the Self Is Empty," *American Psychologist,* May 1990, pp 599–611.

[8] See D C Barnlund, "Public and Private Self in Communicating with Japan," *Business Horizons,* March–April 1989, pp 32–40.

[9] Based in part on a definition found in Gecas, "The Self Concept." Also see J Adler, "Hey, I'm Terrific!" *Newsweek,* February 17, 1992, pp 46–51.

[10] B Nussbaum, "Downward Mobility," *Business Week,* March 23, 1992, p 57.

[11] For related research, see R C Liden, L Martin, and C K Parsons, "Interviewer and Applicant Behaviors in Employment Interviews," *Academy of Management Journal,* April 1993, pp 372–86; and M B Setterlund and P M Niedenthal, "'Who Am I? Why Am I Here?': Self-Esteem, Self-Clarity, and Prototype Matching," *Journal*

of Personality and Social Psychology, October 1993, pp 769–80.

[12] Details may be found in B R Schlenker, M F Weigold, and J R Hallam, "Self-Serving Attributions in Social Context: Effects of Self-Esteem and Social Pressure," *Journal of Personality and Social Psychology,* May 1990, pp 855–63.

[13] See J A Stein, M D Newcomb, and P M Bentler, "The Relative Influence on Vocational Behavior and Family Involvement on Self-Esteem: Longitudinal Analyses of Young Adult Women and Men," *Journal of Vocational Behavior,* June 1990, pp 320–38.

[14] Based on data in F L Smoll, R E Smith, N P Barnett, and J J Everett, "Enhancement of Children's Self-Esteem through Social Support Training for Youth Sports Coaches," *Journal of Applied Psychology,* August 1993, pp 602–10.

[15] B O'Reilly, "Why Grade 'A' Execs Get an 'F' as Parents," *Fortune,* January 1, 1990, pp 36–37.

[16] See J R Hollenbeck and A P Brief, "The Effects of Individual Differences and Goal Origin on Goal Setting and Performance," *Organizational Behavior and Human Decision Processes,* December 1987, pp 392–414.

[17] Details may be found in J Brockner and T Hess, "Self-Esteem and Task Performance in Quality Circles," *Academy of Management Journal,* September 1986, pp 617–23.

[18] The tendency of low self-esteem people to be attracted to more decentralized and larger companies is documented in D B Turban and T L Keon, "Organizational Attractiveness: An Interactionist Perspective," *Journal of Applied Psychology,* April 1993, pp 184–93.

[19] J L Pierce, D G Gardner, L L Cummings, and R B Dunham, "Organization-Based Self-Esteem: Construct Definition, Measurement, and Validation," *Academy of Management Journal,* September 1989, p 625. Also see J L Pierce, D G Gardner, R B Dunham, and L L Cummings, "Moderation by Organization-Based Self-Esteem of Role Condition-Employee Response Relationships," *Academy of Management Journal,* April 1993, pp 271–88.

[20] Practical steps are discussed in M Kaeter, "Basic Self-Esteem," *Training,* August 1993, pp 31–35.

[21] Adapted from discussion in J K Matejka and R J Dunsing, "Great Expectations," *Management World,* January 1987, pp 16–17.

[22] M E Gist, "Self-Efficacy: Implications for Organizational Behavior and Human Resource Management," *Academy of Management Review,* July 1987, p 472. Also see A Bandura, "Self-Efficacy: Toward a Unifying Theory of Behavioral Change," *Psychological Review,* March 1977, pp 191–215; and M E Gist and T R Mitchell, "Self-Efficacy: A Theoretical Analysis of Its Determinants and Malleability," *Academy of Management Review,* April 1992, pp 183–211.

[23] D Rader, "'I Knew What I Wanted To Be,'" *Parade Magazine,* November 1, 1992, p 4.

[24] See, for example, V Gecas, "The Social Psychology of Self-Efficacy," in *Annual Review of Sociology,* eds W R Scott and J Blake (Palo Alto, CA: Annual Reviews, Inc., 1989), vol. 15, pp 291–316; and C K Stevens, A G Bavetta, and M E Gist, "Gender Differences in the Acquisition of Salary Negotiation Skills: The Role of Goals, Self-Efficacy, and Perceived Control," *Journal of Applied Psychology,* October 1993, pp 723–35.

[25] For more on learned helplessness, see Gecas, "The Social Psychology of Self-Efficacy," and M J Martinko and W L Gardner, "Learned Helplessness: An Alternative Explanation for Performance Deficits," *Academy of Management Review,* April 1982, pp 195–204.

[26] Research on this connection is reported in R B Rubin, M M Martin, S S Bruning, and D E Powers, "Test of a Self-Efficacy Model of Interpersonal Communication Competence," *Communication Quarterly,* Spring 1993, pp 210–20.

[27] For details, see J Barling and R Beattie, "Self-Efficacy Beliefs and Sales Performance," *Journal of Organizational Behavior Management,* Spring 1983, pp 41–51.

[28] Based in part on discussion in Gecas, "The Social Psychology of Self-Efficacy."

[29] The positive relationship between self-efficacy and readiness for retraining is documented in L A Hill and J Elias, "Retraining Midcareer Managers: Career History and Self-Efficacy Beliefs," *Human Resource Management,* Summer 1990, pp 197–217.

[30] See P C Earley and T R Lituchy, "Delineating Goal and Efficacy Effects: A Test of Three Models," *Journal of Applied Psychology,* February 1991, pp 81–98.

[31] For evidence of the stability of adult personality dimensions, see R R McCrae, "Moderated Analyses of Longitudinal Personality Stability," *Journal of Personality and Social Psychology,* September 1993, pp 577–85.

[32] For details, see L M Keller, T J Bouchard, Jr., R D Arvey, N L Segal, and R V Dawis, "Work Values: Genetic and Environmental Influences," *Journal of Applied Psychology,* February 1992, pp 79–88.

[33] See J Leo, "Exploring the Traits of Twins," *Time,* January 12, 1987, p 63; and D T Lykken, T J Bouchard, Jr., M McGue, and A Tellegen, "Heritability of Interests: A Twin Study," *Journal of Applied Psychology,* August 1993, pp 649–61.

[34] For interesting discussion, see S Begley, "One Pill Makes You Large, And One Makes You Small . . . ," *Newsweek,* February 7, 1994, pp 36–40.

[35] See G Cowley, "The Culture of Prozac," *Newsweek,* February 7, 1994, pp 41–42.

[36] The landmark report is J M Digman, "Personality Structure: Emergence of the Five-Factor Model," *Annual*

Review of Psychology, vol. 41, 1990, pp 417–40. Also see M R Barrick and M K Mount, "Autonomy as a Moderator of the Relationships between the Big Five Personality Dimensions and Job Performance," *Journal of Applied Psychology,* February 1993, pp 111–18; J A Johnson and F Ostendorf, "Clarification of the Five-Factor Model with the Abridged Big Five Dimensional Circumplex," *Journal of Personality and Social Psychology,* September 1993, pp 563–76; and M Zuckerman, D M Kuhlman, J Joireman, P Teta, and M Kraft, "A Comparison of Three Structural Models for Personality: The Big Three, the Big Five, and the Alternative Five," *Journal of Personality and Social Psychology,* October 1993, pp 757–68.

[37] For a review of research on the relationship between introversion–extroversion, motivation, and performance, see M S Humphreys and W Revelle, "Personality, Motivation, and Performance: A Theory of the Relationship between Individual Differences and Information Processing," *Psychological Review,* April 1984, pp 153–84.

[38] See M R Barrick and M K Mount, "The Big Five Personality Dimensions and Job Performance: A Meta-Analysis," *Personnel Psychology,* Spring 1991, pp 1–26. Also see R P Tett, D N Jackson, and M Rothstein, "Personality Measures as Predictors of Job Performance: A Meta-Analytic Review," *Personnel Psychology,* Winter 1991, pp 703–42.

[39] Barrick and Mount, "The Big Five Personality Dimensions and Job Performance: A Meta-Analysis," p 18.

[40] Ibid., p 21.

[41] See the discussion in Ibid., pp 21–22. Also see J M Cortina, M L Doherty, N Schmitt, G Kaufman, and R G Smith, "The 'Big Five' Personality Factors in the IPI and MMPI: Predictors of Police Performance," *Personnel Psychology,* Spring 1992, pp 119–40.

[42] For an instructive update, see J B Rotter, "Internal versus External Control of Reinforcement: A Case History of a Variable," *American Psychologist,* April 1990, pp 489–93. A critical review of locus of control and a call for a meta-analysis can be found in R W Renn and R J Vandenberg, "Differences in Employee Attitudes and Behaviors Based on Rotter's (1966) Internal-External Locus of Control: Are They All Valid?" *Human Relations,* November 1991, p 1161–77.

[43] See E A Ward, "Motivation of Expansion Plans of Entrepreneurs and Small Business Managers," *Journal of Small Business Management,* January 1993, pp 32–38.

[44] For an overall review of research on locus of control, see P E Spector, "Behavior in Organizations as a Function of Employee's Locus of Control," *Psychological Bulletin,* May 1982, pp 482–97; the relationship between locus of control and performance and satisfaction is examined in D R Norris and R E Niebuhr, "Attributional Influences on the Job Performance–Job Satisfaction Relationship," *Academy of Management Journal,* June 1984, pp 424–31;

salary differences between internals and externals were examined by P C Nystrom, "Managers' Salaries and Their Beliefs about Reinforcement Control," *The Journal of Social Psychology,* August 1983, pp 291–92.

[45] See S R Hawk, "Locus of Control and Computer Attitude: The Effect of User Involvement," *Computers In Human Behavior,* no. 3, 1989, pp 199–206.

[46] These recommendations are from Spector, "Behavior in Organizations as a Function of Employee's Locus of Control."

[47] F L Schmidt and J E Hunter, "Employment Testing: Old Theories and New Research Findings," *American Psychologist,* October 1981, p 1128.

[48] For interesting reading on the subject of intelligence, see J Q Wilson, "Uncommon Sense about the IQ Debate," *Fortune,* January 11, 1993, pp 99–100; and L Shaper Walters, "An Evolving Theory of Intelligence," *The Christian Science Monitor,* March 29, 1993, p 11.

[49] For an excellent update on intelligence, including definitional distinctions and a historical perspective of the IQ controversy, see R A Weinberg, "Intelligence and IQ," *American Psychologist,* February 1989, pp 98–104.

[50] Ibid.

[51] For related research, see M J Ree and J A Earles, "Predicting Training Success: Not Much More Than g," *Personnel Psychology,* Summer 1991, pp 321–32.

[52] See Schmidt and Hunter, "Employment Testing: Old Theories and New Research Findings." For evidence of the economic impact of using cognitive ability tests to select employees, see J E Hunter and F L Schmidt, "Quantifying the Effects of Psychological Interventions on Employee Job Performance and Work-Force Productivity," *American Psychologist,* April 1983, pp 473–78.

[53] See I Briggs Myers (with P B Myers), *Gifts Differing* (Palo Alto, CA: Consulting Psychologists Press, 1980).

[54] For a complete discussion of each cognitive style, see J W Slocum, Jr., and D Hellriegel, "A Look at How Managers' Minds Work," *Business Horizons,* July–August 1983, pp 58–68; and W Taggart and D Robey, "Minds and Managers: On the Dual Nature of Human Information Processing and Management," *Academy of Management Review,* April 1981, pp 187–95.

[55] See B K Blaylock and L P Rees, "Cognitive Style and the Usefulness of Information," *Decision Sciences,* Winter 1984, pp 74–91.

[56] Additional material on cognitive styles may be found in F A Gul, "The Joint and Moderating Role of Personality and Cognitive Style on Decision Making," *The Accounting Review,* April 1984, pp 264–77; B H Kleiner, "The Interrelationship of Jungian Modes of Mental Functioning with Organizational Factors: Implications for Management Development," *Human Relations,* November 1983, pp 997–1012; and J L McKenney and P G W Keen, "How

Managers' Minds Work,'' *Harvard Business Review,* May–June 1974, pp 79–90.

[57] See G H Rice, Jr., and D P Lindecamp, ''Personality Types and Business Success of Small Retailers,'' *Journal of Occupational Psychology,* June 1989, pp 177–82.

[58] Taken from R M Kidder, ''The Three E's of the 1990s,'' *The Christian Science Monitor,* March 19, 1990, p 12.

[59] For example, see A Stark, ''What's the Matter with Business Ethics?'' *Harvard Business Review,* May–June 1993, pp 38–48.

[60] M Rokeach, *The Nature of Human Values* (New York: Free Press, 1973), p 5.

[61] Ibid.

[62] See S H Schwartz and W Bilsky, ''Toward a Theory of the Universal Content and Structure of Values: Extensions and Cross-Cultural Replications,'' *Journal of Personality and Social Psychology,* May 1990, pp 878–91.

[63] M Fishbein and I Ajzen, *Belief, Attitude, Intention and Behavior: An Introduction to Theory and Research* (Reading, MA: Addison-Wesley Publishing, 1975), p 6.

[64] For a discussion of the difference between values and attitudes, see B W Becker and P E Connor, ''Changing American Values—Debunking the Myth,'' *Business,* January–March 1985, pp 56–59.

[65] ''A Bit of the '60s Lives on at Lotus,'' *Business Week,* July 2, 1984, p 59.

[66] For survey evidence of the importance of ''honesty'' to US high school and college students, see R Morin, ''Honesty May No Longer Be the Best Policy,'' *The Washington Post National Weekly Edition,* December 7–13, 1992, p 36.

[67] An alternative list of 24 instrumental values can be found in Exhibit 2 of P McDonald and J Gandz, ''Getting Value from Shared Values,'' *Organizational Dynamics,* Winter 1992, pp 64–77.

[68] See A J DeVito, J F Carlson, and J Kraus, ''Values in Relation to Career Orientation, Gender, and Each Other,'' *Counseling and Values,* July 1984, pp 202–6.

[69] Ibid.

[70] Data from M Rokeach and S J Ball-Rokeach, ''Stability and Change in American Value Priorities, 1968–1981,'' *American Psychologist,* May 1989, pp 775–84. Also see B Z Posner and W H Schmidt, ''Values and the American Manager: An Update Updated,'' *California Management Review,* Spring 1992, pp 80–94.

[71] Based on D E Rosenbaum, ''All Roads Lead to Washington and Politics in S&L Calamity,'' *The Arizona Republic,* June 10, 1990, pp F1, F3–F5.

[72] R M Kidder, ''A Yardstick for Business Ethics,'' *The Christian Science Monitor,* February 26, 1990, p 14.

[73] For a review of this research, see P V Lewis, ''Defining 'Business Ethics': Like Nailing Jello to the Wall,'' *Journal of Business Ethics,* October 1985, pp 377–83.

[74] K Kelly, ''How Did Sears Blow This Gasket?'' *Business Week,* June 29, 1992, p 38.

[75] Based on R B Morgan, ''Self- and Co-Worker Perceptions of Ethics and Their Relationships to Leadership and Salary,'' *Academy of Management Journal,* February 1993, pp 200–14.

[76] Adapted from G F Cavanagh, D J Moberg, and M Velasquez, ''The Ethics of Organizational Politics,'' *Academy of Management Review,* July 1981, pp 363–74. Also see B P Niehoff and R H Moorman, ''Justice as a Mediator of the Relationship between Methods of Monitoring and Organizational Citizenship Behavior,'' *Academy of Management Journal,* June 1993, pp 527–56.

[77] See chapter 6 in K Hodgson, *A Rock and a Hard Place: How To Make Ethical Business Decisions when the Choices Are Tough* (New York: AMACOM, 1992), pp 66–77. Also see D Vogel, ''The Globalization of Business Ethics: Why America Remains Distinctive,'' *California Management Review,* Fall 1992, pp 30–49.

[78] Adapted from W E Stead, D L Worrell, and J Garner Stead, ''An Integrative Model for Understanding and Managing Ethical Behavior in Business Organizations,'' *Journal of Business Ethics,* March 1990, pp 233–42.

[79] For an excellent discussion of integrity testing and personality tests, see D P O'Meara, ''Personality Tests Raise Questions of Legality and Effectiveness,'' *HRMagazine,* January 1994, pp 97–100.

[80] See J G Frierson, ''New Polygraph Test Limits,'' *Personnel Journal,* December 1988, pp 84–92.

[81] Data from W H Wagel, ''A New Focus on Business Ethics at General Dynamics,'' *Personnel,* August 1987, pp 4–8. Corporate ethics officers are discussed in J Amparano Lopez, ''More Big Businesses Set Up Ethics Offices,'' *The Wall Street Journal,* May 10, 1993, p B1.

[82] The questionnaire and scoring key are excerpted from J W Slocum, Jr., and D Hellriegel, ''A Look at How Managers' Minds Work,'' *Business Horizons,* July–August 1983, pp 58–68.

PERCEPTION AND ATTRIBUTIONS

Learning OBJECTIVES

When you finish studying the material in this chapter, you should be able to:

1. Describe perception in terms of social information processing.

2. Identify and briefly explain five managerial implications of social perception.

3. Discuss stereotypes and the process of stereotype formation.

4. Summarize the managerial challenges and recommendations of sex-role, age, and race stereotypes.

5. Discuss how the self-fulfilling prophecy is created and how it can be used to improve individual and group productivity.

6. Explain, according to Kelley's model, how external and internal causal attributions are formulated.

7. Review Weiner's model of attribution.

8. Contrast the fundamental attribution bias and the self-serving bias.

Asian-Americans Confront Stereotypes

Sharon Hoogstraten

As a Japanese-American growing up on the Eastside of Los Angeles, Don Nakanishi dreaded going to school on Dec. 7.

"Inevitably, some teacher would mention that Japan bombed Pearl Harbor and all the eyes in the class would turn to me," said Nakanishi, director of the Asian-American Studies Center at UCLA.

He thought that part of his life was over when he enrolled at Yale University, which he believed to be a great center of liberalism and tolerance. He was wrong. Late on the night of Dec. 7, 1967, as the freshman Nakanishi was studying in his room—relieved that no one had reminded him of the day—a throng of dormitory mates marched in and threw water balloons at him, shouting: "Bomb Pearl Harbor! Bomb Pearl Harbor!"

As Nakanishi sat in his chair, stunned and dripping wet, not knowing whether to laugh or to cry, a classmate began to recite by memory President Franklin D. Roosevelt's speech declaring war against Japan and calling Dec. 7, 1941, "a date which will live in infamy." . . .

But he has learned over the years that American images of Asians change slowly, if at all.

Just this week, his 10-year-old son told him that last Dec. 7, a fourth-grade teacher had mentioned Japan's bombing of Pearl Harbor in class.

When Nakanishi asked the boy how he felt, the child replied: "I felt like everybody was looking at me. I don't know why."

For nearly 8 million people of Asian ancestry in the United States—40% of them in California—life often means reflecting images from two worlds. . . .

No matter how many generations Asian-Americans live in this country, many people continue to think of them as foreigners, contends Jon Funabiki, director of the Center for Integration and Improvement of Journalism at San Francisco State University. "You can never be a full-blooded American citizen as long as you look different from the classic white Anglo."

Funabiki—who is sansei, third-generation Japanese-American—says he has been verbally harassed more frequently in recent years as US trade frictions with Japan accelerated. During a business trip to the Midwest, he recalls, a stranger stopped him on the street and said: "Why are you trying to buy up all the farms here?"

His experience is not uncommon, according to a new Times poll, which found that the most prevalent form of discrimination reported by Asians comes from strangers in a public place. This is in contrast to African-Americans, Latinos, and Anglos, who most commonly report discrimination in the workplace.

The poll, which surveyed 1,232 Southern California residents, also found that 72% of the respondents believe that movies and TV distort Asian characters.

But 60% said Asians are treated fairly by the news media. Even among Asians, more (50%) believe that the news media treat them fairly than say they get negative treatment (32%).

Still, such findings do not mean that all is well, say Asian-American media watchers.

In 1991, the Center for Integration and Improvement of Journalism, working with the Asian-American Journalists Assn., launched Project Zinger, a watchdog for Asian-American coverage in the news media.

In its report on 1992 coverage, Project Zinger identified 10 editorial cartoons depicting Asians with buckteeth, slanted eyes, and with thick glasses—a image straight out of US World War II propaganda.

One cartoon—by Paul Szep in the Jan. 12, 1992, Boston Globe—showed four Japanese car dealers helping an

As human beings, we constantly strive to make sense of the world around us. The resulting knowledge influences our behavior and helps us navigate our way through life. Think of the perceptual process that occurs when meeting someone for the first time. Your attention is drawn to the individual's physical appearance, mannerisms, actions, and reactions to what you say and do. You ultimately arrive at conclusions based on your perceptions of this social interaction. The brown-haired,

OPENING CASE

(continued)

American car salesman who has fainted, an allusion to President George Bush's trip to Japan. The four Japanese characters have slits for eyes and buckteeth, and three wear large glasses. . . .

Even children's literature is not immune. The July/August issue of Jack and Jill, a nationally distributed children's magazine, drew complaints after a story included an exchange in pidgin English.

"The tiny, ancient master stroked the hair on his chin.

"Not end of world, young Freddie. Master Hojo teach you *seclet* weapon.

"A *secret* weapon, Master Hojo?"

"Wong Fong. Ancient Oriental art of *tickring*."

"What exactly is '*tickring*' Master?"

"Everybody *tickrish* some *prace* or other. Watch *carefurry*. Wong Fong will show you how to find most *tickrish* spot on whole human body."

"I have not seen such a stereotype in years," Oakland resident Teri Lee wrote in a letter to the publication, canceling her 7-year-old's subscription. "I had hoped our country was getting beyond portrayals of inscrutable Oriental karate sages who speak broken English and cannot pronounce *l* and *r* sounds." . . .

Ever since Chinese, Japanese, then Koreans, Filipinos, and Asian-Indians began immigrating last century, they have been met by bizarre stereotypes.

When the first Chinese came to California about the time of the Gold Rush, they were called *celestials*— peculiar beings from another world. Later they were depicted as heathens who frequented opium and gambling dens.

In the early decades of the 20th Century, American admiration of Japan's might tended to soften scapegoating—until World War II, when Japanese in this country became the "yellow peril," and California newspapers promoted the internment of Japanese-Americans.

In the early '40s, when the United States supported Chiang Kai-shek, Chinese here and abroad enjoyed a period of good feelings from Americans. But with the triumph of the Communist government on the mainland in 1949, the Chinese for the most part once again were seen as evil enemies.

Pre-1970 portrayals in Hollywood were mostly negative: sly and sinister Fu Manchu; bumbling Charlie Chan, whose bogus "Confucius say" fortune cookie aphorisms denigrated the great Chinese sage; exotic geisha images; and subservient women being used as exotic playthings for white males.

The Korean and Vietnam wars contributed their share of negative images. . . .

With the great Asian influx into the United States in the 1970s and '80s,

the images changed. The country's Asian population more than doubled, and new stereotypes began to rise. Popular portrayals cast Asians as model minorities who excel academically and economically at the expense of others, as greedy inner-city merchants, or as boat people who are a drain on social services. . . .

Some, including Asian-Americans, view the model minority image as flattering. But Stanford University law professor Bill Hing said it can be harmful.

"There are a lot of Asian-Americans who have psychological and mental problems because their academic performance is not measuring up to the expectations of their parents or of their teachers," said Hing, author of the book "Making and Remaking Asian-America Through Immigration Policy."

For Discussion

Have you ever been unfairly stereotyped? Explain.

■ Additional discussion questions linking this case with the following material appear at the end of this chapter.

Source: Excerpted from Kang, "Separate, Distinct—and Equal," *Los Angeles Times*, August 20, 1993, pp A1, A20. Copyright 1993, *Los Angeles Times*. Excerpted by permission.

green-eyed individual turns out to be friendly and fond of outdoor activities. You further conclude that you like this person and then ask him or her to go to a concert.

This reciprocal process of perception, interpretation, and behavioral response also applies at work. A field study illustrates this relationship. Researchers wanted to know whether employee's perceptions of how much an organization valued them affected their behavior and attitudes. The researchers asked samples of high school teachers, brokerage-firm clerks, manufacturing workers, insurance representatives, and police officers to indicate their perception of the extent to which their organization valued their contributions and their well-being. Employees who perceived that their organization cared about them reciprocated with reduced absenteeism, increased performance, innovation, and positive work attitudes.[1] As another example, consider Monette Paparotti, a customer service representative for Giro Sport Design, a manufacturer of bicycle helmets in Soquel, California.

> Although the company attracts its share of hard-core cyclists, Paparotti was not among them. ''As far as I was concerned, if there was air in my tires, that was fine,'' she says. Giro offers each employee a helmet at a discount, a perk Paparotti took advantage of. By the end of her first year at Giro—after rubbing elbows with fellow employees who were former world-class athletes and having designers seek her opinion (Do you like this color? Would you wear this?)—Paparotti was a convert to the helmets and to mountain-bike racing. When she is out cycling, she finds herself hailing those wearing battered non-Giro helmets and telling them about Giro's guarantee to replace damaged helmets for a nominal fee. ''Here I am, out on the trails doing PR work for Giro!'' she says.[2]

Ms. Paparotti acquired new behaviors because of her altered self-perception about mountain-biking and wearing helmets. This chapter explores these perceptual processes.

To guide our discussion, Figure 5–1 provides an overview of the perception process. As shown, the perceptual process is instigated by the presence of environmental stimuli. These stimuli are selectively perceived and interpreted. In turn, there are perceptual outcomes of stereotypes, self-fulfilling prophecies, and attributions formed, and reinforced, by interpretations of environmental stimuli. Finally, perceptual outcomes directly affect attitudes, motivation, and behavior.

In this chapter we focus on: (1) a social information processing model of perception, (2) stereotypes, (3) the self-fulfilling prophecy, and (4) how causal attributions are used to interpret behavior.

A SOCIAL INFORMATION PROCESSING MODEL OF PERCEPTION

perception   Process of interpreting one's environment.

Perception is a mental and cognitive process that enables us to interpret and understand our surroundings. Recognition of objects is one of this process's major functions. For example, both people and animals recognize familiar objects in their environments. You would recognize a picture of your best friend; dogs and cats can recognize their food dishes or a favorite toy. Reading involves recognition of visual patterns representing letters in the alphabet. People must recognize objects to meaningfully interact with their environment. But since OB's principal focus is on people, the following discussion emphasizes *social* perception rather than object perception.

The study of how people perceive one another has been labeled *social cognition* and *social information processing*. In contrast to the perception of objects:

• FIGURE 5–1
An Overview of the Perception Process

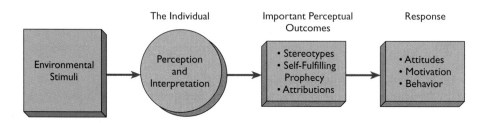

	The Individual	Important Perceptual Outcomes	Response
Environmental Stimuli	Perception and Interpretation	• Stereotypes • Self-Fulfilling Prophecy • Attributions	• Attitudes • Motivation • Behavior

Social cognition is the study of how people make sense of other people and themselves. It focuses on how ordinary people think about people and how they think they think about people. . . .

Research on social cognition also goes beyond naive psychology. The study of social cognition entails a fine-grained analysis of how people think about themselves and others, and it leans heavily on the theory and methods of cognitive psychology.[3]

Moreover, while general theories of perception date back many years, the study of social perception is relatively new, having originated about 1976.[4]

Four-Stage Sequence and a Working Example

Social perception involves a four-stage information processing sequence (hence, the label "social information processing"). Figure 5–2 illustrates a basic social information processing model. Three of the stages in this model—selective attention/comprehension, encoding and simplification, and storage and retention— describe how specific social information is observed and stored in memory. The fourth and final stage, retrieval and response, involves turning mental representations into real-world judgments and decisions.

Keep the following everyday example in mind as we look at the four stages of social perception. Suppose you were thinking of taking a course in, say, personal finance. Three professors teach the same course, using different types of instruction and testing procedures. Through personal experience, you have come to prefer good professors who rely on the case method of instruction and essay tests. According to social perception theory, you would likely arrive at a decision regarding which professor to take as follows:

Stage 1: Selective Attention/Comprehension

People are constantly bombarded by physical and social stimuli in the environment. Since they do not have the mental capacity to fully comprehend all this information, they selectively perceive subsets of environmental stimuli. This is where attention plays a role. **Attention** is the process of becoming consciously aware of something or someone. Attention can be focused on information either from the environment or from memory. Regarding the latter situation, if you sometimes find yourself thinking about totally unrelated events or people while reading a textbook, your memory is the focus of your attention. Research has shown that people tend to pay attention to salient stimuli.

attention Being consciously aware of something or someone.

• ↙ FIGURE 5–2   Social Perception: A Social Information Processing Model

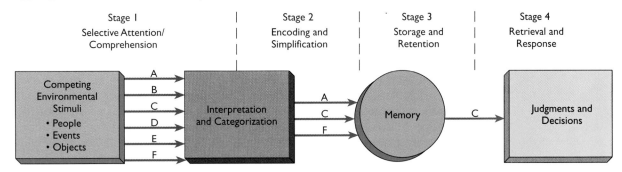

Salient Stimuli   Something is *salient* when it stands out from its context. For example, a 250-pound man would certainly be salient in a women's aerobics class but not at a meeting of the National Football League Players' Association. Social salience is determined by several factors, including

- Being novel (the only person in a group of that race, gender, hair color, or age).
- Being bright (wearing a yellow shirt).
- Being unusual for that person (behaving in an unexpected way, like a person with a fear of heights climbing a steep mountain).
- Being unusual for a person's social category (like a company president driving a motorcycle to work).
- Being unusual for people in general (driving 20 miles per hour in a 55-mph speed zone).
- Being extremely positive (a noted celebrity) or negative (the victim of a bad traffic accident).
- Being dominant in the visual field (sitting at the head of the table).[5]

One's needs and goals often dictate which stimuli are salient. For a driver whose gas gauge is on empty, an Exxon or Mobil sign is more salient than a McDonald's or Burger King sign. The reverse would be true for a hungry driver with a full gas tank.

Back to Our Example   You begin your search for the "right" personal finance professor by asking friends who have taken classes from the three professors. Because you are concerned about the method of instruction and testing procedures, information in those areas is particularly salient to you. Perhaps you even interview the professors to gather still more relevant information. Meanwhile, thousands of competing stimuli fail to get your attention.

Stage 2: Encoding and Simplification

Observed information is not stored in memory in its original form. Encoding is required; raw information is interpreted or translated into mental representations. To accomplish this, perceivers assign pieces of information to **cognitive categories.** "By *category* we mean a number of objects that are considered equivalent. Categories are generally designated by names, e.g., *dog, animal.*"[6] People, events, and objects are interpreted and categorized by comparing their characteristics with *schemata* (or *schema* in singular form).

cognitive categories
Mental depositories for storing information.

schemata   Mental picture of an event or object.

Schemata   According to social information processing theory, a **schema** represents a person's mental picture or summary of a particular event or type of stimulus.[7] For example, your restaurant schema probably is quite similar to the description provided in Table 5–1.

Cognitive-category labels are needed to make schemata meaningful. For example, read the passage in the OB Exercise *now* and determine how comprehensive it is by using the scale at the bottom of the table. Having done this, find the label for this schema in reference note 8.[8] Read the passage again and rate it for comprehensiveness. Your comprehension improved because the cognitive-category label bridged the gap between the description and the laundry schema in your memory.

• ➤ **TABLE 5~1**
Restaurant Schema

Schema: Restaurant.

Characters: Customers, hostess, waiter, chef, cashier.

Scene 1: Entering.
    Customer goes into restaurant.
    Customer finds a place to sit.
      He may find it himself.
      He may be seated by a hostess.
        He asks the hostess for a table.
        She gives him permission to go to the table.

Scene 2: Ordering.
    Customer receives a menu.
    Customer reads it.
    Customer decides what to order.
    Waiter takes the order.
      Waiter sees the customer.
      Waiter goes to the customer.
      Customer orders what he wants.
    Chef cooks the meal.

Scene 3: Eating.
    After some time the waiter brings the meal from the chef.
    Customer eats the meal.

Scene 4: Exiting.
    Customer asks the waiter for the check.
    Waiter gives the check to the customer.
    Customer leaves a tip.
      The size of the tip depends on the goodness of the service.
    Customer pays the cashier.
    Customer leaves the restaurant.

Source: From *Memory, Thought and Behavior* by R W Weisberg. Copyright © 1980 by Oxford University Press, Inc. Reprinted by permission.

OB EXERCISE

How Comprehensive Is This Passage?

The procedure is actually quite simple. First you arrange things into different groups. Of course, one pile may be sufficient depending on how much there is to do. If you have to go somewhere else due to lack of facilities that is the next step, otherwise you are pretty well set. It is important not to overdo things. That is, it is better to do too few things at once than too many. In the short run this may not seem important but complications can easily arise. A mistake can be expensive as well. At first the whole procedure will seem complicated. Soon, however, it will become just another facet of life. It is difficult to foresee any end to the necessity for this task in the immediate future, but then one never can tell. After the procedure is completed one arranges the materials into different groups again. Then they can be put into their appropriate places. Eventually they will be used once more, and the whole cycle will then have to be repeated. However, that is part of life.

	Comprehensive Scale					
Very uncomprehensive			**Neither**			**Very comprehensive**
	1	2	3	4	5	

Source: J D Bransford and M K Johnson, "Contextual Prerequisite for Understanding: Some Investigations of Comprehension and Recall," *Journal of Verbal Learning and Verbal Behavior*, December 1972, p 722. Used with permission.

Long-term memory can be thought of as an apartment complex similar to the one in this photograph, with different memories stored separately yet connected within the building.

Jon Ortner/Tony Stone Images

Back to Our Example   Having collected relevant information about the three personal finance professors and their approaches, your mind creates a mental picture of each by drawing upon your relevant schemata. Thus, by selectively attending to environmental and mental information, you have created simplified mental representations of what it would be like to take a class from each of the three professors. This enables you to render a good decision, as opposed to your life being dictated by random chance.

Stage 3: Storage and Retention

This phase involves storage of information in long-term memory. Long-term memory is like an apartment complex consisting of separate units connected to one another. Although different people live in each apartment, they sometimes interact. In addition, large apartment complexes have different wings (like A, B, and C). Long-term memory similarly consists of separate but related categories. Like the individual apartments inhabited by unique residents, the connected categories contain different types of information. Information also passes among these categories. Finally, long-term memory is made up of three compartments (or wings) containing categories of information about events, semantic materials, and people (see Figure 5–3).[9]

Event Memory   This compartment is composed of categories containing information about both specific and general events. These memories describe appropriate sequences of events in well-known situations, such as going to a restaurant (refer back to Table 5–1), going on a job interview, going to a food store, and going to a movie.

Semantic Memory   Semantic memory refers to general knowledge about the world. In so doing, it functions as a mental dictionary of concepts. Each concept contains a definition (e.g., a good leader) and associated traits (outgoing), emotional states (happy), physical characteristics (tall), and behaviors (works hard). Just as there are schemata for general events, concepts in semantic memory are stored as schemata.

Given our previous discussion of international OB in Chapter 2 and managing diversity in Chapter 3, it should come as no surprise that there are cultural

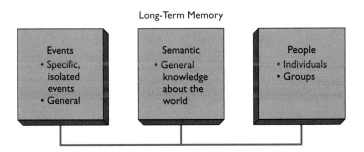

INTERNATIONAL OB

Visual Perceptions Vary by Culture

When Westerners conjure up an image of a car, he [Hirshberg], says it's a side view. With the Japanese, it's the front. "The Japanese read personality and expression into the 'face' of the car," he says.

All the negotiations between Tokyo and San Diego centered on whether the "eyes" were sleepy or awake, and whether the "mouth" gesture was appropriate. "We don't even think of headlights as 'eyes' or the grill as a 'mouth,'" Hirshberg says. In the end, San Diego beat out the Tokyo team and got to do the Infiniti—after a compromise: The headlights and grill were redesigned to make for bigger, more expressive "eyes" and a smaller "mouth."

Source: Excerpted from L Armstrong, "It Started with an Egg," *Business Week,* December 2, 1991, p 142.

---

differences in the type of information stored in semantic memory. Gerald Hirshberg, vice-president at Nissan Design International Inc., the Japanese auto maker's San Diego design shop, learned this lesson when the American Nissan designers competed against the home team in Tokyo for the right to design the J30 Infiniti automobile (see the International OB).

Person Memory   Categories within this compartment contain information about a single individual (your supervisor) or groups of people (managers).

Back to Our Example   As the time draws near for you to decide which personal finance professor to take, your schemata of them are stored in the three categories of long-term memory. These schemata are available for immediate comparison and/or retrieval.

Stage 4: Retrieval and Response

People retrieve information from memory when they make judgments and decisions. Our ultimate judgments and decisions are the product of drawing on, interpreting, and integrating categorical information stored in long-term memory.[10]

Concluding our example, it is registration day and you have to choose which professor to take for personal finance. After retrieving from memory your schemata-based impressions of the three professors, you select a good one who uses the case method and gives essay tests.

Managerial Implications

Social cognition is the window through which we all observe, interpret, and prepare our responses to people and events. A wide variety of managerial activities, organizational processes, and quality-of-life issues are thus affected by perception. Consider, for example, the following implications.

Performance Appraisal   Faulty schemata about what constitutes good versus poor performance can lead to inaccurate performance appraisals, which erode work motivation, commitment, and loyalty. Therefore, it is important for managers to accurately identify the behavioral characteristics and results indicative of good performance at the beginning of a performance review cycle. These characteristics then can serve as the benchmarks for evaluating employee performance. Furthermore, because memory for specific instances of employee performance deteriorates over time, managers need a mechanism for accurately recalling employee behavior. Research reveals that groups remember behaviors more accurately over time than individuals, and individuals can be trained to be more accurate raters of performance.[11]

Hiring   Interviewers make hiring decisions based on their impression of how an applicant fits the perceived requirements of a job. Inaccurate impressions in either direction produce poor hiring decisions. Moreover, interviewers with racist or sexist schemata can undermine the accuracy and legality of hiring decisions. Those invalid schemata need to be confronted and improved through coaching and training. In this regard, a team of researchers demonstrated that a structured behavioral interview reduced race and sex bias and was predictive of successful performers.[12]

Leadership   Research demonstrates that employees' evaluations of leader effectiveness are influenced strongly by their schemata of good and poor leaders. A leader will have a difficult time influencing employees when he or she exhibits behaviors contained in employees' schemata of poor leaders.

Motivation   Perceptions of pay inequity reduce employee motivation and increase employee turnover. Chapter 7 provides a thorough discussion of how equity perceptions affect employee motivation.

Communication   Managers need to remember that social perception is a screening process that can distort communication, both coming and going. Messages are interpreted and categorized according to schemata developed through past experiences and influenced by one's age, gender, and ethnic, geographic, and cultural orientations. Effective communicators try to tailor their messages to the receiver's perceptual schemata. This requires well-developed listening and observation skills and cross-cultural sensitivity.

STEREOTYPES: PERCEPTIONS ABOUT GROUPS OF PEOPLE

While it is often true that beauty is in the eye of the beholder, perception does result in some predictable outcomes. Managers aware of the perception process and its outcomes enjoy a competitive edge. The Walt Disney Company, for instance, takes full advantage of perceptual tendencies to influence customers' reactions to waiting in long lines at its theme parks:

In order to make the experience less psychologically wearing, the waiting times posted by each attraction are generously overestimated, so that one comes away mysteriously grateful for having hung around 20 minutes for a 58-second twirl in the Alice in Wonderland teacups. ("I used the same trick when I was trying to sell sitcoms to the networks," says [Chairman and CEO Michael D.] Eisner. "I showed them a 23-minute 'Happy Days' pilot and told them it was a half hour. They thought it was the fastest-paced show they'd ever seen.")

The lines, moreover, are always moving, even if what looks like the end is actually the start of a second set of switchbacks leading to—oh, no!—a pre-ride waiting area. Those little tricks of the theme park mean a lot.[13]

Likewise, managers can use knowledge of perceptual outcomes to help them interact more effectively with employees. For example, Table 5–2 describes five common perceptual errors. Since these perceptual errors often distort the evaluation of job applicants and of employee performance, managers need to guard against them. This section examines one of the most important and potentially harmful perceptual outcomes associated with person perception: stereotypes. After exploring the process of stereotype formation and maintenance, we discuss sex-role stereotypes, age stereotypes, race stereotypes, and the managerial challenge to avoid stereotypical biases.

Stereotype Formation and Maintenance

stereotype   Beliefs about the characteristics of a group.

"A **stereotype** is an individual's set of beliefs about the characteristics or attributes of a group."[14] Stereotypes are not always negative. For example, the belief that engineers are good at math is certainly part of a stereotype. Stereotypes may or may

• ⟋ TABLE 5~2   Commonly Found Perceptual Errors

Perceptual Error	Description	Example
Halo	A rater forms an overall impression about an object and then uses that impression to bias ratings about the object.	Rating a professor high on the teaching dimensions of ability to motivate students, knowledge, and communication because we like him or her.
Leniency	A personal characteristic that leads an individual to consistently evaluate other people or objects in an extremely positive fashion.	Rating a professor high on all dimensions of performance regardless of his or her actual performance. The rater who hates to say negative things about others.
Central tendency	The tendency to avoid all extreme judgments and rate people and objects as average or neutral.	Rating a professor average on all dimensions of performance regardless of his or her actual performance.
Recency effects	The tendency to remember recent information. If the recent information is negative, the person or object is evaluated negatively.	Although a professor has given good lectures for 12 to 15 weeks, he or she is evaluated negatively because lectures over the last three weeks were done poorly.
Contrast effects	The tendency to evaluate people or objects by comparing them with characteristics of recently observed people or objects.	Rating a good professor as average because you compared his or her performance with three of the best professors you have ever had in college. You are currently taking courses from the three excellent professors.

not be accurate. Engineers may in fact be better at math than the general population. In general, stereotypic characteristics are used to differentiate a particular group of people from other groups.

Consider walking into a business meeting with 10 people situated around a conference table. You notice a male at the head of the table and a woman seated immediately to his right, taking notes. Due to ingrained stereotypes, you are likely to assume that the man is the top-ranking person in the room and the woman, his secretary. This example highlights how people use stereotypes to interpret their environment and to make judgments about others.[15]

Unfortunately, stereotypes can lead to poor decisions, can create barriers for women and people of color, and can undermine employee loyalty and job satisfaction. For example, a recent national survey of 2,958 workers indicated that more than one-fifth of the minority workers had been discriminated against. Employees of all kinds also agreed that women and people of color had lower chances of advancement than whites. Finally, respondents who saw little opportunity for advancement tended to be less loyal, less committed, and less satisfied with their jobs.[16]

Stereotyping is a four-step process. It begins by categorizing people into groups according to various criteria, such as gender, age, race, and occupation. Next, we infer that all people within a particular category possess the same traits or characteristics (e.g., all women are nurturing, older people have more job-related accidents, all blacks are good athletes, all professors are absentminded). Then, we form expectations of others and interpret their behavior according to our stereotypes. Finally, stereotypes are maintained by (1) overestimating the frequency of stereotypic behaviors exhibited by others, (2) incorrectly explaining expected and unexpected behaviors, and (3) differentiating minority individuals from oneself.[17] Let us now take a look at different types of stereotypes.

Sex-Role Stereotypes

sex-role stereotype Beliefs about appropriate roles for men and women.

A **sex-role stereotype** is the belief that differing traits and abilities make men and women particularly well suited to different roles. This perceptual tendency was documented in a classic 1972 study. After administering a sex-role questionnaire to 383 women and 599 men, the researchers drew the following conclusion: ''Our research demonstrates the contemporary existence of clearly defined sex-role stereotypes for men and women contrary to the phenomenon of 'unisex' currently touted in the media.''[18] They further explained:

> Women are perceived as relatively less competent, less independent, less objective, and less logical than men; men are perceived as lacking interpersonal sensitivity, warmth, and expressiveness in comparison to women. Moreover, stereotypically masculine traits are more often perceived to be desirable than are stereotypically feminine characteristics. Most importantly, both men and women incorporate both the positive and negative traits of the appropriate stereotype into their self-concepts. Since more feminine traits are negatively valued than are masculine traits, women tend to have more negative self-concepts than do men.[19]

Although more recent research indicates that men and women do not systematically differ in the manner suggested by traditional stereotypes,[20] these stereotypes still persist. Consider the case of Ann Hopkins.

> In the spring of 1982, Price Waterhouse, an international accounting firm with a large management consulting business, was considering 88 candidates for partnerships. Ann

Hopkins was the only woman among the candidates. . . . She had garnered more than $34 million worth of consulting contracts for the firm during her tenure and billed more hours than any of the other 87 candidates in the fiscal year prior to the partnership nominations. At the time of her nomination, Price Waterhouse had 662 senior partners, of which seven were women. . . .

Subsequently, Hopkins' candidacy was placed on a one-year hold, ostensibly on the basis of her poor interpersonal skills and "unfeminine" behavior. This decision was relayed to Hopkins by her male supervisor, who suggested that she should walk more femininely, talk more femininely, dress more femininely, wear makeup, and have her hair styled.[21]

After all appeals were exhausted, the courts held that Price Waterhouse engaged in illegal sex stereotyping. Ms. Hopkins was apparently denied a partnership because of inappropriate stereotyping in the way partners were reviewed and evaluated and not because of job-related reasons. This case highlights that women and men need to be judged as individuals, when making personnel decisions, not as members of supposedly homogeneous groups. (The same holds true for racial and ethnic minorities.) Findings from laboratory research suggest that managers may be following this recommendation.

A meta-analysis of 24 experimental studies revealed that men and women received similar performance ratings for the same level of task performance. Stated differently, there was no pro-male bias. Further, a second meta-analysis of 19 studies found no significant relationships between applicant gender and hiring recommendations.[22] These results are encouraging. They are also consistent with recent evaluations of employee's attitudes toward women managers. Two OB researchers administered the "Women as Managers Scale" to 284 human resource professionals in the Midwest. Not only did this sample have positive attitudes toward women managers, but results were much more positive than findings obtained in 1970 from the same survey.[23]

What are your attitudes toward women executives? To find out, complete the survey in the OB Exercise. Compute your score by adding your nine responses. (Revised norms for comparison purposes are: Total score of 9–20 = Unfavorable attitude toward female executives; 21–33 = Middle of the road; 34–45 = Favorable.) What are the organizational and career implications of your attitudes toward women executives?

Age Stereotypes

Age stereotypes reinforce age discrimination because of their negative orientation. For example, long-standing age stereotypes depict older workers as less satisfied, not as involved with their work, less motivated, not as committed, less productive than their younger co-workers, and more apt to be absent from work. Older employees are also perceived as being more accident prone. As with sex-role stereotypes, these age stereotypes are more fiction than fact.

OB researcher Susan Rhodes sought to determine whether age stereotypes were supported by data from 185 different studies. She discovered that as age increases so do employees' job satisfaction, job involvement, internal work motivation, and organizational commitment. Moreover, older workers were not more accident prone.[24]

Results are not as clear cut regarding job performance. A meta-analysis of 96 studies representing 38,983 people and a cross section of jobs revealed that age and job performance were unrelated.[25] Some OB researchers, however, believe that this

---

OB Exercise

What Are Your Attitudes toward Women Executives?

Read each question and mark your answer by circling whether you:

  1 = Strongly disagree
  2 = Disagree
  3 = Neither disagree nor agree
  4 = Agree
  5 = Strongly agree

Females have the capabilities for responsible managerial positions	1	2	3	4	5
A female executive merits the same trust and respect as a male executive.	1	2	3	4	5
Women in responsible managerial positions must have the capabilities for their positions and therefore men should honor their decisions.	1	2	3	4	5
It's about time we had some women executives in organizations.	1	2	3	4	5
Women executives are not ignorant when it comes to highly technical subjects.	1	2	3	4	5
It is unfair to say women became top executives by using sexual favors.	1	2	3	4	5
A man is not better suited for handling executive responsibility than a woman is.	1	2	3	4	5
There are no problems with a male working for a female executive if both are dedicated, competent, and learned workers.	1	2	3	4	5
Women are not taking men's positions nowadays.	1	2	3	4	5

Total score =

Source: Based on P Dubno, J Costas, H Cannon, C Wankel, and H Emin, "An Empirically Keyed Scale for Measuring Managerial Attitudes toward Women Executives," *Psychology of Women Quarterly*, Summer 1979, pp 360–61. (Copyrighted by and reprinted with the permission of Cambridge University Press.)

---

finding does not reflect the true relationship between age and performance. They propose that the relationship between age and performance changes as people grow older.[26] This idea was tested on data obtained from 24,219 individuals. In support of this hypothesis, results revealed that age was positively related to performance for younger employees (25–30 years of age) and then plateaued: Older employees were not less productive. Age and experience also predicted performance better for more complex jobs than other jobs, and job experience had a stronger relationship with performance than age.[27]

What about absenteeism? Do older employees miss more days of work? A recent meta-analysis of 34 studies encompassing 7,772 workers indicated that age was inversely related to both voluntary (a day at the beach) and involuntary (sick day) absenteeism.[28] Contrary to stereotypes, older workers are ready and able to meet their job requirements. Moreover, results from the meta-analysis suggest managers should focus more attention on absenteeism among younger workers than among older workers.

Race Stereotypes

There is not a large percentage of Hispanic, black, and Asian managers in the United States. Negative racial stereotypes are one of several potential explanations for this state of affairs. Consider women of color. There appears to be a stereotype that minority women are frequently hired to fulfill equal employment opportunity requirements. "Personnel executives sometimes call them 'twofers' because they fulfill two equal opportunity obligations, and that label undercuts their credibility on the job."[29] This is precisely what happened to 40-year-old Charleyse Pratt.

> As an assistant personnel director at a Midwest electronics company, she gave seminars to senior executives on sexual and racial harassment. One day, after a four-hour presentation to 20 white male senior managers, one of the men, whose last name was pronounced "coon," stood up and said, "Do you mean the coons can't stick together?" All the men, including her boss, broke into laughter. . . .
>
> More recently, at a Midwestern manufacturer, she was told outright that she was hired to meet affirmative action goals. And not long ago, she found herself teaching her job to a white man who had been promoted over her. "He told me, 'You're going to have to learn to subordinate yourself to me,' " says Mrs. Pratt.[30]

Some research supports Mrs. Pratt's experience. A recent study attempted to determine whether there was a relationship between being labeled an "affirmative action" hire and perceptions of an employee's competence. Results from an experiment using college students and a field test using 184 white men both supported the conclusion that a stigma of incompetence arises when people are hired for supposed "affirmative action" reasons. Another study examined the relationship of race to employee attitudes across 814 black managers and 814 white managers. Results demonstrated that blacks, when compared with whites, felt less accepted by their peers, perceived lower managerial discretion on their jobs, reached career plateaus more frequently, noted lower levels of career satisfaction, and received lower performance ratings.[31] Negative findings like these prompted researchers to investigate if race stereotypes actually bias performance ratings and hiring decisions.

Performance ratings were found to be unbiased in two studies that used large samples of 21,547 and 39,537 rater–ratee pairs of black and white employees, respectively, from throughout the United States. These findings revealed that black and white managers did not differentially evaluate their employees based on race.[32] In contrast to the presumed negative bias against people of color, a recent study of 2,805 interview decisions uncovered a same-race bias for Hispanics and blacks. That is, Hispanic and black interviewers evaluated applicants of their own race more favorably than applicants of other races. For white applicants, interviewer race did not differentially affect interview evaluations.[33] Given the increasing number of people of color that will enter the workforce over the next 10 years (recall our discussion in Chapter 3), employers should focus on nurturing and developing women and people of color as well as increasing managers' sensitivities to invalid racial stereotypes.

Managerial Challenges and Recommendations

The key managerial challenge is to make decisions that are blind to gender, age, and race. To do so, organizations first need to educate themselves about the problem of stereotyping through employee training. The next step entails engaging in a broad effort to reduce stereotypes throughout the organization. This can be done by increasing the amount of contact among members of different gender, age, and racial groups. Social scientists believe that mixed-group contact is the best technique for reducing stereotypes because it provides people with more accurate data about the characteristics of other groups of people.[34] As such, organizations should create opportunities for diverse employees to meet and work together in cooperative groups of equal status.

Another recommendation is for managers to identify valid individual differences (discussed in Chapter 4) that differentiate between successful and unsuccessful performers. As previously discussed, for instance, research reveals experience is a better predictor of performance than age. Research also shows that managers can be trained to use these valid criteria when hiring applicants and evaluating employee performance.[35]

Removing promotional barriers for men and women and for people of color is another viable solution to alleviating the stereotyping problem. This can be accomplished by minimizing the differences in job experience across groups of people. Similar experience, coupled with the accurate evaluation of performance, helps managers to make gender, age, and racially blind decisions.

There are several recommendations that can be pursued based on the documented relationship between age and performance.

1. Because performance plateaus with age for noncomplex jobs, organizations may use the variety of job design techniques discussed in Chapter 6 to increase employees' intrinsic motivation.

2. Organizations may need to consider using incentives to motivate employees to upgrade their skills and abilities. This will help avoid unnecessary plateaus.

3. It may be advisable to hire older people in order to acquire their accumulated experience. This is especially useful for highly complex jobs. Moreover, hiring older workers is a good solution for reducing turnover, providing role models for younger employees, and coping with the current shortage of qualified entry-level workers. Results from a meta-analysis and actual corporate experience both support this recommendation.[36]

   A good example is the opening of a new store in Macclesfield, England, by B&Q PLC, Britain's largest home-improvement chain. The store was staffed entirely with workers 50 and older. The International OB illustrates the results obtained from comparing the Macclesfield store with five B&Q stores with similar employment and sales levels.

It is important to obtain top management's commitment and support to eliminate the organizational practices that support or reinforce stereotyping and discriminatory decisions. Research clearly demonstrates that top management support is essential to successful implementation of the types of organizational changes being recommended.[37]

SELF-FULFILLING PROPHECY: THE PYGMALION EFFECT

Historical roots of the self-fulfilling prophecy are found in Greek mythology. According to mythology, Pygmalion was a sculptor who hated women yet fell in love with an ivory statue he carved of a beautiful woman. He became so infatuated with the statue that he prayed to the goddess Aphrodite to bring her to life. The

INTERNATIONAL OB

B&Q PLC's Macclesfield, England, Store Is Staffed Entirely with Workers 50 and Older

- Macclesfield was 18 percent more profitable than the average of the five comparison B&Q stores.

- Employee turnover at Macclesfield was nearly six times lower than the average of the comparison stores.

- The older workers at Macclesfield were absent 39 percent less than

workers in the other stores.

- Leakage, which is the difference between stock expected in the store and stock actually in the store because of theft, damage, and inventory not received, at Macclesfield is less than half the average of the five comparison stores.

- Extra training has not been required for older workers.

Source: "Studies Refute Myths about Older Workers," *Society for Human Resource Management/HRNews,* July 1991, p 8.

goddess heard his prayer, granted his wish, and Pygmalion's statue came to life. The essence of the **self-fulfilling prophecy,** or Pygmalion effect, is that people's expectations or beliefs determine their behavior and performance, thus serving to make their expectations come true. In other words, we strive to validate our *perceptions* of reality, no matter how faulty they may be. Thus, the self-fulfilling prophecy is an important perceptual outcome we need to better understand.

self-fulfilling prophecy
People's expectations determine behavior and performance.

For example, the self-fulfilling prophecy can dramatically affect customer satisfaction and quality. Art Mulwitz, vice-president for operations at Perstorp Components, an auto supplier of noise-insulation sheets, observed that employees' low performance expectations adversely affected operations.

> Once, a maintenance worker told Perstorp's Mulwitz that he considered 80% to 85% uptime acceptable for the plant's machinery. "What uptime do you expect from your Chevy Blazer?" Mulwitz replied. Uptime now averages 94% to 97%. All this pays tangible dividends. At Perstorp, waste is down to 0.7% of sales from 2.5% a few years ago, and the company has become a model of quality control for its Parent, Perstorp AB, a Swedish chemical concern.[38]

Research and an Explanatory Model

The self-fulfilling prophecy was first demonstrated in an academic environment. After giving a bogus test of academic potential to students from grades 1 to 6, researchers informed teachers that certain students had high potential for achievement. In reality, students were randomly assigned to the "high potential" and "control" (normal potential) groups. Results showed that children designated as having high potential obtained significantly greater increases in both IQ scores and reading ability than did the control students.[39] The teachers of the supposedly high potential group got better results because their high expectations caused them to give harder assignments, more feedback, and more recognition of achievement. Students in the normal potential group did not excel because their teachers did not expect outstanding results.

Research similarly has shown that by raising instructors' and managers' expectations for individuals performing a wide variety of tasks, higher levels of achievement/productivity can be obtained.[40] Subjects in these field studies included airmen at the United States Air Force Academy Preparatory School,

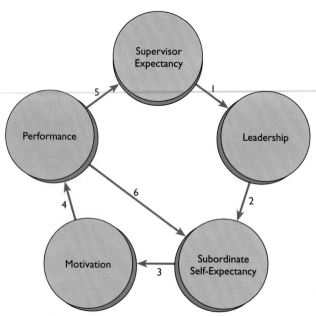

Source: D Eden, "Self-Fulfilling Prophecy as a Management Tool: Harnessing Pygmalion," *Academy of Management Review,* January 1984, p 67. Used with permission.

disadvantaged people in job-training programs, electronics assemblers, trainees in a military command course, and US naval personnel.

Figure 5–4 presents a model of the self-fulfilling prophecy that helps explain these results. This model attempts to outline how supervisory expectations affect employee performance. As indicated, high supervisory expectancy produces better leadership (linkage 1), which subsequently leads employees to develop higher self-expectations (linkage 2). Higher expectations motivate workers to exert more effort (linkage 3), ultimately increasing performance (linkage 4) and supervisory expectancies (linkage 5). Successful performance also improves an employee's self-expectancy for achievement (linkage 6).

Putting the Self-Fulfilling Prophecy to Work

Largely due to the Pygmalion effect, managerial expectations powerfully influence employee behavior and performance. Consequently, managers need to harness the Pygmalion effect by building a hierarchical framework that reinforces positive performance expectations throughout the organization.

Employees' self-expectations are the foundation of this framework. In turn, positive self-expectations improve interpersonal expectations by encouraging people to work toward common goals. This cooperation enhances group-level productivity and promotes positive performance expectations within the work group. At Microsoft Corporation, for example, employees routinely put in 75-hour weeks, especially when work groups are trying to meet shipment deadlines for new products. Because Microsoft is known for meeting its deadlines, positive group-level expectations help create and reinforce an organizational culture of high expectancy for success. This process then excites people about working for the organization, thereby reducing turnover. Microsoft's turnover is well below industry standards, even for highly marketable computer programmers.[41]

At Microsoft, the Pygmalion effect is countered via a culture that promotes and rewards shared group goals and excellence in all aspects of job performance.

Courtesy Microsoft

Because positive self-expectations are the foundation for creating an organization-wide Pygmalion effect, let us consider how managers can create positive performance expectations. This task may be accomplished by using various combinations of the following:

1. Recognize that everyone has the potential to increase his or her performance.
2. Instill confidence in your staff.
3. Set high performance goals.
4. Positively reinforce employees for a job well done.
5. Provide constructive feedback when necessary.
6. Help employees advance through the organization.
7. Introduce new employees as if they have outstanding potential.
8. Become aware of your personal prejudices and nonverbal messages that may discourage others.[42]

CAUSAL ATTRIBUTIONS

Attribution theory is based on the premise that people attempt to infer causes for observed behavior. Rightly or wrongly, we constantly formulate cause-and-effect explanations for our own and others' behavior. Attributional statements such as the following are common: ''Joe drinks too much because he has no willpower; but I need a couple of drinks after work because I'm under a lot of pressure.'' Formally defined, **causal attributions** are suspected or inferred causes of behavior. Even

causal attributions
Suspected or inferred causes of behavior.

though our causal attributions tend to be self-serving and are often invalid, it is important to understand how people formulate attributions because they profoundly affect organizational behavior. For example, a supervisor who attributes an employee's poor performance to a lack of effort might reprimand that individual. However, training might be deemed necessary if the supervisor attributes the poor performance to a lack of ability.

Generally speaking, people formulate causal attributions by considering the events preceding an observed behavior. This section introduces and explores two different widely cited attribution models proposed by Harold Kelley and Bernard Weiner. Attributional tendencies, research, and related managerial implications also are discussed.

Kelley's Model of Attribution

internal factors Personal characteristics that cause behavior.

external factors Environmental characteristics that cause behavior.

Current models of attribution, such as Kelley's, are based on the pioneering work of the late Fritz Heider. Heider, the founder of attribution theory, proposed that behavior can be attributed either to **internal factors** within a person (such as ability) or to **external factors** within the environment (such as a difficult task). This line of thought parallels the idea of an internal versus external locus of control, as discussed in Chapter 4. Building on Heider's work, Kelley attempted to pinpoint major antecedents of internal and external attributions. Kelley hypothesized that people make causal attributions after gathering information about three dimensions of behavior: consensus, distinctiveness, and consistency.[43] These dimensions vary independently, thus forming various combinations and leading to differing attributions.

Figure 5–5 presents performance charts showing low versus high consensus, distinctiveness, and consistency. These charts are now used to help develop a working knowledge of all three dimensions in Kelley's model.

- *Consensus* involves a comparison of an individual's behavior with that of his or her peers. There is high consensus when one acts like the rest of the group and low consensus when one acts differently. As shown in Figure 5–5, high consensus is indicated when persons A, B, C, D, and E obtain similar levels of individual performance. In contrast, person C's performance is low in consensus because it significantly varies from the performance of persons A, B, D, and E.

- *Distinctiveness* is determined by comparing a person's behavior on one task with his or her behavior on other tasks. High distinctiveness means the individual has performed the task in question in a significantly different manner than he or she has performed other tasks. Low distinctiveness means stable performance or quality from one task to another. Figure 5–5 reveals that the employee's performance on task 4 is highly distinctive because it significantly varies from his or her performance on tasks 1, 2, 3, and 5.

- *Consistency* is determined by judging if the individual's performance on a given task is consistent over time. High consistency implies that a person performs a certain task the same, time after time. Unstable performance of a given task over time would mean low consistency. The downward spike in performance depicted in the consistency graph of Figure 5–5 represents low consistency. In this case, the employee's performance on a given task varied over time.

It is instructive to remember that consensus relates to other *people*, distinctiveness relates to other *tasks*, and consistency relates to *time*. The question now is: How

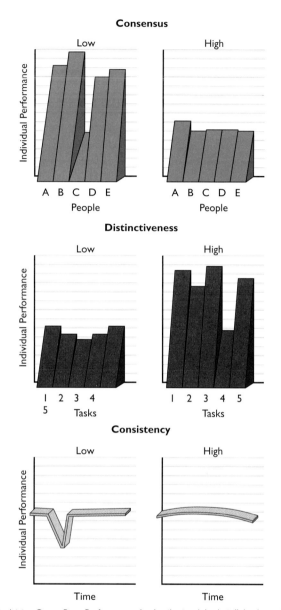

• ➤ FIGURE 5~5
Performance Charts Showing
Low and High Consensus,
Distinctiveness, and
Consistency Information

Source: K A Brown, "Explaining Group Poor Performance: An Attributional Analysis," *Academy of Management Review,* January 1984, p 56. Used with permission.

does information about these three dimensions of behavior lead to internal or external attributions?

Kelley hypothesized that people attribute behavior to *external* causes (environmental factors) when they perceive high consensus, high distinctiveness, and low consistency. *Internal* attributions (personal factors) tend to be made when observed behavior is characterized by low consensus, low distinctiveness, and high consistency. So, for example, when all employees are performing poorly (high consensus), when the poor performance occurs on only one of several tasks (high distinctiveness), and the poor performance occurs during only one time period (low consistency), a supervisor will probably attribute an employee's poor performance to an external source such as peer pressure or an overly difficult task. In contrast, performance will be attributed to an employee's personal characteristics (an internal attribution) when only the individual in question is performing poorly (low consensus), when the inferior performance is found across several tasks (low distinctiveness), and when the low performance has persisted over time (high consistency). Many studies supported this predicted pattern of attributions.[44]

Weiner's Model of Attribution

Bernard Weiner, a noted motivation theorist, developed an attribution model to explain achievement behavior and to predict subsequent changes in motivation and performance. In his model, Weiner proposes that ability, effort, task difficulty, luck, and help from others are the primary causes of achievement behavior (see Figure 5–6). In turn, these attributions for success and failure influence how individuals feel about themselves. For instance, a meta-analysis of 104 studies involving almost 15,000 subjects found that people who attributed failure to their lack of ability (as opposed to bad luck) experienced psychological depression. The exact opposite attributions (to good luck rather than to high ability) tended to trigger depression in people experiencing positive events. In short, perceived bad luck took the sting out of a negative outcome, but perceived good luck reduced the joy associated with success.[45]

In further support of Weiner's model, a recent study examined the attributional processes of 126 employees who were permanently displaced by a plant closing. Consistent with the model, as the explanation for job loss was attributed to internal and stable causes, life satisfaction, self-esteem, and expectations for reemployment diminished. Furthermore, research also shows that when individuals attribute their success to internal rather than external factors, they (1) have higher expectations for future success, (2) report a greater desire for achievement, and (3) set higher performance goals.[46]

Attributional Tendencies

Researchers have uncovered two attributional tendencies that distort one's interpretation of observed behavior—*fundamental attribution bias* and *self-serving bias.*

• FIGURE 5–6   A Modified Version of Weiner's Attribution Model

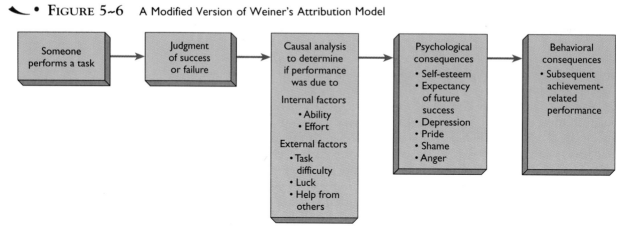

Source: Based in part on B Weiner, "An Attributional Theory of Achievement Motivation and Emotion," *Psychological Review*, October 1985, pp 548–73.

Fundamental Attribution Bias The **fundamental attribution bias** reflects one's tendency to attribute another person's behavior to his or her personal characteristics, as opposed to situational factors. This bias causes perceivers to ignore important environmental forces that often significantly affect behavior. For example, a recent study of 145 manufacturing employees demonstrated that upper management attributed the causes of industrial back pain to the individual involved rather than the environment. In contrast, hourly workers attributed back pain to the work environment and not the individual.[47]

fundamental attribution bias Ignoring environmental factors that affect behavior.

Self-Serving Bias The **self-serving bias** represents one's tendency to take more personal responsibility for success than for failure. Referring again to Figure 5–6, employees tend to attribute their successes to internal factors (high ability and/or hard work) and their failures to uncontrollable external factors (tough job, bad luck, unproductive co-workers, or an unsympathetic boss).[48] This self-serving bias is evident in how students typically analyze their performance on exams. "A" students are likely to attribute their grade to high ability or hard work. "D" students, meanwhile, tend to pin the blame on factors like an unfair test, bad luck, or unclear lectures. Because of self-serving bias, it is very difficult to pin down personal responsibility for mistakes in today's complex organizations.

self-serving bias Taking more personal responsibility for success than failure.

Managerial Application and Implications

Attribution models can be used to explain how managers handle poorly performing employees. One study revealed that managers had negative impressions of employees, administered lower levels of rewards, and blamed employees when they attributed their poor performance to internal causes. A second study indicated that managers tended to transfer employees whose poor performance was attributed to a lack of ability. These same managers also decided to take no immediate action when poor performance was attributed to external factors beyond an individual's control.[49]

The preceding situations have several important implications for managers. First, managers tend to disproportionately attribute behavior to *internal* causes. This can result in inaccurate evaluations of performance, leading to reduced employee motivation. No one likes to be blamed because of factors they perceive to be beyond their control. Further, since managers' responses to employee performance vary according to their attributions, attributional biases may lead to inappropriate managerial actions, including promotions, transfers, layoffs, and so forth. This can dampen motivation and performance. Attributional training sessions for managers are in order. Basic attributional processes can be explained, and managers can be taught to detect and avoid attributional biases. Finally, an employee's attributions for his or her own performance have dramatic effects on subsequent motivation, performance, and personal attitudes such as self-esteem. For instance, people tend to give up, develop lower expectations for future success, and experience decreased self-esteem when they attribute failure to a lack of ability. Fortunately, attributional retraining can improve both motivation and performance. Research shows that employees can be taught to attribute their failures to a lack of effort rather than to a lack of ability.[50] This attributional realignment paves the way for improved motivation and performance.

In summary, managers need to keep a finger on the pulse of employee attributions if they are to make full use of the motivation concepts in the next two chapters.

SUMMARY OF KEY CONCEPTS

1. *Describe perception in terms of social information processing.* Perception is a mental and cognitive process that enables us to interpret and understand our surroundings. Social perception, also known as social cognition and social information processing, is a four-stage process. The four stages are selective attention/comprehension, encoding and simplification, storage and retention, and retrieval and response. During social cognition, salient stimuli are matched with schemata, assigned to cognitive categories, and stored in long-term memory for events, semantic materials, or people.

2. *Identify and briefly explain five managerial implications of social perception.* Social perception affects performance appraisal, hiring decisions, leadership perceptions, motivation, and communication processes. Faulty schemata about what constitutes good versus poor performance can lead to inaccurate performance appraisals. Similarly, inaccurate schemata, or racist and sexist schemata, may be used to evaluate job applicants. Invalid schemata need to be identified and replaced with appropriate schemata through coaching and training. With respect to leadership, a leader will have a difficult time influencing employees when he or she exhibits behaviors contained in employees' schemata of poor leaders. Because perceptions of pay inequity affect employee motivation, managers need to be aware of employees' perceptions. Finally, communication is influenced by schemata used to interpret any message. Effective communicators try to tailor their messages to the receiver's perceptual schemata.

3. *Discuss stereotypes and the process of stereotype formation.* Stereotypes represent grossly oversimplified beliefs or expectations about groups of people. Stereotyping is a four-step process that begins by categorizing people into groups according to various criteria. Next, we infer that all people within a particular group possess the same traits or characteristics. Then, we form expectations of others and interpret their behavior according to our stereotypes. Finally, stereotypes are maintained by (1) overestimating the frequency of stereotypic behaviors exhibited by others, (2) incorrectly explaining expected and unexpected behaviors, and (3) differentiating minority individuals from oneself.

4. *Summarize the managerial challenges and recommendations of sex-role, age, and race stereotypes.* The key managerial challenge is to make decisions that are blind to gender, age, and race. Training can be used to educate employees about the problem of stereotyping. Because mixed-group contact reduces stereotyping, organizations should create opportunities for diverse employees to meet and work together in cooperative groups of equal status. Hiring decisions should be based on valid individual differences, and managers can be trained to use valid criteria when evaluating employee performance. Minimizing differences in job opportunities and experiences across groups of people can help alleviate promotional barriers. Job design techniques can be used to reduce performance plateaus associated with age. Organizations also may need to use incentives to motivate employees to

upgrade their skills and abilities, and hiring older workers has many potential organizational benefits. It is critical to obtain top management's commitment and support to eliminate stereotyping and discriminatory decisions.

5. *Discuss how the self-fulfilling prophecy is created and how it can be used to improve individual and group productivity.* The self-fulfilling prophecy, also known as the Pygmalion effect, describes how people behave so their expectations come true. High managerial expectations foster high employee self-expectations. These in turn lead to greater effort and better performance, and yet higher expectations. Conversely, a downward spiral of expectations-performance may occur. Managers are encouraged to harness the Pygmalion effect by building a hierarchical framework that reinforces positive performance expectations throughout the organization.

6. *Explain, according to Kelley's model, how external and internal causal attributions are formulated.* Attribution theory attempts to describe how people infer causes for observed behavior. According to Kelley's model of causal attribution, external attributions tend to be made when consensus and distinctiveness are high and consistency is low. Internal (personal responsibility) attributions tend to be made when consensus and distinctiveness are low and consistency is high.

7. *Review Weiner's model of attribution.* Weiner's model of attribution predicts achievement behavior in terms of causal attributions. Attributions of ability, effort, task difficulty, luck, and help from others affect how individuals feel about themselves. In turn, these feelings directly influence subsequent achievement-related performance.

8. *Contrast the fundamental attribution bias and the self-serving bias.* Fundamental attribution bias involves emphasizing personal factors more than situational factors while formulating causal attributions for the behavior of others. Self-serving bias involves personalizing the causes of one's successes and externalizing the causes of one's failures.

DISCUSSION QUESTIONS

1. Why is it important for managers to have a working knowledge of perception and attribution?

2. When you are sitting in class, what stimuli are salient? What is your schema for classroom activity?

3. Have you ever been the victim of a sex-role stereotype? Discuss.

4. Which type of stereotype (sex-role, age, or race) is more pervasive and negative in organizations? Why?

5. What evidence of self-fulfilling prophecies have you seen lately?

6. How might the Pygmalion effect be applied in this class?

7. How would you formulate an attribution, according to Kelley's model, for the behavior of a classmate who starts arguing in class with your professor?

8. In what situations do you tend to attribute your successes/failures to luck? How well does Weiner's attributional model in Figure 5–6 explain your answers? Explain.

9. Are poor people victimized by a fundamental attribution bias? Explain.

10. What evidence of the self-serving bias have you observed lately?

EXERCISE

Objectives

1. To gain experience determining the causes of performance.

2. To decide on corrective action for employee performance.

Introduction

Attributions are typically made to internal and external factors. Perceivers arrive at their assessments by using various informational cues or antecedents. To determine the types of antecedents people use, we have developed a case containing various informational cues about an individual's performance. You will be asked to read the case and make attributions about the causes of performance. To assess the impact of attributions on managerial behavior, you will also be asked to recommend corrective action.

Instructions

Presented below is a case that depicts the performance of Mary Martin, a computer programmer. Please read the case and then identify the causes of her behavior by answering the questions following the case. After completing this task, decide on the appropriateness of various forms of corrective action. A list of potential recommendations has been developed. The list is divided into four categories. Read each action, and evaluate its appropriateness by using the scale provided. Next, compute a total score for each of the four categories.

The Case of Mary Martin

Mary Martin, 30, received her baccalaureate degree in computer science from a reputable state school in the Midwest. She also graduated with above-average grades. Mary is currently working in the computer support/analysis department as a programmer for a nationally based firm. During the past year, Mary has missed 10 days of work. She seems unmotivated and rarely has her assignments completed on time. Mary is usually given the harder programs to work on.

Past records indicate Mary, on the average, completes programs classified as "routine" in about 45 hours. Her co-workers, on the other hand, complete "routine" programs in an average time of 32 hours. Further, Mary finishes programs considered "major problems," on the average, in about 115 hours.

Her co-workers, however, finish these same "major problem" assignments, on the average, in about 100 hours. When Mary has worked in programming teams, her peer performance reviews are generally average to negative. Her male peers have noted she is not creative in attacking problems and she is difficult to work with.

The computer department recently sent a questionnaire to all users of its services to evaluate the usefulness and accuracy of data received. The results indicate many departments are not using computer output because they cannot understand the reports. It was also determined that the users of output generated from Mary's programs found the output chaotic and not useful for managerial decision making.[51]

Causes of Performance

To what extent was each of the following a cause of Mary's performance? Use the following scale:

```
   Very little                          Very much
   1————————2—————————3————————4—————————5
         a. High ability            1  2  3  4  5
         b. Low ability             1  2  3  4  5
         c. Low effort              1  2  3  4  5
         d. Difficult job           1  2  3  4  5
         e. Unproductive co-workers 1  2  3  4  5
         f. Bad luck                1  2  3  4  5
```

Appropriateness of Corrective Action

Evaluate the following courses of action by using the scale below:

Very inappropriate				Very appropriate
1	2	3	4	5

Coercive actions

a. Reprimand Mary for her performance   1 2 3 4 5

b. Threaten to fire Mary if her performance does not improve   1 2 3 4 5

Change job

c. Transfer Mary to another job   1 2 3 4 5

d. Demote Mary to a less demanding job   1 2 3 4 5

Nonpunitive actions

e. Work with Mary to help her do the job better   1 2 3 4 5

f. Offer Mary encouragement to help her improve   1 2 3 4 5

No immediate action

g. Do nothing   1 2 3 4 5

h. Promise Mary a pay raise if she improves   1 2 3 4 5

Compute a score for the four categories:[52]

Coercive actions = a + b =

Change job = c + d =

Nonpunitive actions = e + f =

No immediate actions = g + h =

Questions for Consideration/Class Discussion

1. How would you evaluate Mary's performance in terms of consensus, distinctiveness, and consistency?

2. Is Mary's performance due to internal or external causes?

3. What did you identify as the top two causes of Mary's performance? Are your choices consistent with Weiner's classification of internal and external factors? Explain.

4. Which of the four types of corrective action do you think is most appropriate? Explain. Can you identify any negative consequences of this choice?

NOTES

[1] Details may be found in R Eisenberger, P Fasolo, and V Davis–LaMastro, ''Perceived Organizational Support and Employee Diligence, Commitment, and Innovation,'' *Journal of Applied Psychology,* February 1990, pp 51–59.

[2] A Bianchi, ''True Believers,'' *Inc.,* July 1993, p 72.

[3] S T Fiske and S E Taylor, *Social Cognition,* 2nd ed (Reading, MA: Addison-Wesley Publishing, 1991), pp 1–2.

[4] For a review of historical research on social cognition, see S T Fiske, ''Social Cognition and Social Perception,'' in *Annual Review of Psychology,* eds L W Porter and M R Rosenzweig (Palo Alto, CA: Annual Reviews Inc., 1993), vol. 44, pp 155–94.

[5] Adapted from discussion in Fiske and Taylor, *Social Cognition,* 2nd ed, pp 247–50.

[6] E Rosch, C B Mervis, W D Gray, D M Johnson, and

P Boyes-Braem, ''Basic Objects in Natural Categories,'' *Cognitive Psychology*, July 1976, p 383.

[7] A thorough discussion of schema and their role in information processing is presented by S T Fiske and S L Neuberg, ''A Continuum of Impression Formation, from Category-Based to Individuating Processes: Influences of Information and Motivation on Attention and Interpretation,'' in *Advances in Experimental Social Psychology*, ed M P Zanna (New York: Academic Press, 1990), vol. 23, pp 1–74.

[8] Washing clothes.

[9] For a thorough discussion about the structure and organization of memory, see L R Squire, B Knowlton, and G Musen, ''The Structure and Organization of Memory,'' in *Annual Review of Psychology*, eds L W Porter and M R Rosenzweig (Palo Alto, CA: Annual Reviews Inc., 1993), vol. 44, pp 453–95.

[10] A detailed discussion of the retrieval process of past events is provided by W J Friedman, ''Memory for the Time of Past Events,'' *Psychological Bulletin*, January 1993, pp 44–66.

[11] The rating accuracy of groups versus individuals was investigated by R F Martell and M R Borg, ''A Comparison of the Behavioral Rating Accuracy of Groups and Individuals,'' *Journal of Applied Psychology*, February 1993, pp 43–50; the effectiveness of rater training was examined L M Sulsky and D V Day, ''Frame-of-Reference Training and Cognitive Categorization: An Empirical Investigation of Rater Memory Issues,'' *Journal of Applied Psychology*, August 1992, pp 501–10.

[12] Results from a comprehensive study can be found in S J Motowidlo, G W Cater, M D Dunnette, N Tippins, S Werner, J R Burnett, and M J Vaughan, ''Studies of the Structured Behavioral Interview,'' *Journal of Applied Psychology*, October 1992, p 571–87.

[13] C Leerhsen, ''How Disney Does It,'' *Newsweek*, April 3, 1989, p 52.

[14] C M Judd and B Park, ''Definition and Assessment of Accuracy in Social Stereotypes,'' *Psychological Review*, January 1993, p 110.

[15] For a thorough discussion of stereotypes, see Ibid, pp 109–28; and J M Olson and M P Zanna, ''Attitudes and Attitude Change,'' in *Annual Review of Psychology*, eds L W Porter and M R Rosenzweig (Palo Alto, CA: Annual Reviews Inc., 1993), vol. 44, pp 117–54.

[16] For complete details, see S Shellenbarger, ''Work-Force Study Finds Loyalty Is Weak, Division of Race and Gender Are Deep, *The Wall Street Journal*, September 3, 1993, pp B1, B9.

[17] The process of maintaining stereotypes is discussed by L Falkenberg, ''Improving the Accuracy of Stereotypes within the Workplace,'' *Journal of Management*, March 1990, pp 107–18.

[18] I K Broverman, S Raymond Vogel, D M Broverman, F E Clarkson, and P S Rosenkrantz, ''Sex-Role Stereotypes: A Current Appraisal,'' *Journal of Social Issues*, 1972, p 75.

[19] Ibid.

[20] See Shellenbarger, ''Work-Force Study Finds Loyalty Is Weak,'' Divisions of Race and Gender Are Deep.''

[21] E P Kelly, A Oakes Yound, and L S Clark, ''Sex Stereotyping in the Workplace: A Manager's Guide,'' *Business Horizons*, March–April 1993, p 25.

[22] Results from the meta-analyses are discussed in K P Carson, C L Sutton, and P D Corner, ''Gender Bias in Performance Appraisals: A Meta-Analysis,'' paper presented at the 49th Annual Academy of Management Meeting, Washington, DC: 1989; and J D Olian, D P Schwab, and Y Haberfeld, ''The Impact of Applicant Gender Compared to Qualifications on Hiring Recommendations: A Meta-Analysis of Experimental Studies,'' *Organizational Behavior and Human Decision Processes*, April 1988, pp 180–95.

[23] Details may be found in C L Owen and W D Todor, ''Attitudes Toward Women as Managers: Still the Same,'' *Business Horizons*, March–April 1993, pp 12–15.

[24] For a complete review, see S R Rhodes, ''Age-Related Differences in Work Attitudes and Behavior: A Review and Conceptual Analysis,'' *Psychological Bulletin*, March 1983, pp 38–367. Supporting evidence was also provided by K B Ang, C T Goh, and H C Koh, ''The Impact of Age on the Job Satisfaction of Accountants,'' *Personnel Review*, 1993, pp 31–39.

[25] See G M McEvoy, ''Cumulative Evidence of the Relationship between Employee Age and Job Performance,'' *Journal of Applied Psychology*, February 1989, pp 11–17.

[26] A thorough discussion of the relationship between age and performance is contained in D A Waldman and B J Avolio, ''Aging and Work Performance in Perspective: Contextual and Developmental Considerations,'' in *Research in Personnel and Human Resources Management*, ed G R Ferris (Greenwich, CT: JAI Press, 1993), vol. 11, pp 133–62.

[27] For details, see B J Avolio, D A Waldman, and M A McDaniel, ''Age and Work Performance in Nonmanagerial Jobs: The Effects of Experience and Occupational Type,'' *Academy of Management Journal*, June 1990, pp 407–22.

[28] This study was conducted by J J Martocchio, ''Age-Related Differences in Employee Absenteeism: A Meta-Analysis,'' *Psychology and Aging*, December 1989, pp 409–14.

[29] K L Alexander, ''Both Racism and Sexism Block the Path to Management for Minority Women,'' *The Wall Street Journal,* July 25, 1990, p B1.

[30] Ibid.

[31] The affirmative action study was conducted by M E Heilman, C J Block, and J A Lucas, ''Presumed Incompetent? Stigmatization and Affirmative Action Efforts,'' *Journal of Applied Psychology,* August 1992, pp 536–44. Details of the study on race and attitudes may be found in J H Greenhaus, S Parasuraman, W M Wormley, ''Effects of Race on Organizational Experiences, Job Performance Evaluations, and Career Outcomes,'' *Academy of Management Journal,* March 1990, pp 64–86.

[32] See D A Waldman and B J Avolio, ''Race Effects in Performance Evaluations: Controlling for Ability, Education, and Experience,'' *Journal of Applied Psychology,* December 1991, pp 897–901; and E D Pulakos, L A White, S H Oppler, and W C Borman, ''Examination of Race and Sex Effects on Performance Ratings,'' *Journal of Applied Psychology,* October 1989, pp 770–80.

[33] See T-R Lin, G H Dobbins, and J-L Farh, ''A Field Study of Race and Age Similarity Effects on Interview Ratings in Conventional and Situational Interviews,'' *Journal of Applied Psychology,* June 1992, pp 363–71.

[34] See C M Judd and B Park, ''Definition and Assessment of Accuracy in Social Stereotypes;'' and J M Olson and M P Zanna, ''Attitudes and Attitude Change.''

[35] Supporting studies were conducted by A J Kinicki, C A Lockwood, P W Hom, and R W Griffeth, ''Interviewer Predictions of Applicant Qualifications and Interviewer Validity,'' *Journal of Applied Psychology,* October 1990, pp 477–86; and L Sulsky and D V Day, ''Frame-of-Reference Training and Cognitive Categorization: An Empirical Investigation of Rater Memory Issues,'' *Journal of Applied Psychology,* August 1992, pp 501–10.

[36] Results from the meta-analysis may be found in P W Hom and R W Griffeth, *Employee Turnover* (Cincinnati, OH: Southwestern, 1994).

[37] Research is reviewed by R Rodgers, J E Hunter, and D L Rogers, ''Influence of Top Management Commitment on Management Program Success,'' *Journal of Applied Psychology,* February 1993, pp 151–55.

[38] J B Treece, ''A Little Bit of Smarts, A Lot of Hard Work,'' *Business Week,* November 30, 1992, p 71.

[39] The background and results for this study are presented in R Rosenthal and L Jacobson, *Pygmalion in the Classroom: Teacher Expectation and Pupils' Intellectual Development* (New York: Holt, Rinehart & Winston, 1968).

[40] Research on the Pygmalion effect is summarized in D Eden, *Pygmalion in Management: Productivity as a Self-Fulfilling Prophecy* (Lexington, MA: Lexington Books, 1990), chapter 2.

[41] See B Schlender, ''How Bill Gates Keeps the Magic Going,'' *Fortune,* June 18, 1990, pp 82–89.

[42] These recommendations were adapted from R W Goddard, ''The Pygmalion Effect,'' *Personnel Journal,* June 1985, p 10.

[43] Kelley's model is discussed in detail in H H Kelley, ''The Processes of Causal Attribution,'' *American Psychologist,* February 1973, pp 107–28.

[44] For a recent example, see J T Johnson, K R Boyd, and P S Magnani, ''Causal Reasoning in the Attribution of Rare and Common Events,'' *Journal of Personality and Social Psychology,* February 1994, pp 229–42; and J C Fredricks and S J Arenson, ''Physical Attractiveness Stereotype in Causal Attributions for Socially Undesirable Behavior,'' *Psychological Reports,* February 1992, pp 115–23.

[45] See P D Sweeney, K Anderson, and S Bailey, ''Attributional Style in Depression: A Meta-Analytic Review,'' *Journal of Personality and Social Psychology,* May 1986, pp 974–91.

[46] Results can be found in G E Prussia, A J Kinicki, and J S Bracker, ''Psychological and Behavioral Consequences of Job Loss: A Covariance Structure Analysis Using Weiner's (1985) Attribution Model,'' *Journal of Applied Psychology,* June 1993, pp 382–94; N M Ashkanasy, ''Causal Attribution and Supervisors' Response to Subordinate Performance: The Green and Mitchell Model Revisited,'' *Journal of Applied Social Psychology,* March 1989, pp 309–30; and T I Chacko and J C McElroy, ''The Cognitive Component in Locke's Theory of Goal Setting: Suggestive Evidence for a Causal Attribution Interpretation,'' *Academy of Management Journal,* March 1983, pp 104–18.

[47] Results can be found in S J Linton and L-E Warg, ''Attributions (Beliefs) and Job Satisfaction Associated with Back Pain in an Industrial Setting,'' *Perceptual and Motor Skills,* February 1993, pp 51–62. The fundamental attribution bias was also demonstrated by M Schaller and M O'Brien, ''Intuitive Analysis of Covariance and Group Stereotype Formation,'' *Personality and Social Psychology Bulletin,* December 1992, pp 776–85.

[48] The effect of the self-serving bias was tested and supported by G Johns, ''Absenteeism Estimates by Employees and Managers: Divergent Perspectives and Self-Serving Perceptions,'' *Journal of Applied Psychology,* April 1994, pp 229–39; and P E Levy, ''Self-Appraisal and Attributions: A Test of a Model,'' *Journal of Management,* Spring 1993, pp 51–62.

[49] Details may be found in J M Crant and T S Bateman,

"Assignment of Credit and Blame for Performance Outcomes," *Academy of Management Journal,* February 1993, pp 7–27; and E C Pence, W C Pendelton, G H Dobbins, and J A Sgro, "Effects of Causal Explanations and Sex Variables on Recommendations for Corrective Actions Following Employee Failure," *Organizational Behavior and Human Performance,* April 1982, pp 227–40.

[50] For a review of attributional retraining, see F Forsterling, "Attributional Retraining: A Review," *Psychological Bulletin,* November 1985, pp 496–512.

[51] Adapted from A J Kinicki and R W Griffeth, "The Impact of Sex-Role Stereotypes on Performance Ratings and Causal Attributions of Performance," *Journal of Vocational Behavior,* April 1985, pp 155–70.

[52] Based on Pence, Pendleton, Dobbins, and Sgro, "Effects of Causal Explanations and Sex Variables on Recommendations for Corrective Actions Following Employee Failure," pp 227–40.

MOTIVATION THROUGH NEEDS, JOB DESIGN, AND SATISFACTION

Learning OBJECTIVES

When you finish studying the material in this chapter, you should be able to:

1. Define the term *motivation.*

2. Discuss the job performance model of motivation.

3. Highlight the evolution of modern motivation theory.

4. Contrast Maslow's and McClelland's need theories.

5. Demonstrate your familiarity with scientific management, job enlargement, job rotation, and job enrichment.

6. Explain the practical significance of Herzberg's distinction between motivators and hygiene factors.

7. Describe how internal work motivation is increased by using the job characteristics model.

8. Put the job satisfaction controversy into proper perspective.

OPENING CASE

Fast-Growing Companies Use a Variety of Motivation Techniques

Sharon Hoogstraten

Chances are, Prospect Associates Ltd. won't ever offer Drew Melton a corner office and his pick of the company art collection; he started out as a copy-machine operator three years ago, and that's exactly what he is today.

A dead-end job? In a different company, maybe. Two weeks after he was hired at the Rockville, Md., health-communications-policy consultancy, Melton went to its president, Laura Henderson, and told her how he could run document production better and faster. "I think in terms of efficiency," says Melton. So does Henderson, who gave Melton carte blanche to do things his way. "They're listening to my ideas,

and that's where I'm making changes and contributing to the company," says Melton. Today he runs a virtual Xerox fiefdom, dispensing advice to Prospect's harried consultants, who rely on his painstaking attention to detail to give their proposals a professional look.

Has Melton advanced? You bet. He hasn't climbed a corporate ladder, but he has increased his contribution to the company by honing his skills and expanding the scope of his job. His salary has increased by more than 40%, he's respected by the company's professional staff, and there's no pressure on him to "move up." . . .

Like most "best company" CEOs, Henderson took into account the nature of her business and the needs of her employees and created a system of "advancement" that makes sense for both. As a player in the highly competitive government-consulting business, Prospect relies on all employees not only to generate ideas but to market them, too. Marisa Arbona, for example, has been given the freedom to parlay her special interest—communications about Native American health issues—into new business

for Prospect, something she wasn't allowed to do by her former employer. "As long as I can present my ideas and make them work, I don't think there are any limitations for me here," says Arbona, who won a National Cancer Institute Recognition Award last year. "That was very fulfilling," she says. "It wouldn't have come if I hadn't been working at Prospect." . . .

Nowhere are the opportunities for advancement as dramatic as in fast-growing companies. "There's no ladder to climb," says Jon Goodman, director of the Entrepreneur Program at the University of Southern California in Los Angeles. "They're building the ladder as they grow." So the challenge is to hire the kinds of employees that will help build the ladder. "You don't want to advance—you want to enlarge," adds Goodman. "Your technical skills become greater; you build your résumé in terms of span of control and responsibility."

Such is the case in Stonyfield Farm Inc., in Londonderry, N.H., which has seen annual sales growth average over 60% for the past three years. "A year ago we had 9 supervisors," says

E ffective employee motivation has long been one of management's most difficult and important duties. Success in this endeavor is becoming a more difficult challenge in light of organizational trends to downsize and difficulties associated with managing a diverse workforce, as discussed in Chapter 3. As revealed in the chapter opening case, managers like Laura Henderson, Gary Hirshberg, Pam Reynolds, and David Kelley met this challenge. They learned that employees are more motivated, committed, and satisfied when they feel as if they are significantly contributing to their company's success. The purpose of this chapter, as well as the next, is to

OPENING CASE

(continued)

Stonyfield CEO Gary Hirshberg. "Now we have 22, and only 3 of those were new hires." In other words, 10 Stonyfield employees have been promoted to supervisor level. That's what happened to former limo driver Edward Souza, who knew nothing about the dairy business when he applied for a job at Stonyfield, five years ago. "But they emphasized that there was plenty of room to advance for people willing to learn as much as they could," he says. Souza started as a yogurt checker but soon learned how to clean equipment and process milk. A year later he became head processor, and six months after that he was promoted to production supervisor and then to production manager. Souza, who now supervises 40 people, has helped grow production capacity from 9,000 to 60,000 cases a week in only three and a half years. . . .

But even at Phoenix [St. Louis's Phoenix Textile Corp.], which, says [Pam] Reynolds [CEO], "has a very structured system where people have specific jobs," there is plenty of room for "horizontal" advancement. Kim Roussin, for example, ran Phoenix's data-processing division for several

years before she finally concluded that she wouldn't succeed if she stayed in that position. Roussin expressed an interest in sales, so the company moved her into sales support. "That might sound like a demotion, but to me it was a different form of advancing," she says.

David Kelley would agree. In fact, he founded IDEO Product Development, in Palo Alto, Calif., on that principle. "I set out to make a company that was a great place for my friends to work," says Kelley. He had worked for big companies, but, he says, they took the spark out of his life. So he decided to start his own product-design company, eschewing the hierarchy he so disdained. At IDEO, no one has a title, or a "boss," for that matter. Designers form teams around specific projects; each of those teams has a leader whose authority lasts only as long as the project, so today's manager may be tomorrow's subordinate.

So what's the measure of success in such an unstructured environment? "We're talking about climbing the self-fulfillment ladder," says Kelley. "For some employees here, self-fulfillment comes from how technical they are.

For others, it means climbing a ladder based on how big a project you run, or how many you can run." Employees get a fix on their progress with regular peer reviews. They select their own reviewers; most choose someone who they know is especially critical, because that person's praise is valued more.

Would the same motivational techniques used at Prospect, Stonyfield Farm, Phoenix Textile, and IDEO work in larger organizations? Explain.

- Additional discussion questions linking this case with the following material appear at the end of this chapter.

Source: Excerpted from D Fenn, "Bottoms Up: Boosting Careers Is Not About Corporate Ladders or Organizational Charts; It's About Paying Attention to How People Can Grow in the Jobs They Already Have," *Inc.*, July 1993, pp 58, 60. Reprinted with permission *Inc.* magazine, (July, 1993). Copyright 1993 by Goldhirsh Group, Inc., 38 Commercial Wharf, Boston, MA 02110.

provide you with a foundation for understanding the complexities of employee motivation.

Specifically, this chapter provides a definitional and theoretical foundation for the topic of motivation so a rich variety of motivation theories and techniques can be introduced and discussed. Coverage of employee motivation extends to Chapter 7. After providing a conceptual model for understanding motivation, this chapter focuses on: (1) need theories of motivation, (2) an overview of job design methods used to motivate employees, (3) a job characteristics approach to job design, and (4) causes and consequences of job satisfaction. In the next chapter attention turns to equity, expectancy, and goal-setting theory, research, and practice.

WHAT DOES MOTIVATION INVOLVE?

motivation Psychological processes that arouse and direct goal-directed behavior.

The term *motivation* derives from the Latin word *movere,* meaning "to move." In the present context, **motivation** represents "those psychological processes that cause the arousal, direction, and persistence of voluntary actions that are goal directed."[1] Managers need to understand these psychological processes if they are to successfully guide employees toward accomplishing organizational objectives. After considering a conceptual framework for understanding motivation, this section examines the historical roots of motivational concepts and the relationship between motivations and performance.

A Job Performance Model of Motivation

A conceptual model for understanding motivation (Figure 6–1) was created by integrating elements from several of the theories we discuss in this book. The foundation of the model is based on systems theory and reinforcement theory. Systems theory suggests that good performance results from a process of combining effort and technology to transform inputs into desired outputs. Systems theory further implies that people do not perform in isolation. Rather, employees frequently work on interdependent tasks and rely on each other's output as their input. Reinforcement theory, the other component of the model, is discussed in Chapter 8. Reinforcement theory involves improving performance with feedback and contingent consequences. Now let us take a closer look at Figure 6–1.

Figure 6–1 shows four types of inputs that affect employee effort and performance: individual differences and needs, supervisory support and coaching, performance goals, and job characteristics. As you may recall from Chapter 4, individual differences are the self-concepts, ethics, skills, abilities, personality

FIGURE 6–1   A Job Performance Motivation System

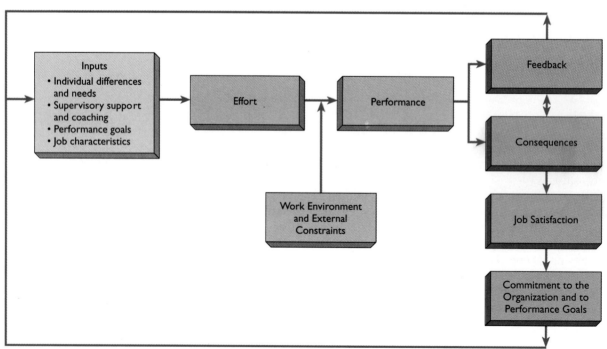

characteristics, values, and needs that vary among people. These differences can significantly affect employee performance. Need theories of motivation are discussed in the next section of this chapter.

Managers use support and coaching as input to employee performance. Support entails supplying employees with adequate resources to get the job done. In addition, coaching involves providing employees with direction, advice, and guidance. These behaviors include effective listening (discussed in Chapter 13), furnishing employees with successful role models, showing employees how to complete complex tasks, and helping them maintain high self-efficacy and self-esteem (recall the discussion in Chapter 4).

Because behavior is geared toward accomplishing end results, performance goals are a critical input to employee performance. Goals and action plans provide employees with direction and guidance about how to spend their time on specific tasks. Chapter 7 reviews how challenging goals lead to higher performance. Job characteristics, the final input variable, represent the types of tasks completed by employees. The role of job characteristics in employee motivation is discussed later in this chapter.

Returning to Figure 6–1, you can see that the relationship between employee effort and performance is affected by work environment and external constraints. These constraints, which include such things as defective raw materials, broken equipment, poor management, and economic considerations, can impair employees' ability to transform their inputs into desired performance outcomes. It is management's responsibility to manage and remove such performance roadblocks.[2] In addition, managers dramatically affect employee effort and performance by providing feedback and by reinforcing employee behavior with consequences.

For example, an individual's self-esteem, self-efficacy, and achievement orientation are enhanced by positive performance feedback. Moreover, managers can increase employee motivation by administering appropriate rewards, such as praise or a pay raise. These processes are thoroughly discussed in Chapters 8 and 14. Job satisfaction is affected by how positively employees evaluate the rewards they receive for a given level of performance. In general, people are more satisfied and committed to the organization and its goals when they receive equitable rewards that they value. Satisfied employees are less likely to quit, join unions, engage in substance abuse or theft, or put forth less effort.[3]

Historical Roots of Modern Motivation Theories

Most contemporary theories of motivation are rooted partially in the principle of **hedonism,** which states that people are motivated to consciously seek pleasure and avoid pain. Hedonism dates to the Greek philosophers. As a separate and self-contained theory of human motivation, hedonism proved unsatisfactory for two reasons: First, hedonism failed to adequately reconcile the relationship between short-term and long-term consequences. For example, hedonism cannot explain why some people choose to become professional football players who willingly risk their health during bruising Sunday afternoon games. Obviously, the football players are sustaining short-term pain in order to attain longer term rewards such as recognition and lucrative contracts. Second, due to the rich variation among people, hedonists could not neatly categorize hundreds of different activities and consequences into distinct pleasure and pain categories. Writing, for example, may be a

hedonism Belief that people seek pleasure and avoid pain.

pleasure for professional writers, but it is definitely a pain for many college students. Let us now examine the historical development of subsequent theories of motivation.[4]

Four ways of explaining behavior—needs, reinforcement, cognition, and job characteristics—underlie the evolution of modern theories of human motivation. As we proceed through this review, remember the objective of each alternative motivation theory is to explain and predict purposeful or goal-directed behavior. As will become apparent, the differences between theoretical perspectives lie in the causal mechanisms used to explain behavior.

Needs   Needs theories are based on the premise that individuals are motivated by unsatisfied needs. Dissatisfaction with your social life, for example, should motivate you to participate in more social activities. Henry Murray, a 1930s psychologist, was the first behavioral scientist to propose a list of needs thought to underlie goal-directed behavior. From Murray's work sprang a wide variety of need theories, some of which remain influential today. Recognized need theories of motivation are explored in the next section of this chapter.

Reinforcement   Reinforcement theorists, such as Edward L Thorndike and B F Skinner, proposed that behavior is controlled by its consequences, not by the result of hypothetical internal states such as instincts, drives, or needs. This proposition is based on research data demonstrating that people repeat behaviors followed by favorable consequences and avoid behaviors resulting in unfavorable consequences. Few would argue with the statement that organizational rewards have a motivational impact on job behavior. However, behaviorists and cognitive theorists do disagree over the role of internal states and processes in motivation.

Cognitions   Uncomfortable with the idea that behavior is shaped completely by environmental consequences, cognitive motivation theorists contend that behavior is a function of beliefs, expectations, values, and other mental cognitions. Behavior is therefore viewed as the result of rational and conscious choices among alternative courses of action. In Chapter 7, we discuss cognitive motivation theories involving equity, expectancies, and goal setting.

Job Characteristics   According to this most recent addition to the evolution of motivation theory, the task itself is said to be the key to employee motivation. Specifically, a boring and monotonous job stifles motivation to perform well, whereas a challenging job enhances motivation. Three ingredients of a more challenging job are variety, autonomy, and decision authority. Two popular ways of adding variety and challenge to routine jobs are job enrichment (or job redesign) and job rotation. These techniques are discussed later in this chapter.

A Motivational Puzzle   Motivation theory presents managers with a psychological puzzle composed of alternative explanations and recommendations. There is not any one motivation theory that is appropriate in all situations. Rather, managers need to use a contingency framework to pick and choose the motivational techniques best suited to the people and situation involved. The matrix in Figure 6–2 was created to help managers make these decisions.

Because managers face a variety of motivational problems that can be solved with different theories of motivation, the matrix crosses outcomes of interest with

• ✎ FIGURE 6~2   Motivation Theories and Workplace Outcomes: A Contingency Approach

Motivation Theories

Outcome of Interest	Need	Reinforcement	Equity	Expectancy	Goal Setting	Job Characteristics
• Choice to Pursue a Course of Action				X		
• Effort	X	X	X	X	X	X
• Performance		X	X		X	X
• Satisfaction	X		X			X
• Absenteeism		X	X			X
• Turnover		X	X	X		X

Source: Adapted and extended from F J Landy and W S Becker, "Motivation Theory Reconsidered," in L L Cummings and B M Staw (eds), *Research in Organizational Behavior* (Greenwich, CT: JAI Press, 1987), vol. 9, p 33.

six major motivation theories.[5] Entries in the matrix indicate which theories are best suited for explaining each outcome. For instance, each motivation theory can help managers determine how to increase employee effort. In contrast, need, equity, and job characteristics theories are most helpful in developing programs aimed at increasing employees' job satisfaction. Managers faced with high turnover are advised to use the reinforcement, equity, expectancy, or job characteristics theory to correct the problem.

You will be better able to apply this matrix after reading the material in this chapter and Chapters 7 and 8. This chapter covers theories related to needs and job characteristics, Chapter 7 focuses on equity, expectancy, and goal setting, and reinforcement theory is reviewed in Chapter 8.

Motivation Is Only One Factor in the Performance Equation

All too often, motivation and performance are assumed to be one and the same. This faulty assumption can lead to poor managerial decisions. The following formula for performance helps put motivation into proper perspective:

$$\text{Performance} = (\text{Ability} \times \text{Motivation})$$

Thus, we see motivation is a necessary but insufficient contributor to job performance. The multiplication sign is used to emphasize how a weakness in one factor can negate the other. Drawing a distinction between performance and motivation has its advantages. According to one motivation expert:

> The implication is that there probably are some jobs for which trying to influence motivation will be irrelevant for performance. These circumstances can occur in a variety of ways. There may be situations in which ability factors or role expectation factors are simply more important than motivation. For example, the best predictor of high school grades typically is intellectual endowment, not hours spent studying. . . .
>
> Another circumstance may occur in which performance is controlled by technological factors. For example, on an assembly line, given that minimally competent and attentive people are there to do the job, performance may not vary from individual to individual. Exerting effort may be irrelevant for performance.[6]

Managers are better able to identify and correct performance problems when they recognize that poor performance is not due solely to inadequate motivation. This awareness can foster better interpersonal relations in the workplace.

NEED THEORIES OF MOTIVATION

Needs Physiological or psychological deficiencies that arouse behavior.

Need theories attempt to pinpoint internal factors that energize behavior. **Needs** are physiological or psychological deficiencies that arouse behavior. They can be strong or weak and are influenced by environmental factors. Thus, human needs vary over time and place. Two popular need theories are discussed in this section: Maslow's need hierarchy theory and McClelland's need theory.

Maslow's Need Hierarchy Theory

In 1943, psychologist Abraham Maslow published his now-famous need hierarchy theory of motivation. Although the theory was based on his clinical observation of a few neurotic individuals, it has subsequently been used to explain the entire spectrum of human behavior. Maslow proposed that motivation is a function of five basic needs—physiological, safety, love, esteem, and self-actualization (see Figure 6–3).

Maslow said these five need categories are arranged in a prepotent hierarchy. In other words, he believed human needs generally emerge in a predictable stair-step fashion. Accordingly, when one's physiological needs are relatively satisfied, one's safety needs emerge, and so on up the need hierarchy, one step at a time. Once a need is satisfied it activates the next higher need in the hierarchy. This process continues until the need for self-actualization is activated.[7] Unfortunately, many people living in Bosnia are not enjoying the satisfaction of higher order needs.

FIGURE 6~3   Maslow's Need Hierarchy

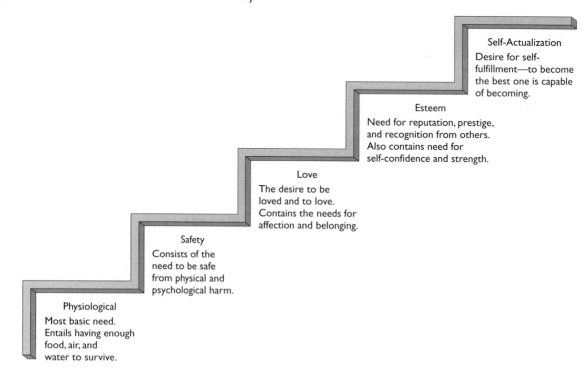

Source: Adapted from descriptions provided by A H Maslow, "A Theory of Human Motivation," *Psychological Review,* July 1943, pp 370–96.

They are stuck at lower levels on the need hierarchy trying to survive (see the International OB).

Research Findings on Maslow's Theory Research does not clearly support this theory because results from studies testing the need hierarchy are difficult to interpret. A well-known motivation scholar summarized the research evidence as follows:

> In balance, Maslow's theory remains very popular among managers and students of organizational behavior, although there are still very few studies that can legitimately confirm (or refute) it. . . . It may be that the dynamics implied by Maslow's theory of needs are too complex to be operationalized and confirmed by scientific research. If this is the case, we may never be able to determine how valid the theory is, or—more precisely—which aspects of the theory are valid and which are not.[8]

Managerial Implications of Maslow's Theory A satisfied need may lose its motivational potential. Therefore, managers are advised to motivate employees by devising programs or practices aimed at satisfying emerging or unmet needs. For example, in the face of technological displacement and mass layoffs (US employers dismissed 4.3 million people between 1985 and 1989, and 1.6 million more people between June 1990 and July 1991), employers can boost motivation by giving workers a job-security pledge.[9] Further, because layoffs create stress and feelings of job insecurity, organizations like Pittsburgh-based Aluminum Company of America attempt to satisfy employees' needs following a cutback by conducting support programs and focus groups to listen to employee concerns.[10] Once employees feel secure in their jobs, management might attempt to satisfy esteem needs. This can be done using status symbols, participative management, and positive performance feedback. When employees' esteem needs are satisfied, management can enhance motivation by redesigning jobs to provide more autonomy and responsibility.

INTERNATIONAL OB

Living Low on the Need Hierarchy in Bosnia

Shivering as her life goes up in smoke, Elza Vukmanovic, 65, weeps while she feeds the pages of a book into her tiny stove. She is trying to stay warm.

Her husband, Branko, 72 is out on the apartment balcony, doing what he does every day—cutting up furniture for firewood. Now he is sawing through a white cupboard. The day before, it was a bed frame.

The stove, about the size of a hatbox, keeps the Vukmanovic living room heated to 45 degrees during daylight hours. The couple goes to bed—fully clothed under a pile of blankets—at about 7 PM, and as the embers die out the temperature falls to near freezing. . . .

There is no running water in Sarajevo—and no electricity or central heating, either—so apartment dwellers must fetch water in buckets from a well two miles away and then haul it stair by stair up to their icy kitchens and bathrooms.

Source: P Maass, "Losing the Battle to Stay Warm and Clean," *The Washington Post National Weekly Edition,* January 25–31, 1993, p 18.

This Bosnian woman is weeping at the grave of her son, who was killed in a mortar attack. Unlike most Americans, who live comparatively high on Maslow's need hierarchy, war-torn Bosnians struggle at the survival level.

Reuters/Bettmann

McClelland's Need Theory

David McClelland, a well-known psychologist, has been studying the relationship between needs and behavior since the late 1940s. Although he is most recognized for his research on the need for achievement, he also investigated the needs for affiliation and power. Before discussing each of these needs, let us consider the typical approach used to measure the strength of an individual's needs.

Measuring Need Strength   The Thematic Apperception Test (TAT) is frequently used to measure an individual's motivation to satisfy various needs. In completing the TAT, people are asked to write stories about ambiguous pictures. These descriptions are then scored for the extent to which they contain achievement, power, and affiliation imagery. A recent meta-analysis of 105 studies demonstrated that the TAT is a valid measure of the need for achievement.[11] At this time, we would like you to examine the picture in the OB Exercise and then write a brief description of what you think is happening to the people in the picture and what you think will happen to them in the future. Use the scoring guide to determine your need strength. What is your most important need?

The Need for Achievement   Achievement theories propose that motivation and performance vary according to the strength of one's need for achievement. For example, a field study of 222 life insurance brokers found a positive correlation between the number of policies sold and the brokers' need for achievement. McClelland's research supported an analogous relationship for societies as a whole. His results revealed that a country's level of economic development was positively related to its overall achievement motivation.[12] The **need for achievement** is defined by the following desires:

need for achievement
Desire to accomplish something difficult.

> To accomplish something difficult. To master, manipulate, or organize physical objects, human beings, or ideas. To do this as rapidly and as independently as possible. To overcome obstacles and attain a high standard. To excel one's self. To rival and surpass others. To increase self-regard by the successful exercise of talent.[13]

OB EXERCISE

Assess Your Need Strength with a Thematic Apperception Test (TAT)

What is happening in this picture?

	Low	Moderate	High
• Achievement motivation	1 ——— 2 ——— 3 ——— 4 ——— 5		
• Power motivation	1 ——— 2 ——— 3 ——— 4 ——— 5		
• Affiliation motivation	1 ——— 2 ——— 3 ——— 4 ——— 5		

Score *achievement* motivation high if:

- A goal, objective, or standard of excellence is mentioned.
- Words such as good, better, or best are used to evaluate performance.
- Someone in your story is striving for a unique accomplishment.
- Reference is made to career status or being a success in life.

Score *power* motivation high if:

- There is emotional concern for influencing someone else.
- Someone is actively striving to gain or keep control over others by ordering, arguing, demanding, convincing, threatening, or punishing.
- Clear reference is made to a superior–subordinate relationship and the superior is taking steps to gain or keep control over the subordinate.

Score *affiliation* motivation high if:

- Someone is concerned about establishing or maintaining a friendly relationship with another.
- Someone expresses the desire to be liked by someone else.
- There are references to family ties, friendly discussions, visits, reunions, parties, or informal get-togethers.

This definition reveals that the need for achievement overlaps Maslow's higher order needs of esteem and self-actualization. Let us now consider the characteristics of high achievers.

Characteristics of High Achievers   Achievement-motivated people share three common characteristics. One is a preference for working on tasks of *moderate* difficulty. For example, when high achievers are asked to stand wherever they like while tossing rings at a peg on the floor, they tend to stand about 10 to 20 feet from the peg. This distance presents the ring tosser with a challenging but not impossible task. People with a low need for achievement, in contrast, tend to either walk up to the peg and drop the rings on or gamble on a lucky shot from far away. The high achiever's preference for moderately difficult tasks reinforces achievement behavior by reducing the frequency of failure and increasing the satisfaction associated with successfully completing challenging tasks.

Achievers also like situations in which their performance is due to their own efforts rather than to other factors, such as luck. A third identifying characteristic of high achievers is that they desire more feedback on their successes and failures than do low achievers. Given these characteristics, McClelland proposed that high achievers are more likely to be successful entrepreneurs. A recent study supported this proposition. Data obtained from 118 entrepreneurs indicated that the growth of their firms was positively related to their achievement orientation.[14] Interestingly, research also documented a positive correlation between the achievement motivation of chief executive officers from 50 of the largest US industrial firms and their company's growth in sales.[15]

need for affiliation   Desire to spend time in social relationships and activities.

The Need for Affiliation   People with a high **need for affiliation** prefer to spend more time maintaining social relationships, joining groups, and wanting to be loved. Individuals high in this need are not the most effective managers or leaders because they have a hard time making difficult decisions without worrying about being disliked.

need for power   Desire to influence, coach, teach, or encourage others to achieve.

The Need for Power   The **need for power** reflects an individual's desire to influence, coach, teach, or encourage others to achieve. People with a high need for power like to work and are concerned with discipline and self-respect. There is a positive and negative side to this need. The negative face of power is characterized by an "if I win, you lose" mentality. Consider John Borowski, owner of a small defense contractor in Burlington, Massachusetts.

> Using buckets, his workers would scoop fuming nitric acid and nickel wastes out of vats and pour them down a sink. When workers questioned the practice, Mr. Borowski told them not to worry because it wouldn't hurt anyone, former employees say. He knew the dumping was illegal but considered it "like not counting tips for income tax," says Peter Kruczynski, a former manager at Mr. Borowski's Borjohn Optical Technology, Inc. . . .
>
> Thousands of gallons of wastes went down Mr. Borowski's sink over the past decade, from there finding their way into Boston Harbor. Some of the workers in his bucket brigade developed rashes and other ailments, but Mr. Borowski attributed the problems to drinking or laziness, former employees testified at his trial. "If I had to follow every rule on the books, I'd be out of business," one worker testified Mr. Borowski told him.[16]

In contrast, people with a positive orientation to power focus on accomplishing group goals and helping employees obtain the feeling of competence. More is said about the two faces of power in Chapter 10.

McClelland now believes that individuals with high achievement motivation are *not* best suited for top management positions. Because effective managers must positively influence others, McClelland proposes that top managers should have a high need for power coupled with a low need for affiliation. Several studies support these propositions.[17]

Managerial Implications   Given that adults can be trained to increase their achievement motivation,[18] organizations should consider the benefits of providing achievement training for employees. Moreover, achievement, affiliation, and power needs can be considered during the selection process, for better placement. For example, a recent study revealed that individuals' need for achievement affected their preference to work in different companies. People with a high need for achievement were more attracted to companies that had a pay-for-performance environment than were those with a low achievement motivation.[19] Finally, managers should create challenging task assignments or goals because the need for achievement is positively correlated with goal commitment, which in turn influences performance.[20] Moreover, challenging goals should be accompanied with a more autonomous work environment and employee empowerment to capitalize on the characteristics of high achievers.

HISTORICAL APPROACHES TO JOB DESIGN

job design   Changing the content and/or process of a specific job to increase job satisfaction and performance.

Job design, also referred to as job redesign, "refers to any set of activities that involve the alteration of specific jobs or interdependent systems of jobs with the intent of improving the quality of employee job experience and their on-the-job productivity."[21] There are two very different routes, one traditional and one modern, that can be taken when deciding how to design jobs. Each is based on a different assumption about people.

The first route entails *fitting people to jobs.* It is based on the assumption that people will gradually adjust and adapt to any work situation. Thus, employee attitudes toward the job are ignored, and jobs are designed to produce maximum economic and technological efficiency. This approach uses the principles of scientific management and work simplification (recall our discussion in Chapter 1). In contrast, the second route involves *fitting jobs to people.* It assumes that people are underutilized at work and that they desire more challenges and responsibility. This philosophy is part of the driving force behind the widespread implementation of work teams across the United States. Techniques such as job enlargement, job rotation, job enrichment, and job characteristics are used when designing jobs according to this second alternative.

The remainder of this section discusses the first four methods of job design to be widely used in industry. They are scientific management, job enlargement, job rotation, and job enrichment. The next section explores the job characteristics approach to job design.

Scientific Management

Developed by Frederick Taylor, scientific management relied on research and experimentation to determine the most efficient way to perform jobs (recall our discussion in Chapter 1). Jobs are highly specialized and standardized when they are designed according to the principles of scientific management. This technique was the impetus for the development of assembly line technology and currently is used in many manufacturing and production-oriented firms throughout the United States.

Designing jobs according to the principles of scientific management has both positive and negative consequences. Positively, employee efficiency and productivity are increased. On the other hand, research reveals that simplified, repetitive jobs also lead to job dissatisfaction, poor mental health, and low sense of accomplishment and personal growth.[22] Further, the principles of scientific management do not apply to professional ''knowledge'' workers, and they are not consistent with the trend to empower both employees and work teams (see the International OB).[23] These negative consequences paved the way for the development of other job designs. Newer approaches attempt to design intrinsically satisfying jobs.

Job Enlargement

job enlargement Putting more variety into a job.

This technique was first used in the late 1940s in response to complaints about tedious and overspecialized jobs. **Job enlargement** involves putting more variety into a worker's job by combining specialized tasks of comparable difficulty. Some call this *horizontally loading* the job. For instance, the job of installing television picture tubes could be enlarged to include installation of the circuit boards.

Proponents of job enlargement claim it can improve employee satisfaction, motivation, and quality of production. Unfortunately, research reveals that job enlargement, by itself, does not have a significant and lasting positive impact on job performance. Researchers recommend using job enlargement as part of a broader approach that uses multiple job design techniques.[24]

Job Rotation

job rotation Moving employees from one specialized job to another.

As with job enlargement, job rotation's purpose is to give employees greater variety in their work. **Job rotation** calls for moving employees from one specialized job to another. Rather than performing only one job, workers are trained and given the opportunity to perform two or more separate jobs on a rotating basis. By rotating employees from job to job, managers believe they can stimulate interest and motivation while providing employees with a broader perspective of the organization.

Other proposed advantages of job rotation include increased worker flexibility and easier scheduling because employees are cross trained to perform different

---

INTERNATIONAL OB

The East and West Have Different Views toward Scientific Management

Konosuke Matsushita, founder of the giant Matsushita Co., once stated: "We are going to win and the industrial West is going to lose out; there is not much you can do about it because the reasons for your failures are within yourselves. Your firms are built on the Taylor idea—and even worse—so are your minds. Your bosses do the thinking, your workers wield the screwdrivers. . . . We are beyond the Taylor model. The continued existence of business depends on the day-to-day mobilization of every ounce of intelligence."

Source: R N Steck, "The First Efficiency Expert," *D&B Reports,* January/February 1992, p 40.

jobs. In turn, this cross training requires employees to learn new skills, which can assist them in upward or lateral mobility. Job rotation is also a cornerstone of creating work teams aimed at improving customer satisfaction and quality. Consider the examples at General Motors and Aid Association for Lutherans, an insurance and financial services company.

> At General Motors' Cadillac Motor Car Division . . . teams came first, quickly followed by cross-training. In 1988 the company organized its maintenance, engineering, and environmental engineering employees into teams responsible for serving a wide range of needs for specific internal customers. Maintenance workers, for example, were no longer specifically pipe fitters, plumbers or heating/ventilation/air conditioning experts. Instead they belonged to a team responsible for those and many other functions. . . .
>
> At Aid Association for Lutherans . . . instead of doing one job, an employee at the Appleton, WI, home office would become part of a service team of 20 to 30 employees that would handle all the needs a sales representative might have. The teams were further divided into smaller groups of five to 10 people who concentrate on underwriting, servicing the account, or paying claims for accounts in one geographic area.[25]

Although these examples support the use of job rotation, the promised benefits associated with job rotation programs have not been adequately researched. Thus, it is difficult to draw any empirical conclusions about their effectiveness.

Job Enrichment

Job enrichment is the practical application of Frederick Herzberg's motivator–hygiene theory of job satisfaction.[26] After reviewing the foundation of Herzberg's theory, we will discuss its application through job enrichment.

The Legacy of Herzberg's Motivator~Hygiene Theory

Herzberg's theory is based on a landmark study in which he interviewed 203 accountants and engineers. These interviews sought to determine the factors responsible for job satisfaction and dissatisfaction. Herzberg found separate and distinct clusters of factors associated with job satisfaction and dissatisfaction. Job satisfaction was more frequently associated with achievement, recognition, characteristics of the work, responsibility, and advancement. These factors were all related to outcomes associated with the *content* of the task being performed. Herzberg labeled these factors **motivators** because each was associated with strong effort and good performance. He hypothesized that motivators cause a person to move from a state of no satisfaction to satisfaction (see Figure 6–4). Therefore, Herzberg's theory predicts managers can motivate individuals by incorporating ''motivators'' into an individual's job.

motivators   Job characteristics associated with job satisfaction.

Herzberg found job *dissatisfaction* to be associated primarily with factors in the work *context* or environment. Specifically, company policy and administration, technical supervision, salary, interpersonal relations with one's supervisor, and working conditions were most frequently mentioned by employees expressing job dissatisfaction. Herzberg labeled this second cluster of factors **hygiene factors.** He further proposed that they were not motivational. At best, according to Herzberg's interpretation, an individual will experience no job dissatisfaction when he or she has no grievances about hygiene factors (refer to Figure 6–4).[27]

hygiene factors   Job characteristics associated with job dissatisfaction.

A Zero Midpoint

The key to adequately understanding Herzberg's motivator–hygiene theory is recognizing that he does not place dissatisfaction and satisfaction on opposite ends of a single, unbroken continuum. Instead, he believes there is a

● FIGURE 6~4   Herzberg's Motivator–Hygiene Model

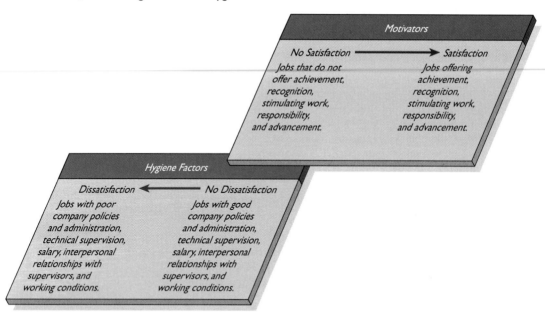

Source: Adapted in part from D A Whitsett and E K Winslow, "An Analysis of Studies Critical of the Motivator–Hygiene Theory," *Personnel Psychology*, Winter 1967, pp 391–415.

zero midpoint between dissatisfaction and satisfaction. Conceivably, an organization member who has good supervision, pay, and working conditions but a tedious and unchallenging task with little chance of advancement would be at the zero midpoint. That person would have no dissatisfaction (because of good hygiene factors) and no satisfaction (because of a lack of motivators). Consequently, Herzberg warns managers that it takes more than good pay and good working conditions to motivate today's employees. It takes an "enriched job" that offers the individual opportunity for achievement and recognition, stimulation, responsibility, and advancement.

Research on the Motivator~Hygiene Theory   Herzberg's theory generated a great deal of research and controversy. The controversy revolved around whether studies supporting the theory were flawed, and thus invalid.[28] A motivation scholar attempted to sort out the controversy by concluding:

> In balance, when we combine all of the evidence with all of the allegations that the theory has been misinterpreted, and that its major concepts have not been assessed properly, one is left, more than twenty years later, not really knowing whether to take the theory seriously, let alone whether it should be put into practice in organizational settings. . . . There is support for many of the implications the theory has for enriching jobs to make them more motivating. But the two-factor aspect of the theory—the feature that makes it unique—is not really a necessary element in the use of the theory for designing jobs, per se.[29]

job enrichment Building achievement, recognition, stimulating work, responsibility, and advancement into a job.

Applying Herzberg's Model through Vertical Loading   Job enrichment is based on the application of Herzberg's ideas. Specifically, **job enrichment** entails modifying a job such that an employee has the opportunity to experience achieve-

● ✏ TABLE 6–1   Principles of Vertically Loading a Job

Principle	Motivators Involved
A. Removing some controls while retaining accountability	Responsibility and personal achievement
B. Increasing the accountability of individuals for their own work	Responsibility and recognition
C. Giving a person a complete natural unit of work (module, division, area, and so on)	Responsibility, achievement, and recognition
D. Granting additional authority to an employee in his activity; job freedom	Responsibility, achievement, and recognition
E. Making periodic reports directly available to the worker himself rather than to the supervisor	Internal recognition
F. Introducing new and more difficult tasks not previously handled	Growth and learning
G. Assigning individuals specific or specialized tasks, enabling them to become experts	Responsibility, growth, and advancement

Source: Reprinted by permission of the *Harvard Business Review*. An exhibit from "One More Time: How Do You Motivate Employees?" by F Herzberg (January/February 1968). Copyright © 1968 by the President and Fellows of Harvard College; all rights reserved.

ment, recognition, stimulating work, responsibility, and advancement. These characteristics are incorporated into a job through vertical loading.

Rather than giving employees additional tasks of similar difficulty (horizontal loading), *vertical loading* consists of giving workers more responsibility. In other words, employees take on chores normally performed by their supervisors. Managers are advised to follow seven principles when vertically loading jobs (see Table 6–1). As an example, consider how Mickey Zaldivar and Chava Sanchez, two managers at Leegin Creative Leather Products, used vertical loading to enrich the jobs of employees making leather belts.

> Since belts require a lot of hand labor, Leegin's factory is in many ways old-fashioned. Workers toil over cutters, punch presses, and sewing machines. In the past, employees stayed in one functional department. They cut or sewed or punched or dyed all manner of belts as they came through, and collected a wage determined by a complicated system of piece rates. Wanting to change all that—and brimming with up-to-the-minute ideas of empowerment and teamwork—Zaldivar and Sanchez handpicked 20 experienced workers and put them in charge of a complete belt line. From then on, . . . those workers would own that category of belts and would monitor their own production. All would be paid an hourly wage, based on what they were earning before.[30]

● ✏

JOB CHARACTERISTICS APPROACH TO JOB DESIGN

The job characteristics model is a more recent approach to job design. It is a direct outgrowth of job enrichment and attempts to pinpoint those situations and those individuals for which job design is most effective. In this regard, the job characteristics model represents a contingency approach.

Overview of the Job Characteristics Model

Two OB researchers, J Richard Hackman and Greg Oldham, played a central role in developing the job characteristics approach. These researchers tried to determine how work can be structured so that employees are internally (or intrinsically) motivated. **Internal motivation** occurs when an individual is "turned on to one's work because of the positive internal feelings that are generated by doing well, rather than being dependent on external factors (such as incentive pay or compliments from the boss) for the motivation to work effectively."[31] These positive

internal motivation
Motivation caused by positive internal feelings.

● **FIGURE 6–5**   The Job Characteristics Model

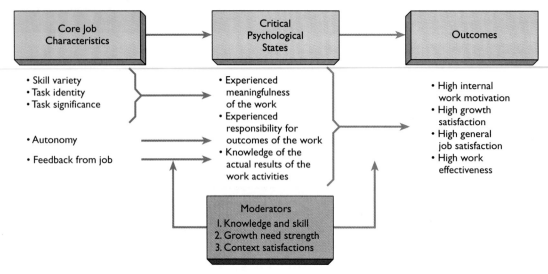

Source: J R Hackman and G R Oldham, *Work Redesign*, © 1980, Addison-Wesley Publishing Co., Reading, MA, p 90. Reprinted with permission.

feelings power a self-perpetuating cycle of motivation. As shown in Figure 6–5, internal work motivation is determined by three psychological states. In turn, these psychological states are fostered by the presence of five core job dimensions. As you can see in Figure 6–5, the object of this approach is to promote high internal motivation by designing jobs that possess the five core job characteristics. Let us examine the major components of this model to see how it works.

Critical Psychological States   A group of management experts described the conditions under which individuals experienced the three critical psychological states. They are:

experienced meaningfulness Feeling that one's job is important and worthwhile.

experienced responsibility Believing that one is accountable for work outcomes.

knowledge of results Feedback about work outcomes.

1. **Experienced meaningfulness.**   The individual must perceive his work as worthwhile or important by some system of value he accepts.
2. **Experienced responsibility.**   He must believe that he personally is accountable for the outcomes of his efforts.
3. **Knowledge of results.**   He must be able to determine, on some fairly regular basis, whether or not the outcomes of his work are satisfactory.[32]

These psychological states generate internal work motivation. Moreover, they encourage job satisfaction and perseverance because they are self-reinforcing. Consider, for example, the important role the three psychological states no doubt played in Angela Azzaretti's decision to pass up two lucrative promotions in favor of her present job that offered more responsibility and challenge.

> Angela Azzaretti, 25, the daughter of Italian immigrants, was graduated from the University of Illinois and took a job at Caterpillar's headquarters in Peoria. . . . Her work played well in Mossville, near Peoria, and soon she was offered a promotion to Caterpillar's headquarters staff. Angela turned it down. Then she was offered another promotion, entailing a move to a different plant. Once again she said no. "Job satisfaction is the most important thing to me," says Angela. "In those other jobs, I would have had less responsibility, less of a challenge. The only benefit was more money. I know it sounds crazy, but I evaluated the situation."[33]

Angela Azzaretti cared more about job satisfaction than money or power. She turned down two promotions at Caterpillar in order to continue doing work she enjoyed.

Alen MacWeeney

If one of the three psychological states is shortchanged, motivation diminishes. For example, if an individual is completely responsible for outcomes associated with a meaningful job but receives no feedback (knowledge of results) about performance, he or she will not experience the positive feelings that create internal motivation.

Core Job Dimensions In general terms, **core job dimensions** are common characteristics found to a varying degree in all jobs. Once again, five core job characteristics elicit the three psychological states (see Figure 6–5). Three of those job characteristics combine to determine experienced meaningfulness of work. They are:

core job dimensions Job characteristics found to various degrees in all jobs.

- *Skill variety.* The extent to which the job requires an individual to perform a variety of tasks that require him or her to use different skills and abilities.
- *Task identity.* The extent to which the job requires an individual to perform a whole or completely identifiable piece of work. In other words, task identity is high when a person works on a product or project from beginning to end and sees a tangible result.
- *Task significance.* The extent to which the job affects the lives of other people within or outside the organization.

Experienced responsibility is elicited by the job characteristic of autonomy, defined as follows:

- *Autonomy.* The extent to which the job enables an individual to experience freedom, independence, and discretion in both scheduling and determining the procedures used in completing the job.

Finally, knowledge of results is fostered by the job characteristic of feedback, defined as follows:

- *Feedback.* The extent to which an individual receives direct and clear information about how effectively he or she is performing the job.[34]

Motivating Potential of a Job Hackman and Oldham devised a self-report instrument to assess the extent to which a specific job possesses the five core job characteristics. With this instrument, which is discussed in the next section, it is possible to calculate a motivating potential score for a job. The **motivating potential score** (MPS) is a summary index that represents the extent to which the job characteristics foster internal work motivation. Low scores indicate that an individual will not experience high internal work motivation from the job. Such a job is a prime candidate for job redesign. High scores reveal that the job is capable of stimulating internal motivation. The MPS is computed as follows:

motivating potential score
The amount of internal work
motivation associated with a
specific job.

$$\text{MPS} = \frac{\text{Skill variety} + \text{Task identity} + \text{Task significance}}{3} \times \text{Autonomy} \times \text{Feedback}$$

Judging from this equation, which core job characteristic do you think is relatively more important in determining the motivational potential of a job? Since MPS equals zero when autonomy or feedback are zero, you are correct if you said both experienced autonomy and feedback.

Does the Theory Work for Everyone? As previously discussed, not all people may want enriched work. Hackman and Oldham incorporated this conclusion into their model by identifying three attributes that affect how individuals respond to jobs with a high MPS. These attributes are concerned with the individual's knowledge and skill, growth need strength (representing the desire to grow and develop as an individual), and context satisfactions (see Figure 6–5). Context satisfactions represent the extent to which employees are satisfied with various aspects of their job, such as satisfaction with pay, co-workers, or supervision.

Hackman and Oldham proposed that people will respond positively to jobs with a high MPS when (1) they have the knowledge and skills necessary to do the job, (2) they have high growth needs, and (3) they are satisfied with various aspects of the work context, such as pay and co-workers. Although these recommendations make sense, two recent studies did not support the moderating influence of an employee's growth needs and context satisfaction.[35] The model worked equally well for employees with high and low growth needs and context satisfaction. Future research needs to examine whether an employee's knowledge and skills are an important moderator of the model's effectiveness.

Applying the Job Characteristics Model There are three major steps to follow when applying Hackman and Oldham's model. Since the model seeks to increase employee motivation and satisfaction, the first step consists of diagnosing the work environment to determine if a problem exists. Hackman and Oldham developed a self-report instrument for managers to use called the *job diagnostic survey* (JDS).

Diagnosis begins by determining if motivation and satisfaction are lower than desired. If they are, a manager then assesses the MPS of the jobs being examined. National norms are used to determine whether the MPS is low or high.[36] If the MPS is low, an attempt is made to determine which of the core job characteristics is causing the problem. If the MPS is high, managers need to look for other factors eroding motivation and satisfaction. (You can calculate your own MPS in the exercise at the end of this chapter.) Potential factors may be identified by considering other motivation theories discussed in this book.

Step two consists of determining whether job redesign is appropriate for a given group of employees. Job redesign is most likely to work in a participative environment in which employees have the necessary knowledge and skills.

In the third step, managers need to consider how to redesign the job. The focus of this effort is to increase those core job characteristics that are lower than national norms. Managers may want to gain employees' input during this step.

Some Practical Implications   Since a meta-analysis covering 15,542 people indicated a moderately strong relationship between job characteristics and job satisfaction, managers may want to use this model to increase employee satisfaction.[37] Unfortunately, job redesign appears to reduce the quantity of output just as often as it has a positive impact. Caution and situational appropriateness are advised. For example, one study demonstrated that job redesign works better in less complex organizations (small plants or companies).[38] Nonetheless, managers are likely to find noticeable increases in the quality of performance after a job redesign program. Results from 21 experimental studies revealed that job redesign resulted in a median increase of 28 percent in the quality of performance.[39]

Moreover, two separate meta-analyses support the practice of using the job characteristics model to help managers reduce absenteeism and turnover.[40] In conclusion, managers need to realize that job redesign is not a panacea for all their employee satisfaction and motivation problems. To enhance their chances of success with this approach, managers need to remember that a change in one job or department can create problems of perceived inequity in related areas or systems within the organization. Managers need to take an open systems perspective when implementing job redesign, as was suggested by Hackman and Oldham. They wrote:

> Our observations of work redesign programs suggest that attempts to change jobs frequently run into—and sometimes get run over by—other organizational systems and practices, leading to a diminution (or even a reversal) of anticipated outcomes. . . .
>
> The ''small change'' effect, for example, often develops as managers begin to realize that radical changes in work design will necessitate major changes in other organizational systems as well.[41]

Job satisfaction is one of the most frequently studied variables in OB. A team of OB scholars estimated there were more than 5,000 articles written on the subject between 1957 and 1992.[42] A good measure of this preoccupation with job satisfaction stems from Herzberg's motivator–hygiene theory. As just discussed, Herzberg's theory assumes there is a causal linkage from job satisfaction to motivation, and ultimately to job performance. This suggests that the best way to increase performance is to improve job satisfaction. Unfortunately, subsequent research has found the job satisfaction→performance relationship to be less than clear cut. Consequently, we need to sort out the various causes and consequences of job satisfaction.

UNRAVELING THE CONTROVERSY SURROUNDING JOB SATISFACTION

The Causes of Job Satisfaction

Job satisfaction is an affective or emotional response toward various facets of one's job. This definition means job satisfaction is not a unitary concept. Rather, a

job satisfaction   An affective or emotional response to one's job.

person can be relatively satisfied with one aspect of his or her job and dissatisfied with one or more other aspects. For example, researchers at Cornell University developed the Job Descriptive Index (JDI) to assess one's satisfaction with the following job dimensions: work, pay, promotions, co-workers, and supervision.[43] Taking a more analytical approach, researchers at the University of Minnesota concluded there are 20 different dimensions underlying job satisfaction. Selected Minnesota Satisfaction Questionnaire (MSQ) items measuring satisfaction with recognition, compensation, and supervision are listed in the OB Exercise. Please take a moment now to determine how satisfied you are with these three aspects of your present or most recent job. (Comparative norms for each dimension of job satisfaction are: Total score of 3–6 = Low job satisfaction; 7–11 = Moderate satisfaction; 12 and above = High satisfaction.)[44] How do you feel about your job?

Five predominant models of job satisfaction specify its causes. They are need fulfillment, discrepancy, value attainment, equity, and trait/genetic components. A brief review of these models will provide insight into the complexity of this seemingly simple concept.

Need Fulfillment   These models propose that satisfaction is determined by the extent to which the characteristics of a job allow an individual to fulfill his or her needs. Although these models generated a great degree of controversy, it is generally accepted that need fulfillment is correlated with job satisfaction.[45]

met expectations The extent to which one receives what he or she expects from a job.

Discrepancies   These models propose that satisfaction is a result of met expectations. **Met expectations** represent the difference between what an individual expects to receive from a job, like good pay and promotional opportunities, and what he or she actually receives. When expectations are greater than what is received, a person will be dissatisfied. In contrast, this model predicts the individual will be satisfied when he or she attains outcomes above and beyond expectations. A recent meta-analysis of 31 studies that included 17,241 people demonstrated that met expectations were significantly related to job satisfaction.[46]

OB EXERCISE

How Satisfied Are You with Your Present Job?

1. The way I am noticed when I do a good job	Very dissatisfied	1 2 3 4 5 Very satisfied
2. The recognition I get for the work I do	Very dissatisfied	1 2 3 4 5 Very satisfied
3. The praise I get for doing a good job	Very dissatisfied	1 2 3 4 5 Very satisfied
4. How my pay compares with that for similar jobs in other companies	Very dissatisfied	1 2 3 4 5 Very satisfied
5. My pay and the amount of work I do	Very dissatisfied	1 2 3 4 5 Very satisfied
6. How my pay compares with that of other workers	Very dissatisfied	1 2 3 4 5 Very satisfied
7. The way my boss handles employees	Very dissatisfied	1 2 3 4 5 Very satisfied
8. The way my boss takes care of complaints brought to him/her by employees	Very dissatisfied	1 2 3 4 5 Very satisfied
9. The personal relationship between my boss and his/her employees	Very dissatisfied	1 2 3 4 5 Very satisfied

Total score for satisfaction with recognition (add questions 1–3), compensation (add questions 4–6), and supervision (add questions 7–9).

Source: Adapted from D J Weiss, R V Dawis, G W England, and L H Lofquist, *Manual for the Minnesota Satisfaction Questionnaire,* (Minneapolis: Industrial Relations Center, University of Minnesota, 1967). Used with permission.

Value Attainment   The idea underlying **value attainment** is that satisfaction results from the perception that a job allows for fulfillment of an individual's important work values.[47] In general, research consistently supports the prediction that value fulfillment is positively related to job satisfaction. However, results from one study indicate that fulfillment of important values leads to satisfaction only in certain situations.[48] Therefore, managers do not have to concentrate solely on satisfying an employee's most important values. Gains in satisfaction can be obtained by providing workers with outcomes of lesser value.

value attainment   The extent to which a job allows fulfillment of one's work values.

Equity   In this model, satisfaction is a function of how "fairly" an individual is treated at work. Satisfaction results from one's perception that work outcomes, relative to inputs, compares favorably with a significant other's outcomes/inputs. A recent meta-analysis involving data from 30 different organizations and 12,979 people supported this model. Employees perceived fairness of pay and promotions were significantly correlated with job satisfaction.[49] Chapter 7 explores this promising model in more detail.

Trait/Genetic Components   Have you ever noticed that some of your co-workers or friends appear to be satisfied across a variety of job circumstances, whereas others always seem dissatisfied? This model of satisfaction attempts to explain this pattern. Specifically, the trait/genetic model is based on the belief that job satisfaction is partly a function of both personal traits and genetic factors. As such, this model implies that stable individual differences are just as important in explaining job satisfaction as are characteristics of the work environment. Although only a few studies have tested these propositions, results support a positive, significant relationship between personal traits and job satisfaction over a period of time from 2 to 50 years.[50] Genetic factors also were found to significantly predict both general job satisfaction and intrinsic satisfaction.[51] Additional research is needed to test this new model of job satisfaction.

The Consequences of Job Satisfaction

This area has significant managerial implications. As previously mentioned, thousands of studies have examined the relationship between job satisfaction and other organizational variables. Since it is impossible to examine them all, we will consider a subset of the more important variables from the standpoint of managerial relevance.

Table 6–2 summarizes the pattern of results. The relationship between job satisfaction and these other variables is either positive or negative. The strength of the relationship ranges from weak (very little relationship) to strong. Strong relationships imply that managers can significantly influence the variable of interest by increasing job satisfaction. Let us now consider several of the key correlates of job satisfaction.

Absenteeism   Absenteeism is costly and managers are constantly on the lookout for ways to reduce it. One recommendation has been to increase job satisfaction. If this is a valid recommendation, there should be a strong negative relationship (or negative correlation) between satisfaction and absenteeism. In other words, as satisfaction increases, absenteeism should decrease. A researcher tracked this prediction by synthesizing three separate meta-analyses containing a total of 74

Variables Related with Satisfaction	Direction of Relationship	Strength of Relationship
Absenteeism	Negative	Weak
Tardiness	Negative .	Weak
Turnover	Negative	Moderate
Heart disease	Negative	Moderate
Stress	Negative	Moderate
Pro-union voting	Negative	Moderate
Organizational citizenship behavior	Positive	Moderate
Organizational commitment	Positive	Strong
Job performance	Positive	Weak
Life satisfaction	Positive	Moderate
Mental health	Positive	Moderate

studies. Results revealed a weak negative relationship between satisfaction and absenteeism.[52] It is unlikely, therefore, that managers will realize any significant decrease in absenteeism by increasing job satisfaction.

Turnover   Turnover is important to managers because it both disrupts organizational continuity and is very costly. A meta-analysis of 49 studies covering 13,722 people demonstrated a moderate negative relationship between satisfaction and turnover.[53] (See Table 6–2.) Given the strength of this relationship, managers would be well advised to try to reduce turnover by increasing employee job satisfaction.

Organizational Citizenship Behavior   Organizational citizenship behaviors consist of employee behaviors that are beyond the call of duty. Examples include "such gestures as constructive statements about the department, expression of personal interest in the work of others, suggestions for improvement, training new people, respect for the spirit as well as the letter of housekeeping rules, care for organizational property, and punctuality and attendance well beyond standard or enforceable levels."[54] Managers certainly would like employees to exhibit these behaviors. Because organizational citizenship behaviors are moderately related to job satisfaction, managers can increase the frequency of such behaviors by increasing employee job satisfaction.[55] This may, in turn, enhance an employee's productivity. Research reveals that organizational citizenship behaviors are positively correlated with performance ratings.[56]

Organizational Commitment   Organizational commitment reflects the extent to which an individual identifies with an organization and is committed to its goals. A recent meta-analysis of 68 studies and 35,282 individuals uncovered a significant and strong relationship between organizational commitment and satisfaction.[57] Managers are advised to increase job satisfaction in order to elicit higher levels of commitment. In turn, higher commitment can facilitate higher productivity (recall Figure 6–1).[58]

Job Performance   One of the biggest controversies within organizational research centers on the relationship between satisfaction and job performance. Some, such as Herzberg, argue that satisfaction leads to higher performance while others contend that high performance leads to satisfaction. In an attempt to resolve this controversy, a meta-analysis accumulated results from 74 studies. Overall, the relationship between job satisfaction and job performance was examined for 12,192 people. It was discovered that satisfaction and performance were only slightly related.[59]

Some researchers claim that this result is misleading and that it understates the true relationship between performance and satisfaction. The rationale for this claim revolves around the accuracy of measuring an individual's performance. If performance ratings do not reflect the actual interactions and interdependencies at work, weak meta-analytic results are partially due to incomplete measures of individual-level performance.[60] Examining the relationship between *aggregate* measures of job satisfaction and organizational performance is one solution to correct this problem. In support of these ideas, a recent study found a significant, positive correlation between organizational performance and employee satisfaction for data collected from 298 schools and 13,808 teachers.[61] Thus, it appears that managers can positively affect performance by increasing employee job satisfaction.

Pro-Union Voting   Results from 11 studies revealed a significant negative correlation between job satisfaction and pro-union voting.[62] In other words, people tend to vote for unions when they are dissatisfied with their jobs. Union organizers have taken advantage of this reality for decades. This suggests organizations may want to monitor employee satisfaction if they desire to maintain a nonunionized status.

Broader Implications   In a general sense, job satisfaction has important implications because it affects an individual's quality of work life. The term *quality of work life* refers to the overall quality of an individual's experiences at work. As suggested by research results listed in Table 6–2, job dissatisfaction is associated with increased heart disease, increased stress, and poor mental health.[63] It is hoped that enlightened managers will develop an interest in reducing these negative work-related outcomes by improving job satisfaction.

BACK TO THE OPENING CASE

Now that you have read Chapter 6, you should be able to answer the following questions about the case involving fast-growing companies.

1. Using the job performance model of motivation in Figure 6–1, why do you think the motivational programs at Prospect, Stonyfield Farm, Phoenix Textile, and IDEO are working?

2. Using need theories, what is likely to happen to the motivation of Drew Melton at Prospect, Edward Souza at Stonyfield Farms, Kim Roussin at Phoenix Textile, and employees at IDEO?

3. How did the top executives from each company use the principles of job enrichment?

4. Using the job characteristics model in Figure 6–5, describe how the different companies fostered intrinsic motivation by increasing the three critical psychological states.

5. Which of the relationships outlined in Table 6–2 are supported by information in the case? Provide detailed examples to support your conclusions.

SUMMARY OF KEY CONCEPTS

1. *Define the term "motivation."* Motivation is defined as those psychological processes that cause the arousal, direction, and persistence of voluntary, goal-oriented actions. Managers need to understand these psychological processes if they are to successfully guide employees toward accomplishing organizational objectives.

2. *Discuss the job performance model of motivation.* The foundation of the model is based on systems theory and reinforcement theory. Four types of inputs affect employee effort and performance: individual differences and needs, supervisory support and coaching, performance goals, and job characteristics. The relationship between employee effort and performance is affected by work environment and external constraints. It is management's responsibility to manage and remove such performance roadblocks. In addition, managers affect employee effort and performance by providing feedback and by reinforcing employee behavior with consequences.

3. *Highlight the evolution of modern motivation theory.* Historically, motivation theory has evolved from hedonism to needs, to reinforcement, to cognitions, and finally to job characteristics. Some theories of motivation focus on internal energizers of behavior such as needs and satisfaction. Other motivation theories, which deal in terms of reinforcement, cognitions, and job characteristics, focus on more complex person–environment interactions. There is no single, universally accepted theory of motivation. Each alternative theory holds important managerial lessons.

4. *Contrast Maslow's and McClelland's need theories.* Two well-known need theories of motivation are Maslow's need hierarchy and McClelland's need theory. Maslow's notion of a prepotent or stair-step hierarchy of five levels of needs has not stood up well under research. McClelland believes that motivation and performance vary according to the strength of an individual's need for achievement. High achievers prefer moderate risks and situations where they can control their own destiny. Top managers should have a high need for power coupled with a low need for affiliation.

5. *Demonstrate your familiarity with scientific management, job enlargement, job rotation, and job enrichment.* Each of these techniques is used in the process of job design. Job design involves altering jobs with the intent of increasing employee job satisfaction and productivity. Scientific management designs jobs by using research and experimentation to identify the most efficient way to perform tasks. Jobs are horizontally loaded in job enlargement by giving workers more than one specialized task to complete. Job rotation increases workplace variety by moving employees from one specialized job to another. Job enrichment vertically loads a job by giving employees administrative duties normally performed by their superiors.

6. *Explain the practical significance of Herzberg's distinction between motivators and hygiene factors.* Herzberg believes job satisfaction motivates better job performance. His *hygiene* factors, such as policies, supervision, and salary, erase sources of dissatisfaction. On the other hand, his *motivators,* such as achievement, responsibility, and recognition, foster job satisfaction. Although Herzberg's motivator–hygiene theory of job satisfaction has been criticized on methodological grounds, it has practical significance for job enrichment.

7. *Describe how internal work motivation is increased by using the job characteristics model.* The psychological states of experienced meaningfulness, experienced responsibility, and knowledge of results produce internal work motivation. These psychological states are fostered by the presence of five core job characteristics. People respond positively to jobs containing these core job characteristics when they have the knowledge and skills necessary to perform the job, high growth needs, and high context satisfactions.

8. *Put the job satisfaction controversy into proper perspective.* Owing to Herzberg's work, the satisfaction–performance relationship has stirred much controversy in OB circles. Actually, job satisfaction has a complex web of causes and consequences. The correlation between job satisfaction and turnover, heart disease, stress, and pro-union voting is moderately negative. A moderately positive relationship has been found between job satisfaction and organizational citizenship behavior, organizational commitment, life satisfaction, and mental health.

DISCUSSION QUESTIONS

1. Why should the average manager be well versed in the various motivation theories?
2. From a practical standpoint, what is a major drawback of theories of motivation based on internal factors such as needs and satisfaction?
3. Are you a high achiever? How can you tell? How will this help or hinder your path to top management?
4. If you were redesigning a job, would you use one or more of the methods of job design we discussed? Explain your rationale.
5. How have hygiene factors and motivators affected your job satisfaction and performance?
6. How might the job characteristics model be used to increase your internal motivation to study?
7. Do you know anyone who would not respond positively to an enriched job? Describe this person.
8. Do you believe that job satisfaction is partly a function of both personal traits and genetic factors? Explain.
9. Do you think job satisfaction leads directly to better job performance? Explain.
10. What are the three most valuable lessons about employee motivation that you have learned from this chapter?

EXERCISE

Objectives

1. To assess the motivating potential score (MPS) of your current or former job.
2. To determine which core job characteristics need to be changed.
3. To explore how you might redesign the job.

Introduction

The first step in calculating the MPS of a job is to complete the job diagnostic survey (JDS). Since the JDS is a long questionnaire, we would like you to complete a subset of the instrument. This will enable you to calculate the MPS, identify deficient job characteristics, and begin thinking about redesigning the job.

Instructions

Indicate whether each of the following statements in the JDS is an accurate or inaccurate description of your present or most recent job. Please select one number from the following scale for each statement. After completing the instrument, use the scoring key to compute a total score for each of the core job characteristics.

1 = Very inaccurate	5 = Slightly accurate
2 = Mostly inaccurate	6 = Mostly accurate
3 = Slightly inaccurate	7 = Very accurate
4 = Uncertain	

_____ 1. Supervisors often let me know how well they think I am performing the job.

_____ 2. The job requires me to use a number of complex or high-level skills.

_____ 3. The job is arranged so that I have the chance to do an entire piece of work from beginning to end.

_____ 4. Just doing the work required by the job provides many chances for me to figure out how well I am doing.

_____ 5. The job is not simple and repetitive.

_____ 6. This job is one where a lot of other people can be affected by how well the work gets done.

_____ 7. The job does not deny me the chance to use my personal initiative or judgment in carrying out the work.

_____ 8. The job provides me the chance to completely finish the pieces of work I begin.

_____ 9. The job itself provides plenty of clues about whether or not I am performing well.

_____ 10. The job gives me considerable opportunity for independence and freedom in how I do the work.

_____ 11. The job itself is very significant or important in the broader scheme of things.

_____ 12. The supervisors and co-workers on this job almost always give me "feedback" about how well I am doing in my work.

Scoring Key

Compute the *average* of the two items that measure each job characteristic.

Skill variety (#2 and #5)	_____
Task identity (#3 and #8)	_____

Task significance (#6 and #11)   ———
Autonomy (#7 and #10)   ———
Feedback from job itself (#4 and #9)   ———
Feedback from others (#1 and #12)   ———

Now you are ready to calculate the MPS. First, you need to compute a total score for the feedback job characteristic. This is done by computing the average of the job characteristics entitled "feedback from job itself" and "feedback from others." Second, use the MPS formula presented earlier in this chapter. Finally, norms are provided below to help you interpret the relative status of the MPS and each individual job characteristic.[64]

Questions for Consideration/Class Discussion

1. What is the MPS of your job? Is it high, average, or low?
2. Using the norms, which job characteristics are high, average, or low?
3. Which job characteristics would you change? Why?
4. How would you specifically redesign your job?

Norms

	Type of Job			
	Professional/Technical	Clerical	Sales	Service
Skill variety	5.4	4.0	4.8	5.0
Task identity	5.1	4.7	4.4	4.7
Task significance	5.6	5.3	5.5	5.7
Autonomy	5.4	4.5	4.8	5.0
Feedback from job itself	5.1	4.6	5.4	5.1
Feedback from others	4.2	4.0	3.6	3.8
MPS	154	106	146	152

Notes

1 T R Mitchell, "Motivation: New Direction for Theory, Research, and Practice," *Academy of Management Review,* January 1982, p 81.

2 For a discussion of management's role in managing performance roadblocks, see T Koentop, "Can We Motivate Without a Pyramid?," *PIMA Magazine,* March 1993, p 8; and M Walton, *The Deming Management Method* (New York: Perigee Books, 1986).

3 See C J Cranny, P Cain Smith, and E F Stone, *Job Satisfaction* (New York: Lexington Books, 1992).

4 For a thorough discussion of the historical development of motivation theories, see E L Deci, "On the Nature and Functions of Motivation Theories," *Psychological Science,* May 1992, pp 167–71; and R Katzell and D E Thompson, "Work Motivation: Theory and Practice," *American Psychologist,* February 1990, pp 144–53.

5 For a complete discussion of the organizational criterion of interest to managers and researchers, see J T Austin and P Villanova, "The Criterion Problem: 1917–

1992," *Journal of Applied Psychology,* December 1992, pp 836–74.

6 Mitchell, "Motivation: New Direction for Theory, Research, and Practice," p 83. A meta-analysis of the relationship between ability and performance was conducted by W M Coward and P R Sackett, "Linearity of Ability-Performance Relationships: A Reconfirmation," *Journal of Applied Psychology,* June 1990, pp 297–300.

7 For a complete description of Maslow's theory, see A H Maslow, "A Theory of Human Motivation," *Psychological Review,* July 1943, pp 370–96.

8 C C Pinder, *Work Motivation: Theory, Issues, and Applications* (Glenview, IL: Scott, Foresman, 1984), p 52.

9 Layoff statistics are discussed by D E Herz, "Worker Displacement Still Common in the Late 1980s," *Monthly Labor Review,* May 1991, pp 3–9.

10 See "Labor Letter: A Special News Report on People

and Their Jobs in Offices, Fields, and Factories," *The Wall Street Journal,* October 5, 1993, p A1.

[11] Results can be found in W D Spangler, "Validity of Questionnaire and TAT Measures of Need for Achievement: Two Meta-Analyses," *Psychological Bulletin,* July 1992, pp 140–54.

[12] Results can be found in S D Bluen, J Barling, and W Burns, "Predicting Sales Performance, Job Satisfaction, and Depression by Using the Achievement Strivings and Impatience–Irritability Dimensions of Type A Behavior," *Journal of Applied Psychology,* April 1990, pp 212–16; and D C McClelland, *The Achieving Society* (New York: Free Press, 1961).

[13] H A Murray, *Explorations in Personality* (New York: John Wiley & Sons, 1938), p. 164.

[14] Results are presented in J B Miner, N R Smith, and J S Bracker, "Role of Entrepreneurial Task Motivation in the Growth of Technologically Innovative Firms," *Journal of Applied Psychology,* August 1989, pp 554–60.

[15] See L H Chusmir and A Azevedo, "Motivation Needs of Sampled Fortune-500 CEOs: Relation to Organization Outcomes," *Perceptual and Motor Skills,* October 1992, pp 595–612.

[16] D Stipp, "Toxic Turpitude: Environmental Crime Can Land Executives in Prison These Days," *The Wall Street Journal,* September 10, 1990.

[17] See the following series of research reports: A M Harrell and M J Stahl, "A Behavioral Decision Theory Approach for Measuring McClelland's Trichotomy of Needs," *Journal of Applied Psychology,* April 1981, pp 242–47; M J Stahl and A M Harrell, "Evolution and Validation of a Behavioral Decision Theory Measurement Approach to Achievement, Power, and Affiliation," *Journal of Applied Psychology,* December 1982, pp 744–51; and M J Stahl, "Achievement, Power and Managerial Motivation: Selecting Managerial Talent with the Job Choice Exercise," *Personnel Psychology,* Winter 1983, pp 775–89.

[18] For a review of the foundation of achievement motivation training, see D C McClelland, "Toward a Theory of Motive Acquisition," *American Psychologist,* May 1965, pp 321–33. Evidence for the validity of motivation training can be found in H Heckhausen and S Krug, "Motive Modification," in *Motivation and Society,* ed A J Stewart (San Francisco: Jossey-Bass, 1982).

[19] Results can be found in D B Turban and T L Keon, "Organizational Attractiveness: An Interactionist Perspective," *Journal of Applied Psychology,* April 1993, pp 184–93.

[20] See D Steele Johnson and R Perlow, "The Impact of Need for Achievement Components on Goal Commitment and Performance," *Journal of Applied Social Psychology,* November 1992, pp 1711–20.

[21] J L Bowditch and A F Buono, *A Primer on Organizational Behavior* (New York: John Wiley & Sons, 1985), p 210.

[22] Research on scientific management is reviewed by T D Wall and R Martin, "Job and Work Design," in *International Review of Industrial and Organizational Psychology,* eds C L Cooper and I T Robertson (New York: John Wiley & Sons, 1987), pp 61–91.

[23] The inconsistency between scientific management and the job responsibilities of current day knowledge workers is discussed by M Maccoby, "Managers Must Unlearn the Psychology of Control," *Research Technology Management,* January–February 1993, pp 49–51.

[24] This type of program was developed and tested by M A Campion and C L McClelland, "Follow-Up and Extension of the Interdisciplinary Costs and Benefits of Enlarged Jobs," *Journal of Applied Psychology,* June 1993, pp 339–51.

[25] M Kaeter, "Cross-Training the Tactical View," *Training,* March 1993, pp 35–36.

[26] See F Herzberg, B Mausner, and B B Snyderman, *The Motivation to Work* (New York: John Wiley & Sons, 1959).

[27] Two recent tests of Herzberg's theory can be found in I O Adigun and G M Stephenson, "Sources of Job Motivation and Satisfaction Among British and Nigerian Employees," *The Journal of Social Psychology,* June 1992, pp 369–76; and E A Maidani, "Comparative Study of Herzberg's Two-Factor Theory of Job Satisfaction Among Public and Private Sectors," *Public Personnel Management,* Winter 1991, pp 441–48.

[28] Both sides of the Herzberg controversy are discussed by N King, "Clarification and Evaluation of the Two-Factor Theory of Job Satisfaction," *Psychological Bulletin,* July 1970, pp 18–31; and B Grigaliunas and Y Weiner, "Has the Research Challenge to Motivation–Hygiene Theory Been Conclusive? An Analysis of Critical Studies," *Human Relations,* December 1974, pp 839–71.

[29] Pinder, *Work Motivation: Theory, Issues, and Applications,* p 28.

[30] J Case, "A Business Transformed," *Inc.,* June 1993, p 90.

[31] J R Hackman, G R Oldham, R Janson, and K Purdy, "A New Strategy for Job Enrichment," *California Management Review,* Summer 1975, p 58.

[32] Ibid., p 58. (Emphasis added.)

33 A Deutschman, "What 25-Year-Olds Want," *Fortune,* August 27, 1990, p 42.

34 Definitions of the job characteristics were adapted from J R Hackman and G R Oldham, "Motivation through the Design of Work: Test of a Theory," *Organizational Behavior and Human Performance,* August 1976, pp 250–79.

35 Results can be found in R B Tiegs, L E Tetrick, and Y Fried, "Growth Need Strength and Context Satisfactions as Moderators of the Relations of the Job Characteristics Model," *Journal of Management,* September 1992, pp 575–93; and G Johns, J L Xie, and Y Fang, "Mediating and Moderating Effects in Job Design," *Journal of Management,* December 1992, pp 657–76.

36 The complete JDS and norms for the MPS are presented in J R Hackman and G R Oldham, *Work Redesign* (Reading, MA: Addison-Wesley Publishing, 1980). Studies that revised the JDS were conducted by J L Cordery and P P Sevastos, "Responses to the Original and Revised Job Diagnostic Survey: Is Education a Factor in Responses to Negatively Worded Items?," *Journal of Applied Psychology,* February 1993, pp 141–43; and J R Idaszak and F Drasgow, "A Revision of the Job Diagnostic Survey: Elimination of a Measurement Artifact," *Journal of Applied Psychology,* February 1987, pp 69–74.

37 See B T Loher, R A Noe, N L Moeller, and M P Fitzgerald, "A Meta-Analysis of the Relation of Job Characteristics to Job Satisfaction," *Journal of Applied Psychology,* May 1985, pp 280–89.

38 Results can be found in M R Kelley, "New Process Technology, Job Design, and Work Organization: A Contingency Model," *American Sociological Review,* April 1990, pp 191–208.

39 Productivity studies are reviewed in R E Kopelman, *Managing Productivity in Organizations* (New York: McGraw-Hill, 1986).

40 Absenteeism results are discussed in Y Fried and G R Ferris, "The Validity of the Job Characteristics Model: A Review and Meta-Analysis," *Personnel Psychology,* Summer 1987, pp 287–322. The turnover meta-analysis was conducted by G M McEvoy and W F Cascio, "Strategies for Reducing Turnover: A Meta-Analysis," *Journal of Applied Psychology,* May 1985, pp 342–53.

41 G R Oldham and J R Hackman, "Work Design in the Organizational Context," in *Research in Organizational Behavior,* eds B M Staw and L L Cummings (Greenwich, CT: JAI Press, 1980), pp 248–49.

42 See Part One from C J Cranny, P Cain Smith, and E F Stone, *Job Satisfaction: How People Feel About Their Jobs and How It Affects Their Performance* (New York: Lexington Books, 1992), pp 1–3.

43 For a review of the development of the JDI, see P C Smith, L M Kendall, and C L Hulin, *The Measurement of Satisfaction in Work and Retirement* (Skokie, IL: Rand McNally, 1969).

44 For norms on the MSQ, see D J Weiss, R V Dawis, G W England, and L H Lofquist, *Manual for the Minnesota Satisfaction Questionnaire* (Minneapolis: Industrial Relations Center, University of Minnesota, 1967).

45 For a review of need satisfaction models, see E F Stone, "A Critical Analysis of Social Information Processing Models of Job Perceptions and Job Attitudes," in *Job Satisfaction: How People Feel about Their Jobs and How It Affects Their Performance,* eds C J Cranny, P Cain Smith, and E F Stone (New York: Lexington Books, 1992), pp 21–52.

46 See J P Wanous, T D Poland, S L Premack, and K S Davis, "The Effects of Met Expectations on Newcomer Attitudes and Behaviors: A Review and Meta-Analysis," *Journal of Applied Psychology,* June 1992, pp 288–97.

47 A complete description of this model is provided by E A Locke, "Job Satisfaction," in *Social Psychology and Organizational Behavior,* eds M Gruneberg and T Wall (New York: John Wiley & Sons, 1984).

48 For a test of the value fulfillment model, see J K Butler, Jr., "Value Importance as a Moderator of the Value Fulfillment—Job Satisfaction Relationship: Group Differences," *Journal of Applied Psychology,* August 1983, pp 420–28. For a review of earlier research, see Locke, "The Nature and Causes of Job Satisfaction."

49 Results from the meta-analysis can be found in L A Witt and L G Nye, "Gender and the Relationship between Perceived Fairness of Pay or Promotion and Job Satisfaction," *Journal of Applied Psychology,* December 1992, pp 910–17.

50 See the following series of studies: D Watson and A Keltner Slack, "General Factors of Affective Temperament and Their Relation to Job Satisfaction over Time," *Organizational Behavior and Human Decision Processes,* March 1993, pp 181–202; T A Judge, "Does Affective Disposition Moderate the Relationship between Job Satisfaction and Voluntary Turnover?," *Journal of Applied Psychology,* June 1993, pp 395–401; and B M Staw and J Ross, "Stability in the Midst of Change: A Dispositional Approach to Job Attitudes," *Journal of Applied Psychology,* August 1985, pp 469–80.

51 This interesting study was conducted by R D Arvey, T J Bouchard, Jr., N L Segal, and L M Abraham, "Job Satisfaction: Environmental and Genetic Components," *Journal of Applied Psychology,* April 1989, pp 187–92.

52 See R D Hackett, ''Work Attitudes and Employee Absenteeism: A Synthesis of the Literature,'' *Journal of Occupational Psychology,* 1989, pp 235–48.

53 The results can be found in R P Tett and J P Meyer, ''Job Satisfaction, Organizational Commitment, Turnover Intention, and Turnover: Path Analysis Based on Meta-Analytic Findings,'' *Personnel Psychology,* Summer 1993, pp 259–93.

54 D W Organ, ''The Motivational Basis of Organizational Citizenship Behavior,'' in *Research in Organizational Behavior,* eds B M Staw and L L Cummings (Greenwich, CT: JAI Press, 1990), p 46.

55 This research is summarized by C D Fisher and E A Locke, ''The New Look in Job Satisfaction Research and Theory,'' in *Job Satisfaction: How People Feel about Their Jobs and How It Affects Their Performance,* eds C J Cranny, P Cain Smith, and E F Stone (New York: Lexington Books, 1992), pp 165–94.

56 For a review of research on organizational citizenship, see P M Podsakoff, S B Mackenzic, and C Hui, ''Organizational Citizenship Behaviors and Managerial Evaluations of Employee Performance: A Review and Suggestions for Future Research,'' in *Research in Personnel and Human Resources Management,* ed G Ferris (Greenwich, CT: JAI Press, 1993), pp 1–40.

57 See Tett and Meyer, ''Job Satisfaction, Organizational Commitment, Turnover Intention, and Turnover: Path Analysis Based on Meta-Analytic Findings.''

58 See J E Mathieu and D Zajac, ''A Review and Meta-analysis of the Antecedents, Correlates, and Consequences of Organizational Commitment,'' *Psychological Bulletin,* September 1990, pp 171–94.

59 The relationship between performance and satisfaction was reviewed by M T Iaffaldano and P M Muchinsky, ''Job Satisfaction and Job Performance: A Meta-Analysis,'' *Psychological Bulletin,* March 1985, pp 251–73.

60 These issues are discussed by C Ostroff, ''The Relationship between Satisfaction, Attitudes, and Performance: An Organizational Level Analysis,'' *Journal of Applied Psychology,* December 1992, pp 963–74; and R A Katzell, D E Thompson, and R A Guzzo, ''How Job Satisfaction and Job Performance Are and Are Not Linked,'' in *Job Satisfaction: How People Feel about Their Jobs and How It Affects Their Performance,* eds C J Cranny, P Cain Smith, and E F Stone (New York: Lexington Books, 1992), pp 195–217.

61 See Ostroff, ''The Relationship between Satisfaction, Attitudes, and Performance: An Organizational Level Analysis.''

62 For an overall review of the satisfaction–pro-union voting relationship, see H G Heneman III and M H Sandver, ''Predicting the Outcome of Union Certification Elections: A Review of the Literature,'' *Industrial and Labor Relations Review,* July 1983, pp 537–59. Two more recent studies were conducted by S Mellor, ''The Relationship between Membership Decline and Union Commitment: A Field Study of Local Unions in Crisis,'' *Journal of Applied Psychology,* June 1990, pp 258–67; and B Klandermans, ''Union Commitment: Replications and Tests in the Dutch Context,'' *Journal of Applied Psychology,* December 1989, pp 869–75.

63 See T A Judge and C L Hulin, ''Job Satisfaction as a Reflection of Disposition: A Multiple Source Causal Analysis,'' *Organizational Behavior and Human Decision Processes,* December 1993, pp 388–421; and J M Ivancevich and M T Matteson, *Stress and Work: A Managerial Perspective* (Glenview, IL: Scott, Foresman, 1980). For a review of the causes of heart disease, see C D Jenkins, ''Psychologic and Social Precursors of Coronary Disease,'' *The New England Journal of Medicine,* February 1971, pp 307–16.

64 The JDS and its norms were adapted from J R Hackman and G R Oldham, *Work Redesign* (Reading, MA: Addison-Wesley Publishing, 1980), pp 280–81, 317.

MOTIVATION THROUGH EQUITY, EXPECTANCY, AND GOAL SETTING

Learning OBJECTIVES

When you finish studying the material in this chapter, you should be able to:

1. Discuss the role of perceived inequity in employee motivation.

2. Distinguish between positive and negative inequity.

3. Explain Vroom's expectancy theory.

4. Discuss Porter and Lawler's expectancy theory of motivation.

5. Describe the practical implications of expectancy theory of motivation.

6. Explain how goal setting motivates an individual.

7. Identify five practical lessons from goal-setting research.

8. Specify issues that should be addressed before implementing a motivational program.

OPENING CASE

Cypress Semiconductor Corporation Uses a Computerized Management System to Monitor and Motivate Employees

Sharon Hoogstraten

TJ Rodgers, CEO, says: "Most companies don't fail for lack of talent or strategic vision. They fail for lack of execution—the mundane blocking and tackling that the great companies consistently do well and strive to do better.

At Cypress, our management systems track corporate, departmental, and individual performance so regularly and in such detail that no manager, including me, can plausibly claim to be in the dark about critical problems. . . .

All of Cypress's 1,400 employees

have goals, which, in theory, makes them no different from employees at most other companies. What does make our people different is that every week they set their own goals, commit to achieving them by a specific date, enter them into a database, and report whether or not they completed prior goals. Cypress's computerized goal system is an important part of our managerial infrastructure. It is a detailed guide to the future and an objective record of the past. In any given week, some 6,000 goals in the database come due. Our ability to meet those goals ultimately determines our success or failure.

Most of the work in our company is organized by project rather than along strict functional lines. Members of a project team may be (and usually are) from different parts of the organization. Project managers need not be (and often aren't) the highest ranking member of the group. Likewise, the goal system is organized by project and function. In Monday project meetings,

employees set short-term goals and rank them in priority order. Short-term goals take from one to six weeks to complete, and different employees have different numbers of goals. At the beginning of a typical week, for example, a member of our production-control staff initiated seven new goals in connection with three different projects. He said he would, among other things, report on progress with certain minicomputer problems (two weeks), monitor and report on quality rejection rates for certain products (three weeks), update killer software for the assembly department (two weeks), and assist a marketing executive with a forecasting software enhancement (four weeks).

On Monday night, the project goals are fed back into a central computer. On Tuesday mornings, functional managers receive a printout of their direct reports' new and pending project goals. These printouts are the basis of Tuesday afternoon meetings in which managers work with their people to

---

This chapter explores three cognitive process theories of work motivation: equity, expectancy, and goal setting. Each theory is based on the premise that employees' cognitions are the key to understanding their motivation. To help you apply what you have learned, we conclude the chapter by highlighting the prerequisites of successful motivational programs.

Defined generally, **equity theory** is a model of motivation that explains how people strive for *fairness* and *justice* in social exchanges or give-and-take relationships. Equity theory is based on cognitive dissonance theory, developed by social psychologist Leon Festinger in the 1950s.[1]

According to Festinger's theory, people are motivated to maintain consistency between their cognitive beliefs and their behavior. Perceived inconsistencies create

ADAMS' EQUITY THEORY OF MOTIVATION

equity theory Holds that motivation is a function of fairness in social exchanges.

(continued)

anticipate overload and conflicting goals, sort out priorities, organize work, and make mutual commitments about what's going to get done. This is a critical step. The failure mode in our company (and I suspect in most growing companies) is that people overcommit themselves rather than establish unchallenging goals. By 5 PM Tuesday, the revised schedule is fed back into the central database.

This 'two pass' system generates the work program that coordinates the mostly self-imposed activities of every Cypress employee. It allows the organization to be project driven, which helps us emphasize speed and agility, as well as functionally accurate, which works against burnout and failure to execute. On Wednesday morning, our eight vice presidents receive goal printouts for their people and the people below them—another conflict-resolution mechanism. . . .

On Wednesday afternoons at my weekly staff meeting, I review various database reports with my vice presidents. We talk about what's going wrong and how to help managers who are running into problems. The following reports typically serve as the basis for discussion: progress with goals on critical projects; percentage of delinquent goals sorted by managers (their goals plus those of their subordinates); percentage of delinquent goals sorted by vice president (the percentage of pending goals that are delinquent for all people reporting up the chain of command to each vice president); all employees without goals (something I do not tolerate); all goals five or more weeks delinquent; and all employees with two or more delinquent goals, sorted by manager.

As we've refined the goal system and used it more extensively, I've developed some general principles. First, people are going to have goals they don't achieve on time; the key is to sense when a vice president or a manager is losing control of the operation. My rule of thumb is that vice presidents should not have delinquency rates above 20 percent, and managers should not let more than 30 percent of their goals become delinquent. When managers do have a delinquency problem, I usually intervene with a short note: 'Your delinquency rate is running at 35 percent, what can I do to help?' I often get back requests for specific assistance. Part of my role is to hold people accountable. But it is also to identify problems before they become crises and to provide help in getting them fixed.

Second, people need positive feedback. Every month we issue a Completed Goal Report for every person in the company. The report lists all goals completed over the past four weeks as well as those that have yet to come due. 'Individual Monthly Goal Report,' an excerpt from a monthly report for a production-control staffer, lists all goals completed in workweek 45 of last year. The entire report consists of 49 goals, 28 of which were completed on time, 4 of which were completed late, and 17 of which were pending—an outstanding record.

The completed goal report is also a

cognitive dissonance (or psychological discomfort), which in turn motivates corrective action. For example, a cigarette smoker who sees a heavy-smoking relative die of lung cancer probably would be motivated to quit smoking if he or she attributes the death to smoking. Accordingly, when victimized by unfair social exchanges, our resulting cognitive dissonance prompts us to correct the situation. Corrective action may range from a slight change in attitude or behavior to the extreme case of trying to harm someone. Consider the case of David Burke, who was fired from his position as a US Air agent: "He smuggled a .44 magnum aboard a US Air flight carrying the supervisor who had fired him. After the plane took off, Burke shot the supervisor, the pilot, and the co-pilot."[2]

Psychologist J Stacy Adams pioneered application of the equity principle to the workplace. Central to understanding Adams' equity theory of motivation is an awareness of key components of the individual–organization exchange relationship. This relationship is pivotal in the formation of employees' perceptions of equity and inequity.

(concluded)

valuable tool for performance evaluation. . . . At Cypress, the completed goal report triggers a performance minireview; each month managers read through their people's printouts and prepare brief, factual evaluations. At year end, managers have a dozen such objective reviews to refresh their memories and fight the proximity effect.

Managers shouldn't expect outstanding performance unless they're prepared to reward outstanding performers. Yet evaluation and reward systems remain an organizational black hole for three reasons.

First, managers aren't very scientific about rating their people. They may be able to identify the real stars and the worst laggards, but the vast majority of people (who must still be ranked) get lost somewhere in the middle. Second, even if they evaluate people correctly, managers like to spread raises around evenly to keep the troops happy. This is a deadly policy that saps the morale of standouts who deserve more and sends the

wrong signal to weak performers. Third, managers are totally incapable of distinguishing between 'merit' and 'equity' when awarding increases. Merit refers to that portion of a raise awarded for the quality of past performance. Equity refers to adjustments in that raise to more closely align salaries of equally ranked peers. Merit and equity both have a place in the incentive mix, but confusing the two makes for mushy logic, counterproductive results, and dissatisfied people. . . .

As with all our resource-allocation systems, the focal-review system starts with policies at the top and forces middle management decisions to be consistent with that thinking. Senior management and the board of directors review our annual revenue forecasts, survey compensation trends among our competitors, and settle on a total corporate allowance for raises. The 'raise budget' is not negotiable, and it drives raises throughout the company. If the corporate budget is 8 percent, then every department must

meet a weighted-average salary increase of 8 percent. It's up to managers to distribute the 8 percent pool, which is where the focal-review system comes in. . . .

Only after they have awarded percentage increases based strictly on merit can managers make adjustments for salary inequities created by personal circumstances and historical accidents."

For Discussion

Why is Cypress so successful in meeting its goals?

- Additional discussion questions linking this case with the following material appear at the end of this chapter.

The Individual~Organization Exchange Relationship

Adams points out that two primary components are involved in the employee–employer exchange, *inputs* and *outcomes*. An employee's inputs, for which he or she expects a just return, include education, experience, skills, and effort. On the outcome side of the exchange, the organization provides such things as pay, fringe benefits, and recognition. These outcomes vary widely, depending on one's organization and rank. Table 7–1 presents a list of on-the-job inputs and outcomes employees consider when making equity comparisons.

Negative and Positive Inequity

On the job, feelings of inequity revolve around a person's evaluation of whether he or she receives adequate rewards to compensate for his or her contributive inputs. People perform these evaluations by comparing the perceived fairness of their employment exchange to that of relevant others. This comparative process, which

• TABLE 7–1

Factors Considered When
Making Equity Comparisons

Inputs	Outcomes
Time	Pay/bonuses
Education/training	Fringe benefits
Experience	Challenging assignments
Skills	Job security
Creativity	Career advancement/promotions
Seniority	Status symbols
Loyalty to organization	Pleasant/safe working environment
Age	Opportunity for personal growth/development
Personality traits	Supportive supervision
Effort expended	Recognition
Personal appearance	Participation in important decisions

Source: Based in part on J S Adams, "Toward an Understanding of Inequity," *Journal of Abnormal and Social Psychology*, November 1963, pp 422–36.

is based on an equity norm, was found to generalize across countries.[3] OB scholar Robert Vecchio identified three major categories of relevant others that people use when making equity comparisons:

(1) *Other* (including referent others inside and outside the organization, and referent others in similar or different jobs), (2) *self* (self-comparisons over time and against one's ideal ratio), and (3) *system* (based on exchanges between an individual and the organization). In addition to these categorizations, it should be noted that a group or even multiple groups can serve as referents.[4]

People tend to compare themselves to similar others—such as people performing the same job or individuals of the same gender or educational level—rather than dissimilar others.[5]

Three different equity relationships are illustrated in Figure 7–1; equity, negative inequity, and positive inequity. Assume the two people in each of the equity relationships in Figure 7–1 have equivalent backgrounds (equal education, seniority, and so forth) and perform identical tasks. Only their hourly pay rates differ. Equity exists for an individual when his or her ratio of perceived outcomes to inputs is equal to the ratio of outcomes to inputs for a relevant co-worker (see part A in Figure 7–1). Since equity is based on comparing *ratios* of outcomes to inputs, inequity will not necessarily be perceived just because someone else receives greater rewards. If the other person's additional outcomes are due to his or her greater inputs, a sense of equity may still exist. However, if the comparison person enjoys greater outcomes for similar inputs, **negative inequity** will be perceived (see part B in Figure 7–1). On the other hand, a person will experience **positive inequity** when his or her outcome to input ratio is greater than that of a relevant co-worker (see part C in Figure 7–1).

negative inequity
Comparison in which another person receives greater outcomes for similar inputs.

positive inequity
Comparison in which another person receives lesser outcomes for similar inputs.

Dynamics of Perceived Inequity

Managers can derive practical benefits from Adams' equity theory by recognizing that (1) negative inequity is less tolerable than positive inequity and (2) inequity can be reduced in a variety of ways.

Thresholds of Inequity   People have a lower tolerance for negative inequity than they do for positive inequity. Those who are shortchanged are more powerfully motivated to correct the situation than those who are excessively rewarded.

A. An Equitable Situation

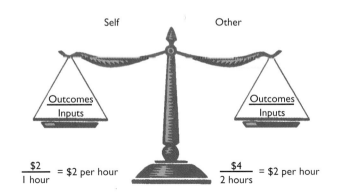

$$\frac{\$2}{1 \text{ hour}} = \$2 \text{ per hour} \qquad \frac{\$4}{2 \text{ hours}} = \$2 \text{ per hour}$$

• ➛ **FIGURE 7–1**
Negative and Positive
Inequity

B. Negative Inequity

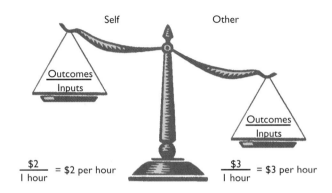

$$\frac{\$2}{1 \text{ hour}} = \$2 \text{ per hour} \qquad \frac{\$3}{1 \text{ hour}} = \$3 \text{ per hour}$$

C. Positive Inequity

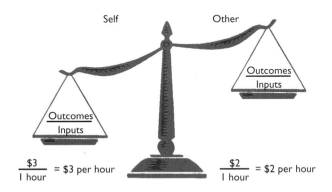

$$\frac{\$3}{1 \text{ hour}} = \$3 \text{ per hour} \qquad \frac{\$2}{1 \text{ hour}} = \$2 \text{ per hour}$$

For example, if you have ever been overworked and underpaid, you know how negative inequity can erode your job satisfaction and performance. Perhaps you put forth less effort or quit the job to escape the negative inequity. Hence, it takes much more positive than negative inequity to produce the same degree of motivation. Moreover, a recent meta-analysis of 12,979 people demonstrated that males and females had equal reactions to negative inequity. There were no gender differences in response to perceived inequity.[6]

Reducing Inequity   Table 7–2 lists eight possible ways to reduce inequity. It is important to note that equity can be restored by altering one's equity ratios behaviorally and/or cognitively. Equity theorists propose that the many possible combinations of behavioral and cognitive adjustments are influenced by the following tendencies:

1. An individual will attempt to maximize the amount of positive outcomes he or she receives.
2. People resist increasing inputs when it requires substantial effort or costs.
3. People resist behavioral or cognitive changes in inputs important to their self-concept or self-esteem.
4. Rather than change cognitions about oneself, an individual is more likely to change cognitions about the comparison other's inputs and outcomes.
5. Leaving the field (quitting) is chosen only when severe inequity cannot be resolved through other methods.[7]

Equity Research Findings

Different managerial insights have been gained from laboratory and field studies.

Insights from Laboratory Studies   The basic approach used in laboratory studies is to pay an experimental subject more (overpayment) or less (underpayment) than the standard rate for completing a task. People are paid on either an hourly or piece-rate basis. Research findings supported equity theory. Overpaid subjects on a piece-rate system lowered the quantity of their performance and increased the quality of their performance. In contrast, underpaid subjects increased the quantity and decreased the quality of their performance.[8] A recent study extended this stream of research by examining the effect of underpayment inequity on ethical behavior. A total of 102 undergraduate students were either equitably

TABLE 7–2
Eight Ways to Reduce Inequity

Methods	Examples
1. Person can increase his or her inputs.	Work harder; attend school or a specialized training program.
2. Person can decrease his or her inputs.	Don't work as hard; take longer breaks.
3. Person can attempt to increase his or her outcomes.	Ask for a raise; ask for a new title; seek outside intervention.
4. Person can decrease his or her outcomes.	Ask for less pay.
5. Leave the field.	Absenteeism and turnover.
6. Person can psychologically distort his or her inputs and outcomes.	Convince self that certain inputs are not important; convince self that he or she has a boring and monotonous job.
7. Person can psychologically distort the inputs or outcomes of comparison other.	Conclude that other has more experience or works harder; conclude that other has a more important title.
8. Change comparison other.	Pick a new comparison person; compare self to previous job.

Source: Adapted from J S Adams, "Toward an Understanding of Inequity," *Journal of Abnormal and Social Psychology,* November 1963, pp 422–36.

paid or underpaid for performing a clerical task. Results indicated that underpaid students stole money to compensate for their negative inequity.[9]

Insights from Field Studies   Field studies of equity theory are on the rise. Overall, results support propositions derived from the theory. For example, perceptions of pay equity were significantly related to the performance and turnover of major league baseball players and to the quality of products produced in 102 different organizations.[10] Several studies further revealed that employees reported greater levels of job satisfaction, organizational commitment, and lower absenteeism and turnover when they felt "fairly" rewarded for their effort and performance.[11] Thus, it appears to be beneficial for managers to equitably distribute monetary rewards and promotions. Moreover, employees also responded with greater organizational commitment and lower intentions to quit when they believed their organizations used "fair" procedures when making decisions about them.[12] Therefore, it seems obvious that organizations should attempt to use managerial decision-making processes that are fair and equitable.

Practical Lessons from Equity Theory

Equity theory has at least seven important practical implications. First, equity theory provides managers with yet another explanation of how beliefs and attitudes affect job performance (recall the discussion of attitudes and values in Chapter 4). According to this line of thinking, the best way to manage job behavior is to adequately understand underlying cognitive processes. Indeed, we are motivated powerfully to correct the situation when our ideas of fairness and justice are offended. Consider the case of a longtime Walt Disney Company employee who felt inequity after being passed over for a promotion she thought she deserved.

> Knowing that her new boss faced pressure to vastly improve the work he supervised, the woman began taking much longer than usual to complete projects. When he wrote a negative job evaluation, without even talking to her, and placed it in her employment file, she responded with a lengthy memo—and sent copies to the division's top brass. She also made nasty comments about his actions to a few colleagues behind his back.
>
> "This was vengeful, and I did it purposely," she admits. "But I felt totally justified. I knew it would really hurt my boss and destroy his credibility." And it did. "All hell broke loose," she recounts. Within months her boss was fired—and she got his job.[13]

Second, research on equity theory emphasizes the need for managers to pay attention to employees' perceptions of what is fair and equitable. No matter how fair management thinks the organization's policies, procedures, and reward system are, each employee's *perceptions* of the equity of those factors are what counts. For example, a recent study examined gender differences in perceptions about the fairness in promoting equally qualified females and males. Results demonstrated that women and men viewed a decision to promote a person of the opposite gender instead of a member of their own gender as significantly less fair.[14] This finding underscores the need for managers to make promotion decisions based on merit-based, job-related information.

Third, managers benefit by allowing employees to participate in making decisions about important work outcomes. For example, employees are more likely to perceive pay plans as fair when they provide input in developing the plan. Fourth, employees should be given the opportunity to appeal decisions that affect their welfare. Being able to appeal a decision promotes the belief that management treats employees fairly.[15] In turn, perceptions of fair treatment promote job satisfaction and organizational commitment, and help to reduce absenteeism and turnover.

Fifth, employees are more likely to accept and support organizational change when they believe it is implemented fairly and when it produces equitable outcomes. For example, two recent studies revealed that employees supported corporate strategic decisions and profit-sharing programs when they were perceived as equitable.[16] Sixth, managers can promote cooperation and teamwork among group members by treating them equitably. Research reveals that people are just as concerned with fairness in group settings as they are with their own personal interests.[17] Finally, treating employees inequitably can lead to litigation and costly court settlements. Employees denied justice at work are turning increasingly to arbitration and the courts. Managers' knowledge about equity theory can keep things from getting that far out of hand.

Managers can attempt to follow these practical implications by monitoring equity perceptions through informal conversations, interviews, or attitude surveys. Please take a moment now to complete the brief equity/fairness questionnaire in the OB Exercise. If you perceive your work organization as unfair, you are probably dissatisfied and have contemplated quitting. In contrast, your organiza-

---

OB EXERCISE

Measuring Perceived Organizational Equity/Fairness

Instructions

Evaluate your present (or most recent) job according to the following five dimensions.

Dimensions	Item	Score
		False True
1. Pay rules	The rules for granting pay raises in my organization are fair.	1—2—3—4—5—6—7
2. Pay administration	My supervisor rates everyone fairly when considering them for promotion.	1—2—3—4—5—6—7
3. Pay level	My employer pays me more for my work than I would receive from other organizations in this area.	1—2—3—4—5—6—7
4. Work pace	My supervisor makes everyone meet their performance standards.	1—2—3—4—5—6—7
5. Rule administration	My supervisor makes everyone come to work on time and adhere to the same rules of conduct.	1—2—3—4—5—6—7
		Total score = _____

Norms

Very fair organization = 26–35
Moderately fair organization = 15–25
Unfair organization = 5–14

Source: Adapted in part from J E Dittrich and M R Carrell, "Organizational Equity Perceptions, Employee Job Satisfaction, and Departmental Absence and Turnover Rates," *Organizational Behavior and Human Performance*, August 1979, pp 29–40.

tional loyalty and attachment are likely greater if you believe you are treated fairly at work.

Expectancy theory holds that people are motivated to behave in ways that produce desired combinations of expected outcomes. Perception plays a central role in expectancy theory because it emphasizes cognitive ability to anticipate likely consequences of behavior. Embedded in expectancy theory is the principle of hedonism. As mentioned in Chapter 6, hedonistic people strive to maximize their pleasure and minimize their pain. Generally, expectancy theory can be used to predict behavior in any situation in which a choice between two or more alternatives must be made. For example, it can be used to predict whether to quit or stay at a job; whether to exert substantial or minimal effort at a task; and whether to major in management, computer science, accounting, or finance.

EXPECTANCY THEORY OF MOTIVATION

expectancy theory Holds that people are motivated to behave in ways that produce valued outcomes.

This section introduces and explores two expectancy theories of motivation: Vroom's expectancy theory and Porter and Lawler's expectancy theory. Understanding these cognitive process theories can help managers develop organizational policies and practices that enhance rather than inhibit employee motivation.

Vroom's Expectancy Theory

Victor Vroom formulated a mathematical model of expectancy theory in his 1964 book *Work and Motivation.*[18] Vroom's theory has been summarized as follows:

> The strength of a tendency to act in a certain way depends on the strength of an expectancy that the act will be followed by a given consequence (or outcome) and on the value or attractiveness of that consequence (or outcome) to the actor.[19]

Motivation, according to Vroom, boils down to the decision of how much effort to exert in a specific task situation. This choice is based on a two-stage sequence of expectations (effort→performance and performance→outcome). First, motivation is affected by an individual's expectation that a certain level of effort will produce the intended performance goal. For example, if you do not believe increasing the amount of time you spend studying will significantly raise your grade on an exam, you probably will not study any harder than usual. Motivation also is influenced by the employee's perceived chances of getting various outcomes as a result of accomplishing his or her performance goal. Finally, individuals are motivated to the extent that they value the outcomes received.

Vroom used a mathematical equation to integrate these concepts into a predictive model of motivational force or strength. For our purposes, however, it is sufficient to define and explain the three key concepts within Vroom's model—*expectancy, instrumentality,* and *valence.*

Expectancy An **expectancy,** according to Vroom's terminology, represents an individual's belief that a particular degree of effort will be followed by a particular level of performance. In other words, it is an effort→performance expectation. Expectancies take the form of subjective probabilities. As you may recall from a course in statistics, probabilities range from zero to one. An expectancy of zero indicates effort has no anticipated impact on performance.

expectancy Belief that effort leads to a specific level of performance.

For example, suppose you do not know how to use a typewriter. No matter how much effort you exert, your perceived probability of typing 30 error-free words per minute likely would be zero. An expectancy of one suggests that performance is totally dependent on effort. If you decided to take a typing course as well as practice a couple of hours a day for a few weeks (high effort), you should be able to type 30 words per minute without any errors. In contrast, if you do not take a typing course and only practice an hour or two per week (low effort), there is a very low probability (say, a 20 percent chance) of being able to type 30 words per minute without any errors.

The following factors influence an employee's expectancy perceptions:

- Self-esteem.
- Self-efficacy.
- Previous success at the task.
- Help received from a supervisor and subordinates.
- Information necessary to complete the task.
- Good materials and equipment to work with.[20]

instrumentality   A performance→outcome perception.

Instrumentality   An **instrumentality** is a performance→outcome perception. It represents a person's belief that a particular outcome is contingent on accomplishing a specific level of performance. Performance is instrumental when it leads to something else. For example, passing exams is instrumental to graduating from college.

Instrumentalities range from −1.0 to 1.0. An instrumentality of 1.0 indicates attainment of a particular outcome is totally dependent on task performance. For instance, Aspect Telecommunications, in San Jose, California, bases every employee's bonus on scores received from an annual customer satisfaction survey. The amount of bonus received depends on the level of customer satisfaction.[21] An instrumentality of zero indicates there is no relationship between performance and outcome. For example, most companies link the number of vacation days to seniority, not job performance. Finally, an instrumentality of −1.0 reveals that high performance reduces the chance of obtaining an outcome while low performance increases the chance. For example, the more time you spend studying to get an A (high performance) on an exam, the less time you will have for enjoying leisure activities. Similarly, as you lower the amount of time spent studying (low performance), you increase the amount of time that may be devoted to leisure activities.

valence   The value of a reward or outcome.

Valence   As Vroom used the term, **valence** refers to the positive or negative value people place on outcomes. Valence mirrors our personal preferences.[22] For example, most employees have a positive valence for receiving additional money or recognition. In contrast, job stress and being laid off would likely be negatively valent for most individuals. In Vroom's expectancy model, *outcomes* refer to different consequences that are contingent on performance, such as pay, promotions, or recognition. An outcome's valence depends on an individual's needs and can be measured for research purposes with scales ranging from a negative value to a positive value. For example, an individual's valence toward more recognition can be assessed on a scale ranging from −2 (very undesirable) to 0 (neutral) to +2 (very desirable).

Vroom's Expectancy Theory in Action   Vroom's expectancy model of motivation can be used to analyze a real-life motivation program. Consider the following performance problem described by Frederick W Smith, founder and chief executive officer of Federal Express Corporation.

> . . . we were having a helluva problem keeping things running on time. The airplanes would come in, and everything would get buuked up. We tried every kind of control mechanism that you could think of, and none of them worked. Finally, it became obvious that the underlying problem was that it was in the interest of the employees at the cargo terminal—they were college kids, mostly—to run late, because it meant that they made more money. So what we did was given them all a minimum guarantee and say, ''Look, if you get through before a certain time, just go home, and you will have beat the system.'' Well, it was unbelievable. I mean, in the space of about 45 days, the place was way ahead of schedule. And I don't even think it was a conscious thing on their part.[23]

How did Federal Express get its college-age cargo handlers to switch from low effort to high effort? According to Vroom's model, the student workers originally exerted low effort because they were paid on the basis of time, not output. It was in their best interest to work slowly and accumulate as many hours as possible. By offering to let the student workers *go home early if and when they completed their assigned duties,* Federal Express prompted high effort. This new arrangement created two positively valued outcomes: guaranteed pay plus the opportunity to leave early. The motivation to exert high effort became greater than the motivation to exert low effort.

Judging from the impressive results, the student workers had both high effort→performance expectancies and positive performance→outcome instrumentalities. Moreover, the guaranteed pay and early departure opportunity evidently had strongly positive valences for the student workers.

Porter and Lawler's Extension

Two OB researchers, Lyman Porter and Edward Lawler III, developed an expectancy model of motivation that extended Vroom's work. This model attempted to (1) identify the source of people's valences and expectancies and (2) link effort with performance and job satisfaction. The model is presented in Figure 7–2.[24]

Predictors of Effort   Effort is viewed as a function of the perceived value of a reward (the reward's valence) and the perceived effort→reward probability (an expectancy). Employees should exhibit more effort when they believe they will receive valued rewards for task accomplishment.

Predictors of Performance   Performance is determined by more than effort. Figure 7–2 indicates that the relationship between effort and performance is moderated by an employee's abilities and traits and role perceptions. That is, employees with higher abilities attain higher performance for a given level of effort than employees with less ability.[25] Similarly, effort results in higher performance when employees clearly understand and are comfortable with their roles. This occurs because effort is channeled into the most important job activities or tasks. For example, stage fright can render an otherwise well prepared actor or speaker ineffective.

Predictors of Satisfaction   Employees receive both intrinsic and extrinsic rewards for performance. Intrinsic rewards are self-granted and consist of intangibles such as a sense of accomplishment and achievement. Extrinsic rewards are

◦ **FIGURE 7~2** Porter and Lawler's Expectancy Model

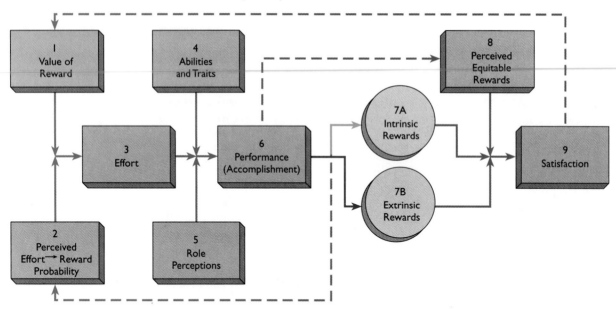

Source: L W Porter and E E Lawler III, *Managerial Attitudes and Performance* (Homewood, IL: Richard D. Irwin, 1968), p 165.

tangible outcomes such as pay and public recognition. In turn, job satisfaction is determined by employees' perceptions of the equity of the rewards received. Employees are more satisfied when they feel equitably rewarded. Figure 7–2 further shows that job satisfaction affects employees' subsequent valence of rewards. Finally, employees' future effort→reward probabilities are influenced by past experience with performance and rewards.

Research on Expectancy Theory and Managerial Implications

Many researchers have tested expectancy theory. A summary of 16 studies revealed that expectancy theory correctly predicted occupational or organizational choice 63.4 percent of the time; this was significantly better than chance predictions. Further, expectancy theory accurately predicted job satisfaction, decisions to retire (80 percent accuracy), voting behavior in union representation elections (over 75 percent accuracy), reenlistment in the National Guard (66 percent accuracy), and the frequency of drinking alcohol.[26]

Nonetheless, expectancy theory has been criticized for a variety of reasons. For example, the theory is difficult to test, and the measures used to assess expectancy, instrumentality, and valence have questionable validity.[27] In the final analysis, however, expectancy theory has important practical implications for individual managers and organizations as a whole (see Table 7–3).

Managers are advised to enhance effort→performance expectancies by helping employees accomplish their performance goals. Managers can do this by serving as role models, providing adequate resources, and increasing employees' self-efficacy by using the methods suggested in Chapter 4. It also is important for managers to influence employees' instrumentalities and to monitor valences for various rewards.

• ⬅ TABLE 7~3   Managerial and Organizational Implications of Expectancy Theory

Implications for Managers	Implications for Organizations
Determine the outcomes employees value.	Reward people for desired performance, and do not keep pay decisions secret.
Identify good performance so appropriate behaviors can be rewarded.	Design challenging jobs.
Make sure employees can achieve targeted performance levels.	Tie some rewards to group accomplishments to build team-work and encourage cooperation.
Link desired outcomes to targeted levels of performance.	Reward managers for creating, monitoring, and maintaining expectancies, instrumentalities, and outcomes that lead to high effort and goal attainment.
Make sure changes in outcomes are large enough to motivate high effort.	Monitor employee motivation through interviews or anonymous questionnaires.
Monitor the reward system for inequities.	Accommodate individual differences by building flexibility into the motivation program.

With respect to instrumentalities and valences, managers should attempt to link employee performance and valued rewards. A recent study of 313 Fortune 1000 companies demonstrated that they were following this recommendation. Results showed that 90 percent of the sample were using individual incentive systems to link performance and pay. Interestingly, 59 percent used team incentives to encourage teamwork.[28] There are four prerequisites to linking performance and rewards, as we discuss in the following paragraphs.

1. Managers need to develop and communicate performance standards to employees. For instance, a recent survey of 487 managers indicated that they were not held accountable for increasing quality. In turn, these managers did not set or enforce high performance standards among their employees.[29] Without question, increased motivation will not result in higher performance unless employees know how and where to direct their efforts.

2. Managers need valid and accurate performance ratings with which to compare employees.[30] Inaccurate ratings create perceptions of inequity and thereby erode motivation.

3. Managers should use the performance ratings to differentially allocate rewards among employees. That is, it is critical that managers allocate significantly different amounts of rewards for various levels of performance. As illustrated in the International OB, this practice is just beginning to take hold in Japan.

4. Managers need to offer rewards or outcomes valued by employees. Motivation is not increased when employees believe they will receive rewards for their effort and performance that they do not value.

• ➤

Regardless of the nature of their specific achievements, successful people tend to have one thing in common. Their lives are goal-oriented. This is as true for politicians seeking votes as it is for rocket scientists probing outer space. In Lewis Carroll's delightful tale of *Alice's Adventures in Wonderland,* the smiling Cheshire

**MOTIVATION
THROUGH GOAL
SETTING**

Japanese Organizations Begin to Reward Output Instead of Seniority

Other mantras of "Japanese management"—consensus building, seniority promotion, and pay—are also being challenged, at companies small and large. When Hiromichi Kimura became president of Pharmacia Biotech K.K. four years ago, he says the company's rigid promotion system yielded diligent but uninspired executives who were compensated "more by seniority than output."

The 43-year old biochemist . . . put his 140 employees on performance-related compensation. Those who didn't meet goals were demoted and their salaries cut. The notion behind the plan was to emphasize personal accountability, not group results.

"I told people they would be rewarded for performance. They performed," he recalls.

Source: J M Schlesinger, M Williams, and C Forman, "Japan Inc., wracked by Recession, Takes Stock of Its Methods," *The Wall Street Journal*, September 29, 1993, p. A10.

---

cat advised the bewildered Alice, "If you don't know where you're going, any road will take you there." Goal-oriented managers tend to find the right road because they know where they are going. Within the context of employee motivation, this section explores the theory, research, and practice of goal setting.

Goals: Definition and Background

goal   What an individual is trying to accomplish.

Edwin Locke, a leading authority on goal setting, and his colleagues define a **goal** as "what an individual is trying to accomplish; it is the object or aim of an action."[31] Expanding this definition, they add:

> The concept is similar in meaning to the concepts of purpose and intent. . . . Other frequently used concepts that are also similar in meaning to that of goal include performance standard (a measuring rod for evaluating performance), quota (a minimum amount of work or production), work norm (a standard of acceptable behavior defined by a work group), task (a piece of work to be accomplished), objective (the ultimate aim of an action or series of actions), deadline (a time limit for completing a task), and budget (a spending goal or limit).[32]

management by objectives Management system incorporating participation in decision making, goal setting, and feedback.

The motivational impact of performance goals and goal-based reward plans has been recognized for a long time. At the turn of the century, Frederick Taylor attempted to scientifically establish how much work of a specified quality an individual should be assigned each day. He proposed that bonuses be based on accomplishing those output standards. More recently, goal setting has been promoted through a widely used management technique called management by objectives (MBO). **Management by objectives** is a management system that incorporates participation in decision making, goal setting, and objective feedback.[33] A meta-analysis of MBO programs showed productivity gains in 68 of 70 different organizations. Specifically, results uncovered an average gain in productivity of 56 percent when top-management commitment was high. The average gain was only 6 percent when commitment was low. A second meta-analysis of 18 studies further demonstrated that employees' job satisfaction was significantly related to top-management's commitment to a MBO implementation.[34] These impressive results highlight the positive benefits of implementing MBO and setting goals. To further understand how MBO programs can increase both productivity and satisfaction, let us examine the process by which goal setting works.

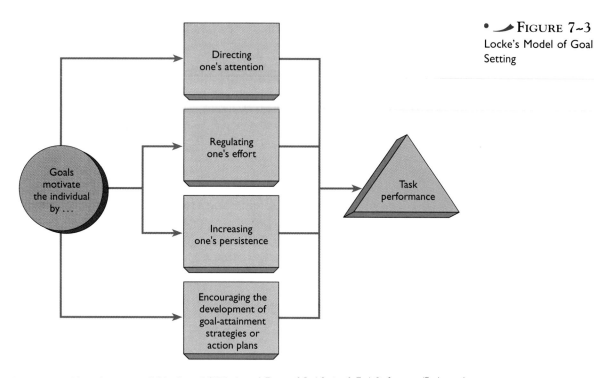

• ➤ **FIGURE 7~3**
Locke's Model of Goal
Setting

Source: Adapted from discussion in E A Locke and G P Latham, *A Theory of Goal Setting & Task Performance* (Englewood Cliffs, NJ: Prentice-Hall, 1990). Reprinted by permission of Prentice Hall, Inc.

How Does Goal Setting Work?

Despite abundant goal-setting research and practice, goal-setting theories are surprisingly scarce. An instructive model was formulated by Locke and his associates (see Figure 7–3). According to Locke's model, goal setting has four motivational mechanisms.[35]

Goals Direct Attention   Goals that are personally meaningful tend to focus one's attention on what is relevant and important. If, for example, you have a term project due in a few days, your thoughts tend to revolve around completing that project. Similarly, the members of a home appliance sales force who are told they can win a trip to Hawaii for selling the most refrigerators will tend to steer customers toward the refrigerator display.

Goals Regulate Effort   Not only do goals make us selectively perceptive, they also motivate us to act. The instructor's deadline for turning in your term project would prompt you to complete it, as opposed to going out with friends, watching television, or studying for another course. Generally, the level of effort expended is proportionate to the difficulty of the goal.

Goals Increase Persistence   Within the context of goal setting, **persistence** represents the effort expended on a task over an extended period of time. It takes effort to run 100 meters; it takes persistence to run a 26-mile marathon. Persistent people tend to see obstacles as challenges to be overcome rather than as reasons to fail. A difficult goal that is important to the individual is a constant reminder to keep exerting effort in the appropriate direction.

Goals Foster Strategies and Action Plans   If you are here and your goal is out there somewhere, you face the problem of getting from here to there. For example, the person who has resolved to lose 20 pounds must develop a plan for getting from ''here'' (his or her present weight) to ''there'' (20 pounds lighter). Goals can help because they encourage people to develop strategies and action plans that enable them to achieve their goals.[36] By virtue of setting a weight-reduction goal, the dieter may choose a strategy of exercising more, eating less, or some combination of the two. For a work-related example, consider the strategies and plans developed by Cindy Ransom's employees at Clorox after receiving a complex, broad goal.

> Three years ago Ransom asked her workers at a 100-person plant in Fairfield, California, to redesign the plant's operations. As she watched, intervening only to answer the occasional question, a team of hourly workers established training programs, set work rules for absenteeism, and reorganized the once traditional factory into five customer-focused business units.[37]

These planned changes were instrumental in Ransom's plant being recognized as the most improved plant in Clorox's household products division in 1992.

Insights from Goal-Setting Research

Research consistently has supported goal setting as a motivational technique. Setting performance goals increases individual, group, and organizational performance. Further, the positive effects of goal setting were found in six other countries or regions: Australia, Canada, the Caribbean, England, West Germany, and Japan.[38] Goal setting works in different cultures. Reviews of the many goal-setting studies conducted over the last couple of decades have given managers five practical insights:

goal difficulty   The amount of effort required to meet a goal.

1. *Difficult goals lead to higher performance.*   **Goal difficulty** reflects the amount of effort required to meet a goal. It is more difficult to sell nine cars a month than it is to sell three cars a month. An extensive review of goal-setting studies by Locke and his associates led them to conclude that performance tends to increase as goals become more difficult, but only to a point. As illustrated in Figure 7–4, the positive relationship between goal difficulty and performance breaks down when goals are perceived to be impossible. Of 57 research studies, 48 demonstrated that performance goes up when employees are given hard goals as opposed to easy or moderate goals (section A of Figure 7–4).[39] However, as the difficulty of a goal increases, performance plateaus (section B) and eventually decreases when the goal becomes impossible (section C). Rick Hess, chief operating officer of M/A-Comm, a Lowell, Massachusetts, defense company, believes in setting challenging yet attainable goals.

   > To motivate his people, Hess constantly tries to get them to challenge themselves, . . . ''Don't rule people out because they don't have experience,'' he says. ''Don't trap people in cubbies. Give people a reach if they have potential. Let a technical guy go and talk with customers and grow.''[40]

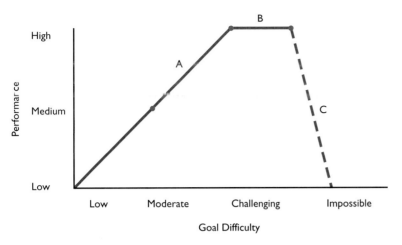

Relationship between Goal Difficulty and Performance

A Performance of committed individuals with adequate ability
B Performance of committed individuals who are working at capacity
C Performance of individuals who lack commitment to high goals

Source: E A Locke and G P Latham, *Goal Setting: A Motivational Technique That Works!* © 1984, p 22. Reprinted by permission of Prentice Hall, Inc., Englewood Cliffs, NJ.

2. *Specific, difficult goals may or may not lead to higher performance.* **Goal specificity** pertains to the quantifiability of a goal. For example, a goal of selling nine cars a month is more specific than telling a salesperson to do his or her best. In the Locke review of goal-setting research, 99 of 110 studies (90 percent) found that specific, hard goals led to better performance than did easy, medium, do-your-best, or no goals. This result was confirmed in a meta-analysis of 70 studies conducted between 1966 and 1984, involving 7,407 people.[41]

   In contrast to these positive effects, several recent studies demonstrated that setting specific, difficult goals leads to poorer performance under certain circumstances. For example, a meta-analysis of 125 studies indicated that goal-setting effects were strongest for easy tasks and weakest for complex tasks.[42] There are two explanations for this finding. First, employees are not likely to put forth increased effort to achieve complex goals unless they "buy-in" or support them.[43] Thus, it is important for managers to obtain employee buy-in to the goal-setting process. Second, accomplishing complex goals requires more planning. If employees fail to develop effective goal-attainment action plans, they are less likely to accomplish their desired goals.[44] Managers need to ensure that employees are properly trained to develop action plans.

   Finally, positive effects of goal setting also were reduced when people worked on novel decision-making tasks and interdependent tasks.[45]

3. *Feedback enhances the effect of specific, difficult goals.* Feedback plays a key role in all of our lives. For example, consider the role of feedback in bowling. Imagine going to the bowling lanes only to find that someone had hung a sheet from the ceiling to the floor in front of the pins. How likely is it that you would reach your goal score or typical bowling average? Not likely, given your inability to see the pins. Regardless of your goal, you would have

goal specificity
Quantifiability of a goal.

Feedback is a potent management tool because it taps the
human capacity for learning from
experience.

Frank Herholdt/Tony Stone Images

to guess where to throw your second ball if you did not get a strike on your first shot. The same principles apply at work.

Feedback lets people know if they are headed toward their goals or if they are off course and need to redirect their efforts. Goals plus feedback is the recommended approach.[46] Goals inform people about performance standards and expectations so that they can channel their energies accordingly. In turn, feedback provides the information needed to adjust direction, effort, and strategies for goal accomplishment.

4. *Participative goals, assigned goals, and self-set goals are equally effective.*   Both managers and researchers are interested in identifying the best way to set goals. Should goals be participatively set, assigned, or set by the employee him- or herself? Bob Frees, CEO of Alphatronix Inc., in Research Triangle Park, North Carolina, believes employees should be allowed to set their own goals. "We let employees tell us when they can accomplish a project and what resources they need," he says. "Virtually always, they set higher goals than we would ever set for them."[47] Contrary to Mr. Frees's experience, a recent summary of goal-setting research indicates that no single approach was consistently more effective than others in increasing performance.[48]

Managers are advised to use a contingency approach by picking a method that seems best suited for the individual and situation at hand. For example, employees' preferences for participation should be considered. Some employees desire to participate in the process of setting goals, whereas others do not. Employees are also more likely to respond positively to the opportunity to participate in goal setting when they have greater task information, higher levels of experience and training, and greater levels of task involvement.[49] Finally, a participative approach helps reduce employees' resistance to goal setting.

5. *Goal commitment and monetary incentives affect goal-setting outcomes.*
Goal commitment is the extent to which an individual is personally committed to achieving a goal. In general, an individual is expected to persist in attempts to accomplish a goal when he or she is committed to it. Researchers are currently debating the process by which goal commitment affects performance.[50] Some contend that goal commitment moderates the relationship between the difficulty of a goal and performance. That is,

goal commitment   Amount of commitment to achieving a goal.

difficult goals lead to higher performance only when employees are committed to their goals. Conversely, difficult goals lead to lower performance when people are not committed to their goals. Other researchers contend that goal commitment directly affects performance. Although evidence can be presented to support both positions, recent research supports the prediction that goal commitment moderates the relationship between goal level and performance.[51] A recent meta-analysis of 78 studies covering 17,607 people also demonstrated that goal commitment did not directly influence performance.[52]

Like goal setting, the use of monetary incentives to motivate employees is seldom questioned. Unfortunately, recent research uncovered some negative consequences when goal achievement is linked to individual incentives. Case studies, for example, reveal that pay should not be linked to goal achievement unless (*a*) performance goals are under the employees' control; (*b*) goals are quantitative and measurable; and (*c*) frequent, relatively large payments are made for performance achievement.[53] Goal-based incentive systems are more likely to produce undesirable effects if these three conditions are not satisfied.

Moreover, recent empirical studies demonstrated that goal-based bonus incentives produced higher commitment to easy goals and lower commitment to difficult goals. People were reluctant to commit to difficult goals that were tied to monetary incentives. People with high goal commitment also offered less help to their co-workers when they received goal-based bonus incentives to accomplish difficult individual goals. Individuals neglected aspects of the job that were not covered in the performance goals.[54] As another case in point, several studies revealed that quality suffered when employees were given quantity goals.[55]

These findings underscore some of the dangers of using goal-based incentives, particularly for employees in complex, interdependent jobs requiring cooperation. Managers need to consider the advantages, disadvantages, and dilemmas of goal-based incentives prior to implementation. These issues are more thoroughly discussed in Chapter 14.

Practical Application of Goal Setting

There are three general steps to follow when implementing a goal-setting program (see Figure 7–5). Serious deficiencies in one step cannot make up for strength in the other two. The three steps need to be implemented in a systematic fashion.

Step 1: Goal Setting A number of sources can be used as input during this goal-setting stage.[56] Time and motion studies are one source. Goals also may be based on the average past performance of job holders. Third, the employee and his or her manager may set the goal participatively, through give-and-take negotiation. Fourth, goal setting often is constrained by external factors. For example, the production schedule of a firm with a government contract may be dictated largely by the terms of that agreement. Finally, the overall strategy of a company (e.g., become the lowest-cost producer) may affect the goals set by employees at various levels in the organization.

In accordance with available research evidence, goals should be specific and difficult, yet attainable through persistent effort. For complex tasks however,

— • FIGURE 7~5

Three Key Steps in
Implementing a Goal-Setting
Program

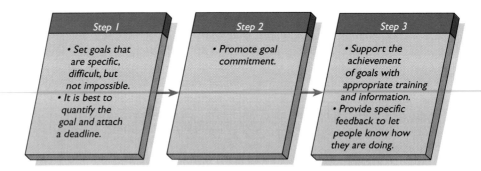

Step 1	Step 2	Step 3
• Set goals that are specific, difficult, but not impossible. • It is best to quantify the goal and attach a deadline.	• Promote goal commitment.	• Support the achievement of goals with appropriate training and information. • Provide specific feedback to let people know how they are doing.

managers should set slightly less difficult goals because difficult goals lead to lower performance than do easier goals. Specificity can be achieved by stating goals in quantitative terms (e.g., units of output, dollars, or percent of desired increase or decrease). With respect to measuring performance, it is important to achieve a workable balance between quantity and quality. Well-conceived goals also have a built-in time limit or deadline. Priorities need to be established in multiple-goal situations.

Finally, because of individual differences in skills and abilities, it may be necessary to establish different goals for employees performing the same job. For example, a recent study of 91 sales representatives revealed that individuals high in conscientiousness set more difficult goals, were more committed to goals, and achieved greater sales volume than employees low in conscientiousness. A second study demonstrated that more difficult goals were set by individuals with high rather than low task abilities.[57] If an employee has low conscientiousness or lacks the ability to perform the job, then progressively harder developmental goals may be in order. But this practice may create feelings of inequity among co-workers, necessitating other alternatives. For example, inability to perform at the standard may suggest a training deficiency or the need to transfer the individual to another job. In any event, managers need to keep in mind that motivation diminishes when people continually fail to meet their goals.

Step 2: Goal Commitment   Obtaining goal commitment is important because employees are more motivated to pursue goals they view as reasonable, obtainable, and fair. Goal commitment may be increased by using one or more of the following techniques:

1. Provide an explanation for why the organization is implementing a goal-setting program.
2. Present the corporate goals, and explain how and why an individual's personal goals support them.
3. Have employees establish their own goals and action plans. Encourage them to set challenging, stretch goals. Goals should not be impossible.
4. Train managers in how to conduct participative goal-setting sessions, and train employees in how to develop effective action plans.
5. Be supportive, and do not use goals to threaten employees.
6. Set goals that are under the employees' control, and provide them with the necessary resources.
7. Provide monetary incentives or other rewards for accomplishing goals.

Tough challenge + skills + goal commitment = success. These tired and happy climbers put it all together.

Gilles Guittard/The Image Bank

Step 3: Support and Feedback   Step 3 calls for providing employees with the necessary support elements or resources to get the job done. This includes ensuring that each employee has the necessary abilities and information to reach his or her goals. As a pair of goal-setting experts succinctly stated: ''Motivation without knowledge is useless.''[58] Training often is required to help employees achieve difficult goals. Moreover, managers should pay attention to employees' perceptions of effort→performance expectancies, self-efficacy, and valence of rewards. A recent study demonstrated that all three of these cognitions significantly affected employees' performance on multiple goals.[59] Finally, as discussed in detail in Chapter 14, employees should be provided with timely, specific feedback (knowledge of results) on how they are doing.

Successfully designing and implementing motivational programs is not easy. Managers cannot simply take one of the theories discussed in this book and apply it word for word. Dynamics within organizations interfere with applying motivation theories in ''pure'' form. According to management scholar Terence Mitchell:

PUTTING MOTIVATIONAL THEORIES TO WORK

There are situations and settings that make it exceptionally difficult for a motivational system to work. These circumstances may involve the kinds of jobs or people present, the technology, the presence of a union, and so on. The factors that hinder the application of motivational theory have not been articulated either frequently or systematically.[60]

With Mitchell's cautionary statement in mind, this section uses the conceptual model of motivation introduced in Chapter 6, which is shown once again in Figure 7–6, to raise issues that need to be addressed before implementing a motivational program. Our intent here is not to discuss all relevant considerations, but rather to highlight a few important ones.

Assuming a motivational program is being considered to improve productivity, the first issue revolves around the difference between motivation and performance. As pointed out in Chapter 6, motivation and performance are not one and the same. Motivation is only one of several factors that influence performance. For example, poor performance may be more a function of a lack of ability, poor supervisory support and coaching, not having goals to direct one's efforts, or a variety of job and work environment characteristics. Job characteristics, discussed in Chapter 6 (autonomy and responsibility), work environment characteristics (teamwork and conflict), organizational characteristics (reward systems and organizational structure), and external environmental characteristics (technological advances and economic cycles) similarly affect job performance. Motivation cannot make up for deficient individual characteristics or negative supervisory and job/work environment characteristics. Managers, therefore, need to gauge the degree to which motivation significantly affects performance.

• **FIGURE 7–6**   A Job Performance Motivation System, Revisited

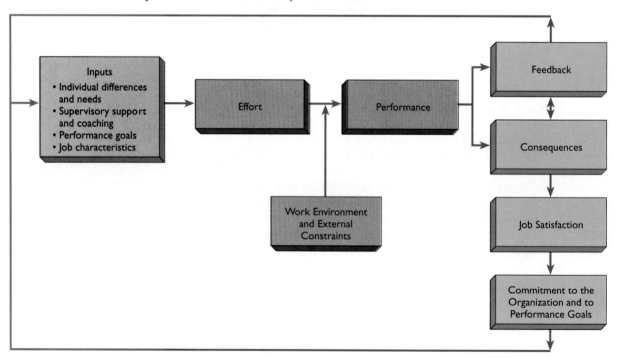

Importantly, managers should not ignore the individual differences discussed in Chapter 4. Figure 7–6 clearly indicates that individual differences and needs influence performance. Therefore, managers should develop and nurture positive employee characteristics, such as self-esteem, self-efficacy, and need for achievement.

Because motivation is goal directed, the process of developing and setting goals should be consistent with our previous discussion. Moreover, the method used to evaluate performance also needs to be considered. Without a valid performance appraisal system, it is difficult, if not impossible, to accurately distinguish good and poor performers. Managers need to keep in mind that both equity and expectancy theory suggest that employee motivation is squelched by inaccurate performance ratings. Inaccurate ratings also make it difficult to evaluate the effectiveness of any motivational program, so it is beneficial for managers to assess the accuracy and validity of their appraisal systems.

Consistent with expectancy theory and the principles of behavior modification discussed in Chapter 8, managers should make rewards contingent on performance. In doing so, it is important that managers consider the accuracy and fairness of the reward system. As discussed under expectancy theory, the promise of increased rewards will not prompt higher effort and good performance unless those rewards clearly are tied to performance. Moreover, equity theory tells us that motivation is influenced by employee perceptions about the fairness of reward allocations. Motivation is decreased when employees believe rewards are inequitably allocated. Rewards also need to be integrated appropriately into the appraisal system. If performance is measured at the individual level, individual achievements need to be rewarded. On the other hand, when performance is the result of group effort, rewards should be allocated to the group.

Figure 7–6 indicates that feedback also should be linked with performance. Feedback provides the information and direction needed to keep employees focused on relevant tasks, activities, and goals. Managers should strive to provide specific, timely, and accurate feedback to employees. Chapter 14 provides a thorough discussion of feedback.

Finally, managers need to use a contingency approach when developing motivational programs. Recalling our discussion in Chapter 6, theories of motivation selectively explain various organizational outcomes (see Figure 6–2). Managers need to use motivation techniques that are best suited to the individuals and situation at hand.

BACK TO THE OPENING CASE

Now that you have read Chapter 7, you should be able to answer the following questions about the Cypress case:

1. Does Cypress treat its employees equitably?
2. To what extent is Cypress's management system consistent with expectancy theory?
3. How does Cypress use goal setting to motivate employees?
4. Which of the five insights from goal-setting research is Cypress following?

SUMMARY OF KEY CONCEPTS

1. *Discuss the role of perceived inequity in employee motivation.* Equity theory is a model of motivation that explains how people strive for fairness and justice in social exchanges. On the job, feelings of inequity revolve around a person's evaluation of whether he or she receives adequate rewards to compensate for his or her contributive inputs. People perform these evaluations by comparing the perceived fairness of their employment exchange with that of relevant others. Perceived inequity creates motivation to restore equity.

2. *Distinguish between positive and negative inequity.* Equity exists for an individual when his or her ratio of perceived outcomes to inputs is equal to the ratio of outcomes to inputs for a relevant co-worker. If the comparison co-worker enjoys greater outcomes for similar inputs, negative inequity will be perceived. Positive inequity is experienced when an individual's outcome to input ratio is greater than that of a relevant co-worker. People have a lower tolerance for negative inequity than they do for positive inequity.

3. *Explain Vroom's expectancy theory.* Expectancy theory assumes motivation is determined by one's perceived chances of achieving valued outcomes. Vroom's expectancy model of motivation reveals how effort→performance expectancies and performance→outcome instrumentalities influence the degree of effort expended to achieve desired (positively valent) outcomes.

4. *Discuss Porter and Lawler's expectancy theory of motivation.* Porter and Lawler developed a model of expectancy that expanded upon the theory proposed by Vroom. This model specifies (1) the source of people's valences and expectancies and (2) the relationship between performance and satisfaction.

5. *Describe the practical implications of expectancy theory of motivation.* Managers are advised to enhance effort→performance expectancies by helping employees accomplish their performance goals. With respect to instrumentalities and valences, managers should attempt to link employee performance and valued rewards. There are four prerequisites to linking performance and rewards: (1) managers need to develop and communicate performance standards to employees, (2) managers need valid and accurate performance ratings, (3) performance ratings should be used to differentially allocate rewards among employees, and (4) managers need to offer rewards valued by employees.

6. *Explain how goal setting motivates an individual.* Four motivational mechanisms of goal setting are: (1) goals direct one's attention, (2) goals regulate effort, (3) goals increase one's persistence, and (4) goals encourage development of goal-attainment strategies and action plans.

7. *Identify five practical lessons to be learned from goal-setting research.* Difficult goals lead to higher performance than easy or moderate goals: goals should not be impossible to achieve. Second, specific, difficult goals may or may not lead to higher performance. Third, feedback enhances the effect of specific, difficult goals. Fourth, participative goals, assigned goals, and self-set goals are equally effective. Fifth, goal commitment and monetary incentives affect goal-setting outcomes.

8. *Specify issues that should be addressed before implementing a motivational program.* When implementing a motivational program, managers should consider the key determinants of performance, the desired goals to be achieved, and the validity of the performance appraisal system. Also requiring careful consideration are the performance-reward linkages, the equity of rewards allocated, and the adequacy of feedback. Managers should use motivation techniques that are best suited to the individuals and situation at hand.

DISCUSSION QUESTIONS

1. Have you experienced positive or negative inequity at work? Describe the circumstances in terms of the inputs and outcomes of the comparison person and yourself.

2. Could a manager's attempt to treat his or her employees equally lead to perceptions of inequity? Explain.

3. What work outcomes (refer to Table 7–1) are most

important to you? Do you think different age groups value different outcomes? What are the implications for managers who seek to be equitable?

4. Relative to Table 7–2, what techniques have you relied on recently to reduce either positive or negative inequity?

5. What is your definition of studying hard? What is your expectancy for earning an A on the next exam in this course? What is the basis of this expectancy?

6. If someone who reported to you at work had a low expectancy for successful performance, what could you do to increase this person's expectancy?

7. Do goals play an important role in your life? Explain.

8. How would you respond to a manager who said, "Goals must be participatively set."

9. Goal-setting research suggests that people should be given difficult goals. How does this prescription mesh with expectancy theory? Explain.

10. How could a professor use equity, expectancy, and goal-setting theory to motivate students?

EXERCISE

Objectives

1. To determine how accurately you perceive the outcomes that motivate nonmanagerial employees.

2. To examine the managerial implications of inaccurately assessing employee motivators.

Introduction

One thousand employees were given a list of 10 outcomes people want from their work. They were asked to rank these items from most important to least important.[61] We are going to have you estimate how you think these workers ranked the various outcomes. This will enable you to compare your perceptions with the average rankings documented by a researcher. Since the results are presented at the end of this exercise, please do not read them until indicated.

Instructions

Below is a list of 10 outcomes people want from their work. Read the list, and then rank each item according to how you think the typical nonmanagerial employee would rank them. Rank the outcomes from 1 to 10; 1 = Most important and 10 = Least important. (Please do this now before reading the rest of these instructions.) After you have completed your ranking, calculate the discrepancy between your perceptions and the actual results. Take the absolute value of the difference between your ranking and the actual ranking for each item, and then add them to get a total discrepancy score. For example, if you gave job security a ranking of 1, your discrepancy score would be 3 because the actual ranking was 4. The lower your discrepancy score, the more accurate your perception of the typical employee's needs. The actual rankings are shown below under the heading *Survey Results*.

How do you believe the typical nonmanagerial employee would rank these outcomes?

———— Full appreciation of work done
———— Job security
———— Good working conditions
———— Feeling of being in on things
———— Good wages
———— Tactful discipline
———— Personal loyalty to employees
———— Interesting work
———— Sympathetic help with personal problems
———— Promotion and growth in the organization

Questions for Consideration/Class Discussion

1. Were your perceptions accurate? Why or why not?

2. What would expectancy theory suggest you should do?

3. Based on the size of your discrepancy, what does the job performance motivation system in Figure 7–6 suggest will happen to satisfaction and commitment?

4. Would you generalize the actual survey results to all nonmanagerial employees? Why or why not?

Survey Results—Employee Ranking

1. Interesting work
2. Full appreciation of work done
3. Feeling of being in on things
4. Job security
5. Good wages
6. Promotion and growth in the organization
7. Good working conditions
8. Personal loyalty to employees
9. Tactful discipline
10. Sympathetic help with personal problems

NOTES

1. See L Festinger, *A Theory of Cognitive Dissonance* (Stanford, CA: Stanford University Press, 1957).

2. H F Bensimon, "Violence in the Work Place," *Training & Development,* January 1994, p 28.

3. The generalizability of the equity norm was examined by K I Kim, H-J Park, and N Suzuki, "Reward Allocations in the United States, Japan, and Korea: A Comparison of Individualistic and Collectivistic Cultures," *Academy of Management Journal,* March 1990, pp 188–98.

4. R P Vecchio, "Models of Psychological Inequity, *Organizational Behavior and Human Performance,* October 1984, p 268. (Emphasis added.)

5. The choice of a comparison person is discussed by J Greenberg and C L McCarty, "Comparable Worth: A Matter of Justice," in *Research in Personnel and Human Resources Management,* eds G R Ferris and K M Rowland (Greenwich, CT: JAI Press, Inc., 1990), vol. 8, pp 265–303; and J V Wood, "Theory and Research Concerning Social Comparisons of Personal Attributes," *Psychological Bulletin,* September 1989, pp 231–48.

6. See L A Witt and L G Nye, "Gender and the Relationship between Perceived Fairness of Pay or Promotion and Job Satisfaction," *Journal of Applied Psychology,* December 1992, pp 910–17.

7. Adapted from a discussion in R L Opsahl and M D Dunnette, "The Role of Financial Compensation in Industrial Motivation," *Psychological Bulletin,* August 1966, pp 94–118.

8. Results can be found in R W Griffeth, R P Vecchio, and J W Logan, Jr., "Equity Theory and Interpersonal Attraction," *Journal of Applied Psychology,* June 1989, pp 394–401; and R P Vecchio, "Predicting Worker Performance in Inequitable Settings," *Academy of Management Review,* January 1982, pp 103–10.

9. See J Greenberg, "Stealing in the Name of Justice: Informational and Interpersonal Moderators of Theft Reactions to Underpayment Inequity," *Organizational Behavior and Human Decision Processes,* February 1993, pp 81–103.

10. Results can be found in R D Bretz, Jr., and S L Thomas, "Perceived Equity, Motivation, and Final-Offer Arbitration in Major League Baseball," *Journal of Applied Psychology,* June 1992, pp 280–87; and D M Cowherd and D I Levine, "Product Quality and Pay Equity between Lower-Level Employees and Top Management: An Investigation of Distributive Justice Theory," *Administrative Science Quarterly,* June 1992, pp 302–20.

11. Supporting studies were conducted by P D Sweeney and D B McFarlin, "Workers' Evaluations of the "Ends" and the "Means": An Examination of Four Models of Distributive and Procedural Justice," *Organizational Behavior and Human Decision Processes,* June 1993, pp 23–40; and J Schwarzwald, M Koslowsky, and B Shalit, "A Field Study of Employees' Attitudes and Behaviors After Promotion Decisions," *Journal of Applied Psychology,* August 1992, pp 511–14.

12. See Sweeney and McFarlin, "Workers' Evaluations of the "Ends" and the "Means": An Examination of Four Models of Distributive and Procedural Justice;" R C Dailey and D J Kirk, "Distributive and Procedural Justice as Antecedents of Job Dissatisfaction and Intent to Turnover," *Human Relations,* March 1992, pp 305–18; and D B McFarlin and P D Sweeney, "Distributive and Procedural Justice As Predictors of Satisfaction with Personal and Organizational Outcomes," *Academy of Management Journal,* August 1992, pp 626–37.

13. L A Winokur, "Sweet Revenge Is Souring the Office."

14. See F E Saal and S C Moore, "Perceptions of Promotion Fairness and Promotion Candidates' Qualifications," *Journal of Applied Psychology,* February 1993, pp 105–10.

15. Managerial techniques for promoting perceptions of fairness are discussed by J Greenberg, "Using Socially Fair Treatment to Promote Acceptance of a Work Site Smoking Ban," *Journal of Applied Psychology,* April 1994, pp 288–97; and J Greenberg, "Looking Fair vs. Being Fair: Managing Impressions of Organizational Justice," in *Research in Organizational Behavior,* eds B M Staw and L L Cummings (Greenwich, CT: JAI Press, Inc., 1990), vol. 12, pp 111–58.

16. Results from these studies can be found in W C Kim and R A Mauborgne, "Procedural Justice, Attitudes, and Subsidiary Top Management Compliance with Multinationals' Corporate Strategic Decisions," *Academy of Management Journal,* June 1993, pp 502–26; and G W Florkowski and M H Schuster, "Support for Profit Sharing and Organizational Commitment: A Path Analysis," *Human Relations,* May 1992, pp 507–24.

17. A study of equity in a group setting was conducted by

E van Dijk and H Wilke, "Differential Interest, Equity, and Public Good Provision," *Journal of Experimental Social Psychology,* January 1993, pp 1–16.

18 For a complete discussion of Vroom's theory, see V H Vroom, *Work and Motivation* (New York: John Wiley & Sons, 1964).

19 E E Lawler III, *Motivation in Work Organizations* (Belmont, CA: Wadsworth, 1973), p 45.

20 See J Chowdhury, "The Motivational Impact of Sales Quotas on Effort," *Journal of Marketing Research,* February 1993, pp 28–41; and C C Pinder, *Work Motivation* (Glenview, IL: Scott, Foresman, 1984), chapter 7.

21 Examples of companies that link pay to performance are presented in T Ehrenfeld, "Cashing In," *Inc.,* July 1993, pp 69–70.

22 For a discussion of the definition and measurement of valence, see A Pecotich and G A Churchill, Jr., "An Examination of the Anticipated-Satisfaction Importance Valence Controversy," *Organizational Behavior and Human Performance,* April 1981, pp 213–26.

23 Excerpted from "Federal Express's Fred Smith," *Inc.,* October 1986, p 38.

24 For a thorough discussion of the model, see L W Porter and E E Lawler III, *Managerial Attitudes and Performance* (Homewood, IL: Richard D. Irwin, 1968).

25 The relationship between ability and performance was examined by W M Coward and P R Sackett, "Linearity of Ability–Performance Relationships: A Reconfirmation," *Journal of Applied Psychology,* June 1990, pp 297–300.

26 These results are based on the following studies: J P Wanous, T L Keon, and J C Latack, "Expectancy Theory and Occupational/Organizational Choices: A Review and Test," *Organizational Behavior and Human Performance,* August 1983, pp 66–86; E D Pulakos and N Schmitt, "A Longitudinal Study of a Valence Model Approach for the Prediction of Job Satisfaction of New Employees," *Journal of Applied Psychology,* May 1983, p 307–12; A J Kinicki, "Predicting Occupational Role Choices for Involuntary Job Loss," *Journal of Vocational Behavior,* October 1989, pp 204–18; T A DeCotiis and J-Y LeLouarn, "A Predictive Study of Voting Behavior in a Representation Election Using Union Instrumentality and Work Perceptions," *Organizational Behavior and Human Performance,* February 1981, pp 103–18; P W Hom, "Expectancy Prediction of Reenlistment in the National Guard," *Journal of Vocational Behavior,* April 1980, pp 235–48; D F Parker and L Dyer, "Expectancy Theory as a Within-Person Behavioral Choice Model: An Empirical Test of Some Conceptual and Methodological Refinements," *Organizational Behavior and Human Performance,* October 1976, pp 97–117; and A W Stacy, K F Widaman, and G A Marlatt, "Expectancy Models of Alcohol Use," *Journal of Personality and Social Psychology,* May 1990, pp 918–28.

27 For reviews of the criticisms of expectancy theory, see F J Landy and W S Becker, "Motivation Theory Reconsidered," in *Research in Organizational Behavior,* vol. 9, eds L L Cummings and B M Staw (Greenwich, CT: JAI Press, 1987), pp 1–38; and T R Mitchell, "Expectancy Models of Job Satisfaction, Occupational Preference and Effort: A Theoretical, Methodological, and Empirical Appraisal," *Psychological Bulletin,* December 1974, pp 1053–77.

28 Details of this study can be found in E E Lawler III, S Albers Mohrman, and G E Ledford, Jr., *Employee Involvement and Total Quality Management: Practices and Results in Fortune 1000 Companies* (San Francisco: Jossey-Bass 1992).

29 P Ancona, "Nice Bosses Often Don't Get Quality They Want," *The Arizona Daily Star,* February 8, 1993, p 9.

30 The relationship between performance appraisal systems and organizational pay is thoroughly discussed by G T Milkovich and A K Wigdor, *Pay for Performance: Evaluating Performance Appraisal and Merit Pay* (Washington, DC: National Academy Press, 1991).

31 E A Locke, K N Shaw, L M Saari, and G P Latham, "Goal Setting and Task Performance: 1969–1980," *Psychological Bulletin,* July 1981, p 126.

32 Ibid.

33 A thorough discussion of MBO is provided by P F Drucker, *The Practice of Management* (New York: Harper, 1954); and P F Drucker, "What Results Should You Expect? A User's Guide to MBO," *Public Administration Review,* January/February 1976, pp 12–19.

34 Results from both studies can be found in R Rodgers and J E Hunter, "Impact of Management by Objectives on Organizational Productivity," *Journal of Applied Psychology,* April 1991, pp 322–36; and R Rodgers, J E Hunter, and D L Rogers, "Influence of Top Management Commitment on Management Program Success," *Journal of Applied Psychology,* February 1993, pp 151–55.

35 A complete review of goal-setting theory and research is presented by E A Locke and G P Latham, *A Theory of Goal Setting & Task Performance* (Englewood Cliffs, NJ: Prentice-Hall, 1990).

36 A summary of this research may be found in R Cropanzano, K James, and M Citera, "A Goal Hierarchy Model of Personality, Motivation, and Leadership," in *Research in Organizational Behavior,* vol. 15, eds L L Cummings and B M Staw (Greenwich, CT: JAI Press, 1993), pp 267–322.

37 B Dumaine, "The New Non-Manager Managers," *Fortune,* February 22, 1993, p 81.

38 See Locke and Latham, *A Theory of Goal Setting & Task Performance.*

39 Drawn from Locke, Shaw, Saari, and Latham, "Goal Setting and Task Performance: 1969–1980." Supportive results from a more recent study can be found in I R Gellatly and J P Meyer, "The Effects of Goal Difficulty on Physiological Arousal, Cognition, and Task Performance," *Journal of Applied Psychology,* October 1992, pp 694–704.

40 Dumaine, "The New Non-Manager Managers," p 84.

41 See Locke, Shaw, Saari, and Latham, "Goal Setting and Task Performance: 1969–1980"; and A J Mento, R P Steel, and R J Karren, "A Meta-Analytic Study of the Effects of Goal Setting on Task Performance: 1966–1984," *Organizational Behavior and Human Decision Processes,* February 1987, pp 52–83.

42 Results from the meta-analysis can be found in R E Wood, A J Mento, and E A Locke, "Task Complexity as a Moderator of Goal Effects: A Meta-Analysis," *Journal of Applied Psychology,* August 1987, pp 416–25.

43 See E L Deci, "On the Nature and Functions of Motivation Theories," *Psychological Science,* May 1992, pp 167–71.

44 See results contained in S W Gilliland and R S Landis, "Quality and Quantity Goals in a Complex Decision Task: Strategies and Outcomes," *Journal of Applied Psychology,* October 1992, pp 672–81; and L R Weingart, "Impact of Group Goals, Task Component Complexity, Effort, and Planning on Group Performance," *Journal of Applied Psychology,* October 1992, pp 682–93.

45 See studies conducted by T R Mitchell and W S Silver, "Individual and Group Goals when Workers Are Interdependent: Effects on Task Strategies and Performance," *Journal of Applied Psychology,* April 1990, pp 185–93; and B M Staw and R D Boettger, "Task Revision: A Neglected Form of Work Performance," *Academy of Management Journal,* September 1990, pp 534–59.

46 The positive effects of feedback are supported by M E Tubbs, D M Boehne, and J G Dahl, "Expectancy Valence, and Motivational Force Functions in Goal-Setting Research: An Empirical Test," *Journal of Applied Psychology,* June 1993, pp 361–73; and Mento, Steel, and Karren, "A Meta-Analytic Study of the Effects of Goal Setting on Task Performance: 1966–1984."

47 J Finegan, "People Power: More and More Companies Are Realizing That Employees Know Things That Bosses Simply Can't. The Best Businesses Are Capitalizing On It," *Inc.,* July 1993, p 63.

48 See Locke and Latham, *A Theory of Goal Setting & Task Performance.*

49 The relationship between goal-setting mode and performance is discussed by J C Wofford, V L Goodwin, and S Premack, "Meta-Analysis of the Antecedents of Personal Goal Level and of the Antecedents and Consequences of Goal Commitment," *Journal of Management,* September 1992, pp 595–615.

50 For a thorough discussion of this debate, see M E Tubbs, "Commitment as a Moderator of the Goal-Performance Relation: A Case for Clearer Construct Definition," *Journal of Applied Psychology,* February 1993, pp 86–97. Also see D A Harrison and L Z Liska, "Promoting Regular Exercise in Organizational Fitness Programs: Health-Related Differences in Motivational Building Blocks," *Personnel Psychology,* Spring 1994, pp 47–72.

51 See Tubbs, "Commitment as a Moderator of the Goal-Performance Relation: A Case for Clearer Construct Definition."

52 Results are presented in Wofford, Goodwin, and Premack, "Meta-Analysis of the Antecedents of Personal Goal Level and of the Antecedents and Consequences of Goal Commitment."

53 These conclusions were derived from Milkovich and Wigdor, *Pay for Performance: Evaluating Performance Appraisal and Merit Pay.*

54 See P M Wright, J M George, S R Farnsworth, and G C McMahan, "Productivity and Extra-Role Behavior: The Effects of Goals and Incentives on Spontaneous Helping," *Journal of Applied Psychology,* June 1993, pp 374–81; and P M Wright, "An Examination of the Relationships among Monetary Incentives, Goal Level, Goal Commitment, and Performance," *Journal of Management,* December 1992, pp 677–93.

55 Supporting results can be found in Gilliland and Landis, "Quality and Quantity Goals in a Complex Decision Task: Strategies and Outcomes;" and J Bavelas and E Lee, "Effects of Goal Level on Performance: A Trade-Off of Quantity and Quality," *Canadian Journal of Psychology,* December 1978, pp 219–39.

56 These recommendations are taken from G P Latham and E A Locke, "Goal Setting—A Motivational Tech-

nique That Works!'' *Organizational Dynamics,* Autumn 1979, pp 68–80.

57 The relationship between conscientiousness and goal setting was examined by M R Barrick, M K Mount, and J P Strauss, ''Conscientiousness and Performance of Sales Representatives: Test of the Mediating Effects of Goal Setting,'' *Journal of Applied Psychology,* October 1993, pp 715–22. Ability and goal difficulty was investigated by R J Vance and A Colella, ''Effects of Two Types of Feedback on Goal Acceptance and Personal Goals,'' *Journal of Applied Psychology,* February 1990, pp 68–76.

58 These recommendations are adapted from E A Locke and G P Latham, *Goal Setting: A Motivational Tech-*

nique That Works! (Englewood Cliffs, NJ: Prentice-Hall, 1984), p 79.

59 Results are shown in A J Mento, E A Locke, and H J Klein, ''Relationship of Goal Level to Valence and Instrumentality,'' *Journal of Applied Psychology,* August 1992, pp 395–405.

60 T R Mitchell ''Motivation: New Directions for Theory, Research, and Practice,'' *Academy of Management Review,* January 1982, p 81.

61 Results from this study are reported in K A Kovach, ''What Motivates Employees? Workers and Supervisors Give Different Answers,'' *Business Horizons,* September–October 1987, pp 58–65.

BEHAVIOR MODIFICATION AND SELF-MANAGEMENT

Learning OBJECTIVES

When you finish studying the material in this chapter, you should be able to:

1. State Thorndike's "law of effect" and explain Skinner's distinction between respondent and operant behavior.

2. Define the term *behavior modification* and explain the A→B→C model.

3. Demonstrate your knowledge of positive reinforcement, negative reinforcement, punishment, and extinction.

4. Distinguish between continuous and intermittent schedules of reinforcement and specify which schedules are most resistant to extinction.

5. Demonstrate your knowledge of behavior shaping.

6. Identify and briefly explain each step in the four-step B Mod process.

7. Specify the six guidelines for managing consequences during B Mod.

8. Explain the social learning model of self-management.

OPENING CASE

Triad's Culture of Success

Sharon Hoogstraten

*F*our or five of us were lounging around the lobby of the Doubletree Resort Hotel located on the Monterey, Calif., peninsula. Every employee working the registration desk wore a three-inch diameter white button that said "Welcome Triad."

Triad Systems Corp. is a 20-year-old, $150 million in sales, computer hardware and software company based in Livermore, Calif. It serves about 12,000 customers primarily in the automotive aftermarket and the retail hardgoods industry (Triad's customers are retail operations that sell

automobile parts or general hardware store merchandise.)

All in our group, except me, were Triad's customer service representatives or field engineers, most of them 10 to 20 years my junior. They were there to participate in technical training and attend Triad's trade show and awards banquet. I was there conducting training workshops for the management team.

At the moment, Joe was on center stage. "Yeah, he got so many awards I couldn't get any sleep. Every few minutes there was someone pounding on the door delivering something else to him," said one of the service reps.

In an attempt to shorten the awards banquet—which had run for about four hours the night before—Triad had decided to distribute much of the $40,000 in cash, plaques, and other mementos to the rooms after the main ceremony. Ralph Montelius, vice president for customer services, had told me the change was necessary, because they had so much achievement to recognize that the distribution

of each individual prize was taking too much time.

"How many awards did you get, Joe?" I asked.

"Not sure, seven, maybe nine." He grew just a bit taller.

And then someone else joined in, "You know, I didn't even know I was in the running for tops-in-sales for surge suppressors."

Triad was building folklore. . . .

That night, about 600 Triad employees and their guests came to the banquet along with Triad's senior management. Like Joe, many people didn't get much sleep after the banquet because of all the door pounding at the Doubletree.

Rewards and Then Some

There were lots of awards.

There were the expected awards for tenure with the company, but there was also the Ralph C Montelius Award for Personal Development given to anyone who completed a college degree. It was named after Mon-

*I*magine you are the general manager of the public transportation authority in a large city, and one of your main duties is overseeing the city's bus system. During the past several years, you have noted with growing concern the increasing number and severity of bus accidents. In the face of mounting public and administrative pressure, it is clear that a workable accident-prevention program must be enacted. Large pay raises for the bus drivers and other expensive options are impossible because of a tight city budget. Based on what you have read about motivation, what remedial action do you propose? (Please take a moment now to jot down some ideas.)

Since these facts have been drawn from a real-life field study, we can see what happened.[1] Management tried to curb the accident rate with some typical programs, including yearly safety awards, stiffer enforcement of a disciplinary code, complimentary coffee and doughnuts for drivers who had a day without an accident, and a comprehensive training program. Despite these remedial actions, the accident rate kept climbing. Finally, management agreed to a behavior modification experiment that directly attacked unsafe driver behavior.

(continued)

telius because he earned his master's degree after age 55. And there was the George Anderson Memorial Award, named after one of Triad's first hard-goods customers. Triad liked Anderson's dedication to his customers, so they named an award for him.

The Jan Gay Award for Valor, a rare award, was presented this year. Triad doesn't like to give out this award—and really, given a choice, no one wants to be in the competition for it.

The Jan Gay Award is presented only to those employees who display exceptional courage in the face of personal adversity. Jan Gay, wife of one company founder, suffers from multiple sclerosis. Even wheelchair-bound, she still travels widely and participates fully. Her dignity has worked its way into Triad folklore. She never lets the disease stop her from living a quality life. When in town and health permitting, she presents the award herself.

There were other awards—Outstanding Achievement, Special Recognition, and President's Club. All the service people were in technical classes during the conference and

were tested on the training they received. High scores meant more awards.

Of course, awards as part of Triad's "We Care" and "Instant Recognition" programs can be given at any time. And there are other awards: The Quality Award for the quarter, the Service Award for the quarter, Customer Support Representative for the quarter, and so on.

Not all recognition is award-based. President and Chief Executive Officer James R Porter finds time to invite new hires over to his home for dinner. Montelius and other senior executives find time to do the same.

Groups within the customer service division have their own award programs, and many of these awards aren't even mentioned at the annual banquet. For example, the Learning Products Group gives away 13 or so awards, which include the Nose to the Grindstone Award for "individuals who most consistently demonstrate initiative, focus, dedication, and persistence"; the Innovator Award to "those who conceive and carry out innovative ideas"; and one I especially like, the

Bustin' the Boundaries Award, given to "those who work most effectively across departmental and divisional boundaries to accomplish their work."

Building Folklore

With lots of training, a big show, and an abundance of awards, Triad works hard to build folklore, culture, and community. How many awards in total does Triad give away annually, company-wide? "Perhaps more than 700, give or take a 100," according to Montelius. Triad has fewer than 1,500 employees.

The award criteria, more substance than style, suggest that the award program has evolved over time—16 years, according to Montelius.

The criteria could have been developed by B F Skinner himself. The award criteria documents are filled with words like "for employees who receive a recognition letter or note from another employee" and "for employees who receive a letter from a customer acknowledging significantly high levels of performance."

Employees are involved in the

One hundred of the city's 425 drivers were randomly divided into four experimental teams of 25 each. The remaining drivers served as a control group. During an 18-week period, the drivers received daily feedback on their safety performance on a chart posted in their lunchroom. An accident-free day was noted on the chart with a green dot, while a driver involved in an accident found a red dot posted next to his or her name. At two-week intervals, members of the team with the best competitive safety record received their choice of incentives averaging $5 in value (e.g., cash, free gas, free bus passes). Teams that went an entire two-week period without an accident received double incentives.

Unlike previous interventions, the behavior modification program reduced the accident rate. Compared with the control group, the experimental group recorded a 25 percent lower accident rate. During an 18-week period following termination of

(concluded)

overall program too, because there are plenty of words like, "peer vote must consider team player criteria (such as) timeliness, availability for consultation, attitude and professionalism, sharing of information, effectiveness of work habits."

Some award recipients are chosen by committees who base decisions on whether the contribution was essential to Triad's success, involvement of nominee, global impact, significant financial impact, and time devoted.

Resisting Short-Term Thinking

Since Skinner taught the importance of positive reinforcement some 40 years ago, why aren't more companies acting like Triad? Cost justification is one answer.

I understand the concept of "short-term thinking" very well, because I own a few shares in mutual funds, and I put pressure on fund managers for instant returns. Directly or indirectly, so do you, and surely some other managers are putting pressure on Triad's board of directors.

When asked how they got around all the financial justification stuff, both Porter and Montelius used all the right words—"long-term view," "investment in the future," and so forth. But it all comes down to their fundamental view of inspirational leadership; they just do it and withstand the short-term thinking pressure, because they believe that building culture and constructive work teams is what quality leadership is all about. They believe that the recognition, the education, the shows, the hoopla, and all the rest are the best ways to build positive folklore and a productive culture. . . .

Perhaps Skinner and those who followed him did us a disservice when they invented clinical terms such as "operant conditioning" and "behavior modification" to describe their early research on recognition. Who wants to think we are like white mice? Maybe if the behaviorists back then had used terms like "team building" or "positive support system," their work would be more readily accepted today.

For those who might be thinking that guys like Porter and his generals are just building a giant maze for human-form white mice out in Liver-

more, here are two points to consider.

- A couple of years ago, Triad received the first-ever Total Quality Award from the Information Technology Association of America. The award recognizes Triad's achievement in quality results and customer satisfaction.
- Although the computer business [had] been lousy for more than a year, Triad exceeded all of its sales forecasts [during] the heart of the [1991–1992] recession.

For Discussion

Have the managers at Triad gone overboard with their reward system? Explain your rationale.

- Additional discussion questions linking this case with the following material appear at the end of this chapter.

Source: Excerpted from M Ramundo, "Service Awards Build Culture of Success," *HRMagazine*, August 1992, pp 61–62, 66. Copyright held by Michael Ramundo of MCR Marketing, Inc. Cincinnati, Ohio.

the incentive program, the experimental group's accident rate remained a respectable 16 percent better than the control group's. This indicated a positive, long-term effect. Moreover, the program was cost effective. The incentives cost the organization $2,033.18, while it realized a savings of $9,416.25 in accident settlement expenses (a 1 to 4.6 cost/benefit ratio).

Why did this particular program work, while earlier attempts failed? It worked because a specific behavior (safe driving) was modified through *systematic* management of the drivers' work environment. If the posted feedback, team competition, and rewards had been implemented in traditional piecemeal fashion, they probably would have failed to reduce the accident rate. However, when combined in a coordinated and systematic fashion, these common techniques produced favorable results.

This chapter introduces two systematic ways to manage job *behavior:* behavior modification and behavioral self-management. Both areas have a common theoretical heritage, behaviorism.

WHAT IS BEHAVIOR MODIFICATION?

behavior modification Making specific behavior occur more or less often by managing its cues and consequences.

Behavior modification (or B Mod) involves making specific behavior occur more or less often by systematically managing its cues and consequences.[2] On-the-job behavior modification has been alternatively labeled *organizational behavior modification* (OB Mod), *organizational behavior management,* and *performance management.* The generic term *behavior modification* is used here to avoid unnecessary confusion. B Mod traces back to the work of two pioneering psychologists, E L Thorndike and B F Skinner.

Thorndike's Law of Effect

During the early 1900s, Edward L Thorndike observed in his psychology laboratory that a cat would behave randomly and wildly when placed in a small box with a secret trip lever that opened a door. However, once the cat accidentally tripped the lever and escaped, the animal would go straight to the lever when placed back in the box. Hence, Thorndike formulated his famous **law of effect,** which says *behavior with favorable consequences tends to be repeated, while behavior with unfavorable consequences tends to disappear.*[3] This was a dramatic departure from the prevailing notion nearly a century ago that behavior was the product of inborn instincts.

law of effect Behavior with favorable consequences is repeated; behavior with unfavorable consequences disappears.

Skinner's Operant Conditioning Model

Skinner refined Thorndike's conclusion that behavior is controlled by its consequences. Skinner's work became known as *behaviorism* because he dealt strictly with observable behavior. As a behaviorist, Skinner believed it was pointless to explain behavior in terms of unobservable inner states such as needs, drives, attitudes, or thought processes.[4] He similarly put little stock in the idea of self-determination.

respondent behavior Skinner's term for unlearned stimulus–response reflexes.

operant behavior Skinner's term for learned, consequence-shaped behavior.

In his 1938 classic, *The Behavior of Organisms,* Skinner drew an important distinction between the two types of behavior: respondent and operant behavior.[5] He labeled unlearned reflexes or stimulus–response (S–R) connections **respondent behavior.** This category of behavior was said to describe a very small proportion of adult human behavior. Examples of respondent behavior would include shedding tears while peeling onions and reflexively withdrawing one's hand from a hot stove. Skinner attached the label **operant behavior** to behavior that is learned when one "operates on" the environment to produce desired consequences. Some call this the response–stimulus (R–S) model. Years of controlled experiments with pigeons in "Skinner boxes" helped Skinner develop a sophisticated technology of behavior control, or operant conditioning. For example, he taught pigeons how to pace figure-eights and how to bowl by reinforcing the underweight (and thus hungry) birds with food whenever they more closely approximated target behaviors. Skinner's work has significant implications for OB because the vast majority of organizational behavior falls into the operant category.

"Now, for my next trick." Years of experiments with pigeons in "Skinner boxes" helped B F Skinner develop the system of behavior control known as operant conditioning.

R. Epstein

Antecedent→	Behavior→	Consequence	Behavior outcome
Manager: "I suppose you haven't finished the payroll report yet."	*Payroll clerk:* "No way! I'm behind schedule because the supervisors didn't submit their payroll cards on time."	*Manager:* "I'm sure everyone will enjoy getting their pay-checks late again!"	The payroll clerk continues to make excuses while missing important deadlines because of the manager's negative antecedents and sarcastic consequences.
Manager: "How are you coming along on this week's payroll report?"	*Payroll clerk:* "I'm a little behind schedule. But if I work during my lunch hour, I'll have it in on time."	*Manager:* "I appreciate the extra effort! How would you like to spend tomorrow working on that bonus-pay project you suggested last week?"	The payroll clerk continues to meet important deadlines because of the manager's nonthreatening antecedents and rewarding consequences.

FIGURE 8~1

Productive Job Behavior Requires Supportive Antecedents and Consequences

Although B Mod interventions in the workplace often involve widely used techniques such as goal setting, feedback, and rewards, B Mod is unique in its adherence to Skinner's operant model of learning.[6] To review, operant theorists assume it is more productive to deal with observable behavior and its environmental determinants than with personality traits, perception, or inferred internal causes of behavior such as needs or cognitions. The purpose of this section is to introduce important concepts and terminology associated with B Mod. Subsequent sections explore B Mod application and research and some issues, pro and con.

A→B→C Contingencies

To adequately understand the operant learning process, one needs a working knowledge of **behavioral contingencies,** as characterized by the A→B→C model. The initials stand for Antecedent→Behavior→Consequence. When person–environment interaction is reduced to A→B→C terms (as in Figure 8–1), a **functional analysis** has taken place.[7]

PRINCIPLES OF BEHAVIOR MODIFICATION

behavioral contingencies
Antecedent→behavior→ consequence (A→B→C) relationships.

functional analysis
Reducing person–environment interaction to A→B→C terms.

Within the context of B Mod, *contingency* means the antecedent, behavior, and consequence in a given A→B→C relationship are connected in "if-then" fashion. If the antecedent is present, then the behavior is more likely to be displayed. If the behavior is displayed, then the consequence is experienced. Furthermore, as learned from Thorndike's law of effect, if the consequence is pleasing, the behavior will be strengthened (meaning it will occur more often). According to a pair of writers, one a clinical psychologist and the other a manager:

> Some contingencies occur automatically; others we set up by linking our behavior with the behavior of others in an attempt to design an environment that will best serve our purposes. Setting up a contingency involves designating behaviors and assigning consequences to follow. We design contingencies for children fairly simply ("If you finish your homework, I'll let you watch television"), but influencing the behavior of people in the work force is more difficult.
>
> As a result, managers often fail to use contingencies to their full advantage.[8]

Let us look more closely at antecedents, behavior, and consequences to fully understand A→B→C contingencies.

The Role of Antecedents   Unlike the S in the reflexive stimulus–response (S–R) model, antecedents *cue* rather than cause behavior. For example, in classic S–R fashion, a blistering hot piece of pizza *causes* you to quickly withdraw it from your mouth. In contrast, a yellow traffic light *cues* rather than causes you to step on the brake. Because many motorists step on the gas when green traffic signals change to yellow, traffic signals have probable rather than absolute control over driving behavior. Antecedents get the power to cue certain behaviors from associated consequences. For instance, if you have just received a ticket for running a red light, you will probably step on the brake when encountering the next few yellow traffic signals.

Focusing on Behavior   True to Skinnerian behaviorism, B Mod proponents emphasize the practical value of focusing on *behavior*. They caution against references to unobservable psychological states and general personality traits when explaining job performance (e.g., see Table 8–1). Phil's behavioral descriptions (the italicized portions in the bottom half of the table) give him a solid foundation for modifying Joe's behavioral performance problems.

When managers focus exclusively on behavior, without regard for personality traits or cognitive processes, their approach qualifies as radical behaviorism.[9] As one might suspect, this extreme perspective has stirred debate and controversy, complete with philosophical and ethical implications.

Contingent Consequences

Contingent consequences, according to Skinner's operant theory, control behavior in four ways: positive reinforcement, negative reinforcement, punishment, and extinction.[10] These contingent consequences are managed systematically in B Mod programs. To avoid the all-too-common mislabeling of these consequences, let us review some formal definitions.

The Wrong Way: **Subjective appraisal of the *person*, rather than objective information about *performance*.**

Phil Oaks, the department manager, describes his subordinate, Joe Scott, as follows:

> Well, Joe is just not easy to get along with. He's so disagreeable and negative all the time. He's very aggressive and disruptive. When he's unhappy he just sulks a lot, and he daydreams. He's also insubordinate and doesn't follow the rules. I don't know if he's immature, not intelligent, or irrational. Overall, his motivation is very low. He lacks drive and is generally hostile. I suspect that there may be a home problem also.

The Right Way: **Objective information about *observable performance behaviors*, rather than subjective appraisal of the person.**

In contrast, if Phil had training in pinpointing behaviors, he might describe Joe as follows:

> Well, whenever Joe is given some direction, he responds by immediately *telling you why it can't be done*. He frequently *threatens* other employees and has even been in one or two *fights*. He *leaves his own work area to tell jokes* to other workers. Sometimes he just *sits in a corner, or stares out the window* for several minutes.
>   He has violated several company rules such as *smoking in a nonsmoking zone, working without safety goggles*, and *parking in a fire lane*. He can't seem to *tell right-handed prints from left-handed prints*. Also, he *arrived late for work* ten times in the last month, and *returned from his break late* on twelve occasions.

Source: Performance descriptions excerpted from C C Manz and H P Sims, Jr., *SuperLeadership: Leading Others to Lead Themselves* (New York: Prentice-Hall, 1989), pp 66–67.

• ⤳ **TABLE 8~1**
Behaviorists Explain How Managers Should Describe Job Behavior: A Brief Case Study

Positive Reinforcement Strengthens Behavior **Positive reinforcement** is the process of strengthening a behavior by contingently presenting something pleasing. (Remember that a behavior is strengthened when it increases in frequency and weakened when it decreases in frequency.) A young design engineer who works overtime because of praise and recognition from the boss is responding to positive reinforcement. Similarly, people tend to return to restaurants where they are positively reinforced with good food and friendly, high-quality service.[11]

positive reinforcement Making behavior occur more often by contingently presenting something positive.

Negative Reinforcement Also Strengthens Behavior **Negative reinforcement** is the process of strengthening a behavior by contingently withdrawing something displeasing. For example, an army sergeant who stops yelling when a recruit jumps out of bed has negatively reinforced that particular behavior. Similarly, the behavior of clamping our hands over our ears when watching a jumbo jet take off is negatively reinforced by relief from the noise. Negative reinforcement is often confused with punishment. But the two strategies have opposite effects on behavior. Negative reinforcement, as the word *reinforcement* indicates, strengthens a behavior because it provides relief from an unpleasant situation.

negative reinforcement Making behavior occur more often by contingently withdrawing something negative.

Punishment Weakens Behavior **Punishment** is the process of weakening behavior through either the contingent presentation of something displeasing (see the International OB) or the contingent withdrawal of something positive. A manager assigning a tardy employee to a dirty job exemplifies the first type of punishment. Docking a tardy employee's pay is an example of the second type of punishment, called ''response cost'' punishment. Legal fines involve response cost punishment. Salespeople who must make up any cash register shortages out of their own pockets are being managed through response cost punishment. Ethical questions can and should be raised about this type of on-the-job punishment.

punishment Making behavior occur less often by contingently presenting something negative or withdrawing something positive.

INTERNATIONAL OB

Canadians Modify Behavior with Classical Music!

Music can do magical things, especially in Canada. First there was the 7-Eleven store in British Columbia that piped Muzak into the parking lot to keep teenagers from loitering. Out blasted the Mantovani and the kids scattered, leaving only a wake of Slurpee cups. Now downtown businesses in Edmonton, Alberta, are playing Bach and Mozart in a city park to drive away drug dealers and their clients. Police say drug activity in the park has dropped dramatically since Johann and Wolfgang arrived.

Source: "Let's Split!," *Newsweek,* August 20, 1990, p 2.

extinction Making behavior occur less often by ignoring or not reinforcing it.

Extinction Also Weakens Behavior   **Extinction** is the weakening of a behavior by ignoring it or making sure it is not reinforced. Getting rid of a former boyfriend or girlfriend by refusing to answer their phone calls is an extinction strategy. A good analogy for extinction is to imagine what would happen to your houseplants if you stopped watering them. Like a plant without water, a behavior without occasional reinforcement eventually dies. Although very different processes, both punishment and extinction have the same weakening effect on behavior.

How to Properly Categorize Contingent Consequences   In B Mod, consequences are defined in terms of their demonstrated impact on behavior (see Figure 8–2), not subjectively or by their intended impact. For example, notice how one expert in the field distinguishes between reinforcement and rewards:

> Reinforcement is distinguished from reward in that a reward is something that is perceived to be desirable and is delivered to an individual after performance. An increase in pay, a promotion, and a comment on good work performance may all be rewards. But rewards are not necessarily reinforcers. Reinforcers are defined by the increase in the rate of behavior.[12]

A promotion is both a reward and a positive reinforcer if the individual's performance subsequently improves.[13] On the other hand, *apparent* rewards may turn out to be the opposite. For example, consider Tampa Electric Company's successful "positive discipline" program, which gives misbehaving employees *a paid day off!*

> It works like this: Employees who come in late, do a sloppy job, or mistreat a colleague first get an oral "reminder" rather than a "reprimand." Next comes a written reminder, then the paid day off—called a "decision-making leave day."
>
> After a pensive day on the beach, naughty employees must agree in writing—or orally, at some union shops—that they will be on their best behavior for the next year. The paid day off is a one-shot chance at reform. If the employee doesn't shape up, it's curtains. The process is documented, so employees often have little legal recourse.[14]

Contingent consequences are always categorized "after the fact" by answering the following two questions: (1) Was something contingently presented or withdrawn? and (2) Did the target behavior subsequently occur more or less often? Using these two diagnostic questions, can you figure out why Tampa Electric's apparent reward turned out to be punishment for employees? Referring to the

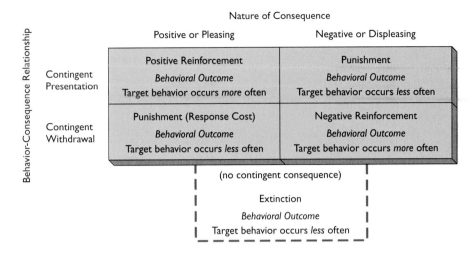

• ↗**FIGURE 8~2**
Contingent Consequences in
Behavior Modification

upper-right-hand quadrant in Figure 8–2, something was contingently presented, and the target behavior (tardiness, sloppy work, etc.) was weakened. Hence, it was a punishment contingency.

Schedules of Reinforcement

As just illustrated, contingent consequences are an important determinant of future behavior. The *timing* of behavioral consequences can be even more important. Based on years of tedious laboratory experiments with pigeons in highly controlled environments, Skinner and his colleagues discovered distinct patterns of responding for various schedules of reinforcement.[15] Although some of their conclusions can be generalized to negative reinforcement, punishment, and extinction, it is best to think only of positive reinforcement when discussing schedules.

Continuous Reinforcement   As indicated in Table 8–2, every instance of a target behavior is reinforced when a **continuous reinforcement** (CRF) schedule is in effect. For instance, when your television set is operating properly, you are reinforced with a picture every time you turn it on (a CRF schedule). But, as with any CRF schedule of reinforcement, the behavior of turning on the television will undergo rapid extinction if the set breaks.

continuous reinforcement
Reinforcing every instance of a behavior.

Intermittent Reinforcement   Unlike CRF schedules, **intermittent reinforcement** involves reinforcement of some but not all instances of a target behavior. Four subcategories of intermittent schedules, described in Table 8–2, are fixed and variable ratio schedules and fixed and variable interval schedules. Reinforcement in *ratio* schedules is contingent on the number of responses emitted. *Interval* reinforcement is tied to the passage of time. Some common examples of the four types of intermittent reinforcement are:

intermittent reinforcement
Reinforcing some but not all instances of behavior.

- *Fixed ratio.*   Piece-rate pay; bonuses tied to the sale of a fixed number of units.
- *Variable ratio.*   Slot machines that pay off after a variable number of lever pulls; lotteries that pay off after the purchase of a variable number of tickets.

✏ • TABLE 8-2
Schedules of Reinforcement

Schedule	Description	Probable Effects on Responding
Continuous (CRS)	Reinforcer follows every response.	Steady high rate of performance as long as reinforcement continues to follow every response. High frequency of reinforcement may lead to early satiation. Behavior weakens rapidly (undergoes extinction) when reinforcers are withheld. Appropriate for newly emitted, unstable, or low-frequency responses.
Intermittent	Reinforcer does not follow every response.	Capable of producing high frequencies of responding. Low frequency of reinforcement precludes early satiation. Appropriate for stable or high-frequency responses.
Fixed ratio (FR)	A fixed number of responses must be emitted before reinforcement occurs.	A fixed ratio of 1:1 (reinforcement occurs after every response) is the same as a continuous schedule. Tends to produce a high rate of response which is vigorous and steady.
Variable ratio (VR)	A varying or random number of responses must be emitted before reinforcement occurs.	Capable of producing a high rate of response which is vigorous, steady, and resistant to extinction.
Fixed interval (FI)	The first response after a specific period of time has elapsed is reinforced.	Produces an uneven response pattern varying from a very slow, unenergetic response immediately following reinforcement to a very fast, vigorous response immediately preceding reinforcement.
Variable interval (VI)	The first response after varying or random periods of time have elapsed is reinforced.	Tends to produce a high rate of response which is vigorous, steady, and resistant to extinction.

Source: F Luthans and R Kreitner, *Organizational Behavior Modification and Beyond: An Operant and Social Learning Approach* (Glenview, IL: Scott, Foresman, 1985), p 58. Used with permission.

- *Fixed interval.* Hourly pay; annual salary paid on a regular basis.
- *Variable interval.* Random supervisory praise and pats on the back for employees who have been doing a good job. (See the OB Exercise.)

Scheduling Is Critical   The schedule of reinforcement can more powerfully influence behavior than the magnitude of reinforcement. Although this proposition grew out of experiments with pigeons, subsequent on-the-job research confirmed it. Consider, for example, a field study of 12 unionized beaver trappers employed by a lumber company to keep the large rodents from eating newly planted tree seedlings.[17]

The beaver trappers were randomly divided into two groups that alternated weekly between two different bonus plans. Under the first schedule, each trapper earned his regular $7 per hour wage plus $1 for each beaver caught. Technically, this bonus was paid on a CRF schedule. The second bonus plan involved the regular $7 per hour wage plus a one-in-four chance (as determined by rolling the dice) of receiving $4 for each beaver trapped. This second bonus plan qualified as a variable ratio (VR-4) schedule. In the long run, both incentive schemes averaged out to a $1-per-beaver bonus. Surprisingly, however, when the trappers were under

---

OB EXERCISE

A Test of How Well You Know the Schedules of Reinforcement

Company: Drakenfeld Colors, Ciba-Geigy Corporation, Washington, Pennsylvania.
Target behavior: Absenteeism

Instructions:

Read the following case incident, select one of the answers listed below, and then check the interpretation in footnote 16 at the end of this chapter.

Drakenfeld had a population of about 250 employees with an absenteeism rate of only 0.89 percent. In fact, a full 44 percent of its employees had perfect attendance records in 1987. . . .

Because of the significant population of perfect attendees, it was decided to capitalize upon the strengths and to not only reward these people but to showcase them to the organization-at-large. This included a monetary bonus of $50 at six months and again at 12, with an additional $25 bonus for a full-calendar year of perfect attendance. Such an incentive alone may not sound as though it would induce someone to crawl out of bed on a day he or she might not otherwise do so, but the majority of the work force already had a strong work ethic and that root behavior was still dominant.

In order to make the program visible and exciting, employees with perfect attendance were entered into a sweepstakes drawing to take place at a special awards banquet with employees, spouses, and management. The winner would receive an all-expenses paid trip for two to a resort location. The cost/benefit ratio of this incentive is obvious. . . .

Response to . . . [this] aspect of the program was extremely well received, with perfect attendance increasing from an already impressive 44 percent to a new high of 62 percent in the first year (1988).

Which schedules of reinforcement were used in this case?

   a. Fixed interval plus variable interval.

   b. Variable ratio plus variable interval.

   c. Fixed ratio plus fixed interval.

   d. Variable interval plus fixed ratio.

   e. Fixed ratio plus variable ratio.

Source: Case incident excerpted from J Putzier and F T Nowak, "Attendance Management and Control," *Personnel Administrator*, August 1989, pp 59–60.

---

the VR-4 schedule, they were 58 percent more productive than under the CRF schedule, despite the fact that the net amount of pay averaged out the same for the two groups during the 12-week trapping season.

Work Organizations Typically Rely on the Weakest Schedule   Generally, variable ratio and variable interval schedules of reinforcement produce the strongest behavior that is most resistant to extinction. As gamblers will attest, variable schedules hold the promise of reinforcement after the next target response. For example, the following drama at a Laughlin, Nevada, gambling casino is one more illustration of the potency of variable ratio reinforcement:

An elderly woman with a walker had lost her grip on the slot [machine] handle and had collapsed on the floor.

''Help,'' she cried weakly.

The woman at the machine next to her interrupted her play for a few seconds to try to help her to her feet, but all around her the army of slot players continued feeding coins to the machines.

A security man arrived to soothe the woman and take her away.

''Thank you,'' she told him appreciatively.

''But don't forget my winnings.''[18]

Organizations without at least some variable reinforcement are less likely to prompt this sort of dedication to task. Unfortunately, time-based pay schemes such as hourly wages and yearly salaries that have become predominant in today's service economy are the weakest schedule of reinforcement (fixed interval).

Behavior Shaping

Have you ever wondered how trainers at aquarium parks manage to get bottlenosed dolphins to do flips, killer whales to carry people on their backs, and seals to juggle balls? The results are seemingly magical. Actually, a mundane learning process called shaping is responsible for the animals' antics.

Two-ton killer whales, for example, have a big appetite, and they find buckets of fish very reinforcing. So if the trainer wants to ride a killer whale, he or she reinforces very basic behaviors that will eventually lead to the whale being ridden. The killer whale is contingently reinforced with a few fish for coming near the trainer, then for being touched, then for putting its nose in a harness, then for being straddled, and eventually for swimming with the trainer on its back. In effect, the trainer systematically raises the behavioral requirement for reinforcement. Thus, **shaping** is defined as the process of reinforcing closer and closer approximations to a target behavior.

Shaping works very well with people, too, especially in training. Praise, recognition, and instructive and credible feedback cost managers little more than moments of their time.[19] Yet, when used in conjunction with a behavior-shaping program, these consequences can efficiently foster significant improvements in job performance.[20] The key to successful behavior shaping lies in reducing a complex target behavior to easily learned steps and then faithfully (and patiently) reinforcing any improvement. Table 8–3 lists practical tips on shaping.

shaping Reinforcing closer and closer approximations to a target behavior.

1. *Accommodate the process of behavioral change.* Behaviors change in gradual stages, not in broad, sweeping motions.
2. *Define new behavior patterns specifically.* State what you wish to accomplish in explicit terms and in small amounts that can be easily grasped.
3. *Give individuals feedback on their performance.* A once-a-year performance appraisal is not sufficient.
4. *Reinforce behavior as quickly as possible.*
5. *Use powerful reinforcements.* In order to be effective, rewards must be important to the employee—not to the manager.
6. *Use a continuous reinforcement schedule.* New behaviors should be reinforced every time they occur. This reinforcement should continue until these behaviors become habitual.
7. *Use a variable reinforcement schedule for maintenance.* Even after behavior has become habitual, it still needs to be rewarded, though not necessarily every time it occurs.
8. *Reward teamwork—not competition.* Group goals and group rewards are one way to encourage cooperation in situations in which jobs and performance are interdependent.
9. *Make all rewards contingent on performance.*
10. *Never take good performance for granted.* Even superior performance, if left unrewarded, will eventually deteriorate.

TABLE 8-3
Ten Practical Tips for Shaping Job Behavior

Source: Adapted from A T Hollingsworth and D Tanquay Hoyer, "How Supervisors Can Shape Behavior," *Personnel Journal,* May 1985, pp 86, 88.

Someone once observed that children and pets are the world's best behavior modifiers. In fact, one of your authors responds obediently to his cats, while the other jumps to satisfy contingencies arranged by his dogs! Despite their ignorance of operant theory, children and pets are good behavior modifiers because they (1) know precisely what behavior they want to elicit, (2) provide clear antecedents, and (3) wield situationally appropriate and powerful contingent consequences. Let us learn from these ''masters'' of behavior modification and examine a four-step B Mod process for managing on-the-job behavior[21] (see Figure 8–3). A review of practical implications follows.

A MODEL FOR MODIFYING JOB BEHAVIOR

Step 1: Identify Target Behavior

Managers who strictly follow the operant principle of focusing on observable behavior rather than on inferred internal states, have two alternatives in step 1. They can pinpoint a *desirable* behavior that occurs too *seldom* (e.g., contributing creative ideas at staff meetings), or they can focus on an *undesirable* behavior that occurs too *often* (e.g., making disruptive comments at staff meetings). Organizational behavior modification proponents prefer the first alternative because it requires managers to see things in a positive, growth-oriented manner instead of in a negative, punitive manner. As a case in point, researchers have documented the benefits of ''well pay'' versus the costs of traditional sick pay.[22] In short, every undesirable behavior has a desirable opposite. Just a few of many possible examples are: being absent/being on time, having an accident/working safely, remaining aloof/participating actively, procrastinating/completing assignments on time, competing destructively/being a team player.

Pointers for Identifying Behavior   According to the former editor of the *Journal of Organizational Behavior Management,* a journal devoted to the study of

FIGURE 8–3
Modifying On-the-Job
Behavior

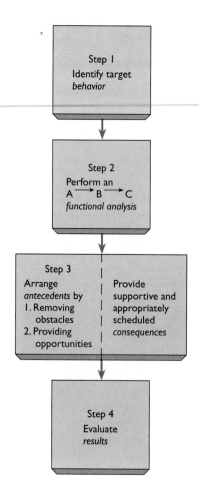

Step 1
Identify target
behavior

Step 2
Perform an
A → B → C
functional analysis

Step 3
Arrange
antecedents by
1. Removing
obstacles
2. Providing
opportunities

Provide
supportive and
appropriately
scheduled
consequences

Step 4
Evaluate
results

B Mod in the workplace, too many B Mod programs focus on process (rule following) rather than on accomplishments. Thus, he offers the following three pointers for identifying target behaviors:

1. The primary focus should be on accomplishments or outcomes. These accomplishments should have *significant* organizational impact.
2. The targeting of process behaviors (rule adherence, etc.) should only occur when that behavior can be functionally related to a significant organizational accomplishment.
3. There should be broad participation in the development of behavioral targets.[23]

These pointers are intended to prevent managers from falling victim to charges of unethical manipulation.

A Word of Caution about Shifting the Focus from Behavior to Results   In laboratory settings or highly controlled situations such as classrooms or machine shops, it is possible to directly observe and record the frequency of specific behaviors. Asking a question in class, arriving late at work, and handing in an error-free report are all observable behavioral events. However, in today's complex organizations, it is not always possible (or desirable) to observe and record work behaviors firsthand. For example, top-level managers and technical specialists often spend time alone in closed offices. When work behavior cannot be monitored

Remove Obstacles	Provide Opportunities
Eliminate unrealistic plans, schedules, and deadlines.	Formulate difficult but attainable goals.
Identify and remedy skill deficiencies through training.	Provide clear instructions.
Eliminate confusing or contradictory rules.	Give friendly reminders, constructive suggestions, and helpful tips.
Avoid conflicting orders and priorities.	Ask nonthreatening questions about progress.
Remove distracting co-workers.	Display posters with helpful advice.
	Rely on easy-to-use forms.
	Build enthusiasm and commitment through participation and challenging work assignments.
	Promote personal growth and development through training.

TABLE 8–4

Paving the Way for Good Job Performance with Helpful Antecedents

firsthand, the next-best alternative is to track results. Examples include number of units sold, number of customer complaints, degree of goal attainment, and percent of projects completed. Managers who build contingencies around results need to keep in mind that those contingencies will be less precise than ones anchored to observable behavioral events.[24] For instance, the wrong person could be reinforced because organizational politicians sometimes take credit for others' results.

Step 2: Functionally Analyze the Situation

Any behaviors occurring on a regular basis necessarily have their own supportive cues and consequences. Thus, it is important for managers to identify existing A→B→C contingencies before trying to rearrange things. For example, it is important to know that a recently uncooperative employee is being pressured by co-workers to vote yes in an upcoming union certification election.

Step 3: Arrange Antecedents and Provide Consequences

In this step, analysis gives way to action. An instructive way to discuss step 3 is to explore separately antecedent management and consequence management. In practice, antecedent and consequence management are closely intertwined.

Managing Antecedents   As specified in step 3 of Figure 8–3, antecedent management involves two basic strategies: (1) removing obstacles and/or (2) providing opportunities. Some practical suggestions are listed in Table 8–4. Based on the discussion of goal setting in Chapter 7, challenging objectives that specify what and when something is to be accomplished are probably the most potent antecedent management tool. For instance, supervisors in one study handed in their weekly reports more promptly when they were given specific target dates.[25]

By rearranging apparently insignificant antecedents, significant results can be achieved. Importantly, these must be *contingent* antecedents, as identified through an A→B→C functional analysis. For example, a telephone company was losing an estimated $250,000 annually because its telephone installers were not reporting the installation of ''ceiling drops.'' A ceiling drop involves installing extra wiring to compensate for a lowered ceiling. Despite comprehensive training on how to install and report ceiling drops, a large percentage of ceiling drops remained unreported and thus unbilled by the company. The following turn of events then took place.

A specialist in training design was called in to find out why the training had failed. She noted a curious thing. The form that the installers were required to fill out was extremely complicated and the part dealing with ceiling drops was even more complicated. . . .

One small change was made by adding a box where the installer could merely check ''ceiling drop installed.'' Now the installer no longer had to fill out an extensive explanation of what took place in the house. Within one week after the change in the form, the number of ceiling drops reported and charged back to the customers had increased dramatically, far above what it was immediately after the training sessions.[26]

Summarizing, from a B Mod perspective the telephone installers did not have an attitude or motivation problem. Nor did they have a knowledge deficiency requiring more training. They simply did not report ceiling drops because it was too complicated to do so. The streamlined reporting form presented the installers with an opportunity to behave properly, whereas the old form was an obstacle to good performance. In A→B→C terms, the streamlined reporting form became an antecedent that efficiently cued the desired behavior.

Managing Consequences   Step 3 in Figure 8–3 calls for providing supportive and appropriately scheduled consequences. Six guidelines for successfully managing consequences during B Mod are as follows:

1. *Reinforce improvement, not just final results.*   Proper shaping cannot occur if the behavioral requirement for reinforcement is too demanding. Behavior undergoes extinction when it is not shaped in achievable step-by-step increments.

2. *Fit the consequences to the behavior.*   A pair of B Mod scholars interpreted this guideline as follows:

    > Overrewarding a worker may make him feel guilty and certainly reinforces his current performance level. If the performance level is lower than that of others who get the same reward, he has no reason to increase his output. When a worker is underrewarded, he becomes angry with the system. His behavior is being extinguished and the company may be forcing the good employee (underrewarded) to seek employment elsewhere while encouraging the poor employee (overrewarded) to stay on.[27]

    Note how this recommendation is consistent with the discussion of equity theory in Chapter 7.

natural rewards   Normal social interactions such as praise or recognition.

3. *Emphasize natural rewards over contrived rewards.*   **Natural rewards** are potentially reinforcing consequences derived from day-to-day social and administrative interactions. Typical natural rewards include supervisory praise, assignment to favored tasks, early time off with pay, flexible work schedules, and extended breaks. Contrived rewards include money and other tangible rewards. Regarding this distinction, it has been pointed out that

    > Natural social rewards are potentially the most powerful and universally applicable reinforcers. In contrast to contrived rewards, they do not generally lead to satiation (people seldom get tired of compliments, attention, or recognition) and can be administered on a very contingent basis.[28]

4. *Provide individuals with objective feedback whenever possible.*   As discussed in Chapter 14, objective feedback can have a positive impact on

future behavior. This is particularly true when people have the opportunity to keep track of their own performance.[29] The three-way marriage of goal setting, objective feedback, and positive reinforcement for improvement can be fruitful indeed. For example, a field study of college hockey players demonstrated that a B Mod intervention of goal setting, feedback, and praise increased the team's winning percentage by almost 100 percent for two consecutive years.[30]

5. *Emphasize positive reinforcement; de-emphasize punishment.* Proponents of B Mod in the workplace, as mentioned earlier, recommend building up good behavior with positive reinforcement instead of tearing down bad behavior with punishment.[31] For instance, the authors of the best-seller, *The One Minute Manager,* told their readers to "catch them doing something right!"[32] In other words, managers who focus on what's right with job performance unavoidably end up emphasizing positive reinforcement.

Regarding the use of punishment, operant researchers found it tends to suppress undesirable behavior only temporarily while prompting emotional side effects. For example, a computer programmer who is reprimanded publicly for failing to "debug" an important program may get even with the boss by skillfully sabotaging another program. Moreover, those punished come to fear and dislike the person administering the punishment.[33] Thus, it is unlikely that punitive managers can build the climate of trust so necessary for success in today's TQM-oriented organizations. For example, the "giant retailer W T Grant, which went bankrupt in 1975, made it a practice to cut the tie of any sales manager who did not meet his quota."[34]

Constructive and positive feedback is a proven alternative to punishment (e.g., see the International OB).

6. *Schedule reinforcement appropriately.* Once again, immature behavior requires the nurture of continuous reinforcement. Established or habitual behavior, in contrast, can be maintained with fixed or variable schedules of intermittent reinforcement.

Step 4: Evaluate Results

B Mod intervention is effective if (1) a desirable target behavior occurs more often or (2) an undesirable target behavior occurs less often. Since *more* or *less* are relative terms, managers need a measurement tool that provides an objective basis for comparing preintervention with postintervention data. This is where baseline data and behavior charting can make a valuable contribution.

Baseline data are preintervention behavioral data collected without the target person's knowledge. This "before" measure later provides a basis for assessing an intervention's effectiveness.

A **behavior chart** is a B Mod program evaluation tool that includes both preintervention baseline data and postintervention data. The vertical axis of a behavior chart can be expressed in terms of behavior frequency, percent, or results attained. A time dimension is typically found on the horizontal axis of a behavior chart. When a goal is included, as shown in Figure 8–4, a behavior chart quickly tells the individual where his or her performance has been, is, and should be. As the

baseline data
Preintervention data collected by someone other than the target person.

behavior chart   Program evaluation graph with baseline and intervention data.

INTERNATIONAL OB

Organizational Behavior Modification (OB Mod) Successfully Exported to Russia

The Setting:*

The study was conducted at the largest textile mill in Russia. The mill employed about 8,000 employees at the time of the study, late spring of 1990. This was after Gorbachev's perestroika (economic and political restructuring) had been implemented, but before the breakup of the Soviet Union. The factory is located in Tver (formerly Kalinin), about 96 miles northwest of Moscow.

The Intervention:**

The supervisors were instructed on examples of specific functional and dysfunctional performance behaviors and were encouraged to ask clarifying questions. The researchers then instructed the supervisors to administer recognition and praise when workers performed the functional behaviors and to provide specific feedback to them about these behaviors. The supervisors were also instructed to give reminders and make corrections when they observed the dysfunctional behaviors but were specifically told not to give negative reprimands or punishment.

The Results:*

First, the introduction of an OB Mod intervention led to an increase in functional behavior and a decrease in dysfunctional behavior among the [33] workers in this study. Second, the impact was more immediate and distinctive for eliminating undesired behaviors than for increasing desired behaviors. Third, both the functional and dysfunctional behaviors failed to reverse after the withdrawal of the intervention.

Sources: * Excerpted from D H B Welsh, F Luthans, and S M Sommer, "Organizational Behavior Modification Goes to Russia: Replicating an Experimental Analysis Across Cultures and Tasks," *Journal of Organizational Behavior Management*, no. 2, 1993, pp 15–35.
** Excerpted from D H B Welsh, F Luthans, and S M Sommer, "Managing Russian Factory Workers: The Impact of US-Based Behavioral and Participative Techniques," *Academy of Management Journal*, February 1993, pp 58–79.

• **FIGURE 8~4**

Behavior Charts Help
Evaluate B Mod Programs
and Provide Feedback

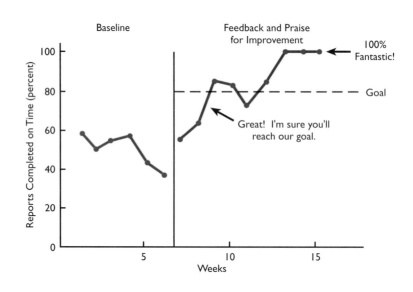

successful bus driver safety program discussed at the opening of this chapter illustrates, posted feedback can be a very effective management tool. Moreover, a behavior chart provides an ongoing evaluation of a B Mod program.

Some Practical Implications

Some believe B Mod does not belong in the workplace.[35] They see it as blatantly manipulative and demeaning. Although even the severest critics admit it works, they rightly point out that on-the-job applications of B Mod have focused on superficial rule-following behavior such as getting to work on time. Indeed, B Mod is still in transition from highly controlled and simple laboratory and clinical settings to loosely controlled and complex organizational settings.[36] Despite the need for more B Mod research and application in complex organizations, some practical lessons already have been learned.

First, it is very difficult and maybe impossible to change organizational behavior without systematically managing antecedents and contingent consequences. Second, even the best-intentioned reward system will fail if it does not include clear behavior–consequence contingencies. Third, behavior shaping is a valuable developmental technique. Fourth, goal setting, objective feedback, and positive reinforcement for improvement, when combined in systematic A→B→C fashion, are a powerful management tool. Finally, because formal program evaluation is fundamental to B Mod, those who use it on the job can be held accountable.

Judging from the number of diet books appearing on best-seller lists each year, self-control seems to be in rather short supply. Historically, when someone sought to wage the war of self-control, he or she was told to exercise willpower, be self-disciplined, resist temptation, or seek divine guidance. Although well-intentioned, this advice gives the individual very little to go on relative to actually changing one's behavior. Fortunately, behavioral scientists formulated step-by-step self-management models that have helped individuals conquer serious behavioral problems. Typical among those problems are alcohol and drug abuse, overeating, cigarette smoking, phobias, and antisocial behavior. True to its interdisciplinary nature, the field of OB has recently translated self-management theory and techniques from the clinic to the workplace.

Formally defined, **behavioral self-management** (BSM) is the process of modifying one's own behavior by systematically managing cues, cognitive processes, and contingent consequences. The term *behavioral* signifies that BSM focuses primarily on modifying behavior, rather than on changing values, attitudes, or personalities. At first glance, BSM appears to be little more than self-imposed B Mod. But BSM differs from B Mod in that cognitive processes are considered in BSM, while ignored in B Mod. This adjustment reflects the influence of Albert Bandura's extension of operant theory into social learning theory.

In this section, we discuss Bandura's social learning theory, from which BSM has evolved. Next, a brief overview of the managerial context for BSM is presented. A social learning model of self-management is then introduced and explored, followed by some practical implications of relevant research findings.

BEHAVIORAL SELF-MANAGEMENT

behavioral self-management
Modifying one's own behavior by managing cues, cognitive processes, and consequences.

Bandura's Social Learning Theory

Albert Bandura built on Skinner's work by initially demonstrating how people acquire new behavior by imitating role models (called vicarious learning) and later exploring the cognitive processing of cues and consequences. (Recall our discussion of the Stanford psychologist's ideas about self-efficacy in Chapter 4.) Like Skinner's operant model, Bandura's approach makes observable behavior the primary unit of analysis. Bandura also goes along with Skinner's contention that behavior is controlled by environmental cues and consequences. However, Bandura has extended Skinner's operant model by emphasizing that cognitive or mental processes affect how one responds to surroundings. In short, Bandura considers factors *inside* the individual, whereas the operant model stays outside the person. This extension is called social learning theory.[37]

A Managerial Context for Behavioral Self-Management

OB scholars Fred Luthans and Tim Davis developed the managerial context for BSM as follows:

> Research and writing in the management field have given a great deal of attention to managing societies, organizations, groups, and individuals. Strangely, almost no one has paid any attention to managing oneself more effectively. . . . Self-management seems to be a basic prerequisite for effective management of other people, groups, organizations, and societies.[38]

Moreover, some have wrapped BSM in ethical terms: "Proponents of self-control contend that it is more ethically defensible than externally imposed behavior control techniques when used for job enrichment, behavior modification, management by objectives, or organization development."[39] Others have placed self-management within a managerial context by discussing it as a substitute for hierarchical leadership.[40] Behavioral self-management also meshes well with today's emphasis on empowerment, self-managed teams, and total quality management (TQM).[41] Recall that *everyone* is responsible for product and service quality in a TQM environment.

Social Learning Model of Self-Management

Bandura has put self-management into a social learning context by noting the following:

> [A] distinguishing feature of social learning theory is the prominent role it assigns to self-regulatory capacities. By arranging environmental inducements, generating cognitive supports, and producing consequences for their own actions people are able to exercise some measure of control over their own behavior.[42]

In other words, to the extent that you can control your environment and your cognitive representations of your environment, you are the master of your own behavior. The practical BSM model displayed in Figure 8–5 is derived from social learning theory. Reflecting Bandura's extension of Skinner's basic A→B→C model, the BSM model includes the person's psychological self. The two-headed arrows reflect Bandura's contention, discussed previously, that the individual has a degree of control over his or her own antecedent cues, behavior, and consequences. Each of the four major components of this BSM model requires a closer look. Since this is a *behavioral* model, let us begin our examination with the behavior component in the center of the triangle.

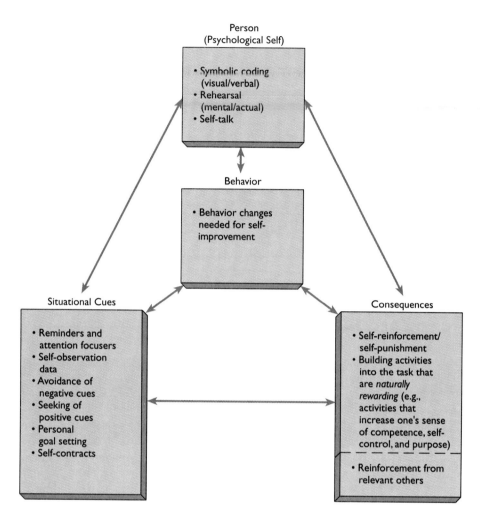

• ⟶ FIGURE 8~5
A Social Learning Model of
Self-Management

An Agenda for Self-Improvement   Stephen R Covey, in his best-selling book *The Seven Habits of Highly Effective People,* has given managers a helpful agenda for improving themselves (see Table 8–5). Covey refers to the seven habits, practiced by truly successful people, as "principle-centered, character-based."[43] The first step for those practicing BSM is to pick one or more of the seven habits that are personal trouble spots and translate them to specific behaviors. For example, "think win/win" might remind a conflict-prone manager to practice cooperative teamwork behaviors with co-workers. Habit number five might prompt another manager to stop interrupting others during conversations.

As a procedural note, behavior charts can be used in BSM to evaluate progress toward one's goals, but baseline data ideally should be collected by someone else to ensure objectivity.

Managing Situational Cues   When people try to give up a nagging habit like smoking, the cards are stacked against them. Many people (friends who smoke) and situations (after dinner, when under stress at work, or when relaxing) serve as subtle yet powerful cues telling the individual to light up. If the behavior is to be changed, the cues need to be rearranged so as to trigger the alternative behavior.

TABLE 8~5

Covey's Seven Habits: An Agenda for Managerial Self-Improvement

1. *Be proactive.* Choose the right means and ends in life, and take personal responsibility for your actions. Make timely decisions and make positive progress.

2. *Begin with the end in mind.* When all is said and done, how do you want to be remembered? Be goal oriented.

3. *Put first things first.* Establish firm priorities that will help you accomplish your mission in life. Strike a balance between your daily work and your potential for future accomplishments.

4. *Think win/win.* Cooperatively seek creative and mutually beneficial solutions to problems and conflicts.

5. *Seek first to understand, then to be understood.* Strive hard to become a better listener.

6. *Synergize.* Because the whole is greater than the sum of its parts, you need to generate teamwork among individuals with unique abilities and potential. Value interpersonal differences.

7. *Sharpen the saw.* "This is the habit of self-renewal, which has four elements. The first is mental, which includes reading, visualizing, planning, and writing. The second is spiritual, which means value clarification and commitment, study, and meditation. Third is social/emotional, which involves service, empathy, synergy, and intrinsic security. Finally, the physical element includes exercise, nutrition, and stress management."

Sources: Adapted from discussion in S R Covey, *The Seven Habits of Highly Effective People* (New York: Simon & Schuster, 1989). Excerpt from "Q & A with Stephen Covey," *Training,* December 1992, p 38.

Six techniques for managing situational cues are listed in the left-hand column of Figure 8–5.

Reminders and attention focusers do just that. For example, many students and managers cue themselves about deadlines and appointments with yellow Post-it™ notes stuck all over their work areas, refrigerators, and dashboards. Self-observation data, when compared against a goal or standard, can be a potent cue for improvement. Those who keep a weight chart near their bathroom scale will attest to the value of this tactic. Successful self-management calls for avoiding negative cues while seeking positive cues. Managers in Northwestern Mutual Life Insurance Company's new business department appreciate the value of avoiding negative cues: "On Wednesdays, the department shuts off all incoming calls, allowing workers to speed processing of new policies. On those days, the unit averages 23 percent more policies than on other days."[44]

Goals, as repeatedly mentioned in this text, are the touchstone of good management. So it is with challenging yet attainable personal goals and effective self-management. Goals simultaneously provide a target and a measuring stick of progress.[45] Finally, a self-contract is an "if-then" agreement with oneself. For example, if you can define all the key terms in this chapter, treat yourself to something special.

Arranging Cognitive Supports   This component makes BSM distinctly different from conventional behavior modification. Referring to the *person* portion of the self-management model in Figure 8–5, three cognitive supports for behavior change are symbolic coding, rehearsal, and self-talk. These amount to psychological, as opposed to environmental, cues. Yet, according to Bandura, they prompt appropriate behavior in the same manner. Each requires brief explanation:

- *Symbolic coding:* From a social learning theory perspective, the human brain stores information in visual and verbal codes. For example, a sales manager could use the visual picture of a man chopping down a huge tree to remember Woodman, the name of a promising new client. In contrast, people commonly rely on acronyms to recall names, rules for behavior, and other information. An acronym (or verbal code) that is often heard in managerial circles is the KISS principle, standing for "Keep It Simple, Stupid."

■ *Rehearsal.* While it is true that practice often makes perfect, mental rehearsal of challenging tasks also can increase one's chances of success. Importantly, experts draw a clear distinction between systematic visualization of how one should proceed and daydreaming about success.

> The big difference between daydreaming and visualizing is that "visualizing is much more specific and detailed," says Philadelphia consultant Judith Schuster. "A day-dream typically has gaps in it—we jump immediately to where we want to wind up. In visualization, we use building blocks and, step-by-step, construct the result we want."[46]

This sort of visualization has been recommended for use in managerial planning.[47]

Managers stand to learn a great deal about mental rehearsal and visualization from successful athletes. Mary Lou Retton, 1984 Olympic gold medal gymnast, is an inspiring example:

> "Before I dropped off to sleep inside the Olympic Village, I did what I always do before a major competition—mind-scripted it completely. I mentally ran through each routine, every move, imagining everything done perfectly," recalls Retton.[48]

Job-finding seminars are very popular on college campuses today because they typically involve mental and actual rehearsal of tough job interviews. This sort of manufactured experience can build the confidence and self-efficacy necessary for real-world success.

■ *Self-talk:* According to an expert on the subject, "**self-talk** is the set of evaluating thoughts that you give yourself about facts and events that happen to you."[49] Personal experience tells us that self-talk tends to be a self-fulfilling prophecy (recall the discussion in Chapter 5). Negative self-talk tends to pave the way for failure, whereas positive self-talk often facilitates success. Replacing negative self-talk ("I'll never get a raise") with positive self-talk ("I deserve a raise and I'm going to get it") is fundamental to better self-management.[50]

self-talk Evaluating thoughts about oneself.

Self-Reinforcement The satisfaction of self-contracts and other personal achievements calls for self-reinforcement. According to Bandura, three criteria must be satisfied before self-reinforcement can occur:

1. The individual must have *control over desired reinforcers.*
2. Reinforcers must be *self-administered on a conditional basis.* Failure to meet the performance requirement must lead to self-denial.
3. *Performance standards must be adopted* to establish the quantity and quality of target behavior required for self-reinforcement.[51]

In view of the following realities, self-reinforcement strategies need to be resourceful and creative:

> Self-granted rewards can lead to self-improvement. But as failed dieters and smokers can attest, there are short-run as well as long-run influences on self-reinforcement. For the overeater, the immediate gratification of eating has more influence than the promise of a new wardrobe. The same sort of dilemma plagues procrastinators. Consequently, one needs to weave a powerful web of cues, cognitive supports, and internal and external

consequences to win the tug-of-war with status-quo payoffs. Primarily because it is so easy to avoid, self-punishment tends to be ineffectual. As with managing the behavior of others, positive instead of negative consequences are recommended for effective self-management.[52]

In addition, it helps to solicit positive reinforcement for self-improvement from supportive friends, co-workers, and relatives.

Research and Managerial Implications

There is ample evidence that behavioral self-management works. For example, in one controlled study of 20 college students, 17 were able to successfully modify their own behavior problems involving smoking, lack of assertiveness, poor study habits, overeating, sloppy housekeeping, lack of exercise, and moodiness.[53] Research on **self-monitoring,** a personality trait involving the "ability to monitor and control one's expressive behaviors," may help explain why BSM works for some but not for others.[54] High self-monitors likely have an advantage over low self-monitors because they are more concerned about their social behavior and tend to be more adaptable.

Because BSM has only recently been transplanted from clinical and classroom applications to the workplace, on-the-job research evidence is limited. One pair of researchers reported successful BSM interventions with managerial problems, including overdependence on the boss, ignoring paperwork, leaving the office without notifying anyone, and failing to fill out expense reports.[55] Also, absenteeism of unionized state government employees was significantly reduced with BSM training.[56] A survey of 36 organization development consultants found positive applications of mental imagery and visualization for organizational problem solving.[57] These preliminary studies need to be supplemented by research of how, why, and under what conditions BSM does or does not work. In the meantime, present and future managers can fine-tune their own behavior by taking lessons from proven self-management techniques.[58]

self-monitoring Degree to which people observe and control their own expressive behavior.

BACK TO THE OPENING CASE

Now that you have read Chapter 8, you should be able to answer the following questions about the Triad Systems case:

1. How would you rate Triad's president and CEO James R Porter as a behavior modifier? Explain in technical B Mod terms.

2. In A→B→C terms, why do the recognition awards seem to effectively boost job performance at Triad?

3. Which of the six guidelines for effectively managing consequences are evident in this case.

4. How would you answer a manager who made the following statement? "Eventually, Triad's managers will be sorry for getting tangled up with so many incentive gimmicks."

5. Would you like to work for an incentive-oriented company such as Triad? Why or why not?

SUMMARY OF KEY CONCEPTS

1. *State Thorndike's "law of effect," and explain Skinner's distinction between respondent and operant behavior.* According to Edward L Thorndike's law of effect, behavior with favorable consequences tends to be repeated, while behavior with unfavorable consequences tends to disappear. B F Skinner called unlearned stimulus–response reflexes respondent behavior. He applied the term *operant behavior* to all behavior learned through experience with environmental consequences.

2. *Define the term* behavior modification, *and explain the A→B→C model.* Behavior modification (B Mod) is defined as the process of making specific behavior occur more or less often by systematically managing (1) antecedent cues and (2) contingent consequences. B Mod involves managing person–environment interactions that can be functionally analyzed into antecedent→behavior→consequence (A→B→C) relationships. Antecedents cue rather than cause subsequent behavior. Contingent consequences, in turn, either strengthen or weaken that behavior.

3. *Demonstrate your knowledge of positive reinforcement, negative reinforcement, punishment, and extinction.* Positive and negative reinforcement are consequence management strategies that strengthen behavior, whereas punishment and extinction weaken behavior. These strategies need to be defined objectively in terms of their actual impact on behavior frequency, not subjectively on the basis of intended impact.

4. *Distinguish between continuous and intermittent schedules of reinforcement, and specify which schedules are most resistant to extinction.* Every instance of a behavior is reinforced with a continuous reinforcement (CRF) schedule. Under intermittent reinforcement schedules—fixed and variable ratio or fixed and variable interval—some, rather than all, instances of a target behavior are reinforced. Vari-

able schedules produce the most extinction-resistant behavior.

5. *Demonstrate your knowledge of behavior shaping.* Behavior shaping occurs when closer and closer approximations of a target behavior are reinforced. In effect, the standard for reinforcement is made more difficult as the individual learns. The process begins with continuous reinforcement, which gives way to intermittent reinforcement when the target behavior becomes strong and habitual.

6. *Identify and briefly explain each step in the four-step B Mod process.* On-the-job behavior can be modified with the following four-step model: (1) identify target behavior, (2) functionally analyze the situation, (3) arrange antecedents and provide consequences, and (4) evaluate results. Behavior charts, with baseline data for before-and-after comparison, are a practical way of evaluating the effectiveness of a B Mod program.

7. *Specify the six guidelines for managing consequences during B Mod.* (1) Reinforce improvement, not just final results. (2) Fit the consequences to the behavior. (3) Emphasize natural rewards over contrived rewards. (4) Provide individuals with objective feedback whenever possible. (5) Emphasize positive reinforcement; de-emphasize punishment. (6) Schedule reinforcement appropriately.

8. *Explain the social learning model of self-management.* Behavior results from interaction among four components: (1) situational cues, (2) the person's psychological self, (3) the person's behavior, and (4) consequences. Behavior, such as Covey's seven habits of highly effective people, can be developed by relying on supportive cognitive processes such as mental rehearsal and self-talk. Carefully arranged cues and consequences also help in the self-improvement process.

DISCUSSION QUESTIONS

1. What would an A→B→C functional analysis of your departing your residence *on time* for school or work look like? How about a functional analysis of your leaving late?

2. Why is the term *contingency* central to understanding the basics of B Mod?

3. What real-life examples of positive reinforcement, negative reinforcement, both forms of punishment,

and extinction can you draw from your recent experience? Were these strategies appropriately or inappropriately used?

4. From a schedule of reinforcement perspective, why do people find gambling so addictive?

5. What sort of behavior shaping have you engaged in lately? Explain your success or failure.

6. Regarding the six guidelines for successfully managing consequences, which do you think ranks as the most important? Explain your rationale.

7. Why is valid baseline data essential in a B Mod program?

8. What sort of luck have you had with self-management recently? Which of the self-management techniques discussed in this chapter would help you do better?

9. Do you agree with the assumption that managers need to do a good job with self-management before they can effectively manage others? Explain.

10. What importance would you attach to self-talk in self-management? Explain.

EXERCISE

Objectives

1. To better understand the principles of behavior modification through firsthand experience.

2. To improve your own or someone else's behavior by putting to use what you have learned in this chapter.

Introduction

Because the areas of B Mod and BSM are application oriented, they need to be put to practical use if they are to be fully appreciated. In a general sense, everyone is a behavior modifier. Unfortunately, those without a working knowledge of behavioral principles tend to manage their own and others' behavior rather haphazardly. They tend to unwittingly reinforce undesirable behavior, put desirable behavior on extinction, and rely too heavily on punishment and negative reinforcement. This exercise is designed to help you become a more systematic manager of behavior.

Instructions

Selecting the target behavior of your choice, put the four-step behavior modification model in Figure 8–3 into practice. The target may be your own behavior (e.g., studying more, smoking fewer cigarettes, eating less or eating more nutritionally, or one of Covey's seven habits in Table 8–5) or someone else's (e.g., improving a roommate's house-keeping behavior). Be sure to construct a behavior chart (as in Figure 8–4) with the frequency of the target behavior on the vertical axis and time on the horizontal axis. It is best to focus on a behavior that occurs daily so a three- or four-day baseline period can be followed by a one- to two-week intervention period. Make sure you follow as many of the six consequence management guidelines as possible.

You will find it useful to perform an A→B→C functional analysis of the target behavior to identify its supporting (or hindering) cues and consequences. Then you will be in a position to set a reasonable goal and design an intervention strategy involving antecedent and consequence management. When planning a self-management intervention, give careful thought to how you can use cognitive supports. Make sure you use appropriate schedules of reinforcement.

Questions for Consideration/Class Discussion

1. Did you target a specific behavior (e.g., eating) or an outcome (e.g., pounds lost)? What was the advantage or disadvantage of tracking that particular target?

2. How did your B Mod or BSM program turn out? What did you do wrong? What did you do right?

3. How has this exercise increased your working knowledge of B Mod and/or BSM?

NOTES

[1] Complete details of this field study may be found in R S Haynes, R C Pine, and H G Fitch, "Reducing Accident Rates with Organizational Behavior Modification," *Academy of Management Journal,* June 1982, pp 407–16.

[2] Based on a similar definition in R Kreitner, "The Feedforward and Feedback Control of Job Performance through Organizational Behavior Management (OBM)," *Journal of Organizational Behavior Management,* no. 3, 1982, pp 3–20. Three excellent resources, relative to B Mod in the workplace, are L W Frederiksen, ed, *Handbook of Organizational Behavior Management* (New York: John Wiley & Sons, 1982); F Andrasik, "Organizational Behavior Modification in Business Settings: A Methodological and Content Review," *Journal of Organizational Behavior Management,* no. 1, 1989, pp 59–77; and G A Merwi, Jr., J A Thomason, and E E Sanford, "A Methodology and Content Review of Organizational Behavior Management in the Private Sector: 1978–1986," *Journal of Organizational Behavior Management,* no. 1, 1989, pp 39–57.

[3] See E L Thorndike, *Educational Psychology: The Psychology of Learning, Vol. II* (New York: Columbia University Teachers College, 1913).

[4] For recent discussion, see J W Donahoe, "The Unconventional Wisdom of B F Skinner: The Analysis-Interpretation Distinction," *Journal of the Experimental Analysis of Behavior,* September 1993, pp 453–56.

[5] See B F Skinner, *The Behavior of Organisms* (New York: Appleton-Century-Crofts, 1938).

[6] For an instructive overview of learning, see G S Odiorne, "Four Magic Moments in Changing Behavior," *Training,* June 1991, pp 43–46.

[7] Complete discussion of the A→B→C model may be found in F Luthans and R Kreitner, *Organizational Behavior Modification and Beyond: An Operant and Social Learning Approach* (Glenview, IL: Scott, Foresman, 1985), pp 46–49.

[8] D H Ruben and M J Ruben, "Behavioral Principles on the Job: Control or Manipulation?" *Personnel,* May 1985, p 61.

[9] See P A Lamal, "The Continuing Mischaracterization of Radical Behaviorism," *American Psychologist,* January 1990, p 71.

[10] See Luthans and Kreitner, *Organizational Behavior Modification and Beyond,* pp 49–56.

[11] See D H B Welsh, D J Bernstein, and F Luthans, "Application of the Premack Principle of Reinforcement to the Quality Performance of Service Employees," *Journal of Organizational Behavior Management,* no. 1, 1992, pp 9–32.

[12] L M Miller, *Behavior Management: The New Science of Managing People at Work* (New York: John Wiley & Sons, 1978), p 106.

[13] For a unique psychobiological interpretation of reinforcement, see N M White and P M Milner, "The Psychobiology of Reinforcers," *Annual Review of Psychology,* vol. 43, 1992, pp 443–71.

[14] L Baum, "Punishing Workers with a Day Off," *Business Week,* June 16, 1986, p 80.

[15] See C B Ferster and B F Skinner, *Schedules of Reinforcement* (New York: Appleton-Century-Crofts, 1957).

[16] Our choice is *e.* Of course, the correct answer to this challenging exercise is a matter of interpretation. There is plenty of room for honest disagreement. Our interpretation is based on the belief that the passage of time is *not* the primary criterion for granting reinforcement. The first reinforcement schedule, involving cash bonuses at the end of 6-month and 12-month periods for perfect attendance, is anchored to a specific number of complete work days. Every employee, regardless of his or her attendance record, does not automatically receive the cash bonuses at 6- and 12-month intervals (as would be the case with a fixed interval schedule). Hence, it is a fixed ratio schedule.

The second reinforcement schedule is anchored to whether or not one is eligible to enter the drawing. Again, the criterion is a specific set of behaviors, not the passage of time. This second reinforcement schedule qualifies as variable ratio, because a random number of perfect attendance days must pass before a given employee wins the all-expenses-paid trip. Maintaining perfect attendance to qualify for the drawing each year is just like playing a slot machine. Together, these two schedules of reinforcement are a good incentive for perfect attendance.

[17] See L M Saari and G P Latham, "Employee Reactions to Continuous and Variable Ratio Reinforcement Schedules Involving a Monetary Incentive," *Journal of Applied Psychology,* August 1982, pp 506–8.

[18] P Brinkley-Rogers and R Collier, "Along the Colorado, the Money's Flowing," *The Arizona Republic,* March 4, 1990, p A12.

[19] The topic of managerial credibility is covered in J M Kouzes and B Z Posner, *Credibility* (San Francisco: Jossey-Bass, 1993).

[20] See, for example, J C Bruening, "Shaping Workers' Attitudes toward Safety," *Occupational Hazards,* March 1990, pp 49–51.

[21] An alternative five-step model—pinpoint, record, involve, coach, evaluate—may be found in K Blanchard and R Lorber, *Putting the One Minute Manager to Work* (New York: Berkley Books, 1984), p 58.

[22] For example, see B H Harvey, J A Schultze, and J F Rogers, "Rewarding Employees for Not Using Sick Leave," *Personnel Administrator,* May 1983, pp 55–59. Also see J C Landau, "The Impact of a Change in an Attendance Control System on Absenteeism and Tardiness," *Journal of Organizational Behavior Management,* no. 2, 1993, pp 51–70.

[23] L W Frederiksen, "The Selection of Targets for Organizational Interventions," *Journal of Organizational Behavior Management,* no. 4, 1981–1982, p 4.

24 For related discussion, see W Wilhelm, "Changing Corporate Culture—or Corporate Behavior? How to Change Your Company," *Academy of Management Executive,* November 1992, pp 72–77.

25 See J Conrin, "A Comparison of Two Types of Antecedent Control over Supervisory Behavior," *Journal of Organizational Behavior Management,* Fall–Winter 1982, pp 37–47. For a report of the positive impact of antecedents on consumer behavior, see M J Martinko, J D White, and B Hassell, "An Operant Analysis of Prompting in a Sales Environment," *Journal of Organizational Behavior Management,* no. 1, 1989, pp 93–107. Antecedent control of safety behavior is reported in F M Streff, M J Kalsher, and E S Geller, "Developing Efficient Workplace Safety Programs: Observations of Response Covariation," *Journal of Organizational Behavior Management,* no. 2, 1993, pp 3–14.

26 T K Connellan, *How to Improve Human Performance: Behaviorism in Business and Industry* (New York: Harper & Row, 1978), p 27.

27 W C Hamner and E P Hamner, "Behavior Modification on the Bottom Line," *Organizational Dynamics,* Spring 1976, p 8.

28 Luthans and Kreitner, *Organizational Behavior Modification and Beyond,* p 128. Incentive programs are critiqued in B Filipczak, "Why No One Likes Your Incentive Program," *Training,* August 1993, pp 19–25; and A Kohn, "Why Incentive Plans Cannot Work," *Harvard Business Review,* September–October 1993, pp 54–63.

29 See "At Emery Air Freight: Positive Reinforcement Boosts Performance," *Organizational Dynamics,* Winter 1973, pp 41–50.

30 See D C Anderson, C R Crowell, M Doman, and G S Howard, "Performance Posting, Goal Setting, and Activity-Contingent Praise as Applied to a University Hockey Team," *Journal of Applied Psychology,* February 1988, pp 87–95.

31 An alternative perspective of punishment is presented in L Klebe Trevino, "The Social Effects of Punishment in Organizations: A Justice Perspective," *Academy of Management Review,* October 1992, pp 647–76.

32 K Blanchard and S Johnson, *The One Minute Manager* (New York: Berkley Books, 1982), p 39. Interestingly, managers were given this identical bit of advice, "Catch them doing something right!" five years earlier by R Kreitner, "People Are Systems, Too: Filling the Feedback Vacuum," *Business Horizons,* November 1977, pp 54–58.

33 For a review of this research, see Luthans and Kreitner, *Organizational Behavior Modification and Beyond,* pp 139–44. An alternative view of the benefits of punishment is discussed by R D Arvey and J M Ivancevich, "Punishment in Organizations: A Review, Propositions, and Research Suggestions," *Academy of Management Review,* January 1980, pp 123–32.

34 S Narod, "Off-Beat Company Customs," *Dun's Business Month,* November 1984, p 66.

35 For example, see F L Fry, "Operant Conditioning in Organizational Settings: Of Mice or Men?" *Personnel,* July–August 1974, pp 17–24, and E A Locke, "The Myths of Behavior Mod in Organizations," *Academy of Management Review,* 1977, pp 543–53.

36 Evidence of constructive applications of B Mod in the workplace can be found in K O'Hara, C M Johnson, and T A Beehr, "Organizational Behavior Management in the Private Sector: A Review of Empirical Research and Recommendations for Further Investigation," *Academy of Management Review,* October 1985, pp 848–64. Also see recent issues of *Journal of Organizational Behavior Management,* particularly the special issue: "Promoting Excellence through Performance Management," *Journal of Organizational Behavior Management,* no. 1, 1990.

37 See Bandura, *Social Learning Theory* (Englewood Cliffs, NJ: Prentice-Hall, 1977).

38 F Luthans and T R V Davis, "Behavioral Self-Management—The Missing Link in Managerial Effectiveness," *Organizational Dynamics,* Summer 1979, p 43.

39 Luthans and Kreitner, *Organizational Behavior Modification and Beyond,* p 158.

40 See, for example, C C Manz and H P Sims, Jr., "Self-Management as a Substitute for Leadership: A Social Learning Theory Perspective," *Academy of Management Review,* July 1980, pp 361–67; C C Manz, *The Art of Self-Leadership* (Englewood Cliffs, NJ: Prentice-Hall, 1983); C C Manz, "Self-Leadership: Toward an Expanded Theory of Self-Influence Processes in Organizations," *Academy of Management Review,* July 1986, pp 585–600; and C C Manz and H P Sims, Jr., *SuperLeadership: Leading Others to Lead Themselves* (New York: Prentice-Hall, 1989).

41 For example, see R Kelley and J Caplan, "How Bell Labs Creates Star Performers," *Harvard Business Review,* July–August 1993, pp 128–39; and E E Lawler III, "Total Quality Management and Employee Involvement: Are They Compatible?" *Academy of Management Executive,* February 1994, pp 68–76.

42 Bandura, *Social Learning Theory,* p. 13.

43 S R Covey, *The Seven Habits of Highly Effective People* (New York: Simon & Schuster, 1989), p 42. Also see J Hillkirk, "Golden Rules Promoted for Work Success," *USA Today,* August 20, 1993, pp 1B–2B; and L Bongiorno, "Corporate America, Dr. Feelgood Will See You Now," *Business Week,* December 6, 1993, p 52.

44 "Labor Letter: A Special News Report on People and

their Jobs in Offices, Fields, and Factories," *The Wall Street Journal,* October 15, 1985, p 1.

45 Helpful instructions on formulating career goals may be found in D Heide and E N Kushell, "I Can Improve My Management Skills by: _____," *Personnel Journal,* June 1984, pp 52–54.

46 R McGarvey, "Rehearsing for Success," *Executive Female,* January/February 1990, p 36.

47 See W P Anthony, R H Bennett, III, E N Maddox, and W J Wheatley, "Picturing the Future: Using Mental Imagery to Enrich Strategic Environmental Assessment," *Academy of Management Executive,* May 1993, pp 43–56.

48 McGarvey, "Rehearsing for Success," p 36.

49 C Zastrow, *Talk to Yourself: Using the Power of Self-Talk* (Englewood Cliffs, NJ: Prentice-Hall, 1979), p 60. Also see Manz and Sims, *SuperLeadership* pp 41–43; and C C Manz and C P Neck, "Inner Leadership: Creating Productive Thought Patterns," *Academy of Management Executive,* August 1991, pp 87–95.

50 See C C Manz and C P Neck, "Inner Leadership: Creating Productive Thought Patterns," pp 87–95.

51 Drawn from discussion in A Bandura, "Self-Reinforcement: Theoretical and Methodological Considerations," *Behaviorism,* Fall 1976, pp 135–55.

52 R Kreitner and F Luthans, "A Social Learning Approach to Behavioral Management: Radical Behaviorists 'Mellowing Out,' " *Organizational Dynamics,* Autumn 1984, p 63.

53 See R F Rakos and M V Grodek, "An Empirical Evaluation of a Behavioral Self-Management Course in a College Setting," *Teaching of Psychology,* October 1984, pp 157–62.

54 S J Zaccaro, R J Foti, and D A Kenny, "Self-Monitoring and Trait-Based Variance in Leadership: An Investigation of Leader Flexibility across Multiple Group Situations," *Journal of Applied Psychology,* April 1991, p 309.

55 Luthans and Davis, "Behavioral Self-Management—The Missing Link in Managerial Effectiveness," pp 52–59.

56 Results are presented in C A Frayne and G P Latham, "Application of Social Learning Theory to Employee Self-Management of Attendance," *Journal of Applied Psychology,* August 1987, pp 387–92. Follow-up data are presented in G P Latham and C A Frayne, "Self-Management Training for Increasing Job Attendance: A Follow-Up and a Replication," *Journal of Applied Psychology,* June 1989, pp 411–16.

57 See M A Howe, "Using Imagery to Facilitate Organizational Development and Change," *Group & Organizational Studies,* March 1989, pp 70–82.

58 See C A Frayne and M J Geringer, "Self-Management Training for Joint Venture General Managers," *Human Resource Planning,* no 4, 1992, pp 69–85.

GROUP AND SOCIAL PROCESSES

GROUP DYNAMICS

Learning OBJECTIVES

When you finish studying the material in this chapter, you should be able to:

1. Identify the four criteria of a group from a sociological perspective.
2. Describe the six stages of group development.
3. Distinguish between role conflict and role ambiguity.
4. Contrast roles and norms and specify four reasons norms are enforced in organizations.
5. Distinguish between task and maintenance functions in groups.
6. Summarize the practical contingency management implications for group size and group member ability.
7. Discuss why managers need to carefully handle mixed-gender task groups.
8. Describe groupthink and identify at least four of its symptoms.
9. Define social loafing and explain how managers can prevent it.

OPENING CASE

The Wilderness Lab (Janet W. Long)

Sharon Hoogstraten

I found myself on a bus . . . winding into the Rockies west of Denver toward the base camp used by the Corporate Development Program of the Colorado Outward Bound School. There were 18 other refugees from the white-collar world, all headed for five days of management development in the woods. Outward Bound offers "Reaching Your Management Potential" in conjunction with the University of Denver Center for Management Development. . . .

Our bus carried a diverse group into the mountains. We represented organizations from Washington State to Washington, D.C. . . . from one-person consulting firms to multinational corporations. The participants included wise, understated, seasoned managers as well as bright young travelers on the corporate ladder whose rough edges were softened by the positive energy in their eyes. There were managers whose natural interests in

people and leadership ability had taken them up the ranks, and highly skilled technicians, used to being independent contributors, who had recently found themselves in the uncomfortable position of needing to manage others. Ages ranged from 24 to 44, and disciplines included law, engineering, architecture, marketing, and education, among others. Some participants were veterans of many training programs; others were fairly new to the realm of management development.

Most of us wanted to be there. Some had learned of the program themselves and lobbied to go. Others had been sent by their organizations to learn to work more effectively in groups—either because they were normally reticent in groups, or because they tended to dominate and compete. The outdoor medium had been selected by some because it is a more comfortable setting than the traditional classroom. Others had chosen it because it is a substantial step *beyond* the familiar corporate comfort zone and as such is a ripe environment for testing the ways we plan, solve problems, and work with others.

Most of us were a little scared. Our fears ranged from making fools of ourselves to falling off a cliff. It was hard to determine which of those fears was more serious. . . .

At the top of the hill we found a "trust ladder" nailed to one of the many pines surrounding us. There

appeared to be a little more risk here than looking silly. Eric [the course director] explained that we would need to rely on one another under many circumstances in the coming week, and that the object of this exercise was to climb the ladder and fall off backwards into the arms of the group. He showed us how to line up and join hands to catch our falling teammate, and he headed for the ladder before we could ponder the matter too thoroughly. I was afraid that I wouldn't be able to hold him . . . and, of course, I couldn't have alone. One by one we climbed the ladder and thumped down into the waiting arms.

This was the first activity that we analyzed. We talked about risk taking, trusting one's support system, communicating needs, and checking to be sure that the support system is ready before relying on it . . . and a little about what's involved in supporting someone effectively.

Our most physical group challenge was a 13-foot wall the entire group had to scale. It was sheer and smooth, with a platform behind it on which one could stand at about waist level with the top of the wall. This platform could be occupied by two people (once we got them up and over) to help haul up the rest of the group. A ladder was provided on the back for climbing down to earth. Thirteen feet had never seemed so imposing. We were given a few safety restrictions, and the

f you were a waitress in a restaurant and you wanted to maximize your tips while serving male–female couples, which of the following approaches would you use?

1. Touch the male lightly and briefly on the shoulder while asking if everything was all right.
2. Do not touch either person while asking if everything was all right.

OPENING CASE

(concluded)

stopwatch began ticking. Group planning and problem solving were again germane, with special attention to the first and last people over the wall.

We decided that we needed to boost some strong people up first to help pull the rest up, and keep some powerful boosters on the ground. The middle group would be relatively straightforward, with help from above and below. The final climb appeared to require two key players: someone strong enough to act as a "human rope," facing the wall and hanging with his shoulders looped over the top; and someone light and strong enough to scramble up the wall, using the human rope until he could get a hand from the pullers.

The roles clear, we began to assess our resources. I was proud of the group as we offered up both our strengths *and* limitations. We had walked past THE WALL several times over the previous two days, and it was the culmination of our group challenges. We were hungry to do it well, and the chance to play a key role was tantalizing. But the group interdependence in this exercise took on a more serious note. Despite good safety precautions (such as helmets and "spotters" whose job it would be to break anyone's fall) we really did have one another's safety in our hands. It would not do to play the hero here and be unable to come through. Some of our most athletic team members owned

up to prohibitive injuries that would keep them in the middle of the progression. Others stepped forward to fill the void, each assessing his or her own capabilities with a balance of commitment and responsibility. Soon we all knew our roles, and the adrenaline began to flow.

The scene that followed was an organized frenzy of push, pull, scramble, encourage, and keep those hands in the air in case someone fell. No one spent a moment uninvolved in the process. We all ached for our last two teammates as they completed the grueling climb. It was a tired and happy group that sat in a circle beneath the wall to talk not only about planning and problem solving but also the dynamics of sensible group risk taking, and the strength of being part of a multitalented, interdependent and mutually supportive team.

As I leaned back against the wall and watched all this with an analytical trainer's eye, I became aware of the powerful lesson I was experiencing at gut level. [White-water canoeing had] . . . left me with a shoulder that chronically dislocates, which not only put me in the center of the progression up the wall, but made me feel like a liability to the group. As I stepped up for my boost, I told the pullers what to expect. "All right, Wayne, you can pull for all you're worth. But Mike, I can't extend this right arm very high, and if I call your name, let go in a hurry." I

could feel the spotters move in around me, but I was up and over in a moment with no trouble.

During the debriefing I asked what effect my limitation had on the group, especially Wayne and Mike. "None at all," said Wayne. "None," echoed Mike, "because you told us what your needs were. I could lean down the wall further and put myself into a more vulnerable position with more leverage because I knew you wouldn't be pulling very hard with that arm." I've never been good at making my needs known, but in this situation I felt a responsibility to the group. I thought back to the office and wondered how many projects I had avoided or contributed less than I could have because I didn't give someone the chance to fill in my weak spots.

For Discussion

Why might the wilderness lab be a better learning environment than the classroom?

■ Additional discussion questions linking this case with the following material appear at the end of this chapter.

Source: Excerpted from J W Long, "The Wilderness Lab," *Training and Development Journal,* May 1984, pp 58–69. Used with permission.

---

3. Touch the female lightly and briefly on the shoulder while asking if everything was all right.

Think briefly about why you have selected that answer before reading further.

According to the results of a social psychology field study in a Greensboro, North Carolina, restaurant, the last approach would be your most profitable alternative. This approach produced an average tip of 15 percent, whereas the first and second tactics yielded average tips of 13 percent and 11 percent, respectively.[1] Of course, different results could be expected in cultures where public physical contact is discouraged. The outcome for a male waiter might be different, too. Nonetheless, this little multiple-choice quiz illustrates the curious twists behavior can take when individuals interact. Because the management of organizational behavior is above all else a social endeavor, managers need a working knowledge of *interpersonal* behavior. This point was driven home recently by a survey of 56 recruiters for *Fortune* 500 companies. The number one hiring factor for general management positions was *strong interpersonal skills.*[2]

Let us begin by defining the term *group* as a prelude to examining types of groups, functions of group members, and the group development process. Our attention then turns to group roles and norms, the basic building blocks of group dynamics. Impacts of group structure and member characteristics on group outcomes are explored next. Finally, three serious threats to group effectiveness are discussed.

GROUPS: DEFINITIONS, TYPES, AND FUNCTIONS

Groups are an inescapable aspect of modern life.[3] College students are often teamed with their peers for class projects. Parents serve on community advisory boards at their local high school. Managers find themselves on product planning committees and productivity task forces. Productive organizations simply cannot function without gathering individuals into groups and teams.[4] But, as personal experience shows, group effort can bring out both the best and the worst in people. A marketing department meeting, where several people excitedly brainstorm and refine a creative new advertising campaign, can yield results beyond the capabilities of individual contributors. Conversely, committees have become the butt of jokes (e.g., a committee is a place where they take minutes and waste hours; a camel is a horse designed by a committee) because they all too often are plagued by lack of direction and by conflict. Modern managers need a solid understanding of groups and group processes so as to both avoid their pitfalls and tap their vast potential.

group   Two or more freely interacting people with shared norms and goals and a common identity.

Although other definitions of groups exist, we draw from the field of sociology and define a **group** as two or more freely interacting individuals who share collective norms and goals and have a common identity.[5] Figure 9–1 illustrates how the four criteria in this definition combine to form a conceptual whole. Organizational psychologist Edgar Schein shed additional light on this concept by drawing instructive distinctions between a group, a crowd, and an organization:

> The size of a group is thus limited by the possibilities of mutual interaction and mutual awareness. Mere aggregates of people do not fit this definition because they do not interact and do not perceive themselves to be a group even if they are aware of each other

• FIGURE 9–1
Four Sociological Criteria of a Group

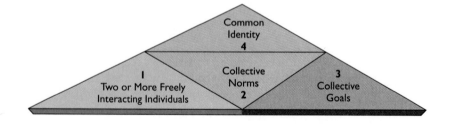

as, for instance, a crowd on a street corner watching some event. A total department, a union, or a whole organization would not be a group in spite of thinking of themselves as ''we,'' because they generally do not all interact and are not all aware of each other. However, work teams, committees, subparts of departments, cliques, and various other informal associations among organizational members would fit this definition of a group.[6]

Take a moment now to think of various groups of which you are a member. Does each of your ''groups'' satisfy the four criteria in Figure 9–1?

Formal and Informal Groups

Individuals join groups, or are assigned to groups, to accomplish various purposes. If the group is formed by a manager to help the organization accomplish its goals, then it qualifies as a **formal group.** Formal groups typically wear such labels as work group, team, committee, quality circle, or task force. An **informal group** exists when the members' overriding purpose of getting together is friendship. Although formal and informal groups often overlap, such as a team of corporate auditors heading for the tennis courts after work, some employees are not friends with their co-workers. The desirability of overlapping formal and informal groups is problematic. Some managers firmly believe personal friendship fosters productive teamwork on the job while others view workplace ''bull sessions'' as a serious threat to productivity. Both situations are common, and it is the manager's job to strike a workable balance, based on the maturity and goals of the people involved.

formal group   Formed by the organization.

informal group   Formed by friends.

Functions of Formal Groups

Researchers point out that formal groups fulfill two basic functions: *organizational* and *individual*.[7] The various functions are listed in Table 9–1. Complex combinations of these functions can be found in formal groups at any given time.

For example, consider what Mazda's new American employees experienced when they spent a month working in Japan before the opening of the firm's Flat Rock, Michigan, plant in 1987.

> After a month of training in Mazda's factory methods, whipping their new Japanese buddies at softball and sampling local watering holes, the Americans were fired

Organizational Functions	Individual Functions
1. Accomplish complex, interdependent tasks that are beyond the capabilities of individuals.	1. Satisfy the individual's need for affiliation.
2. Generate new or creative ideas and solutions.	2. Develop, enhance, and confirm the individual's self-esteem and sense of identity.
3. Coordinate interdepartmental efforts.	3. Give individuals an opportunity to test and share their perceptions of social reality.
4. Provide a problem-solving mechanism for complex problems requiring varied information and assessments.	4. Reduce the individual's anxieties and feelings of insecurity and powerlessness.
5. Implement complex decisions.	5. Provide a problem-solving mechanism for personal and interpersonal problems.
6. Socialize and train newcomers.	

• ➤ **TABLE 9–1**
Formal Groups Fulfill Organizational and Individual Functions

Source: Adapted from E H Schien, *Organizational Psychology*, 3rd ed (Englewood Cliffs, NJ: Prentice Hall, 1980), pp 149–51.

up. . . . [A maintenance manager] even faintly praised the Japanese practice of holding group calisthenics at the start of each working day: "I didn't think I'd like doing exercises every morning, but I kind of like it."[8]

While Mazda pursued the organizational functions it wanted—interdependent teamwork, creativity, coordination, problem solving, and training—the American workers benefited from the individual functions of formal groups. Among those benefits were affiliation with new friends, enhanced self-esteem, exposure to the Japanese social reality, and reduction of anxieties about working for a foreign-owned company. In short, Mazda created a workable blend of organizational and individual group functions by training its newly hired American employees in Japan.

THE GROUP DEVELOPMENT PROCESS

Groups go through a predictable maturation process, such as one would find in any life-cycle situation (e.g., humans, organizations, products). However, while there is general agreement among theorists that the group development process occurs in identifiable stages, they disagree about the exact number, sequence, length, and nature of those stages.[9] An instructive model of group development is depicted in Figure 9–2. Notice how *uncertainty over authority and power* is an overriding obstacle during the first three phases. During the last three phases, *uncertainty over interpersonal relations* becomes the major obstacle.

Six Stages

Let us briefly examine each of the six stages.[10] You can make this process come to life by relating the various stages to your own experiences with work groups, committees, athletic teams, social or religious groups, or class project teams. Some group happenings that surprised you when they occurred may now make sense or strike you as inevitable when seen as part of a developmental process.

• FIGURE 9–2

Six Stages of Group Development

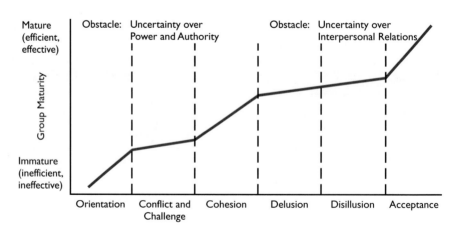

Source: Adapted from L N Jewell and H J Reitz, *Group Effectiveness in Organizations* (Glenview, IL: Scott Foresman, 1981), p 20.

Stage 1: Orientation   During this "ice-breaking" stage, group members tend to be uncertain and anxious about such things as their roles, who is in charge, and the group's goals. Mutual trust is low and there is a good deal of holding back to see who takes charge and how. If the formal leader (e.g., a supervisor) does not assert his or her authority, an emergent leader will eventually step in to fulfill the group's need for leadership and direction. Leaders typically mistake this honeymoon period as a mandate for permanent control. But later problems may force a leadership change.

Stage 2: Conflict and Challenge   This is a time of testing. Individuals test the leader's policies and assumptions as they try to determine how they fit into the power structure.[11] Subgroups take shape, and subtle forms of rebellion, such as procrastination, occur. Many groups stall in stage 2 because power politics erupts into open rebellion.

Stage 3: Cohesion   Groups that make it through stage 2 generally do so because a respected member, other than the leader, challenges the group to resolve its power struggles so something can be accomplished. Questions about authority and power are resolved rather quickly through unemotional, matter-of-fact group discussion. A renewed feeling of team spirit is experienced because members believe they have found their proper roles.

Stage 4: Delusion   Having resolved major disputes over power and authority, the group's members feel a sense of relief over having been "through the worst of it." Unfortunately, pressures build up as the quest for harmony and goodwill causes individuals to stifle their complaints. Participation is very active during this stage.

Stage 5: Disillusion   The unrealistic sense of harmony in stage 4 begins to fray around the edges as some members point out that the group is not fulfilling its potential. Conflict between subgroups may arise over whether or not individuals should reveal their relative strengths and weaknesses. A drop in group cohesiveness is evidenced by increased absenteeism, withheld commitment, and critical remarks.

Stage 6: Acceptance   The hurdle between stages 4 and 5 is much like that between stages 2 and 3. Consequently, it once again falls on an influential member of the group, typically not the leader, to challenge his or her peers to do some reality testing. This exercise promotes greater understanding about the members' expectations for each other and for the group as a whole.

> As a result of overcoming this final obstacle, the group structure can become flexible and adjust to fit the requirements of the situation without causing problems for the members. Influence can shift depending on who has the particular expertise or skills required for the group task or activity. Subgroups can work on special problems or subproblems without posing threats to the authority or cohesiveness of the rest of the group.[12]

These characteristics combine to signal that the group has matured.

Group Development: Research and Practical Implications

A growing body of group development research provides managers with some practical insights.

Feedback   One fruitful study was carried out by a pair of Dutch social psychologists. They hypothesized that interpersonal feedback would vary systematically during the group development process. "The unit of feedback measured was a verbal message directed from one participant to another in which some aspect of behavior was addressed."[13] After collecting and categorizing 1,600 instances of feedback from four different eight-person groups, they concluded the following:

- Interpersonal feedback increases as the group develops through successive stages.
- As the group develops, positive feedback increases and negative feedback decreases.
- Interpersonal feedback becomes more specific as the group develops.
- The credibility of peer feedback increases as the group develops.[14]

These findings hold important lessons for managers. The content and delivery of interpersonal feedback among work group or committee members can be used as a gauge of whether the group is developing properly. For example, the onset of stages 2 (conflict and challenge) and 5 (disillusion) will be signaled by a noticeable increase in *negative* feedback. Effort can then be directed at generating specific, positive feedback among the members so the group's development will not stall. The feedback model discussed in Chapter 14 is helpful in this regard.

Deadlines   Field and laboratory studies found uncertainty about deadlines to be a major disruptive force in both group development and intergroup relations. The practical implications of this finding were summed up by the researcher as follows:

> Uncertain or shifting deadlines are a fact of life in many organizations. Interdependent organizational units and groups may keep each other waiting, may suddenly move deadlines forward or back, or may create deadlines that are known to be earlier than is necessary in efforts to control erratic workflows. The current research suggests that the consequences of such uncertainty may involve more than stress, wasted time, overtime work, and intergroup conflicts. Synchrony in group members' expectations about deadlines may be critical to groups' abilities to accomplish successful transitions in their work.[15]

Thus, effective group management involves clarifying not only tasks and goals, but deadlines as well. When group members accurately perceive important deadlines, the pacing of work and timing of interdependent tasks tends to be more efficient.

Leadership Styles   Along a somewhat different line, experts in the area of leadership contend that different leadership styles are needed as work groups develop.

> In general, it has been documented that leadership behavior that is active, aggressive, directive, structured, and task-oriented seems to have favorable results early in the group's history. However, when those behaviors are maintained throughout the life of the group, they seem to have a negative impact on cohesiveness and quality of work. Conversely, leadership behavior that is supportive, democratic, decentralized, and participative seems to be related to poorer functioning in the early group development stages. However, when these behaviors are maintained throughout the life of the group, more productivity, satisfaction, and creativity result.[16]

The practical punch line here is that managers are advised to shift from a directive and structured leadership style to a participative and supportive style as the group develops. (Leadership is discussed in detail in Chapter 15.)

"All the world's a stage, and all the men and women merely players." William Shakespeare could hardly have imagined that these lines from his play *As You Like It* would foretell a complex theory of human interactions based on roles.

SUPERSTOCK

Work groups transform individuals into functioning organizational members through subtle yet powerful social forces. These social forces, in effect, turn "I" into "we" and "me" into "us." Group influence weaves individuals into the organization's social fabric by communicating and enforcing both role expectations and norms. We need to understand roles and norms if we are to effectively manage group and organizational behavior.

ROLES AND NORMS: SOCIAL BUILDING BLOCKS FOR GROUP AND ORGANIZATIONAL BEHAVIOR

Roles

Four centuries have passed since William Shakespeare had his character Jaques speak the following memorable lines in Act II of *As You Like It:* "All the world's a stage, And all the men and women merely players; They have their exits and their entrances; And one man in his time plays many parts. . . ." This intriguing notion of all people as actors in a universal play was not lost on 20th-century sociologists who developed a complex theory of human interaction based on roles. According to an OB scholar, "**roles** are sets of behaviors that persons expect of occupants of a position."[17] Role theory attempts to explain how these social expectations influence employee behavior. This section explores role theory by analyzing a role episode and defining the terms *role overload, role conflict,* and *role ambiguity.*

roles Expected behaviors for a given position.

Role Episodes   A role episode, as illustrated in Figure 9–3, consists of a snapshot of the ongoing interaction between two people. In any given role episode, there is a role sender and a focal person who is expected to act out the role. Within a broader context, one may be simultaneously a role sender and a focal person. For the sake of social analysis, however, it is instructive to deal with separate role episodes.

Role episodes begin with the role sender's perception of the relevant organization's or group's behavioral requirements. Those requirements serve as a standard for formulating expectations for the focal person's behavior. The role sender then cognitively evaluates the focal person's actual behavior against those expectations. Appropriate verbal and nonverbal messages are then sent to the focal person to pressure him or her into behaving as expected.[18] Consider how Westinghouse used a carrot-and-stick approach to communicate role expectations.

The carrot is a plan, that since 1984, has rewarded 134 managers with options to buy 764,000 shares of stock for boosting the company's financial performance.

FIGURE 9~3

A Role Episode

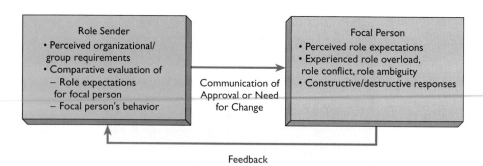

Role Sender		Focal Person

Feedback

Source: Adapted in part from R L Kohn, D M Wolfe, R P Quinn, and J D Snoek, *Organizational Stress: Studies in Role Conflict and Ambiguity,* 1981 edition (Malabar, FL: Robert E. Krieger Publishing, 1964), p 26.

The stick is quarterly meetings that are used to rank managers by how much their operations contribute to earnings per share. The soft-spoken . . . [chairman of the board] doesn't scold. He just charts in green the results of the sectors that have met their goals and charts the laggards in red. Peer pressure does the rest. Shame ''is a powerful tool,'' says one executive.[19]

On the receiving end of the role episode, the focal person accurately or inaccurately perceives the communicated role expectations. Various combinations of role overload, role conflict, and role ambiguity are then experienced. (These three outcomes are defined and discussed in the following sections.) The focal person then responds constructively by engaging in problem solving, for example, or destructively because of undue tension, stress, and strain.[20] Stress is discussed in detail in Chapter 16.

role overload   Others' expectations exceed one's ability.

Role Overload   According to organizational psychologist Edgar Schein, **role overload** occurs when ''the sum total of what role senders expect of the focal person far exceeds what he or she is able to do.''[21] Students who attempt to handle a full course load and maintain a decent social life while working 30 or more hours a week know full well the consequences of role overload. As the individual tries to do more and more in less and less time, stress mounts and personal effectiveness slips.

role conflict   Others have conflicting or inconsistent expectations.

Role Conflict   Have you ever felt like you were being torn apart by the conflicting demands of those around you? If so, you were a victim of role conflict. **Role conflict** is experienced when ''different members of the role set expect different things of the focal person.''[22] Managers often face conflicting demands between work and family, for example.[23] Interestingly, however, women experience greater role conflict between work and family than men because women perform the majority of the household duties and child care responsibilities.[24]

Role conflict also may be experienced when internalized values, ethics, or personal standards collide with others' expectations. For instance, an otherwise ethical production supervisor may be told by a superior to ''fudge a little'' on the quality control reports so an important deadline will be met. The resulting role conflict forces the supervisor to choose between being loyal but unethical or ethical but disloyal. Tough ethical choices such as this mean personal turmoil, interpersonal conflict, and even resignation. Consequently, experts say business schools should do a better job of weaving ethics training into their course requirements.

OB Exercise

Measuring Role Conflict and Role Ambiguity

Instructions:

Step 1. While thinking of your present (or last) job, circle one response for each of the following statements. Please consider each statement carefully because some are worded positively and some negatively.

Step 2. In the space in the far right column, label each statement with either a "C" for role conflict or an "A" for role ambiguity. (See note 26 for a correct categorization.)

Step 3. Calculate separate totals for role conflict and role ambiguity, and compare them with these arbitrary norms: 5–14 = low; 15–25 = moderate; 26–35 = high.

	Very False	Very True	
1. I feel certain about how much authority I have.	7—6—5—4—3—2—1		_____
2. I have to do things that should be done differently.	7—6—5—4—3—2—1		_____
3. I know that I have divided my time properly.	7—6—5—4—3—2—1		_____
4. I know what my responsibilities are.	7—6—5—4—3—2—1		_____
5. I have to buck a rule or policy in order to carry out an assignment.	7—6—5—4—3—2—1		_____
6. I feel certain how I will be evaluated for a raise or promotion.	7—6—5—4—3—2—1		_____
7. I work with two or more groups who operate quite differently.	7—6—5—4—3—2—1		_____
8. I know exactly what is expected of me.	7—6—5—4—3—2—1		_____
9. I do things that are apt to be accepted by one person and not accepted by others.	7—6—5—4—3—2—1		_____
10. I work on unnecessary things.	7—6—5—4—3—2—1		_____

Role conflict score = _____
Role ambiguity store = _____

Source: Adapted from J R Rizzo, R J House, and S I Lirtzman, "Role Conflict and Ambiguity in Complex Organizations," *Administrative Science Quarterly*, June 1970, p 156.

Role Ambiguity Those who experience role conflict may have trouble complying with role demands, but they at least know what is expected of them. Such is not the case with **role ambiguity,** which occurs when "members of the role set fail to communicate to the focal person expectations they have or information needed to perform the role, either because they do not have the information or because they deliberately withhold it."[25] In short, people experience role ambiguity when they do not know what is expected of them. Organizational newcomers often complain about unclear job descriptions and vague promotion criteria. According to role theory, prolonged role ambiguity can foster job dissatisfaction, erode self-confidence, and hamper job performance.

role ambiguity Others' expectations are unknown.

Take a moment now to complete the self-assessment exercise in the OB Exercise. See if you can distinguish between sources of role conflict and sources of role ambiguity, as they affect your working life.

Norms

Norms are more encompassing than roles. While roles involve behavioral expectations for specific positions, norms help organizational members determine right from wrong and good from bad. According to one respected team of management consultants: "A **norm** is an attitude, opinion, feeling, or action—shared by two or more people—that guides their behavior."[27] Although norms are typically unwritten and seldom discussed openly, they have a powerful influence on group and organizational behavior.[28] PepsiCo Inc., for instance, has evolved a norm that equates corporate competitiveness with physical fitness. According to observers:

> Leanness and nimbleness are qualities that pervade the company. When Pepsi's brash young managers take a few minutes away from the office, they often head straight for the company's physical fitness center or for a jog around the museum-quality sculptures outside of PepsiCo's Purchase, New York, headquarters.[29]

At PepsiCo and elsewhere, group members positively reinforce those who adhere to current norms with friendship and acceptance. On the other hand, nonconformists experience criticism and even *ostracism*, or rejection by group members. Anyone who has experienced the "silent treatment" from a group of friends knows what a potent social weapon ostracism can be. Norms can be put into proper perspective by understanding how they develop and why they are enforced.

How Norms Are Developed Experts say norms evolve in an informal manner as the group or organization determines what it takes to be effective. Generally speaking, norms develop in various combinations of the following four ways:

1. *Explicit statements by supervisors or co-workers.* For instance, a group leader might explicitly set norms about not drinking at lunch.
2. *Critical events in the group's history.* At times there is a critical event in the group's history that established an important precedent. [For example, a key recruit may have decided to work elsewhere because a group member said too many negative things about the organization. Hence, a norm against such "sour grapes" behavior might evolve.]
3. *Primacy.* The first behavior pattern that emerges in a group often sets group expectations. If the first group meeting is marked by very formal interaction between supervisors and subordinates, then the group often expects future meetings to be conducted in the same way.
4. *Carryover behaviors from past situations.* Such carryover of individual behaviors from past situations can increase the predictability of group members' behaviors in new settings and facilitate task accomplishment. For instance, students and professors carry fairly constant sets of expectations from class to class.[30]

We would like you to take a few moments and think about the norms that are currently in effect in your classroom. List the norms on a sheet of paper. Do these norms help or hinder your ability to learn? Norms can affect performance either positively or negatively.[31]

Why Norms Are Enforced Norms tend to be enforced by group members when they

∙ TABLE 9-2 Four Reasons Norms Are Enforced

Norm	Reason for Enforcement	Example
"Make our department look good in top management's eyes."	Group/organization survival	After vigorously defending the vital role played by the Human Resources Management Department at a divisional meeting, a staff specialist is complimented by her boss.
"Success comes to those who work hard and don't make waves."	Clarification of behavioral expectations.	A senior manager takes a young associate aside and cautions him to be a bit more patient with co-workers who see things differently.
"Be a team player, not a star."	Avoidance of embarrassment	A project team member is ridiculed by her peers for dominating the discussion during a progress report to top management.
"Customer service is our top priority."	Clarification of central values/unique identity	Two sales representatives are given a surprise Friday afternoon party for having received prestigious best-in-the-industry customer service awards from an industry association.

- Help the group or organization survive.
- Clarify or simplify behavioral expectations.
- Help individuals avoid embarrassing situations.
- Clarify the group's or organization's central values and/or unique identity.[32]

Working examples of each of these four situations are presented in Table 9–2.

Relevant Research Insights and Managerial Implications

Although instruments used to measure role conflict and role ambiguity have questionable validity,[33] two separate meta-analyses indicated that role conflict and role ambiguity negatively affected employees. Specifically, role conflict and role ambiguity were associated with job dissatisfaction, tension and anxiety, lack of organizational commitment, intentions to quit, and, to a lesser extent, poor job performance.[34]

The meta-analyses results hold few surprises for managers. Generally, because of the negative association reported, it makes sense for management to reduce both role conflict and role ambiguity. In this endeavor, managers can use feedback, formal rules and procedures, directive leadership, setting of specific (difficult) goals, and participation. Managers also can use the mentoring process discussed in Chapter 19 to reduce role conflict and ambiguity.

GROUP STRUCTURE AND COMPOSITION

Work groups of varying size are made up of individuals with varying ability and motivation. Moreover, those individuals perform different roles, on either an assigned or voluntary basis. No wonder some work groups are more productive than others. No wonder some committees are tightly knit while others wallow in conflict. In this section, we examine four important dimensions of group structure and composition: (1) functional roles of group members, (2) group size, (3) gender composition, (4) group member ability. Each of these dimensions alternatively can enhance or hinder group effectiveness, depending on how it is managed.

Functional Roles Performed by Group Members

As described in Table 9–3, both task and maintenance roles need to be performed if a work group is to accomplish anything.[35]

task roles Task-oriented group behavior.

maintenance roles Relationship-building group behavior.

Task versus Maintenance Roles   **Task roles** enable the work group to define, clarify, and pursue a common purpose. Meanwhile, **maintenance roles** foster supportive and constructive interpersonal relationships. In short, task roles keep the group *on track* while maintenance roles keep the group *together*. A fraternity or sorority member is performing a task function when he or she stands at a business meeting and says: "What is the real issue here? We don't seem to be getting anywhere." Another individual who says, "Let's hear from those who oppose this plan," is performing a maintenance function. Importantly, each of the various task and maintenance roles may be played in varying combinations and sequences by either the group's leader or any of its members.

Checklist for Managers   The task and maintenance roles listed in Table 9–3 can serve as a handy checklist for managers and group leaders who wish to ensure proper group development. Roles that are not always performed when needed, such

TABLE 9–3
Functional Roles Performed by Group Members

Task Roles	Description
Initiator	Suggests new goals or ideas.
Information seeker/giver	Clarifies key issues.
Opinion seeker/giver	Clarifies pertinent values.
Elaborator	Promotes greater understanding through examples or exploration of implications.
Coordinator	Pulls together ideas and suggestions.
Orienter	Keeps group headed toward its stated goal(s).
Evaluator	Tests group's accomplishments with various criteria such as logic and practicality.
Energizer	Prods group to move along or to accomplish more.
Procedural technician	Performs routine duties (e.g., handing out materials or rearranging seats).
Recorder	Performs a "group memory" function by documenting discussion and outcomes.

Maintenance Roles	Description
Encourager	Fosters group solidarity by accepting and praising various points of view.
Harmonizer	Mediates conflict through reconciliation or humor.
Compromiser	Helps resolve conflict by meeting others "half way."
Gatekeeper	Encourages all group members to participate.
Standard setter	Evaluates the quality of group processes.
Commentator	Records and comments on group processes/dynamics.
Follower	Serves as a passive audience.

Source: Adapted from discussion in K D Benne and P Sheats, "Functional Roles of Group Members," *Journal of Social Issues*, Spring 1948; pp 41–49.

as those of coordinator, evaluator, and gatekeeper, can be performed in a timely manner by the formal leader or assigned to other members.

International managers need to be sensitive to cultural differences regarding the relative importance of task and maintenance roles. In Japan, for example, cultural tradition calls for more emphasis on maintenance roles, especially the roles of harmonizer and compromiser:

> Courtesy requires that members not be conspicuous or disputatious in a meeting or classroom. If two or more members discover that their views differ—a fact that is tactfully taken to be unfortunate—they adjourn to find more information and to work toward a stance that all can accept. They do not press their personal opinions through strong arguments, neat logic, or rewards and threats. And they do not hesitate to shift their beliefs if doing so will preserve smooth interpersonal relations. (To lose is to win.)[36]

Group Size

How many group members is too many? The answer to this deceptively simple question has intrigued managers and academics for years. Folk wisdom says "two heads are better than one" but that "too many cooks spoil the broth." So where should a manager draw the line when staffing a committee? At 3? At 5 or 6? At 10 or more? Researchers have taken two different approaches to pinpointing optimum group size: mathematical modeling and laboratory simulations. Let us briefly review recent findings from these two approaches.

The Mathematical Modeling Approach   This approach involves building a mathematical model around certain desired outcomes of group action such as decision quality. Due to differing assumptions and statistical techniques, the results of this research are inconclusive. Statistical estimates of optimum group size have ranged from 3 to 13.[37]

The Laboratory Simulation Approach   This stream of research is based on the assumption that group behavior needs to be observed firsthand in controlled laboratory settings. A laboratory study by respected Australian researcher Philip Yetton and his colleague, Preston Bottger, provides useful insights about group size and performance.[38]

Five hundred fifty-five subjects (330 managers and 225 graduate management students, of whom 20 percent were female) were assigned to task teams ranging in size from 2 to 6. The teams worked on the National Aeronautics and Space Administration moon survival exercise. (This exercise involves the rank ordering of 15 pieces of equipment that would enable a spaceship crew on the moon to survive a 200-mile trip between a crash-landing site and home base.)[39] After analyzing the relationships between group size and group performance, Yetton and Bottger concluded:

> It would be difficult, at least with respect to decision quality, to justify groups larger than five members. . . . Of course, to meet needs other than high decision quality, organizations may employ groups significantly larger than four or five.[40]

More recent laboratory studies exploring the brainstorming productivity of various size groups (2 to 12 people), in face-to-face versus computer-mediated situations, proved fruitful. In the usual face-to-face brainstorming sessions, productivity of ideas did not increase as the size of the group increased. But brainstorming

productivity increased as the size of the group increased when ideas were typed into networked computers.[41] These results suggest that computer networks could help deliver on the promise of productivity improvement through modern information technology.[42]

Managerial Implications   Within a contingency management framework, there is no hard-and-fast rule about group size. It depends on the manager's objective for the group. If a high-quality decision is the main objective, then a three- to five-member group would be appropriate. However, if the objective is to generate creative ideas, encourage participation, socialize new members, engage in training, or communicate policies, then groups much larger than five could be justified. But managers need to be aware of *qualitative* changes that occur when group size increases. A meta-analysis of eight studies found the following relationships: as group size increased, group leaders tended to become more directive and group member satisfaction tended to decline slightly.[43]

Odd-numbered groups (e.g., three, five, seven members) are recommended if the issue is to be settled by a majority vote. Voting deadlocks (e.g., 2–2, 3–3) too often hamper effectiveness of even-numbered groups. A majority decision rule is not necessarily a good idea. One study found that better group outcomes were obtained by negotiation groups that used a unanimous as opposed to majority decision rule. Individuals' self-interests were more effectively integrated when groups used a unanimous decision criterion.[44]

Effects of Men and Women Working Together in Groups

As pointed out in Chapter 3, the female portion of the US labor force has grown significantly in recent years. This demographic shift brought an increase in the number of organizational committees and teams composed of both men and women. Some profound effects on group dynamics might be expected.[45] Let us see what researchers have found in the way of group gender composition effects and what managers can do about them.

Women Face an Uphill Battle in Mixed-Gender Task Groups   Recent laboratory and field studies paint a picture of inequality for women working in mixed-gender groups. Both women and men need to be aware of these often subtle but powerful group dynamics so corrective steps can be taken.

In a laboratory study of six-person task groups, a clear pattern of gender inequality was found in the way group members interrupted each other. Men interrupted women significantly more often than they did other men. Women, who tended to interrupt less frequently and less successfully than men, interrupted men and women equally.[46]

A field study of mixed-gender police and nursing teams in the Netherlands found another group dynamics disadvantage for women. These two particular professions—police work and nursing—were fruitful research areas because men dominate the former while women dominate the latter. As women move into male-dominated police forces and men gain employment opportunities in the female-dominated world of nursing, who faces the greatest resistance? The answer from this study was the women police officers. As the representation of the minority gender (either female police officers or male nurses) increased in the work groups, the following changes in attitude were observed:

> The attitude of the male majority changes from neutral to resistant, whereas the attitude of the female majority changes from favorable to neutral. In other words, men increasingly want to keep their domain for themselves, while women remain willing to share their domain with men.[47]

Again, managers are faced with the challenge of countering discriminatory tendencies in group dynamics.

Social-sexual behavior was the focus of a random survey of 1,232 working men (n = 405) and women (n = 827) in the Los Angeles area.[48] Both harassing and nonharassing sexual conduct were investigated. One-third of the female employees and one-fourth of the male employees reported being sexually harassed in their present job. Nonharassing sexual behavior was much more common, with 80 percent of the total sample reporting experience with such behavior. Indeed, according to the researchers, increased social contact between men and women in work groups and organizations had led to increased sexualization of the workplace. (To assess the extent of sexualization in your present or former workplace, take a moment to complete the OB Exercise. What are the ethical implications of your score?)[49]

Constructive Managerial Action   Male and female employees can and often do work well together in groups. A survey of 387 male US government employees sought to determine how they were affected by the growing number of female co-workers. The researchers concluded, ''Under many circumstances, including inter-gender interaction in work groups, frequent contact leads to cooperative and supportive social relations.''[50] Still, managers need to take affirmative steps to ensure that the documented sexualization of work environments does not erode into sexual harassment. Whether perpetrated against women or men, sexual harassment is demeaning, unethical, and appropriately called ''work environment pollution.'' Moreover, the US Equal Employment Opportunity Commission holds employers

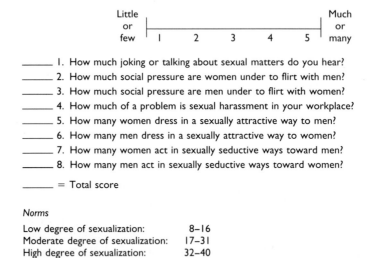

What Is the Degree of Sexualization in Your Work Environment?

Instructions:

Describe the work environment at your present (or last) job by selecting one number along the following scale for each question.

```
Little                                              Much
  or      |———————————————————|                      or
 few      1      2      3      4      5              many
```

_____ 1. How much joking or talking about sexual matters do you hear?
_____ 2. How much social pressure are women under to flirt with men?
_____ 3. How much social pressure are men under to flirt with women?
_____ 4. How much of a problem is sexual harassment in your workplace?
_____ 5. How many women dress in a sexually attractive way to men?
_____ 6. How many men dress in a sexually attractive way to women?
_____ 7. How many women act in sexually seductive ways toward men?
_____ 8. How many men act in sexually seductive ways toward women?

_____ = Total score

Norms

Low degree of sexualization:	8–16
Moderate degree of sexualization:	17–31
High degree of sexualization:	32–40

Source: Adapted from B A Gutek, A Gross Cohen, and A M Konrad, "Predicting Social-Sexual Behavior at Work: A Contact Hypothesis," _Academy of Management Journal_, September 1990, p 577.

legally accountable for behavior it considers sexually harassing. An expert on the subject explains:

> What exactly is sexual harassment? The Equal Employment Opportunity Commission (EEOC) says that unwelcome sexual advances, requests for sexual favors, and other verbal or physical conduct of a sexual nature constitute sexual harassment when submission to such conduct is made a condition of employment; when submission to or rejection of sexual advances is used as a basis for employment decisions; or when such conduct creates an intimidating, hostile, or offensive work environment. These EEOC guidelines interpreting Title VII of the Civil Rights Act of 1964 further state that employers are responsible for the actions of their supervisors and agents and that employers are responsible for the actions of other employees if the employer knows or should have known about the sexual harassment.[51]

In a 1992 nationwide survey by _Training_ magazine, 79 percent of the companies polled had a formal policy on sexual harassment in force.[52]

Beyond avoiding lawsuits by establishing and enforcing anti-discrimination and sexual harassment policies, managers need to take additional steps.[53] Workforce diversity training is a popular approach today. Gender-issue workshops are another option. "Du Pont Co., for example, holds monthly workshops to make managers aware of gender-related attitudes."[54] Phyllis B Davis, a senior vice president at Avon Corporation, has framed the goal of such efforts by saying: "It's a question of consciously creating an environment where everyone has an equal shot at contributing, participating, and most of all advancing."[55] (See the International OB.)

INTERNATIONAL OB

Sexual Harassment Is a Global Issue

Sexual harassment is fast becoming an important world-wide workplace issue, the International Labor Office said.

The ILO, a United Nations affiliate based in Geneva, released a 300-page report, "Combating Sexual Harassment at Work," based on surveys in 23 nations, most of them in the West. The report shows that while there's still a widespread tendency for women to keep silent about being harassed, surveys of the problem have received more attention and many countries have begun taking action to address the problem.

Between 15% and 30% of women in various surveys in the 23 nations say they've experienced such conduct by supervisors or co-workers. Many have left their jobs because of the harassment.

"No longer can governments, trade unions, workers or employers say, 'It's an issue that we don't have to deal with,'" and call it just a U.S. problem, Constance Thomas, an ILO civil rights lawyer, said in an interview.

In Australia, for example, a federal commission found that sexual harassment complaints accounted for 36% of total sex-discrimination filings under a 1984 law. A Czechoslovakian survey showed that from 18% to 36% of surveyed women said they had been sexually harassed, physically or verbally. In a 1986 survey, 84% of Spanish women workers said that sexual remarks or jokes were made to them on the job, 55% experienced sexual looks or gestures, and 27% received strong verbal advances or touching; the Spanish government adopted a 1989 provision against such workplace harassment. . .

[In 1992] in Japan, a court ruled that a publishing company and a company supervisor violated a woman worker's rights because of offensive remarks that caused her to quit. It was the first successful sexual harassment lawsuit under Japan's civil code. The woman charged that the supervisor had spread rumors that she had a promiscuous reputation.

While public discussion of sexual harassment as an issue had been rare, that is changing, the ILO said. In a 1990 survey of 3,131 Japanese women, wide dislike was expressed for touching and for the obligation to serve after-hours alcohol to male colleagues. In the women's opinion, "Once you serve alcohol after hours, you are up for grabs," Ms. Thomas said.

Fully 82% of the women said they had been subjected to "seku hara," which has become the Japanese term for sexual harassment, from superiors, colleagues, customers or others.

Many countries are trying to emulate the U.S. in cracking down on work site harassment, ILO officials said. A few—Canada, Belgium, Sweden and New Zealand—are forging ahead by emphasizing prevention over punishment, Ms. Thomas said.

Only eight nations have laws specifically prohibiting sexual harassment, but two, France and Belgium, enacted laws in recent weeks. The others are Australia, Canada, New Zealand, Spain, Sweden and the U.S. In other countries, sexual harassment is defined by court rulings or in legislation covering other matters such as unfair firing.

Often, Ms. Thomas said, though no legal definition of "sexual harassment" yet exists in such nations as the Netherlands, and there isn't even a phrase for it in Russian, women in countries including Russia quickly recognize the concept when she describes it.

In a 1991 British survey, 47% of women said they had been sexually harassed, and 14% of men said they'd been harassed, too, mostly by women. "It is one of the true international issues," Ms. Thomas said.

Source: A R Karr, "Issue of Sex Harassment at Workplace Is Gaining More Attention World-Wide," *The Wall Street Journal*, December 1, 1992, pp A2, A8. Excerpted by permission of *The Wall Street Journal*, © 1992 Dow Jones & Company, Inc. All Rights Reserved Worldwide.

Individual Ability and Group Effectiveness

Imagine that you are a department manager charged with making an important staffing decision amid the following circumstances. You need to form eight 3-person task teams from a pool of 24 employees. Based on each of the employee's prior work records and their scores on ability tests, you know that 12 have high ability and 12 have low ability. The crux of your problem is how to assign the 12 high-ability employees. Should you spread your best talent around by making sure there are both high- and low-ability employees on each team? Then again, you may want to concentrate your best talent by forming four high-ability teams and four low-ability teams. Or should you attempt to find a compromise between these two extremes? What is your decision? Why? One field experiment provided an instructive and interesting answer.

The Israeli Tank-Crew Study Aharon Tziner and Dov Eden, researchers from Tel Aviv University, systematically manipulated the composition of 208 three-man tank crews. All possible combinations of high- and low-ability personnel were studied (high-high-high; high-high-low; high-low-low; and low-low-low). Ability was a composite measure of (1) overall intelligence, (2) amount of formal education, (3) proficiency in Hebrew, and (4) interview ratings. Successful operation of the tanks required the three-man crews to perform with a high degree of synchronized interdependence.[56] Tank-crew effectiveness was determined by commanding officers during military maneuvers for the Israel Defense Forces.

As expected, the high-high-high ability tank crews performed the best and the low-low-low the worst. But the researchers discovered an important *interaction effect:*

> Each member's ability influenced crew performance effectiveness differently depending on the ability levels of the other two members. A high-ability member appears to achieve more in combination with other uniformly high-ability members than in combination with low-ability members.[57]

The tank crews composed of three high-ability personnel far outperformed all other ability combinations. The interaction effect also worked in a negative direction because the low-low-low ability crews performed far below expected levels. Moreover, as illustrated in Figure 9–4, significantly greater performance gains were achieved by creating high-high-high ability crews than by upgrading low-low-low ability crews with one or two high-ability members.

This returns us to the staffing problem at the beginning of this section. Tziner and Eden recommended the following solution:

> Our experimental results suggest that the most productive solution would be to allocate six highs and all 12 lows to six teams of high-low-low ability and to assign the six remaining highs to two teams of high-high-high ability. This avoids the disproportionately low productivity of the low-low-low ability combination, while leaving some of the highs for high-high-high ability teams where they are most productive. . . . Our results show that talent is used more effectively when concentrated than when spread around.[58]

A Managerial Interpretation While the real-life aspect of the tank-crew study makes its results fairly generalizable, a qualification is in order. Specifically, modern complex organizations demand a more flexible contingency approach. Figure 9–5 shows two basic contingencies. If management seeks to *improve* the performance of *all* groups or train novices, high-ability personnel can be spread around. This option would be appropriate in a high-volume production operation. But if the desired outcome is to *maximize* performance of the *best* group(s), then high-ability personnel should be concentrated. This second option would be advisable in research and development departments, for example, where technological breakthroughs need to be achieved. Extraordinary achievements require clusters of extraordinary talent.[59]

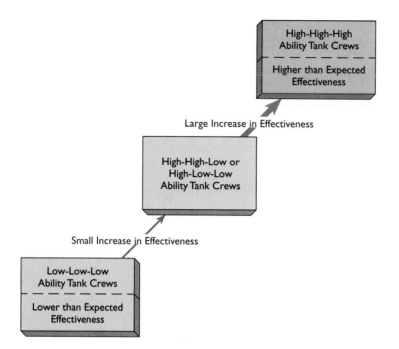

• ➤ **FIGURE 9~4**
Ability of Israeli Tank-Crew
Members and Improvements
in Effectiveness

Source: Based on discussion in A Tziner and D Eden, "Effects of Crew Composition on Crew Performance: Does the Whole Equal the Sum of Its Parts?" *Journal of Applied Psychology*, February 1985, pp 85–93.

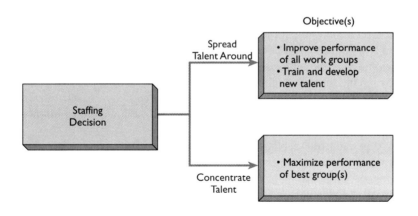

• ➤ **FIGURE 9~5**
A Contingency Model for
Staffing Work Groups:
Effective Use of Available
Talent

Even when managers carefully staff and organize task groups, group dynamics can still go haywire. Forehand knowledge of three major threats to group effectiveness—the Asch effect, groupthink, and social loafing—can help managers take necessary preventive steps. Because the first two problems relate to blind conformity, some brief background work is in order.

Very little would be accomplished in task groups and organizations without conformity to norms, role expectations, policies, and rules and regulations. After all, deadlines, commitments, and product/service quality standards have to be

**THREATS
TO GROUP
EFFECTIVENESS**

established and adhered to if the organization is to survive. But, as pointed out by management consultants Robert Blake and Jane Srygley Mouton, conformity is a two-edged sword:

> Social forces powerful enough to influence members to conform may influence them to perform at a very high level of quality and productivity. All too often, however, the pressure to conform stifles creativity, influencing members to cling to attitudes that may be out of touch with organizational needs and even out of kilter with the times.[60]

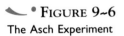

Moreover, excessive or blind conformity can stifle critical thinking, the last line of defense against unethical conduct. Almost daily accounts in the popular media of insider trading scandals, illegal dumping of hazardous wastes, and other unethical practices make it imperative that future managers understand the mechanics of blind conformity.

The Asch Effect

More than 40 years ago, social psychologist Solomon Asch conducted a series of laboratory experiments that revealed a negative side of group dynamics.[61] Under the guise of a "perception test," Asch had groups of seven to nine volunteer college students look at 12 pairs of cards such as the ones in Figure 9–6. The object was to identify the line that was the same length as the standard line. Each individual was told to announce his or her choice to the group. Since the differences among the comparison lines were obvious, there should have been unanimous agreement during each of the 12 rounds. But that was not the case.

A Minority of One   All but one member of each group were Asch's confederates who agreed to systematically select the wrong line during seven of the rounds (the other five rounds were control rounds for comparison purposes). The remaining individual was the naive subject who was being tricked. Group pressure was created by having the naive subject in each group be among the last to announce his or her choice. Thirty-one subjects were tested. Asch's research question was: "How often would the naive subjects conform to a majority opinion that was obviously wrong?"

Only 20 percent of Asch's subjects remained entirely independent; 80 percent yielded to the pressures of group opinion at least once! Fifty-eight percent knuckled under to the "immoral majority" at least twice. Hence, the **Asch effect,** the distortion of individual judgment by a unanimous but incorrect opposition, was documented. (Do you ever turn your back on your better judgment by giving in to group pressure?)

Asch effect Giving in to a unanimous but wrong opposition.

◤• FIGURE 9–6
The Asch Experiment

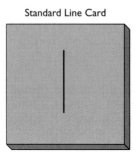

Standard Line Card

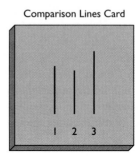

Comparison Lines Card

1 2 3

A Managerial Perspective Asch's experiment has been widely replicated with mixed results. Both high and low degrees of blind conformity have been observed with various situations and subjects. Replications in Japan and Kuwait have demonstrated that the Asch effect is not unique to the United States.[62] But the point is not precisely how great the Asch effect is in a given situation or culture, but rather, managers committed to ethical conduct need to be concerned that the Asch effect exists. Even isolated instances of blind, unthinking conformity seriously threaten the effectiveness and integrity of work groups and organizations. Functional conflict and assertiveness, discussed in Chapters 10 and 13, can help employees respond appropriately when they find themselves facing an immoral majority. Ethical codes mentioning specific practices also can provide support and guidance.

Groupthink

Why did President Lyndon B Johnson and his group of intelligent White House advisers make some very *unintelligent* decisions that escalated the Vietnam War? Those fateful decisions were made despite obvious warning signals, including stronger than expected resistance from the North Vietnamese and withering support at home and abroad. Systematic analysis of the decision-making processes underlying the war in Vietnam and other US foreign policy fiascoes prompted Yale University's Irving Janis to coin the term *groupthink*.[63] Modern managers can all too easily become victims of groupthink, just like President Johnson's staff, if they passively ignore the danger.

Definition and Symptoms of Groupthink Janis defines **groupthink** as "a mode of thinking that people engage in when they are deeply involved in a cohesive in-group, when members' strivings for unanimity override their motivation to realistically appraise alternative courses of action."[64] He adds, "Groupthink refers to a deterioration of mental efficiency, reality testing, and moral judgment that results from in-group pressures."[65] Unlike Asch's subjects, who were strangers to each other, members of groups victimized by groupthink are friendly, tightly knit, and cohesive.

> **groupthink** Janis's term for a cohesive in-group's unwillingness to realistically view alternatives.

The symptoms of groupthink listed in Figure 9–7 thrive in the sort of climate outlined in the following critique of corporate directors in the United States:

> Many directors simply don't rock the boat. "No one likes to be the skunk at the garden party," says [management consultant] Victor H. Palmieri. . . . "One does not make friends and influence people in the boardroom or elsewhere by raising hard questions that create embarrassment or discomfort for management."[66]

In short, policy- and decision-making groups can become so cohesive that strong-willed executives are able to gain unanimous support for poor decisions.[67]

Groupthink Research and Prevention Laboratory studies using college students as subjects validate portions of Janis's groupthink concept. Specifically, it has been found that:

- Groups with a moderate amount of cohesiveness produce better decisions than low- or high-cohesive groups.
- Highly cohesive groups victimized by groupthink make the poorest decisions, despite high confidence in those decisions.[68]

• FIGURE 9-7   Symptoms of Groupthink Lead to Defective Decision Making

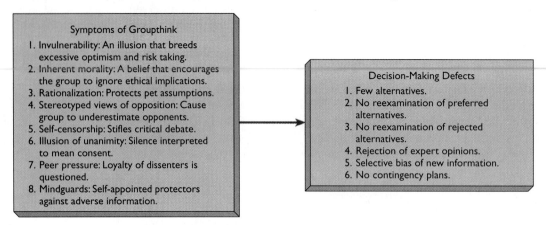

Symptoms of Groupthink
1. Invulnerability: An illusion that breeds excessive optimism and risk taking.
2. Inherent morality: A belief that encourages the group to ignore ethical implications.
3. Rationalization: Protects pet assumptions.
4. Stereotyped views of opposition: Cause group to underestimate opponents.
5. Self-censorship: Stifles critical debate.
6. Illusion of unanimity: Silence interpreted to mean consent.
7. Peer pressure: Loyalty of dissenters is questioned.
8. Mindguards: Self-appointed protectors against adverse information.

Decision-Making Defects
1. Few alternatives.
2. No reexamination of preferred alternatives.
3. No reexamination of rejected alternatives.
4. Rejection of expert opinions.
5. Selective bias of new information.
6. No contingency plans.

Sources: Symptoms adapted from I L Janis, *Groupthink*, 2nd ed (Boston: Houghton Mifflin, 1982), pp 174–75. Defects excerpted from G Moorhead, "Groupthink: Hypothesis in Need of Testing," *Group & Organization Studies*, December 1982, p 434.

Janis believes prevention is better than cure when dealing with groupthink. He recommends the following preventive measures:

1. Each member of the group should be assigned the role of critical evaluator. This role involves actively voicing objections and doubts.
2. Top-level executives should not use policy committees to rubber-stamp decisions that have already been made.
3. Different groups with different leaders should explore the same policy questions.
4. Subgroup debates and outside experts should be used to introduce fresh perspectives.
5. Someone should be given the role of devil's advocate when discussing major alternatives. This person tries to uncover every conceivable negative factor.
6. Once a consensus has been reached, everyone should be encouraged to rethink their position to check for flaws.[69]

These anti-groupthink measures can help cohesive groups produce sound recommendations and decisions.[70] For example, Kenneth A Macke, the chairman and CEO of Dayton Hudson Corporation, has created a corporate board of directors for the department store giant that is unlikely to be victimized by groupthink:

Twelve out of 14 directors are outsiders. A vice-chairman chosen from among the outside directors serves as a special liaison between the board and the CEO. The result is a powerful, independent group of directors—a rare species in boardrooms today. How independent? [In 1991], for instance, the board withheld Macke's bonus, which had totaled almost $600,000 in 1990.[71]

Social Loafing

Is group performance less than, equal to, or greater than the sum of its parts? Can three people, for example, working together accomplish less than, the same as, or more than they would working separately? An interesting study conducted more than a half century ago by a French agricultural engineer named Ringelmann found the answer to be ''less than.''[72] In a rope-pulling exercise, Ringlemann reportedly found that three people pulling together could achieve only two and a half times the average individual rate. Eight pullers achieved less than four times the individual rate. This tendency for individual effort to decline as group size increases has come to be called **social loafing.**[73] Let us briefly analyze this threat to group effectiveness and synergy with an eye toward avoiding it.

Social Loafing Theory and Research   Among the theoretical explanations for the social loafing effect are (1) equity of effort (''Everyone else is goofing off, so why shouldn't I?''), (2) loss of personal accountability (''I'm lost in the crowd, so who cares?''), (3) motivational loss due to the sharing of rewards (''Why should I work harder than the others when everyone gets the same reward?''), and (4) coordination loss as more people perform the task (''We're getting in each other's way.'').

Laboratory studies refined these theories by identifying situational factors that moderated the social loafing effect. Social loafing occurred when

- The task was perceived to be unimportant, simple or not interesting.[74]
- Group members thought their individual output was not identifiable.[75]
- Group members expected their co-workers to loaf.[76]

But social loafing did *not* occur when group members in two laboratory studies expected to be evaluated.[77]

social loafing   Decrease in individual effort as group size increases.

Practical Implications   These findings demonstrate that social loafing is not an inevitable part of group effort. Management can curb this threat to group effectiveness by making sure the task is challenging and perceived as important. Additionally, it is a good idea to hold group members personally accountable for identifiable portions of the group's task. One way to do this is with the *stepladder technique,* a group decision-making process proven effective in recent research (see Table 9–4). Compared with conventional groups, stepladder groups produced significantly better decisions in the same amount of time. ''Furthermore, stepladder

● ▰ TABLE 9~4
How to Avoid Social Loafing in Groups and Teams: The Stepladder Technique

The stepladder technique is intended to enhance group decision making by structuring the entry of group members into a core group. Increasing or decreasing the number of group members alters the number of steps. In a four-person group, the stepladder technique has three steps. Initially, two group members (the initial core group) work together on the problem at hand. Next, a third member joins the core group and presents his or her preliminary solutions for the same problem. The entering member's presentation is followed by a three-person discussion. Finally, the fourth group member joins the core group and presents his or her preliminary solutions. This is followed by a four-person discussion, which has as its goal the rendering of a final group decision.

The stepladder technique has four requirements. First, each group member must be given the group's task and sufficient time to think about the problem before entering the core group. Second, the entering member must present his or her preliminary solutions before hearing the core group's preliminary solutions. Third, with the entry of each additional member to the core group, sufficient time to discuss the problem is necessary. Fourth, a final decision must be purposely delayed until the group has been formed in its entirety.

Source: Excerpted from S G Rogelberg, J L Barnes-Farrell, and C A Lowe, "The Stepladder Technique: An Alternative Group Structure Facilitating Effective Group Decision Making," *Journal of Applied Psychology,* October 1992, p 731.

groups' decisions surpassed the quality of their best individual members' decisions 56 percent of the time. In contrast, conventional groups' decisions surpassed the quality of their best members' decisions only 13 percent of the time."[78] The stepladder technique could be a useful tool for organizations relying on self-managed or total quality management (TQM) teams.

BACK TO THE OPENING CASE

Now that you have read Chapter 9, you should be able to answer the following questions about Janet Long's wilderness lab experience:

1. Did Janet Long's group satisfy the criteria of a sociological group?
2. The trust ladder played a key role relative to which stage of the group development process?
3. Why was social loafing probably not a problem during the wall-climbing exercise?

SUMMARY OF KEY CONCEPTS

1. *Identify the four criteria of a group from a sociological perspective.* Sociologically, a *group* is defined as two or more freely interacting individuals who share collective norms and goals and have a common identity.

2. *Describe the six stages of group development.* Groups mature through six stages of development: orientation, conflict and challenge, cohesion, delusion, disillusion, and acceptance. Interpersonal feedback increases and becomes more positive, specific, and credible as the group matures.

    Uncertainty about deadlines can disrupt the group development process. Leaders need to become more supportive as the group develops.

3. *Distinguish between role conflict and role ambiguity.* Organizational *roles* are sets of behaviors persons expect of occupants of a position. One may experience role overload (too much to do in too little time), role conflict (conflicting role expectations), or role ambiguity (unclear role expectations).

4. *Contrast roles and norms and specify four reasons norms are enforced in organizations.* While roles are specific to the person's position, norms are shared attitudes that differentiate appropriate from inappropriate behavior in a variety of situations. Norms evolve informally and are enforced because they help the group or organization survive, clarify behavioral expectations, help people avoid embarrassing situations, and clarify the group's or organizations central values.

5. *Distinguish between task and maintenance functions in groups.* Members of formal groups need to perform both task (goal-oriented) and maintenance (relationship-oriented) roles if anything is to be accomplished.

6. *Summarize the practical contingency management implications for group size and group member ability.* Laboratory simulation studies suggest decision-making groups should be limited to five or fewer members. Larger groups are appropriate when creativity, participation, or socialization are the main objectives. If majority votes are to be taken, odd-numbered groups are recommended, to avoid deadlocks. Results of the Israeli tank-crew study prompted researchers to conclude that it is better to concentrate high-ability personnel in separate groups. Within a contingency management perspective, however, there are situations in which it is advisable to spread high-ability people around.

7. *Discuss why managers need to carefully handle mixed-gender task groups.* Women face special group dynamics challenges in mixed-gender task groups. Steps need to be taken to make sure increased sexualization of work environments does not erode into illegal sexual harassment.

8. *Describe groupthink and identify at least four of its symptoms.* Groupthink plagues cohesive in-groups that shortchange moral judgment while putting too much emphasis on unanimity. Symptoms of groupthink include invulnerability, inherent morality, rationalization, stereotyped views of opposition, self-

censorship, illusion of unanimity, peer pressure, and mindguards. Critical evaluators, outside expertise, and devil's advocates are among the preventive measures recommended by Irving Janis, who coined the term *groupthink.*

9. *Define social loafing and explain how managers can prevent it.* Social loafing involves the tendency for individual effort to decrease as group size increases.

This problem can be contained if the task is challenging and important, individuals are held accountable for results and group members expect everyone to work hard. The stepladder technique, a structured approach to group decision making, can reduce social loafing by increasing personal effort and accountability.

DISCUSSION QUESTIONS

1. Which of the following would qualify as a sociological group? A crowd watching a baseball game? One of the baseball teams? Explain.

2. What is your opinion about employees being friends with their co-workers (overlapping formal and informal groups)?

3. What is your personal experience with groups that failed to achieve the sixth stage of group development? At which stage did they stall?

4. Considering your present lifestyle, how many different roles are you playing? What sorts of role conflict and role ambiguity are you experiencing?

5. What norms do college students usually enforce in class? How are they enforced?

6. Which roles do you prefer to play in work groups: task or maintenance? How could you do a better job in this regard?

7. How would you respond to a manager who made the following statement? "When it comes to the size of work groups, the bigger the better."

8. Are women typically at a disadvantage in mixed-gender work groups? Give your rationale.

9. Have you ever been a victim of either the Asch effect or groupthink? Explain the circumstances.

10. Have you observed any social loafing recently? What were the circumstances and what could be done to correct the problem?

EXERCISE

Objectives

1. To give you firsthand experience with work group dynamics through a role-playing exercise.[79]

2. To develop your ability to evaluate group effectiveness.

Introduction

Please read the following case before going on:

The Johnny Rocco Case

Johnny has a grim personal background. He is the third child in a family of seven. He has not seen his father for several years, and his recollection is that his father used to come home drunk and beat up every member of the family; everyone ran when his father came staggering home.

His mother, according to Johnny, wasn't much better. She was irritable and unhappy, and she always predicted that Johnny would come to no good end. Yet she worked when her health allowed her to do so in order to keep the family in food and clothing. She always decried the fact that she was not able to be the kind of mother she would like to be.

Johnny quit school in the seventh grade. He had great difficulty conforming to the school routine—he misbehaved often, was truant frequently, and fought with schoolmates. On several occasions he was picked up by the police and, along with members of his group, questioned during several investigations into cases of both petty and grand larceny. The police regarded him as "probably a bad one."

The juvenile officer of the court saw in Johnny some good qualities that no one else seemed to sense. Mr. O'Brien took it on himself to act as a "big brother" to Johnny. He had several long conversations with Johnny, during which he managed to penetrate to some degree Johnny's defensive shell. He represented to Johnny the first semblance of personal interest in his life. Through Mr. O'Brien's efforts, Johnny returned to school and obtained a high school diploma. Afterwards, Mr. O'Brien helped him obtain a job. Now 20, Johnny is a stockroom clerk in one of the laboratories where you are employed. On the whole Johnny's performance has been acceptable, but there have been glaring exceptions. One involved a clear act of insubordination on a fairly unimportant matter. In another, Johnny was accused, on

(continued)

(concluded)

circumstantial grounds, of destroying some expensive equipment. Though the investigation is still open, it now appears the destruction was accidental.

Johnny's supervisor wants to keep him on for at least a trial period, but he wants "outside" advice as to the best way of helping Johnny grow into greater responsibility. Of course, much depends on how Johnny behaves in the next few months. Naturally, his supervisor must follow personnel policies that are accepted in the company as a whole. It is important to note that Johnny is not an attractive young man. He is rather weak and sickly, and he shows unmistakable signs of long years of social deprivation.

A committee is formed to decide the fate of Johnny Rocco. The chairperson of the meeting is Johnny's supervisor and should begin by assigning roles to the group members. These roles (shop steward [representing the union], head of production, Johnny's co-worker, director of personnel, and social worker who helped Johnny in the past) represent points of view the chairperson believes should be included in this meeting. (Johnny is not to be included.) Two observers should also be assigned. Thus, each group will have eight members.

Instructions

After roles have been assigned, each role player should complete the personal preference part of the work sheet, ranking from 1 to 11 the alternatives according to their appropriateness from the vantage point of his or her role.

Once the individual preferences have been determined, the chairperson should call the meeting to order. The following rules govern the meeting: (1) the group must reach a consensus ranking of the alternatives; (2) the group cannot use a statistical aggregation, or majority vote, decision-making process; (3) members should stay "in character" throughout the discussion. Treat this as a committee meeting consisting of members with different backgrounds, orientation, and interests who share a problem.

After the group has completed the assignment, the observers should conduct a discussion of the group process, using the Group Effectiveness Questions here as a guide. Group members should not look at these questions until after the group task has been completed.

Worksheet

Personal Preference	Group Decision	
_____	_____	Warn Johnny that at the next sign of trouble he will be fired.
_____	_____	Do nothing, as it is unclear if Johnny did anything wrong.
_____	_____	Create strict controls (do's and don'ts) for Johnny with immediate strong punishment for any misbehavior.
_____	_____	Give Johnny a great deal of warmth and personal attention and affection (overlooking his present behavior) so he can learn to depend on others.
_____	_____	Fire him. It's not worth the time and effort spent for such a low-level position.
_____	_____	Talk over the problem with Johnny in an understanding way so he can learn to ask others for help in solving his problems.
_____	_____	Give Johnny a well-structured schedule of daily activities with immediate and unpleasant consequences for not adhering to the schedule.
_____	_____	Do nothing now, but watch him carefully and provide immediate punishment for any future behavior.
_____	_____	Treat Johnny the same as everyone else, but provide an orderly routine so he can learn to stand on his own two feet.
_____	_____	Call Johnny in and logically discuss the problem with him and ask what you can do to help him.
_____	_____	Do nothing now, but watch him so you can reward him the next time he does something good.

Group Effectiveness Questions

A. Referring to Table 9–3, what task roles were performed? By whom?

B. What maintenance roles were performed? By whom?

C. Were any important task or maintenance roles ignored? Which?

D. Was there any evidence of the Asch effect, groupthink, or social loafing? Explain.

Questions for Consideration/Class Discussion

1. Did your committee do a good job? Explain.
2. What, if anything, should have been done differently?
3. How much similarity in rankings is there among the different groups in your class? What group dynamics apparently were responsible for any variations in rankings?

NOTES

[1] See R Stephen and R L Zweigenhaft, "The Effect on Tipping of a Waitress's Touching Male and Female Customers," *The Journal of Social Psychology,* February 1986, pp 141–42.

[2] Data from K F Kane, "MBAs: A Recruiter's-Eye View," *Business Horizons,* January–February 1993, pp 65–71.

[3] See L G Bolman and T E Deal, *Reframing Organizations* (San Francisco: Jossey-Bass, 1991), chap. 7.

[4] For instructive research overviews, see K L Bettenhausen, "Five Years of Group Research: What We Have Learned and What Needs To Be Addressed," *Journal of Management,* no. 2, 1991, pp 345–81; and R T Mowday and R I Sutton, "Organizational Behavior: Linking Individuals and Groups to Organizational Contexts," in *Annual Review of Psychology,* vol. 44, eds L W Porter and M R Rosenzweig (Palo Alto, CA: Annual Reviews Inc., 1993), pp 195–229.

[5] This definition is based in part on one found in D Horton Smith, "A Parsimonious Definition of 'Group': Toward Conceptual Clarity and Scientific Utility," *Sociological Inquiry,* Spring 1967, pp 141–67.

[6] E H Schein, *Organizational Psychology,* 3rd ed (Englewood Cliffs, NJ: Prentice-Hall, 1980), p 145.

[7] Ibid., pp 149–53.

[8] J Castro, "Mazda U.," *Time,* October 20, 1986, p 65.

[9] For an instructive overview of five different theories of group development, see J P Wanous, A E Reichers, and S D Malik," Organizational Socialization and Group Development: Toward an Integrative Perspective," *Academy of Management Review,* October 1984, pp 670–83.

[10] Adapted from discussion in L N Jewell and H J Reitz, *Group Effectiveness in Organizations* (Glenview, IL: Scott, Foresman, 1981), pp 15–20.

[11] Practical advice on handling a dominating group member can be found in M Finley, "Belling the Bully," *HRMagazine,* March 1992, pp 82–86.

[12] Jewell and Reitz, *Group Effectiveness in Organizations,* p 19.

[13] D Davies and B C Kuypers, "Group Development and Interpersonal Feedback," *Group & Organizational Studies,* June 1985, p 194.

[14] Ibid., pp 184–208.

[15] C J G Gersick, "Marking Time: Predictable Transitions in Task Groups," *Academy of Management Journal,* June 1989, pp 274–309.

[16] D K Carew, E Parisi-Carew, and K H Blanchard, "Group Development and Situational Leadership: A Model for Managing Groups," *Training and Development Journal,* June 1986, pp 48–49. For evidence linking leadership and group effectiveness, see G R Bushe and A L Johnson, "Contextual and Internal Variables Affecting Task Group Outcomes in Organizations," *Group & Organization Studies,* December 1989, pp 462–82.

[17] G Graen, "Role-Making Processes within Complex Organizations," in *Handbook of Industrial and Organizational Psychology,* ed M D Dunnette (Chicago: Rand McNally, 1976), p 1201.

[18] Other role determinants are explored in H Ibarra "Network Centrality, Power, and Innovation Involvement: Determinants of Technical and Administrative Roles," *Academy of Management Journal,* June 1993, pp 471–501.

[19] Excerpted from G L Miles, "Doug Danforth's Plan to Put Westinghouse in the 'Winner's circle,' " *Business Week,* July 28, 1986, p 75.

[20] For a review of research on the role episode model, see L A King and D W King, "Role Conflict and Role Ambiguity: A Critical Assessment of Construct Validity," *Psychological Bulletin,* January 1990, pp 48–64.

[21] Schein, *Organizational Psychology,* p 198.

[22] Ibid.

[23] See A S Wharton and R J Erickson, "Managing Emotions on the Job and at Home: Understanding the Consequences of Multiple Emotional Roles," *Academy of Management Review,* July 1993, pp 457–86.

[24] See A L Otten, "People Patterns: Wives May Not Benefit When Men Do Chores," *The Wall Street Journal,* October 30, 1989, p B1.

[25] Schein, *Organizational Psychology,* p 198.

[26] 1 = A; 2 = C; 3 = A; 4 = A; 5 = C; 6 = A; 7 = C; 8 = A; 9 = C; 10 = C.

[27] R R Blake and J Srygley Mouton, "Don't Let Group Norms Stifle Creativity," *Personnel,* August 1985, p 28.

[28] See D Kahneman, "Reference Points, Anchors, Norms, and Mixed Feelings," *Organizational Behavior and Human Decision Processes,* March 1992, pp 296–312.

[29] A Dunkin, "Pepsi's Marketing Magic: Why Nobody Does It Better," *Business Week,* February 10, 1986, p 52.

[30] D C Feldman, "The Development and Enforcement of Group Norms," *Academy of Management Review,* January 1984, pp 50–52.

[31] For more on norms, see K L Bettenhausen and K J Murnigham, "The Development of an Intragroup Norm and the Effects of Intrapersonal and Structural Chal-

lenges," *Administrative Science Quarterly,* March 1991, pp 20–35; R I Sutton, "Maintaining Norms about Expressed Emotions; The Case of Bill Collectors," *Administrative Science Quarterly,* June 1991, pp 245–68; and R D Russell and C J Russell, "An Examination of the Effects of Organizational Norms, Organizational Structure, and Environmental Uncertainty on Entrepreneurial Strategy," *Journal of Management,* December 1992, pp 639–56.

[32] Feldman, "The Development and Enforcement of Group Norms."

[33] See R G Netemeyer, M W Johnston, and S Burton, "Analysis of Role Conflict and Role Ambiguity in a Structural Equations Framework," *Journal of Applied Psychology,* April 1990, pp 148–57; and G W McGee, C E Ferguson, Jr., and A Seers, "Role Conflict and Role Ambiguity: Do the Scales Measure These Two Constructs?," *Journal of Applied Psychology,* October 1989, pp 815–18.

[34] See S E Jackson and R S Schuler, "A Meta-Analysis and Conceptual Critique of Research on Role Ambiguity and Role Conflict in Work Settings," *Organizational Behavior and Human Decision Processes,* August 1985, pp 16–78. Also see King and King, "Role Conflict and Role Ambiguity: A Critical Assessment of Construct Validity."

[35] See K D Benne and P Sheats, "Functional Roles of Group Members," *Journal of Social Issues,* Spring 1948, pp 41–49.

[36] A Zander, "The Value of Belonging to a Group in Japan," *Small Group Behavior,* February 1983, pp 7–8. Also see P R Harris and R T Moran, *Managing Cultural Differences,* 3rd ed (Houston: Gulf Publishing, 1991), chap. 7.

[37] For example, see B Grofman, S L Feld, and G Owen, "Group Size and the Performance of a Composite Group Majority: Statistical Truths and Empirical Results," *Organizational Behavior and Human Performance,* June 1984, pp 350–59.

[38] See P Yetton and P Bottger, "The Relationships among Group Size, Member Ability, Social Decision Schemes, and Performance," *Organizational Behavior and Human Performance,* October 1983, pp 145–59.

[39] This copyrighted exercise may be found in J Hall, "Decisions, Decisions, Decisions," *Psychology Today,* November 1971, pp 51–54, 86, 88.

[40] Yetton and Bottger, "The Relationships among Group Size, Member Ability, Social Decision Schemes, and Performance," p 158.

[41] Based on R B Gallupe, A R Dennis, W H Cooper, J S Valacich, L M Bastianutti, and J F Nunamaker, Jr., "Electronic Brainstorming and Group Size," *Academy of Management Journal,* June 1992, pp 350–69.

[42] For encouraging data, see L S Richman, "The Big Payoff from Computers," *Fortune,* March 7, 1994, p 28.

[43] Drawn from B Mullen, C Symons, L-T Hu, and E Salas, "Group Size, Leadership Behavior, and Subordinate Satisfaction," *The Journal of General Psychology,* April 1989, pp 155–69. Also see P Oliver and G Marwell, "The Paradox of Group Size in Collective Action: A Theory of the Critical Mass. II.," *American Sociological Review,* February 1988, pp 1–8.

[44] Details of this study are presented in L L Thompson, E A Mannix, and M H Bazerman, "Group Negotiation: Effects of Decision Rule, Agenda and Aspiration," *Journal of Personality and Social Psychology,* January 1988, pp 86–95.

[45] See G Koretz, "Women in the Workplace: Men Are All Shook Up," *Business Week,* May 18, 1992, p 22.

[46] See L Smith-Lovin and C Brody, "Interruptions in Group Discussions: The Effects of Gender and Group Composition," *American Sociological Review,* June 1989, pp 424–35.

[47] E M Ott, "Effects of the Male–Female Ratio at Work," *Psychology of Women Quarterly,* March 1989, p 53.

[48] Data from B A Gutek, A Groff Cohen, and A M Konrad, "Predicting Social-Sexual Behavior at Work: A Contact Hypothesis," *Academy of Management Journal,* September 1990, pp 560–77.

[49] Sexual harassment is discussed as 1 of 10 ethical landmines in C Cox, "High Explosives," *Business Ethics,* January 1994, pp 33–35.

[50] S J South, C M Bonjean, W T Markham, and J Corder, "Female Labor Force Participation and the Organizational Experiences of Male Workers," *The Sociological Quarterly,* Summer 1983, p 378.

[51] B T Thornton, "Sexual Harassment, 1: Discouraging It in the Work Place," *Personnel,* April 1986, p 18. For research evidence that men and women tend to perceive sexual harassment similarly, see D D Baker, D E Terpstra, and B D Cutler, "Perceptions of Sexual Harassment: A Re-Examination of Gender Differences," *The Journal of Psychology,* July 1990, pp 409–16.

[52] Data from J Gordon, "Social Issues at Work," *Training,* October 1992, pp 50–51.

[53] For practical advice, see A B Fisher, "Sexual Harass-

ment: What to Do," *Fortune,* August 23, 1993, pp 84–88; and R A Thacker, "Innovative Steps to Take in Sexual Harassment Prevention," *Business Horizons,* January–February 1994, pp 29–32.

54 I Pave, "A Woman's Place Is at GE, Federal Express P&G . . . ," *Business Week,* June 23, 1986, p 78.

55 W Konrad, "Welcome to the Woman-Friendly Company," *Business Week,* August 6, 1990, p 50. Also see W E Watson, K Kumar, and L K Michaelsen, "Cultural Diversity's Impact on Interaction Process and Performance: Comparing Homogeneous and Diverse Task Groups," *Academy of Management Journal,* June 1993, pp 590–602.

56 A former Israeli tank commander's first-hand account of tank warfare in the desert can be found in A Kahalani, "Advice from a Desert Warrior," *Newsweek,* September 3, 1990, p 32.

57 A Tziner and D Eden, "Effects of Crew Composition on Crew Performance: Does the Whole Equal the Sum of Its Parts?" *Journal of Applied Psychology,* February 1985, p 91.

58 Ibid.

59 For related research, see R Saavedra, C P Earley, and L Van Dyne, "Complex Interdependence in Task-Performing Groups," *Journal of Applied Psychology,* February 1993, pp 61–72.

60 Blake and Mouton, "Don't Let Group Norms Stifle Creativity," p 29.

61 For additional information, see S E Asch, *Social Psychology* (Englewood Cliffs, NJ: Prentice-Hall, 1952), chap. 16.

62 See T P Williams and S Sogon, "Group Composition and Conforming Behavior in Japanese Students," *Japanese Psychological Research,* no. 4, 1984, pp 231–34; and T Amir, "The Asch Conformity Effect: A Study in Kuwait," *Social Behavior and Personality,* no. 2, 1984, pp 187–90.

63 For an interesting analysis of the presence or absence of groupthink in selected US foreign policy decisions, see C McCauley, "The Nature of Social Influence in Groupthink: Compliance and Internalization," *Journal of Personality and Social Psychology,* August 1989, pp 250–60. Also see G Whyte, "Groupthink Reconsidered," *Academy of Management Review,* January 1989, pp 40–56.

64 I L Janis, *Groupthink,* 2nd ed (Boston: Houghton Mifflin, 1982), p 9.

65 Ibid. For an alternative model, see R J Aldag and S Riggs Fuller, "Beyond Fiasco: A Reappraisal of the Groupthink Phenomenon and a New Model of Group Decision Processes," *Psychological Bulletin,* May 1993, pp 533–52.

66 L Baum, "The Job Nobody Wants," *Business Week,* September 8, 1986, p 60.

67 For an ethical perspective, see R R Sims, "Linking Groupthink to Unethical Behavior in Organizations," *Journal of Business Ethics,* September 1992, pp 651–62.

68 Details of this study may be found in M R Callaway and J K Esser, "Groupthink: Effects of Cohesiveness and Problem-Solving Procedures on Group Decision Making," *Social Behavior and Personality,* no. 2, 1984, pp 157–64. Also see C R Leana, "A Partial Test of Janis's Groupthink Model: Effects of Group Cohesiveness and Leader Behavior on Defective Decision Making," *Journal of Management,* Spring 1985, pp 5–17; and G Moorhead and J R Montanari, "An Empirical Investigation of the Groupthink Phenomenon," *Human Relations,* May 1986, pp 399–410.

69 Adapted from discussion in Janis, *Groupthink,* chap. 11.

70 An illustrative case study is reported in C P Neck and G Moorhead, "Jury Deliberations in the Trial of U.S. v John DeLorean: A Case Analysis of Groupthink Avoidance and an Enhanced Framework," *Human Relations,* October 1992, pp 1077–91.

71 J Flynn, "Giving the Board More Clout," *Business Week,* Bonus Issue: Reinventing America, 1992, p 74.

72 Based on discussion in B Latane, K Williams, and S Harkins, "Many Hands Make Light the Work: The Causes and Consequences of Social Loafing," *Journal of Personality and Social Psychology,* June 1979, pp 822–32; and D A Kravitz and B Martin, "Ringelmann Rediscovered: The Original Article," *Journal of Personality and Social Psychology,* May 1986, pp 936–41.

73 See J A Shepperd, "Productivity Loss in Performance Groups: A Motivation Analysis," *Psychological Bulletin,* no. 1, 1993, pp 67–81; R E Kidwell, Jr., and N Bennett, "Employee Propensity to Withhold Effort: A Conceptual Model to Intersect Three Avenues of Research," *Academy of Management Review,* July 1993, pp 429–56; and S J Karau and K D Williams, "Social Loafing: Meta-Analytic Review and Theoretical Integration," *Journal of Personality and Social Psychology,* October 1993, pp 681–706.

74 See S J Zaccaro, "Social Loafing: The Role of Task Attractiveness," *Personality and Social Psychology Bulletin,* March 1984, pp 99–106; J M Jackson and K D Williams, "Social Loafing on Difficult Tasks: Working Collectively Can Improve Performance," *Journal of Personality and Social Psychology,* October 1985, pp 937–42;

and J M George, "Extrinsic and Intrinsic Origins of Perceived Social Loafing in Organizations," *Academy of Management Journal,* March 1992, pp 191–202.

75 For complete details, see K Williams, S Harkins, and B Latane, "Identifiability as a Deterrent to Social Loafing: Two Cheering Experiments," *Journal of Personality and Social Psychology,* February 1981, pp 303–11.

76 See J M Jackson and S G Harkins, "Equity in Effort: An Explanation of the Social Loafing Effect," *Journal of Personality and Social Psychology,* November 1985, pp 1199–1206.

77 Both studies are reported in S G Harkins and K Szymanski, "Social Loafing and Group Evaluation," *Journal of Personality and Social Psychology,* June 1989, pp 934–41.

78 S G Rogelberg J L Barnes-Farrell, and C A Lowe, "The Stepladder Technique: An Alternative Group Structure Facilitating Effective Group Decision Making," *Journal of Applied Psychology,* October 1992, p 730.

79 The case and instructions portions of this exercise excerpted from *Developing Management Skills* by D A Whetten and K S Cameron. Copyright © 1984 by Scott, Foresman and Company. Reprinted by permission of Harper Collins Publishers.

POWER, POLITICS, AND CONFLICT

Learning OBJECTIVES

When you finish studying the material in this chapter, you should be able to:

1. Explain the concept of mutuality of interest and identify the three most effective influence tactics.

2. Distinguish between power and authority.

3. Identify and briefly describe French and Raven's five bases of power.

4. Explain why delegation is the highest form of empowerment.

5. Define organizational politics and explain what triggers it.

6. Discuss the management of organizational politics.

7. Define conflict and distinguish between functional and dysfunctional conflict.

8. Explain how managers can stimulate functional conflict.

9. Describe five conflict-handling styles and discuss the contingency approach to managing conflict.

When Sarah Teslik Speaks, Corporate America Listens

Sharon Hoogstraten

Sarah Teslik arrives at work each weekday at 5 a.m. and puts in 15-hour days, breaking only for a 10-mile morning run at the YMCA in downtown Washington. On weekends, she takes it easy, rising at 9 and reaching her office in late morning.

Teslik, a 39-year-old Washington lawyer who often wears seven antique watches on one arm as her trademark, is a woman with a mission. She heads the Council of Institutional Investors, a group of pension funds that controls more than $500 billion, and is harnessing that enormous clout to change the way that Corporate America is governed.

She has been remarkably successful. In [1992–93], for example, the council . . . helped to topple the chief executives of General Motors Corp.,

Westinghouse Electric Corp. and International Business Machines Corp.

Operating with a tiny staff out of a modest office, she furiously works the phones and fax machines at all hours of day and night, praising, cajoling, massaging and inquiring while building one of the most important new financial alliances in the United States.

Her network of contacts stretches from the inner councils of the Securities and Exchange Commission and Capitol Hill to the nation's statehouses, elite law firms and boardrooms of its most powerful corporations.

Business leaders also mention "Sarah and the council" when they talk about the stepped-up pressure for a greater link between executive pay and corporate performance. Teslik was instrumental in supporting and helping craft new SEC rules that have boosted the required disclosures on executive pay and the accountability of directors on the issue.

"They are at the forefront of things," says one prominent attorney whose corporate clients have had extensive dealings with the council and its members. "Their power has increased dramatically. I think she has created something out of next to

nothing and made it into a potent force."

The members of the council hold stakes in thousands of companies on behalf of employees of local and state governments and some corporations.

Teslik is paid something more than $100,000 a year by the council, but money obviously is not what motivates her.

"I can't wait till I get to the office in the morning," she says.

"There is nobody who believes in this more than me. This is people's grocery money. The members own so much of Corporate America that it is also people's jobs. Once pension funds were asleep at the switch. If we had been more on the ball, then we could have saved jobs at GM. It is clear boards are acting differently now and it is partly because we have done our homework."

The pension funds in the council tend to be large and slow to act, but Teslik is possessed by a constant sense of urgency, and the shareholder movement she spearheads has a grass-roots feel, beginning with the way she runs her small office.

"I make the coffee. Everyone brings their lunch. I don't take vacations," she says. . . .

At the very heart of interpersonal dealings in today's work organizations is a constant struggle between individual and collective interests. For example, Sid wants a raise, but his company doesn't make enough money to both grant raises and pay minimum stockholder dividends. Preoccupation with self-interest is understandable. After all, each of us was born, not as a cooperating organization member, but as an individual with instincts for self-preservation. It took socialization in family, school, religious, sports, recreation, and employment settings to introduce us to the notion of mutuality of interest. Basically, **mutuality of interest** involves win-win situations in which one's self-interest is served by cooperating actively and creatively with potential adversaries. A pair of organization development consultants offered this managerial perspective of mutuality of interest:

mutuality of interest
Balancing individual and organizational interests through win-win cooperation.

OPENING CASE

(continued)

Teslik sends musing monthly memos to the council's members and makes sure they are aware of her devotion and strict upbringing as the daughter of a Methodist minister in Walla Walla, Wash.

"I really like the members," Teslik says. "I'm annoyed they don't all have fire in the belly even though they're not all minister's daughters."

Another thing Teslik inherited from her father is a knack for energizing and persuading others through wit and words, charm and persistence. "As you know, Sarah is hard to say no to," says billionaire investor Warren Buffett, explaining his appearance as a speaker at a recent council meeting. . . .

With Teslik encouraging them and helping devise strategy, the biggest pension funds from California and New York began pressing harder in the last year for change at companies that were obviously poor performers, and the results have been dramatic. Instead of ignoring the council, she says, chief executives and nonmanagement directors of major companies return her phone calls to schedule meetings with her and public pension fund chiefs. Increasingly, the companies are agreeing at these sessions

to make changes rather than face fights at their annual meetings.

"Companies are softer targets," she says. "If a number of CEOs have been rolled, it is easier to talk to other companies."

Just as it seems from such tough talk that she may be a radical intent on beheading white men in pinstripe suits, Teslik, who has a master's degree in history from Oxford University and a law degree from Georgetown University, shifts gears, discussing her ties to the Clinton administration and her willingness to help big business on certain issues. Helping management when possible, she says, is the only responsible way for pension funds, as major stockholders of companies, to act.

"We get lots of calls from top people in the administration asking us our opinion on things," she says. "Companies can call us for help. We can now go to the boards with things we can be helpful on too." . . .

Teslik crisscrosses the country by telephone, calling key public pension fund executives in Connecticut, New York, New Jersey, Pennsylvania, Maryland, the District of Columbia, Florida, Ohio, Missouri, Illinois, Iowa, Minnesota, Wisconsin, Colorado, California and Oregon in one four-hour stretch.

She knows who to call to get things done, and when she reaches them, knows who likes straight talk and who likes the early morning fax follow-up (many people say they know how early Teslik gets to the office because they have the 5 a.m. faxes to prove it).

She sprinkles the calls with juicy job tidbits, culling from the morning newspaper that the Rhode Island pension fund job is open and passing that information along to less careful readers who might want the job. ("I'm the main job reference service for public funds. It's a free headhunting service.") She often is asked to provide recommendations when government pension jobs become available, fostering personal relationships and loyalties that make her more effective.

For Discussion

Why is Sarah Teslik so effective as a corporate reformer?

■ Additional discussion questions linking this case with the following material appear at the end of the chapter.

Source: Excerpted by permission from D A Vise, "And in This Corner—Sarah Teslik," *The Washington Post National Weekly Edition,* April 5–11, 1993, pp 11–12.

Nothing is more important than this sense of mutuality to the effectiveness and quality of an organization's products and services. Management must strive to stimulate a strong sense of shared ownership in every employee, because otherwise an organization cannot do its best in the long run. Employees who identify their own personal self-interest with the quality of their organization's output understand mutuality and strive to maintain it in their jobs and work relations.[1]

Figure 10–1 graphically portrays the constant tug-of-war between employees' self-interest and the organization's need for mutuality of interest. It also serves as an overview model for this chapter, dealing with social influence tactics, social power, organizational politics, and conflict management. Notice how political tactics, motivated by self-interest, tend to pull individuals and groups away from mutual self-interest (organizational effectiveness). Oppositely, managers have

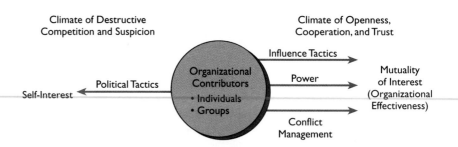

three counteracting interpersonal tools at their disposal: influence tactics, power, and conflict management techniques. At stake in this tug-of-war between individual and collective interests is no less than the ultimate survival of the organization.

ORGANIZATIONAL INFLUENCE TACTICS: GETTING ONE'S WAY AT WORK

How do you get others to carry out your wishes? Do you simply tell them what to do? Or do you prefer a less direct approach, such as promising to return the favor? Whatever approach you use, the crux of the issue is *social influence*. A large measure of interpersonal interaction involves attempts to influence others, including parents, bosses, co-workers, spouses, teachers, friends, and children. Consider how the power of persuasion and a car phone got results in this curious example: "Doug Dusenberg, a Houston businessman, dialed his Jeep Cherokee when he discovered it missing from a parking lot and talked the two young joyriders into returning it; he let them keep the $20 in the glove compartment."[2] Even if managers do not expect to get such dramatic results, they need to sharpen their influence skills. A good starting point is familiarity with the following research insights.

Eight Generic Influence Tactics

A particularly fruitful stream of research, initiated by David Kipnis and his colleagues in 1980, reveals how people influence each other in organizations. The Kipnis methodology involved asking employees how they managed to get either their bosses, co-workers, or subordinates to do what they wanted them to do.[3] Statistical refinements and replications by other researchers over a 10-year period eventually yielded eight influence tactics. The eight tactics, ranked in diminishing order of use in the workplace are

1. *Consultation.* Getting others to participate in decisions and changes.
2. *Rational persuasion.* Trying to convince someone with reason, logic, or facts.
3. *Inspirational appeals.* Trying to build enthusiasm by appealing to others' emotions, ideals, or values.
4. *Ingratiating tactics.* Getting someone in a good mood prior to making a request.
5. *Coalition tactics.* Getting others to support your effort to persuade someone.
6. *Pressure tactics.* Demanding compliance or using intimidation and threats.

7. *Upward appeals.* Trying to persuade someone on the basis of express or implied support from superiors.

8. *Exchange tactics.* Making express or implied promises and trading favors.[4]

These approaches can be considered *generic* influence tactics because they characterize social influence in all directions. Researchers have found this ranking to be fairly consistent regardless of whether the direction of influence is downward, upward, or lateral.

Additional Research Insights

The preceding ranking reflects the self-reported use of influence tactics. But what about the effectiveness of the various tactics from the viewpoint of those being influenced? In short, which tactics actually work? A recent field study found the same top three—consultation, rational persuasion, and inspirational appeals—to be the most effective. Pressure tactics and coalition tactics were the least effective influence tactics.[5] Interestingly, in the same study, managers were not very effective at *downward* influence. They relied most heavily on inspiration (an effective tactic), ingratiation (a moderately effective tactic), and pressure (an ineffective tactic).

A related study recently probed male-female differences in influencing work group members. Many studies have found women to be perceived as less competent and less influential in work groups than men. The researchers had male and female work group leaders engage in either task behavior (demonstrating ability and task competence) or dominating behavior (relying on threats). For both women and men, task behavior was associated with perceived competence and effective influence. Dominating behavior was not effective. The following conclusion by the researchers has important practical implications for all present and future managers who desire to successfully influence others: ''The display of task cues is an effective means to enhance one's status in groups and . . . the attempt to gain influence in task groups through dominance is an ineffective and poorly received strategy for both men and women.''[6]

How to Extend Your Influence by Forming Strategic Alliances

In their useful book, *Influence without Authority,* Allan R Cohen and David L Bradford extended the concept of corporate strategic alliances to interpersonal influence. Hardly a day goes by without another mention in the business press of a new strategic alliance between two global companies intent on staying competitive. These win-win relationships are based on complementary strengths. According to Cohen and Bradford, managers need to follow suit by forming some strategic alliances of their own with anyone who has a stake in their area. This is particularly true given today's rapid change, cross-functional work teams, and diminished reliance on traditional authority structures.

While admitting the task is not an easy one, Cohen and Bradford recommend the following tips for dealing with potential allies:

1. *Mutual respect.* Assume they are competent and smart.

2. *Openness.* Talk straight to them. It isn't possible for any one person to know everything, so give them the information they need to know to help you better.

3. *Trust.* Assume that no one will take any action that is purposely intended to hurt another, so hold back no information that the other could use, even if it doesn't help your immediate position.

4. *Mutual benefit.* Plan every strategy so that both parties win. If that doesn't happen over time, the alliance will break up. When dissolving a partnership becomes necessary as a last resort, try to do it in a clean way that minimizes residual anger. Some day, you may want a new alliance with that person.[7]

reciprocity Widespread belief that people should be paid back for their positive and negative acts.

True, these tactics involve taking some personal risks. But the effectiveness of interpersonal strategic alliances is anchored to the concept of reciprocity. ''**Reciprocity** is the almost universal belief that people should be paid back for what they do—that one good (or bad) turn deserves another.''[8] In short, people tend to get what they give when attempting to influence others.

By demonstrating the rich texture of social influence, the foregoing research evidence and practical advice whet our appetite for learning more about how today's managers can and do reconcile individual and organizational interests. Let us focus on social power.

SOCIAL POWER AND POWER SHARING

The term *power* evokes mixed and often passionate reactions. Citing recent instances of government corruption and corporate misconduct, many observers view power as a sinister force. In an annual nationwide poll, Louis Harris & Associates asks Americans this question: ''Do most people with power try to take advantage of people like yourself?'' Forty-three percent of the respondents said yes in 1972. By 1992, the figure had reached 71 percent.[9] To these skeptics, Lord Acton's time-honored statement that ''power corrupts and absolute power corrupts absolutely'' is as true as ever. However, OB specialists remind us that, like it or not, power is a fact of life in modern organizations. According to one management writer:

> Power must be used because managers must influence those they depend on. Power also is crucial in the development of managers' self-confidence and willingness to support subordinates. From this perspective, power should be accepted as a natural part of any organization. Managers should recognize and develop their own power to coordinate and support the work of subordinates; it is powerlessness, not power, that undermines organizational effectiveness.[10]

social power Ability to get things done with human, informational, and material resources.

Thus, power is a necessary and generally positive force in organizations. As the term is used here, **social power** is defined as ''the ability to marshal the human, informational, and material resources to get something done.''[11]

Dimensions of Power

While power may be an elusive concept to the casual observer, social scientists view power as having reasonably clear dimensions. Three dimensions of power that deserve our attention are (1) the distinction between power and authority, (2) socialized versus personalized power, and (3) the five bases of power.

Power and Authority   In our definition of power, emphasis must be placed on the word *ability* because it sets power apart from the concept of authority.[12]

Authority is the "right" or the "obligation" to seek compliance; power is the "demonstrated ability" to achieve compliance. As illustrated in Figure 10–2, three classic situations can arise because power and authority often do not overlap. Effective managers are able to back up their authority with power (the middle portion of Figure 10–2).

authority   The official right or obligation to seek compliance.

This distinction between power and authority may appear to be a simple one, but those who fail to appreciate the difference can unwittingly commit career suicide. For instance, nonmanagerial employees who have no official authority may wield a great deal of power because of who or what they know. Staff assistants, who have no real authority in the formal chain of command, often are very powerful. For example:

> At Intel Corp., Jean C Jones, executive secretary to Chairman Gordon E Moore, is curator of Intel's high-tech museum. But most of her influence—as well as the power most executive assistants wield—derives from many of those old-fashioned secretarial duties. Each week, she decides how much of the 30-in. stack of mail her boss will see and how many of the 125 telephone calls will gain his ear. Jones deflects 80 percent of those calls, weeding out the insurance salesmen and the stockbrokers. By scheduling Moore's calendar, she helps determine who gets to see the boss in person.[13]

Part of the organizational socialization process discussed in Chapter 19 involves teaching newcomers where the real power lies.

Two Types of Power   Behavioral scientists such as David McClelland contend that one of the basic human needs is the need for power (n Pwr). Because this need is learned and not innate, the need for power has been extensively studied. Historically, need for power was scored when subjects interpreted TAT pictures in terms of one person attempting to influence, convince, persuade, or control another, as discussed in Chapter 6. More recently, however, researchers have drawn a distinction between **socialized power** and **personalized power.**

socialized power   Directed at helping others.

personalized power   Directed at helping oneself.

> There are two subscales or "faces" in n Pwr. One face is termed "socialized" (s Pwr) and is scored in the Thematic Apperception Test (TAT) as "plans, self-doubts, mixed outcomes and concerns for others, . . ." while the second face is "personalized" power (p Pwr), in which expressions of power for the sake of personal aggrandizement become paramount.[14]

This distinction between socialized and personalized power helps explain why power has a negative connotation for many people. Managers and others who

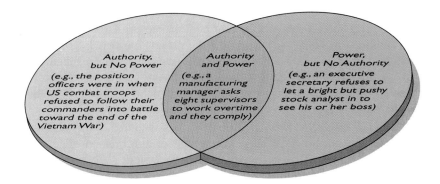

•   FIGURE 10–2
Power and Authority Are Not Necessarily the Same Thing

Socialized power is power that is directed at helping others. US Senator Carol Moseley Braun of Illinois is an elected official who has a strong preference for this unselfish kind of power.

Reuters/Bettmann

pursue personalized power for their own selfish ends give power a bad name. But a recent series of interviews with 25 American women elected to public office found a strong preference for socialized power. The following comments illustrate their desire to wield power effectively and ethically:

- "Power in itself means nothing. . . . I think power is the opportunity to really have an impact on your community."
- "My goal is to be a powerful advocate on the part of my constituents."[15]

Five Bases of Power   A popular classification scheme for social power traces back more than 30 years to the work of John French and Bertram Raven. They proposed that power arises from five different bases: reward power, coercive power, legitimate power, expert power, and referent power.[16] Each involves a different approach to influencing others.

reward power   Obtaining compliance with promised or actual rewards.

- *Reward power:*   A manager has **reward power** to the extent that he or she obtains compliance by promising or granting rewards. On-the-job behavior modification, for example, relies heavily on reward power.

coercive power   Obtaining compliance through threatened or actual punishment.

- *Coercive power:*   Threats of punishment and actual punishment give an individual **coercive power.** A sales manager who threatens to fire any salesperson who uses a company car for family vacations is relying on coercive power.

legitimate power   Obtaining compliance through formal authority.

- *Legitimate power:*   This base of power is anchored to one's formal position or authority. Thus, individuals who obtain compliance primarily because of their formal authority to make decisions have **legitimate power.** Legitimate power may express itself in either a positive or negative manner in managing people. Positive legitimate power focuses constructively on job performance. Negative legitimate power tends to be threatening and demeaning to those being influenced. Its main purpose is to build the power holder's ego.

expert power   Obtaining compliance through one's knowledge or information.

- *Expert power:*   Valued knowledge or information gives an individual **expert power** over those who need such knowledge or information. The power of supervisors is enhanced because they know about work schedules and assignments before their subordinates do.

OB EXERCISE

What Is Your Self-Perceived Power?

Instructions:

Score your various bases of power for your present (or former) job, using the following scale:

1 = Strongly disagree	4 = Agree
2 = Disagree	5 = Strongly agree
3 = Slightly agree	

Reward Power Score = _____
1. I can reward persons at lower levels. _____
2. My review actions affect the rewards gained at lower levels. _____
3. Based on my decisions, lower level personnel may receive a bonus. _____

Coercive Power Score = _____
1. I can punish employees at lower levels. _____
2. My work is a check on lower level employees. _____
3. My diligence reduces error. _____

Legitimate Power Score = _____
1. My position gives me a great deal of authority. _____
2. The decisions made at my level are of critical importance. _____
3. Employees look to me for guidance. _____

Expert Power Score = _____
1. I am an expert in this job. _____
2. My ability gives me an advantage in this job. _____
3. Given some time, I could improve the methods used on this job. _____

Referent Power Score = _____
1. I attempt to set a good example for other employees. _____
2. My personality allows me to work well in this job. _____
3. My fellow employees look to me as their informal leader. _____

Source: Adapted and excerpted in part from D L Dieterly and B Schneider, "The Effect of Organizational Environment on Perceived Power and Climate: A Laboratory Study," *Organizational Behavior and Human Performance,* June 1974, pp 316–37.

- *Referent power:*   Also called charisma, **referent power** comes into play when one's personality becomes the reason for compliance. Role models have referent power over those who identify closely with them.

referent power   Obtaining compliance through charisma or personal attraction.

To further your understanding of these five bases of power and to assess your self-perceived power, please take a moment to complete the questionnaire in the OB Exercise. Think of your present job or your most recent job when responding to the various items. Arbitrary norms for each of the five bases of power are: 3–6 = Weak power base; 7–11 = Moderate power base; 12–15 = Strong power base. What is your power profile?

Research Insights about Social Power

In one study, a sample of 94 male and 84 female nonmanagerial and professional employees in Denver, Colorado, completed TAT tests. The researchers found that the male and female employees had similar needs for power (n Pwr) and personalized power (p Pwr). But the women had a significantly higher need for socialized power (s Pwr) than did their male counterparts.[17] This bodes well for today's work organizations where women are playing an ever greater administrative role. Unfortunately, as women gain power in the workplace, greater tension between men and women has been observed. *Training* magazine recently offered this perspective:

> . . . observers view the tension between women and men in the workplace as a natural outcome of power inequities between the genders. Their argument is that men still have most of the power and are resisting any change as a way to protect their power base. [Consultant Susan L] Webb asserts that sexual harassment has far more to do with exercising power in an unhealthy way than with sexual attraction. Likewise, the glass ceiling, a metaphor for the barriers women face in climbing the corporate ladder to management and executive positions, is about power and access to power.[18]

A reanalysis of 18 field studies that measured French and Raven's five bases of power uncovered "severe methodological shortcomings."[19] After correcting for these problems, the researchers identified the following relationships between power bases and work outcomes such as job performance, job satisfaction, and turnover:

- Expert and referent power had a generally positive impact.
- Reward and legitimate power had a slightly positive impact.
- Coercive power had a slightly negative impact.

The same researcher, in a 1990 follow-up study involving 251 employed business seniors, looked at the relationship between influence styles and bases of power. This was a bottom-up study. In other words, subordinate perceptions of managerial influence and power were examined. Rational persuasion was found to be a highly acceptable managerial influence tactic. Why? Because subordinates perceived it to be associated with the three bases of power they viewed positively: legitimate, expert, and referent.[20]

In summary, expert and referent power appear to get the best *combination* of results and favorable subordinate reactions.[21]

Responsible Management of Power

If managers are to use their various bases of power effectively and ethically, they need to understand the differences between compliance and internalization and power sharing and power distribution.

From Compliance to Internalization   Responsible managers strive for socialized power while avoiding personalized power. This, in addition to being aware of the relative strengths of their bases of power, can help managers use their power effectively. It is important to recognize, however, that the various power bases tend to produce two very different modes of behavior change. Reward, coercive, and negative legitimate power tend to produce *compliance.* On the other hand, positive legitimate, expert, and referent power tend to foster *internalization.* Internalization is superior to compliance because it is driven by internal or intrinsic motivation. Employees who merely comply require frequent ''jolts'' of power from the boss to keep them headed in a productive direction. Those who internalize the task at hand tend to become self starters who do not require close supervision.

According to the research cited earlier, expert and referent power have the greatest potential for improving job performance and satisfaction and reducing turnover. Formal education, training, and self-development can build a manager's expert power. At the same time, one's referent power base can be strengthened by forming and developing the strategic alliances discussed earlier under the heading of influence tactics.

Empowerment: From Power Sharing to Power Distribution   Before leaving the topic of social power, we need to briefly highlight a very exciting trend in today's organizations. Some call it **empowerment** or power sharing.[22] Others use traditional labels such as participative management, participative decision making, and delegation. Regardless of the term one prefers, the underlying process is the same. Namely, the decentralization of power. Where power once resided solely in the hands of managers, it now is being shifted to the hands of nonmanagers (see Figure 10–3). The overriding goal is to increase productivity and competitiveness in leaner organizations. Each step in this evolution increases the power of organizational contributors who traditionally had little or no legitimate power. Participative decision making and leadership are discussed in later chapters. So here we will describe the highest degree of empowerment—delegation—as a foundation concept for later chapters.

Delegation is the process of granting decision-making authority to subordinates. Importantly, delegation gives nonmanagerial employees more than simply a voice in decisions. It empowers them to make their own decisions. A prime example is the Ritz-Carlton Hotel chain:

empowerment   Sharing power with nonmanagers through participative management.

delegation   Granting decision-making authority to people at lower levels.

➧ FIGURE 10~3   The Evolution of Power: From Domination to Delegation

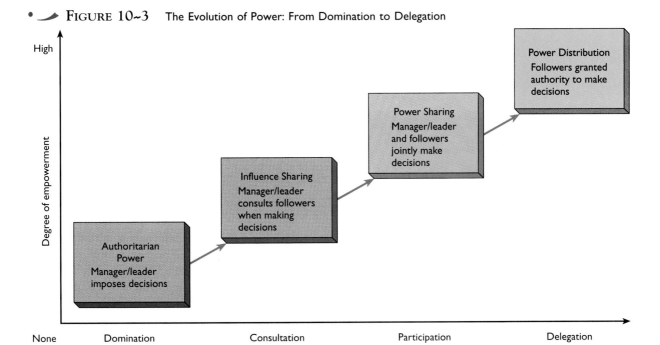

Degree of empowerment

High

Authoritarian Power
Manager/leader imposes decisions

Influence Sharing
Manager/leader consults followers when making decisions

Power Sharing
Manager/leader and followers jointly make decisions

Power Distribution
Followers granted authority to make decisions

None   Domination   Consultation   Participation   Delegation

At Ritz-Carlton, every worker is authorized to spend up to $2,000 to fix any problem a guest encounters. Employees do not abuse the privilege. ''When you treat people responsibly, they act responsibly,'' said Patrick Mene, the hotel chain's director of quality.[23]

Not surprising, then, that Ritz-Carlton has won national service quality awards. Delegation has long been the recommended way to lighten the busy manager's load while at the same time developing employees' abilities. Unfortunately, research support for testimonial claims[24] stemming from the human relations movement was slow in coming. But, according to Carrie Leana's landmark field study of 26 insurance claims supervisors, subordinates who enjoyed a greater degree of delegation processed more insurance claims at lower cost.[25] Power distribution via delegation does indeed seem to work.

The promising area of empowerment is explored further in Chapter 12 under the heading of autonomous (self-managed) work teams.

ORGANIZATIONAL POLITICS

Most students of OB find the study of organizational politics intriguing. Perhaps this topic owes its appeal to the antics of Hollywood's corporate villains who get their way by stepping on anyone and everyone. As we will see, however, organizational politics includes, but is not limited to, dirty dealing. Organizational politics is an ever-present and sometimes annoying feature of modern work life. In a recent survey of 1,000 American employees, office politics turned out to be the leading cause of ''a bad day'' at work.[26] On the other hand, organizational politics is often a positive force in modern work organizations.

Roberta Bhasin, a district manager for US West, put organizational politics into perspective by observing:

> Most of us would like to believe that organizations are rationally structured, based on reasonable divisions of labor, a clear hierarchical communication flow, and well-defined lines of authority aimed at meeting universally understood goals and objectives.
>
> But organizations are made up of *people* with personal agendas designed to win power and influence. The agenda—the game—is called corporate politics. It is played by avoiding the rational structure, manipulating the communications hierarchy, and ignoring established lines of authority. The rules are never written down and seldom discussed.
>
> For some, corporate politics are second nature. They instinctively know the unspoken rules of the game. Others must learn. Managers who don't understand the politics of their organizations are at a disadvantage, not only in winning raises and promotions, but even in getting things *done.*[27]

We explore this important, interesting area by (1) defining the term *organizational politics,* (2) identifying three levels of political action, (3) discussing eight specific political tactics, and (4) examining relevant research and practical implications.

Definition and Domain of Organizational Politics

organizational politics
Intentional enhancement of self-interest.

''**Organizational politics** involves intentional acts of influence to enhance or protect the self-interest of individuals or groups.''[28] An emphasis on *self-interest* distinguishes this form of social influence. Managers are endlessly challenged to achieve a workable balance between employees' self-interests and organizational interests. When a proper balance exists, the pursuit of self-interest may serve the organization's interests. Political behavior becomes a negative force when self-interests erode or defeat organizational interests. For example, researchers have documented the political tactic of filtering and distorting information flowing up to the boss. This self-serving practice put the reporting employees in the best possible light.[29] Experts say America's global competitiveness is threatened by unmanaged organizational politics (see the International OB).

Uncertainty Triggers Political Behavior   Political maneuvering is triggered primarily by *uncertainty.* Five common sources of uncertainty within organizations are

1. Unclear objectives.
2. Vague performance measures.
3. Ill-defined decision processes.
4. Strong individual or group competition.[30]
5. Any type of change.

Regarding this last source of uncertainty, organization development specialist Anthony Raia noted, "Whatever we attempt to change, the political subsystem becomes active. Vested interests are almost always at stake and the distribution of power is challenged."[31]

Thus, we would expect a field sales representative, striving to achieve an assigned quota, to be less political than a management trainee working on a variety of projects. While some management trainees stake their career success on hard work, competence, and a bit of luck, many do not. These people attempt to gain a competitive edge through some combination of the political tactics discussed below. Meanwhile, the salesperson's performance is measured in actual sales, not in terms of being friends with the boss or taking credit for others' work. Thus, the

---

INTERNATIONAL OB

TQM Is No Match for Organizational Politics

U.S. manufacturers won't win the global competition by simply embracing the hottest management fads.

Instead, a survey concludes, the world's most successful manufacturers triumph by curbing internal politics and taking similar steps to foster cooperation among employees. Using such approaches, the typical Japanese concern develops innovative products faster than U.S. and European rivals, according to the survey of 553 global manufacturers by two Massachusetts consulting firms, Boston Consulting Group and Product Development Consulting Inc.

It takes an average of 17.7 months for a Japanese manufacturer to introduce a product, compared with 19.7 months in the U.S. and 20.6 months in Europe, the study found. Companies grow faster and grab a bigger market share when they "bring the right innovative products to market ahead of the pack," the survey said.

To become more competitive, U.S. executives must address "the politics of [their] organization before [they] install mechanisms to develop products faster," suggests Thomas Hout, a Boston Consulting vice president and the study's co-author. "Politics, if not addressed, will defeat any mechanism known to man," he adds.

The companies surveyed make wide use of popular management tools such as product-development teams, total quality management and com-

puter-aided design. "But no one of these stands out as explaining fast and innovative product development," the survey noted. Japanese manufacturers, for instance, use project teams less frequently than their U.S. or European counterparts.

"The difference doesn't lie in training or tools," the study continued. "It's in how people work together, how decisions get made and how leadership is practiced."

Source: J S Lublin, "Best Manufacturers Found to Triumph by Fostering Cooperation of Employees," *The Wall Street Journal,* July 20, 1993, p A4. Excerpted by permission of *The Wall Street Journal,* © 1993 Dow Jones & Company, Inc. All Rights Reserved Worldwide.

management trainee would tend to be more political than the field salesperson because of greater uncertainty about management's expectations.

Because employees generally experience greater uncertainty during the earlier stages of their careers, are junior employees more political than more senior ones? The answer is yes, according to a survey of 243 employed adults in upstate New York. In fact, one senior employee nearing retirement told the researcher: "I used to play political games when I was younger. Now I just do my job."[32]

Three Levels of Political Action   Although much political maneuvering occurs at the individual level, it also can involve group or collective action. Figure 10–4 illustrates three different levels of political action: the individual level, the coalition level, and the network level.[33] Each level has its distinguishing characteristics. At the individual level, personal self-interests are pursued by the individual. The political aspects of coalitions and networks are not so obvious, however.

People with a common interest can become a political coalition by fitting the following definition. In an organizational context, a **coalition** is an informal group bound together by the *active* pursuit of a *single* issue. Coalitions may or may not coincide with formal group membership. When the target issue is resolved (a sexually harassing supervisor is fired, for example), the coalition disbands. Experts note that political coalitions have "fuzzy boundaries," meaning they are fluid in membership, flexible in structure, and temporary in duration.[34]

Coalitions are a potent political force in organizations. Consider the situation Charles J Bradshaw faced in a finance committee meeting at Transworld Corporation in 1986: Bradshaw, president of the company, opposed the chairman's plan to acquire a $93 million nursing home company.

> [The senior vice president for finance] kicked off the meeting with a battery of facts and figures in support of the deal. "Within two or three minutes, I knew I had lost," Bradshaw concedes. "No one was talking directly to me, but all statements addressed my opposition. I could tell there was a general agreement around the board table." . . .
> Then the vote was taken. Five hands went up. Only Bradshaw voted "no."[35]

After the meeting, Bradshaw resigned his $530,000-a-year position, without as much as a handshake or good-bye from the chairman. In Bradshaw's case, the finance committee was a formal group that temporarily became a political coalition aimed at sealing his fate at Transworld.[36]

A third level of political action involves networks. Unlike coalitions, which pivot on specific issues, networks are loose associations of individuals seeking social support for their general self-interests. Politically, networks are people oriented, while coalitions are issue oriented. Networks have broader and longer

coalition Temporary groupings of people who actively pursue a single issue.

• FIGURE 10–4

Levels of Political Action in Organizations

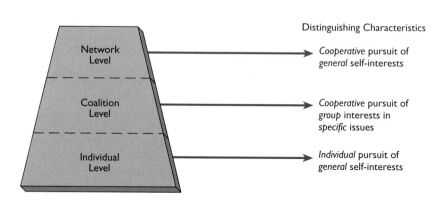

Distinguishing Characteristics

Network Level → *Cooperative* pursuit of *general* self-interests

Coalition Level → *Cooperative* pursuit of *group* interests in *specific* issues

Individual Level → *Individual* pursuit of *general* self-interests

term agendas than do coalitions. For instance, Avon's Hispanic employees have built a network to enhance the members' career opportunities.

Political Tactics

Anyone who has worked in an organization has firsthand knowledge of blatant politicking. Blaming someone else for your mistake is an obvious political ploy. But other political tactics are more subtle. Researchers have identified a range of political behavior.

One landmark study, involving in-depth interviews with 87 managers from 30 electronics companies in Southern California, identified eight political tactics. Top-, middle-, and low-level managers were represented about equally in the sample. According to the researchers: ''Respondents were asked to describe organizational political tactics and personal characteristics of effective political actors based upon their accumulated experience in *all* organizations in which they had worked.''[37] Listed in descending order of occurrence, the eight political tactics that emerged were

1. Attacking or blaming others.
2. Using information as a political tool.
3. Creating a favorable image. (Also known as *impression management*.)[38]
4. Developing a base of support.
5. Praising others (ingratiation).
6. Forming power coalitions with strong allies.
7. Associating with influential people.
8. Creating obligations (reciprocity).

Table 10–1 describes these political tactics and indicates how often each reportedly was used by the interviewed managers.

• ➔ TABLE 10–1   Eight Common Political Tactics in Organizations

Political Tactic	Percentage of Managers Mentioning Tactic	Brief Description of Tactic
1. Attacking or blaming others	54%	Used to avoid or minimize association with failure. Reactive when scapegoating is involved. Proactive when goal is to reduce competition for limited resources.
2. Using information as a political tool	54	Involves the purposeful withholding or distortion of information. Obscuring an unfavorable situation by overwhelming superiors with information.
3. Creating a favorable image (impression management)	53	Dressing/grooming for success. Adhering to organizational norms and drawing attention to one's successes and influence. Taking credit for others' accomplishments.
4. Developing a base of support	37	Getting prior support for a decision. Building others' commitment to a decision through participation.
5. Praising others (ingratiation)	25	Making influential people feel good (''apple polishing'').
6. Forming power coalitions with strong allies	25	Teaming up with powerful people who can get results.
7. Associating with influential people	24	Building a support network both inside and outside the organization.
8. Creating obligations (reciprocity)	13	Creating social debts (''I did you a favor, so you owe me a favor'').

Source: Adapted from R W Allen, D L Madison, L W Porter, P A Renwick, and B T Mayes, ''Organizational Politics: Tactics and Characteristics of Its Actors,'' *California Management Review*, Fall 1979, pp 77–83.

The researchers distinguished between reactive and proactive political tactics. Some of the tactics, such as scapegoating, were *reactive* because the intent was to *defend* one's self-interest. Other tactics, such as developing a base of support, were *proactive* because they sought to *promote* the individual's self-interest.

Find out how political you are with the questionnaire in the OB Exercise. After responding to all 10 items, determine your political tendencies by using the scoring system recommended by the author of this quiz:

> A confirmed organizational politician will answer "true" to all 10 questions. Organizational politicians with fundamental ethical standards will answer "false" to Questions 5 and 6, which deal with deliberate lies and uncharitable behavior. Individuals who regard manipulation, incomplete disclosure, and self-serving behavior as unacceptable will answer "false" to all or almost all of the questions.[39]

Research Evidence on Organizational Politics

Field research evidence in the area of organizational politics is slowly accumulating. Three particularly insightful studies are discussed in this section. Two are

---

OB EXERCISE

How Political Are You? A Self-Quiz

The Political Behavior Inventory

To determine your political appreciation and tendencies, please answer the following questions. Select the answer that best represents your behavior or belief, even if that particular behavior or belief is not present all the time.

1. You should make others feel important through an open appreciation of their ideas and work. _____ True _____ False
2. Because people tend to judge you when they first meet you, always try to make a good first impression. _____ True _____ False
3. Try to let others do most of the talking, be sympathetic to their problems, and resist telling people that they are totally wrong. _____ True _____ False
4. Praise the good traits of the people you meet and always give people an opportunity to save face if they are wrong or make a mistake. _____ True _____ False
5. Spreading false rumors, planting misleading information, and backstabbing are necessary, if somewhat unpleasant, methods to deal with your enemies. _____ True _____ False
6. Sometimes it is necessary to make promises that you know you will not or cannot keep. _____ True _____ False
7. It is important to get along with everybody, even with those who are generally recognized as windbags, abrasive, or constant complainers. _____ True _____ False
8. It is vital to do favors for others so that you can call in these IOUs at times when they will do you the most good. _____ True _____ False
9. Be willing to compromise, particularly on issues that are minor to you, but important to others. _____ True _____ False
10. On controversial issues, it is important to delay or avoid your involvement if possible. _____ True _____ False

Source: J F Byrnes, "Connecting Organizational Politics and Conflict Resolution," *Personnel Administrator*, June 1986, p 49. Used with author's permission.

based on self-report questionnaires, the third on direct observation of managers in action.

A follow-up research report on the sample of Southern California electronics industry managers, discussed earlier, provided the following insights:

- Sixty percent of the managers reported organizational politics was a frequent occurrence.
- The larger the organization, the greater the perceived political activity.
- Ambiguous roles and goals and increased conflict were associated with increased political activity.
- Marketing staffs and members of corporate boards of directors were rated as the most political, while production, accounting, and finance personnel were viewed as the least political.
- Reorganizations and personnel changes prompted the most political activity.[40]

Another study analyzed 330 brief reports written by 90 middle managers from a variety of industries. Those reports dealt with how the managers had ''taken a position on a decision'' or ''resisted a decision.'' The researchers concluded that middle managers, often acting in coalitions, are a formidable barrier to implementing strategic plans they consider contrary to their self-interests.[41] This helps explain why middle managers have been particularly hard hit by the recent wave of corporate downsizings.[42]

A more recent observational study of 248 managers, employed by a variety of organizations, found a curious relationship between the amount of time spent networking and career success and managerial effectiveness. The University of Nebraska research team, directed by Fred Luthans, defined networking as socializing, interacting with outsiders, and politicking. Career success was determined by how fast the individual was promoted up the managerial ladder. Managerial effectiveness was assessed in terms of subunit performance and subordinates' satisfaction and commitment. It turned out that only 10 percent of the managers were both successful and effective. Among the other 90 percent, those who enjoyed career success devoted the largest share of their time to networking. In contrast, the effective managers devoted the *least* amount of their time to networking. This evidence prompted Luthans to ask:

> Could this finding explain some of the performance problems facing American organizations today? Could it be that the successful managers, the politically savvy ones who are being rapidly promoted into responsible positions, may not be the effective managers, the ones with satisfied, committed subordinates turning out quantity and quality performance in their units?[43]

Luthans then called for a concerted effort to create more *balanced* managers who are *both successful and effective*. One likely approach is to teach effective managers career management and networking skills.

Managing Organizational Politics

Organizational politics cannot be eliminated. A manager would be naive to expect such an outcome. But political maneuvering can and should be managed to keep it constructive and within reasonable bounds. Harvard's Abraham Zaleznik put the issue this way: ''People can focus their attention on only so many things. The more it lands on politics, the less energy—emotional and intellectual—is available to attend to the problems that fall under the heading of real work.''[44] Perhaps this

TABLE 10–2

Some Practical Advice on Managing Organizational Politics

To Reduce System Uncertainty

Make clear what are the bases and processes for evaluation.

Differentiate rewards among high and low performers.

Make sure the rewards are as immediately and directly related to performance as possible.

To Reduce Competition

Try to minimize resource competition among managers.

Replace resource competition with externally oriented goals and objectives.

To Break Existing Political Fiefdoms

Where highly cohesive political empires exist, break them apart by removing or splitting the most dysfunctional subgroups.

If you are an executive, be keenly sensitive to managers whose mode of operation is the personalization of political patronage. First, approach these persons with a directive to "stop the political maneuvering." If it continues, remove them from the positions and, preferably, the company.

To Prevent Future Fiefdoms

Make one of the most important criteria for promotion an apolitical attitude that puts organizational ends ahead of personal power ends.

Source: D R Beeman and T W Sharkey, "The Use and Abuse of Corporate Politics," *Business Horizons*, March–April 1987, p 30.

explains why only 10 percent of the Luthans' sample managed to be promoted rapidly, while at the same time, doing a good job. The successful, but not effective, managers evidently spent too much of their emotional and intellectual energy on politicking. An appropriate middle ground needs to be achieved.

An individual's degree of politicalness is a matter of personal values, ethics, and temperament. People who are either strictly nonpolitical or highly political generally pay a price for their behavior. The former may experience slow promotions and feel left out, while the latter may run the risk of being called self-serving and lose their credibility. People at both ends of the political spectrum may be considered poor team players. A moderate amount of prudent political behavior generally is considered a survival tool in complex organizations.

With this perspective in mind, the practical steps in Table 10–2 are recommended. Notice the importance of reducing uncertainty through standardized performance evaluations and clear performance-reward linkages.[45] Measurable objectives are management's first line of defense against negative expressions of organizational politics. To resolve the conflict between middle managers' self-interests and strategy implementation, top managers need to build commitment to strategic plans through participative strategic goal setting.

MANAGING INTERPERSONAL AND INTERGROUP CONFLICT

Mention the term *conflict* and most people envision fights, riots, or war. In fact, on virtually every day of every year one can find approximately two dozen armed combat situations somewhere in the world.[46] But these extreme situations represent only the most overt and violent expressions of conflict. During the typical workday, managers encounter more subtle and nonviolent types of opposition such as arguments, criticism, and disagreement. Conflict, like power and organizational politics, is an inevitable and sometimes positive force in modern work organizations. For example, a sincere dissenting opinion by a member of an executive planning committee might prevent the group from falling victim to groupthink. OB scholar Stephen Robbins defines **conflict** as "all kinds of opposition or antagonistic interaction. It is based on scarcity of power, resources or social position, and differing value systems."[47] Research reveals that managers spend approximately 21 percent of their time dealing with conflict,[48] so they need to be well grounded in conflict theory, research, and practice.

conflict   All kinds of opposition or antagonistic interaction

Conflict occurs at two levels within organizations: interpersonal and intergroup. This section addresses both levels of conflict by (1) distinguishing between functional and dysfunctional conflict, (2) identifying antecedents of conflict, (3) explaining how to promote functional conflict, (4) examining alternative styles of handling conflict, (5) reviewing relevant research evidence, and (6) discussing a contingency approach to managing conflict.

A Conflict Continuum

Ideas about managing conflict have undergone an interesting evolution during this century. Initially, scientific management experts such as Frederick W Taylor believed all conflict ultimately threatened management's authority and thus had to be avoided or quickly resolved. Later, human relationists recognized the inevitability of conflict and advised managers to learn to live with it. Emphasis remained on resolving conflict whenever possible, however. Beginning in the 1970s, OB specialists realized conflict had both positive and negative outcomes, depending on its nature and intensity. This perspective introduced the revolutionary idea that organizations could suffer from *too little* conflict. Figure 10–5 illustrates the relationship between conflict intensity and outcomes.

Work groups, departments, or organizations that experience too little conflict tend to be plagued by apathy, lack of creativity, indecision, and missed deadlines. Excessive conflict, on the other hand, can erode organizational performance because of political infighting, dissatisfaction, lack of teamwork, and turnover. Appropriate types and levels of conflict energize people in constructive directions.

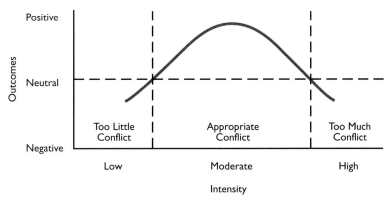

• ↗ **FIGURE 10–5**
The Relationship between Conflict Intensity and Outcomes

Source: L D Brown, *Managing Conflict of Organizational Interfaces*, © 1986, Addison-Wesley Publishing Co., Inc., Reading, Massachusetts. Figure 1.1 on page 8. Reprinted with permission.

Functional versus Dysfunctional Conflict

The distinction between **functional conflict** and **dysfunctional conflict** pivots on whether or not the organization's interests are served. According to Robbins:

> Some [types of conflict] support the goals of the organization and improve performance; these are functional, constructive forms of conflict. They benefit or support the main purposes of the organization. Additionally, there are those types of conflict that hinder organizational performance; these are dysfunctional or destructive forms. They are undesirable and the manager should seek their eradication.[49]

Functional conflict is commonly referred to in management circles as constructive or cooperative conflict.[50]

Richard (Skip) LeFauve, President of General Motors's successful Saturn Corporation, relies on functional conflict to energize his team-based organization that requires intense union-management cooperation.

> Everyone eats at the same cafeterias, and UAW [United Auto Workers union] members helped pick Saturn's dealers and its advertising agency. That might be controversial elsewhere within General Motors, but the soft-spoken LeFauve doesn't care. "A lot of people try to avoid controversy and conflict," he says. But he contends that conflict often fuels creativity.[51]

In contrast, managers such as Fred Ackman, former chairman of Superior Oil Corporation, foster dysfunctional conflict by dealing with personalities rather than with issues.

> Employees say Ackman proved thoroughly autocratic, refusing even to discuss staff suggestions. He tended to treat disagreement as disloyalty. Many were put off by Ackman's abusive temper, which together with his stature (5 feet 8½ inches) and red hair earned him the nickname "Little Red Fred." Says a former subordinate, "He couldn't stand it when somebody disagreed with him, even in private. He'd eat you up alive, calling you a dumb S.O.B. or asking if you had your head up your ass. It happened all the time."[52]

Not surprisingly, of 13 top executives at Superior Oil, 9 left within one year after Ackman joined the company.

Antecedents of Conflict

Certain situations produce more conflict than others. By knowing the antecedents of conflict, managers are better able to anticipate conflict and take steps to resolve it if it becomes dysfunctional. Among the situations that tend to produce either functional or dysfunctional conflict are

- Incompatible personalities or value systems.
- Overlapping or unclear job boundaries.
- Competition for limited resources.
- Inadequate communication.
- Interdependent tasks (for example, one person cannot complete his or her assignment until others have completed their work).
- Organizational complexity (conflict tends to increase as the number of hierarchical layers and specialized tasks increase).
- Unreasonable or unclear policies, standards, or rules.

- Unreasonable deadlines or extreme time pressure.
- Collective decision making (the greater the number of people participating in a decision, the greater the potential for conflict).
- Decision making by consensus (100 percent agreement often is impossible to achieve without much arguing).
- Unmet expectations (employees who have unrealistic expectations about job assignments, pay, or promotions are more prone to conflict).
- Unresolved or suppressed conflicts.[53]

Proactive managers carefully read these early warnings and take appropriate action. For example, group conflict can be reduced by making decisions on the basis of a majority vote rather than seeking a consensus.

Stimulating Functional Conflict

Sometimes committees and decision-making groups become so bogged down in details and procedures that nothing substantive is accomplished. Carefully monitored functional conflict can help get the creative juices flowing once again. Managers basically have two options. They can fan the fires of naturally occurring conflict—but this approach can be unreliable and slow. Alternatively, managers can resort to programmed conflict. Experts in the field define **programmed conflict** as "conflict that raises different opinions *regardless of the personal feelings of the managers.*"[54] The trick is to get contributors to either defend or criticize ideas based on relevant facts rather than on the basis of personal preference or political interests. This requires disciplined role playing. Two programmed conflict techniques with proven track records are devil's advocacy and the dialectic method. Let us explore these two ways of stimulating functional conflict.

> **programmed conflict** Encourages different opinions without protecting management's personal feelings.

Devil's Advocacy   This technique gets its name from a traditional practice within the Roman Catholic Church. When someone's name came before the College of Cardinals for elevation to sainthood, it was absolutely essential to ensure that he or she had a spotless record. Consequently, one individual was assigned the role of *devil's advocate* to uncover and air all possible objections to the person's canonization. In accordance with this practice, **devil's advocacy** in today's organizations involves assigning someone the role of critic.[55] Recall from the last chapter, Irving Janis recommended the devil's advocate role for preventing groupthink.

> **devil's advocacy** Assigning someone the role of critic.

In the left half of Figure 10–6 note how devil's advocacy alters the usual decision-making process in steps 2 and 3. This approach to programmed conflict is intended to generate critical thinking and reality testing.[56] It is a good idea to rotate the job of devil's advocate so no one person or group develops a strictly negative reputation. Moreover, periodic devil's advocacy role-playing is good training for developing analytical and communicative skills.

The Dialectic Method   Like devil's advocacy, the dialectic method is a time-honored practice. This particular approach to programmed conflict traces back to the dialectic school of philosophy in ancient Greece. Plato and his followers attempted to synthesize truths by exploring opposite positions (called thesis and antithesis). Court systems in the United States and elsewhere rely on directly opposing points of view for determining guilt or innocence. Accordingly, today's

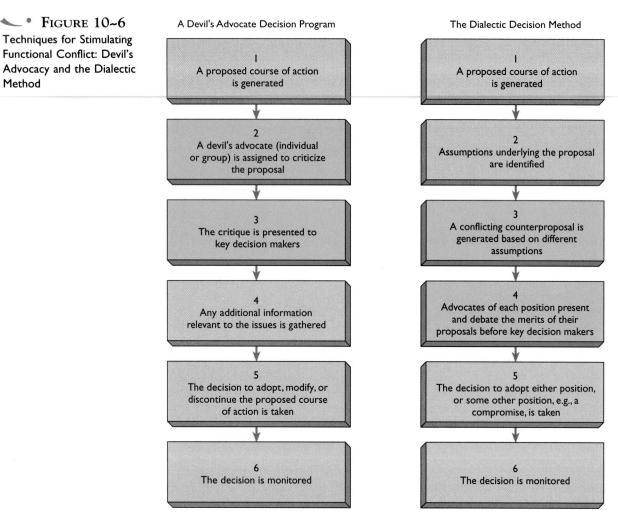

• FIGURE 10–6

Techniques for Stimulating Functional Conflict: Devil's Advocacy and the Dialectic Method

A Devil's Advocate Decision Program

1
A proposed course of action is generated

2
A devil's advocate (individual or group) is assigned to criticize the proposal

3
The critique is presented to key decision makers

4
Any additional information relevant to the issues is gathered

5
The decision to adopt, modify, or discontinue the proposed course of action is taken

6
The decision is monitored

The Dialectic Decision Method

1
A proposed course of action is generated

2
Assumptions underlying the proposal are identified

3
A conflicting counterproposal is generated based on different assumptions

4
Advocates of each position present and debate the merits of their proposals before key decision makers

5
The decision to adopt either position, or some other position, e.g., a compromise, is taken

6
The decision is monitored

Source: R A Cosier and C R Schwenk, "Agreement and Thinking Alike: Ingredients for Poor Decisions," *Academy of Management Executive*, February 1990, pp 72–73. Used with permission.

dialectic method Fostering a debate of opposing viewpoints to better understand an issue.

dialectic method calls for managers to foster a structured debate of opposing viewpoints prior to making a decision. Steps 3 and 4 in the right half of Figure 10–6 set the dialectic approach apart from the normal decision-making process. Here is how Anheuser-Busch's corporate policy committee uses the dialectic method:

> When the policy committee . . . considers a major move—getting into or out of a business, or making a big capital expenditure—it sometimes assigns teams to make the case for each side of the question. There may be two teams or even three. Each is knowledgeable about the subject; each has access to the same information. Occasionally someone in favor of the project is chosen to lead the dissent, and an opponent to argue for it. Pat Stokes, who heads the company's beer empire, describes the result: "We end up with decisions and alternatives we hadn't thought of previously," sometimes representing a synthesis of the opposing views. "You become a lot more anticipatory, better able to see what might happen, because you have thought through the process."[57]

A major drawback of the dialectic method is that "winning the debate" may overshadow the issue at hand. Also, the dialectic method requires more skill

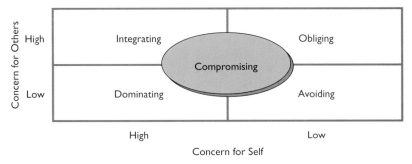

FIGURE 10–7
Five Conflict-Handling Styles

Source: M A Rahim, "A Strategy for Managing Conflict in Complex Organizations, *Human Relations,* January 1985, p 84. Used with author's permission.

training than does devil's advocacy. Regarding the comparative effectiveness of these two approaches to stimulating functional conflict, however, a laboratory study ended in a tie. Compared with groups that strived to reach a consensus, decision-making groups using either devil's advocacy or the dialectic method yielded equally higher quality decisions.[58] In light of this evidence, managers have some latitude in using either devil's advocacy or the dialectic method for pumping creative life back into stalled deliberations. Personal preference and the role players' experience may well be the deciding factors in choosing one approach over the other. The important thing is to actively stimulate functional conflict when necessary (such as when the risk of blind conformity or groupthink is high).

Alternative Styles for Handling Dysfunctional Conflict

People tend to handle negative conflict in patterned ways referred to as *styles.* Several conflict styles have been categorized over the years. According to conflict specialist Afzalur Rahim's model, five different conflict-handling styles can be plotted on a 2 × 2 grid. High to low concern for *self* is found on the horizontal axis of the grid while low to high concern for *others* forms the vertical axis (see Figure 10–7). Various combinations of these variables produce the five different conflict-handling styles: integrating, obliging, dominating, avoiding, and compromising.

There is no single best style; each has strengths and limitations and is subject to situational constraints.

Integrating (Problem Solving)   In this style, interested parties confront the issue and cooperatively identify the problem, generate and weigh alternative solutions, and select a solution. Integrating is appropriate for complex issues plagued by misunderstanding. However, it is inappropriate for resolving conflicts rooted in opposing value systems. Its primary strength is its longer lasting impact because it deals with the underlying problem rather than merely with symptoms. The primary weakness of this style is that it is very time consuming.

Obliging (Smoothing)   "An obliging person neglects his or her own concern to satisfy the concern of the other party."[59] This style, often called smoothing, involves playing down differences while emphasizing commonalities. Obliging may be an appropriate conflict-handling strategy when it is possible to eventually get something in return. But it is inappropriate for complex or worsening problems. Its primary strength is that it encourages cooperation. Its main weakness is that it's a temporary fix that fails to confront the underlying problem.

Dominating (Forcing)   High concern for self and low concern for others encourages "I win, you lose" tactics. The other party's needs are largely ignored. This style is often called forcing because it relies on formal authority to force compliance. Dominating is appropriate when an unpopular solution must be implemented, the issue is minor, or a deadline is near. It is inappropriate in an open and participative climate. Speed is its primary strength. The primary weakness of this domineering style is that it often breeds resentment.

Avoiding   This tactic may involve either passive withdrawal from the problem or active suppression of the issue. Avoidance is appropriate for trivial issues or when the costs of confrontation outweigh the benefits of resolving the conflict. It is inappropriate for difficult and worsening problems. The main strength of this style is that it buys time in unfolding or ambiguous situations. The primary weakness is that the tactic provides a temporary fix that sidesteps the underlying problem.

Compromising   This is a give-and-take approach involving moderate concern for both self and others. "Each party is required to give up something of value. Includes external or third party interventions, negotiation, and voting."[60] Compromise is appropriate when parties have opposite goals or possess equal power (such as labor-management contract negotiations).[61] But compromise is inappropriate when overuse would lead to inconclusive action (e.g., failure to meet production deadlines). The primary strength of this tactic is that the democratic process has no losers, but it's a temporary fix that can stifle creative problem solving.

To reinforce your knowledge of these conflict styles and learn more about yourself, take a few moments to complete the self-quiz in the OB Exercise. The instrument from which this quiz was drawn was validated through a factor analysis of responses from 1,219 managers from across the United States.[62] Are the results what you expected or are they a surprise?

With the antecedents of conflict, the stimulation of functional conflict, and the five conflict-handling styles in mind, let us probe the relevant research for instructive insights.

OB EXERCISE

What Is Your Primary Conflict-Handling Style?

Instructions:

For each of the 15 items, indicate how often you rely on that tactic by circling the appropriate number. After you have responded to all 15 items, complete the scoring key below.

Conflict-Handling Tactics	Rarely Always
1. I argue my case with my co-workers to show the merits of my position.	1—2—3—4—5
2. I negotiate with my co-workers so that a compromise can be reached.	1—2—3—4—5
3. I try to satisfy the expectations of my co-workers.	1—2—3—4—5
4. I try to investigate an issue with my co-workers to find a solution acceptable to us.	1—2—3—4—5
5. I am firm in pursuing my side of the issue.	1—2—3—4—5
6. I attempt to avoid being "put on the spot" and try to keep my conflict with my co-workers to myself.	1—2—3—4—5
7. I hold on to my solution to a problem.	1—2—3—4—5
8. I use "give and take" so that a compromise can be made.	1—2—3—4—5
9. I exchange accurate information with my co-workers to solve a problem together.	1—2—3—4—5
10. I avoid open discussion of my differences with my co-workers.	1—2—3—4—5
11. I accommodate the wishes of my co-workers.	1—2—3—4—5
12. I try to bring all our concerns out in the open so that the issues can be resolved in the best possible way.	1—2—3—4—5
13. I propose a middle ground for breaking deadlocks.	1—2—3—4—5
14. I go along with the suggestions of my co-workers.	1—2—3—4—5
15. I try to keep my disagreements with my co-workers to myself in order to avoid hard feelings.	1—2—3—4—5

Scoring Key:

Integrating		**Obliging**		**Dominating**	
Item	Score	Item	Score	Item	Score
4.	_____	3.	_____	1.	_____
9.	_____	11.	_____	5.	_____
12.	_____	14.	_____	7.	_____
Total = _____		Total = _____		Total = _____	

Avoiding		**Compromising**	
Item	Score	Item	Score
6.	_____	2.	_____
10.	_____	8.	_____
15.	_____	13.	_____
Total = _____		Total = _____	

Your primary conflict-handling style is: _____
  (The category with the highest total.)

Your backup conflict-handling style is: _____
  (The category with the second highest total.)

Source: Adapted and excerpted in part from M A Rahim, "A Measure of Styles of Handling Interpersonal Conflict," *Academy of Management Journal,* June 1983, pp 368–76.

Conflict Research Evidence

Laboratory studies, relying on college students as subjects, uncovered the following insights about organizational conflict:

- People with a high need for affiliation tended to rely on a smoothing (obliging) style while avoiding a forcing (dominating) style.[63] Thus, personality traits affect how people handle conflict.
- Disagreement expressed in an arrogant and demeaning manner produced significantly more negative effects than the same sort of disagreement expressed in a reasonable manner.[64] In other words, *how* you disagree with someone is very important in conflict situations.
- Threats and punishment, by one party in a disagreement, tended to produce intensifying threats and punishment from the other party.[65] In short, aggression breeds aggression.
- As conflict increased, group satisfaction decreased. An integrative style of handling conflict led to higher group satisfaction than did an avoidance style.[66]

Field studies involving managers and real organizations have given us the following insights:

- Both intradepartmental and interdepartmental conflict decreased as goal difficulty and goal clarity increased. Thus, as was the case with politics, challenging and clear goals can defuse conflict.
- Higher levels of conflict tended to erode job satisfaction and internal work motivation.[67]
- Men and women at the same managerial level tended to handle conflict similarly. In short, there was no gender effect.[68]
- Conflict tended to move around the organization in a case study of a public school system.[69] Thus, managers need to be alerted to the fact that conflict often originates in one area or level and becomes evident somewhere else. Conflict needs to be traced back to its source if there is to be lasting improvement.

Conflict Management: A Contingency Approach

Three realities dictate how organizational conflict should be managed. First, conflict is inevitable because it is triggered by a wide variety of antecedents. Second, too little conflict may be as counterproductive as too much. Third, there is no single best way of resolving conflict. Consequently, conflict specialists recommend a contingency approach to managing conflict. Antecedents of conflict and actual conflict need to be monitored. If signs of too little conflict such as apathy or lack of creativity appear, then functional conflict needs to be stimulated. This can be done by nurturing appropriate antecedents of conflict and/or programming conflict with techniques such as devil's advocacy and the dialectic method. On the other hand, when conflict becomes dysfunctional, the appropriate conflict-handling style needs to be enacted. Realistic training involving role playing can prepare managers to try alternative conflict styles.

Managers can keep from getting too deeply embroiled in conflict by applying three lessons from recent research: (1) establish challenging and clear goals, (2) disagree in a constructive and reasonable manner, and (3) refuse to get caught in the aggression-breeds-aggression spiral.

BACK TO THE OPENING CASE

Now that you have read Chapter 10, you should be able to answer the following questions about the Sarah Teslik case:

1. What influence tactics are evident in this case? Which tactic (or tactics) does Sarah Teslik appear to use most effectively? Explain.

2. How is it possible that Teslik, a person who has no official authority in America's corporate boardrooms, can capture the close attention of corporate leaders?

3. What is Teslik's primary base (or bases) of power? Explain.

4. Is Teslik's power socialized or personalized? Explain.

5. Does Teslik use her power ethically and responsibly? Explain.

6. Is Teslik stimulating functional or dysfunctional conflict in corporate America? Explain the implications of your answer.

SUMMARY OF KEY CONCEPTS

1. *Explain the concept of mutuality of interest and identify the three most effective influence tactics.* Managers are constantly challenged to foster mutuality of interest (a win-win situation) between individual and organizational interests. Organization members need to actively and creatively cooperate with potential adversaries. The three most commonly used and most effective influence tactics are consultation, rational persuasion, and inspirational appeals.

2. *Distinguish between power and authority.* Social power is the *ability* to get things done, whereas authority is the *right* to seek compliance. Socialized power embraces a concern for the welfare of others. Personalized power is rooted in self-interest.

3. *Identify and briefly describe French and Raven's five bases of power.* French and Raven's five bases of power are reward power (rewarding compliance), coercive power (punishing noncompliance), legitimate power (relying on formal authority), expert power (providing needed information), and referent power (relying on personal attraction).

4. *Explain why delegation is the highest form of empowerment.* An exciting and promising trend in today's organizations is the decentralization of power. In short, power is shifting to nonmanagerial employees as a way of boosting productivity and competitiveness. The highest evolution of power is delegation. Delegation gives employees more than a participatory role in decision making. It allows them to make their own work-related decisions.

5. *Define organizational politics and explain what triggers it.* Organizational politics is defined as intentional acts of influence to enhance or protect the self-interests of individuals or groups. Uncertainty triggers most politicking in organizations. Political action occurs at individual, coalition, and network levels. Coalitions are informal, temporary, and single-issue alliances.

6. *Discuss the management of organizational politics.* Since organizational politics cannot be eliminated, managers need to learn to deal with it. Uncertainty can be reduced by evaluating performance and linking rewards to performance. Measurable objectives are key. Participative management also helps.

7. *Define conflict and distinguish between functional and dysfunctional conflict.* Conflict is defined as all kinds of opposition or antagonistic interaction. It is inevitable and not necessarily destructive. Too little conflict, as evidenced by apathy or lack of creativity, can be as great a problem as too much conflict. Functional conflict enhances organizational interests while dysfunctional conflict is counterproductive.

8. *Explain how managers can stimulate functional conflict.* There are many antecedents of conflict—including incompatible personalities, competition for limited resources, and unrealized expectations—that need to be monitored. Functional conflict can be stimulated by permitting selected antecedents of conflict to persist and/or programming conflict during decision making with devil's advocates or the dialectic method.

9. *Describe five conflict-handling styles and discuss the*

contingency approach to managing conflict. Five alternative conflict-handling styles are integrating (problem solving), obliging (smoothing), dominating (forcing), avoiding, and compromising (negotiating). There is no single best style. Antecedents of conflict need to be monitored and stimulated if too little conflict is a problem. Functional conflict can be programmed with techniques such as devil's advocacy and the dialectic method. An appropriate conflict-handling style needs to be employed when conflict becomes dysfunctional.

DISCUSSION QUESTIONS

1. Of the eight generic influence tactics, which do you use the most when dealing with friends, parents, your boss, or your professors? Would other tactics be more effective?

2. Before reading this chapter, did the term *power* have a negative connotation for you? Do you view it differently now? Explain.

3. What base(s) of power do you rely on in your daily affairs? (Use the OB Exercise to assess your power bases at work.) Do you handle power effectively and responsibly?

4. What are the main advantages and drawbacks of the trend toward increased delegation?

5. Why do you think organizational politics is triggered primarily by uncertainty?

6. What personal experiences have you had with coalitions? Explain any positive or negative outcomes.

7. How political are you prepared to be at work? (Use the self-quiz in the OB Exercise as an assessment tool.) What are the career implications of your behavior?

8. What examples of functional and dysfunctional conflict have you encountered?

9. What has been your experience with playing the devil's advocate role?

10. According to the OB Exercise, what is your primary conflict-handling style? Would this help or hinder your effectiveness as a manager?

EXERCISE

Objectives

1. To further your knowledge of interpersonal conflict and conflict-handling styles.

2. To give you a firsthand opportunity to try the various styles of handling conflict.

Introduction

This is a role-playing exercise intended to develop your ability to handle conflict. There is no single best way to resolve the conflict in this exercise. One style might work for one person, while another gets the job done for someone else.

Instructions

Read the following short case, "Can Larry Fit In?" Pair up with someone else and decide which of you will play the role of Larry and which will play the manager. Pick up the action from where the case leaves off. Try to be realistic and true to the characters in the case. The manager is primarily responsible for resolving this conflict situation. Whoever plays Larry should resist any unreasonable requests or demands and cooperate with any personally workable solution. *Note:* To conserve time, try to resolve this situation in less than 15 minutes.

Case: "Can Larry Fit In?"[70]

> You are the manager of an auditing team for a major accounting firm. You are sitting in your office reading some complicated new reporting procedures that have just arrived from the home office. Your concentration is suddenly interrupted by a loud knock on your door. Without waiting for an invitation to enter, Larry, one of your auditors, bursts into your office. He is obviously very upset, and it is not difficult for you to surmise why he is in such a nasty mood. You have just posted the audit assignments for the next month, and you scheduled Larry for a job you knew he wouldn't like. Larry is one of your senior auditors, and the company norm is that they get the better assignments. This particular job will require him to spend

two weeks away from home, in a remote town, working with a company whose records are notorious for being a mess.

Unfortunately, you have had to assign several of these less desirable audits to Larry recently because you are short of personnel. But that's not the only reason. You have received several complaints from the junior staff members recently about Larry's treating them in an obnoxious manner. They feel he is always looking for an opportunity to boss them around, as if he were their supervisor instead of a member of the audit team. As a result, your whole operation works smoothly when you can send Larry out of town on a solo project for several days. It keeps him from coming into your office telling you how to do your job, and the morale of the rest of the auditing staff is significantly higher.

Larry slams the door and proceeds to express his anger over this assignment. He says you are deliberately trying to undermine his status in the group by giving him all the dirty assignments. He accuses you of being insensitive to his feelings and says that if things don't change, he is going to register a formal complaint with your boss.

Questions for Consideration/ Class Discussion

1. What antecedents of conflict appear to be present in this situation? What can be done about them?

2. Having heard how others handled this conflict, did one particular style seem to work better than the others?

3. Did influence tactics, power, and politics enter into your deliberations? Explain.

NOTES

[1] H Malcolm and C Sokoloff, "Values, Human Relations, and Organization Development," in *The Emerging Practice of Organizational Development,* eds W Sikes, A Drexler, and J Gant (San Diego: University Associates, 1989), p 64.

[2] "Push-Button Age," *Newsweek,* July 9, 1990, p 57.

[3] See D Kipnis, S M Schmidt, and I Wilkinson, "Intraorganizational Influence Tactics: Explorations in Getting One's Way," *Journal of Applied Psychology,* August 1980, pp 440–52. Also see C A Schriesheim and T R Hinkin, "Influence Tactics Used by Subordinates: A Theoretical and Empirical Analysis and Refinement of the Kipnis, Schmidt, and Wilkinson Subscales," *Journal of Applied Psychology,* June 1990, pp 246–57.

[4] Based on G Yukl and C M Falbe, "Influence Tactics and Objectives in Upward, Downward, and Lateral Influence Attempts," *Journal of Applied Psychology,* April 1990, pp 132–40.

[5] Data from G Yukl and J B Tracey, "Consequences of Influence Tactics Used with Subordinates, Peers, and the Boss," *Journal of Applied Psychology,* August 1992, pp 525–35. Also see C M Falbe and G Yukl, "Consequences for Managers of Using Single Influence Tactics and Combinations of Tactics," *Academy of Management Journal,* August 1992, pp 638–52.

[6] J E Driskell, B Olmstead, and E Salas, "Task Cues, Dominance Cues, and Influence in Task Groups," *Journal of Applied Psychology,* February 1993, p 51.

[7] A R Cohen and D L Bradford, *Influence Without Authority* (New York: John Wiley & Sons, 1990), pp 23–24.

[8] Ibid., p. 28. Another excellent source on this subject is R B Cialdini, *Influence* (New York: William Morrow, 1984).

[9] Based on H Collingwood, "That Shut-Out Feeling," *Business Week,* January 18, 1993, p 40.

[10] D Tjosvold, "The Dynamics of Positive Power," *Training and Development Journal,* June 1984, p 72.

[11] M W McCall, Jr., *Power, Influence, and Authority: The Hazards of Carrying a Sword,* Technical Report No. 10 (Greensboro, NC: Center for Creative Leadership, 1978), p 5. For an excellent update on power, see E P Hollander and L R Offermann, "Power and Leadership in Organizations," *American Psychologist,* February 1990, pp 179–89.

[12] For alternative models of authority, see W A Kahn and K E Kram, "Authority at Work: Internal Models and Their Organizational Consequences," *Academy of Management Review,* January 1994, pp 17–50.

[13] L Baum and J A Byrne, "Executive Secretary: A New Rung on the Corporate Ladder," *Business Week,* April 21, 1986, p 74.

[14] L H Chusmir, "Personalized versus Socialized Power Needs among Working Women and Men," *Human Relations,* February 1986, p 149.

[15] D W Cantor and T Bernay, *Women in Power: The*

Secrets of Leadership (Boston: Houghton Mifflin, 1992), p 40.

[16] See J R P French and B Raven, "The Bases of Social Power," in *Studies in Social Power*, ed D Cartwright (Ann Arbor: University of Michigan Press, 1959), pp 150–67.

[17] Details may be found in Chusmir, "Personalized vs. Socialized Power Needs among Working Women and Men," pp 149–59. For a review of research on individual differences in the need for power, see R J House, "Power and Personality in Complex Organizations," in *Research in Organizational Behavior*, ed B M Staw and L L Cummings (Greenwich, CT: JAI Press, 1988), pp 305–57.

[18] B Filipczak, "Is It Getting Chilly in Here?" *Training*, February 1994, p 27.

[19] P M Podsakoff and C A Schriesheim, "Field Studies of French and Raven's Bases of Power: Critique, Reanalysis, and Suggestions for Future Research," *Psychological Bulletin*, May 1985, p 388. Also see M A Rahim and G F Buntzman, "Supervisory Power Bases, Styles of Handling Conflict with Subordinates, and Subordinate Compliance and Satisfaction," *Journal of Psychology*, March 1989, p 195–210; D Tjosvold, "Power and Social Context in Superior-Subordinate Interaction," *Organizational Behavior and Human Decision Processes*, June 1985, pp 281–93; and C A Schriesheim, T R Hinkin, and P M Podsakoff, "Can Ipsative and Single-Item Measures Produce Erroneous Results in Field Studies of French and Raven's (1950) Five Bases of Power? An Empirical Investigation," *Journal of Applied Psychology*, February 1991, pp 106–14.

[20] See T R Hinkin and C A Schriesheim, "Relationships between Subordinate Perceptions and Supervisor Influence Tactics and Attributed Bases of Supervisory Power," *Human Relations*, March 1990, pp 221–37. Also see D J Brass and M E Burkhardt, "Potential Power and Power Use: An Investigation of Structure and Behavior," *Academy of Management Journal*, June 1993, pp 441–70.

[21] See H E Baker III, " 'Wax On—Wax Off:' French and Raven at the Movies," *Journal of Management Education*, November 1993, pp 517–19.

[22] For background and examples, see M Levinson, "When Workers Do the Hiring," *Newsweek*, June 21, 1993, p 48; R Frey, "Empowerment or Else," *Harvard Business Review*, September–October 1993, pp 80–94; and L Holpp, "Applied Empowerment," *Training*, February 1994, pp 39–44.

[23] M Memmott, "Managing Government Inc.," *USA Today*, June 28, 1993, p 2B.

[24] For example, see L Baum, "Delegating Your Way to Job Survival," *Business Week*, November 2, 1987, p 206.

[25] For complete details, see C R Leana, "Power Relinquishment versus Power Sharing: Theoretical Clarification and Empirical Comparison of Delegation and Partici-

pation," *Journal of Applied Psychology*, May 1987, pp 228–33.

[26] Data from "Got Those White-Collar Blues," *Business Week*, January 17, 1994, p 8.

[27] R Bhasin, "On Playing Corporate Politics," *Pulp & Paper*, October 1985, p 175.

[28] R W Allen, D L Madison, L W Porter, P A Renwick, and B T Mayes, "Organizational Politics: Tactics and Characteristics of Its Actors," *California Management Review*, Fall 1979, p 77. Also see K M Kacmar and G R Ferris, "Politics at Work: Sharpening the Focus of Political Behavior in Organizations," *Business Horizons*, July–August 1993, pp 70 –74.

[29] See P M Fandt and G R Ferris, "The Management of Information and Impressions: When Employees Behave Opportunistically," *Organizational Behavior and Human Decision Processes*, February 1990, pp 140–58.

[30] First four based on discussion in D R Beeman and T W Sharkey, "The Use and Abuse of Corporate Politics," *Business Horizons*, March–April 1987, pp 26–30.

[31] A Raia, "Power, Politics, and the Human Resource Professional," *Human Resource Planning*, no. 4, 1985, p 203.

[32] A J DuBrin, "Career Maturity, Organizational Rank, and Political Behavioral Tendencies: A Correlational Analysis of Organizational Politics and Career Experience," *Psychological Reports*, October 1988, p 535.

[33] This three-level distinction comes from A T Cobb, "Political Diagnosis: Applications in Organizational Development," *Academy of Management Review*, July 1986, pp 482–96.

[34] An excellent historical and theoretical perspective of coalitions can be found in W B Stevenson, J L Pearce, and L W Porter, "The Concept of 'Coalition' in Organization Theory and Research," *Academy of Management Review*, April 1985, pp 256–68.

[35] L Baum, "The Day Charlie Bradshaw Kissed Off Transworld," *Business Week*, September 29, 1986, p 68.

[36] Accounts of other corporate boardroom dramas can be found in B D Fromson, "The Coup at American Express," *The Washington Post National Weekly Edition*, February 22–28, 1993, pp 11–13; and J Amparano Lopez, "CEOs Find that Closest Chums on Board Are the Ones Most Likely to Plot a Revolt," *The Wall Street Journal*, March 26, 1993, p B1.

[37] Allen, Madison, Porter, Renwick, and Mayes, "Organizational Politics: Tactics and Characteristics of Its Actors," p 77.

[38] See W L Gardner III, "Lessons in Organizational Dramaturgy: The Art of Impression Management," *Organizational Dynamics*, Summer 1992, pp 33–46.

[39] J F Byrnes, "Connecting Organizational Politics and

Conflict Resolution,'' *Personnel Administrator,* June 1986, pp 49–50. An alternative 50-item questionnaire may be found in A J DuBrin, ''Winning at Office Politics,'' *Success,* September 1981, pp 26–28, 46.

[40] See D L Madison, R W Allen, L W Porter, P A Renwick, and B T Mayes, ''Organizational Politics: An Exploration of Managers' Perceptions,'' *Human Relations,* February 1980, pp 79–100.

[41] For additional details, see W D Guth and I C Macmillan, ''Strategy Implementation versus Middle Management Self-Interest,'' *Strategic Management Journal,* July–August 1986, pp 313–27.

[42] See R Henkoff, ''Getting Beyond Downsizing,'' *Fortune,* January 10, 1994, pp 58–64; and J A Byrne, ''The Pain of Downsizing,'' *Business Week,* May 9, 1994, pp 60–68.

[43] F Luthans, ''Successful versus Effective Real Managers,'' *Academy of Management Executive,* May 1988, p 127.

[44] A Zaleznik, ''Real Work,'' *Harvard Business Review,* January–February 1989, p 60.

[45] The management of organizational politics also is discussed in S L Payne and B F Pettingill, ''Coping with Organizational Politics,'' *Supervisory Management,* April 1986, pp 28–31; C O Longenecker, ''Truth or Consequences: Politics and Performance Appraisals,'' *Business Horizons,* November–December 1989, pp 76–82; and J B Harvey, ''Some Thoughts about Organizational Backstabbing: Or, How Come Every Time I Get Stabbed in the Back My Fingerprints Are on the Knife?'' *Academy of Management Executive,* November 1989, pp 271–77.

[46] Data from M Ingwerson, ''Clinton Will Inherit Bush Legacy of Military Use 'Without Formulas,' '' *The Christian Science Monitor,* January 7, 1993, pp 1, 4.

[47] S P Robbins, *Managing Organizational Conflict: A Nontraditional Approach* (Englewood Cliffs, NJ: Prentice-Hall, 1974), p 23.

[48] See K W Thomas and W H Schmidt, ''A Survey of Managerial Interests with Respect to Conflict,'' *Academy of Management Journal,* June 1976, pp 315–18.

[49] S P Robbins, '' 'Conflict Management' and 'Conflict Resolution' Are Not Synonymous Terms,'' *California Management Review,* Winter 1978, p 70.

[50] Cooperative conflict is discussed in D Tjosvold, *Learning to Manage Conflict: Getting People to Work Together Productively* (New York: Lexington Books, 1993).

[51] J B Treece, ''Richard LeFauve,'' *The 1990 Business Week 1000,* April 13, 1990, p 130.

[52] S Flax, ''The Toughest Bosses in America,'' *Fortune,* August 6, 1984, p 21.

[53] Adapted in part from discussion in A C Filley, *Interpersonal Conflict Resolution* (Glenview, IL: Scott, Foresman, 1975), pp 9–12; and B Fortado, ''The Accumulation of Grievance Conflict,'' *Journal of Management Inquiry,* December 1992, pp 288–303.

[54] R A Cosier and C R Schwenk, ''Agreement and Thinking Alike: Ingredients for Poor Decisions,'' *Academy of Management Executive,* February 1990, p 71.

[55] For example, see ''Facilitators as Devil's Advocates,'' *Training,* September 1993, p 10.

[56] Good background reading on devil's advocacy can be found in C R Schwenk, ''Devil's Advocacy in Managerial Decision Making,'' *Journal of Management Studies,* April 1984, pp 153–68.

[57] W Kiechel III, ''How to Escape the Echo Chamber,'' *Fortune,* June 18, 1990, p 130.

[58] See D M Schweiger, W R Sandberg, and P L Rechner, ''Experiential Effects of Dialectical Inquiry, Devil's Advocacy, and Consensus Approaches to Strategic Decision Making,'' *Academy of Management Journal,* December 1989, pp 745–72.

[59] M A Rahim, ''A Strategy for Managing Conflict in Complex Organizations,'' *Human Relations,* January 1985, p 84.

[60] Robbins, '' 'Conflict Management' and 'Conflict Resolution' Are Not Synonymous Terms,'' p 73. Also see D E Conlon and W H Ross, ''The Effects of Partisan Third Parties on Negotiator Behavior and Outcome Perceptions,'' *Journal of Applied Psychology,* April 1993, pp 280–90; and M H Bazerman and M A Neale, *Negotiating Rationally* (New York: The Free Press, 1992).

[61] An empirically derived list of 43 third-party mediation tactics can be found in R G Lim and P J D Carnevale, ''Contingencies in the Mediation of Disputes,'' *Journal of Personality and Social Psychology,* February 1990, pp 259–72.

[62] The complete instrument may be found in M A Rahim, ''A Measure of Styles of Handling Interpersonal Conflict,'' *Academy of Management Journal,* June 1983, pp 368–76. A validation study of Rahim's instrument may be found in E Van De Vliert and B Kabanoff, ''Toward Theory-Based Measures of Conflict Management,'' *Academy of Management Journal,* March 1990, pp 199–209.

[63] See R E Jones and B H Melcher, ''Personality and the Preference for Modes of Conflict Resolution,'' *Human Relations,* August 1982, pp 649–58.

[64] See R A Baron, ''Reducing Organizational Conflict: An Incompatible Response Approach,'' *Journal of Applied Psychology,* May 1984, pp 272–79.

[65] See G A Youngs, Jr., ''Patterns of Threat and Punishment Reciprocity in a Conflict Setting,'' *Journal of Personality and Social Psychology,* September 1986, pp 541–46.

[66] For more details, see V D Wall, Jr., and L L Nolan,

"Small Group Conflict: A Look at Equity, Satisfaction, and Styles of Conflict Management," *Small Group Behavior,* May 1987, pp 188–211.

[67] See M E Schnake and D S Cochran, "Effect of Two Goal-Setting Dimensions on Perceived Intraorganizational Conflict," *Group & Organization Studies,* June 1985, pp 168–83.

[68] Drawn from L H Chusmir and J Mills, "Gender Differences in Conflict Resolution Styles of Managers: At Work and at Home," *Sex Roles,* February 1989, pp 149–63.

[69] See K K Smith, "The Movement of Conflict in Organizations: The Joint Dynamics of Splitting and Triangulation," *Administrative Science Quarterly,* March 1989, pp 1–20.

[70] This case is quoted from *Developing Management Skills* by D A Whetten and K S Cameron. Copyright © 1984 by Scott, Foresman and Company. Reprinted by permission.

INDIVIDUAL AND GROUP DECISION MAKING

Learning OBJECTIVES

When you finish studying the material in this chapter, you should be able to:

1. Distinguish between programmed and nonprogrammed decisions.
2. Discuss the four steps in the rational model of decision making.
3. Contrast Simon's normative model and the garbage can model of decision making.
4. Discuss the contingency relationships that influence the three primary strategies used to select solutions.
5. Describe the model of escalation of commitment.

6. Summarize the pros and cons of involving groups in the decision-making process.
7. Explain how participative management affects performance.
8. Review Vroom and Jago's decision-making model.
9. Contrast brainstorming, the nominal group technique, the Delphi technique, and computer-aided decision making.
10. Describe the stages of the creative process and specify at least five characteristics of creative people.

Ford Motor Company Uses Creative Decision Making to Develop and Deliver the New Mustang

Sharon Hoogstraten

Ford Motor Co. today [September 21, 1993] will begin showing off a new Mustang coupe and convertible, heirs to one of the best-loved names in the American auto business. Ford will act as though there was never a doubt that the Mustang would gallop along into the next century. . . .

Enter the members of a group known inside Ford as "Team Mustang." In just three years, this group of about 400 people scrambled to save their beloved car and solve a riddle for the 1990s: How do you make a product that stirs the soul on a skinflint budget?

To find an answer, the Mustang team broke many of the rules that govern product development in the rigidly disciplined corporation and, in the process, survived some close calls. More than once, they struggled to reconcile the conflicting forces of finance

and feeling. . . . But Ford officials say the Mustang was redone in three years for about $700 million. That is 25% less time and 30% less money than for any comparable new car program in Ford's recent history. . . .

The fanfare comes as quite a relief to Mr. Coletti [a founding member of the group], to Will Boddie, the engineer who led the Mustang development team, and to chief engineer Michael Zevalkink and program manufacturing boss Dia Hothi. Not long ago, it seemed, their careers were riding on a horse that wouldn't go the distance. . . .

The last straw was a federal safety rule requiring all cars sold after Sept. 1, 1993, to have "passive restraints." That meant a major overhaul to accommodate air bags. Skeptics in Ford management said the cost wasn't justified for a niche vehicle. In August 1989, Mr. Coletti and a small group of managers got the task of proving them wrong. They formed a "skunk works" development team and set out on a quest.

"Some of us were on the team just to save the Mustang," says Mr. Coletti. But his pride had been challenged, too. "I'd heard enough that the Japanese can do this, or the Japanese can do that. They're not superhumans."

His pride didn't stop the team from making Japan one of the first stops on a

six-month global brainstorming tour. From Hiroshima, where Mazda is based, to Ford's operations in Australia to the industrial centers of Germany and Italy, the crew searched for clues to how rivals brought out new cars for hundreds of millions of dollars less than Ford had been spending. . . .

But first, the skunk-works team had to have a plan. That came together one night in early 1990 when Messrs. Coletti and Hothi were flying home from Germany after a round of fact-finding interviews. They compared notes, and ideas began to gel. As they hurtled over Iceland, they began drafting a plan for saving the Mustang in just three years, using a new product-development approach. A normal new car project at Ford took four years to complete.

As the Mustang team fleshed out the plan in mid-1990, it agreed that the Mustang effort would need unprecedented freedom to make decisions without waiting for approval from headquarters or other departments. Team members wanted to think of themselves as independent stockholders of a "Mustang Car Co.," which happened to be financed by Ford.

The plan called for putting everyone involved under one roof—draftsmen sitting next to "bean counters," engineers one room away from stylists. That meant breaching the bud-

---

D ecision making is one of the primary responsibilities of being a manager. The quality of a manager's decisions is important for two principal reasons. First, the quality of a manager's decisions directly affects his or her career opportunities, rewards, and job satisfaction. Second, managerial decisions contribute to the success or failure of an organization.

OPENING CASE

(concluded)

getary walls that divided departments and persuading department managers to cede some control over their subordinates. One of the boldest decisions was that Mr. Hothi, the program's manufacturing chief, would get veto power over changes to the body that threatened to derail his efforts to build the car with many of the factory tools used for the old one. All this cut sharply against the grain of Ford's corporate culture. . . .

They also did away with the arduous bidding process most Ford programs endure when selecting suppliers. With no time for that "rain dance," Mr. Boddie and the Mustang team leaders agreed to pick the best available suppliers and simply ask them to join the Mustang process, from the start. Among suppliers nominated to bring the "All-American car" to life: Ogihara Tool Works, the Japanese maker of sheet metal stamping dies.

The decision to bring in suppliers that way proved crucial, particularly during the days last year when the convertible almost died.

Mr. Zevalkink grins when he remembers the trials, but at the time they were no cause for mirth. To save time and money, most of the convertible's designs were tested first on computer images, not on actual cars. Unfortunately, what happened on the screen didn't match what happened on the road. In July 1991, Mr. Zevalkink test-drove the first convertible prototype and discovered that it shimmied and shook. With Mr. Boddie's approval, he ordered a crash program to fix it. About a year later, in August 1992, Mr. Zevalkink took another test drive in another prototype convertible. To his dismay, it still shook. Images danced and wiggled in the rearview mirror.

Mr. Zevalkink felt queasy. Without a convertible, the Mustang line would lack its "image car" and miss out on sales. It had to be fixed. But that would mean ordering new reinforcement parts, new tooling. It might also require redesigning wiring and hoses under the hood. All that could make the car miss its September 1993 start-of-production target and overshoot the budget. The team went into a crisis drill. Mr. Boddie assembled a special team of about 50 people to attack the convertible's problems. Suppliers were called in, and round-the-clock work began. . . .

For eight weeks, the team ran a blitz of re-engineering work, computer manipulations and tough budget sessions. Engineers slept on the floors at the Allen Park warehouse. Although the crisis was known to senior Ford executives, they stuck to their promise not to meddle.

"There was a great temptation to overrule a program," admits Mr. Ressler, the vehicle engineering chief. But he says he resisted. And by October, the Mustang team had found solutions for the convertible's shakes. They installed extra bracing, and redesigned the rearview mirror so it would be less prone to wiggling.

Mr. Boddie was even emboldened to go further. After seeing a new Mercedes-Benz convertible parked in front of a restaurant, he instructed his engineers to get one and take it apart to find the secrets of its smooth ride. The result: Mustang engineers bolted a 25-pound steel cylinder to a spot behind the front fender. On the Mercedes, a similar "damper" muffled vibrations like a finger on a tuning fork.

For Discussion

Would you like to have been a member of "Team Mustang"? Explain.

■ Additional discussion questions linking this case with the following material appear at the end of this chapter.

Source: J B White and O Suris, "How a 'Skunk Works' Kept the Mustang Alive—On a Tight Budget," *The Wall Street Journal,* September 21, 1993, pp A1, A12. Excerpted by permission of *The Wall Street Journal,* © 1993 Dow Jones & Company, Inc. All Rights Reserved Worldwide.

Decision making is a means to an end. It entails identifying and choosing alternative solutions that lead to a desired state of affairs. The process begins with a problem and ends when a solution has been chosen. To gain an understanding of how managers can make better decisions, this chapter focuses on: (1) the types of decisions managers make, (2) models of decision making, (3) the dynamics of decision making, (4) group decision making, and (5) creativity.

decision making   Identifying and choosing solutions that lead to a desired end result.

⟋ • TABLE 11~1
Techniques for Dealing with
Two Types of Decisions

Types of Decisions	Decision-Making Techniques	
	Traditional	**Modern**
Programmed Routine, repetitive decisions Organization develops specific processes for handling them	1. Habit 2. Clerical routine: Standard operating procedures 3. Organization structure: Common expectations A system of subgoals Well-defined informational channels	1. Operations research Mathematical analysis Models Computer simulation 2. Electronic data processing
Nonprogrammed One-shot, ill-structured, novel policy decisions Handled by general problem-solving processes	1. Judgment, intuition, and creativity 2. Rules of thumb 3. Selection and training of executives	Heuristic problem-solving techniques applied to: a. Training human decision makers b. Constructing heuristic computer programs

Source: H A Simon, *The New Science of Management Decision,* © 1977, p 48. Reprinted by permission of Prentice-Hall, Inc., Englewood Cliffs, NJ.

TYPES OF MANAGERIAL DECISIONS

Decision theorists have identified two types of managerial decisions: programmed and nonprogrammed.[1] It is important to distinguish between these two types because different techniques are used to deal with them (see Table 11–1).

Programmed Decisions

programmed decisions
Repetitive and routine decisions.

Programmed decisions tend to be repetitive and routine. Through time and experience, organizations develop specific procedures for handling these decisions. Getting dressed in the morning or driving to school involve personal programmed decisions. Through habit, you are likely to act on a similar chain of decisions each day. Work-related examples are determining how much vacation time to give an employee, deciding when to send customers a bill, and ordering office supplies. Habit and standard operating procedures are the most frequently used techniques for making these decisions. Today, computers handle many programmed decisions. For example, computerized job interviews are one method being used to select entry-level employees. American General, an insurance company, and Younkers Inc., a Des Moines-based department store chain, significantly reduced turnover by hiring people on the basis of computerized job interviews.[2]

Nonprogrammed Decisions

nonprogrammed decisions
Novel and unstructured decisions.

Nonprogrammed decisions are novel and unstructured. Hence, there are no cut-and-dried procedures for dealing with the problem at hand. These decisions also tend to have important consequences. Hospitals throughout the United States are good examples of nonprogrammed decision making in action. They are being driven to cut costs and simultaneously increase quality. How can these seemingly opposite objectives be met? Consider an experiment being conducted at Intermountain Healthcare's LDS Hospital in Salt Lake City, Utah.

Doctors routinely prescribe antibiotics before and after surgery to prevent infections that can imperil patients and double their hospital stay. LDS researchers found that the best

Programmed decisions are repetitive and routine. Nonprogrammed decisions are unique and unfamiliar. These Southern California Edison technicians are making both types of decisions during a difficult and dangerous troubleshooting task.

(*Courtesy Southern California Edison Company*)

time for the treatment was within two hours before an operation. In 1985, just 40% of LDS surgical patients got the antibiotic during that two hours, and the hospital's infection rate was 1.8%. In 1991, 96% of patients got the medication on time, reducing the infection rate to 0.4%—a 78% drop—and saving more than $700,000.[3]

As highlighted by this example, a hospital's future success depends on its response to the novel and unstructured problems associated with the current health care crisis.

To solve nonprogrammed decisions, managers tend to rely on judgment, intuition, and creativity. As demonstrated in the chapter opening case on Ford Motor Company, companies also are forming decision-making teams or using computer simulations to help solve these problems. Du Pont, for instance, used computer simulations to develop business strategies that are expected to increase the organization's value by $175 million.[4]

MODELS OF DECISION MAKING

There are several models of decision making. Each is based on a different set of assumptions and offers unique insight into the decision-making process. This section reviews three key historical models of decision making. They are (1) the rational model, (2) Simon's normative model, and (3) the garbage can model. Each successive model assumes that the decision-making process is less and less rational. Let us begin with the most orderly or rational explanation of managerial decision making.

The Rational Model

The **rational model** proposes that managers use a rational, four-step sequence when making decisions: (1) identifying the problem, (2) generating alternative solutions, (3) selecting a solution, and (4) implementing and evaluating the

rational model   Logical four-step approach to decision making.

solution. According to this model, managers are completely objective and possess complete information to make a decision. Despite criticism for being unrealistic, the rational model is instructive because it analytically breaks down the decision-making process and serves as a conceptual anchor for newer models. Let us now consider each of these four steps.

problem Gap between an actual and desired situation.

Identifying the Problem   A **problem** exists when the actual situation and the desired situation differ. For example, a problem exists when you have to pay rent at the end of the month and don't have enough money. Your problem is not that you have to pay rent. Your problem is obtaining the needed funds. Similarly, the problem for a sales manager who has orders for 100 personal computers, but only 80 units in stock, is the 20 units unavailable (the gap between actual and desired). One expert proposed that managers use one of three methods to identify problems: historical cues, planning, and other people's perceptions:[5]

1. Using historical cues to identify problems assumes that the recent past is the best estimate of the future. Thus, managers rely on past experience to identify discrepancies (problems) from expected trends. For example, a sales manager may conclude that a problem exists because the first-quarter sales are less than they were a year ago. This method is prone to error because it is highly subjective.

2. A planning approach is more systematic and can lead to more accurate results. This method consists of using projections or scenarios to estimate what is expected to occur in the future. A time period of one or more years is generally used. Companies are increasingly using this scenario technique as a planning tool. The **scenario technique** is a speculative, conjectural forecasting tool used to identify future states, given a certain set of environmental conditions. Royal Dutch/Shell, for example, has conducted scenario planning for more than 19 years and currently uses two 20-year scenarios to make decisions. The company is very pleased with the outcomes of scenario planning.

scenario technique Speculative forecasting method.

> Group planning coordinator Peter Hadfield believes that scenario planning has helped Shell be better prepared than its competitors for external shocks. In the early Eighties, for example, while most forecasters were predicting a steadily increasing price for crude oil, Shell, in one of its scenarios, had entertained the possibility that the price would slide to $15 a barrel. As a hedge against such an eventuality, the company began looking into cost-saving exploration technologies. When the slump hit, Shell was able to sustain a higher level of drilling activity than many of its competitors. Shell realizes that its two scenarios don't encompass everything that might happen in the future, and that neither will be a perfect predictor. Says Hadfield: "They're there to condition the organization to think."[6]

3. A final approach to identifying problems is to rely on the perceptions of others. A restaurant manager may realize that his or her restaurant provides poor service when a large number of customers complain about how long it takes to receive food after placing an order. In other words, customers' comments signal that a problem exists. Similarly, automobile manufacturers are sometimes forced to recall cars because of consumer complaints about product safety or quality.

Generating Solutions   After identifying a problem, the next logical step is generating alternative solutions. For programmed decisions, alternatives are readily available through decision rules. This is not the case for nonprogrammed decisions. For nonprogrammed decisions, this step is the creative part of problem solving. Managers can use a number of techniques to stimulate creativity. Techniques to increase creative thinking are discussed later in this chapter.

Selecting a Solution   Optimally, decision makers want to choose the alternative with the greatest value. Decision theorists refer to this as maximizing the expected utility of an outcome. This is no easy task. First, assigning values to alternatives is complicated and prone to error. Not only are values subjective, but they also vary according to the preferences of the decision maker. For example, research demonstrates that people vary in their preferences for safety or risk when making decisions.[7] Further, evaluating alternatives assumes they can be judged according to some standards or criteria. This further assumes that (1) valid criteria exist, (2) each alternative can be compared against these criteria, and (3) the decision maker actually uses the criteria. As you know from making your own key life decisions, people frequently violate these assumptions.

Implementing and Evaluating the Solution   Once a solution is chosen, it needs to be implemented. Before implementing a solution, though, managers need to do their homework. For example, three ineffective managerial tendencies have been observed frequently during the initial stages of implementation (see Table 11–2). Skillful managers try to avoid these tendencies. Table 11–2 indicates that to promote necessary understanding, acceptance, and motivation, managers should involve implementors in the choice-making step.

After the solution is implemented, the evaluation phase assesses its effectiveness. If the solution is effective, it should reduce the difference between the actual and desired states that created the problem. If the gap is not closed, the implementation was not successful, and one of the following is true: Either the problem was

TABLE 11–2   Three Managerial Tendencies Reduce the Effectiveness of Implementation

Managerial Tendency	Recommended Solution
The tendency not to ensure that people understand what needs to be done.	Involve the implementators in the choice-making step. When this is not possible, a strong and explicit attempt should be made to identify any misunderstanding, perhaps by having the implementor explain what he or she thinks needs to be done and why.
The tendency not to ensure the acceptance or motivation for what needs to be done.	Once again, involve the implementators in the choice-making step. Attempts should also be made to demonstrate the payoffs for effective implementation and to show how completion of various tasks will lead to successful implementation.
The tendency not to provide appropriate resources for what needs to be done.	Many implementations are less effective than they could be because adequate resources, such as time, staff, or information, were not provided. In particular, the allocations of such resources across departments and tasks are assumed to be appropriate because they were appropriate for implementing the previous plan. These assumptions should be checked.

Source: Modified from G P Huber, *Managerial Decision Making* (Glenview, IL: Scott, Foresman, 1980), p 19.

incorrectly identified, or the solution was inappropriate. Assuming the implementation was unsuccessful, management can return to the first step, problem identification. If the problem was correctly identified, management should consider implementing one of the previously identified, but untried, solutions. This process can continue until all feasible solutions have been tried or the problem has changed.

optimizing   Choosing the best possible solution.

Summarizing the Rational Model   The rational model is based on the premise that managers optimize when they make decisions. **Optimizing** involves solving problems by producing the best possible solution. This assumes that managers:

- Have knowledge of all possible alternatives.
- Have complete knowledge about the consequences that follow each alternative.
- Have a well-organized and stable set of preferences for these consequences.
- Have the computational ability to compare consequences and to determine which one is preferred.[8]

As noted by Herbert Simon, a decision theorist who in 1978 earned the Nobel Prize for his work on decision making, ''The assumptions of perfect rationality are contrary to fact. It is not a question of approximation; they do not even remotely describe the processes that human beings use for making decisions in complex situations.''[9] Thus, the rational model is at best an instructional tool. Since decision makers do not follow these rational procedures, Simon proposed a normative model of decision making.

Simon's Normative Model

This model attempts to identify the process that managers actually use when making decisions. The process is guided by a decision maker's bounded rationality. **Bounded rationality** represents the notion that decision makers are ''bounded'' or restricted by a variety of constraints when making decisions. These constraints include any personal or environmental characteristics that reduce rational decision making. Examples are the limited capacity of the human mind, problem complexity and uncertainty, amount and timeliness of information at hand, criticality of the decision, and time demands.[10] Consider how these constraints affected ethical decision making at Syntex Corporation.

bounded rationality   Constraints that restrict decision making.

> Back in 1985, Syntex Corp. figured it was onto something big: a new ulcer drug that promised to relieve the misery of millions—and earn the company big profits. In its annual report Syntex showed capsules of the drug spilling forth as shining examples of research. It pictured the drug's inventor, Gabriel Garay, at work in his lab. . . .
>
> Critics are charging that the company, after investing millions in the drug's development, played down—and even suppressed—potentially serious safety problems that could hinder its approval.
>
> Mr. Garay says it was he who sounded alarms internally over enprostil, warning it could cause dangerous blood clots and actually prompt new ulcers. Even when an outside researcher agreed there were potential dangers, Syntex executives dismissed the findings as preliminary. Mr. Garay says Syntex then forced him out.[11]

Although decision makers at Syntex may have desired the best solution to problems identified by Mr. Garay, bounded rationality precluded its identification. How then do managers make decisions?[12]

As opposed to the rational model, Simon's normative model suggests that decision making is characterized by (1) limited information processing, (2) the use of rules of thumb or shortcuts, and (3) satisficing. Each of these characteristics is now explored.

Limited Information Processing   Managers are limited by how much information they process because of bounded rationality. This results in the tendency to acquire manageable rather than optimal amounts of information. In turn, this practice makes it difficult for managers to identify all possible alternative solutions. In the long run, the constraints of bounded rationality cause decision makers to fail to evaluate all potential alternatives.

Use of Rules of Thumb or Shortcuts   Decision makers use rules of thumb or shortcuts to reduce information-processing demands. Since these shortcuts represent knowledge gained from past experience, they help decision makers evaluate current problems. For example, recruiters may tend to hire applicants receiving degrees from the same university attended by other successful employees. In this case, the ''school attended'' criterion is used to facilitate complex information processing associated with employment interviews. Unfortunately, these shortcuts can result in biased decisions.[13]

Satisficing   People satisfice because they do not have the time, information, or ability to handle the complexity associated with following a rational process. This is not necessarily undesirable. **Satisficing** consists of choosing a solution that meets some minimum qualifications, one that is ''good enough.'' Satisficing resolves problems by producing solutions that are satisfactory, as opposed to optimal.[14] Although a discounted, blue, two-door automobile may satisfice for purchasing your new sports car, shopping around may locate the red, two-seat convertible you prefer.

satisficing   Choosing a solution that meets a minimum standard of acceptance.

The Garbage Can Model

As true of Simon's normative model, this approach grew from the rational model's inability to explain how decisions are actually made. It assumes that decision making does not follow an orderly series of steps. In fact, organizational decision making is said to be such a sloppy and haphazard process that the garbage can label is appropriate. This contrasts sharply with the rational model, which proposed that decision makers follow a sequential series of steps beginning with a problem and ending with a solution. According to the **garbage can model,** decisions result from a complex interaction between four independent streams of events: problems, solutions, participants, and choice opportunities.[15] The interaction of these events creates ''a collection of choices looking for problems, issues and feelings looking for decision situations in which they might be aired, solutions looking for issues to which they might be the answer, and decision makers looking for work.''[16] The garbage can model attempts to explain how these events interact and lead to a decision. After discussing the streams of events and how they interact, this section highlights managerial implications of the garbage can model.

garbage can model   Holds that decision making is sloppy and haphazard.

Streams of Events   The four streams of events—problems, solutions, participants, and choice opportunities—represent independent entities that flow into and out of organizational decision situations (see Figure 11–1). Because decisions are a function of the interaction among these independent events, the stages of problem

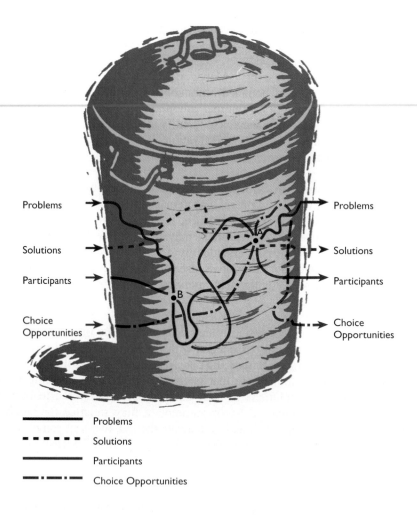

```
Problems    →                                        →  Problems

Solutions   →   ·····                           →  Solutions

Participants →                                   →  Participants

Choice      →                                   ─·─·→ Choice
Opportunities                                        Opportunities
```

─────────── Problems

▬ ▬ ▬ ▬ Solutions

─────────── Participants

─·─ ─·─ ·─ Choice Opportunities

identification and problem solution may be unrelated. For instance, a solution may be proposed for a problem that does not exist. This can be observed when students recommend that a test be curved, even though the average test score is a comparatively high 85 percent. On the other hand, some problems are never solved. Each of the four events in the garbage can model deserves a closer look.

■ *Problems:* As defined earlier, problems represent a gap between an actual situation and a desired condition. But problems are independent from alternatives and solutions. The problem may or may not lead to a solution.

■ *Solutions:* Solutions are answers looking for questions. They represent ideas constantly flowing through an organization. Contrary to the classical model, however, solutions are used to formulate problems rather than vice versa. This is predicted to occur because managers often do not know what they want until they have some idea of what they can get.

■ *Participants:* Participants are the organizational members who come and go throughout the organization. They bring different values, attitudes, and experiences to a decision-making situation. Time pressures limit the extent to which participants are involved in decision making.

opportunities are occasions in which an organi-
tion. While some opportunities, such as hiring
regularly, others do not because they result
e situation.

Events   Because of the independent nature
ct in a random fashion. This implies decision
encounters than a rational process. Thus, the
garbage can" in which problems, solutions,
s are all mixed together (see Figure 11–1).
ts happen to connect, such as at point A in
ce these connections randomly occur among
events, decision quality generally depends on
ck.) In other words, good decisions are made
act at the proper time. This explains why
solutions (point B in Figure 11–1) and why
ns. In support of the garbage can model, one
n the textbook publishing industry followed a
vledge of this process helped the researchers
extbooks.[17]

bage can model of organizational decision
making has four practical implications.[18] First, many decisions will be made by
oversight or the presence of a salient opportunity. Second, political motives
frequently guide the process by which participants make decisions. Participants
tend to make decisions that promise to increase their status. (Recall the discussion
of organizational politics in Chapter 10.) Third, the process is sensitive to load.
That is, as the number of problems increases, relative to the amount of time
available to solve them, problems are less likely to be solved. Finally, important
problems are more likely to be solved than unimportant ones because they are more
salient to organizational participants.[19]

Decision making is part science and part art. Accordingly, this section examines
two dynamics of decision making—contingency considerations and the problem of
escalation of commitment—that affect the "science" component. An understanding of these dynamics can help managers make better decisions.

**DYNAMICS OF
DECISION MAKING**

Selecting Solutions: A Contingency Perspective

The previous discussion of decision-making models noted that managers typically
satisfice when they select solutions. However, we did not probe how managers
actually evaluate and select solutions. Let us explore the model in Figure 11–2 to
better understand how individuals make decisions.

Strategies for Selecting a Solution   What procedures do decision makers use to
evaluate the costs and benefits of alternative solutions? According to management
experts Lee Roy Beach and Terence Mitchell, one of three approaches is used:

● FIGURE 11~2

A Contingency Model for
Selecting a Solution

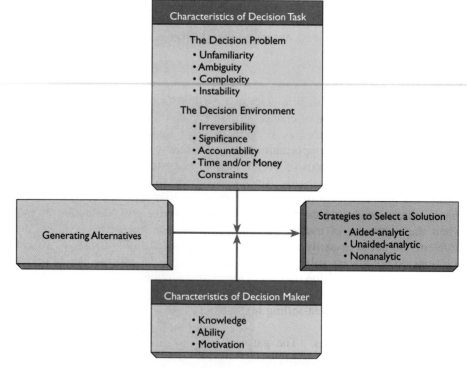

Source: Based on L R Beach and T R Mitchell, "A Contingency Model for the Selection of Decision Strategies," *Academy of Management Review,* July 1978, pp 439–44.

aided-analytic, unaided-analytic, and nonanalytic.[20] Decision makers systematically use tools such as mathematical equations, calculators, or computers to analyze and evaluate alternatives within an **aided-analytic** approach. Technicians also may be commissioned to conduct a formal study. In contrast, decision makers rely on the confines of their minds when using an **unaided-analytic** strategy. In other words, the decision maker systematically compares alternatives, but the analysis is limited to evaluating information that can be directly processed in his or her head. Decision-making tools such as a personal computer are not used. Finally, a **nonanalytic** strategy consists of using a simple preformulated rule to make a decision. Examples are flipping a coin, habit, normal convention (''we've always done it that way''), using a conservative approach (''better safe than sorry''), or following procedures offered in instruction manuals. Both the cost and level of sophistication decrease as one moves from an aided-analytic to a nonanalytic strategy.

Determining which approach to use depends on two sets of contingency factors: characteristics of the decision task and characteristics of the decision maker (refer again to Figure 11–2).

Characteristics of the Decision Task   This set of contingency factors reflects the demands and constraints a decision maker faces. In general, the greater these demands and constraints, the higher the probability that an aided-analytic approach will be used. These characteristics are divided into two components: those pertaining to the specific problem and those related to the general decision environment.

aided-analytic   Using tools to make decisions.

unaided-analytic   Analysis is limited to processing information in one's mind.

nonanalytic   Using preformulated rules to make decisions.

1. Analytic strategies are used when the decision problem is unfamiliar, ambiguous, complex, or unstable.
2. Nonanalytic methods are employed when the problem is familiar, straightforward, or stable.
3. Assuming there are no monetary or time constraints, analytic approaches are used when the solution is irreversible and significant and when the decision maker is accountable.
4. Nonanalytic strategies are used when the decision can be reversed and is not very significant or when the decision maker is not held accountable.
5. As the probability of making a correct decision goes down, analytic strategies are used.
6. As the probability of making a correct decision goes up, nonanalytic strategies are employed.
7. Time and money constraints automatically exclude some strategies from being used.
8. Analytic strategies are more frequently used by experienced and educated decision makers.
9. Nonanalytic approaches are used when the decision maker lacks knowledge, ability, or motivation to make a good decision.

Source: Adapted from L R Beach and T R Mitchell, "A Contingency Model for the Selection of Decision Strategies," *Academy of Management Review,* July 1978, pp 439–44.

Unfamiliar, ambiguous, complex, or unstable problems are more difficult to solve and typically require more sophisticated analysis.

The environment also restricts the type of analysis used. For instance, a recent study of 75 MBA students revealed that they purchased and used less information for decision making as the cost of information increased. In contrast, they purchased and used more information when they were rewarded for making good decisions. These results suggest that both the cost of information and one's accountability for a decision affect the type of analysis used to solve a problem.[21] Moreover, time constraints influence selection of a solution. Poorer decisions are bound to be made in the face of severe time pressure.

Characteristics of the Decision Maker   Chapter 4 highlighted a variety of individual differences that affect employee behavior and performance. In the present context, knowledge, ability, and motivation affect the type of analytical procedure used by a decision maker. In general, research supports the prediction that aided-analytic strategies are more likely to be used by competent and motivated individuals.[22]

Contingency Relationships   There are many ways in which characteristics of the decision task and decision maker can interact to influence the strategy used to select a solution.[23] In choosing a strategy, decision makers compromise between their desire to make correct decisions and the amount of time and effort they put into the decision-making process. Table 11–3 lists contingency relationships that help reconcile these competing demands. As shown in this table, analytic strategies are more likely to be used when the problem is unfamiliar and irreversible. In contrast, nonanalytic methods are employed on familiar problems or problems in which the decision can be reversed.

Escalation of Commitment

Prior to reading any further, we would like you to read the scenario in the OB Exercise and answer the diagnostic question. The scenario describes an escalation situation. Escalation situations involve circumstances in which things have gone wrong but where the situation can possibly be turned around by investing additional

OB EXERCISE

Making a Decision in an Escalation Situation

As the president of an airline company, you have invested 10 million dollars of the company's money into a research project. The purpose was to build a plane that would not be detected by conventional radar, in other words, a radar-blank plane. When the project is 90 percent completed, another firm begins marketing a plane that cannot be detected by radar. Also, it is apparent that their plane is much faster and far more economical than the plane your company is building. The question is: Should you invest the last 10 percent of the research funds to finish your radar-blank plane?

    Answer: Yes, invest the money.

              No, drop the project.

Source: H R Arkes and C Blumer, "The Psychology of Sunk Cost," *Organizational Behavior and Human Decision Processes*, February 1985, p 129.

time, money, or effort.[24] Consider the situation faced by Lyndon Johnson during the early stages of the Vietnam war. Johnson received the following memo from George Ball, then Undersecretary of State:

> The decision you face now is crucial. Once large numbers of US troops are committed to direct combat, they will begin to take heavy casualties in a war they are ill-equipped to fight in a noncooperative if not downright hostile countryside. Once we suffer large casualties, we will have started a well-nigh irreversible process. Our involvement will be so great that we cannot—without national humiliation—stop short of achieving our complete objectives. Of the two possibilities I think humiliation will be more likely than the achievement of our objectives—even after we have paid terrible costs.[25]

Unfortunately, President Johnson's increased commitment to the war helped make George Ball's prediction come true.

Let us return to the scenario in the OB Exercise. What was your answer? If you responded yes, you experienced what researchers call escalation of commitment: So did Lyndon Johnson. **Escalation of commitment** refers to the tendency to stick to an ineffective course of action when it is unlikely that the bad situation can be reversed. Personal examples include investing more money into an old or broken car, waiting an extremely long time for a bus to take you somewhere that you could have walked just as easily, or trying to save a disruptive interpersonal relationship that has lasted 10 years. Case studies also indicate that escalation of commitment is partially responsible for some of the worst financial losses experienced by organizations. For example, from 1966 to 1989 the Long Island Lighting Company's investment in the Shoreham nuclear power plant escalated from $65 million to $5 billion, despite a steady flow of negative feedback. The plant was never opened.[26]

OB researchers Jerry Ross and Barry Staw identified four reasons for escalation of commitment (see Figure 11–3). They involve psychological and social determinants, organizational determinants, project characteristics, and contextual determinants.[27]

escalation of commitment
Sticking to an ineffective course of action too long.

Psychological and Social Determinants   Ego defense and individual motivations are the key psychological contributors to escalation of commitment. Individuals "throw good money after bad" because they tend to (1) bias facts so that they

• ✒ FIGURE 11~3   A Model of Escalation of Commitment

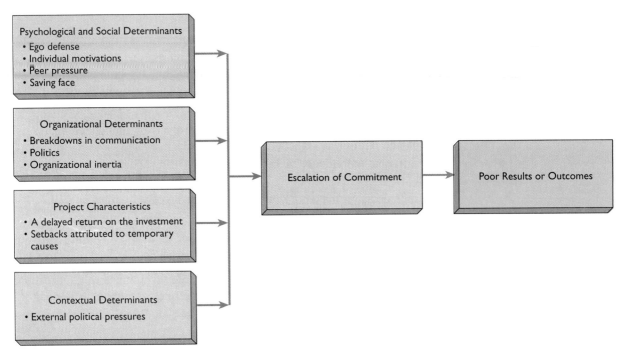

FIGURE 11~3   A Model of Escalation of Commitment

Based on discussion in J Ross and B M Staw, "Organizational Escalation and Exit: Lessons from the Shoreham Nuclear Power Plant." *Academy of Management Journal.* August 1993, pp 701–32.

support previous decisions, (2) take more risks when a decision is stated in negative terms (to recover losses) rather than positive ones (to achieve gains), and (3) get too ego-involved with the project. Because failure threatens an individual's self-esteem or ego, people tend to ignore negative signs and push forward.[28]

Social pressures can make it difficult for a manager to reverse a course of action. For instance, peer pressure makes it difficult for an individual to drop a course of action when he or she publicly supported it in the past. Further, managers may continue to support bad decisions because they don't want their mistakes exposed to others.

Organizational Determinants   Breakdowns in communication, workplace politics, and organizational inertia cause organizations to maintain bad courses of action.

Project Characteristics   Project characteristics involve the objective features of a project. They have the greatest impact on escalation decisions. For example, because most projects do not reap benefits until some delayed time period, decision makers are motivated to stay with the project until the end. Thus, there is a tendency to attribute setbacks to temporary causes that are correctable with additional expenditures.[29]

Contextual Determinants   These causes of escalation are due to external political forces outside an organization's control. For instance, the continuance of the previously discussed Shoreham nuclear power plant was partially influenced by pressures from other public utilities interested in nuclear power, representatives of the nuclear power industry, and people in the federal government pushing for the development of nuclear power.[30]

Reducing Escalation of Commitment   It is important to reduce escalation of commitment because it leads to poor decision making for both individuals and groups.[31] Barry Staw and Jerry Ross, the researchers who originally identified the phenomenon of escalation, recommended several ways to reduce it:

- Set minimum targets for performance and have decision makers compare their performance with these targets.
- Have different individuals make the initial and subsequent decisions about a project.
- Encourage decision makers to become less ego-involved with a project.
- Provide more frequent feedback about project completion and costs.
- Reduce the risk or penalties of failure.
- Make decision makers aware of the costs of persistence.[32]

Although a few studies have supported some of these recommendations, additional research on the causes and reduction of escalation of commitment is needed.[33]

GROUP DECISION MAKING

Chapter 9 examined the unique dynamics that arise when individuals work together in groups. Groups such as committees, task forces, or review panels often play a key role in the decision-making process. For example, the Opening Case on Ford Motor Company indicated that group decision making was used to manage all aspects of redesigning the Mustang.

Are two or more heads always better than one? Do all employees desire to have a say in the decision-making process? When and how should a manager use group decision making? This section provides the background for answering these questions, essential for gaining maximum benefits from group decision making. We discuss (1) advantages and disadvantages of group-aided decision making, (2) participative management, (3) when to use groups in decision making, and (4) group problem-solving techniques.

Advantages and Disadvantages of Group-Aided Decision Making

Including groups in the decision-making process has both pros and cons (see Table 11–4). On the positive side, groups contain a greater pool of knowledge, provide more varied perspectives, create more comprehension of decisions, increase decision acceptance, and create a training ground for inexperienced employees. These advantages must be balanced, however, with the disadvantages listed in Table 11–4. In doing so, managers need to determine the extent to which the advantages and disadvantages apply to the decision situation. The following three guidelines may then be applied to help decide whether groups should be included in the decision-making process:

1. If additional information would increase the quality of the decision, managers should involve those people who can provide the needed information.

Advantages	Disadvantages
1. *Greater pool of knowledge.* A group can bring much more information and experience to bear on a decision or problem than can an individual acting alone.	1. *Social pressure.* Unwillingness to "rock the boat" and pressure to conform may combine to stifle the creativity of individual contributors.
2. *Different perspectives.* Individuals with varied experience and interests help the group see decision situations and problems from different angles.	2. *Minority domination.* Sometimes the quality of group action is reduced when the group gives in to those who talk the loudest and longest.
3. *Greater comprehension.* Those who personally experience the give-and-take of group discussion about alternative courses of action tend to understand the rationale behind the final decision.	3. *Logrolling.* Political wheeling and dealing can displace sound thinking when an individual's pet project or vested interest is at stake.
4. *Increased acceptance.* Those who play an active role in group decision making and problem solving tend to view the outcome as "ours" rather than "theirs."	4. *Goal displacement.* Sometimes secondary considerations such as winning an argument, making a point, or getting back at a rival displace the primary task of making a sound decision or solving a problem.
5. *Training ground.* Less experienced participants in group action learn how to cope with group dynamics by actually being involved.	5. *"Groupthink."* Sometimes cohesive "ingroups" let the desire for unanimity override sound judgment when generating and evaluating alternative courses of action.

• ➔ TABLE 11~4

Advantages and Disadvantages of Group-Aided Decision Making

Source: R Kreitner, *Management*, 4th ed (Boston: Houghton Mifflin, 1989) p 238.

2. If acceptance is important, managers need to involve those individuals whose acceptance and commitment are important. Consider Drypers, a small but growing maker of disposable diapers.

> This profitable Houston company, whose sales last fiscal year grew 24% to $140 million, operates with an office of the chief executive that consists of five managing directors, all with equal power. The five, each of whom has a functional responsibility like finance, marketing, and manufacturing, work much like a middle management team, sharing information and kicking around ideas. No major decision is made until the five managing directors arrive at consensus. A lone CEO might be able to make a decision faster, but at Drypers, once a decision is made, all functions feel they own it, which helps wonderfully their inclination to put it into effect swiftly.[34]

3. If people can be developed through their participation, managers may want to involve those whose development is most important.[35]

Group versus Individual Performance   Before recommending that managers involve groups in decision making, it is important to examine whether groups perform better or worse than individuals. After reviewing 61 years of relevant research, a decision-making expert concluded that "Group performance was generally qualitatively and quantitatively superior to the performance of the average individual."[36] Although a recent review of small group decision making generally supported this conclusion, a few drawbacks to group decision making were uncovered.[37]

1. Groups were less efficient than individuals. This suggests that time constraints are an important consideration in determining whether to involve groups in decision making.

2. Groups were more confident about their judgments and choices than individuals. Because group confidence is not a surrogate for group decision quality, this overconfidence can fuel groupthink—recall the discussion in Chapter 9—and a resistance to consider alternative solutions proposed by individuals outside the group.

3. Group size affected decision outcomes. Decision quality was negatively related to group size.

4. Additional research suggests that managers should use a contingency approach when determining whether to include others in the decision-making process.

Let us consider these practical contingency recommendations.

Practical Contingency Recommendations   If the decision occurs frequently, such as deciding on promotions or who qualifies for a loan, use groups because they tend to produce more consistent decisions than do individuals.[38] Given time constraints, let the most competent individual, rather than a group, make the decision. In the face of environmental threats such as time pressure and potential serious impact of a decision, groups use less information and fewer communication channels. This increases the probability of a bad decision.[39] This conclusion underscores a general recommendation that managers should keep in mind: Because the quality of communication strongly affects a group's productivity, on complex tasks it is essential to devise mechanisms to enhance communication effectiveness.

Participative Management

Confusion exists about the exact meaning of participative management (PM). One management expert clarified this situation by defining **participative management** as the process whereby employees play a direct role in (1) setting goals, (2) making decisions, (3) solving problems, and (4) making changes in the organization. Without question, participative management entails much more than simply asking employees for their ideas or opinions.[40]

Advocates of PM claim employee participation increases employee satisfaction, commitment, and performance. Practical experience at Childress Buick Company, a Phoenix auto dealership, supports this view.

> Childress began empowering employees in 1988 as part of his "crisis management" plan. Customer satisfaction had dropped drastically—retention was down to 30%. To improve it, he disassembled the company's autocratic management style. Today he stresses that he wants his employees to use their judgment and initiative from day one. The message is getting through; recently, a team from the service department decided to run a shuttle-bus service to a local horse-race track for customers who had cars in the shop.
>
> In the showroom, salesman Jim Lather finds the latitude a big asset. "We all work our own deals from start to finish," he says. "Customers are more relaxed when they know they're dealing with someone who doesn't have to go ask the manager for a price every two minutes." These days Childress enjoys retention rates of up to 70%, remarkable in the car business.[41]

To get a fuller understanding of how and when participative management works, we begin by discussing a model of participative management.

participative management
Involving employees in various forms of decision making.

A Model of Participative Management   Consistent with both Maslow's need theory and the job characteristics model of job design (see Chapter 6), participative management is predicted to increase motivation because it helps employees fulfill three basic needs: (1) autonomy, (2) meaningfulness of work, and (3) interpersonal contact. Satisfaction of these needs enhances feelings of acceptance and commitment, security, challenge, and satisfaction. In turn, these positive feelings supposedly lead to increased innovation and performance.[42]

Participative management does not work in all situations. The design of work, the level of trust between management and employees, and the employees' readiness to participate represent three factors that influence the effectiveness of PM. With respect to the design of work, individual participation is counterproductive when employees are highly interdependent on each other, as on an assembly line. The problem with individual participation in this case is that interdependent employees generally do not have a broad understanding of the entire production process. Participative management also is less likely to succeed when employees do not trust management. Finally, PM is more effective when employees are properly trained, prepared, and interested in participating.[43]

Research and Practical Suggestions for Managers   Participative management can significantly increase employee job involvement, organizational commitment, and creativity. It can also lower role conflict and ambiguity.[44] A recent meta-analysis further demonstrates that participation only has a small but significant impact on both job performance and job satisfaction. This finding questions the practical value of using participative management to influence performance or satisfaction at work.[45]

So what is a manager to do? We believe that PM is not a quick-fix solution for low productivity and motivation, as some enthusiastic supporters claim.[46] Nonetheless, since participative management is effective in certain situations, managers can increase their chances of obtaining positive results by using once again a contingency approach.[47] For example, the effectiveness of participation depends on the type of interactions between managers and employees as they jointly solve problems. Effective participation requires a constructive interaction that fosters cooperation and respect, as opposed to competition and defensiveness.[48] Managers are advised not to use participative programs when they have destructive interpersonal interactions with their employees.

Experiences of companies implementing participative management programs suggest two additional practical recommendations. First, supervisors and middle managers tend to resist participative management because it reduces their power and authority. It is important to gain the support and commitment from employees who have managerial responsibility. Second, the process of implementing participative management must be monitored and managed by top management.[49]

When to Have Groups Participate in Decision Making: The Vroom/Yetton/Jago Model

Victor Vroom and Philip Yetton developed a model in 1973 to help managers determine the degree of group involvement in the decision-making process. It was later expanded by Vroom and Arthur Jago.[50] The model is prescriptive in that it specifies decision-making styles that should be effective in different situations.

TABLE 11-5

Management Decision Styles

AI	You solve the problem or make the decision yourself, using information available to you at that time.
AII	You obtain the necessary information from your subordinate(s), then decide on the solution to the problem yourself. You may or may not tell your subordinates what the problem is in getting the information from them. The role played by your subordinates in making the decision is clearly one of providing the necessary information to you rather than generating or evaluating solutions.
CI	You share the problem with relevant subordinates individually, getting their ideas and suggestions without bringing them together as a group. Then you make the decision that may or may not reflect your subordinates' influence.
CII	You share the problem with your subordinates as a group, collectively obtaining their ideas and suggestions. Then you make the decision that may or may not reflect your subordinates' influence.
GII	You share a problem with your subordinates as a group. Together you generate and evaluate alternatives and attempt to reach agreement (consensus) on a solution. Your role is much like that of a chairman. You do not try to influence the group to adopt "your" solution, and you are willing to accept and implement any solution that has the support of the entire group.

Source: Reprinted by permission of the publisher, from "A New Look at Managerial Decision Making," V H Vroom, *Organizational Dynamics*, Spring 1973, p 67, © 1973 American Management Association, New York. All rights reserved.

Vroom and Jago's model is represented as a decision tree. The manager's task is to move from left to right along the various branches of the tree. A specific decision-making style is prescribed at the end point of each branch. Before we apply the model, however, it is necessary to consider the different decision styles managers ultimately choose from and an approach for diagnosing the problem situation.

Five Decision-Making Styles Vroom and Yetton identified five distinct decision-making styles. In Table 11-5, each style is represented by a letter. The letter indicates the basic thrust of the style. For example, A stands for *autocratic*, C for *consultive*, and G for *group*. There are several important issues to consider as one moves from an AI style to a GII style:

- The problem or decision is discussed with more people.
- Group involvement moves from merely providing data to recommending solutions.
- Group "ownership" and commitment to the solution increases.
- As group commitment increases, so does the time needed to arrive at a decision.[51]

Style choice is dependent on the type of problem situation.

Matching the Situation to Decision-Making Style Vroom and Jago developed eight problem attributes that managers can use to diagnose a situation. They are shown at the top of the decision tree presented in Figure 11-4 and are expressed as questions. Answers to these questions lead managers along different branches, pointing the way to potentially effective decision-making styles.

Applying the Model Because Vroom and Jago developed four decision trees, the first step is to choose one of the trees. Each tree represents a generic type of problem that managers frequently encounter. They are (1) an individual-level

• ⟍ FIGURE 11–4   Vroom and Jago's Decision-Making Model

QR	Quality Requirement	How important is the technical quality of this decision?
CR	Commitment Requirement	How important is subordinate commitment to the decision?
LI	Leader's Information	Do you have sufficient information to make a high-quality decision?
ST	Problem Structure	Is the problem well structured?
CP	Commitment Probability	If you were to make the decision by yourself, is it reasonably certain that your subordinate(s) would be committed to the decision?
GC	Goal Congruence	Do subordinates share the organizational goals to be attained in solving this problem?
CO	Subordinate Conflict	Is conflict among subordinates over preferred solutions likely?
SI	Subordinate Information	Do subordinates have sufficient information to make a high-quality decision?

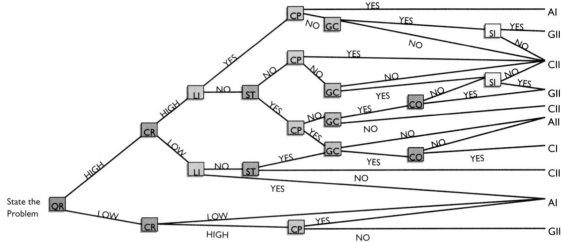

Source: V H Vroom and A G Jago, *The New Leadership: Managing Participation in Organizations* (Englewood Cliffs, NJ: Prentice-Hall, 1988), p 184.

problem with time constraints, (2) an individual-level problem in which the manager wants to develop an employee's decision-making abilities, (3) a group-level problem in which the manager wants to develop employees' decision-making abilities, and (4) a time-driven group problem[52] (illustrated in Figure 11–4).

To use the model in Figure 11–4, start at the left side and move toward the right by asking yourself the questions associated with each decision point (represented by a box in the figure) encountered. A decision-making style is prescribed at the end of each branch.

Let us track a simple example through Figure 11–4. Suppose you have to determine the work schedule for a group of part-time workers who report to you. The first question is "How important is the technical quality of this decision?" It seems rather low. This leads us to the second question: "How important is subordinate commitment to the decision?" Assuming acceptance is important, this takes us along the branch leading to the question about commitment probability (CP). If you were to make the decision by yourself, is it reasonably certain that your subordinate(s) would be committed to the decision? A yes answer suggests you should use an AI decision-making style (see Table 11–5) and a GII style if you answered no.

Research Insights and Managerial Implications   Because this model is relatively new, very little research has tested its prescriptive accuracy. Nonetheless, research does support the earlier model developed by Vroom and Yetton in 1973.[53] For example, a study of 36 departments in a large retail department store indicated that group productivity was higher when managers used decision-making styles consistent with the model.[54] Managers thus are advised to use different decision-making styles to suit situational demands.

Also, the model can help managers determine when, and to what extent, they should involve employees in decision making. By simply being aware of the eight diagnostic questions, managers can enhance their ability to structure ambiguous problems. This should ultimately enhance the quality of managerial decisions.

Group Problem-Solving Techniques

consensus   Presenting opinions and gaining agreement to support a decision.

Using groups to make decisions generally requires that they reach a consensus. According to a decision-making expert, a **consensus** "is reached when all members can say they either agree with the decision or have had their 'day in court' and were unable to convince the others of their viewpoint. In the final analysis, everyone agrees to support the outcome."[55] This definition indicates that consensus does not necessarily represent unanimous agreement.

Groups can experience roadblocks when trying to arrive at a consensus decision. For one, groups may not generate all relevant alternatives to a problem because an individual dominates or intimidates other group members. This is both overt and/or subtle. For instance, group members who possess power and authority, such as a CEO, can be intimidating, regardless of interpersonal style, simply by being present in the room. Moreover, shyness inhibits the generation of alternatives. Shy individuals may withhold their input for fear of embarrassment or lack of confidence. Satisficing is another hurdle to effective group decision making. As previously noted, groups satisfice due to limited time, information, or ability to handle large amounts of information.[56]

Decision-making experts have developed three group problem-solving techniques—brainstorming, the nominal group technique, and the Delphi technique—to reduce the above roadblocks. Knowledge of these techniques can help present and future managers to more effectively use group-aided decision making. Further, the advent of computer-aided decision making enables managers to use these techniques to solve complex problems with large groups of people.

brainstorming   Process to generate a quantity of ideas.

Brainstorming   Brainstorming was developed by A F Osborn, an advertising executive, to increase creativity.[57] **Brainstorming** is used to help groups generate multiple ideas and alternatives for solving problems. This technique is effective because it helps reduce interference caused by critical and judgmental reactions to one's ideas from other group members.

When brainstorming, a group is convened, and the problem at hand is reviewed. Individual members then are asked to silently generate ideas/alternatives for solving the problem. Next, these ideas/alternatives are solicited and written on a board or flip chart. A second session is used to critique and evaluate the alternatives. Managers are advised to follow four rules when brainstorming:

1. Freewheeling is encouraged. Group members are advised to offer any and all ideas they have. The wilder, the better.
2. Criticism is discouraged. Don't criticize during the initial stage of idea generation. Phrases such as "we've never done it that way," "it won't

work," "it's too expensive," and "the boss will never agree" should not be used.

3. Quantity of ideas is encouraged. Managers should try to generate and write down as many ideas as possible.

4. Combination and improvement of ideas is pursued. Group members are advised to "piggyback" onto the ideas of others.

Brainstorming is an effective technique for generating new ideas/alternatives. It is not appropriate for evaluating alternatives or selecting solutions.[58]

The Nominal Group Technique The **nominal group technique** (NGT) helps groups to generate ideas and evaluate and select solutions. NGT is more comprehensive than brainstorming. This technique is primarily used during the decision-making stage of evaluating and selecting solutions. NGT is a structured group meeting that follows this format:[59]

A group is convened to discuss a particular problem or issue. After the problem is understood, individuals silently generate ideas in writing. Each individual, in round-robin fashion, then offers one idea from his or her list. Ideas are recorded on a blackboard or flip chart; they are not discussed at this stage of the process. Once all ideas are elicited, the group discusses them. Anyone may criticize or defend any item. During this step, clarification is provided as well as general agreement or disagreement with the idea. Finally, group members anonymously vote for their top choices with a weighted voting procedure (e.g., 1st choice = 3 points; 2nd choice = 2 points; 3rd choice = 1 point). The group leader then adds the votes to determine the group's choice. Prior to making a final decision, the group may decide to discuss the top ranked items and conduct a second round of voting.

The nominal group technique reduces the roadblocks to group decision making by (1) separating brainstorming from evaluation, (2) promoting balanced participation among group members, and (3) incorporating mathematical voting techniques in order to reach consensus. NGT has been successfully used in many different decision-making situations.

The Delphi Technique This problem-solving method was originally developed by the Rand Corporation for technological forecasting.[60] It now is used as a multipurpose planning tool. The **Delphi technique** is a group process that anonymously generates ideas or judgments from physically dispersed experts. Unlike the NGT, experts' ideas are obtained from questionnaires as opposed to face-to-face group discussions.

A manager begins the Delphi process by identifying the issue(s) he or she wants to investigate. For example, a manager might want to inquire about customer demand, customers' future preferences, or the impact of locating a plant in a certain region of the country. Next, participants are identified and a questionnaire is developed. The questionnaire is sent to participants and returned to the manager. The manager then summarizes the responses and sends feedback to the participants. At this stage, participants are asked to (1) review the feedback, (2) prioritize the issues being considered, and (3) return the survey within a specified time period. This cycle repeats until the manager obtains the necessary information.

The Delphi technique is useful when face-to-face discussions are impractical, when disagreements and conflict are likely to impair communication, when certain

nominal group technique Process to generate ideas and evaluate solutions.

Delphi technique Process to generate ideas from physically dispersed experts.

In many companies, computer-aided decision making is proving to be a highly effective way of generating ideas and building needed support for key decisions.

(Michael Gillespie/The Image Bank)

individuals might severely dominate group discussion, and when groupthink is a probable outcome of the group process (recall our discussion in Chapter 9).[61]

Computer-Aided Decision Making   The purpose of computer-aided decision making is to reduce consensus roadblocks while collecting more information in a shorter period of time. There are two types of computer-aided decision making systems: chauffeur driven and group driven.[62] Chauffeur-driven systems ask participants to answer predetermined questions on electronic keypads or dials. Live television audiences on shows such as ''Love Connection'' and ''America's Funniest Home Videos'' are frequently polled with this system. The computer system tabulates participants' responses in a matter of seconds.

Group-driven meetings are conducted in special facilities equipped with individual computer workstations that are networked to each other. Instead of talking, participants type their input, ideas, comments, reactions, or evaluations on their keyboards. The input simultaneously appears on a large projector screen at the front of the room, thereby enabling all participants to see all input. This computer-driven process reduces consensus roadblocks because input is anonymous, everyone gets a chance to contribute, and no one can dominate the process. Research demonstrated that computer-aided decision making produced greater quality and quantity of ideas than either traditional brainstorming or the nominal group technique for large groups of people. There were no significant advantages to group-aided decision making with groups of 4 to 6 people.[63]

CREATIVITY

In light of today's fast-paced decisions, an organization's ability to stimulate the creativity and innovation of its employees is becoming increasingly important. Some organizations are successfully meeting this challenge. Others are not. For example, the decline of the US steel industry is partly due to its inability to successfully innovate. To gain further insight into managing the creative process, we begin by defining creativity and highlighting stages of the creative process. This section then reviews the characteristics of creative people and discusses the management of creative individuals.

• ➔ FIGURE 11–5 Stages of the Creative Process

| Preparation | → | Concentration | → | Incubation | → | Illumination | → | Verification |

Definition and Stages

Although many definitions have been proposed, the essence of **creativity** is development of something new, something that has never existed before. It can be as simple as developing a new flavor of the month for an ice cream store or as complex as developing a pocket-size microcomputer. This definition highlights three broad types of creativity. One can create something new (creation), one can combine or synthesize things (synthesis), or one can improve or change things (modification).[64]

Early approaches to explaining creativity were based on differences between the left and right hemispheres of the brain. Researchers thought the right side of the brain was responsible for creativity. More recently, however, researchers have questioned this explanation.

> "The left brain/right brain dichotomy is simplified and misleading," says Dr. John C Mazziotta, a researcher at the University of California at Los Angeles School of Medicine.
>
> What scientists have found instead is that creativity is a feat of mental gymnastics engaging the conscious and subconscious parts of the brain. It draws on everything from knowledge, logic, imagination, and intuition to the ability to see connections and distinctions between ideas and things.[65]

Let us now examine a model of the creativity process.

Researchers are not absolutely certain how creativity takes place. Nonetheless, we do know that creativity involves "making remote associations" between unconnected events, ideas, information stored in memory (recall our discussion in Chapter 5), or physical objects. Figure 11–5 depicts five stages underlying this process.[66]

The *preparation* stage reflects the notion that creativity starts from a base of knowledge. Preparation includes the amount of time an individual engages in schooling, reading, on-the-job training, attending workshops, or just paying attention to one's environment. Consider how Karen Monte Calvo, creative team leader in the marketing communications department at Microsoft Corporation, prepares for creative ideas.

> Monte Calvo is proof that creativity isn't just something you're born with. Behind her mental index file of great ideas is a lot of hard work. . . . The best way to find ideas is to surround yourself with them, Monte Calvo says. At home, she reads 20 magazines a month, and her department at work subscribes to more—journals as varied as *Communication Arts, Mondo 2000,* and *Interview.* Creative people always have their antennae up, she points out. Writers are either voracious readers or TV connoisseurs, she says, always in search of a perfect line.[67]

During the *concentration* stage, an individual focuses on the problem at hand. Interestingly, Japanese companies are noted for encouraging this stage as part of a quality improvement process much more than American companies. The International OB presents data indicating that the average number of suggestions per

creativity Development of something that never existed before.

Japanese Companies Generate More Process Improvement Ideas Than Their American Counterparts

Company	Number of Suggestions	Number of Employees	Percentage per Employee
Matsushita	6,446,935	81,000	79.6
Hitachi	3,618,014	57,051	63.4
Mazda	3,025,853	23,929	126.5
Toyota	2,648,710	55,578	47.6
Nissan	1,393,745	48,849	38.5
Nippon Denso	1,393,745	33,192	41.6
Canon	1,076,356	13,788	78.1
Fuji Electric	1,022,340	10,226	99.6
Tohoku Oki	734,044	881	833.2
JVC	728,529	15,000	48.6
Typical leading US company	21,000	9,000	2.3

Source: Data taken from Table 1 in M Basadur, "Managing Creativity: A Japanese Model," *Academy of Management Executive*, May 1992, p 32.

employee for improving quality and productivity is significantly lower in the typical US company than in comparable Japanese firms.

Incubation is done unconsciously. During this stage, people engage in daily activities while their minds simultaneously mull over information and make remote associations. These associations ultimately are generated in the *illumination* stage. Finally, *verification* entails going through the entire process to verify, modify, or try out the new idea.

Let us reconsider the data presented in the International OB. Why do Japanese organizations propose and implement so many more ideas than do American companies? To answer this question, a creativity expert visited and extensively interviewed employees from five major Japanese companies. He observed that Japanese firms have created a management infrastructure that encourages and reinforces creativity. People were taught to identify problems (discontents) on their first day of employment. In turn, discontents were referred to as "golden eggs" to reinforce the notion that it is good to identify problems.

These organizations also promoted the stages of incubation, illumination, and verification through teamwork and incentives. For example, some companies posted the golden eggs on large wall posters in the work area; employees were then encouraged to interact with each other to execute the final three stages of the creative process. Employees eventually received monetary awards for any suggestions that passed all five phases of this process.[68] This research underscores the conclusion that creativity can be enhanced by effectively managing the creativity process.[69]

Characteristics of Creative People

Creative people typically march to the beat of a different drummer. They are highly motivated individuals who spend many years mastering their chosen field or

1.	Knowledge	Creative people spend a great number of years mastering their chosen field.	
2.	Education	Education does not increase creativity. Education that stresses logic tends to inhibit creativity.	
3.	Intelligence	Creative people do not necessarily have high IQs. The threshold for IQ is around 130. After that, IQ does not really matter. Creative people have been found to possess the following intellectual abilities: sensitivity to problems, flexibility in forming fluid association between objects, thinking in images rather than words, and synthesizing information.	
4.	Personality	Creative people are typically risk takers who are independent, persistent, highly motivated, skeptical, open to new ideas, able to tolerate ambiguity, self-confident, and able to tolerate isolation. They also have a strong sense of humor and are hard to get along with.	
5.	Childhood	Creative people have usually had a childhood marked by adversity. Experiences such as family strains, financial ups and downs, and divorces are common occurrences.	
6.	Social habits	Contrary to stereotypes, creative people are not introverted nerds. Creative people tend to be outgoing and enjoy exchanging ideas with colleagues.	

TABLE 11-6

Characteristics of Creative People

Source: Based in part on R G Godfrey, "Tapping Employees' Creativity," *Supervisory Management,* February 1986, pp 16–20; and "Mix Skepticism, Humor, a Rocky Childhood—and Presto! Creativity," *Business Week,* September 30, 1985, p 81.

occupation. But contrary to stereotypes, creative people are not necessarily geniuses or introverted nerds. In addition, they are not *adaptors.* "Adaptors are those who seek to solve problems by 'doing things better.' They prefer to resolve difficulties or make decisions in such a way as to have the least impact upon the assumptions, procedures, and values of the organization. . . ."[70] In contrast, creative individuals are dissatisfied with the status quo. They look for new and exciting solutions to problems. Because of this, creative organizational members can be perceived as disruptive and hard to get along with. Further, research indicates that male and female managers do not differ in levels of creativity, and creative people are more open to experiencing new and different activities.[71] Table 11–6 presents additional characteristics of creative individuals.

Research also reveals that creativity seems to peak in early adulthood and then steadily declines. For example, Albert Einstein was 26 when he came up with his theory of relativity, and Isaac Newton figured out the laws of gravity at 24. Moreover, creativity seems to peak at different ages for people in different professions. "People who rely on pure bursts of creativity—for example physicists, theoretical mathematicians, and poets—tend to produce their most original work in their late twenties and early thirties. The output of novelists, engineers, and medical researchers, on the other hand, tends to rise more slowly, peaking in the late thirties and early forties, and then falling steadily until retirement."[72] Researchers currently are trying to figure out why these patterns occur.

Managing Creative Employees

Today's competitive pressures challenge managers to develop an environment that supports creative behavior. Kodak, for example, created a humor room where employees can relax and have creative brainstorming sessions. The room contains joke books, videotapes of comedians, stress-reducing toys, and software for creative decision making.[73] Table 11–7 lists some specific managerial recommendations to spark creativity.

After a supportive environment has been created, managers may want to consider creativity training for employees. Since each of us has the potential to be

◤ • TABLE 11~7
Suggestions for Improving Employee Creativity

Develop an environment that supports creative behavior.
Try to avoid using an autocratic style of leadership.
Encourage employees to be more open to new ideas and experiences.
Keep in mind that people use different strategies, like walking around or listening to music, to foster their creativity.
Provide employees with stimulating work that creates a sense of personal growth.
Encourage employees to view problems as opportunities.
Don't let your decision-making style stifle those employees who have a different style.
Guard against employees being too involved with putting out fires and dealing with urgent short-term problems.
Make sure creative people are not bogged down with specific tasks all day long.
Allow employees to have fun and play around.
Encourage an open environment that is free from defensive behavior.
Treat errors and mistakes as opportunities for learning.
Let employees occasionally try out their pet ideas. Provide a margin of error.
Be a catalyst instead of an obstacle.
Avoid using a negative mind-set when an employee approaches you with a new idea.
Encourage creative people to communicate with one another.
Welcome diverse ideas and opinions.
Send yourself and your employees to creativity training.
Reward creative behavior.

Source: Adapted from discussion in E Raudsepp, "101 Ways to Spark Your Employees' Creative Potential," *Office Administration and Automation*, September 1985, pp 38, 39–43, 56.

creative, training gives everyone a chance to participate in the creative process. This training should help people to overcome the mental locks that stifle creativity.

Roger von Oech, a creativity consultant in Silicon Valley, identified 10 mental locks or hang-ups that interfere with creativity:

1. Searching for the "right" answer.
2. Always trying to be logical.
3. Looking for solutions that "follow the rules."
4. Trying to be too practical.
5. Avoiding ambiguity.
6. Fearing failure.
7. Not playing or having fun at work.
8. Ignoring problems outside one's specialty.
9. Not wanting to look foolish.
10. Believing you are not creative.[74]

To demonstrate how these mental locks inhibit creativity, try the two exercises in the OB Exercise. After completing these exercises, look at the solutions provided in endnote 75. (Which mental lock may have reduced your creativity?) In an organizational context, managers need to help employees identify and confront these mental locks. Finally, managers will need to modify their own behavior and attitudes (the ideas in Table 11–7 point the way).

OB Exercise

Creativity Exercises

Exercise 1

In the line of letters listed below, cross out six letters so the remaining letters spell a familiar English word. You may not alter the sequence of the letters.

B S A I N X L E A T N T E A R S

Try to solve the exercise for a while before proceeding.

Exercise 2

What is this figure? Come up with as many interpretations as you can.

Source: Reprinted by permission of Warner Books/New York, from *A Whack on the Side of the Head.* Copyright © 1983 by R von Oech, pp 76–78.

BACK TO THE OPENING CASE

Now that you have read Chapter 11, you should be able to answer the following questions about decision making in Team Mustang:

1. Are Team Mustang's decision-making processes more characteristic of the rational or garbage can model of decision making? Discuss your rationale.

2. How does the team try to control escalation of commitment?

3. To what extent does Team Mustang rely on group-aided decision making? Explain.

4. What examples of creative decision making can you identify within Team Mustang?

Summary of Key Concepts

1. *Distinguish between programmed and nonprogrammed decisions.* There are two types of managerial decisions: programmed and nonprogrammed. Programmed decisions are repetitive and routine. Habit and standard operating procedures are most frequently used to make these decisions. Nonprogrammed decisions are novel, unstructured, and tend to have important consequences. To make these decisions, managers rely on judgment, intuition, and creativity.

2. *Discuss the four steps in the rational model of decision making.* The rational decision-making model consists of identifying the problem, generating alternative solutions, evaluating and selecting a solution, and implementing and evaluating the solution. Research indicates that decision makers do not follow the series of steps outlined in the rational model.

3. *Contrast Simon's normative model and the garbage can model of decision making.* Simon's normative model is guided by a decision maker's bounded rationality. Bounded rationality means that decision makers are bounded or restricted by a variety of constraints when making decisions. The normative model suggests that decision making is characterized by (1) limited information processing, (2) the use of rules of thumb or shortcuts, and (3) satisficing.

    The garbage can model of decision making assumes that decision making does not follow an orderly series of steps. In a garbage can process, decisions result from interaction among four independent streams of events: problems, solutions, participants, and choice opportunities.

4. *Discuss the contingency relationships that influence the three primary strategies used to select solutions.* Decision makers use either an aided-analytic, unaided-analytic, or nonanalytic strategy when selecting a solution. The choice of a strategy depends on the characteristics of the decision task and the characteristics of the decision maker. In general, the greater the demands and constraints faced by a decision maker, the higher the probability that an aided-analytic approach will be used. Aided-analytic strategies are more likely to be used by competent and motivated individuals. Ultimately, decision makers compromise between their desire to make correct decisions and the amount of time and effort they put into the decision-making process.

5. *Describe the model of escalation of commitment.* Escalation of commitment refers to the tendency to stick to an ineffective course of action when it is unlikely that a bad situation can be reversed. Psychological and social determinants, organizational determinants, project characteristics, and contextual determinants cause managers to exhibit this decision-making error.

6. *Summarize the pros and cons of involving groups in the decision-making process.* There are both pros and cons of involving groups in the decision-making process. Although research shows that groups typically outperform the average individual, managers are encouraged to use a contingency approach when determining whether to include others in the decision-making process.

7. *Explain how participative management affects performance.* Participative management reflects the extent to which employees participate in setting goals, making decisions, solving problems, and making changes in the organization. Participative management is expected to increase motivation because it helps employees fulfill three basic needs: (1) autonomy, (2) meaningfulness of work, and (3) interpersonal contact. Participative management does not work in all situations. The design of work, level of trust between management and employees, and employees' readiness to participate represent three factors that influence the effectiveness of participative management.

8. *Review Vroom and Jago's decision-making model.* Vroom, Yetton, and Jago developed a model to help managers determine the extent to which they should include groups in the decision-making process. Through the use of decision trees, the model identifies appropriate decision-making styles for various types of managerial problems. The styles range from autocratic to highly participative.

9. *Contrast brainstorming, the nominal group technique, the Delphi technique, and computer-aided decision making.* Group problem-solving techniques facilitate better decision making within groups. Brainstorming is used to help groups generate multiple ideas and alternatives for solving problems. The nominal group technique assists

groups both to generate ideas and to evaluate and select solutions. The Delphi technique is a group process that anonymously generates ideas or judgments from physically dispersed experts. The purpose of computer-aided decision making is to reduce consensus roadblocks while collecting more information in a shorter period of time.

10. *Describe the stages of the creative process and specify at least five characteristics of creative*

people. Creativity is the development of something new. It is not adequately explained by differences between the left and right hemispheres of the brain. There are five stages of the creative process. They are preparation, concentration, incubation, illumination, and verification. Several characteristics differentiate creative people from average individuals. Table 11–6 summarizes the characteristics of creative people.

DISCUSSION QUESTIONS

1. Identify both a programmed and a nonprogrammed decision you made recently. How did you arrive at a solution for each one?

2. Do you think people are rational when they make decisions? Under what circumstances would an individual tend to follow a rational process?

3. Describe a situation in which you satisficed when making a decision. Why did you satisfice instead of optimize?

4. Do you think the garbage can model is a realistic representation of organizational decision making? Explain your rationale.

5. What is the most valuable lesson about selecting solutions through a contingency perspective? Explain.

6. Describe a situation in which you exhibited escalation of commitment. Why did you escalate a losing situation?

7. Do you prefer to solve problems in groups or by yourself? Why?

8. Given the intuitive appeal of participative management, why do you think it fails as often as it succeeds? Explain.

9. Do you think you are creative? Why or why not?

10. What advice would you offer a manager who was attempting to improve the creativity of his or her employees? Explain.

EXERCISE

Objectives

1. To promote understanding of the Vroom, Yetton, and Jago decision-making model.

2. To develop and assess your ability to use the model.

Introduction

Vroom and Jago extended an earlier model by Vroom and Yetton to help managers determine the extent to which they should include groups in the decision-making process. To enhance your understanding of this model, we would like you to use it to analyze a brief case. You will be asked to read the case and use the information to determine an appropriate decision-making style. This will enable you to compare your solution with that recommended by Vroom and Jago. Since their analysis is pre-

sented at the end of this exercise, please do not read it until indicated.

Instructions

Presented below is a case depicting a situation faced by the manufacturing manager of an electronics plant.[76] Read the case and then use Vroom and Jago's model (refer to Figure 11–4 and Table 11–5) to arrive at a solution. At this point, it might be helpful to reread the material that explains how to apply the model. Keep in mind that you move toward a solution by asking yourself the questions (at the top of Figure 11–4) associated with each relevant decision point. After completing your analysis, we would like you to compare your solution with the one offered by Vroom and Jago.

Leadership Case

You are a manufacturing manager in a large electronics plant. The company's management has recently installed new machines and put in a new simplified work system, but to the surprise of everyone, yourself included, the expected increase in productivity was not realized. In fact, production has begun to drop, quality has fallen off, and the number of employee separations has risen.

You do not believe that there is anything wrong with the machines. You have had reports from other companies that are using them, and they confirm this opinion. You have also had representatives from the firm that built the machines go over them, and they report that they are operating at peak efficiency.

You suspect that some parts of the new work system may be responsible for the change, but this view is not widely shared among your immediate subordinates, who are four first-line supervisors, each in charge of a section, and your supply manager. The drop in production has been variously attributed to poor training of the operators, lack of an adequate system of financial incentives, and poor morale. Clearly, this is an issue about which there is considerable depth of feeling within individuals and potential disagreement among your subordinates.

This morning you received a phone call from your division manager. He had just received your production figures for the last six months and was calling to express his concern. He indicated that the problem was yours to solve in any way that you think best, but that he would like to know within a week what steps you plan to take.

You share your division manager's concern with the falling productivity and know that your [people] are also concerned. The problem is to decide what steps to take to rectify the situation.

Questions for Consideration/ Class Discussion

1. What decision-making style from Table 11–5 do you recommend?
2. Did you arrive at the same solution as Vroom and Jago? If not, what do you think caused the difference?
3. Based on this experience, what problems would a manager encounter in trying to apply this model?

Vroom and Jago's Analysis and Solution

Question:

(QR:	quality requirement)	= Critical/high importance
(CR:	commitment requirement)	= High importance
(LI:	leader's information)	= Probably no
(ST:	problem structure)	= No
(CP:	commitment probability)	= Probably no
(GC:	goal congruence)	= Probably yes
(CO:	subordinate conflict)	= Not a consideration for this problem.
(SI:	subordinate information)	= Maybe [but probably not]

Decision-making style = CII

NOTES

[1] A thorough discussion is provided by H A Simon, *The New Science of Management Decision* (Englewood Cliffs, NJ: Prentice-Hall, 1977), pp 39–81.

[2] The use of computerized job interviews is discussed by S Oliver, "Slouches Makes Better Operators," *Forbes,* August 16, 1993, pp 104–105.

[3] R Winslow, "Health-Care Providers Try Industrial Tactics to Reduce Their Costs," *The Wall Street Journal,* November 3, 1993, p A1.

[4] For an example of using computer simulations to solve nonprogrammed decisions, see F V Krum and C F Rolle, "Management and Application of Decision and Risk Analysis in Du Pont," *Interfaces,* November–December 1992, pp 84–93; and P Coy, "Oh, What a Lovely War Game," *Business Week,* February 1, 1993, p 34.

[5] See W F Pounds, "The Process of Problem Finding," *Industrial Management Review,* Fall 1969, pp 1–19.

[6] R Henkoff, "How to Plan for 1995," *Fortune,* December 31, 1990, p 79.

[7] For a thorough review of this research, see R P Larrick, "Motivational Factors in Decision Theories: The Role of Self-Protection," *Psychological Bulletin,* May 1993, pp 440–50; and E U Weber, C J Anderson, and M H Birnbaum, "A Theory of Perceived Risk and Attractiveness," *Organizational Behavior and Human Decision Processes,* August 1992, pp 492–523.

[8] For a review of these assumptions, see H A Simon, "A Behavioral Model of Rational Choice," *The Quarterly Journal of Economics,* February 1955, pp 99–118.

[9] H A Simon, "Rational Decision Making in Business

Organizations," *The American Economic Review,* September 1979, p 510.

10 For a complete discussion of bounded rationality, see H A Simon, *Administrative Behavior,* 2nd ed (New York: Free Press, 1957); J G March and H A Simon, *Organizations* (New York: John Wiley, 1958); and H A Simon, "Altruism and Economics," *American Economic Review,* May 1993, pp 156–61.

11 M Chase, "A Matter of Candor: Did Syntex Withhold Data on Side Effects of a Promising Drug?" *The Wall Street Journal,* January 8, 1991, p A1.

12 The concept of bounded rationality was recently challenged by D A Skidd, "Revisiting Bounded Rationality," *Journal of Management Inquiry,* December 1992, pp 343–47; and D K Mumby and L L Putnam, "The Politics of Emotion: A Feminist Reading of Bounded Rationality," *Academy of Management Review,* July 1992, pp 465–86.

13 Biases associated with using shortcuts in decision making are discussed by A Tversky and D Kahneman, "Judgment under Uncertainty: Heuristics and Biases," *Science,* September 1974, pp 1124–31; and E Creyer and W T Ross, Jr., "Hindsight Bias and Inferences in Choice: The Mediating Effect of Cognitive Effort," *Organizational Behavior and Human Decision Processes,* June 1993, pp 61–77.

14 Satisficing is discussed by D Schmidtz, "Rationality Within Reason," *The Journal of Philosophy,* September 1992, pp 445–66; and J Bowen and Z-L Qui, "Satisficing when Buying Information," *Organizational Behavior and Human Decision Processes,* April 1992, pp 471–81.

15 The model is discussed in detail in M D Cohen, J G March, and J P Olsen, "A Garbage Can Model of Organizational Choice," *Administrative Science Quarterly,* March 1971, pp 1–25.

16 Ibid., p 2.

17 Results can be found in B Levitt and C Nass, "The Lid on the Garbage Can: Institutional Constraints on Decision Making in the Technical Core of College-Text Publishers," *Administrative Science Quarterly,* June 1989, pp 190–207.

18 This discussion is based on material presented by J G March and R Weissinger-Baylon, *Ambiguity and Command* (Marshfield, MA: Pitman Publishing, 1986), pp 11–35.

19 Simulated tests of the garbage can model were conducted by M Masuch and P LaPotin, "Beyond Garbage Cans: An AI Model of Organizational Choice," *Administrative Science Quarterly,* March 1989, pp 38–67; and M B Mandell, "The Consequences of Improving Dissemination in Garbage-Can Decision Processes," *Knowledge: Creation, Diffusion, Utilization,* March 1988, pp 343–61.

20 For a complete discussion, see L R Beach and T R Mitchell, "A Contingency Model for the Selection of Decision Strategies," *Academy of Management Review,* July 1978, pp 439–44.

21 Results from this study can be found in S W Gilliland, N Schmitt, and L Wood, "Cost-Benefit Determinants of Decision Process and Accuracy," *Organizational Behavior and Human Decision Processes,* November 1993, pp 308–30.

22 See P E Johnson, S Graziolo, K Jamal, and I A Zualkernan, "Success and Failure in Expert Reasoning," *Organizational Behavior and Human Decision Processes,* November 1992, pp 173–203.

23 This research is summarized by T R Mitchell and L R Beach, "'. . . Do I Love Thee? Let Me Count . . .' Toward an Understanding of Intuitive and Automatic Decision Making," *Organizational Behavior and Human Decision Processes,* October 1990, pp 1–20.

24 A thorough discussion of escalation situations can be found in B M Staw and J Ross, "Behavior in Escalation Situations: Antecedents, Prototypes, and Solutions," in *Research in Organizational Behavior,* vol. 9, eds L L Cummings and B M Staw (Greenwich, CT: JAI Press, 1987), pp 39–78.

25 *The New York Times* (based on the investigative reporting of N Sheehan), *The Pentagon Papers* (New York: Bantam Books, 1971), p 450.

26 The details of this case are discussed in J Ross and B M Staw, "Organizational Escalation and Exit: Lessons from the Shoreham Nuclear Power Plant," *Academy of Management Journal,* August 1993, pp 701–32.

27 Ibid.

28 Psychological determinants of escalation are discussed by J Brockner, "The Escalation of Commitment to a Failing Course of Action: Toward Theoretical Progress," *Academy of Management Review,* January 1992, pp 39–61; and J Schaubroeck and S Williams, "Type A Behavior Pattern and Escalating Commitment," *Journal of Applied Psychology,* October 1993, pp 862–67.

29 See H Garland, C A Sandefur, and A C Rogers, "De-Escalation of Commitment in Oil Exploration: When Sunk Costs and Negative Feedback Coincide," *Journal of Applied Psychology,* December 1990, pp 721–27; and H Garland, "Throwing Good Money after Bad: The Effect of Sunk Costs on the Decision to Escalate Commitment to an Ongoing Project," *Journal of Applied Psychology,* December 1990, pp 728–32.

[30] See Ross and Staw, "Organizational Escalation and Exit: Lessons from the Shoreham Nuclear Power Plant."

[31] Escalation among individuals and groups was examined by J Schaubroeck and E Davis, "Prospect Theory Predictions When Escalation Is Not the Only Chance to Recover Sunk Costs," *Organizational Behavior and Human Decision Processes,* January 1994, pp 59–82; and G Whyte, "Escalating Commitment in Individual and Group Decision Making: A Prospect Theory Approach," *Organizational Behavior and Human Decision Processes,* April 1993, pp 430–55.

[32] See B M Staw and J Ross, "Behavior in Escalation Situations: Antecedents, Prototypes, and Solutions"; and W S Silver and T R Mitchell, "The Status Quo Tendency in Decision Making," *Organizational Dynamics,* Spring 1990, pp 34–36.

[33] A recent study of techniques to reduce escalation was conducted by I Simonson and B M Staw, "Deescalation Strategies: A Comparison of Techniques for Reducing Commitment to Losing Courses of Action," *Journal of Applied Psychology,* August 1992, pp 419–26.

[34] B Dumaine, "The New Non-Manager Managers," *Fortune,* February 22, 1993, p 81.

[35] These guidelines were derived from G P Huber, *Managerial Decision Making* (Glenview, IL: Scott, Foresman, 1980), p 149.

[36] G W Hill, "Group versus Individual Performance: Are N + 1 Heads Better than One?" *Psychological Bulletin,* May 1982, p 535.

[37] These conclusions were based on the following studies: J H Davis, "Some Compelling Intuitions about Group Consensus Decisions, Theoretical and Empirical Research, and Interpersonal Aggregation Phenomena: Selected Examples, 1950–1990," *Organizational Behavior and Human Decision Processes,* June 1992, pp 3–38; and J A Sniezek, "Groups Under Uncertainty: An Examination of Confidence in Group Decision Making," *Organizational Behavior and Human Decision Processes,* June 1992, pp 124–55.

[38] This finding was obtained by P Chalos and S Pickard, "Information Choice and Cue Use: An Experiment in Group Information Processing," *Journal of Applied Psychology,* November 1985, pp 634–41.

[39] See D L Gladstein and N P Reilly, "Group Decision Making under Threat: The Tycoon Game," *Academy of Management Journal,* September 1985, pp 613–27.

[40] See M Sashkin, "Participative Management Is an Ethical Imperative," *Organizational Dynamics,* Spring 1984, pp 4–22. Different forms of participation are discussed by D R Lee, "Competitive Success: Supporting Operational Level Participation," *Industrial Management,* July/August 1990, pp 29–32.

[41] J Finegan, "People Power: More and More Companies Are Realizing that Employees Know Things that Bosses Simply Can't. The Best Businesses Are Capitalizing on It," *Inc.,* July 1993, p 63.

[42] For an expanded discussion of this model, see Sashkin, "Participative Management Is an Ethical Imperative."

[43] Contingency factors affecting the success of participative management are discussed by W A Pasmore and M R Fagans, "Participation, Individual Development, and Organizational Change: A Review and Synthesis," *Journal of Management,* June 1992, pp 375–97; and W N Cooke, "Product Quality Improvement Through Employee Participation: The Effects of Unionization and Joint Union-Management Administration," *Industrial and Labor Relations Review,* October 1992, pp 119–34.

[44] Supporting results can be found in C R Leana, R S Ahlbrandt, and A J Murrell, "The Effects of Employee Involvement Programs on Unionized Workers' Attitudes, Perceptions, and Preferences in Decision Making," *Academy of Management Journal,* October 1992, pp 861–73; and D Plunkett, "The Creative Organization: An Empirical Investigation of the Importance of Participation in Decision Making," *The Journal of Creative Behavior,* Second Quarter 1990, pp 140–48. Results pertaining to role conflict and ambiguity can be found in C S Smith and M T Brannick, "A Role and Expectancy Model of Participative Decision Making: A Replication and Theoretical Extension," *Journal of Organizational Behavior,* March 1990, pp 91–104.

[45] J A Wagner III, "Participation's Effects on Performance and Satisfaction: A Reconsideration of Research Evidence," *Academy of Management Review,* April 1994, pp 312–330.

[46] See Sashkin, "Participative Management Is an Ethical Imperative."

[47] See E A Locke, D M Schweiger, and G R Latham, "Participation in Decision Making: When Should It Be Used?" *Organizational Dynamics,* Winter 1986, pp 65–79.

[48] The influence of culture on participative techniques was investigated by D H B Welsh, F Luthans, and S M Sommer, "Managing Russian Factory Workers: The Impact of US-Based Behavioral and Participative Techniques," *Academy of Management Journal,* February 1993, pp 58–79; and P Boreham, "The Myth of Post-Fordist Management: Work Organization and Employee

Discretion in Seven Countries," *Employee Relations,* 1992, pp 13–24.

49 See R Rodgers, J E Hunter, and D L Rogers, "Influence of Top Management Commitment on Management Program Success," *Journal of Applied Psychology,* February 1993, pp 151 55.

50 See V H Vroom and P W Yetton, *Leadership and Decision Making* (Pittsburgh, PA: University of Pittsburgh Press, 1973); and V H Vroom and A G Jago, *The New Leadership: Managing Participation in Organizations* (Englewood Cliffs, NJ: Prentice-Hall, 1988), p 184.

51 See N B Wright, "Leadership Styles: Which Are Best When?" *Business Quarterly,* Winter 1984, pp 20–23.

52 For a complete discussion of these decision trees, see Vroom and Jago, *The New Leadership: Managing Participation in Organizations.*

53 Supportive results can be found in R H G Field and R J House, "A Test of the Vroom–Yetton Model Using Manager and Subordinate Reports," *Journal of Applied Psychology,* June 1990, pp 362–66; and A Crouch and P Yetton, "Manager Behavior, Leadership Style, and Subordinate Performance: An Empirical Extension of the Vroom–Yetton Conflict Rule," *Organizational Behavior and Human Decision Processes,* June 1987, pp 384–96.

54 See R J Paul and Y M Ebadi, "Leadership Decision Making in a Service Organization: A Field Test of the Vroom–Yetton Model," *Journal of Occupational Psychology,* September 1989, pp 201–11.

55 G M Parker, *Team Players and Teamwork: The New Competitive Business Strategy* (San Francisco: CA: Jossey-Bass, 1990).

56 Roadblocks to group consensus were studied by P B Paulus and M T Dzindolet, "Social Influence Processes in Group Brainstorming," *Journal of Personality and Social Psychology,* April 1993, pp 575–86.

57 See A F Osborn, *Applied Imagination: Principles and Procedures of Creative Thinking,* 3rd ed (New York: Scribners, 1979).

58 A summary and evaluation of different brainstorming methods is provided by R Zemke, "In Search Of . . .: Are Your Quality Teams Getting Tired of Using Traditional Brainstorming to Solve Problems? It's Not the Only Way to Generate Creative Solutions," *Training,* January 1993, pp 46–52.

59 A complete description of the nominal group technique can be found in A L Delbecq, A H Van de Ven, and D H Gustafson, *Group Techniques for Program Planning: A Guide to Nominal Group and Delphi Processes* (Glenview, IL: Scott, Foresman, 1975).

60 See N C Dalkey, D L Rourke, R Lewis, and D Snyder, *Studies in the Quality of Life: Delphi and Decision Making* (Lexington, MA: Lexington Books: D C Heath and Co, 1972).

61 Benefits of the Delphi technique are discussed by N I Whitman, "The Committee Meeting Alternative: Using the Delphi Technique," *Journal of Nursing Administration,* July/August 1990, pp 30–36.

62 A thorough description of computer-aided decision-making systems is provided by A LaPlante, "Brainstorming," *Forbes,* October 25, 1993, p 45–61; J G Donelan, "Using Electronic Tools to Improve Meetings," *Management Accounting,* March 1993, pp 42–45; and J Cavarretta, "Computer-Aided Decisions," *Association Management,* December 1992, pp 12, 14.

63 Results can be found in R B Gallupe, W H Cooper, M Grise, and L M Bastianutti, "Blocking Electronic Brainstorms, *Journal of Applied Psychology,* February 1994, pp 77–86; A R Dennis and J S Valacich, "Computer Brainstorms: More Heads Are Better than One," *Journal of Applied Psychology,* August 1993, pp 531–37; and R B Gallupe, A R Dennis, W H Cooper, J S Valacich, L M Bastianutti, and J F Nunamaker, Jr., "Electronic Brainstorming and Group Size," *Academy of Management Journal,* June 1992, pp 350–69.

64 Types of creativity are thoroughly discussed by J V Anderson, "Weirder than Fiction: The Reality and Myths of Creativity," *Academy of Management Executive,* November 1992, pp 40–47.

65 E T Smith, "Are You Creative?" *Business Week,* September 30, 1985, pp 81–82. For a review of research about the left and right hemispheres of the brain, see T Hines, "Left Brain/Right Brain Mythology and Implications for Management and Training," *Academy of Management Review,* October 1987, pp 600–606.

66 These stages are thoroughly discussed by E Glassman, "Creative Problem Solving," *Supervisory Management,* January 1989, pp 21–26. Another model of the creativity process is presented by R W Woodman, J E Sawyer, and R W Griffin, "Toward a Theory of Organizational Creativity," *Academy of Management Review,* April 1993, pp 293–321.

67 E Winninghoff, "Something Borrowed, Something New," *Executive Female,* January/February 1993, p 47.

68 Details of this study can be found in M Basadur, "Managing Creativity: A Japanese Model," *Academy of Management Executive,* May 1992, pp 29–42.

69 See S G Scott and R A Bruce, "Determinants of Innovative Behavior: A Path Model of Individual Innova-

tion in the Workplace,'' *Academy of Management Journal,* June 1994, pp 580–607.

[70] T A Matherly and R E Goldsmith, ''The Two Faces of Creativity,'' *Business Horizons,* September–October 1985, p 9.

[71] See Woodman, Sawyer, and Griffin, ''Toward a Theory of Organizational Creativity''; and R W Woodman and L F Schoenfeldt, ''An Interactionist Model of Creative Behavior,'' *Journal of Creative Behavior,* First Quarter 1990, pp 10–13.

[72] M Gladwell, ''Over the Hill at Twentysomething,'' *The Washington Post National Weekly Edition,* April 23–29, 1990, p 38.

[73] See S Caudron, ''Humor Is Healthy in the Workplace,'' *Personnel Journal,* June 1992, pp 63–66.

[74] A detailed discussion is provided by R von Oech, *A Whack on the Side of Head* (New York: Warner, 1983).

[75] Exercise I: One way to solve this problem is to interpret the instructions in an ambiguous fashion. Instead of crossing out six letters, you can literally cross out the S, and the I, and the X, and L, and the E, and so on until you have crossed out the word *six letters.* If you did this, you would have found the word *BANANA.* Another solution to this exercise would be to choose six different letters—say, B, S, A, I, N, and X—and cross them out every time they appear. You would end up with the word *LETTER.* Exercise 2: If you look at it one way, it's a bird; it could also be a question mark; if you turn it upside down, it's a seal juggling a ball on its nose.

[76] Reprinted, by permission of the publisher, ''A New Look at Managerial Decision Making,'' V H Vroom, *Organizational Dynamics,* Spring 1973, p 72, © 1973 American Management Association, New York. All rights reserved.

12 TEAMS AND TEAMWORK

Learning OBJECTIVES

When you finish studying the material in this chapter, you should be able to:

1. Explain how a work group becomes a team.

2. Identify and describe the four types of work teams.

3. Explain the ecological model of work team effectiveness.

4. List at least three things managers can do to build trust.

5. Distinguish two different types of cohesiveness.

6. Contrast quality circles and self-managed teams.

7. Discuss what must be done to set the stage for self-managed teams.

8. Describe high-performance teams.

How Thermos Grilled the Competition with Teamwork

Sharon Hoogstraten

When Monte Peterson took over as CEO of Thermos in 1990, he faced the toughest task in business. Says he: "We needed to totally reinvent the company." Famous for its Thermos bottles and lunch boxes, the Schaumburg, Illinois, corporation is also a major maker of gas and electric cookout grills, competing neck and neck with brands like Sunbeam, Char-Broil, and Weber. But growth at Thermos (1992 sales: $225 million) had been lukewarm. The $1-billion-a-year barbecue grill market produced a significant portion of company sales, but the fire had gone out of it. The product had become a commodity, with department stores selling many brands of black, look-alike, coffin-shaped gas boxes.

To reignite Thermos's growth, Peterson felt he had to find a new product. This meant changing the conventional thinking at the company, or in today's management-speak, break-ing the paradigm. Now, after three years of hard work, Peterson, 49, has taken a bureaucratic culture organized by function—marketing, manufacturing, engineering—and replaced it with flexible, interdisciplinary teams. How he and his colleagues at Thermos did this is a textbook lesson for any manager looking to use teamwork to revitalize a corporation, division, department, or even a small business.

What drove Thermos to such radical change was Peterson's recognition that the marketplace is experiencing a revolution as extraordinary as the one inspired by Henry Ford's mass production. Today's intelligent and demanding consumers cannot be tricked by clever advertising or slick packaging into buying a so-so, me-too product. To survive in this brutal environment, companies must constantly innovate, creating goods that give their customers high quality at the right price—in a word, value.

The first fruit of Peterson's discovery is the new Thermos Thermal Electric Grill, a sleek, ecologically sound cookout stove that looks like something the Jetsons might use. So far, sales of the cool-looking cooker, which was introduced in the fall of 1992, have been sizzling. Retailers like Kmart and Target Stores have been unloading them faster than ribs at a rodeo. . . .

[When] faced with the daunting task of creating an all-new product, Peterson wisely chose the team approach. Here are the steps Thermos, owned by Japanese manufacturer Nippon Sanso, took to achieve its breakthrough electric grill:

. . . In the fall of 1990, Peterson assembled a product-development team of six Thermos middle managers from various disciplines like engineering, marketing, manufacturing, and finance. The idea was to build a network around markets—in this case, for grills—rather than around functions. At first some employees resisted working this new way, but Peterson patiently reminded his troops they had a great opportunity to make their market grow, and he emphasized how important the project could be to all aspects of the company's business. Says he: "Like a politician, you provide a platform for change and then paint a picture of the difference between winning and losing. After that, the old barriers break down, and teamwork becomes infectious."

The team christened itself not the electric grill team or even the new grill team, but the Lifestyle team. Their assignment was to go into the field, learn all about people's cookout needs, and invent a product to meet them. This point is key. If the team had focused on the product rather than on the customer, the project would have generated yet another slightly improved, ho-hum gas grill. . . .

Teams and teamwork are popular terms in management circles these days. A cynic might dismiss teamwork as just another management fad or quick-fix gimmick. But a close look reveals that much more than catchy buzz words are involved here. The team approach to managing organizations is having diverse and substantial impacts on organizations and individuals. Teams promise to be a cornerstone of progressive management for the foreseeable future. According to management expert Peter Drucker, tomorrow's organization's will be flatter, information based, and orga-

OPENING CASE

(concluded)

To enhance harmony, Peterson made sure no single team leader rode roughshod over the others. Rather, leadership rotated based on who had the most pressing task. When the team needed to do field research, for example, the marketing person would take the lead. When technical developments became the issue, the R&D person took over, and so on.

From the beginning, the team agreed on a rock-solid deadline. Every August, the grill industry presents its goods at the National Hardware Show in Chicago. The team wanted to have a product ready for the August 1992 show, meaning they would have to plan, design, and build a new grill in a little less than two years.

In setting up the team, Peterson avoided a mistake that many managers make: He made sure the project was the primary responsibility of his key team members. He had seen too many undertakings fail because team members were spread too thin, working on three or four projects simultaneously. . . .

One of the biggest obstacles to any team project is getting the members to resolve disputes. In most cases they can work out differences among themselves, but sometimes they are at loggerheads, and no matter how empowered the group, the boss has to step in. Some of Thermos's marketing people, for instance, thought the grill's price—$299 retail for the base

model—was too high to sell at Kmart and Target. The wrangling went nowhere, so Peterson finally said, "Give me a reason why you *can't* sell it at that price level." No one could, so the price stuck. . . .

By now it was late 1991, and with the August deadline looming, the engineering team members stepped in and temporarily took the lead. Don't think, though, that engineering had been idle all this time. While marketing was out in the field doing research, engineering had been hunched over computers playing with ways to improve electric grill technology. Manufacturing had been making sure that any ideas kicked around for a new grill could be produced economically. . . .

By bringing the manufacturing people into the process from the start, the team avoided some costly mistakes later on. At one meeting in the winter of 1992, the designers said they wanted tapered legs on the grill. Manufacturing explained that tapered legs would have to be custom-made—an expensive undertaking—and eventually persuaded the team to make them straight. Under the old system, manufacturing wouldn't have known about the tapered legs until production time, and by then they would have caused a big cramp. Says R&D director [Frederick] Mather: "If that mistake hadn't been caught, we would have lost three to four months doing rework on the design."

After the first batch of grills rolled off the assembly line in the early summer of 1992, the team gave 100 of them to Thermos employees for testing, with instructions to use them hard. The outdoor Escoffers cooked in the rain and loaded up the grill's shelves with heavy food platters. That's how the team discovered that the shelves broke easily and needed to be made of stronger plastic. Says Mather: "I'd rather our people tell us the product has flaws than the customers at Target." . . .

Motivated by the Lifestyle project, the company is now using teams in all its other product lines. Early next year, for example, Thermos will introduce improved gas grills that, like the electric version, cook food faster and cleanly; they will also sport a radically new design. Says Peterson: "We needed to reinvent our product lines, and teamwork is doing it for us."

For Discussion

Why was the Lifestyle team so successful?
■ Additional discussion questions linking this case with the following material appear at the end of the chapter.

Source: Excerpted from B Dumaine, "Payoff from the New Management," *Fortune*, December 13, 1993, pp 103–10. © 1993 Time Inc. All rights reserved.

nized around teams.[1] This means managers will need to polish their team skills. General Electric's director of corporate management development, James Baughman, put it this way: "The people who will excel will be those who can build a team and integrate it with other teams."[2] Examples of the trend toward teams and teamwork abound.

Hospitals, for example, are installing health care teams to control runaway costs and improve quality of care. Team policing is a growing practice in public safety departments.[3] Commercial airline pilots are attending team-building seminars to improve cockpit communication and coordination skills.[4] Swedish carmaker Volvo has replaced some of its assembly lines with self-managed teams. Industrial giants such as Boeing have adopted cross-functional teams to speed product design and delivery by better coordinating the work of technical specialists. This is how the world's largest airplane manufacturer plans to get its next-generation Boeing 777 jetliner to market by 1995.

> In a major departure, it has handed the 777 over to Japanese-style design-build teams. The idea: Bunch marketing, engineering, manufacturing, finance, and service representatives on teams so that each department knows what the other is doing. Boeing also plans to arm the teams with "digital preassembly" design technology so that the 777 can be conceived, engineered, and "assembled" in three-dimensional computer models. Before a single piece of metal is cut, Boeing people in all disciplines will know if each phase of the design is feasible.[5]

Like Thermos, Boeing has staked its future competitiveness on teams and total quality management.

Emphasis in this chapter is on tapping the full and promising potential of work groups. We will (1) identify different types of work teams, (2) introduce a model of team effectiveness, (3) discuss keys to effective teamwork—such as trust, (4) explore applications of the team concept, and (5) review team-building techniques.

WORK TEAMS: DEFINITION, TYPES, AND EFFECTIVENESS

team Small group with complementary skills who hold themselves mutually accountable for common purpose, goals, and approach.

Jon R Katzenbach and Douglas K Smith, management consultants at McKinsey & Company, say it is a mistake to use the terms *group* and *team* interchangeably. After studying many different kinds of teams—from athletic to corporate to military—they concluded that successful teams tend to take on a life of their own. Katzenbach and Smith define a **team** as "a small number of people with complementary skills who are committed to a common purpose, performance goals, and approach for which they hold themselves mutually accountable."[6] Relative to the six-stage group development process discussed in Chapter 9, teams are task groups that have matured to the sixth stage. Because of conflicts over power and authority and unstable interpersonal relations, many work groups never qualify as a real team.[7] Katzenbach and Smith clarified the distinction this way: "The essence of a team is common commitment. Without it, groups perform as individuals; with it, they become a powerful unit of collective performance."[8] (See Table 12–1.)

When Katzenbach and Smith refer to "a small number of people" in their definition, they mean between 2 and 25 team members. They found effective teams to typically have fewer than 10 members.

TABLE 12–1

The Evolution of a Team

A work group becomes a team when
1. *Leadership* becomes a shared activity.
2. *Accountability* shifts from strictly individual to both individual and collective.
3. The group develops its own *purpose* or mission.
4. *Problem solving* becomes a way of life, not a part-time activity.
5. *Effectiveness* is measured by the group's collective outcomes and products.

Source: Condensed and adapted from J R Katzenbach and D K Smith, *The Wisdom of Teams: Creating the High-Performance Organization* (Boston: Harvard Business School Press, 1993), p 214.

A team
that has no prejudice
has no limits.

XEROX

The strongest team, the strongest business, the strongest country, is one where there is freedom to be yourself without inequality or prejudice.

We have seen prejudice hurt all those who participate in it. And we've seen togetherness and equality give power and joy.

That's why, at Xerox, we are dedicated to working towards a world where there is only one race... the human race.

Starting in 1968 we began a major effort, both within Xerox and in the communities around us, to make the concept of equal opportunity a reality.

In a 1968 memo, Xerox president Joseph Wilson said: "We, like all other Americans, share the responsibility for a color-blind nation and, in all honesty, we need not look beyond our own doorstep to find out why. But we can and will change."

And we did. Xerox developed programs in every phase of its structure, from pre-entry training up through the top of upper management.

Our minority programs in those 20 years made so much progress that we were awarded the Department of Labor Exemplary Voluntary Effort Award for affirmative action.

We've created a team that we believe is the strongest possible, without the

constraints of prejudice, to serve our clients proudly and productively.

But to us at Team Xerox, it's just the beginning. Until the whole world is a team that works together with respect, fairness and equality; until all of us are without prejudice; until we have only just begun.

**Team Xerox.
We document the world.**

Effective work teams are characterized by a shared commitment to a common purpose. It has been said, "There is no 'I' in the word 'team'."

(Courtesy Xerox Corporation)

A General Typology of Work Teams

Work teams are created for various purposes and thus face different challenges. Managers can deal more effectively with those challenges when they understand how teams differ. A helpful way of sorting things out is to consider a typology of work teams developed by Eric Sundstrom and his colleagues.[9] Four general types of work teams listed in Table 12–2 are (1) advice, (2) production, (3) project, and (4) action. Each of these labels identifies a basic *purpose*. For instance, advice teams generally make recommendations for managerial decisions. Less commonly do they actually make final decisions. In contrast, production and action teams carry out management's decisions.

Four key variables in Table 12–2 deal with technical specialization, coordination, work cycles, and outputs. Technical specialization is low when the team draws upon members' general experience and problem-solving ability. It is high when team members are required to apply technical skills acquired through higher education and/or extensive training. The degree of coordination with other work units is determined by the team's relative independence (low coordination) or interdependence (high coordination). Work cycles are the amount of time teams need to discharge their missions. The various outputs listed in Table 12–2 are intended to illustrate real-life impacts. A closer look at each type of work team is in order.[10]

Advice Teams As their name implies, advice teams are created to broaden the information base for managerial decisions. Quality circles, discussed later, are a prime example because they facilitate suggestions for improvement from volunteer production or service workers. Advice teams tend to have a low degree of technical specialization. Coordination also is low because advice teams work pretty much on their own. Ad hoc committees (e.g., the annual picnic committee) have shorter life cycles than standing committees (e.g., the grievance committee).

• TABLE 12~2   Four General Types of Work Teams and Their Outputs

Types and Examples	Degree of Technical Specialization	Degree of Coordination with Other Work Units	Work Cycles	Typical Outputs
Advice Committees Review panels, boards Quality circles Employee involvement groups Advisory councils	Low	Low	Work cycles can be brief or long; one cycle can be team life span.	Decisions Selections Suggestions Proposals Recommendations
Production Assembly teams Manufacturing crews Mining teams Flight attendant crews Data processing groups Maintenance crews	Low	High	Work cycles typically repeated or continuous process; cycles often briefer than team life span.	Food, chemicals Components Assemblies Retail sales Customer service Equipment repairs
Project Research groups Planning teams Architect teams Engineering teams Development teams Task forces	High	Low (for traditional units) or High (for cross-functional units)	Work cycles typically differ for each new project; one cycle can be team life span.	Plans, designs Investigations Presentations Prototypes Reports, findings
Action Sports team Entertainment groups Expeditions Negotiating teams Surgery teams Cockpit crews Military platoons and squads	High	High	Brief performance events, often repeated under new conditions, requiring extended training and/or preparation.	Combat missions Expeditions Contracts, lawsuits Concerts Surgical operations Competitive events

Source: Excerpted and adapted from E Sundstrom, K P De Meuse, and D Futrell, "Work Teams," *American Psychologist*, February 1990, p 125.

Production Teams   This second type of team is responsible for performing day-to-day operations. Minimal training for routine tasks accounts for the low degree of technical specialization. But coordination typically is high because work flows from one team to another. For example, railroad maintenance crews require fresh information about needed repairs from train crews.

Project Teams   Projects require creative problem solving, often involving the application of specialized knowledge. The Boeing 777 team discussed earlier, for example, has a high degree of technical specialization. It also requires a high degree of coordination among organizational subunits because it is cross functional. A pharmaceutical research team of biochemists, on the other hand, would interact less with other work units because it is relatively self-contained.

Action Teams   This last type of team is best exemplified by a Major League Baseball club. High specialization is combined with high coordination. Nine highly trained athletes play specialized defensive positions. But good defensive play is not enough because effective hitting is necessary. Moreover, coordination between the manager, base runners, base coaches, and the bull pen needs to be precise. So it is with airline cockpit crews, hospital surgery teams, mountain-climbing expeditions, rock music groups, labor contract negotiating teams, and police SWAT teams, among others. A unique challenge for action teams is to exhibit peak performance on demand.

This four-way typology of work teams is dynamic and changing, not static. Some teams evolve from one type to another. Other teams represent a combination of types. For example, consider the work of a team at General Foods: "About five years ago the company launched a line of ready-to-eat desserts by setting up a team of nine people with the freedom to operate like entrepreneurs starting their own business. The team even had to oversee construction of a factory with the technology required to manufacture their product."[11] This particular team was a combination advice-project-action team. In short, the General Foods team did everything but manufacture the end product themselves (that was done by production teams).

Work Team Effectiveness: An Ecological Model

The effectiveness of athletic teams is a straightforward matter of wins and losses. Things become more complicated, however, when the focus shifts to work teams in today's organizations.[12] Figure 12–1 lists two effectiveness criteria for work teams: performance and viability. According to Sundstrom and his colleagues: "*Performance* means acceptability of output to customers within or outside the organization who receive team products, services, information, decisions, or performance events (such as presentations or competitions)."[13] While the foregoing relates to satisfying the needs and expectations of outsiders such as clients, customers, and fans, another team-effectiveness criterion arises. Namely, **team viability,** defined as team member satisfaction and continued willingness to contribute. Are the team members better or worse off for having contributed to the team effort? A work team is not truly effective if it gets the job done but self-destructs in the process.[14]

Figure 12–1 is an *ecological* model because it portrays work teams within their organizational environment. In keeping with the true meaning of the word *ecology*—the study of interactions between organisms and their environments—this model emphasizes that work teams need an organizational life-support system. Six critical organizational context variables are listed in Figure 12–1. Work teams have a much greater chance of being effective if they are nurtured and facilitated by the organization. The team's purpose needs to be in concert with the organization's strategy. Similarly, team participation and autonomy require an organizational culture that values those processes. Team members also need appropriate technological tools and training. Teamwork needs to be reinforced by the organizational reward system. Such is not the case when pay and bonuses are tied solely to individual output. Phillips–Van Heusen, the clothing manufacturer, is a striking example of a company that rewards teamwork. The firm's founder, Lawrence S Phillips, offered each of the top 11 executives the chance to earn a $1 million bonus over a four-year period. *Fortune* explained the deal as follows: "The first $500,000 can be earned incrementally by meeting earnings-per-share goals for each year. If the company makes the combined target in the fourth year, each of the 11 receives

team viability   team members satisfied and willing to contribute.

• FIGURE 12~1

An Ecological Model of
Work Team Effectiveness

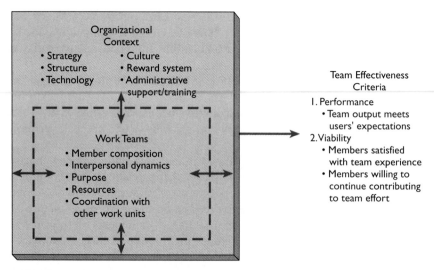

Source: Adapted in part from E Sundstrom, K P De Meuse, and D Futrell, "Work Teams," *American Psychologist*, February 1990, pp 120–33.

the second $500,000 as a kicker."[15] Thus, each executive has a strong *personal* incentive to help reach *collective* goals.

Regarding the internal processes of work teams, five important factors are listed in Figure 12–1. Chapters 9 and 10 provided a good background for dealing with these factors. Additional insights lie ahead as we turn our attention to cooperation, trust, and cohesiveness.

EFFECTIVE TEAMWORK THROUGH COOPERATION, TRUST, AND COHESIVENESS

As competitive pressures intensify, organizational success increasingly will depend on teamwork rather than individual stars. In fact, companies such as Microsoft and Xerox have gone so far as to fill the position of corporate president with a team of executives instead of an individual. According to Xerox's Chairman Paul Allaire, cooperation from top to bottom is the goal:

"I would hope that we have been clear enough that one of the criteria of this new organization is working together," he says. To underscore the issue, he says future Xerox leaders will be drawn only from those who can cooperate: "Anyone who isn't a team player would be automatically excluded from succession," he says.[16]

If this sort of commitment to teamwork has a familiar ring, it is because World Series baseball and Super Bowl football champions generally say they owe their success to it. Whether in the athletic arena or the world of business, three components of teamwork receiving the greatest attention are cooperation, trust, and cohesiveness. Let us explore the contributions each can make to effective teamwork.

Cooperation

Individuals are said to be cooperating when their efforts are systematically *integrated* to achieve a collective objective. The greater the integration, the greater the degree of cooperation.

Cooperation versus Competition   A widely held assumption among American managers is that "competition brings out the best in people." From an economic standpoint, business survival depends on staying ahead of the competition. But from an interpersonal standpoint, critics contend competition has been over-emphasized, primarily at the expense of cooperation.[17] According to Alfie Kohn, a strong advocate of greater emphasis on cooperation in our classrooms, offices, and factories:

> My review of the evidence has convinced me that there are two . . . important reasons for competition's failure. First, success often depends on sharing resources efficiently, and this is nearly impossible when people have to work against one another. Cooperation takes advantage of all the skills represented in a group as well as the mysterious process by which that group becomes more than the sum of its parts. By contrast, competition makes people suspicious and hostile toward one another and actively discourages this process. . . .
>
>   Second, competition generally does not promote excellence because trying to do well and trying to beat others simply are two different things. Consider a child in class, waving his arm wildly to attract the teacher's attention, crying, "Oooh! Oooh! Pick me!" When he is finally recognized, he seems befuddled. "Um, what was the question again?" he finally asks. His mind is focused on beating his classmates, not on the subject matter.[18]

Research Support for Cooperation   After conducting a meta-analysis of 122 studies encompassing a wide variety of subjects and settings, one team of researchers concluded:

1. Cooperation is superior to competition in promoting achievement and productivity.
2. Cooperation is superior to individualistic efforts in promoting achievement and productivity.
3. Cooperation without intergroup competition promotes higher achievement and productivity than cooperation with intergroup competition.[19]

Given the size and diversity of the research base, these findings strongly endorse cooperation in modern organizations. Cooperation can be encouraged by reward systems that reinforce teamwork as well as individual achievement.

   Another study involving 84 male US Air Force trainees uncovered an encouraging link between cooperation and favorable race relations. After observing the subjects interact in three-man teams during a management game, the researchers concluded: "[Helpful] teammates, both black and white, attract greater respect and liking than do teammates who have not helped. This is particularly true when the helping occurs voluntarily."[20] These findings suggest that managers can enhance equal employment opportunity and diversity programs by encouraging *voluntary* helping behavior in interracial work teams. Accordingly, it is reasonable to conclude that voluntary helping behavior could build cooperation in mixed-gender teams and groups as well.

   A more recent study involving 72 health care professionals in a US Veterans Affairs Medical Center found a negative correlation between cooperation and team size. In other words, cooperation diminished as the health-care team became larger.[21] Managers thus need to restrict the size of work teams if they desire to facilitate cooperation.

Trust

These have not been good times for trust in corporate America. Years of mergers, downsizings, layoffs, and broken promises have left many employees justly cynical about trusting management. According to one recent study in the United States, "only 12% of survey respondents trust public statements made by corporations."[22] Clearly, managers need to take constructive action to close what *Fortune* magazine has called "the trust gap."[23] Jack Welch, General Electric's chief executive officer, recently framed the challenge this way:

> Trust is enormously powerful in a corporation. People won't do their best unless they believe they'll be treated fairly—that there's no cronyism and everybody has a real shot. The only way I know to create that kind of trust is by laying out your values and then walking the talk. You've got to do what you say you'll do, consistently, over time.[24]

In this section, we examine the concept of trust and introduce six practical guidelines for building trust.

trust Reciprocal faith in others' intentions and behavior.

A Cognitive Leap   **Trust** is defined as reciprocal faith in others' intentions and behavior. Experts on the subject explain the reciprocal (give-and-take) aspect of trust as follows:

> When we see others acting in ways that imply that they trust us, we become more disposed to reciprocate by trusting in them more. Conversely, we come to distrust those whose actions appear to violate our trust or to distrust us.[25]

In short, we tend to give what we get: trust begets trust; distrust begets distrust. (Take a few moments now to complete the OB Exercise.)

Trust involves "a cognitive 'leap' beyond the expectations that reason and experience alone would warrant"[26] (see Figure 12–2). For example, suppose a member of a newly formed class project team works hard, based on the assumption that her teammates also are working hard. That assumption, on which her trust is based, is a cognitive leap that goes beyond her actual experience with her teammates. When you trust someone, you have *faith* in their good intentions. The act of trusting someone, however, carries with it the inherent risk of betrayal.[27] Progressive managers believe that the benefits of interpersonal trust far outweigh any risks of betrayed trust.

How to Build Trust   Management professor/consultant Fernando Bartolomé offers the following six guidelines for building and maintaining trust.

1. *Communication.*   Keep team members and employees informed by explaining policies and decisions and providing accurate feedback. Be candid about one's own problems and limitations.
2. *Support.*   Be available and approachable. Provide help, advice, coaching, and support for team members' ideas.
3. *Respect.*   Delegation, in the form of real decision-making authority, is the most important expression of managerial respect. Actively listening to the ideas of others is a close second.
4. *Fairness.*   Be quick to give credit and recognition to those who deserve it. Make sure all performance appraisals and evaluations are objective and impartial.

OB EXERCISE

Measuring Interpersonal Trust

Instructions:

Think of a specific individual who plays an important role in your present life (e.g., present or future spouse, friend, supervisor, co-worker, team member, etc.) and rate his/her trustworthiness for each statement according to the following scale.

Strongly   Strongly
Disagree   Agree
1—2—3—4—5—6—7—8—9—10

Score

Overall Trust

1. I can expect this person to play fair. _____
2. I can confide in this person and know she or he desires to listen. _____
3. I can expect this person to tell me the truth. _____

Emotional Trust

4. This person would never intentionally misrepresent my point of view to other people. _____
5. I can confide in this person and know that he or she will not discuss it with others. _____

Reliability

6. If this person promised to do me a favor, she or he would carry out that promise. _____
7. If I had an appointment with this person, I could count on him or her showing up. _____
8. I could lend this person money and count on getting it back as soon as possible. _____

Total score = _____

Trustworthiness Scale

65–80 = High (Trust is a precious thing.)
24–64 = Moderate (Be careful; get a rearview mirror.)
8–23 = Low (Lock up your valuables!)

Source: Adapted from C Johnson-George and W C Swap, "Measurement of Specific Interpersonal Trust: Construction and Validation of a Scale to Assess Trust in a Specific Other," *Journal of Personality and Social Psychology,* December 1982, pp 1306–17.

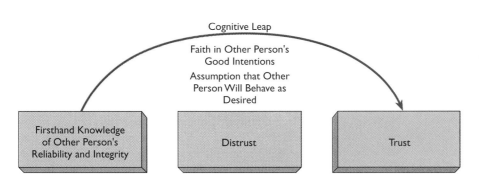

FIGURE 12–2
Interpersonal Trust Involves a Cognitive Leap

5. *Predictability.* As mentioned previously, be consistent and predictable in your daily affairs. Keep both expressed and implied promises.

6. *Competence.* Enhance your credibility by demonstrating good business sense, technical ability, and professionalism.[28]

Trust needs to be earned; it cannot be demanded.[29]

Cohesiveness

cohesiveness A sense of "we-ness" helps group stick together.

Cohesiveness is a process whereby "a sense of 'we-ness' emerges to transcend individual differences and motives."[30] Members of a cohesive group stick together. They are reluctant to leave the group. Cohesive group members stick together for one or both of the following reasons: (1) because they enjoy each others' company or (2) because they need each other to accomplish a common goal. Accordingly, two types of group cohesiveness, identified by sociologists, are socio-emotional cohesiveness and instrumental cohesiveness.[31]

socio-emotional cohesive-ness Sense of togetherness based on emotional satisfaction.

instrumental cohesiveness Sense of togetherness based on mutual dependency needed to get the job done.

Socio-Emotional and Instrumental Cohesiveness **Socio-emotional cohesive-ness** is a sense of togetherness that develops when individuals derive emotional satisfaction from group participation. Most general discussions of group cohesiveness are limited to this type. However, from the standpoint of getting things accomplished in task groups and teams, we cannot afford to ignore instrumental cohesiveness. **Instrumental cohesiveness** is a sense of togetherness that develops when group members are mutually dependent on one another because they believe they could not achieve the group's goal by acting separately. A feeling of "we-ness" is *instrumental* in achieving the common goal. Both types of cohesiveness are essential to productive teamwork.

Lessons from Group Cohesiveness Research After reviewing the relevant research literature, a Texas A&M University scholar concluded:

- Highly cohesive groups have greater member satisfaction than groups with low cohesiveness.
- High-cohesion groups are more effective than low-cohesion groups.
- Members of highly cohesive groups communicate more frequently and more positively than members of low-cohesion groups.[32]

In a second study of 125 groups with interaction problems, trained observers found lack of cohesiveness to be the number one problem. Leadership was the next greatest problem.[33]

The relationship between cohesiveness and performance remains ambiguous. Studies have found a mixture of positive, negative, and neutral relationships. This unexpected trend is partially due to researchers using inconsistent measures of cohesiveness.[34]

Putting Cohesiveness to Work Because cohesiveness has proved to be an important component of effective teamwork, managers need to take constructive steps to foster both types (see Table 12–3). A good example is Westinghouse's highly automated military radar electronics plant in College Station, Texas. Compared with their counterparts at a traditional factory in Baltimore, each of the Texas plant's 500 employees produces eight times more, at half the per-unit cost.

Socio-Emotional Cohesiveness

Keep the group relatively small.

Strive for a favorable public image to increase the status and prestige of belonging.

Encourage interaction and cooperation.

Emphasize members' common characteristics and interests.

Point out environmental threats (e.g., competitors' achievements) to rally the group.

Instrumental Cohesiveness

Regularly update and clarify the group's goal(s).

Give every group member a vital "piece of the action."

Channel each group member's special talents toward the common goal(s).

Recognize and equitably reinforce every member's contributions.

Frequently remind group members they need each other to get the job done.

• ↗ TABLE 12–3

Steps Managers Can Take to Enhance the Two Types of Group Cohesiveness

The key, says Westinghouse, is not the robots but the people. Employees work in teams of 8 to 12. Members devise their own solutions to problems. Teams measure daily how each person's performance compares with that of other members and how the team's performance compares with the plant's. Joseph L Johnson, 28, a robotics technician, says that is a big change from a previous hourly factory job where he cared only about ''picking up my paycheck.'' Here, peer pressure ''makes sure you get the job done.''[35]

Self-selected work teams (in which people pick their own teammates) and off-the-job social events can stimulate socio-emotional cohesiveness.[36] The fostering of socio-emotional cohesiveness needs to be balanced with instrumental cohesiveness. The latter can be encouraged by making sure everyone in the group recognizes and appreciates each member's vital contribution to the group goal. While balancing the two types of cohesiveness, managers need to remember that group-think theory and research, discussed in Chapter 9, cautions against too much cohesiveness.

This section strives to bring the team approach to life for present and future managers. It does so by exploring two different team formats found in the workplace today: quality circles and self-managed teams. We have chosen these two particular applications of teamwork, out of a growing variety, for three reasons: First, they are sharply contrasting approaches to teamwork. Managers can gain valuable insights about work teams by understanding their basic differences. Second, each is established enough to be generally recognizable. Third, both approaches have been evaluated by OB researchers.

Table 12–4 provides a conceptual foundation for this section by highlighting important distinctions between quality circles and self-managed teams. Quality circles involve limited empowerment in the form of consultation (recall our discussion in Chapter 10). Thus, they qualify as *advice* teams (as described in Table 12–2). Self-managed teams, in contrast, enjoy a high degree of empowerment through delegation. Production, project, and/or action teams may be self-managed because decision authority can be delegated to teams in virtually any part of the organization. Regarding membership, quality circles rely on volunteers while employees are assigned to self-managed teams or selected by the team itself. Another vital distinction involves the team's relationship to the organization's

TEAMS IN ACTION: FROM QUALITY CIRCLES TO SELF-MANAGED TEAMS

TABLE 12~4
Some Basic Distinctions
between Quality Circles and
Self-Managed Teams

	Quality Circles	**Self-Managed Teams**
Type of team (see Table 12–2)	Advice	Production, project, or action
Type of empowerment (see Figure 10–3)	Consultation	Delegation
Basis of membership	Voluntary	Assigned
Relationship to organization structure	Parallel	Integrated
Focus of influence	Lower level operations	Possibly all organizational levels and functions, depending upon makeup of team

structure and hierarchy. Quality circles are called parallel structures[37] because they exist outside normal channels of authority and communication. Self-managed teams, on the other hand, are integrated into the basic organizational structure. Quality circles make recommendations to management which retains all decision-making authority. Self-managed teams, meanwhile, make and implement their own decisions. Finally, quality circles primarily influence production and service operations at the lowest levels. Self-managed teams tend to have much broader influence because of greater reliance on technical and staff specialists throughout the organization.

Keeping these conceptual distinctions in mind, let us examine quality circles and self-managed teams more closely.

Quality Circles

quality circles Small groups of volunteers who strive to solve quality-related problems.

Quality circles are small groups of people from the same work area who voluntarily get together to identify, analyze, and recommend solutions for problems related to quality, productivity, and cost reduction. Some prefer the term *quality control circles*. With an ideal size of 10 to 12 members, they typically meet for about 60 to 90 minutes on a regular basis. Some companies allow meetings during work hours, others encourage quality circles to meet after work on employees' time. Once a week or twice a month are common schedules. Management facilitates the quality circle program through skills training and listening to periodic presentations of recommendations. Monetary rewards for suggestions tend to be the exception rather than the rule. Intrinsic motivation, derived from learning new skills and meaningful participation, is the primary payoff for quality circle volunteers.

The Quality Circle Movement   American quality control experts helped introduce the basic idea of quality circles to Japanese industry soon after World War II. The idea eventually returned to the United States and reached fad proportions during the 1970s and 1980s. Proponents made zealous claims about how quality circles were the key to higher productivity, lower costs, employee development, and improved job attitudes. At its zenith during the mid-1980s, the quality circle movement claimed millions of employee participants around the world. Hundreds of US companies and government agencies adopted the idea under a variety of labels.[38] Dramatic growth of quality circles in the United States has been attributed to (1) a desire to replicate Japan's industrial success, (2) America's penchant for business fads, and (3) the relative ease of installing quality circles without restruc-

● FIGURE 12~3   A Life-Cycle Model of Quality Circle Programs

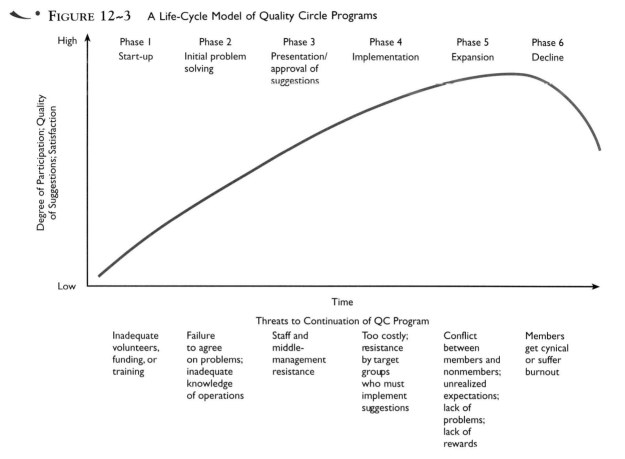

Source: Adapted from G E Ledford, Jr, E E Lawler III, and S A Mohrman, "The Quality Circle and Its Variations," in *Productivity in Organizations,* eds J P Campbell, R J Campbell and Associates (San Francisco: Jossey-Bass, 1988), pp 255–94.

turing the organization.[39] All too often, however, early enthusiasm gave way to disappointment, apathy, and abandonment.[40]

But quality circles, if properly administered and supported by management, can be much more than a management fad seemingly past its prime. According to USC researchers Edward E Lawler and Susan A Mohrman, "quality circles can be an important first step toward organizational effectiveness through employee involvement."[41] As we will see later, quality circles can be a stepping-stone to self-managed teams.

A life-cycle perspective of quality circles helps us better appreciate their promises and pitfalls.

A Life-Cycle Perspective of Quality Circle Programs   The six-phase life-cycle model in Figure 12–3 makes two important contributions to management's thinking. First, it portrays an organization's quality circle program as a step-by-step evolution rather than a one-shot deal. Second, it warns of potentially fatal problems during each phase. By systematically anticipating and addressing each set of problems along the bottom of Figure 12–3, managers can reach and prolong phase 5 (the expansion phase).

Management's first significant hurdle is to sell the idea to suspicious and possibly mistrusting employees. Remember, *volunteers* are the lifeblood of quality circles. This can be a particularly hard sell with militant union members. Imagine yourself as a manager at Scott Paper Company in Chester, Pennsylvania, trying to win over John Brodie, the president of United Paperworkers Local 448. *Business Week* quoted Brodie as saying:

> What the company wants is for us to work like the Japanese. Everybody go out and do jumping jacks in the morning and kiss each other when they go home at night. You work as a team, rat on each other, and lose control of your destiny. That's not going to work in this country.[42]

This sort of opposition to quality circles or any other form of teamwork needs to be overcome with training, honesty, and patience.[43] Monetary rewards can help, too. Beyond overcoming resistance, quality circle members need to be adequately trained in problem-solving and presentation skills. A good working knowledge of company operations also is a must. Otherwise, unrealistic recommendations will be made. Resistance from supervisors and middle managers, who sometimes view employee participation as a threat to their authority, needs to be neutralized. This can be accomplished through their personal involvement and recognition of benefits for management.

Another problem, encountered in phase 4, relates to quality circles being outside the normal hierarchy. Just because one group of managers has endorsed a proposal made during a quality circle presentation, prompt implementation by other managers does not automatically follow. The parallel or ad hoc structure of quality circles makes implementation very problematic. In phase 5, a whole host of problems can arise. Not the least being that the quality circle can work itself out of business by running out of problems. If the threats to success during phases 1 through 5 are allowed to accumulate, then cynicism and burnout will eventually kill the program.

Insights from Field Research on Quality Circles   A body of objective field research on quality circles is growing. Still, much of what we know comes from testimonials and case histories from managers and consultants who have a vested interest in demonstrating the technique's success. Although documented failures are scarce, one expert concluded that quality circles have failure rates of more than 60 percent.[44] Poor implementation is probably more at fault than the quality circle concept itself.[45]

To date, field research on quality circles has been inconclusive. Lack of standardized variables is the main problem, as it typically is when comparing the results of field studies.[46] Team participation programs of all sizes and shapes have been called quality circles. Here's what we have learned to date. A case study of military and civilian personnel at a US Air Force base found a positive relationship between quality circle participation and desire to continue working for the organization. The observed effect on job performance was slight. A longitudinal study spanning 24 months revealed that quality circles had only a marginal impact on employee attitudes but had a positive impact on productivity. In a more recent study, utility company employees who participated in quality circles received significantly better job performance ratings and were promoted more frequently than nonparticipants. This suggests that quality circles live up to their billing as a good employee development technique.[47]

Overall, quality circles are a promising participative management tool, *if they are carefully implemented and supported by all levels of management during the first five phases of the program life cycle.*

Strengthening Quality Circles   In addition to doing a better job of implementing and supporting quality circles during later phases of the life cycle, management can take other constructive steps as well. Lawler and Mohrman recommend the following changes:

> The most important of the changes is probably the development of a gainsharing formula that will let everyone participate in the benefits of performance improvement. Other possible approaches include improved information and education for circle members and the use of training, appraisal, and rewards to develop participative supervision. The suggested reward, information, and education system changes involve changing the work organization in some important ways. In essence, they call for making it a more active organization for lower-level participants by giving them new kinds of knowledge, information, supervision, and rewards. This reinforces the fact that an organization that wants to sustain a participative parallel structure must become more participative in its day-to-day business.[48]

The call for a linkage between quality circles and gainsharing strikes an important cultural cord. American workers, more so than their Japanese counterparts, expect to share directly in the fruits of their suggestions and recommendations.

Self-Managed Teams

Have you ever thought you could do a better job than your boss? Well, if the trend toward self-managed work teams continues to grow as predicted, you just may get your chance. Entrepreneurs and artisans often boast of not having a supervisor. The same generally cannot be said for employees working in organizational offices and factories. But things are changing. For example, consider the following situations:

> At a General Mills cereal plant in Lodi, California, teams . . . schedule, operate, and maintain machinery so effectively that the factory runs with no managers present during the night shift.[49]

> [Teams of United Steel Worker's Union members] run Inland Steel Industries Inc. and Nippon Steel Corp.'s $1.1 billion joint venture in New Carlisle, Ind.—with no foremen. Workers share profits and production bonuses, and all make the same pay—about $50,000 . . . [in 1992].[50]

General Mills has found that, when it comes to management, less can mean more. At the Lodi plant, some of the self-managed teams have set higher production goals for themselves than those formerly set by management. Self-managed teamwork does have its price tag, however. "Training alone costs $70,000 per worker"[51] at the New Carlisle steel plant. This section explores self-managed teams by looking at their past, present, and future.

What Are Self-Managed Teams?   Something much more complex is involved than this apparently simple label suggests. The term *self-managed* does not mean simply turning workers loose to do their own thing. Indeed, as we will see, an organization embracing self-managed teams should be prepared to undergo revolutionary changes in management philosophy, structure, staffing and training practices, and reward systems. Moreover, the traditional notions of managerial

While self-managed teams are not yet the norm in most companies, these workers at General Mills' Lodi, California, plant operate the night shift without a single manager being present.

(Copyright 1990 Doug Menuez/Reportage)

authority and control are turned on their heads. Not surprisingly, many managers strongly resist giving up the reins of power to people they view as subordinates. Another potential stumbling block worth watching is US labor laws, which are based on an adversarial relationship between management and organized labor. According to *Business Week,* ''the best insurance may be truly to empower employees on teams, even if they represent only themselves.''[52]

self-managed teams
Groups of employees granted administrative oversight for their work.

Self-managed teams are defined as groups of workers who are given administrative oversight for their task domains. Administrative oversight involves delegated activities such as planning, scheduling, monitoring, and staffing. These are chores normally performed by managers. In short, employees in these unique work groups act as their own supervisor.[53] Self-managed teams are variously referred to as semiautonomous work groups, autonomous work groups, and superteams. A common feature of self-managed teams, particularly among those above the shop-floor or clerical level, is **cross-functionalism.** In other words, specialists from

cross-functionalism Team made up of technical specialists from different areas.

different areas are put on the same team. Amgen, a rapidly growing biotechnology company in Thousand Oaks, California, is literally run by cross-functional, self-managed teams.

> There are two types: product development teams, known as PDTs, which are concerned with everything that relates to bringing a new product to market, and task forces, which do everything else. The members of both come from all areas of the company, including marketing and finance as well as the lab bench. The groups range from five or six employees up to 80 and usually report directly to senior management. In a reversal of the normal process, department heads called facilitators don't run teams; they work for them, making sure they have the equipment and money they need. Teams may meet weekly, monthly, or whenever the members see fit.[54]

Extensive coverage in the popular media in recent years has created the impression that self-managed teams have become the norm. The fact is they still are not very far beyond the experimental stage. According to *Training* magazine's 1993 survey of organizations of all types across the United States, only 29 percent

Among organizations* with self-directed teams, percent indicating that teams perform these functions on their own . . .	
Set work schedules	72
Training	65
Set production quotas/performance targets	57
Deal directly with external customers	58
Performance appraisals	47
Deal with vendors/suppliers	45
Purchase equipment or services	42
Budgeting	36
Hiring	29
Firing	22

• ➤ TABLE 12–5
Survey Evidence: What Self-Managing Teams Manage

* US organizations with 100 or more employees.
Source: Excerpted from P Froiland, "The Teaming of America," *Training*, October 1993, pp 58–59. Reprinted with permission from the October 1993 issue of *Training* Magazine. Copyright 1993. Lakewood Publications, Minneapolis, MN. All rights reserved. Not for resale.

reportedly had at least one self-managed or semiautonomous work team.[55] Among the companies with self-managed teams, the task most commonly delegated to the teams was work scheduling (see Table 12–5). The least common team chores were hiring and firing. Most of today's self-managed teams remain bunched at the shop-floor level in factory settings. Experts predict growth of the practice in the managerial ranks and in service operations.[56]

Historical and Conceptual Roots of Self-Managed Teams Self-managed teams are an outgrowth of a blend of behavioral science and management practice.[57] Group dynamics research of variables such as cohesiveness initially paved the way. A later stimulus was the socio-technical systems approach in which first British, and then American researchers, tried to harmonize social and technical factors. Their goal was to simultaneously increase productivity and employees' quality of work life. More recently, the idea of self-managed teams has gotten a strong boost from job design and participative management advocates. Recall our discussion of Hackman and Oldham's job characteristics model in Chapter 6. According to their model, internal motivation, satisfaction, and performance can be enhanced through five core job characteristics. Of those five core factors, increased *autonomy* is a major benefit for members of self-managed teams. Three types of autonomy are method, scheduling, and criteria autonomy (see the OB Exercise). Members of self-managed teams score high on group autonomy. Autonomy empowers those who are ready and able to handle added responsibility. How did you score? Finally, the social learning theory of self-management, as discussed in Chapter 8, has helped strengthen the case for self-managed teams.

The net result of this confluence is the continuum in Figure 12–4. The traditional clear-cut distinction between manager and managed is being blurred as subordinates are delegated greater authority and granted increased autonomy. Importantly, self-managed teams do not eliminate the need for all managerial control (see the upper right-hand corner of Figure 12–4). Semiautonomous work teams represent a balance between managerial and group control.

Are Self-Managed Teams Effective? Research Evidence As with quality circles, much of what we know about self-managed teams comes from testimonials and case studies. Fortunately, a body of higher quality field research is slowly

OB EXERCISE

Measuring Work Group Autonomy

Instructions:

Think of your present (or past) job and work groups. Characterize the group's situation by circling one number on the following scale for each statement. Add your responses for a total score:

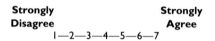

Strongly Disagree						Strongly Agree
1—2—3—4—5—6—7						

Work Method Autonomy

1. My work group decides how to get the job done. _____
2. My work group determines what procedures to use. _____
3. My work group is free to choose its own methods when carrying out its work. _____

Work Scheduling Autonomy

4. My work group controls the scheduling of its work. _____
5. My work group determines how its work is sequenced. _____
6. My work group decides when to do certain activities. _____

Work Criteria Autonomy

7. My work group is allowed to modify the normal way it is evaluated so some of our activities are emphasized and some deemphasized. _____
8. My work group is able to modify its objectives (what it is supposed to accomplish). _____
9. My work group has some control over what it is supposed to accomplish. _____

Total score = _____

Norms
9–26 = Low autonomy
27–45 = Moderate autonomy
46–63 = High autonomy

Source: Adapted from an individual autonomy scale in J A Breaugh, "The Work Autonomy Scales: Additional Validity Evidence," *Human Relations,* November 1989, pp 1033–56.

⤙ • FIGURE 12~4
The Evolution of Self-Managed Work Teams

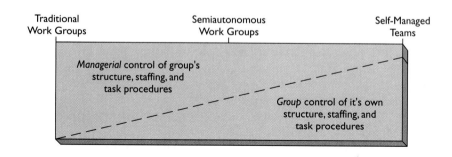

Traditional Work Groups

Semiautonomous Work Groups

Self-Managed Teams

Managerial control of group's structure, staffing, and task procedures

Group control of it's own structure, staffing, and task procedures

developing. A review of three meta-analyses covering 70 individual studies concluded that self-managed teams had

- A positive impact on productivity.
- A positive impact on specific attitudes relating to self-management (e.g., responsibility and control).
- No significant impact on general attitudes (e.g., job satisfaction and organizational commitment).
- No significant impact on absenteeism or turnover.[58]

Although encouraging, these results do not qualify as a sweeping endorsement of self-managed teams. Nonetheless, experts say the trend toward self-managed work teams will continue upward in the United States because of a strong cultural bias in favor of direct participation. Managers need to be prepared for the resulting shift in organizational administration.

Setting the Stage for Self-Managed Teams   Experience shows that it is better to build a new production or service facility around self-managed teams than to attempt to convert an existing one. The former approach involves so-called ''green field sites.'' General Foods, for example, pioneered the use of autonomous work teams in the United States in 1971 by literally building its Topeka, Kansas, Gravy Train pet food plant around them.[59] Green field sites give management the advantage of selecting appropriate technology and carefully screening job applicants likely to be good team players.

But the fact is, most organizations are not afforded green field opportunities. They must settle for introducing self-managed teams into an existing organization structure.[60] This is where Lawler and Mohrman's transitional model is helpful (see Figure 12–5). Even though their model builds a bridge specifically from quality circles to team organization, their recommendations apply to transition from any sort of organization structure to teams. As mentioned earlier, quality circles are a good stepping-stone from a nonparticipative organization to one driven by self-managed teams. A brief overview of each transition program is in order.

Making the Transition to Self-Managed Teams   Extensive *management training and socialization* are required to deeply embed Theory Y and participative management values in the organization's culture. This new logic necessarily has to start with top management and filter down. Otherwise, resistance among middle- and lower-level managers will block the transition to teams.[61] Some turnover can be expected among managers who refuse to adjust to broader empowerment. Both *technical and organizational redesign* are necessary. Self-managed teams may require special technology. Volvo's team-based auto assembly plant, for example, relies on portable assembly platforms rather than traditional assembly lines. Structural redesign of the organization must take place because self-managed teams are an integral part of the organization, not patched onto it as in the case of quality circles. For example, in one of Texas Instruments' computer chip factories a hierarchy of teams operates within the traditional structure. Four levels of teams are responsible for different domains. Reporting to the steering team that deals with strategic issues are quality-improvement, corrective-action, and effectiveness teams. TI's quality-improvement and corrective-action teams are cross-functional teams made up of middle managers and functional specialists such as accountants

• FIGURE 12~5

Making the Transition between Quality Circles and Self-Managed Teams

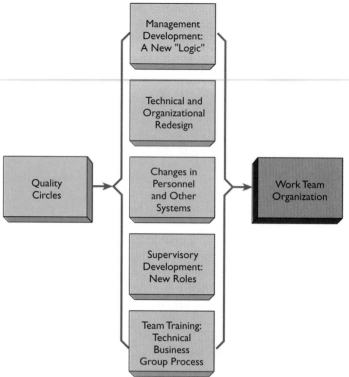

Source: E E Lawler III and S A Mohrman, "Quality Circles: After the Honeymoon," *Organizational Dynamics,* Spring 1987, p 50. Reprinted, by permission of publisher, from *Organizational Dynamics,* Spring 1987 © 1987, American Management Association, New York. All Rights Reserved.

and engineers. Production workers make up the effectiveness teams. The corrective-action teams are unique because they are formed to deal with short-term problems and are disbanded when a solution is found. All the other teams are long-term assignments.[62]

In turn, *personnel and reward systems* need to be adapted to encourage teamwork. Staffing decisions may shift from management to team members who hire their own co-workers. Individual bonuses must give way to team bonuses. *Supervisory development workshops* are needed to teach managers to be facilitators rather than order givers.[63] Finally, extensive *team training* is required to help team members learn more about technical details, the business as a whole, and how to be team players. This is where team building enters the picture.

TEAM BUILDING

team building Experiential learning aimed at better internal functioning of groups.

Team building is a catchall term for a whole host of techniques aimed at improving the internal functioning of work groups. Whether conducted by company trainers or outside consultants, team-building workshops strive for greater cooperation, better communication, and less dysfunctional conflict. Experiential learning techniques such as interpersonal trust exercises, conflict-handling role play sessions, and interactive games are common. For example, Germany's Opel uses Lego blocks to teach its auto workers the tight teamwork necessary for just-in-time production.[64] Meanwhile, in the United States, the Target department store chain has its salesclerks learn cooperation and teamwork with this exercise: "employees linked in a human chain must each wriggle through two Hula-Hoops moving in opposite directions, without breaking the chain or letting the hoops touch the ground.''[65] Rote memorization and lecture/discussion are discouraged by team-building experts who prefer this sort of *active* versus passive learning. Greater emphasis is placed on *how* work groups get the job done than on the job itself. Team building generally is carried out in the name of organization development (OD). The extensive use of team building appears to be justified. In a survey of human resource development managers from 179 Fortune 500 companies, team building reportedly was the most successful management technique.[66]

Complete coverage of the many team-building techniques would require a separate book. Consequently, the scope of our present discussion is limited to the purposes of team building and the day-to-day development of self-management skills. This foundation is intended to give you a basis for selecting appropriate team-building techniques from the many you are likely to encounter in the years ahead.[67]

The Purpose of Team Building/High-Performance Teams

According to Richard Beckhard, a respected authority on organization development, the four purposes of team building are

- To set goals and/or priorities.
- To analyze or allocate the way work is performed.
- To examine the way a group is working and its processes (such as norms, decision making, and communication).
- To examine relationships among the people doing the work.[68]

Trainers achieve these objectives by allowing team members to wrestle with simulated or real-life problems. Outcomes are then analyzed by the group to determine what group processes need improvement. Learning stems from recognizing and addressing faulty group dynamics. Perhaps one subgroup withheld key information from another, thereby hampering group progress. With cross-cultural teams becoming commonplace in today's global economy, team building is more important than ever. (see the International OB).

A nationwide survey of team members from many organizations, by Wilson Learning Corporation, provides a useful model or benchmark of what OD specialists expect of teams. The researchers' question was simply: ''What is a high-performance team?''[69] The respondents were asked to describe their peak experiences in work teams. Analysis of the survey results yielded the following eight attributes of high-performance teams:

1. *Participative leadership.* Creating an interdependency by empowering, freeing up, and serving others.
2. *Shared responsibility.* Establishing an environment in which all team members feel as responsible as the manager for the performance of the work unit.
3. *Aligned on purpose.* Having a sense of common purpose about why the team exists and the function it serves.
4. *High communication.* Creating a climate of trust and open, honest communication.
5. *Future focused.* Seeing change as an opportunity for growth.
6. *Focused on task.* Keeping meetings focused on results.
7. *Creative talents.* Applying individual talents and creativity.
8. *Rapid response.* Identifying and acting on opportunities.[70]

INTERNATIONAL OB

The Wild World of Cross-Cultural Team Building

Brussels—Anyone can talk about cultural differences. Fons Trompenaars tries to make his students feel them.

To do that, the Dutch leader of workshops on "multicultural" management teaches his students (mostly executives) to play a game invented by one of his colleagues, L J P Brug. The object: building towers made of paper.

Mr. Trompenaars, a 39-year-old former Royal Dutch/Shell executive, divides a group of several dozen Swedish managers into two groups. Four are designated as "international experts" in building paper towers, Everyone else becomes a native of a make-believe village called Derdia.

"Your culture loves towers but doesn't know how to build them," Mr. Trompenaars tells the Derdians. "It's a bit like the British car industry."

The experts are sent out of the room to learn to make paper towers and prepare to pass that skill on to Derdia. Meanwhile, Mr. Trompenaars initiates the Swedes into the strange customs of Derdia.

Derdians' greetings involve kissing one another on the shoulder. Holding out a hand to someone means "Please go away." If they disagree, Derdians say "Yes!" and nod their heads vigorously.

What's more, Derdian women have a taboo against using paper or scissors in the presence of men, while men would never use a pencil or a ruler in front of women.

The Swedes, reserved a moment ago, throw themselves into the task of acting like Derdians. They merrily tap one another, kiss shoulders and bray "Yessss!"

Soon, two "experts" are allowed back into the room for a brief study of Derdian culture. The Derdians flock to the experts and gleefully kiss their shoulders. The experts turn red. They seem lost already.

"Would you please sit?" asks Hans Olav Friberg, a young "expert" who, back home in Sweden, works for a company that makes flooring.

"Yessss!" the Derdians say in a chorus. But they don't sit down.

"Who is in charge here?" Mr. Friberg inquires. "Yessss!" the Derdians reply.

Mr. Friberg leaves the room to confer with his fellow experts. "They didn't understand us," he tells them. But fellow expert Hakan Kalmermo isn't about to be deterred by strange habits. He is taking charge. As he briskly practices making a paper tower, Mr. Kalmermo says firmly to the other experts: "The target is to have them produce one tower."

The four experts carry paper and other supplies to the adjoining room, now known às Derdia. They begin to explain the process to the Derdians very slowly, as if speaking to small children. When one of the Derdians

shows he understands the workings of a scissors, Mr. Kalmermo exclaims: "Good boy!"

Although Mr. Kalmermo works hard at making himself clear, the Derdians' customs and taboos obstruct progress. The men won't use rulers as long as women are around but don't explain this behavior to the experts. The answer to every question seems to be "yes." At the end of 30 minutes, no tower has been completed.

The game is over; now comes the self-criticism. "They treated us like idiots," protests one of the Derdians.

The lessons are clear, but Mr. Trompenaars drives them home: If you don't figure out basics of a foreign culture, you won't get much accomplished. And if your biases lead you to think of foreign ways as childish, the foreigners may well respond by acting childish.

Still, Mr. Kalmermo, the take-charge expert, thinks his team was on the right track. "If we'd had another hour," he says, "I think we would have had 15 towers built."

Source: B Hagerty, "Learning to Turn the Other Shoulder," *The Wall Street Journal*, June 14, 1993, pp B1, B3. Reprinted by permission of *The Wall Street Journal*, © 1993 Dow Jones & Company, Inc. All Rights Reserved Worldwide.

These eight attributes effectively combine many of today's most progressive ideas on management. Among them being participation, empowerment, service ethic, individual responsibility and development, self-management, trust, active listening, and envisioning. But patience and diligence are required. According to a manager familiar with work teams, "high-performance teams may take three to five years to build."[71] Let us keep this inspiring model of high-performance teams in mind as we conclude our discussion of team building.

Developing Team Members' Self-Management Skills

A promising dimension of team building has emerged in recent years. It is an extension of the behavioral self-management approach discussed in Chapter 8. Proponents call it **self-management leadership,** defined as the process of leading others to lead themselves. An underlying assumption is that self-managed teams likely will fail if team members are not expressly taught to engage in self-management behaviors. This makes sense because it is unreasonable to expect employees who are accustomed to being managed and led to suddenly manage and lead themselves. Transition training is required, as discussed in the prior section. A key transition to self-management involves *current managers* engaging in self-management leadership behaviors. This is team building in the fullest meaning of the term.

self-management leadership
Process of leading others to lead themselves.

Six self-management leadership behaviors were isolated in a field study of a manufacturing company organized around self-managed teams. The observed behaviors were

1. *Encourages self-reinforcement* (e.g., getting team members to praise each other for good work and results).
2. *Encourages self-observation/evaluation* (e.g., teaching team members to judge how well they are doing).
3. *Encourages self-expectation* (e.g., encouraging team members to expect high performance from themselves and the team).
4. *Encourages self-goal-setting* (e.g., having the team set its own performance goals).
5. *Encourages rehearsal* (e.g., getting team members to think about and practice new tasks).
6. *Encourages self-criticism* (e.g., encouraging team members to be critical of their own poor performance).[72]

According to the researchers, Charles Manz and Henry Sims, this type of leadership is a dramatic departure from traditional practices such as giving orders and/or making sure everyone gets along. Empowerment, not domination, is the overriding goal.

BACK TO THE OPENING CASE

Now that you have read Chapter 12, you should be able to answer the following questions about the Thermos/Lifestyle team case:

1. Using Table 12–1 as a guide, was the Lifestyle team simply a work group or really a *team?* Explain.
2. Was the Lifestyle team effective, according to the ecological model in Figure 12–1? Explain.
3. How important was trust in this case? Explain.
4. Why did Monte Peterson's transition to self-managed teams work out so well?
5. Based on the available evidence, was the Lifestyle team a "high-performance team?" Explain.

SUMMARY OF KEY CONCEPTS

1. *Explain how a work group becomes a team.*   A team is a mature group where leadership is shared, accountability is both individual and collective, the members have developed their own purpose, problem solving is a way of life, and effectiveness is measured by collective outcomes.

2. *Identify and describe the four types of work teams.*   Four general types of work teams are advice, production, project, and action teams. Each type has its characteristic degrees of specialization and coordination, work cycle, and outputs.

3. *Explain the ecological model of work team effectiveness.*   According to the ecological model, two effectiveness criteria for work teams are performance and viability. The performance criterion is met if the group satisfies its clients/customers. A work group is viable if its members are satisfied and continue contributing. An ecological perspective is appropriate because work groups require an organizational life-support system. For instance, group participation is enhanced by an organizational culture that values employee empowerment.

4. *List at least three things managers can do to build trust.*   Six recommended ways to build trust are through communication, support, respect (especially delegation), fairness, predictability, and competence.

5. *Distinguish two different types of cohesiveness.* Cohesive groups have a shared sense of togetherness or a ''we'' feeling. Socio-emotional cohesiveness involves emotional satisfaction. Instrumental cohesiveness involves goal-directed togetherness. Despite methodological inconsistencies, research is generally supportive of cohesiveness.

6. *Contrast quality circles and self-managed teams.*   Quality circles are groups of volunteers, usually at the lowest operating levels, who meet periodically to identify and solve quality and productivity problems. Based on Japan's success with quality circles, the practice grew to fad proportions in the United States during the 1970s and 1980s. Sloppy implementation too often led to unrealized expectations and disappointment.

   Self-managed teams, barely beyond the experimentation stage, hold great promise for tapping the full potential of today's employees by increasing their autonomy. They call for nonmanagerial employees to take over traditional managerial duties such as planning, scheduling, and even hiring.

7. *Discuss what must be done to set the stage for self-managed teams.*   Management must embed a new Theory Y logic in the organization's culture. Technology and the organization need to be redesigned to accommodate self-managed teams. Personnel changes and reward systems that reinforce teamwork are necessary. Supervisory training helps managers learn to be facilitators rather than traditional order givers. Team members need lots of training and team building to make them cooperative team players.

8. *Describe high-performance teams.*   Eight attributes of high-performance teams are (1) participative leadership, (2) shared responsibility, (3) aligned on purpose, (4) high communication, (5) future focused for growth, (6) focused on task, (7) creative talents applied, and (8) rapid response.

DISCUSSION QUESTIONS

1. Do you agree or disagree with Drucker's vision of more team-oriented organizations? Explain your assumptions and reasoning.

2. Which of the factors listed in Table 12–1 is most crucial to a successful team? Explain.

3. Why bother taking an ecological perspective of work team effectiveness?

4. In your personal friendships, how do you come to trust someone? How fragile is that trust? Explain.

5. Why is delegation so important to building organizational trust?

6. Why should a group leader strive for both socio-emotional and instrumental cohesiveness?

7. Which threats during the life cycle of the quality circle program deserve management's closest attention? Explain.

8. Would you like to work on a self-managed team? Explain.

9. How would you respond to a manager who said, "Why should I teach my people to manage themselves and work myself out of a job?"

10. Have you ever been a member of a high-performing team? If so, explain the circumstances and success factors.

EXERCISE

Objectives

1. To help you better understand the components of teamwork.
2. To give you a practical diagnostic tool to assess the need for team building.

Introduction

Teamwork is essential in modern organizations. Virtually all administrative activity is group oriented. The more present and future managers know about effective teamwork the better.

Instructions

If you currently have a full-time or part-time job, think of your immediate work group and circle an appropriate response for each of the following five questions. If you are not currently employed, think of your work group in your last job. Alternatively, you might want to evaluate a class project team, sorority, fraternity, or club to which you belong. Compute a total score and use the scoring key for interpretation.

Questionnaire[73]

1. To what extent do I feel "under wraps," that is, have private thoughts, unspoken reservations, or unexpressed feelings and opinions that I have not felt comfortable bringing out into the open?

1	2	3	4	5
Almost completely under wraps	Under wraps many times	Slightly more free and expressive than under wraps	Quite free and expressive much of the time	Almost completely free and expressive

2. How effective are we, in our team, in getting out and using the ideas, opinions, and information of all team members in making decisions?

1	2	3	4	5
We don't really encourage everyone to share their ideas, opinions, and information with the team in making decisions.	Only the ideas, opinions, and information of a few members are really known and used in making decisions.	Sometimes we hear the views of most members before making decisions and sometimes we disregard most members.	A few are sometimes hesitant about sharing their opinions, but we generally have good participation in making decisions.	Everyone feels his or her ideas, opinions, and information are given a fair hearing before decisions are made.

3. How well does the team work at its tasks?

1	2	3	4	5
Coasts, loafs, makes no progress	Makes a little progress; most members loaf	Progress is slow, spurts of effective work	Above average in progress and pace of work	Works well; achieves definite progress

4. How are differences or conflicts handled in our team?

1	2	3	4	5
Differences or conflicts are denied, suppressed, or avoided at all cost.	Differences or conflicts are recognized, but remain unresolved mostly.	Differences or conflicts are recognized and some attempts are made to work them through by some members, often outside the team meetings.	Differences and conflicts are recognized and some attempts are made to deal with them in our team.	Differences and conflicts are recognized and the team usually is working them through satisfactorily.

5. How do people relate to the team leader, chairman, or "boss"?

1	2	3	4	5
The leader dominates the team and people are often fearful or passive.	The leader tends to control the team, although people generally agree with the leader's direction.	There is some give and take between the leader and the team members.	Team members relate easily to the leader and usually are able to influence leader decisions.	Team members respect the leader, but they work together as a unified team with everyone participating and no one dominant.

Total score = _____

Questions for Consideration/ Class Discussion

1. Having analyzed your work group, is it a stronger or weaker team than you originally thought? Explain.

2. Which factor is your work group's biggest barrier to cooperative and productive teamwork?

3. What needs to be done to prepare your team for self-management?

NOTES

[1] See P F Drucker, "The Coming of the New Organization," *Harvard Business Review,* January–February 1988, 45–53.

[2] J Huey, "Where Managers Will Go," *Fortune,* January 27, 1992, p 51.

[3] See B Geber, "A New Kind of Police Department," *Training,* October 1993, pp 66–72.

[4] For example, see C Bovier, "Teamwork: The Heart of an Airline," *Training,* June 1993, pp 53–58.

[5] D Jones Yang and M Oneal, "How Boeing Does It," *Business Week,* July 9, 1990, p 49. Also see D Jones Yang, "Grace Robertson: Piloting a Superfast Rollout at Boeing," *Business Week,* August 30, 1993, p 77.

[6] J R Katzenbach and D K Smith, *The Wisdom of Teams: Creating the High-Performance Organization* (Boston: Harvard Business School Press, 1993), p 45.

[7] See L G Bolman and T E Deal, "What Makes a Team Work?" *Organizational Dynamics,* Autumn 1992, pp 34–44.

[8] J R Katzenbach and D K Smith, "The Discipline of Teams," *Harvard Business Review,* March–April 1993, p 112.

[9] See E Sundstrom, K P De Meuse, and D Futrell, "Work Teams," *American Psychologist,* February 1990, pp 120–33.

[10] For an alternative typology of teams, see S G Cohen, "New Approaches to Teams and Teamwork," in *Organizing for the Future: The New Logic for Managing Complex Organizations,* eds J R Galbraith, E E Lawler III and Associates (San Francisco: Jossey-Bass, 1993), chap. 8, pp 194–226.

[11] P King, "What Makes Teamwork Work?" *Psychology Today,* December 1989, p 16.

[12] An instructive overview of group effectiveness models can be found in P S Goodman, E Ravlin, and M Schminke, "Understanding Groups in Organizations," in *Research in Organizational Behavior,* eds L L Cummings and B M Staw (Greenwich, CT: JAI Press, 1987), vol. 9, pp 121–73.

[13] Sundstrom, De Meuse, and Futrell, "Work Teams," p 122.

[14] For a winning football coach's advice on teamwork, see R Rapaport, "To Build a Winning Team: An Interview with Head Coach Bill Walsh," *Harvard Business Review,* January–February 1993, pp 111–20.

[15] C Knowlton, "11 Men's Million-Dollar Motivator," *Fortune,* April 9, 1990, p 65.

[16] A Bennett, "Firms Run by Executive Teams Can Reap Rewards, Incur Risks," *The Wall Street Journal,* February 5, 1992, p B1.

[17] See "Work Teams Have Their Work Cut Out for Them," *HR Focus,* January 1993, p 24; W F Fechter, "The Competitive Myth," *Quality Progress,* May 1993, pp 87–88; and K G Salwen, "To Some Small Firms, Idea of Cooperating with Labor Is Foreign," *The Wall Street Journal,* July 27, 1993, pp A1–A6.

[18] A Kohn, "How to Succeed without Even Vying," *Psychology Today,* September 1986, pp 27–28.

[19] D W Johnson, G Maruyama, R Johnson, D Nelson, and L Skon, "Effects of Cooperative, Competitive, and Individualistic Goal Structures on Achievement: A Meta-Analysis," *Psychological Bulletin,* January 1981, pp 56–57. An alternative interpretation of the foregoing study that emphasizes the influence of situational factors can be found in J L Cotton and M S Cook, "Meta-Analysis and the Effects of Various Reward Systems: Some Different Conclusions from Johnson et al.," *Psychological Bulletin,* July 1982, pp 176–83.

[20] S W Cook and M Pelfrey, "Reactions to Being Helped in Cooperating Interracial Groups: A Context Effect," *Journal of Personality and Social Psychology,* November 1985, p 1243.

[21] See A J Stahelski and R A Tsukuda, "Predictors of Cooperation in Health Care Teams," *Small Group Research,* May 1990, pp 220–33.

[22] S Sherman, "A Brave New Darwinian Workplace," *Fortune,* January 25, 1993, p 51.

[23] See A Farnham, "The Trust Gap," *Fortune,* December 4, 1989, pp 56–78.

[24] "Jack Welch's Lessons for Success," *Fortune,* January 25, 1993, p 92.

[25] J D Lewis and A Weigert, "Trust as a Social Reality," *Social Forces,* June 1985, p 971.

[26] Ibid., p 970.

[27] For an interesting trust exercise, see G Thompson and P F Pearce, "The Team-Trust Game," *Training & Development Journal,* May 1992, pp 42–43.

[28] Adapted from F Bartolomé, "Nobody Trusts the Boss Completely—Now What?" *Harvard Business Review,* March–April 1989, pp 135–42.

[29] Personal and social consequences of trust are discussed in J B Rotter, "Interpersonal Trust, Trustworthiness, and Gullibility," *American Psychologist,* January 1980, pp 1–7.

[30] W Foster Owen, "Metaphor Analysis of Cohesiveness in Small Discussion Groups," *Small Group Behavior,* August 1985, p 416. Also see J Keyton and J Springston, "Redefining Cohesiveness in Groups," *Small Group Research,* May 1990, pp 234–54.

[31] This distinction is based on discussion in A Tziner, "Differential Effects of Group Cohesiveness Types: A Clarifying Overview," *Social Behavior and Personality,* no. 2, 1982, pp 227–39.

[32] See Owen, "Metaphor Analysis of Cohesiveness in Small Discussion Groups."

[33] Details may be found in S B Weinberg, S H Rovinski, L Weiman, and M Beitman, "Common Group Problems: A Field Study," *Small Group Behavior,* February 1981, pp 81–92.

[34] For a summary of cohesiveness research, see Goodman, Ravlin, and Schminke, "Understanding Groups in Organizations," in *Research in Organizational Behavior.* See also P E Mudrack, "Group Cohesiveness and Productivity: A Closer Look," *Human Relations,* September 1989, pp 771–85.

[35] G L Miles, "The Plant of Tomorrow Is in Texas Today," *Business Week,* July 28, 1986, p 76.

[36] See, for example, P Jin, "Work Motivation and Productivity in Voluntarily Formed Work Teams: A Field Study in China," *Organizational Behavior and Human Decision Processes,* 1993, pp 133–155.

[37] Based on discussion in E E Lawler III and S A Mohrman, "Quality Circles: After the Honeymoon," *Organizational Dynamics,* Spring 1987, pp 42–54. Also see B Sheehy, "Understanding Q Levels—From Quality Circles to Federal Budgets," *National Productivity Review,* Winter 1992–93, pp 3–7.

[38] The historical development of quality circles is discussed by C Stohl, "Bridging the Parallel Organization: A Study of Quality Circle Effectiveness," in *Organizational Communication,* ed M L McLaughlin (Beverly Hills, CA: Sage Publications, 1987), pp 416–30; T Li-Ping Tang, P Smith Tollison, and H D Whiteside, "The Effect of Quality Circle Initiation on Motivation to Attend Quality Circle Meetings and on Task Performance," *Personnel Psychology,* Winter 1987, pp 799–814; and N Kano, "A Perspective on Quality Activities in American Firms," *California Management Review,* Spring 1993, pp 12–31.

[39] Based on discussion in K Buch and R Spangler, "The Effects of Quality Circles on Performance and Promotions," *Human Relations,* June 1990, pp 573–82.

[40] See G R Ferris and J A Wagner III, "Quality Circles in the United States: A Conceptual Reevaluation," *The Journal of Applied Behavioral Science,* no. 2, 1985, pp 155–67.

[41] Lawler and Mohrman, "Quality Circles: After the Honeymoon," p 43. Also see E E Lawler III, "Total Quality Management and Employee Involvement: Are They Compatible?" *Academy of Management Executive,* February 1994, pp 68–76.

[42] J Hoerr, "The Payoff from Teamwork," *Business Week,* July 10, 1989, p 56.

[43] A good case study of resistance to team empowerment can be found in M Levinson, "Playing with Fire," *Newsweek,* June 21, 1993, pp 46–48.

[44] See M L Marks, "The Question of Quality Circles," *Psychology Today,* March 1986, pp 36–38, 42, 44, 46.

[45] See A K Naj, "Some Manufacturers Drop Effort to

Adopt Japanese Techniques," *The Wall Street Journal,* May 7, 1993, p A1.

[46] See E E Adam, Jr., "Quality Circle Performance," *Journal of Management,* March 1991, pp 25–39.

[47] See R P Steel and R F Lloyd, "Cognitive, Affective, and Behavioral Outcomes of Participation in Quality Circles: Conceptual and Empirical Findings," *The Journal of Applied Behavioral Science,* no. 1, 1988, pp 1–17; M L Marks, P H Mirvis, E J Hackett, and J F Grady, Jr., "Employee Participation in a Quality Circle Program: Impact on Quality of Work Life, Productivity, and Absenteeism," *Journal of Applied Psychology,* February 1986, pp 61–69; and Buch and Spangler, "The Effects of Quality Circles on Performance and Promotions."

[48] Lawler and Mohrman, "Quality Circles: After the Honeymoon," p. 52.

[49] B Dumaine, "Who Needs a Boss?" *Fortune,* May 7, 1990, p 52.

[50] S Baker and T Buell, Jr., "Buddy-Buddy at the Steel Smelter," *Business Week,* April 5, 1993, p 27.

[51] Ibid.

[52] For details, see A Bernstein, "Making Teamwork Work—and Appeasing Uncle Sam," *Business Week,* January 25, 1993, p 101; J Shiver, Jr., "NLRB Orders DuPont to Deal Directly with Union," *Los Angeles Times,* June 8, 1993, pp D1, D11; and J Case, "When Teamwork Is Un-American," *Inc.,* November 1993, pp 29–30.

[53] For example, see M Selz, "Testing Self-Managed Teams, Entrepreneur Hopes to Lose Job," *The Wall Street Journal,* January 11, 1994, pp B1–B2.

[54] A Erdman, "How to Keep that Family Feeling," *Fortune,* April 6, 1992, p 95.

[55] Data from P Froiland, "The Teaming of America," *Training,* October 1993, pp 58–59.

[56] See P S Goodman, R Devadas, and T L Griffith Hughson, "Groups and Productivity: Analyzing the Effectiveness of Self-Managing Teams," in *Productivity in Organizations,* eds J P Campbell, R J Campbell and Associates (San Francisco: Jossey-Bass, 1988), pp 295–327.

[57] Good background discussions can be found in work cited in note 56 and in C Lee, "Beyond Teamwork," *Training,* June 1990, pp 25–32.

[58] Drawn from Goodman, Devadas, and Hughson, "Groups and Productivity: Analyzing the Effectiveness of Self-Managing Teams."

[59] See R E Walton, "Work Innovations at Topeka: After Six Years," *The Journal of Applied Behavioral Science,* 1977, pp 422–33.

[60] For useful tips, see L Holpp, "Five Ways to Sink Self-Managed Teams," *Training,* September 1993, pp 38–42.

[61] See B Dumaine, "The New Non-Manager Managers," *Fortune,* February 22, 1993, pp 80–84. Also see "Easing the Fear of Self-Directed Teams," *Training,* August 1993, pp 14, 55–56.

[62] See Dumaine, "Who Needs a Boss?", pp 55, 58; and J Hillkirk, "Self-Directed Work Teams Give TI Lift," *USA Today,* December 20, 1993, p 8B.

[63] For an instructive case study on this topic, see C C Manz, D E Keating, and A Donnellon, "Preparing for an Organizational Change to Employee Self-Management: The Managerial Transition," *Organizational Dynamics,* Autumn 1990, pp 15–26.

[64] Based on K Lowry Miller, "GM's German Lessons," *Business Week,* December 20, 1993, pp 67–68.

[65] R Henkoff, "Companies that Train Best," *Fortune,* March 22, 1993, p 73.

[66] Data from E Stephan, G E Mills, R W Pace, and L Ralphs, "HRD in the Fortune 500: A Survey," *Training and Development Journal,* January 1988, pp 26–32.

[67] A good resource book on team building is W G Dyer, *Team Building: Issues and Alternatives,* 2nd ed (Reading, MA: Addison-Wesley Publishing, 1987). Also see Exhibit 3 in M L Marks and P M Mirvis, "Rebuilding After the Merger: Dealing with 'Survivor Sickness,'" *Organizational Dynamics,* Autumn 1992, pp 18–32.

[68] R Beckhard, "Optimizing Team-Building Efforts," *Journal of Contemporary Business,* Summer 1972, p 24.

[69] S Bucholz and T Roth, *Creating the High-Performance Team* (New York: John Wiley & Sons, 1987), p xi.

[70] Ibid., p 14.

[71] P King, "What Makes Teamwork Work?" *Psychology Today,* December 1989, p 17.

[72] Adapted from C C Manz and H P Sims, Jr., "Leading Workers to Lead Themselves: The External Leadership of Self-Managing Work Teams," *Administrative Science Quarterly,* March 1987, pp 106–29. Also see C C Manz, "Beyond Self-Managing Work Teams: Toward Self-Leading Teams in the Workplace," in *Research in Organizational Change and Development,* vol. 4, eds R W Woodman and W A Pasmore (Greenwich, CT: JAI Press, 1990), pp 273–99; C C Manz, "Self-Leading Work Teams: Moving Beyond Self-Management Myths," *Human Relations,* no. 11, 1992, pp 1119–40; and C C Manz, *Mastering Self-Leadership: Empowering Yourself for Personal Excellence* (Englewood Cliffs, NJ: Prentice-Hall, 1992).

[73] Excerpted from Dyer, *Team Building,* pp 69–71. Reprinted by permission of the publisher.

ORGANIZATIONAL PROCESSES

PART IV

ORGANIZATIONAL COMMUNICATION PROCESSES

Learning OBJECTIVES

When you finish studying the material in this chapter, you should be able to:

1. Describe the perceptual process model of communication.

2. Explain the contingency approach to media selection.

3. Contrast the communication styles of assertiveness, aggressiveness, and nonassertiveness.

4. Discuss the primary sources of both nonverbal communication and listener comprehension.

5. Identify and give examples of the three different listening styles.

6. Review the 10 keys to effective listening.

7. Discuss patterns of hierarchical communication and the grapevine.

8. Demonstrate your familiarity with four antecedents of communication distortion between managers and employees.

9. Explain collaborative computing and the related use of video conferencing and telecommuting.

10. Describe the process, personal, physical, and semantic barriers to effective communication.

Collaborative Computing Dramatically Affects Organizational Communication

Sharon Hoogstraten

Employees of Chemical Banking Corp. had been shaken by work-force cuts, reorganizations and a pending merger. Rumors often raced through the ranks, sapping productivity and morale.

But Bruce Hasenyager found a way to squelch the gossip in the bank's corporate-systems division: The senior vice president let employees post anonymous questions on an electronic bulletin board, accessible to anyone who was on the office computer network. Then he responded to the questions on-line.

"It became a powerful tool for building trust," Mr. Hasenyager says. "We could kill off the crazy rumors. When it was whispered around the water cooler that part of our group's work might be contracted out to IBM, I had a way to tell everyone at once that it was baloney."

But Chemical's electronic water cooler soon spun out of control. When Mr. Hasenyager resigned last year, following the completion of Chemical's merger with Manufacturers Hanover Trust, his successor became

uncomfortable with this unruly forum. After barbed criticism of management began appearing on the system, the new executive pulled the plug.

Computer networks—and the sticky management issues they present—are spreading across the workplace. In the first wave of desktop computerization, workers generally used their machines to perform tasks in isolation, such as writing, creating a financial spreadsheet, or designing graphics or products. But as more and more office computers are tied together in networks—using cables or phone lines, "servers" that store data and direct traffic, and a new class of software called groupware—the nature of personal computing is changing. And office life is changing along with it.

Electronic mail is probably the simplest and most familiar form of groupware, in which notes are zapped across a network between two desktop PCs. More sophisticated groupware programs connect many people together at the same time, often functioning like a suite of electronic conference rooms where many conversations can take place at the same time. The programs can also collect these silent conversations and create an electronic transcript. And they are not limited to words: Some groupware programs can sift, sort, and transmit scanned images, sound, and even video.

Because they enable hundreds of workers to share information simultaneously, groupware networks can

give lowly office workers intelligence previously available only to their bosses. Networks also can give the rank-and-file new access: the ability to join in on-line discussions with senior executives. In these interactions, people are judged more by what they say than by their rank on the corporate ladder.

"The cultural effect is enormous," says Bill Wilson, a manager at Johnson & Higgins, a New York insurance brokerage firm that links its professional staff with new network software. "It's helping to dissolve the old corporate hierarchy." . . .

But the proliferation of networks can also bring unintended tensions. In a corporate culture where information is already jealously guarded, some companies are finding employees unwilling to share their best work in network discussions. Managers like the ones at Chemical often feel the need to control what goes out across the network. . . .

This new electronic landscape can foster an egalitarian sense of empowerment among employees. Or it can be a tool of authoritarian managers, leading to loss of workplace privacy. For better or worse, "it's a powerful means of amplifying the style and character of a company and its managers," Mr. Hasenyager says.

At MTV Networks, groupware became a new weapon for the affiliate sales force. When the Viacom Inc. unit was battling last summer against rival Turner Broadcasting System Inc.'s Cartoon Channel, trying to get cable

very managerial function and activity involves some form of direct or indirect communication. Whether planning and organizing or directing and leading, managers find themselves communicating with and through others. Managerial decisions and organizational policies are ineffective unless they are understood by those respon-

OPENING CASE

(concluded)

operators to carry MTV's new Comedy Central network instead, salesmen in some areas were meeting unexpected resistance. Then a saleswoman in Chicago discovered that a cable system in her territory had been offered a special two-year, rock-bottom price by Cartoon Channel.

She typed this intelligence into a groupware network that tracks most day-to-day activity of the sales force. Others noticed that another salesman in Florida had also heard something about a new, more aggressive deal from the competition. "Suddenly it clicked; we'd figured out their game," says Kris Bagwell, the young MTV salesman who helped design the new network. Top MTV executives were told of the tactic and were able to counterattack by changing their own pricing and terms, saving several pending deals, according to Mr. Bagwell.

He says groupware gives management a better tool to follow what's going on in the field. "Let's say we need to know about every sales call last month on a Cox system where Nickelodeon was discussed," he says. "Or we need to know what people were hearing about Comedy Central's local ad sales in the Southeast last quarter. With a couple of mouse clicks, you can drill in and find what you need."

At Coopers & Lybrand's Atlanta office, William Jennings, director of fraud investigation services, used groupware to win a contract that he says he wouldn't have known about otherwise. Using a system that elec-

tronically clips and categorizes news wires, he came across a report of a food-service company in Hawaii that had an inventory-theft problem, apparently covered up by fraud. He quickly turned to an in-house Notes database and discovered that people in Coopers & Lybrand's Los Angeles office knew people at the victimized company.

After on-line consultations, he decided to offer Coopers & Lybrand's services to ferret out the fraud. Clicking into another groupware database, which cross-indexed the background and skills of 900 auditors, he searched for someone with prior law-enforcement experience, a C.P.A., and familiarity with food-service inventories. "We found him in Dallas, and put him on a plane the next day. Coopers got the contract, and the client got the right man for the job."

In some organizations, networks and groupware breach the lines of command. At Wright-Patterson Air Force Base in Ohio, which uses network software made by Quality Decision Management, of Taunton, Mass., "rank doesn't really matter when you're on-line," says Lt. Col. Donald Potter. "An enlisted man could send a message to a colonel." Five years ago, he says, "there wouldn't have been an easy way for a sergeant to share an idea with a colonel short of making a formal appointment to go see him in his office." . . .

But at some organizations, knowledge is power, and sharing doesn't come easily. This became clear at Price

Waterhouse, which uses Notes to connect 18,000 professionals. In an MIT study of an unnamed company—which others confirm was the big accounting firm—Prof. Wanda Orlikowsky found evidence that some junior employees wouldn't share information on the network because of the firm's intensely competitive culture.

As one explained to Ms. Orlikowsky: "The corporate psychology makes the use of Notes difficult, particularly in the consultant career path, which creates a back-stabbing, aggressive environment." Another said: "I'm trying to develop an area of expertise that makes me stand out. If I shared that with you, you'd get the credit and not me . . . . Power in this firm is client base and technical ability. Now if you put this information in a Notes database, you lose power." Price Waterhouse says it is happy with Notes.

For Discussion

Would you like to be networked to your peers at work? Explain.

- Additional discussion questions linking this case with the following material appear at the end of this chapter.

Source: J R Wilke, "Shop Talk: Computer Links Erode Hierarchical Nature of Workplace Culture," *The Wall Street Journal,* December 12, 1993, p A1, A9. Excerpted by permission of *The Wall Street Journal,* © 1993 Dow Jones & Company, Inc. All Rights Reserved Worldwide.

sible for enacting them. Management experts also note that effective communication is a cornerstone of ethical organizational behavior.

Communication by top executives keeps the firm on its ethical course, and top executives must ensure that the ethical climate is consistent with the company's overall objectives. Communication is important in providing guidance for ethical standards and activities that provide integration between the functional areas of the business. A vice president of marketing, for example, must communicate and work with regional sales managers and other marketing employees to make sure that all agree on what constitutes certain unethical activities such as bribery, price collusion, and deceptive sales techniques. Top corporate executives must also communicate with managers at the operations level (in production, sales, and finance, for example) and enforce overall ethical standards within the organization.[1]

Moreover, effective communication is critical for both managerial and organizational success. For example, a study involving 65 savings and loan employees and 110 manufacturing employees revealed that employee satisfaction with organizational communication was positively and significantly correlated with both job satisfaction and performance.[2] Two additional studies demonstrated that the quality of managerial communication was directly related to organizational innovation and overall organizational performance.[3] The importance of these findings is underscored by the fact that managers reportedly spend between 70 and 87 percent of their time communicating.[4]

Even though managers spend the majority of their time communicating, they are not necessarily effective communicators. Robert Levinson, a banking industry executive, summed up the state of managerial communication by describing the typical manager as follows: "He talks too much, expresses himself poorly, and has an uncanny ability for evading the point." Levinson further concluded that most managers cannot "write a coherent letter, make a compelling presentation, dictate a concise memo, or put together a speech that doesn't have half his audience looking at their watches."[5] While some might call this appraisal too harsh, it highlights the need for better managerial communication.

This chapter will help you better understand how managers can both improve their communication skills and design more effective communication programs. We discuss (1) basic dimensions of the communication process, focusing on a perceptual process model and a contingency approach to selecting media; (2) interpersonal communication; (3) organizational communication patterns; and (4) barriers to effective communication.

BASIC DIMENSIONS OF THE COMMUNICATION PROCESS

communication
Interpersonal exchange of information and understanding.

Communication is defined as "the exchange of information between a sender and a receiver, and the inference (perception) of meaning between the individuals involved."[6] Analysis of this exchange reveals that communication is a two-way process consisting of consecutively linked elements (see Figure 13–1). Managers who understand this process can analyze their own communication patterns as well as design communication programs that fit organizational needs. This section reviews a perceptual process model of communication and discusses a contingency approach to choosing communication media.

A Perceptual Process Model of Communication

The communication process historically has been described in terms of a *conduit* model. This traditional model depicts communication as a pipeline in which information and meaning are transferred from person to person. Recently, however, communication scholars have criticized the conduit model for being based on unrealistic assumptions. For example, the conduit model assumes communication

• ↙ FIGURE 13~1   A Perceptual Model of Communication

Feedback Loop

transfers *intended meanings* from person to person.[7] If this assumption was true, miscommunication would not exist and there would be no need to worry about being misunderstood. We could simply say or write what we want and assume the listener or reader accurately understands our intended meaning.

As we all know, communicating is not that simple or clear-cut. Communication is fraught with miscommunication. In recognition of this, researchers have begun to examine communication as a form of social information processing (recall the discussion in Chapter 5) in which receivers interpret messages by cognitively processing information. This view led to development of a **perceptual model of communication** that depicts communication as a process in which receivers create meaning in their own minds. Let us briefly examine the elements of the perceptual process model shown in Figure 13–1.

perceptual model of communication Consecutively linked elements within the communication process.

Sender   The sender is an individual, group, or organization that desires or attempts to communicate with a particular receiver. Receivers may be individuals, groups, or organizations.

Encoding   Communication begins when a sender encodes an idea or thought. Encoding translates mental thoughts into a code or language that can be understood by others. Managers typically encode using words, numbers, gestures, nonverbal cues such as facial expressions, or pictures. A recent study of 12 male and 12 female undergraduates revealed women were better at encoding emotions like pleasantness, disgust, distress, fear, and anger, while men were better senders of guilt.[8] Moreover, different methods of encoding can be used to portray similar ideas. The following short exercise highlights this point.

On a piece of paper, draw a picture of the area currently surrounding you. Now, write a verbal description of the same area. Does the pictorial encoding portray the same basic message as the verbal description? Which mode was harder to use and which more effective? Interestingly, a growing number of management consultants recommend using visual communication, such as drawings, to analyze and improve group interaction and problem solving and to reduce stress.

The Message   The output of encoding is a message. There are two important points to keep in mind about messages. First, they contain more than meets the eye. Messages may contain hidden agendas as well as trigger affective or emotional reactions. The second point to consider about messages is that they need to match the medium used to transmit them. For example, a routine memo is a poor way to announce an emotional issue such as a large layoff.

Selecting a Medium   Managers can communicate through a variety of media. Potential media include face-to-face conversations, telephone calls, electronic mail, written memos or letters, photographs or drawings, meetings, bulletin boards, computer output, and charts or graphs. Choosing the appropriate media depends on many factors, including the nature of the message, its intended purpose, the type of audience, proximity to the audience, time horizon for disseminating the message, and personal preferences.

   All media have advantages and disadvantages. Face-to-face conversations, for instance, are useful for communicating about sensitive or important issues and those requiring feedback and intensive interaction. Telephones are convenient, fast, and private, but lack nonverbal information. Although writing memos or letters is time consuming, it is a good medium when it is difficult to meet with the other person, when formality and a written record are important, and when face-to-face interaction is not necessary to enhance understanding. More is said later in this chapter about choosing media.

Decoding   Decoding is the receiver's version of encoding. Decoding consists of translating verbal, oral, or visual aspects of a message into a form that can be interpreted. Receivers rely on social information processing to determine the meaning of a message during decoding. Decoding is a key contributor to misunderstanding in intercultural communication because decoding by the receiver is subject to social values and cultural variables that may not be understood by the sender.[9] Learning about cultural values and norms is the key to improving communication across diverse cultures.

Creating Meaning   In contrast to the conduit model's assumption that meaning is directly transferred from sender to receiver, the perceptual model is based on the belief that a receiver creates the meaning of a message in his or her mind. A receiver's interpretation of a message often will differ from that intended by the sender. In turn, receivers act according to their own interpretations, not the communicator's. A communication expert concluded the following after considering this element of the communication process:

> Miscommunication and unintentional communication are to be expected, for they are the norm. Organizational communicators who take these ideas seriously would realize just how difficult successful communication truly is. Presumably, they would be conscious of the constant effort needed to communicate in ways most closely approximating their intentions. . . . Communication is fraught with unintentionality and, thereby, great difficulty for communicators.[10]

Managers are encouraged to rely on *redundancy* of communication to reduce this unintentionality. This can be done by transmitting the message over multiple media. For example, a production manager might follow up a phone conversation about a critical schedule change with a memo.

Feedback   The receiver's response to a message is the crux of the feedback loop. At this point in the communication process, the receiver becomes a sender. Specifically, the receiver encodes a response and then transmits it to the original sender. This new message is then decoded and interpreted. As you can see from this discussion, feedback is used as a comprehension check. It gives senders an idea of how accurately their message is understood.

Noise   **Noise** represents anything that interferes with the transmission and understanding of a message. It affects all linkages of the communication process. Noise includes factors such as a speech impairment, poor telephone connections, illegible handwriting, inaccurate statistics in a memo or report, poor hearing and eyesight, and physical distance between sender and receiver. Managers can improve communication accuracy by reducing noise. Growing diversity in the workforce is one example of a significant source of noise that managers need to manage. Progressive companies like Datatec have relied on training to improve the communication process among diverse employees.

> When Datatec, a $40-million computer installer, decided to bring manufacturing in-house at its Fairfield, N.J., location, a language barrier loomed. Seventy percent of the work force there, which had done light assembly of parts until that time, was foreign born: most of the workers were Hispanic and didn't speak English. They struggled to understand their new, more technical job descriptions.
>
> Vice-President of manufacturing Larry Tourjee decided that giving English lessons would be cheaper than losing longtime employees, so he told the employees that Datatec would pay for lessons on Company time. . . .
>
> Errors from misinterpreting verbal instruction on the production line have since decreased dramatically, says Tourjee. And supervisors don't have to check up on assembly as frequently, since team leaders can now write in English the instruction notes that follow each project. Turnover has been nonexistent since the program was introduced, Tourjee claims.[11]

noise   Interference with the transmission and understanding of a message

Choosing Media: A Contingency Perspective

Managers need to determine which media to use for both obtaining and disseminating information. If an inappropriate medium is used, managerial decisions may be based on inaccurate information and/or important messages may not reach the intended audience. Media selection therefore is a key component of communication effectiveness. This section explores a contingency model designed to help managers select communication media in a systematic and effective manner. Media selection in this model is based on the interaction between information richness and complexity of the problem/situation at hand.

Information Richness   Respected organizational theorists Richard Daft and Robert Lengel define **information richness** in the following manner:

> Richness is defined as the potential information-carrying capacity of data. If the communication of an item of data, such as a wink, provides substantial new understanding, it would be considered rich. If the datum provides little understanding, it would be low in richness.[12]

information richness Information-carrying capacity of data.

As this definition implies, alternative media possess levels of information richness that vary from high to low.

⌣ • FIGURE 13–2   Characteristics of Information Richness for Different Media

Information Richness	Medium	Feedback	Channel	Type of Communication	Language Source
High	Face-to-face	Immediate	Visual, audio	Personal	Body, natural
↑	Telephone	Fast	Audio	Personal	Natural
	Personal written	Slow	Limited visual	Personal	Natural
	Formal written	Very slow	Limited visual	Impersonal	Natural
Low	Formal numeric	Very slow	Limited visual	Impersonal	Numeric

Source: Adapted from R Daft and R H Lengel, "Information Richness: A New Approach to Managerial Behavior and Organization Design," in *Research in Organizational Behavior*, ed B M Staw and L L Cummings (Greenwich, CT: JAI Press, 1984), p 197.

Information richness is determined by four factors: (1) feedback (ranging from immediate to very slow), (2) channel (ranging from a combined visual and audio to limited visual), (3) type of communication (personal versus impersonal), and (4) language source (body, natural, or numeric). In Figure 13–2, the information richness of five different media is categorized in terms of these four factors.

Face-to-face is the richest form of communication. It provides immediate feedback, which serves as a comprehension check. Moreover, it allows for the observation of multiple language cues, such as body language and tone of voice, over more than one channel. Although high in richness, the telephone is not as informative as the face-to-face medium. Formal numeric media such as quantitative computer printouts or video displays possess the lowest richness. Feedback is very slow, the channel involves only limited visual information, and the numeric information is impersonal.

Complexity of the Managerial Problem/Situation   Managers face problems and situations that range from low to high in complexity. Low-complexity situations are routine, predictable, and managed by using objective or standard procedures. Calculating an employee's paycheck is an example of low complexity. Highly complex situations, like a corporate reorganization, are ambiguous, unpredictable, hard to analyze, and often emotionally laden. Managers spend considerably more time analyzing these situations because they rely on more sources of information during their deliberations. There are no set solutions to complex problems or situations.

Contingency Recommendations   The contingency model for selecting media is graphically depicted in Figure 13–3. As shown, there are three zones of communication effectiveness. Effective communication occurs when the richness of the medium is matched appropriately with the complexity of the problem or situation. Media low in richness—formal numeric or formal written—are better suited for simple problems, while media high in richness—telephone or face-to-face—are appropriate for complex problems or situations. Consider, for example, how Federal Express adheres to this recommendation by using its own TV network to communicate about complex problems.

In 1991, when fog at the Memphis airport stranded thousands of Federal Express Corp. packages, the company's TV network gave detailed live reports to workers throughout

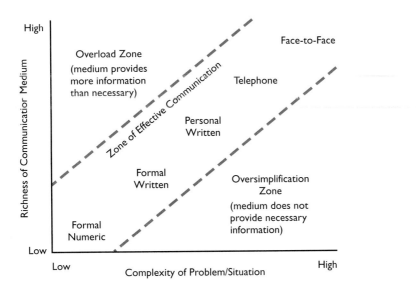

A Contingency Model for Selecting Communication Media

Source: Adapted from R L Daft and R H Lengel, "Information Richness: A New Approach to Managerial Behavior and Organization Design," in *Research in Organizational Behavior*, ed B M Staw and L L Cummings (Greenwich, CT: JAI Press, 1984), p 199. Used with permission.

the day. As a result, remote locations were able to adjust staff levels and delivery routes. . . . Federal Express also uses its TV networks to deliver bad news to employees. When the company decided to drop package delivery between European countries last year [1992] and dismiss 4,000 European employees, the company went on television to inform its U.S. workers of the move and assure them that their jobs were secure. (European workers got the bad news in person.)[13]

Conversely, ineffective communication occurs when the richness of the medium is either too high or too low for the complexity of the problem or situation. Extending the preceding example, a district sales manager would fall into the *overload zone* if he or she communicated monthly sales reports through richer media. Conducting face-to-face meetings or telephoning each salesperson would provide excessive information and take more time than necessary to communicate monthly sales data. The oversimplification zone represents another ineffective choice of communication medium. In this situation, media with inadequate richness are used to communicate complicated problems. An example would be announcing a major reorganization via a formal memo. Effective communicators use rich media to prepare employees for reorganizations.

Research Evidence   The relationship between media richness and problem/situation complexity has not been researched extensively because the underlying theory is relatively new. Available evidence indicates that managers used richer sources when confronted with ambiguous and complicated events.[14] Moreover, a meta-analysis of over 40 studies revealed that media usage was significantly different across organizational levels. Upper-level executives/managers spent more time in face-to-face meetings than did lower-level managers.[15] This finding is consistent with recommendations derived from the contingency model just discussed.

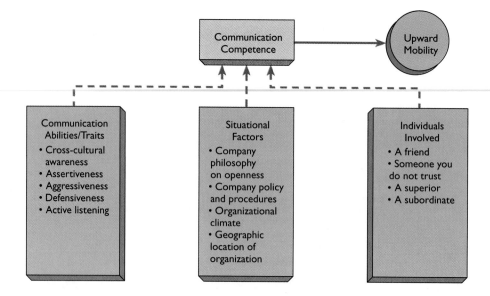

FIGURE 13–4
Communication
Competence Affects
Upward Mobility

INTERPERSONAL COMMUNICATION

communication competence
Ability to effectively use language in a social context.

The quality of interpersonal communication within an organization is very important. People with good communication skills helped groups make better decisions and were promoted more frequently than individuals with less developed abilities.[16] Although there is no universally accepted definition of **communication competence,** it is a performance-based index of an individual's knowledge of "when and how to use language in the social context."[17]

Communication competence is determined by three components: communication abilities and traits, situational factors, and the individuals involved in the interaction (see Figure 13–4). Cross-cultural awareness, for example, is an important communication ability/trait. As a case in point, the International OB illustrates how a lack of cross-cultural awareness affected business negotiations between an American manager and a group of Japanese buyers.

Individuals involved in an interaction also affect communication competence. For example, people are likely to withhold information and react emotionally or defensively when interacting with someone they dislike or do not trust. You can improve your communication competence through five communication styles/abilities/traits under your control: assertiveness, aggressiveness, nonassertiveness, nonverbal communication, and active listening.

Assertiveness, Aggressiveness, and Nonassertiveness

assertive style Expressive and self-enhancing, but does not take advantage of others.

The saying, "You can attract more bees with honey than with vinegar," captures the difference between using an assertive communication style and an aggressive style. Research studies indicate that assertiveness is more effective than aggressiveness in both work-related and consumer contexts.[18] An **assertive style** is expressive and self-enhancing and is based on the "ethical notion that it is not right or good to violate our own or others' basic human rights, such as the right to self-

INTERNATIONAL OB

Cross-Cultural Awareness Affects Business Negotiations

After a lengthy and very thorough sales presentation, the American concluded by offering what he felt was a fair price. The Japanese buyers followed with silence. After several moments, the American, anticipating rejection, said that he could perhaps cut the price a little more, and offered a second price. More silence followed. Exasperated, the visiting businessman said that he could make one final offer of his very lowest price. After a brief silence, the Japanese agreed to accept the price. One of the Japanese buyers later related that the first price offered was within an acceptable range for them. It was, however, their custom to consider the proposal silently before reaching and announcing their decision. The American businessman, automatically responding in a manner appropriate for his own culture, believed that silence meant an unacceptable price had been tendered and countered again and again with lower prices.

Source: Excerpted from R Maddox, *Cross-Cultural Problems in International Business* (Westport CT: Quorum Books, 1993), pp 21–22.

expression or the right to be treated with dignity and respect.''[19] In contrast, an **aggressive style** is expressive and self-enhancing and strives to take unfair advantage of others. A **nonassertive style** is characterized by timid and self-denying behavior. Nonassertiveness is ineffective because it gives the other person an unfair advantage.

aggressive style Expressive and self-enhancing, but takes unfair advantage of others.

nonassertive style Timid and self-denying behavior.

Managers may improve their communication competence by trying to be more assertive and less aggressive or nonassertive. This can be achieved by using the appropriate nonverbal and verbal behaviors listed in Table 13–1. For instance, managers should attempt to use the nonverbal behaviors of good eye contact, a strong, steady, and audible voice, and selective interruptions. They should avoid nonverbal behaviors such as glaring or little eye contact, threatening gestures, slumped posture, and a weak or whiny voice. Appropriate verbal behaviors include direct and unambiguous language and the use of ''I'' statements. Inappropriate behaviors consist of swear words and abusive language, sexist or racist terms, and qualifiers such as ''maybe.''

Remember that nonverbal and verbal behaviors should complement and reinforce each other. James Waters, a communication expert, further recommends that assertiveness can be enhanced by using various combinations of the following assertiveness elements:

1. *Describe* the situation or the behavior of people to which you are reacting.
2. *Express* your feelings, and/or *explain* what impact the other's behavior has on you.
3. *Empathize* with the other person's position in the situation.
4. *Specify* what changes you would like to see in the situation or in another's behavior, and offer to *negotiate* those changes with the other person.
5. *Indicate,* in a nonthreatening way, the possible consequences that will follow if change does not occur.[20]

Waters offers managers the following situational advice when using the various assertiveness elements: (1) *empathize* and *negotiate* with superiors or others on

TABLE 13~1
Communication Styles

Communication Style	Description	Nonverbal Behavior Pattern	Verbal Behavior Pattern
Assertive	Pushing hard without attacking; permits others to influence outcome; expressive and self-enhancing without intruding on others	Good eye contact Comfortable but firm posture Strong, steady, and audible voice Facial expressions matched to message Appropriately serious tone Selective interruptions to ensure understanding	Direct and unambiguous language No attributions or evaluations of other's behavior Use of "I" statements and cooperative "we" statements
Aggressive	Taking advantage of others; expressive and self-enhancing at other's expense	Glaring eye contact Moving or leaning too close Threatening gestures (pointed finger; clenched fist) Loud voice Frequent interruptions	Swear words and abusive language Attributions and evaluations of other's behavior Sexist or racist terms Explicit threats or put-downs
Nonassertive	Encouraging others to take advantage of us; inhibited; self-denying	Little eye contact Downward glances Slumped posture Constantly shifting weight Wringing hands Weak or whiny voice	Qualifiers ("maybe"; "kind of") Fillers ("uh," "you know," "well") Negaters ("It's not really that important"; "I'm not sure")

Source: Adapted in part from J A Waters, "Managerial Assertiveness," *Business Horizons*, September–October 1982, pp 24–29.

whom you are dependent, (2) *specify* with friends and peers, and (3) *describe* to strangers.

Sources of Nonverbal Communication

Nonverbal communication is "Any message, sent or received independent of the written or spoken word . . . [It] includes such factors as use of time and space, distance between persons when conversing, use of color, dress, walking behavior, standing, positioning, seating arrangement, office locations and furnishing."[21] Due to the prevalence of nonverbal communication and its significant impact on organizational behavior (including, but not limited to, perceptions of others, hiring decisions, work attitudes, and turnover),[22] it is important that managers become consciously aware of the sources of nonverbal communication.

nonverbal communication
Messages sent outside of the written or spoken word.

Body Movements and Gestures Body movements, such as leaning forward or backward, and gestures, such as pointing, provide additional nonverbal information. Open body positions such as leaning backward, communicate *immediacy,* a term used to represent openness, warmth, closeness, and availability for communication. *Defensiveness* is communicated by gestures such as folding arms, crossing hands, and crossing one's legs.[23] Judith Hall, a communication researcher, conducted a meta-analysis of gender differences in body movements and gestures.

Body language can reinforce or compete with our spoken message. This manager's body language emphasizes her enthusiasm. But her listeners are sending mixed body language messages about their support for her ideas.

(Jon Riley/Tony Stone Images)

Results revealed that women nodded their heads and moved their hands more than men. Leaning forward, large body shifts, and foot and leg movements were exhibited more frequently by men than women.[24] Although it is both easy and fun to interpret body movements and gestures, it is important to remember that body-language analysis is subjective, easily misinterpreted, and highly dependent on the context and cross-cultural differences.[25] Thus, managers need to be careful when trying to interpret body movements. Inaccurate interpretations can create additional ''noise'' in the communication process.

Touch　Touching is another powerful nonverbal cue. People tend to touch those they like. A meta-analysis of gender differences in touching indicated that women do more touching during conversations than men.[26] Of particular note, however, is the fact that men and women interpret touching differently. Sexual harassment claims might be reduced by keeping this perceptual difference in mind.

Moreover, norms for touching vary significantly around the world. Consider the example of two males walking across campus holding hands. In the Middle East, this behavior would be quite normal for males who are friends or have great respect for each other. In contrast, this behavior is not commonplace in the United States. The International OB presents cross-cultural guidelines for touching.

Facial Expressions　Facial expressions convey a wealth of information. Smiling, for instance, typically represents warmth, happiness, or friendship, whereas frowning conveys dissatisfaction or anger. Do you think these interpretations apply to different cross-cultural groups? If you said yes, it supports the view that there is a universal recognition of emotions from facial expressions. If you said no, this indicates you believe the relationship between facial expressions and emotions varies across cultures. A recent summary of relevant research revealed that the association between facial expressions and emotions varies across cultures.[27] A smile, for example, does not convey the same emotion in different countries. Therefore, managers need to be careful in interpreting facial expressions among diverse groups of employees.

Eye Contact　Eye contact is a strong nonverbal cue that serves four functions in communication. First, eye contact regulates the flow of communication by signaling the beginning and end of conversation. There is a tendency to look away from

INTERNATIONAL OB

Norms for Touching Vary across Countries

Touch	Middle Ground	Don't Touch
Middle East countries	France	Japan
Latin countries	China	United States and Canada
Italy	Ireland	England
Greece	India	Scandinavia
Spain and Portugal		Other Northern European countries
Some Asian countries		Australia
Russia		Estonia

Source: R E Axtell, *Gestures: The Do's and Taboos of Body Language Around the World* (New York: John Wiley & Sons, 1991), p 43. © Copyright 1991. Reprinted by permission of John Wiley & Sons, Inc.

others when beginning to speak and to look at them when done. Second, gazing (as opposed to glaring) facilitates and monitors feedback because it reflects interest and attention. Third, eye contact conveys emotion. People tend to avoid eye contact when discussing bad news or providing negative feedback. Fourth, gazing relates to the type of relationship between communicators.

As is also true for body movements, gestures, and facial expressions, norms for eye contact vary across cultures. Westerners are taught at an early age to look at their parents when spoken to. In contrast, Asians are taught to avoid eye contact with a parent or superior in order to show obedience and subservience.[28] Once again, managers should be sensitive to different orientations toward maintaining eye contact with diverse employees.

Interpersonal Distance Zones Renowned anthropologist Edward Hall studied the impact of social and personal space on human communication and behavior. He identified four distance zones that regulate interpersonal interactions. These zones differ across cultures. The zones and accompanying distances for Americans are as follows:

- *Intimate distance,* the zone for lovemaking, wrestling, comforting, and protecting, is physical contact to 18 inches.
- *Personal distance* is 1.5 to 4 feet and is used for interpersonal interactions with friends or acquaintances.
- *Social distance,* the zone used for business and casual social interactions, spans 4 to 12 feet.
- *Public distance* is used for impersonal and formal interactions and covers 12 to 25 feet.[29]

The important point to remember is that people strive to maintain a distance zone consistent with their cultural expectations and the nature of the interaction. Violating interpersonal distance zones creates discomfort, which can reduce communication effectiveness. This is particularly true in crosscultural dealings.

Practical Tips   A communication expert offers the following advice to improve nonverbal communication skills:

Positive nonverbal actions that help to communicate include:

- Maintaining eye contact.
- Occasionally nodding the head in agreement.
- Smiling and showing animation.
- Leaning toward the speaker.
- Speaking at a moderate rate, in a quiet, assuring tone. . . .

Here are some actions . . . to avoid:

- Looking away or turning away from the speaker.
- Closing your eyes.
- Using an unpleasant voice tone.
- Speaking too quickly or too slowly.
- Yawning excessively.[30]

Practice these tips by turning the sound off while watching television and then trying to interpret emotions and interactions. Honest feedback from your friends about your nonverbal communication style also may help.

Active Listening

Some communication experts contend that listening is the keystone communication skill for today's managers. Estimates suggest that managers typically spend about 9 percent of a working day reading, 16 percent writing, 30 percent talking, and 45 percent listening.[31] Moreover, because listening appears to be effortless—we have the cognitive ability to process information three to four times faster than people speak—it is often neglected or taken for granted. For example, communication experts estimate that most people comprehend about 25 percent of a typical verbal message.[32] Listening involves much more than hearing a message. Hearing is merely the physical component of listening.

   Listening is the process of *actively* decoding and interpreting verbal messages. Listening requires cognitive attention and information processing; hearing does not. With these distinctions in mind, we will examine a model of listener comprehension, listening styles, and some practical advice for becoming a more effective listener.

listening Actively decoding and interpreting verbal messages.

Listener Comprehension Model   Listener comprehension represents the extent to which an individual can recall factual information and draw accurate conclusions and inferences from a verbal message. It is a function of listener, speaker, message, and environmental characteristics (see Figure 13–5). Communication researchers Kittie Watson and Larry Barker conducted a global review of listening behavior research and arrived at the following conclusions. Listening comprehension is positively related to high mental and reading abilities, academic achievements, a large vocabulary, being ego-involved with the speaker, having energy, being female, extrinsic motivation to pay attention, and being able to take good notes. Speakers who talk too fast or too slow, possess disturbing accents or speech patterns, are not visible to the audience, lack credibility, or are disliked have a negative impact on listening comprehension. In contrast, clear messages stated in the active voice increase listening comprehension. The same is true of messages

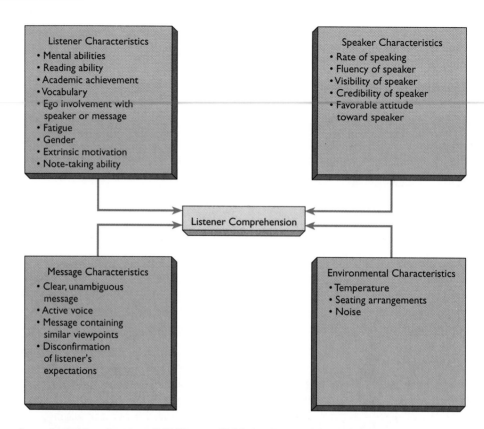

FIGURE 13–5
Listener Comprehension
Model

Source: Adapted from discussion in K W Watson and L L Barker, "Listening Behavior: Definition and Measurement," in *Communication Yearbook* 8, ed R N Bostrom (Beverly Hills, CA: Sage Publications, 1984), pp 178–97.

containing viewpoints similar to the listener's or those that disconfirm expectations. Finally, comfortable environmental characteristics and compact seating arrangements enhance listening comprehension.[33]

Listening Styles   A pair of communication experts identified three different listening styles.[34] Their research indicated that people prefer to hear information that is suited to their own listening style. People also tend to speak in a style that is consistent with their own listening style. Because inconsistent styles represent a barrier to effective listening, it is important for managers to understand and respond to the different listening styles. The three listening styles are called "results," "reasons," and "process."

Results-style listeners don't like any beating around the bush. They are interested in hearing the bottom line or result of the communication message first, and then like to ask questions. These behaviors identify a results-style listener:

- They sound direct. Everything is right out front, so you never have to wonder. They may sound blunt or even rude sometimes.
- They are action oriented.
- They are present oriented.

results style   Interested in hearing the bottom line or result of a message.

- They love to problem solve. Because of their love of fixing things and their action orientation, they are usually good crisis managers.
- Their first interest is the bottom line.[35]

Reasons-style listeners want to know the rationale for what someone is saying or proposing. They must be convinced about a point of view before accepting it. Typical behaviors exhibited by a reasons-style listener include:

reasons style Interested in hearing the rationale behind a message.

- They are most concerned with whether or not a solution is practical, realistic, and reasonable for the situation.
- They weigh and balance everything. . . .
- If asked a direct question, they frequently answer, "It depends."
- They argue, out loud or internally.
- They expect people to present ideas in an organized way. They have little tolerance and no respect for a "disorderly" mind.
- Their first concern is "Why?"[36]

Process-style listeners like to discuss issues in detail. They prefer to receive background information prior to having a thorough discussion and like to know why an issue is important in the first place. You can identify process-style listeners by watching for these behaviors:

process style Likes to discuss issues in detail.

- They are people oriented. They have a high concern for relationships, believing that people and relationships are the keys to long-term success.
- They like to know the whole story before making a decision.
- They have a high concern for quality and will hold out for a quality solution to a problem, even if it seems unrealistic to others.
- They are future oriented. They are not only concerned about the future, but they predict what may happen in the future as a result of decisions made today.
- They have ongoing conversations. They continue subjects from one conversation to the next.
- Their language and messages tend to be indirect. They imply rather than state the bottom line.
- Their primary interests are *how* and *benefits*.[37]

Managers can gain greater acceptance of their ideas and proposals by adapting the *form* and *content* of a message to fit a receiver's listening style:

1. For a results-style listener, for instance, the sender should present the bottom line at the beginning of the discussion.
2. Explain your rationale to a reasons-style listener.
3. For a process-style listener, describe the process and the benefits.

Becoming a More Effective Listener   In addition to following the preceding recommendations, you can improve your listening skills by avoiding the 10 habits of bad listeners while cultivating the 10 good listening habits (see Table 13–2). Importantly, it takes awareness, effort, and practice to improve one's listening comprehension. Is anyone listening?

TABLE 13~2
The Keys to Effective Listening

Keys to Effective Listening	The Bad Listener	The Good Listener
1. Find areas of interest	Tunes out dry subjects	Opportunistic; asks "What's in it for me?"
2. Judge content, not delivery	Tunes out if delivery is poor	Judges content; skips over delivery errors
3. Hold your fire	Tends to enter into arguments	Doesn't judge until comprehension is complete
4. Listen for ideas	Listens for facts	Listens for central themes
5. Be flexible	Takes intensive notes using only one system	Takes fewer notes; uses four or five different systems, depending on speaker
6. Work at listening	Shows no energy output; attention is faked	Works hard; exhibits active body state
7. Resist distractions	Is distracted easily	Fights or avoids distractions; tolerates bad habits; knows how to concentrate
8. Exercise your mind	Resists difficult expository material; seeks light, recreational material	Uses heavier material as exercise for the mind
9. Keep your mind open	Reacts to emotional words	Interprets color words; does not get hung up on them
10. Capitalize on the fact that *thought* is faster than speech	Tends to daydream with slow speakers	Challenges, anticipates, mentally summarizes, weighs the evidence, listens between the lines to tone of voice

Source: L K Steil, "How Well Do You Listen?" *Executive Female,* special issue no. 2 (1986), p 37. Reprinted with permission from *Executive Female,* the bimonthly publication of the National Association for Female Executives.

ORGANIZATIONAL COMMUNICATION PATTERNS

Examining organizational communication patterns is a good way to identify factors contributing to effective and ineffective management. For example, research reveals that effective managers, in contrast to ineffective ones, tend to be (1) more communication oriented and willing to speak up, (2) more receptive to employees, (3) more willing to ask or persuade than to tell, and (4) more open to explaining the "why" of things.[38] With these progressive practices in mind, this section promotes a working knowledge of three important communication patterns: hierarchical communication, the grapevine, and communication distortion.

Hierarchical Communication

hierarchical communication
Exchange of information between managers and employees.

Hierarchical communication is defined as "those exchanges of information and influence between organizational members, at least one of whom has formal (as defined by official organizational sources) authority to direct and evaluate the activities of other organizational members."[39] This communication pattern involves information exchanged downward from manager to employee and upward from employee to manager. Managers provide five types of information through downward communication: job instructions, job rationale, organizational procedures and practices, feedback about performance, and indoctrination of goals. Employees, in turn, communicate information upward about themselves, coworkers and their problems, organizational practices and policies, and what needs to be done and how to do it. Timely and valid hierarchical communication can

THE ARMY TELEGRAPH—SETTING UP THE WIRE DURING AN ACTION.—[Sketched by Mr. A. R. Waud.]

The term *grapevine* derives from the Civil War practice of stringing battlefield telegraph lines between trees.

(North Wind Picture Archives)

promote individual and organizational success. For example, a study of 24 branches of a large East Coast bank revealed that those with a two-way pattern of communication between managers and employees were 70 percent more profitable than branches with a one-way communication pattern.[40] Managers are encouraged to foster two-way communication among all employees.

The Grapevine

The term *grapevine* originated from the Civil War practice of stringing battlefield telegraph lines between trees. Today, the **grapevine** represents the unofficial communication system of the informal organization. Information traveling along the grapevine supplements official or formal channels of communication. Although the grapevine can be a source of inaccurate rumors, it functions positively as an early warning signal for organizational changes, a medium for creating organizational culture, a mechanism for fostering group cohesiveness, and a way of informally bouncing ideas off others.[41] Evidence indicates that the grapevine is alive and well in today's workplaces.

A national survey of the readers of *Industry Week,* a professional management magazine, revealed that employees used the grapevine as their most frequent source of information.[42] Contrary to general opinion, the grapevine is not necessarily counterproductive. Plugging into the grapevine can help employees, managers, and organizations alike achieve desired results. To enhance your understanding of the grapevine, we will explore grapevine patterns and research and managerial recommendations for monitoring this often misunderstood system of communication.

grapevine Unofficial communication system of the informal organization.

Grapevine Patterns   Communication along the grapevine follows predictable patterns (see Figure 13–6). The most frequent pattern is not a single strand or gossip chain, but the cluster pattern.[43] In this case, person A passes along a piece of information to three people, one of whom—person F—tells two others, and then one of those two—person B—tells one other. As illustrated in Figure 13–6, only certain individuals repeat what they hear when the cluster pattern is operating.

• **FIGURE 13~6**

Grapevine Patterns

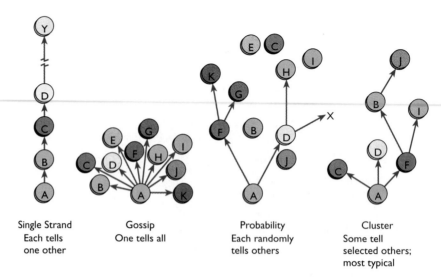

Single Strand
Each tells
one other

Gossip
One tells all

Probability
Each randomly
tells others

Cluster
Some tell
selected others;
most typical

Source: K Davis and J W Newstrom, *Human Behavior at Work: Organizational Behavior,* 7th ed (New York: McGraw-Hill, 1985), p 317. Used with permission.

liaison individuals
Consistently pass along grape-vine information to others.

People who consistently pass along grapevine information to others are called **liaison individuals** or "gossips."

> About 10 percent of the employees on an average grapevine will be highly active participants. They serve as liaisons with the rest of the staff members who receive information but spread it to only a few other people. Usually these liaisons are friendly, outgoing people who are in positions that allow them to cross departmental lines. For example, secretaries tend to be liaisons because they can communicate with the top executive, the janitor, and everyone in between without raising eyebrows.[44]

Effective managers monitor the pulse of work groups by regularly communicating with known liaisons.

Research and Practical Implications Although research activity on this topic has slowed in recent years, past research about the grapevine provided the following insights: (1) it is faster than formal channels; (2) it is about 75 percent accurate; (3) people rely on it when they are insecure, threatened, or faced with organizational changes; and (4) employees use the grapevine to acquire the majority of their on-the-job information.[45]

The key managerial recommendation is to *monitor* and *influence* the grapevine rather than attempt to control it. Effective managers accomplish this by openly sharing relevant information with employees. For example, managers can increase the amount of communication by both keeping in touch with liaison individuals and making sure information travels to people "isolated" from the formal communication system. Providing advance notice of departmental or organizational changes, carefully listening to employees, and selectively sending information along the grapevine are other ways to influence and monitor the grapevine. Keith Davis, who has studied the grapevine for over 30 years, offers this final piece of advice:

> No administrator in his right mind would try to abolish the management grapevine. It is as permanent as humanity is. Nevertheless, many administrators have abolished the grapevine from their own minds. They think and act without giving adequate weight to it

Situational Antecedents

Pattern of Distortion in
Upward Communication

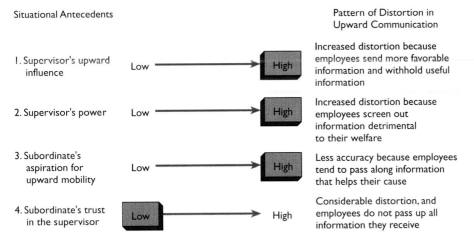

1. Supervisor's upward influence — Low ⟶ High — Increased distortion because employees send more favorable information and withhold useful information

2. Supervisor's power — Low ⟶ High — Increased distortion because employees screen out information detrimental to their welfare

3. Subordinate's aspiration for upward mobility — Low ⟶ High — Less accuracy because employees tend to pass along information that helps their cause

4. Subordinate's trust in the supervisor — Low ⟶ High — Considerable distortion, and employees do not pass up all information they receive

Source: Adapted in part from J Fulk and S Mani, "Distortion of Communication in Hierarchical Relationships," in *Communication Yearbook 9*, ed M L McLaughlin (Beverly Hills, CA: Sage Publications, 1986).

or, worse, try to ignore it. This is a mistake. The grapevine is a factor to be reckoned with in the affairs of management. The administrator should analyze it and should consciously try to influence it.[46]

Communication Distortion between Managers and Employees

Communication distortion occurs when an employee purposely modifies the content of a message, thereby reducing the accuracy of communication between managers and employees. Employees tend to engage in this practice because of workplace politics, a desire to manage impressions, and fear of how a manager might respond to a message.[47] Communication experts point out the organizational problems caused by distortion:

> Distortion is an important problem in organizations because modifications to messages cause misdirectives to be transmitted, nondirectives to be issued, incorrect information to be passed on, and a variety of other problems related to both the quantity and quality of information.[48]

Knowledge of the antecedents or causes of communication distortion can help managers avoid or limit these problems.

Antecedents of Distortion   Studies have identified four situational antecedents of distortion in upward communication (see Figure 13–7). Distortion tends to increase when supervisors have high upward influence and/or power. Employees also tend to modify or distort information when they aspire to move upward and when they do not trust their supervisors.[49] Because managers generally do not want to reduce their upward influence or curb their subordinates' desire for upward mobility, they can reduce distortion in several ways.

1. Managers can de-emphasize power differences between themselves and their subordinates.
2. They can enhance trust through a meaningful performance review process that rewards actual performance.

communication distortion
Purposely modifying the content of a message.

3. Managers can encourage staff feedback by conducting smaller, more informal meetings.
4. They can establish performance goals that encourage employees to focus on problems rather than personalities.
5. Distortion can be limited by encouraging dialogue between those with opposing viewpoints.

What Is Your Potential for Communication Distortion?   To assess the communication pattern between you and your immediate supervisor, please take a moment to complete the survey in the OB Exercise. Think of your present (or last) job when responding to the various items. Do your responses to the first three statements suggest low or high potential for distortion? (Arbitrary norms for each

---

OB EXERCISE

A Self-Assessment of Antecedents and Outcomes of Distortion in Upward Communication

Instructions:

Circle your response to each question by using the following scale:

    1 = Strongly disagree
    2 = Disagree
    3 = Neither agree nor disagree
    4 = Agree
    5 = Strongly agree

Supervisor's upward influence:
In general, my immediate supervisor can have a big impact on my career in this organization.   1 2 3 4 5

Aspiration for upward mobility:
It is very important for me to progress upward in this organization.   1 2 3 4 5

Supervisory trust:
I feel free to discuss the problems and difficulties of my job with my immediate supervisor without jeopardizing my position or having it "held against" me later.   1 2 3 4 5

Withholding information:
I provide my immediate supervisor with a small amount of the total information I receive at work.   1 2 3 4 5

Selective disclosure:
When transmitting information to my immediate supervisor, I often emphasize those aspects that make me look good.   1 2 3 4 5

Satisfaction with communication:
In general, I am satisfied with the pattern of communication between my supervisor and me.   1 2 3 4 5

Source: Adapted and excerpted in part from K H Roberts and C A O'Reilly III, "Measuring Organizational Communication," *Journal of Applied Psychology,* June 1974, p 323.

of the first three items are: Low = 1–2, Moderate = 3, and High = 4–5.) How does this assessment mesh with your responses to the last three statements, which measure three outcomes of distortion?

Effective communication is the cornerstone of survival in today's competitive business environment. This was particularly true for CEOs Jack Welch from General Electric and Michael Walsh from Tenneco when they confronted the need to revolutionize their organizations.[50] Managers who are sensitive to communicating in today's computerized workplace and to various communication barriers are more likely to be successful change agents.

DYNAMICS OF
MODERN
COMMUNICATIONS

Communication in the Computerized Information Age

Organizations are increasingly using information technology as a lever to improve productivity and customer and employee satisfaction. In turn, communication patterns at work are radically changing. Consider how Jay Chiat, chairman of Chiat/Day, a $620 million advertising agency, is using information technology to reorganize his company:

> He plans, first of all, to replace the personal working spaces of his 800 employees with elegant common areas and technically sophisticated meeting, editing, and screening rooms. He is cutting his staff loose from the nine-to-five work schedule, which he considers a throwback to the early Industrial Age, to allow them to be where they need to be when they need to be there—sort of a just-in-time approach to personnel management. . . . Ultimately, it hinges on the technology and software necessary to connect every employee with individual cellular phone numbers and hundreds of e-mail [electronic mail] equipped notebook computers, so they can work and interact wherever they are in the world.[51]

Like other companies, Chiat/Day is using information technology to change the way people work. This section explores three key components of Chiat/Day's new organization: collaborative computing, video conferencing, and telecommuting. All three are elements of communicating in a computerized workplace.

Collaborative Computing   **Collaborative computing** entails using state-of-the-art computer software and hardware to help people work better together. Collaborative systems enable people to share information without the constraints of time and space. This is accomplished by utilizing computer networks to link people across a room or across the globe. Collaborative applications include messaging and E-mail systems, calendar management, video conferencing, computer teleconferencing, electronic whiteboards, and the type of computer-aided decision-making systems discussed in Chapter 11.[52]

collaborative computing
Using computer software and hardware to help people work better together.

Organizations that use full-fledged collaborative systems are referred to as "virtual companies" because people can communicate with anyone at anytime. Take VeriFone Inc., for example:

> New VeriFone employees get laptops . . . before they get desks, and they quickly learn that it is in their best interests to plug into the corporate network at airports, hotel rooms, customers' offices, and if necessary, pay phones on the street. . . . For VeriFone employees, dashing off an informal E-mail note is as natural an act as speaking, but the company's network culture isn't based on merely swapping memos. . . . Virtually all of

its work processes are carved up and electronically distributed to speed things up and garner maximum expertise. For example, the company's salespeople will sometimes excuse themselves from tricky negotiations with a prospective client and . . . go off in search of the nearest phone jack so they can send off a description of their difficulties via laptop. The next time they step out for a break they can read through advice from a range of managers.[53]

As is true at VeriFone, collaborative computing can significantly increase both the speed and quality of delivering products and services.

Video Conferencing   Video conferencing is an application of collaborative computing. It uses video and audio links to connect people at different locations. For example, EDS uses video conferences to simultaneously train its employees at hundreds of locations around the world.[54] This enables employees to conduct long-distance meetings and training classes without leaving their office. The results are substantial cost savings. It, therefore, is not surprising that the use of video conferencing is on the rise. Sales of video systems are predicted to grow from $660 million in 1993 to $10.8 billion in 1997.[55]

telecommuting   Receiving and sending work from home to the office via a computer link.

Telecommuting   **Telecommuting** involves receiving and sending work from home by using a modem to link a home computer to an office computer. Full-time telecommuters generally work two days at home and three at the office. Telecommuting is more common in ''information jobs'' that require analysis, research, writing, typing, or computer programming. An estimated 6.6 million US workers were involved with formal telecommuting programs in 1992, an increase of 20 percent from 1991.[56] Proposed benefits of telecommuting include the following:

1. *Reduction of capital costs.*   JC Penney and Los Angeles County reported lower costs by letting employees work at home.
2. *Increased flexibility and autonomy for workers.*
3. *Competitive edge in recruitment.*   The Traveler's Insurance Company and the federal government used telecommuting to increase their ability to keep and attract qualified personnel.
4. *Increased job satisfaction.*   Employees like telecommuting because it helps resolve work-family conflicts.
5. *Increased productivity.*   Telecommuting resulted in productivity increases of 25 and 35 percent for FourGen Software and Continental Traffic Services, respectively.
6. *Tapping nontraditional labor pools* (such as prison inmates and home-bound disabled persons).[57]

Although telecommuting represents an attempt to accommodate employee needs and desires, it requires adjustments and is not for everybody. According to John Naisbitt, the futurist who wrote the best-seller *Megatrends,* ''not very many of us will be willing to work at home. People want to be with people; people want to go to the office.''[58] It thus appears that the growth of telecommuting will depend more on behavioral than technical limitations.

Barriers to Effective Communication

Communication noise is a barrier to effective communication because it interferes with the accurate transmission and reception of a message. Management awareness of these barriers is a good starting point to improve the communication process. There are four key barriers to effective communication: (1) process barriers, (2) personal barriers, (3) physical barriers, and (4) semantic barriers.

Process Barriers   Every element of the perceptual model of communication shown in Figure 13–1 is a potential process barrier. Consider the following examples.

1. *Sender barrier.*   A customer gets incorrect information from a customer service agent because he or she was recently hired and lacks experience.
2. *Encoding barrier.*   An employee for whom English is a second language has difficulty explaining why a delivery was late.
3. *Message barrier.*   An employee misses a meeting for which he or she never received a confirmation memo.
4. *Medium barrier.*   A salesperson gives up trying to make a sales call when the potential customer fails to return three previous phone calls.
5. *Decoding barrier.*   An employee does not know how to respond to a manager's request to stop exhibiting ''passive aggressive'' behavior.
6. *Receiver barrier.*   A student who is talking to his or her friend during a lecture asks the professor the same question that was just answered.
7. *Feedback barrier.*   The nonverbal head nodding of an interviewer leads an interviewee to think that he or she is doing a great job answering questions.

Barriers in any of these process elements can distort the transfer of meaning. Reducing these barriers is essential but difficult, given the current diversity of the workforce.[59]

Personal Barriers   Carl Rogers, the renowned psychologist, identified two personal characteristics that interfere with interpersonal communication.[60] They are (1) natural tendency to evaluate or judge a sender's message and (2) not listening with understanding. To highlight the natural tendency to evaluate, consider how you might respond to the statement ''I like the book you are reading.'' What would you say? Your likely response is to approve or disapprove the statement. You may say, ''I agree,'' or alternatively, ''I disagree, the book is boring.'' The point is that we all tend to evaluate messages from our own point of view or frame of reference. The tendency to evaluate messages is greatest when one has strong feelings or emotions about the issue being discussed.

An inability to listen with understanding is the second personal barrier to effective communication. *Listening with understanding* occurs when a receiver can ''see the expressed idea and attitude from the other person's point of view, to sense how it feels to him, to achieve his frame of reference in regard to the thing he is talking about.''[61] Listening with understanding reduces defensiveness and improves accuracy in perceiving a message. How can these personal barriers be reduced?

Because one can not totally eliminate the natural tendency to evaluate messages, *awareness of this barrier* is a first step toward improving interpersonal communication. The second step is to have both parties to the communication be able to *come to understand* each other's point of view. This can be initiated by a third party to the exchange, or by one of the parties, independently. Exaggerated perceptions and defensive responses can be reduced by listening with understanding.[62]

Physical Barriers   The distance between employees can interfere with effective communication. It is hard to understand someone who is speaking to you from 20 yards away. Time zone differences between the East and West Coasts also represent physical barriers. Work and office noise are additional barriers. For example, airline baggage handlers must wear ear plugs to protect themselves. Imagine how difficult it would be for two employees to verbally communicate when both of them are wearing ear plugs.

In spite of the general acceptance of physical barriers, they can be reduced. For example, employees on the East Coast can agree to call their West Coast peers prior to leaving for lunch. Distracting or inhibiting walls also can be torn down. It is important that managers attempt to manage this barrier by choosing a medium that optimally reduces the physical barrier at hand.

Semantic Barriers   *Semantics* is the study of words. Semantic barriers show up as encoding and decoding errors because these phases of communication involve transmitting and receiving words and symbols. These barriers occur very easily. Consider the following statement: Crime is ubiquitous.

Do you understand this message? Even if you do, would it not be simpler to say that "crime is all around us" or "crime is everywhere"? Choosing our words more carefully is the easiest way to reduce semantic barriers. This barrier can also be decreased by attentiveness to mixed messages and cultural diversity. Mixed messages occur when a person's words imply one message while his or her actions or nonverbal cues suggest something different. Obviously, understanding is enhanced when a person's actions and nonverbal cues match the verbal message.

BACK TO THE OPENING CASE

Now that you have read Chapter 13, you should be able to answer the following questions about the effect of collaborative computing on organizational communication.

1. How does collaborative computing influence the amount of noise in the communication process? Explain.

2. Is using networked computers to communicate consistent with the contingency model for selecting media? Discuss your rationale.

3. How does collaborative computing affect the grapevine and communication distortion? Explain.

4. What are the major benefits and limitations of collaborative computing? Discuss your conclusions.

5. Do you think people say things on a computer network that they would not say face-to-face? Discuss the implications for organizational behavior.

SUMMARY OF KEY CONCEPTS

1. *Describe the perceptual process model of communication.* Communication is a process of consecutively linked elements. Historically, this process was described in terms of a conduit model. Criticisms of this model led to development of a perceptual process model of communication that

depicts receivers as information processors who create the meaning of messages in their own mind. Because receivers' interpretations of messages often differ from those intended by senders, miscommunication is a common occurrence.

2. *Explain the contingency approach to media selection.* Selecting media is a key component of communication effectiveness. Media selection is based on the interaction between the information richness of a medium and the complexity of the problem/situation at hand. Information richness ranges from low to high and is a function of four factors: speed of feedback, characteristics of the channel, type of communication, and language source. Problems/situations range from simple to complex. Effective communication occurs when the richness of the medium matches the complexity of the problem/situation. From a contingency perspective, richer media need to be used as problems/situations become more complex.

3. *Contrast the communication styles of assertiveness, aggressiveness, and nonassertiveness.* An assertive style is expressive and self-enhancing but does not violate others' basic human rights. In contrast, an aggressive style is expressive and self-enhancing but takes unfair advantage of others. A nonassertive style is characterized by timid and self-denying behavior. An assertive communication style is more effective than either an aggressive or non-assertive style.

4. *Discuss the primary sources of both nonverbal communication and listener comprehension.* There are several identifiable sources of nonverbal communication effectiveness. Body movements and gestures, touch, facial expressions, eye contact, and interpersonal distance zones are important nonverbal cues. The interpretation of these nonverbal cues significantly varies across cultures. Listening is the process of actively decoding and interpreting verbal messages. Listener characteristics, speaker characteristics, message characteristics, and environmental characteristics influence listener comprehension.

5. *Identify and give examples of the three different listening styles.* Communication experts identified three unique types of listening styles. A results-style listener likes to hear the bottom line or result of a communication at the beginning of a conversation. Reasons-style listeners want to know the rationale for what someone is saying or proposing. Process-style listeners like to discuss issues in detail.

6. *Review the 10 keys to effective listening.* Good listeners use the following 10 listening habits: (1)

ask questions to identify areas of interest between the speaker and listener; (2) judge content and not delivery; (3) do not judge until the speaker has completed his or her message; (4) listen for ideas; (5) use multiple systems to take notes; (6) put energy and effort into listening; (7) resist distractions; (8) read or listen to complex material to exercise the mind; (9) do not react to emotional words; and (10) challenge, anticipate, mentally summarize, weigh the evidence, and listen between the lines.

7. *Discuss the patterns of hierarchical communication and the grapevine.* Hierarchical communication patterns describe exchanges of information between managers and the employees they supervise. Managers provide five types of downward communication: job instructions, job rationale, organizational procedures and practices, feedback about performance, and indoctrination of goals. Employees communicate information upward about themselves, co-workers and their problems, organizational practices and policies, and what needs to be done and how to do it.

The grapevine is the unofficial communication system of the informal organization. Communication along the grapevine follows four predictable patterns: single strand, gossip, probability, and cluster. The cluster pattern is the most common.

8. *Demonstrate your familiarity with four antecedents of communication distortion between managers and employees.* Communication distortion is a common problem that consists of modifying the content of a message. Employees distort upward communication when their supervisor has high upward influence and/or power. Distortion also increases when employees aspire to move upward and when they do not trust their supervisor.

9. *Explain collaborative computing and the related use of video conferencing and telecommuting.* Collaborative computing entails using state-of-the-art computer software and hardware to help people work better together. Information is shared across time and space by linking people with computer networks. Video conferencing is an application of collaborative computing. It uses video and audio links to connect people at different locations. Telecommuting involves receiving and sending work from home by using a modem to link a home computer to an office computer.

10. *Describe the process, personal, physical, and semantic barriers to effective communication.* Every element of the perceptual model of communication is a potential process barrier. There are two key

personal characteristics that create important barriers to interpersonal communications: the natural tendency to evaluate or judge a sender's message and the inability to listen with understanding. Physical barriers pertain to distance, physical objects, time, and work and office noise.

Semantic barriers show up as encoding and decoding errors because these phases of communication involve transmitting and receiving words and symbols. Cultural diversity is a key contributor to semantic barriers.

DISCUSSION QUESTIONS

1. Describe a situation where you had trouble decoding a message. What caused the problem?

2. What are some sources of noise that interfere with communication during a class lecture, an encounter with a professor in his or her office, and a movie?

3. Which of the three zones of communication in Figure 13–3 (overload, effective, oversimplification) do you think is most common in today's large organizations? What is your rationale?

4. Would you describe your prevailing communication style as assertive, aggressive, or nonassertive? How can you tell? Would your style help or hinder you as a manager?

5. Are you good at reading nonverbal communication? Give some examples.

6. What is your listening style? Give behavioral examples to support your assessment.

7. What is your personal experience with the grapevine? Do you see it as a positive or negative factor in the workplace? Explain.

8. What steps do you need to take to become a better listener? Explain.

9. Have you ever distorted upward communication? What was your reason? Was it related to one of the four antecedents of communication distortion? Explain.

10. Which barrier to effective communication is more difficult to reduce? Explain.

EXERCISE

Objectives

1. To demonstrate the relative effectiveness of communicating assertively, aggressively, and nonassertively.

2. To give you hands-on experience with different styles of communication.

Introduction

Research shows that assertive communication is more effective than either an aggressive or nonassertive style. This *role-playing exercise* is designed to increase your ability to communicate assertively. Your task is to use different communication styles while attempting to resolve the work-related problems of a poor performer.

Instructions

Divide into groups of three and read the "Poor Performer" and "Store Manager" roles on p. 393. Then decide who will play the poor performer role, who will play the managerial role, and who will be the observer. The observer will be asked to provide feedback to the manager after each role play. When playing the managerial role, you should first attempt to resolve the problem by using an aggressive communication style. Attempt to achieve your objective by using the nonverbal and verbal behavior patterns associated with the aggressive style shown in Table 13–1. Take about four to six minutes to act out the instructions. The observer should give feedback to the manager after completing the role play. The observer should comment on how the employee responded to the aggressive behaviors displayed by the manager.

After feedback is provided on the first role play, the person playing the manager should then try to resolve the problem with a nonassertive style. Observers once again should provide feedback. Finally, the manager should confront the problem with an assertive style. Once again, rely on the relevant nonverbal and verbal behavior patterns presented in Table 13–1 and take four to six minutes to act out each scenario. Observers should try to provide detailed feedback on how effectively the manager exhibited nonverbal and verbal assertive behaviors. Be sure to provide positive and constructive feedback.

After completing these three role plays, switch roles: manager becomes observer, observer becomes poor performer, and poor performer becomes the manager. When these role plays are completed, switch roles once again.

Role: Poor Performer

You sell shoes full-time for a national chain of shoe stores. During the last month you have been absent three times without giving your manager a reason. The quality of your work has been slipping. You have a lot of creative excuses when your boss tries to talk to you about your performance.

When playing this role, feel free to invent a personal problem that you may eventually want to share with your manager. However, make the manager dig for information about this problem. Otherwise, respond to your manager's comments as you normally would.

Role: Store Manager

You manage a store for a national chain of shoe stores. In the privacy of your office, you are talking to one of your salespeople who has had three unexcused absences from work during the last month. (This is excessive, according to company guidelines, and must be corrected.) The quality of his or her work has been slipping. Customers have complained that this person is rude, and co-workers have told you this individual isn't carrying his or her fair share of the work. You are fairly sure this person has some sort of personal problem. You want to identify that problem and get him or her back on the right track.

Questions for Consideration/Class Discussion

1. What drawbacks of the aggressive and nonassertive styles did you observe?
2. What were major advantages of the assertive style?
3. What were the most difficult aspects of trying to use an assertive style?
4. How important was nonverbal communication during the various role plays? Explain with examples.

NOTES

1 O C Ferrell and John Fraedrich, *Business Ethics: Ethical Decision Making and Cases* (Boston: Houghton Mifflin, 1991), p 143.

2 Results can be found in P G Clampitt and C W Downs, "Employee Perceptions of the Relationship between Communication and Productivity: A Field Study," *Journal of Business Communication,* 1993, pp 5–28.

3 Results from the innovation study are discussed in J D Johnson, "Effects of Communicative Factors on Participation in Innovations," *The Journal of Business Communication,* Winter 1990, pp 7–24. For details on the second study, see R A Snyder and J H Morris, "Organizational Communication and Performance," *Journal of Applied Psychology,* August 1984, pp 461–65.

4 Supporting evidence can be found in W L Gardner and M J Martinko, "Impression Management: An Observational Study Linking Audience Characteristics with Verbal Self-Presentations," *Academy of Management Journal,* March 1988, pp 42–65; and F Luthans and J K Larsen, "How Managers Really Communicate," *Human Relations,* February 1986, pp 161–78.

5 R E Levinson, "How's That Again?: Execs: The World's Worst Communicators," *Management World,* July–August 1986, p 40.

6 J L Bowditch and A F Buono, *A Primer on Organizational Behavior* (New York: John Wiley & Sons, 1994), p 132.

7 For a review of these criticisms see J Fulk, "Social Construction of Communication Technology," *Academy of Management Journal,* October 1993, pp 921–50; and S R Axley, "Managerial and Organizational Communication in Terms of the Conduit Metaphor," *Academy of Management Review,* July 1984, pp 428–37.

8 See H L Wagner, R Buck, and M Winterbotham, "Communication of Specific Emotions: Gender Differences in Sending Accuracy and Communication Measures," *Journal of Nonverbal Behavior,* Spring 1993, pp 29–53.

9 For a thorough discussion of decoding in intercultural communication, see F Elashmawi and P R Harris, *Multicultural Management: New Skills for Global Success* (Houston: Gulf Publishing, 1993); and L Beamer, "Learning Intercultural Communication Competence," *Journal of Business Communication,* Summer 1992, pp 285–303.

10 Axley, "Managerial and Organizational Communication in Terms of the Conduit Metaphor," p 432.

11 P Hise, "Training: When English Isn't so Plain," *Inc.,* November 1993, p 127.

12 R L Daft and R H Lengel, "Information Richness: A New Approach to Managerial Behavior and Organizational Design," in *Research in Organizational Behavior,* eds B M Staw and L L Cummings (Greenwich, CT: JAI Press, 1984), p 196.

13 N Templin, "Companies Use TV to Reach Their

Workers," *The Wall Street Journal,* December 7, 1993, p B2.

[14] Supporting results can be found in Fulk, "Social Construction of Communication Technology," pp 921–50; D Murphy, "Electronic Communication in Smaller Organizations: Case Analysis from a Theoretical Perspective," *Technical Communication,* First Quarter 1992, pp 24–32; and Daft and Lengel, "Information Richness: A New Approach to Managerial Behavior and Organization Design," pp 191–233.

[15] See R E Rice and D E Shook, "Relationships of Job Categories and Organizational Levels to Use of Communication Channels, Including Electronic Mail: A Meta-Analysis and Extension," *Journal of Management Studies,* March 1990, pp 195–229.

[16] Results can be found in B Davenport Sypher and T E Zorn, Jr., "Communication-Related Abilities and Upward Mobility: A Longitudinal Investigation," *Human Communication Research,* Spring 1986, pp 420–31.

[17] D J Cegala, "Interaction Involvement: A Cognitive Dimension of Communicative Competence," *Communication Education,* April 1981, p 110.

[18] See E Raudsepp, "Are You Properly Assertive?" *Supervision,* June 1992, pp 17–18; and D A Infante and W I Gorden, "Superiors' Argumentativeness and Verbal Aggressiveness as Predictors of Subordinates' Satisfaction," *Human Communication Research,* Fall 1985, pp 117–25.

[19] J A Waters, "Managerial Assertiveness," *Business Horizons,* September–October 1982, p 25.

[20] Ibid., p 27.

[21] W D St. John, "You Are What You Communicate," *Personnel Journal,* October 1985, p 40.

[22] The impact of nonverbal cues on hiring decisions was examined by R C Liden, C L Martin, and C K Parsons, "Interviewer and Applicant Behaviors in Employment Interviews," *Academy of Management Journal,* April 1993, pp 372–86; and A J Kinicki, C A Lockwood, P W Hom, and R W Griffeth, "Interviewer Predictions of Applicant Qualifications and Interviewer Validity: Aggregate and Individual Analyses," *Journal of Applied Psychology,* October 1990, pp 477–86.

[23] Supporting research is presented in P A Anderson, "Nonverbal Immediacy in Interpersonal Communication," in *Multichannel Integrations of Nonverbal Behavior,* eds A W Siegman and S Feldstein (Hillsdale, NJ: Lawrence Erlbaum, 1985), pp 1–36.

[24] Related research is summarized by J A Hall, "Male and Female Nonverbal Behavior," in *Multichannel Integrations of Nonverbal Behavior,* eds A W Siegman and S Feldstein (Hillsdale, NJ: Lawrence Erlbaum, 1985), pp 195–226.

[25] A thorough discussion of cross-cultural differences is provided by R E Axtell, *Gestures: The Do's and Taboos of Body Language Around the World* (New York: John Wiley & Sons, 1991). Problems with body language analysis also are discussed by C L Karrass, "Body Language: Beware the Hype," *Traffic Management,* January 1992, p 27; and M Everett and B Wiesendanger, "What Does Body Language Really Say?" *Sales & Marketing Management,* April 1992, p 40.

[26] Results can be found in Hall, "Male and Female Nonverbal Behavior."

[27] See J A Russell, "Is There Universal Recognition of Emotion from Facial Expression? A Review of the Cross-Cultural Studies," *Psychological Bulletin,* January 1994, pp 102–41.

[28] Norms for cross-cultural eye contact are discussed by C Engholm, *When Business East Meets Business West: The Guide to Practice and Protocol in the Pacific Rim* (New York: John Wiley & Sons, 1991).

[29] Based on E T Hall, *The Hidden Dimension* (Garden City, NY: Doubleday, 1966).

[30] St. John, "You Are What You Communicate," p 43.

[31] Estimates are provided in both J Hart Seibert, "Listening in the Organizational Context," in *Listening Behavior: Measurement and Application,* ed R N Bostrom (New York: The Guilford Press, 1990), pp 119–27; and D W Caudill and R M Donaldson, "Effective Listening Tips for Managers," *Administrative Management,* September 1986, pp 22–23.

[32] See C G Pearce, "How Effective Are We As Listeners?" *Training & Development,* April 1993, pp 79–80; and R A Luke, Jr., "Improving Your Listening Ability," *Supervisory Management,* June 1992, p 7.

[33] For a summary of supporting research, see K W Watson and L L Barker, "Listening Behavior: Definition and Measurement," in *Communication Yearbook 8,* ed R N Bostrom (Beverly Hills, CA: Sage Publications, 1984); and R W Preiss and L R Wheeles, "Affective Responses in Listening: A Meta-Analysis of Receiver Apprehension Outcomes," in *Listening Behavior: Measurement and Application,* ed R N Bostrom (New York: The Guilford Press, 1990, pp 91–118).

[34] For a thorough discussion of the different listening styles, see R T Bennett and R V Wood, "Effective Communication via Listening Styles," *Business,* April–June 1989, pp 45–48.

[35] Ibid., p 46.

[36] Ibid., p 47.

[37] Ibid., p 46.

[38] C Redding, *Communication within the Organization: An Interpretive Review of Theory and Research* (New York: Industrial Communication Council, 1972).

[39] F M Jablin, "Superior-Subordinate Communication: The State of the Art," *Psychological Bulletin,* November 1979, p 1202.

[40] Results from this study are discussed by D Krackhardt and J R Hanson, "Informal Networks: The Company Behind the Chart," *Harvard Business Review,* July/August 1993, pp 104–11.

[41] Organizational benefits of the grapevine are discussed by R Brody, "Gossip: Pros and Cons," *USAIR Magazine,* November 1989, pp 100–104.

[42] Results can be found in S J Modic, "Grapevine Rated Most Believable," *Industry Week,* May 15, 1989, pp 11, 14.

[43] See K Davis, "Management Communication and the Grapevine," *Harvard Business Review,* September–October 1953, pp 43–49.

[44] H B Vickery III, "Tapping into the Employee Grapevine," *Association Management,* January 1984, pp 59–60.

[45] Earlier research is discussed by Davis, "Management Communication and the Grapevine"; and R Rowan, "Where Did *That* Rumor Come From?" *Fortune,* August 13, 1979, pp 130–31, 134, 137. More recent research is discussed in "Pruning the Company Grapevine," *Supervision,* September 1986, p 11; and R Half, "Managing Your Career: 'How Can I Stop the Gossip?' " *Management Accounting,* September 1987, p 27.

[46] Davis, "Management Communication and the Grapevine," p 49.

[47] See P M Fandt and G R Ferris, "The Management of Information and Impressions: When Employees Behave Opportunistically," *Organizational Behavior and Human Decision Processes,* February 1990, pp 140–58.

[48] J Fulk and S Mani, "Distortion of Communication in Hierarchical Relationships," in *Communication Yearbook 9,* ed M L McLaughlin (Beverly Hills, CA: Sage Publications, 1986), p 483.

[49] For a review of this research, see Fulk and Mani, "Distortion of Communication in Hierarchical Relationships," pp 483–510.

[50] The role of communication in transforming organizations is discussed by J E Davis, "A Master Class in Radical Change," *Fortune,* December 13, 1993, pp 82–90; and E H Schein, "How Can Organizations Learn Faster? The Challenge of Entering the Green Room," *Sloan Management Review,* Winter 1993, pp 85–92.

[51] R Rapaport, "Jay Chiat Tears Down the Walls," *Forbes ASAP,* October 25, 1993, p 26.

[52] Collaborative computing is discussed by P Marshall, "Stay in Touch," *Technology Guide/Inc.,* February 1994, pp 57–62; and J Hsu and T Lockwood, "Collaborative Computing," *Byte,* March 1993, pp 113–20.

[53] D H Freedman, "Culture of Urgency," *Forbes ASAP,* September 13, 1993, p 25.

[54] EDS's system is discussed in D Kirkpatrick, "Making It All Worker-Friendly," *Fortune,* Autumn 1993, pp 44–53.

[55] Video conferencing is discussed by A LaPlante, "TeleConfrontationing," *Forbes ASAP,* September 13, 1993, pp 111–26; and A Kupfer, "Prime Time for Video-conferences," *Fortune,* December 28, 1992, pp 90–95.

[56] See J Cote-O'Hara, "Sending Them Home to Work: Telecommuting," *Business Quarterly,* Spring 1993, pp 104–09.

[57] Supporting evidence is discussed in P Hise, "Telecommuter Tips," *Inc.,* June 1993, p 35; S Alvi and D McIntyre, "The Open-Collar Worker," *Canadian Business Review,* Spring 1993, pp 21–24; and K Christensen, "Managing Invisible Employees: How to Meet the Telecommuting Challenge," *Employment Relations Today,* Summer 1992, pp 133–43.

[58] John Naisbitt, *Megatrends: Ten New Directions Transforming Our Lives* (New York: Warner Books, 1982), p 36.

[59] Barriers to communication are discussed by M Munter, "Cross-Cultural Communication for Managers," *Business Horizons,* May–June 1993, pp 69–77; and J M Lump, "Overcoming Obstacles to Effective Communications," *Employee Benefits,* September 1992, pp 27–31.

[60] For a thorough discussion of these barriers, see C R Rogers and F J Roethlisberger, "Barriers and Gateways to Communication," *Harvard Business Review,* July–August 1952, pp 46–52.

[61] Rogers and Roethlisberger, "Barriers and Gateways to Communication," p 47.

[62] See "Becoming a Better Listener: Energize Your Communication by Becoming an Effective Listener," *Nursing,* February 1993, pp 103–04; and P Wylie and M Grothe, "How to Listen so Your Staff Will Talk," *Executive Female,* July/August 1992, pp 27–31.

PERFORMANCE APPRAISAL, FEEDBACK, AND REWARDS

Learning OBJECTIVES

When you finish studying the material in this chapter, you should be able to:

1. Identify four key components of the performance appraisal process.

2. Explain how the trait, behavioral, and results approaches to performance appraisal vary.

3. Identify three different sources of feedback and discuss how we perceive and cognitively evaluate feedback.

4. List at least three practical lessons from feedback research.

5. Explain the difference between extrinsic and intrinsic rewards.

6. Discuss the impact that incentive bonuses have on employee motivation and performance.

7. Explain how profit sharing and gainsharing differ.

8. Identify at least four ways managers can improve pay-for-performance plans.

OPENING CASE

Business Not as Usual at Granite Rock

Sharon Hoogstraten

When Granite Rock Company in 1988 decided to overhaul its performance appraisal process, top management knew it would be tampering with tradition. After all, most U.S. companies believe that a manager's annual review of a subordinate, with the emphasis skewed toward past missteps, is the surest way to boost performance.

Fear, they figure, is a great motivator.

But executives at the Watsonville, California, supplier of ready-mix concrete and other road treatments, sought something different. They wanted to build an appraisal system that Dave Franceschi, manager of quality support, calls much more "forward-looking than backward-looking."

Called the Individual Professional Development Plan (IPDP), the process encourages employees to set annual, personal education goals that will help them learn new skills and advance in their careers—or establish new ones. The company was betting that a substantial training investment (about $2,000 per worker in 1992) together with a visible concern for employees' futures would produce a more motivated and productive workforce.

So far, the gamble has paid off. Last year, the privately held firm nabbed a Malcolm Baldrige National Quality Award, and according to Franceschi, earnings per employee are running 30 percent higher than the industry average.

Accountability for past performance hasn't disappeared, though; it's just become more immediate. "Someone who is not performing will hear about it as soon as it comes to a manager's attention," Franceschi notes. "We're not going to wait until the end of the year to tell someone they did a lousy job on a project three months ago."

And pay increases are still largely awarded based on where employees, lumped in twenty-one salary categories, land on a five-level performance

Productivity and total quality experts tell us that we need to work smarter, not harder. While it is true that a sound education and appropriate training are needed if one is to work smarter, the process does not end there. Today's employees need instructive performance appraisals, supportive feedback, and desired rewards if they are to translate their knowledge into improved productivity and superior quality. As Figure 14–1 illustrates, constructive performance appraisals, feedback, and rewards

• FIGURE 14–1   Performance Appraisal, Feedback, and Rewards Translate Effort into Strong Performance

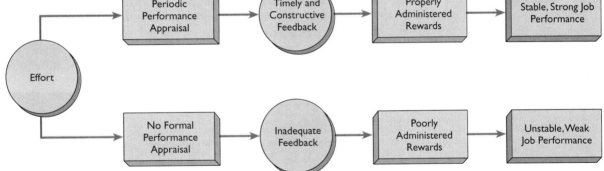

(*continued*)

scale. But Franceschi says this more traditional appraisal discussion now represents only 15 to 20 percent of the time spent on employee development.

The rest is spent on evaluating and developing skills, and setting career goals. Specifically, the process works like this: Both the manager and subordinate draft preliminary IPDP. The form includes a review of the individual's five or six main job responsibilities, summarizes the previous year's IPDP results, identifies the individual's skill strengths on the job, and details developmental objectives for the coming year. The two parties then meet to exchange copies of their first drafts, and review and discuss the contents. That meeting produces a revised

plan agreed upon by both parties.

The manager then presents the consensus plan at a "Roundtable Discussion." The ten-person panel includes Granite Rock division managers, a licensed psychologist, Granite Rock's president, and some peers of the manager presenting the plan. This group generates suggestions on the rough draft of the development plan. A manager from another division might spot a gap in a training plan that would decrease the odds of promotion. It also helps managers develop coaching abilities.

After the roundtable, the manager has a follow-up meeting with the individual being reviewed, either to confirm the plans already made, or to suggest new ideas be added as a result

of roundtable discussions. The final copy is then signed and sent to the personnel office. During the next twelve months the individual and manager meet quarterly—to review progress and "make it a living, constant improvement process," Franceschi says.

The roundtable also serves another vital purpose: It gives employees increased companywide exposure, making it more difficult for managers to squirrel away star performers for their own benefit and keep them from reaching their potential.

For a Granite Rock truck driver who aspires to a branch manager job—perhaps a five-year process—part of the IPDP might include training classes in computer skills, account-

channel effort into stable, strong job performance. These coordinated and systematic human resource management tools give life to the motivation theories presented earlier. On the other hand, a weak or uncoordinated appraisal/feedback/reward system can derail even well-intentioned effort. This chapter will help you integrate and apply concepts you have acquired about individual differences, motivation, behavior modification, and communication.

PERFORMANCE APPRAISAL: DEFINITION AND COMPONENTS

performance appraisal
Judgmental evaluation of one's traits, behavior, or accomplishments as basis for personnel decisions.

In everyday life, it is hard to escape being on the receiving end of some sort of performance appraisal. There are report cards all through school, win-loss records in organized sports, and periodic meetings with one's boss. For managers, who are in the position of both giving and receiving them, performance appraisals are an especially important consideration. As used here, **performance appraisal** involves the judgmental evaluation of a jobholder's traits, behavior, or accomplishments as a basis for making important personnel decisions. A survey of 106 industrial psychologists identified the top 10 uses for performance appraisal data. In diminishing order of importance, they are used for

1. Salary administration.
2. Performance feedback.
3. Identifying individual strengths and weaknesses.
4. Documenting personnel decisions.

(concluded)

ing and management development through Granite Rock University, the company's training program, or maybe a return to college for a management degree. It might also prescribe the "Try Job" program, in which employees can spend a day tagging along with someone in a position they're striving for.

Of course, taking employees away from jobs for large chunks of time (an average of forty hours per employee in 1992) to attend classes or roam around other departments does present some special challenges, Franceschi admits. "There's no doubt it's difficult to cover for people when they're in training, but we've done a lot of cross-training to prepare," he says. "We've found our people even

welcome covering for others because it removes the boredom from jobs."

The plan does not guarantee promotions, but it has certainly made it easier to fill vacancies from within. When IPDP began in 1988, the company filled 30 percent of its vacant positions with internal promotions; in 1992 that number grew to 70 percent.

And management understands full well the potential frustration that could result, even with the no-guarantee policy, if IPDP participants (about 70 percent of the company's 350 employees) begin to outnumber promotion opportunities. With turnover rates shrinking (from 5.6 percent in 1991 to only 4 percent, or less than fifteen openings, last year) Granite Rock's innovative training and ap-

praisal program could create quite a bottleneck at the personnel office. "It's a concern," Franceschi says, "but it hasn't smacked us in the face yet."

For Discussion

Which aspect of this employee development program is most critical to its success?

- Additional discussion questions linking this case with the following material appear at the end of this chapter.

Source: D Zielinski, "Don't Look Back," *Business Ethics,* September–October 1993, p 16.

---

5. Recognition of individual performance.
6. Identifying poor performance.
7. Assisting in goal identification.
8. Promotion decisions.
9. Retention or termination of personnel.
10. Evaluating goal achievement.

Also, performance appraisal information was typically used for *multiple* purposes, rather than for a single purpose.[1] Economic efficiency and the principle of fairness dictate that these decisions be made on the basis of valid and reliable evidence, rather than as the result of prejudice and guesswork.

This section analyzes the key components of the performance appraisal process and summarizes recent research findings relative to those components.

Components of the Performance Appraisal Process

Although formal performance appraisals are practically universal in the managerial ranks (91 percent according to one study),[2] few express satisfaction with them.[3] Appraisers and appraisees alike are unhappy with the process. Much of the problem stems from the complexity of the appraisal process. One writer has captured this issue with the following example:

If you wonder why evaluating an employee's performance can be so difficult, consider a simpler appraisal: one made by the barroom fan who concludes that his team's quarterback is a bum because several of his passes have been intercepted. An objective appraisal would raise the following questions: Were the passes really that bad or did the receivers run the wrong patterns? Did the offensive line give the quarterback adequate protection? Did he call those plays himself, or were they sent in by the coach? Was the quarterback recovering from an injury?

And what about the fan? Has he ever played football himself? How good is his vision? Did he have a good view of the TV set through the barroom's smoky haze? Was he talking to his friends at the bar during the game? How many beers did he down during the game?[4]

Further complicating things are Equal Employment Opportunity laws and guidelines that constrain managers' actions during the appraisal process.[5] Let us begin to sort out the complex appraisal process by examining its key components. Four key components, as shown in Figure 14–2, are the appraiser, the appraisee, the appraisal method, and the outcomes.

The Appraiser   Managers generally express discomfort with playing the role of performance appraiser. After finding that 95 percent of the mid- to lower-level management performance appraisals at 293 U.S. companies were conducted by immediate supervisors, researchers concluded that "most supervisors dislike 'playing God' and that many try to avoid responsibility for providing subordinates with feedback of unflattering appraisal information."[6]

Charges of racism, sexism, and perceptual distortion also have been leveled at appraisers. Common perceptual errors include those discussed in Chapter 5 (halo, leniency, central tendency, recency, and contrast). In a survey of 267 corporations, 62 percent of the respondents reported that leniency error was their number one appraisal problem.[7] Everyday experience and research evidence show how stereotyping and bias can contaminate the appraisal process. For example, combined evidence from a laboratory study and a field study documented how women professors tended to get lower ratings from students with traditional stereotypes of women.[8] Another study monitored the fates of 173 unionized employees who had filed grievances against their supervisors over an eight-year period. Those who had filed grievances tended to receive lower performance ratings from their supervisors than did their co-workers who had not filed grievances. This was especially true when the grievances had been settled in favor of the employee.[9] Thus, in this study at least, supervisors were shown to use performance appraisals as a weapon to get even with disliked subordinates. The ethical implications of this practice are obvious. Moreover, because performance appraisers engage in social cognition (see

• FIGURE 14–2
Components of the Performance Appraisal Process.

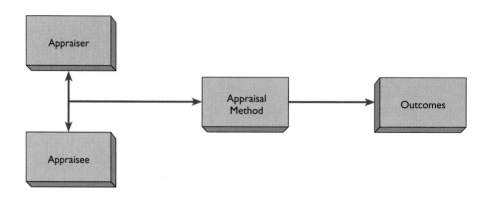

Chapter 5), problems can occur in comprehending, encoding, retaining, or retrieving performance-related information.

Finally, managers typically lack the necessary performance appraisal skills. In fact, according to one recent study, only 25 percent of the managers doing performance appraisals had actually been trained for the task. The researchers added: ''When there is training it often goes little further than to explain how to use the form, administrative procedures, and deadlines for submitting and getting the forms approved.''[10] Experts on the subject have specified four criteria for a willing and able performance appraiser:

> The person doing the assessment must: (1) be in a position to observe the behavior and performance of the individual of interest; (2) be knowledgeable about the dimensions or features of performance; (3) have an understanding of the scale format and the instrument itself; and (4) must be motivated to do a conscientious job of rating.[11]

Managers need to ensure that all four criteria are satisfied if performance appraisals are to be conducted properly.

The Appraisee   Employees play a characteristically passive listening and watching role when their own performance is being appraised. This experience can be demeaning and often threatening. According to a pair of human resource consultants:

> Whatever method is used, performance appraisals are always manager-driven. Managers are in charge of the schedule, the agenda, and the results, and managers are the ones that receive any training and/or rewards concerning performance appraisals. Subordinates generally are given no responsibility or particular preparation for their roles in the process beyond attending the appraisal meetings.[12]

Consequently, these consultants recommend four *proactive* roles (see Table 14–1) for appraisees. They suggest formal *appraisee* training so analyzer, influencer,

Role	Description
Analyzer	Performs self-assessment of goal achievement.
	Identifies performance strengths and weaknesses.
	Makes suggestions for performance improvement.
	Takes personal responsibility for solving performance problems.
Influencer	Improves communication skills (e.g., negotiations, advocating, providing information, advising, soliciting feedback, listening).
	Questions old assumptions and organizational roadblocks.
	Strives for collaborative relationship with boss.
Planner	Develops a clear vision of why his or her job exists.
	Identifies quality-of-service goals relative to "customers" or "clients."
	Understands what his or her job contributes (or does not contribute) to the organization.
Protégé	Learns from high-performing role models without compromising personal uniqueness.
	Learns through personal initiative rather than by waiting for instructions from others.

● ➥ TABLE 14–1

Proactive Appraisee Roles during Performance Appraisal

Source: Adapted from B Jacobson and B L Kaye, "Career Development and Performance Appraisal: It Takes Two to Tango," *Personnel,* January 1986, pp 26–32.

· FIGURE 14~3   Three Basic Approaches to Appraising Job Performance

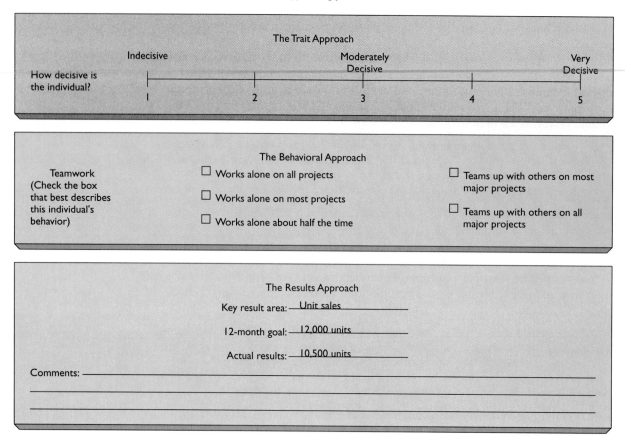

planner, and protégé roles can be performed skillfully. This represents a marked departure from the usual practice of training appraisers only. The goal of this promising approach is to marry performance appraisal and career development through enhanced communication and greater personal commitment.

The Appraisal Method   Three distinct approaches to appraising job performance have emerged over the years—the trait approach, the behavioral approach, and the results approach. Figure 14–3 displays examples of these three approaches. Controversy surrounds the question of which of these three approaches (and a suggested contingency approach) is best.

■ *Trait approach:*   This approach involves rating an individual's personal traits or characteristics. Commonly assessed traits are initiative, decisiveness, and dependability. Although the trait approach is widely used by managers, it is generally considered by experts to be the weakest. Trait ratings are deficient because they are ambiguous relative to actual performance. For instance, rating someone low on initiative tells him or her nothing about how to improve job performance. Also, employees tend to react defensively to feedback about their personality (who or what they are).[13]

■ *Behavioral approach:*   How the person actually behaves, rather than his or her personality, matters in the behavioral approach. As indicated in Figure 14–4, the legal defensibility (in the United States) of performance appraisals is enhanced

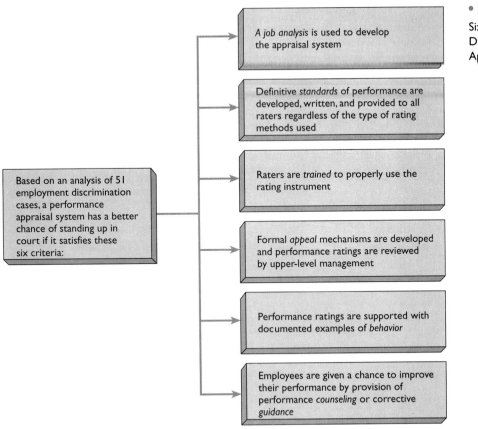

Source: Adapted from G V Barrett and M C Kernan, "Performance Appraisal and Terminations: A Review of Court Decisions since *Brito* v. *Zia* with Implications for Personnel Practices," *Personnel Psychology*, Autumn, 1987, pp 489–503.

when performance ratings are supported with behavioral examples of performance.

- *Results approach:*   Whereas the trait approach focuses on the ''person'' and the behavioral approach focuses on the ''process,'' the results approach focuses on the ''product'' of one's efforts. In other words, what has the individual accomplished? *Management by objectives* (MBO) is the most common format for the results approach.[14]

- *Contingency approach:*   A pair of performance appraisal experts has called the trait-behavioral-results controversy a ''pseudo issue.''[15] They contend that each approach has its appropriate use, depending on the demands of the situation. Thus, they recommend a contingency approach (see Table 14–2). Notice how the poorly regarded trait approach is appropriate when a promotion decision needs to be made for candidates with dissimilar jobs. Although it has widespread applicability, the results approach is limited by its failure to specify why the appraisee's objectives have not been met. Overall, the behavioral approach emerges as the strongest. But it too is subject to situational limitations, such as when employees with dissimilar jobs are being evaluated for a promotion.

Outcomes of the Appraisal   According to a researcher from the Center for Creative Leadership, there are three indicators of a useful performance appraisal. They are

TABLE 14~2
A Contingency Approach to
Performance Appraisals

Function of Appraisal	Appraisal Method	Comments
Promotion decisions	Trait	Appropriate when competing appraisees have *dissimilar* jobs.
	Behavioral	Appropriate when competing appraisees have *similar* jobs.
	Results	Same as above.
Development decisions	Trait	Tends to cause defensiveness among low self-esteem employees.
	Behavioral	Pinpoints specific performance improvement needs.
	Results	Identifies deficient results, but does not tell why.
Pay decisions	Trait	Weak performance-reward linkage.
	Behavioral	Enhances performance-reward linkage.
	Results	Same as above.
Layoff decisions	Trait	Inappropriate, potentially discriminatory.
	Behavioral	Weighted combination of behaviors, results, and seniority is recommended.
	Results	Same as above.

Source: Adapted from K N Wexley and R Klimoski, "Performance Appraisal: An Update," in *Research in Personnel and Human Resources Management*, vol. 2, eds K M Rowland and G R Ferris (Greenwich, CT: JAI Press, 1984), pp 35–79.

- Timely feedback on performance.
- Input for key personnel decisions.
- Individual and organizational planning tool.[16]

To this list, we would add "human resource development tool." These four appraisal outcomes cannot be left to chance. They need to be forethoughts rather than afterthoughts.

Performance Appraisal Research Insights

Researchers have probed many facets of the appraisal process. Resulting insights include the following:

- Appraisers typically rate same-race appraisees higher. A meta-analysis of 74 studies and 17,159 individuals revealed that white superiors tended to favor white subordinates. Similarly, black superiors tended to favor black subordinates in a meta-analysis of 14 studies and 2,248 people.[17]
- Although a great deal of effort has been devoted to creating more precise rating formats, formats account for very little difference (4 to 8 percent) in ratings.
- Performance appraisers tend to give poor performers significantly higher ratings when they have to give the appraisees face-to-face feedback as opposed to anonymous written feedback or no feedback.
- More experienced appraisers tend to render higher quality appraisals. This finding suggests that comprehensive appraiser training and practice can reduce rater errors.[18]

These research insights, along with evidence of rater bias discussed earlier, constitute a bad news–good news situation for management. The *bad* news: performance appraisals can be contaminated by racism, sexism, personal bias, and fear of conflict. The *good* news: managers can be trained to improve their performance appraisal skills.

Employee performance appraisals are conducted in many different ways today. There are weighted checklists, forced distributions, graphic rating scales, written essays, and customer satisfaction surveys, among others. Our purpose here, however, is not to discuss the relative merits of alternative appraisal formats. Not only are there far too many to adequately cover, the particular appraisal format (as indicated in our research insights discussed earlier) tends to have a minor impact on appraisal results. Instead, we will address more fundamental issues that may determine the difference between effective and ineffective appraisals.

Who Should Evaluate Job Performance?

Sheer force of tradition alone almost guarantees a standard answer to this question: One's immediate supervisor, of course. This answer may be the most common one, but some experts contend it is not necessarily the correct one today. Interest is growing in nontraditional appraisals by subordinates, peers, and self. How do these nontraditional approaches to performance appraisal measure up? Should managers use them?

Feedback from subordinates (generally anonymous) effectively turns the performance appraisal process on its head. According to *The Wall Street Journal:*

> Corporate managers increasingly are being put on the hot seat—by the people who work for them. The technique isn't easy to administer and makes many managers uncomfortable. But proponents contend that it can help workers feel more involved in their company. And they argue that subordinates are uniquely situated to observe and evaluate their bosses for leadership, organization, and crisis-management skills. . . .
>
> Indeed, a 1984 study found that subordinates tend to rate their supervisor tougher than the supervisor's boss. One obvious reason, suggests the author, Michael K Mount, a University of Iowa professor, is the setting: Subordinates don't have to evaluate their boss face-to-face.[19]

Amid enthusiastic calls for bottom-up appraisal,[20] the practice is growing slowly. Early adopters of upward evaluations include AT&T, General Mills, Motorola, and Procter & Gamble.[21] Management resistance is strong. Moreover, the results can be readily ignored because they lack hierarchical authority. Even where it is used, subordinate feedback typically is a management development tool rather than the basis for pay and promotion decisions.

Peer- and self-appraisals also are significant affronts to tradition. The main argument in favor of both is the same one offered for subordinate appraisals. Namely, co-workers and the manager himself or herself are closer to the action. They have more opportunities to directly observe job performance. Research builds a stronger case for peer appraisals than for self-appraisals.[22]

So should management bother with subordinate, peer, and self performance appraisals? The answer is a qualified yes. These nontraditional appraisals are an appropriate and useful *supplement* to the traditional top-down variety. They are not an adequate replacement, at least at this time and state of the art. Nontraditional feedback to managers from peers and subordinates should be anonymous. Unfortunately, this requirement destroys the rater accountability found in traditional

360-degree review
Performance evaluation based
on input from one's superior,
peers, and subordinates.

top-down appraisals. A promising compromise is a growing practice called the 360-degree review. A **360-degree review** combines performance evaluation feedback from one's superior, peers, subordinates, and sometimes customers. General Electric's CEO, Jack Welch, explains how his company does it:

> (Every employee is graded on a 1-to-5 scale by his manager, his peers and all his subordinates in areas such as team-building, quality focus and vision.) Some people think it's bureaucratic. But it embodies our values (which came out of years of discussions with employees). And the subordinates clearly provide the best input. Peers are a little more careful, and the boss is always a little more cautious.[23]

Performance Appraisals and TQM

There is a direct conflict between traditional performance appraisals and total quality management (TQM). Why? Traditional appraisals focus on *individual* performance while TQM is *team* oriented. A pair of TQM advocates recently offered this argument:

> When organizations rely on individual appraisal and merit ratings to assign rewards, employees will often forgo opportunities for productive collaboration and cooperation. Instead, they engage in actions that will make them look better as individuals. The individual result is a higher performance rating—and a greater pay increase or bonus. But for the organization the outcome may be low-quality products and lower profits.[24]

Thus, managers who are truly committed to TQM need to shift from individual appraisals and incentives to team-based evaluations and rewards.[25] The focus of the various appraisal techniques covered in this chapter, such as 360-degree reviews, can be shifted from the individual to teams to promote the cooperation and teamwork so vital to TQM.

FEEDBACK

Achievement-oriented students have a hearty appetite for feedback. Following a difficult exam, for instance, students want to know two things: how they did and how their peers did. By letting students know how their work measures up to grading and competitive standards, an instructor's feedback permits the students to adjust their study habits so they can reach their goals. Likewise, managers in well-run organizations follow up goal setting with a feedback program to provide a rational basis for adjustment and improvement. For example, consider how the chief executive officer of electrical equipment maker Square D used feedback to personalize the financial goals of the company:

> [He] installed an outsize scoreboard at corporate headquarters. Up on the board are the quarterly results broken down by profit per employee, sales per employee, and return on equity for Square D and its competitors, among them Emerson Electric, General Electric, and Westinghouse. Square D workers know exactly what they're up against.[26]

Not surprisingly, Square D is an industry leader among electrical equipment manufacturers.

feedback   Objective information about one's performance.

As the term is used here, **feedback** is objective information about the adequacy of one's own job performance. Subjective assessments such as, "You're doing a lousy job," "You're really a jerk," or "We truly appreciate your hard work" do not qualify as objective feedback. But hard data such as units sold, days absent, dollars saved, projects completed, and quality control rejects are all candidates for objective feedback programs. Management consultants Chip Bell and Ron Zemke recently offered this perspective of feedback:

> Feedback is, quite simply, any information that answers those "How am I doing?" questions. *Good* feedback answers them truthfully and productively. It's information people can use either to confirm or correct their performance.
>
> Feedback comes in many forms and from a variety of sources. Some is easy to get and requires hardly any effort to understand. The charts and graphs tracking group and individual performance that are fixtures in many workplaces are an example of this variety. Performance feedback—the numerical type at least—is at the heart of most approaches to total quality management.
>
> Some feedback is less accessible. It's tucked away in the heads of customers and managers. But no matter how well-hidden the feedback, if people need it to keep their performance on track, we need to get it to them—preferably while it's still fresh enough to make an impact.[27]

Experts say feedback serves two functions for those who receive it, one is *instructional* and the other *motivational*. Feedback instructs when it clarifies roles or teaches new behavior. For example, an assistant accountant might be advised to handle a certain entry as a capital item rather than as an expense item. On the other hand, feedback motivates when it serves as a reward or promises a reward.[28] Having the boss tell you that a grueling project you worked on earlier has just been completed can be a rewarding piece of news. As documented in one study, the motivational function of feedback can be significantly enhanced by pairing *specific*, challenging goals with *specific* feedback about results.[29] We expand upon these two functions in this section by analyzing a conceptual model of feedback, and reviewing the practical implications of recent feedback research.

Conceptual Model of the Feedback Process

The influence of objective feedback on job behavior is a much more complex process than one might initially suspect. To begin with, as shown in Figure 14–5, feedback comes from different sources. Moreover, perceptual and cognitive hurdles must be jumped if the desired behavioral outcomes are to be achieved. Let us explore this model to better understand how feedback influences job behavior.

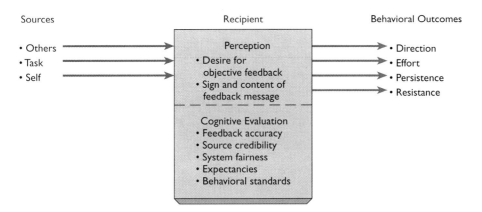

● ⤴ FIGURE 14~5

A Model of Feedback on Job Performance

Source: Based in part on discussion in M S Taylor, C D Fisher, and D R Ilgen, "Individuals' Reactions to Performance Feedback in Organizations: A Control Theory Perspective," in *Research in Personnel and Human Resources Management*, vol. 2, eds K M Rowland and G R Ferris (Greenwich, CT: JAI Press, 1984). pp 81–124.

Sources of Feedback   It almost goes without saying that employees receive objective feedback from others such as peers, supervisors, subordinates, and outsiders. Perhaps less obvious is the fact that the task itself is a ready source of objective feedback. Anyone who has been "hooked into" pumping quarters into a video game can appreciate the power of task-provided feedback. Similarly, skilled tasks such as computer programming or landing a jet airplane provide a steady stream of feedback about how well or poorly one is doing. A third source of feedback is oneself, but self-serving bias and other perceptual problems can contaminate this source. Those high in self-confidence tend to rely on personal feedback more than those with low self-confidence. Although circumstances vary, an employee can be bombarded by feedback from all three sources simultaneously. This is where the gatekeeping functions of perception and cognitive evaluation are needed to help sort things out.

Perception and Cognitive Evaluation of Feedback   As with other stimuli, we selectively perceive feedback. One's desire for objective feedback is an important factor here. Many people ask for objective feedback when it is the last thing they truly want. Restaurant servers who ask, "How was everything?" before presenting the bill, typically turn a deaf ear to constructive criticism. Personality characteristics, such as need for achievement, also can influence one's desire for feedback. In a laboratory study, Japanese psychology students who scored high on need for achievement responded more favorably to feedback than did their classmates who had low need for achievement.[30] This particular relationship likely exists in Western cultures as well. Moreover, 331 employees in the marketing department of a large public utility in the United States were found to seek feedback on important issues or when faced with uncertain situations. Long-tenured employees from this sample also were less likely to seek feedback than employees with little tenure.[31] Consequently, managers need to consider each individual's readiness for objective feedback, based on relevant personality and situational variables.

The *sign* of feedback refers to whether it is positive or negative. Generally, people tend to perceive and recall positive feedback more accurately than they do negative feedback.[32] But feedback with a negative sign (e.g., being told your performance is below average) can have a *positive* motivational impact. In fact, in a recent laboratory study, those who were told they were below average on a creativity test subsequently outperformed those who were led to believe their results were above average. The subjects apparently took the negative feedback as a challenge and set and pursued higher goals. Those receiving positive feedback apparently were less motivated to do better.[33] Nonetheless, feedback with a negative sign or threatening content needs to be administered carefully to avoid creating insecurity and defensiveness.

Upon receiving feedback, people cognitively evaluate factors such as its accuracy, the credibility of the source, the fairness of the system (e.g., performance appraisal system), their performance-reward expectancies, and the reasonableness of the standards. Any feedback that fails to clear one or more of these cognitive hurdles will be rejected or downplayed. Personal experience largely dictates how these factors are weighed. For instance, you would probably discount feedback from someone who exaggerates or from someone who performed poorly on the same task you have just successfully completed. In view of the "trust gap," discussed in Chapter 12, managerial credibility is an ethical matter of central importance today. According to the authors of the book *Credibility: How Leaders*

Gain and Lose It, Why People Demand It, ''without a solid foundation of personal credibility, leaders can have no hope of enlisting others in a common vision.''[34] Managers who have proven untrustworthy and not credible have a hard time improving job performance through feedback.

Feedback from a source who apparently shows favoritism or relies on unreasonable behavior standards would be suspect. Also, as predicted by expectancy motivation theory, feedback must foster high effort→performance expectancies and performance→reward instrumentalities if it is to motivate desired behavior. For example, many growing children have been cheated out of the rewards of athletic competition because they were told by respected adults that they were too small, too short, too slow, too clumsy, and so forth. Feedback can have a profound and lasting impact on behavior.

Behavioral Outcomes of Feedback   In Chapter 7, we discussed how goal setting gives behavior direction, increases expended effort, and fosters persistence. Because feedback is intimately related to the goal-setting process, it involves the same behavioral outcomes: direction, effort, and persistence. However, while the fourth outcome of goal setting involves formulating goal-attainment strategies, the fourth possible outcome of feedback is *resistance.* Feedback schemes, that smack of manipulation or fail one or more of the perceptual and cognitive evaluation tests just discussed, breed resistance. Steve Jobs, the young cofounder of Apple Computer, left the firm amid controversy in 1985 partly because his uneven and heavy-handed feedback bred resistance:

> According to several insiders, Jobs, a devout believer that new technology should supersede the old, couldn't abide the success of the venerable Apple II. Nor did he hide his feelings. He once addressed the Apple II marketing staff as members of the ''dull and boring product division.'' As chairman and largest stockholder, with an 11.3 percent block, Jobs was a disproportionately powerful general manager. And he had disproportionate enthusiasm for the [Macintosh] staff. Says one of them: ''He was so protective of us that whenever we complained about somebody outside the division, it was like unleashing a Doberman. Steve would get on the telephone and chew the guy out so fast your head would spin.''[35]

Practical Lessons from Feedback Research

After reviewing dozens of laboratory and field studies of feedback, a trio of OB researchers cited the following practical implications for managers:

- The acceptance of feedback should not be treated as a given; it is often misperceived or rejected. This is especially true in intercultural situations.
- Managers can enhance their credibility as sources of feedback by developing their expertise and creating a climate of trust.
- Negative feedback is typically misperceived or rejected.
- Although very frequent feedback may erode one's sense of personal control and initiative, feedback is too *infrequent* in most work organizations.
- Feedback needs to be tailored to the recipient.
- While average and below-average performers need extrinsic rewards for performance, high performers respond to feedback that enhances their feelings of competence and personal control.[36]

More recent research insights about feedback include the following:

• TABLE 14~3

Six Common Trouble Signs
for Organizational Feedback
Systems

1. Feedback is used to punish, embarrass, or put down employees.
2. Those receiving the feedback see it as irrelevant to their work.
3. Feedback information is provided too late to do any good.
4. People receiving feedback believe it relates to matters beyond their control.
5. Employees complain about wasting too much time collecting and recording feedback data.
6. Feedback recipients complain about feedback being too complex or difficult to understand.

Source: Adapted from C Bell and R Zemke, "On-Target Feedback," *Training*, June 1992, pp 36–44.

■ Computer-based performance feedback leads to greater improvements in performance when it is received directly from the computer system rather than via an immediate supervisor.[37]

■ Recipients of feedback perceive it to be more accurate when they actively participate in the feedback session, versus passively receiving feedback.[38]

■ Destructive criticism tends to cause conflict and reduce motivation.[39]

■ "The higher one rises in an organization the less likely one is to receive quality feedback about job performance."[40]

Managers who act on these research implications and the trouble signs in Table 14–3 can build credible and effective feedback systems.[41]

Our attention now turns to rewards, a natural follow-up to any discussion of performance appraisal and feedback.

ORGANIZATIONAL REWARD SYSTEMS

Rewards are an ever-present feature of organizational life. Some employees see their jobs as the source of a paycheck and little else. Others derive great pleasure from their jobs and association with co-workers. Even volunteers who donate their time to charitable organizations, such as the Red Cross, walk away with rewards in the form of social recognition and pride of having given unselfishly of their time. Hence, the subject of organizational rewards includes, but goes far beyond, monetary compensation. This section examines key components of organizational reward systems to provide a conceptual background for discussing the timely topic of pay for performance.

Despite the fact that reward systems vary widely, it is possible to identify and interrelate some common components. The model in Figure 14–6 focuses on four important components: (1) types of rewards, (2) reward norms, (3) distribution criteria, and (4) desired outcomes. Let us examine these components.

Types of Rewards

Including the usual paycheck, the variety and magnitude of organizational rewards boggles the mind—from subsidized lunches to college tuition reimbursement to stock options. A US Bureau of Labor Statistics economist offered the following historical perspective of employee compensation:

> One of the more striking developments . . . over the past 75 years has been the growing complexity of employee compensation. Limited at the outbreak of World War I largely to straight-time pay for hours worked, compensation now includes a variety of employer-financed benefits, such as health and life insurance, retirement income, and paid time off. Although the details of each vary widely, these benefits are today standard components of the compensation package, and workers generally have come to expect them.[42]

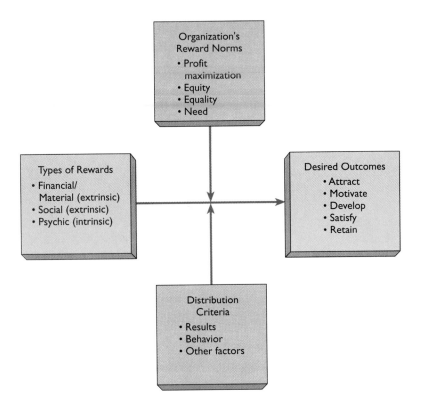

• ↗ FIGURE 14~6

A General Model of
Organizational Reward
Systems

"In 1990, the average cost of benefits as a percentage of total gross pay was 38.4 percent."[43]

In addition to the obvious pay and benefits, there are less obvious social and psychic rewards. Social rewards include praise and recognition from others both inside and outside the organization. Psychic rewards come from personal feelings of self-esteem, self-satisfaction, and accomplishment.

An alternative typology for organizational rewards is the distinction between extrinsic and intrinsic rewards. Financial, material, and social rewards qualify as **extrinsic rewards** because they come from the environment. Psychic rewards, however, are **intrinsic rewards** because they are self-granted. An employee who works to obtain extrinsic rewards, such as money or praise, is said to be extrinsically motivated. One who derives pleasure from the task itself or experiences a sense of competence or self-determination is said to be intrinsically motivated.[44] The relative importance of extrinsic and intrinsic rewards is a matter of personal values and tastes.

extrinsic rewards   Financial, material, or social rewards from the environment.

intrinsic rewards   Self-granted, psychic rewards.

Organizational Reward Norms

As discussed in Chapter 7 under the heading of equity theory, some OB scholars view the employer–employee linkage as an exchange relationship. Employees exchange their time and talent for rewards. Ideally, four alternative norms dictate the nature of this exchange. In pure form, each would lead to a significantly different reward distribution system. They are as follows:

■ *Profit maximization:*   The objective of each party is to maximize its net gain, regardless of how the other party fares. A profit-maximizing company would attempt to pay the least amount of wages for maximum effort. Conversely, a

People experience positive psychic rewards when they receive recognition. These Compaq Corp. employees respond happily to appreciation expressed by top management.

profit-maximizing employee would seek maximum rewards, regardless of the organization's financial well-being, and leave the organization for a better deal.

reward equity norm
Rewards should be tied to contributions.

- *Equity:*   According to the **reward equity norm,** rewards should be allocated proportionate to contributions. Those who contribute the most should be rewarded the most. A cross-cultural study of American, Japanese, and Korean college students led the researchers to the following conclusion: "Equity is probably a phenomenon common to most cultures, but its strength will vary."[45] Basic principles of fairness and justice, evident in most cultures, drive the equity norm.

reward equality norm
Everyone should get the same rewards.

- *Equality:*   The **reward equality norm** calls for rewarding all parties equally, regardless of their comparative contributions.
- *Need:*   This norm calls for distributing rewards according to employees' needs, rather than their contributions.[46]

After defining these exchange norms, a pair of researchers concluded that these contradictory norms are typically intertwined.

> We propose that employer–employee exchanges are governed by the contradictory norms of profit maximization, equity, equality, and need. These norms can coexist; what varies is the extent to which the rules for correct application of a norm are clear and the relative emphasis different managements will give to certain norms in particular allocations.[47]

Conflict and ethical debates often arise over the perceived fairness of reward allocations because of disagreement about reward norms.[48] Stockholders might prefer a profit-maximization norm, while technical specialists would like an equity norm, and unionized hourly workers would argue for a pay system based on equality. A reward norm anchored to need might prevail in a family owned and operated business. Effective reward systems are based on clear and consensual exchange norms.

Reward Distribution Criteria

According to one expert on organizational reward systems, three general criteria for the distribution of rewards are:

- *Performance: results.* Tangible outcomes such as individual, group, or organization performance; quantity and quality of performance.
- *Performance: actions and behaviors.* Such as teamwork, cooperation, risk-taking, creativity.
- *Nonperformance considerations.* Customary or contractual, where the type of job, nature of the work, equity, tenure, level in hierarchy, etc., are rewarded.[49]

Well-managed organizations integrate these reward distribution criteria with the performance appraisal system. For example, a pay-for-performance system facilitates granting rewards for results, while behaviorally specific appraisals help pinpoint rewardable behavior. Nonperformance factors such as seniority are simply taken at face value.

Desired Outcomes of the Reward System

As listed in Figure 14–6, a good reward system should attract talented people and motivate and satisfy them once they have joined the organization. Further, a good reward system should foster personal growth and development and keep talented people from leaving. A prime example is Herman Miller Inc., the profitable office-furniture maker. Not only does the firm maintain a much lower than average ratio between top management and shop-floor pay levels, Herman Miller shares generous productivity bonuses with its employees as well. The net results: low turnover, a strong supportive culture, and excellent employee–management working relationships.[50]

Our discussion of organizational rewards would not be complete without more closely considering the role of *money*. In the workplace, money is the most common reward. Administration of monetary rewards falls into the general category of employee compensation. A comprehensive review and analysis of the hundreds of different compensation plans in use today would require a separate textbook. Instead, let us address this important underlying OB question: How can managers increase the incentive effect of monetary compensation? Managers who adequately comprehend this issue are in a better position to make decisions about specific compensation plans.

PAY FOR PERFORMANCE

Putting Pay for Performance in Perspective

Pay for performance is the popular term for monetary incentives linking at least some portion of the paycheck directly to results or accomplishments. The whole idea behind pay-for-performance schemes—including but not limited to merit pay, bonuses, and profit sharing—is to give employees an incentive for working harder and/or smarter. Pay for performance is something extra, compensation above and beyond basic wages and salaries. Proponents of incentive compensation say something extra is needed because hourly wages and salaries do little more than motivate one to show up at work and put in the requisite hours.[51] The most blatant

pay for performance
Monetary incentives tied to one's results or accomplishments.

Lincoln Electric Company's pay-for-performance system has generated interest among many other companies that are looking for better incentives for their employees.

(Courtesy Lincoln Electric Company, Cleveland, Ohio)

form of pay for performance is the traditional piece rate plan, whereby the employee is paid a specified amount of money for each unit of work. For example, a drill press operator gets 25 cents for every gasket drilled in four places. Sales commissions, whereby a salesperson receives a specified amount of money for each unit sold, is another longstanding example of pay for performance. Today's service economy is forcing management to creatively adapt and go beyond piece rate and sales commission plans to accommodate greater emphasis on product and service quality, interdependence, and teamwork.

A recent survey of more than 2,000 US companies documented one dimension of the trend toward pay for performance: "Since 1988 the number of US concerns offering variable pay, chiefly bonuses, to all salaried employees has jumped from 47% to 68%. Moreover, these companies now pay out far more in incentive compensation than in salary increases."[52] Top executives in the United States are routinely granted multimillion dollar bonuses. For example, in 1993, Chrysler's chairman, Robert Eaton, was granted a $1.9 million bonus because his company exceeded customer satisfaction and quality improvement goals. Eaton's total compensation that year was $3 million.[53] And the US Congress has tackled the issue of merit pay for federal employees. While all this activity is well-intentioned, it too often falls short of its goal of improved job performance. "Experts say that roughly half the incentive plans they see don't work, victims of poor design and administration."[54] Researchers have found only a weak statistical link between large executive bonuses paid out in good years and subsequent improvement in corporate profitability.[55] Also, in a survey of small business owners, more than half said their commission plans failed to motivate extra effort from their salespeople.[56] Clearly, the pay-for-performance movement is in danger of stalling if constructive steps are not taken.

Source: B Graham-Moore and T L Ross, *Gainsharing* (Washington, DC: The Bureau of National Affairs, 1990), p 13 as adapted from T Hammer, "New Developments in Profit Sharing," in *Productivity in Organizations,* eds J Campbell, R Campbell, and Associates (San Francisco: Jossey-Bass, 1988). Reprinted by permission.

Incentive Bonuses and Motivation: A Double-Impact Model

A first important step toward improving pay for performance is to better understand the motivational mechanism of bonuses (see Figure 14–7). As the term is used in Figure 14–7, *bonuses* refers to all forms of incentive compensation (in other words, pay for performance). Notice how *participation* plays a central role in this model. When employees fully participate in developing, implementing, and updating the performance-reward standards, three processes are triggered. First, productivity problems are more readily identified and solved. This is particularly true when teamwork techniques, such as quality circles, discussed in Chapter 12, are in force. Second, intrinsic motivation grows as the employee finds greater personal enjoyment and challenge in her or his work. Third, increased two-way information flow between management and employees empowers the employees. In turn, each of these three processes increases one's chances of earning the promised bonus, via lower costs and/or higher productivity. Intrinsic motivation translates into increased effort. Recalling our discussion of job design in Chapter 6 and expectancy motivation theory in Chapter 7, we can appreciate the motivating potential of properly administered incentive bonuses. This model makes a significant contribution to our thinking about pay for performance by emphasizing the double impact of bonuses. They motivate both when promised and when granted! The feedback loop from bonus to participation likely bolsters the employee's self-efficacy.

With this model in mind as a useful conceptual framework, let us take a closer look at two distinctly different pay-for-performance practices.[57] We then offer some practical recommendations.

Profit Sharing versus Gainsharing

The terms *profit sharing* and *gainsharing* sometimes are used interchangeably. That is not only a conceptual mistake, but a major disservice to gainsharing as well. These two general approaches to pay for performance differ significantly in both method and results.

profit sharing Portion of bottom-line economic profits given to employees.

Profit Sharing   Most of today's corporate pay-for-performance plans are profit sharing schemes. **Profit sharing** occurs when individual employees or work groups are granted a specified portion of any economic profits earned by the business as a whole. These internally distributed profits may be apportioned according to the equality or equity norms discussed earlier. Equity distributions supposedly occur when performance appraisal results are used to gauge who gets how much in the way of merit pay or profit sharing bonuses. Profit sharing bonuses may be paid in cash, deferred until retirement or death, or some combination of both (see the top section of Table 14–4). According to a 20-year study of 500 US companies, "Productivity increases 3.5% to 5% on average after companies adopt profit-sharing programs. . . . Profit sharing lifts productivity more in smaller companies [ones with 775 or fewer employees]."[58]

gainsharing Bonuses tied to measurable productivity increases.

Gainsharing   Perhaps because it tends to be used in smaller companies with 500 or fewer employees, gainsharing is not as popularly known as profit sharing. "**Gainsharing** involves a measurement of productivity combined with the calculation of a bonus designed to offer employees a mutual share of any increases in total organizational productivity. Usually all those responsible for the increase receive the bonus."[59] Gainsharing has been around for more than a half century and typically goes by one of the following names: Improshare®, Rucker® plan, or

⤙• TABLE 14~4
Profit Sharing and Gainsharing Plans

Types of Profit Sharing Plans

Deferred Plan—Credit individuals with periodic earnings, delaying actual distribution until their disability, retirement, or death.

Distribution plan—Fully distributes each period's earned benefits as soon as the profit-sharing pool can be calculated.

Combination plan—Allows employees to receive a portion of each period's earnings in cash, while the remainder awaits future distribution.

Types of Gainsharing Plans

Improshare plans—Based on employees' ability to complete assignments in less time than would be expected given the historical productivity base ratio. Work-hours saved are divided between the firm and plan participants according to a set percentage, such as 50 percent. Individuals receive a corresponding percentage increase in gross pay. Although no structural barriers exist, these plans generally do not provide formal participation in decision making.

Rucker plan—Generally limits decision-making participation to a single screening committee or the interface of a production and a screening committee. The Rucker formula assesses the relationship between the value added to produced goods as they pass through the manufacturing process and total labor costs. Unlike the typical Scanlon ratio, this formula enables workers to benefit from savings in production-related materials, supplies, and services. Bonuses result when the current ratio is better than that for the base period. A reserve pool is established to offset bad months. The reserves left over at the end of the year are paid out to employees as an additional bonus.

Scanlon plan—Uses a dual-committee system to foster companywide participation in decision making. Draws upon a historical productivity base ratio relating adjusted sales to total payroll. A bonus pool is created whenever actual output, as measured by adjusted sales, requires lower labor costs than would be expected using the base ratio. Each month, a percentage of the bonus pool is held in reserve to offset deficit months. The remaining funds are divided between the firm and employees. All of the retained funds remaining at year's end are proportionately shared by the parties.

Source: G W Florkowski, "Analyzing Group Incentive Plans," *HRMagazine,* January 1990, p 37. Reprinted with permission from HRMagazine (formerly *Personnel Administrator*) published by the Society for Human Resource Management, Alexandria, VA.

Scanlon plan (see the bottom section of Table 14–4 for details). Distinguishing characteristics of gainsharing include the following:

■ An organizational culture based on labor–management cooperation, trust, free-flowing information, and extensive participation.

■ Built-in employee involvement structures such as suggestion systems or quality circles.

■ Precise measurement and tracking of cost and/or productivity data for comparison purposes.

■ The sharing with managerial and nonmanagerial employees of the proceeds from any productivity gains.[60]

Ideally, a self-perpetuating cycle develops. Communication and participation generate creative suggestions which foster productivity gains that yield bonuses which build motivation and trust.[61]

How Do Profit Sharing and Gainsharing Measure Up?   Profound differences mark these two general approaches to pay for performance. Gainsharing, by definition, is anchored to hard productivity data; profit sharing typically is more loosely linked to performance appraisal results. Thus profit sharing determinations, like performance appraisals, are readily plagued by bias and misperception. Another significant problem with profit sharing is that bottom-line profits are influenced by many factors beyond the average employee's control. Those factors include strategy, pricing, competition, and fluctuating interest rates, to name just a few. Profit sharing's principal weaknesses are effectively neutralized by gainsharing's major strength, namely, a quantified performance-pay formula.

Critics of profit sharing admit it is generous to share the good times with employees, but they fear profit sharing bonuses are perceived as a reward for past performance, not as an incentive to work harder in the future. Moreover, gainsharing rewards participation and teamwork while profit sharing generally does not. On the other hand, gainsharing formulas are complex and require extensive communication and training commitments.

So, on balance, which is better? Judging by available research evidence, much of which is subjective, the vote goes to gainsharing. One study of 71 managers and professionals in a metals processing company found no significant correlation between individual performance and profit sharing bonuses.[62] Another study of 1,746 manufacturing employees, at seven firms with Scanlon plans and two control firms without Scanlon plans, found higher job satisfaction and commitment among the Scanlon employees. Additionally, participation was a significantly stronger cultural norm in the Scanlon organizations. Scanlon participants quickly passed this norm along to new employees.[63] Gainsharing seems to work best when it becomes embedded in the organization's culture. (e.g., see the International OB).

Making Pay for Performance Work

From a practical "so what" perspective, the real issue is not profit sharing versus gainsharing. Rather, the issue is this: How can managers improve the motivational impact of their present pay-for-performance plan? The fact is, most such plans are not pure types. They are hybrids. They combine features of profit sharing and gainsharing. One option is to hire consultants to establish one of the trademarked gainsharing plans or the Scanlon plan. A second, more broadly applicable, option is

INTERNATIONAL OB

Gainsharing Helps This Swedish-American Joint Venture Thrive

In the early '80s, Ericsson GE was General Electric's Mobile Communications Business and it was in trouble. In 1984 General Electric CEO Jack Welch directed John Trani, then general manager, to close the [Lynchburg, Virginia] division, "fix" it or sell it.

In attempting to fix the business, Trani cut the work force to the bone, laying off some 700 line workers in 1984. He froze salaried and hourly workers' pay. But Trani recognized that cuts alone weren't going to save the division, so he also cast about for some way to improve its performance. The seeds of Winshare were sown when Trani brought in consultant Tim Ross in 1986 to create a gain-sharing plan that would help fix GE Mobile Communications.

According to Ross, currently the director of Ross Gainsharing Institute in Chapel Hill, NC, there are three ways to design a gain-sharing system: The first stresses the gain-sharing bonus (the cash incentive employees receive when the company exceeds a targeted profitability) and includes no employee involvement; the second also stresses the bonus, but includes some form of employee involvement; the third, the one Ross recommended to Ericsson, is built around extensive employee involvement and fundamentally changes the way a company manages its people.

Top executives at Lynchburg weren't enthusiastic about the employee-involvement part of the package at first, says Ross. In fact, he virtually had to push them into it.

The gain-sharing part of Ericsson's program provided for a quarterly bonus based on the company's performance: If profits rose above a cer-tain level, the employees got a bonus. The employee-involvement part of the program rested on the assumption that the line workers knew best how to do—and how to improve—their jobs. Since the average length of tenure of a line employee at Ericsson GE is 22 years, the premise that workers are qualified to come up with ideas for improvement seemed reasonable. Employees were encouraged to suggest ways to improve production processes, reduce waste, or just make their jobs easier. Instead of submitting these ideas to some committee of managers that might respond to them six months later, employee teams—dubbed Win Teams—were given both the power and the budget to implement the ideas themselves.

Membership on Win Teams is voluntary. Currently, there are 50 teams in the plant, each led by an elected line employee. A team has the authority to accept an idea, spend money on equipment to expedite the change, and implement it without management input. The budgetary limit for each team started out at $250 per year, but has since been increased to $6,000. Managers and exempt employees *can* belong to Win Teams, but only as resource people who do some of the interdepartmental legwork and research to see if an idea is feasible. Final approval and authority lie with the Win Team and its leader.

This may sound like a simple suggestion system with a budgetary twist, and indeed, it started out that way. But because employees took this empowerment effort seriously and because management at all levels supported the change, the Winshare program became a permanent part of the company's culture.

As a result of Trani's cuts and the division concentrating on what it did best (i.e., making mobile radios), the unit became profitable in 1986. Profitability and this new way of doing business attracted the attention of Ericsson, a Swedish company whose core business is mobile communications. Ericsson bought a 60 percent share of the company at the end of 1989, and GE Mobile Communications Business became Ericsson GE.

This partnership gave Ericsson an American plant and a foot in the door of the U.S. market. Though its name is well-known in Europe, Ericsson wanted the General Electric label on its radios and cellular phones for the recognition value in the United States. . . .

The now-profitable joint venture had sales of $1.1 billion for 1992 and the Lynchburg plant currently employs about 2,000 people. On paper, Ericsson now owns 80 percent of Ericsson GE while General Electric maintains a 20 percent share. But it is line employees who actually have taken ownership of the business, in feeling if not in fact. As Jimmy Howerton, an associate who works on the Carfone line, puts it, "It doesn't matter what name is on the gate because this is my company."

Source: Excerpted from B Filipczak, "Ericsson General Electric: The Evolution of Empowerment," *Training*, September 1993, pp 21–27. Reprinted with permission of the September 1993 issue of *Training* Magazine. Copyright 1993. Lakewood Publications, Minneapolis, MN. All rights reserved. Not for resale.

to build the best characteristics of profit sharing and gainsharing plans into the organization's pay-for-performance plan. The following practical recommendations can help in this regard:

- Make pay for performance an integral part of the organization's basic strategy (e.g., pursuit of best-in-the-industry product or service quality).[64]
- Base incentive determinations on objective performance data.
- Have all employees actively participate in the development, implementation, and revision of the performance-pay formulas.
- Encourage two-way communication so problems with the pay-for-performance plan will be detected early.
- Build the pay-for-performance plan around participative structures such as suggestion systems or quality circles.
- Reward teamwork and cooperation whenever possible.[65]
- Actively sell the plan to supervisors and middle managers who may view employee participation as a threat to their traditional notion of authority.
- If annual cash bonuses are granted, pay them in a lump sum to maximize their motivational impact.
- Remember that money motivates when it comes in significant amounts, not occasional nickels and dimes.

BACK TO THE OPENING CASE

Now that you have read Chapter 14, you should be able to answer the following questions about the Granite Rock case:

1. What factors account for the apparent success of Granite Rock's performance appraisal/development process?

2. What is the main drawback of this particular system? What recommendations would you make to management?

3. Using the model in Figure 14–5 as a guide, how effective is the employee feedback system at Granite Rock?

SUMMARY OF KEY CONCEPTS

1. *Identify four key components of the performance appraisal process.* They are the appraiser, the appraisee, the appraisal method, and the outcomes.

2. *Explain how the trait, behavioral, and results approaches to performance appraisal vary.* The person's personal traits and characteristics are rated with the trait approach. As the term implies, one's actual behavior is rated with the behavioral approach. Raters use the results approach to judge an employee's results or accomplishments. Within a contingency framework, each approach has its appropriate use.

3. *Identify three different sources of feedback and discuss how we perceive and cognitively evaluate feedback.* Three sources of feedback are others, the task, and oneself. If feedback is to be believed and acted upon, it must clear several perceptual and cognitive hurdles. The recipient must desire positive and/or negative feedback. Cognitively, the recipient must see the feedback as accurate, the source as credible, the system as fair, and the expectations and behavioral standards as reasonable.

4. *List at least three practical lessons from feedback research.* Feedback is not automatically accepted as

intended, especially negative feedback. Managerial credibility can be enhanced through expertise and a climate of trust. Feedback must not be too frequent or too scarce and must be tailored to the individual. Feedback directly from computers is effective. Active participation in the feedback session helps people perceive feedback as more accurate. The quality of feedback received decreases as one moves up the organizational hierarchy.

5. *Explain the difference between extrinsic and intrinsic rewards.* Extrinsic rewards (financial/material/social) come from the environment. Intrinsic rewards (psychic) are self-granted, internally experienced rewards.

6. *Discuss the impact that incentive bonuses have on employee motivation and performance.* Incentive bonuses have a double impact on employee motivation and performance because they are first promised and then delivered. Employee participation plays a key role in this process by generating solutions to productivity problems and prompting intrinsic motivation, information sharing, and employee empowerment.

7. *Explain how profit sharing and gainsharing differ.* Profit sharing plans give employees a specified portion of the business's economic profits. Gainsharing ties bonuses to documented productivity increases.

8. *Identify at least four ways managers can improve pay-for-performance plans.* They need to be strategically anchored, based on quantified performance data, highly participative, actively sold to supervisors and middle managers, and teamwork oriented. Annual bonuses of significant size are helpful.

Discussion Questions

1. How could a weak link in the performance appraisal–feedback–rewards cycle damage the entire process?

2. Would you prefer to have your academic and/or work performance appraised in terms of traits, behavior, or results? Explain.

3. How would you respond to a manager who said, "The format of the performance appraisal instrument is everything?"

4. How has feedback instructed or motivated you lately?

5. Which of the five cognitive evaluation criteria for feedback—feedback accuracy, source credibility, system fairness, expectancies, behavioral standards—do you think ranks as most important? Explain.

6. What is the most valuable lesson feedback research teaches us? Explain.

7. Which of the three organizational reward norms do you prefer? Why?

8. How would you respond to a manager who said, "Employees cannot be motivated with money"?

9. Why does gainsharing appear to have the edge over profit sharing?

10. What do you see as the number one barrier to successful pay-for-performance plans?

Exercise

Objectives

1. To provide actual examples of on-the-job feedback from three primary sources: organization/supervisor, co-workers, and self/task.

2. To provide a handy instrument for evaluating the comparative strength of positive feedback from these three sources.

Introduction

A pair of researchers from Georgia Tech developed and tested a 63-item feedback questionnaire to demonstrate the importance of both the sign and content of feedback messages.[66] Although their instrument contains both positive and negative feedback items, we have extracted 18 positive items for this self-awareness exercise.

Instructions

Thinking of your present job (or your most recent job), circle one number for each of the 18 items. Alternatively, you could ask one or more other employed individuals to complete the questionnaire. Once the questionnaire has been completed, calculate subtotal and total scores by adding the circled numbers. Then try to answer the discussion questions.

Instrument

How frequently do you experience each of the following outcomes in your present (or past) job?

Organizational/Supervisory Feedback

	Rarely	Occasionally	Very Frequently
1. My supervisor complimenting me on something I have done.		1—2—3—4—5	
2. My supervisor increasing my responsibilities.		1—2—3—4—5	
3. The company expressing pleasure with my performance.		1—2—3—4—5	
4. The company giving me a raise.		1—2—3—4—5	
5. My supervisor recommending me for a promotion or raise.		1—2—3—4—5	
6. The company providing me with favorable data concerning my performance.		1—2—3—4—5	

Subscore = _____

Co-Worker Feedback

7. My co-workers coming to me for advice.	1—2—3—4—5
8. My co-workers expressing approval of my work.	1—2—3—4—5
9. My co-workers liking to work with me.	1—2—3—4—5
10. My co-workers telling me that I am doing a good job.	1—2—3—4—5
11. My co-workers commenting favorably on something I have done.	1—2—3—4—5
12. Receiving a compliment from my co-workers.	1—2—3—4—5

Subscore = _____

Self/Task Feedback

13. Knowing that the way I go about my duties is superior to most others.	1—2—3—4—5
14. Feeling I am accomplishing more than I used to.	1—2—3—4—5
15. Knowing that I can now perform or do things which previously were difficult for me.	1—2—3—4—5
16. Finding that I am satisfying my own standards for "good work."	1—2—3—4—5
17. Knowing that what I am doing "feels right."	1—2—3—4—5
18. Feeling confident of being able to handle all aspects of my job.	1—2—3—4—5

Subscore = _____

Total Score = _____

Questions for Consideration/ Class Discussion

1. Which items on this questionnaire would you rate as primarily instructional in function? Are all of the remaining items primarily motivational? Explain.
2. In terms of your own feedback profile, which of the three types is the strongest (has the highest subscore)? Which is the weakest (has the lowest subscore)? How well does your feedback profile explain your job performance and/or satisfaction?
3. How does your feedback profile measure up against those of your classmates? (Arbitrary norms, for comparative purposes, are: Deficient feedback = 18–42; Moderate feedback = 43–65; Abundant feedback = 66–90.)
4. Which of the three sources of feedback is most critical to your successful job performance and/or job satisfaction? Explain.

NOTES

[1] See J N Cleveland, K R Murphy, and R E Williams, "Multiple Uses of Performance Appraisal: Prevalence and Correlates," *Journal of Applied Psychology*, February 1989, pp 130–35.

2 ''Performance Appraisal: Current Practices and Techniques,'' *Personnel,* May–June 1984, p 57.

3 See M L Bowles and G Coates, ''Image and Substance: The Management of Performance as Rhetoric or Reality?'' *Personnel Review,* no. 2, 1993, pp 3–21.

4 B Rice, ''Performance Review: The Job Nobody Likes,'' *Psychology Today,* September 1986, p 32.

5 For discussion of EEOC guidelines for performance appraisals, see W S Swan and P Margulies, *How To Do a Superior Performance Appraisal* (New York: John Wiley, 1991). Also see R D Dickson, ''The Business of Equal Opportunity,'' *Harvard Business Review,* January–February 1992, pp 46–53; and ''Debate: Can Equal Opportunity Be Made More Equal?'' *Harvard Business Review,* March–April 1992, pp 138–58.

6 R I Lazer and W S Wikstrom, *Appraising Managerial Performance: Current Practices and Future Directions,* Report 723 (New York: The Conference Board, 1977), p 26.

7 See ''Performance Appraisals—Reappraised,'' *Management Review,* November 1983, p 5. Eight common performance appraisal errors are discussed in T R Lowe, ''Eight Ways to Ruin a Performance Review,'' *Personnel Journal,* January 1986, pp 60–62. Also see G L Blakely, ''The Effects of Performance Rating Discrepancies on Supervisors and Subordinates,'' *Organizational Behavior and Human Decision Processes,* February 1993, pp 57–80.

8 For details, see G H Dobbins, R L Cardy, and D M Truxillo, ''The Effects of Purpose of Appraisal and Individual Differences in Stereotypes of Women on Sex Differences in Performance Ratings: A Laboratory and Field Study,'' *Journal of Applied Psychology,* August 1988, pp 551–58. A similar finding is reported in P R Sackett, C L Z DuBois, and A Wiggins Noe, ''Tokenism in Performance Evaluation: The Effects of Work Group Representation on Male-Female and White-Black Differences in Performance Ratings,'' *Journal of Applied Psychology,* April 1991, pp 263–67.

9 Data from B Klaas and A S DeNisi, ''Managerial Reactions to Employee Dissent: The Impact of Grievance Activity on Performance Ratings,'' *Academy of Management Journal,* December 1989, pp 705–17.

10 Swan and Margulies, *How To Do a Superior Performance Appraisal,* p 8.

11 K N Wexley and R Klimoski, ''Performance Appraisal: An Update,'' in *Research in Personnel and Human Resources Management,* vol. 2, eds K M Rowland and G R Ferris (Greenwich, CT: JAI Press, 1984), pp 55–56.

12 B Jacobson and B L Kaye, ''Career Development and Performance Appraisal: It Takes Two to Tango,'' *Personnel,* January 1986, p 27.

13 Supporting discussion is provided by K N Wexley, ''Appraisal Interview,'' in *Performance Assessment,* ed R A Berk (Baltimore, MD: The Johns Hopkins Press Ltd., 1986).

14 See, for example, J P Muczyk and B C Reimann, ''MBO as a Complement to Effective Leadership,'' *The Academy of Management Executive,* May 1989, pp 131–38; R Rodgers and J E Hunter, ''Impact of Management by Objectives on Organizational Productivity,'' *Journal of Applied Psychology,* April 1991, pp 322–36; and R Rodgers, J E Hunter, and D L Rogers, ''Influence of Top Management Commitment on Management Program Success,'' *Journal of Applied Psychology,* February 1993, pp 151–55.

15 Indeed, recent research found rater differences to be more important than format differences. See C E J Härtel, ''Rating Format Research Revisited: Format Effectiveness and Acceptability Depend on Rater Characteristics,'' *Journal of Applied Psychology,* April 1993, pp 212–17. Also see T J Maurer, J K Palmer, and D K Ashe, ''Diaries, Checklists, Evaluations, and Contrast Effects in Measurement of Behavior,'' *Journal of Applied Psychology,* April 1993, pp 226–31.

16 See A M Morrison, ''Performance Appraisal: Getting from Here to There,'' *Human Resource Planning,* no. 2, 1984, pp 73–77. Also see C Lee, ''Smoothing Out Appraisal Systems,'' *HRMagazine,* March 1990, pp 72–76.

17 Results are presented in K Kraiger and J K Ford, ''A Meta-Analysis of Ratee Race Effects in Performance Ratings,'' *Journal of Applied Psychology,* February 1985, pp 56–65.

18 Research results extracted from F J Landy and J L Farr, ''Performance Rating,'' *Psychological Bulletin,* January 1980, pp 72–107; Wexley and Klimoski, ''Performance Appraisal: An Update''; Rice, ''Performance Review: The Job Nobody Likes''; J W Hedge and M J Kavangh, ''Improving the Accuracy of Performance Evaluations: Comparisons of Three Methods of Performance Appraiser Training,'' *Journal of Applied Psychology,* February 1988, pp 68–73; and R Klimoski and L Inks, ''Accountability Forces in Performance Appraisal,'' *Organizational Behavior and Human Decision Processes,* April 1990, pp 194–208.

19 L Reibstein, ''Firms Ask Workers to Rate Their Bosses,'' *The Wall Street Journal,* June 13, 1988, p 17.

20 For example, see C Lee, ''Talking Back to the Boss,'' *Training,* April 1990, pp 29–35; and R McGarvey and S Smith, ''When Workers Rate the Boss,'' *Training,* March 1993, pp 31–34.

21 For a complete list, see ''Companies Where Employees Rate Executives,'' *Fortune,* December 27, 1993, p 128.

22 See M M Harris and J Schaubroeck, ''A Meta-

Analysis of Self-Supervisor, Self-Peer, and Peer-Supervisor Ratings,'' *Personnel Psychology,* Spring 1988, pp 43–62, and J Lane and P Herriot, ''Self-Ratings, Supervisor Ratings, Positions and Performance,'' *Journal of Occupational Psychology,* March 1990, pp 77–88. Also see J R Williams and P E Levy, ''The Effects of Perceived System Knowledge on the Agreement between Self-Ratings and Supervisor Ratings,'' *Personnel Psychology,* Winter 1992, pp 835–47; and R F Martell and M R Borg, ''A Comparison of the Behavioral Rating Accuracy of Groups and Individuals,'' *Journal of Applied Psychology,* February 1993, pp 43–50.

23 J Hillkirk, ''Tearing Down Walls Builds GE,'' *USA Today,* July 26, 1993, p 5B.

24 M Sashkin and K J Kiser, *Putting Total Quality Management to Work* (San Francisco: Berrett-Koehler, 1993), p 94.

25 For an interesting alternative to traditional appraisals, see ''Out with Appraisals, In with Feedback,'' *Training,* August 1993, pp 10, 12.

26 R Henkoff, ''Cost Cutting: How To Do It Right,'' *Fortune,* April 9, 1990, p 48.

27 C Bell and R Zemke, ''On-Target Feedback,'' *Training,* June 1992, p 36.

28 Both the definition of feedback and the functions of feedback are based on discussion in D R Ilgen, C D Fisher, and M S Taylor, ''Consequences of Individual Feedback on Behavior in Organizations,'' *Journal of Applied Psychology,* August 1979, pp 349–71; and R E Kopelman, *Managing Productivity in Organizations: A Practical People-Oriented Perspective* (New York: McGraw-Hill, 1986), p 175.

29 See P C Earley, G B Northcraft, C Lee, and T R Lituchy, ''Impact of Process and Outcome Feedback on the Relation of Goal Setting to Task Performance,'' *Academy of Management Journal,* March 1990, pp 87–105.

30 See T Matsui, A Okkada, and T Kakuyama, ''Influence of Achievement Need on Goal Setting, Performance, and Feedback Effectiveness,'' *Journal of Applied Psychology,* October 1982, pp 645–48.

31 S J Ashford, ''Feedback-Seeking in Individual Adaptation: A Resource Perspective,'' *Academy of Management Journal,* September 1986, pp 465–87. Also see D B Fedor, R B Rensvold, and S M Adams, ''An Investigation of Factors Expected to Affect Feedback Seeking: A Longitudinal Field Study,'' *Personnel Psychology,* Winter 1992, pp 779–805.

32 See B D Bannister, ''Performance Outcome Feedback and Attributional Feedback: Interactive Effects on Recipient Responses,'' *Journal of Applied Psychology,* May 1986, pp 203–10.

33 For complete details, see P M Podsakoff and J-L Farh, ''Effects of Feedback Sign and Credibility on Goal Setting

and Task Performance,'' *Organizational Behavior and Human Decision Processes,* August 1989, pp 45–67. Also see S J Ashford and A S Tsui, ''Self-Regulation for Managerial Effectiveness: The Role of Active Feedback Seeking,'' *Academy of Management Journal,* June 1991, pp 251–80.

34 J M Kouzes and B Z Posner, *Credibility: How Leaders Gain and Lost It, Why People Demand It* (San Francisco: Jossey-Bass, 1993), p 25.

35 B Uttal, ''Behind the Fall of Steve Jobs,'' *Fortune,* August 5, 1985, p 22.

36 Based on discussion in Ilgen, Fisher, and Taylor, ''Consequences of Individual Feedback on Behavior in Organizations,'' pp 367–68. Also see J J Martocchio and J Webster, ''Effects of Feedback and Cognitive Playfulness on Performance in Microcomputer Software Training,'' *Personnel Psychology,* Autumn 1992, pp 553–78.

37 See P C Earley, ''Computer-Generated Performance Feedback in the Magazine-Subscription Industry,'' *Organizational Behavior and Human Decision Processes,* February 1988, pp 50–64.

38 See M De Gregorio and C D Fisher, ''Providing Performance Feedback: Reactions to Alternate Methods,'' *Journal of Management,* December 1988, pp 605–16.

39 For details, see R A Baron, ''Countering the Effects of Destructive Criticism: The Relative Efficacy of Four Interventions,'' *Journal of Applied Psychology,* June 1990, pp 235–45. Also see M L Smith, ''Give Feedback, Not Criticism,'' *Supervisory Management,* February 1993, p 4.

40 C O Longenecker and D A Gioia, ''The Executive Appraisal Paradox,'' *Academy of Management Executive,* May 1992, p 18. Also see ''It's Still Lonely at the Top,'' *Training,* April 1993, p 8.

41 Practical tips for giving feedback can be found in E Van Velsor and S J Wall, ''How to Choose a Feedback Instrument,'' *Training,* March 1992, pp 47–52; T Lammers, ''The Effective Employee-Feedback System,'' *Inc.,* February 1993, pp 109–11; and L Smith, ''The Executive's New Coach,'' *Fortune,* December 27, 1993, pp 126–34.

42 W J Wiatrowski, ''Family-Related Benefits in the Workplace,'' *Monthly Labor Review,* March 1990, p 28.

43 M M Markowich, ''25 Ways to Save a Bundle,'' *HRMagazine,* October 1992, p 57. Also see M J Cleary and T J Cleary, ''Designing an Effective Compensation System,'' *Quality Progress,* May 1993, pp 97–99; and the special section on rewards in the Summer 1993 issue of *National Productivity Review,* pp 325–94.

44 For complete discussions, see A P Brief and R J Aldag, ''The Intrinsic-Extrinsic Dichotomy: Toward Conceptual Clarity,'' *Academy of Management Review,* July 1977, pp 496–500; and E L Deci, *Intrinsic Motivation* (New York: Plenum Press, 1975), chap. 2.

[45] See K I Kim, H-J Park, and N Suzuki, "Reward Allocations in the United States, Japan, and Korea: A Comparison of Individualistic and Collectivistic Cultures," *Academy of Management Journal,* March 1990, pp 188–98.

[46] Adapted from J L Pearce and R H Peters, "A Contradictory Norms View of Employer–Employee Exchange," *Journal of Management,* Spring 1985, pp 19–30.

[47] Ibid., p 25.

[48] See D B McFarlin and P D Sweeney, "Distributive and Procedural Justice as Predictors of Satisfaction with Personal and Organizational Outcomes," *Academy of Management Journal,* August 1992, pp 626–37.

[49] M Von Glinow, "Reward Strategies for Attracting, Evaluating, and Retaining Professionals," *Human Resource Management,* Summer 1985, p 193.

[50] See K Labich, "Hot Company, Warm Culture," *Fortune,* February 27, 1989, pp 74–78. For enjoyable reading about the Herman Miller philosophy of managing people, see M De Pree, *Leadership Jazz* (New York: Dell, 1992).

[51] Pros and cons of pay for performance are reviewed in T Rollins, "Pay for Performance: Is It Worth the Trouble?" *Personnel Administrator,* May 1988, pp 42–46; also see B Filipczak, "Why No One Likes Your Incentive Program," *Training,* August 1993, pp 19–25. The case against incentive plans is presented in A Kohn, "Why Incentive Plans Cannot Work," *Harvard Business Review,* September–October 1993, pp 54–63.

[52] S Tully, "Your Paycheck Gets Exciting," *Fortune,* November 1, 1993, p 83. Additional pay-for-performance data are reported in B Leonard, "New Ways to Pay Employees," *HRMagazine,* February 1994, pp 61–62.

[53] Data from M Clements, "Chrysler's Gains Drive Eaton's Pay: $3 Million," *USA Today,* March 18, 1994, p 1B.

[54] Data from N J Perry, "Here Come Richer, Riskier Pay Plans," *Fortune,* December 19, 1988, p 51. More favorable data are reported in "Mixed Reviews on 'Pay-for-Performance,'" *The Christian Science Monitor,* July 20, 1993, p 8.

[55] See M J Mandel, "Those Fat Bonuses Don't Seem to Boost Performance," *Business Week,* January 8, 1990, p 26. Also see M M Petty, B Singleton, and D W Connell, "An Experimental Evaluation of an Organizational Incentive Plan in the Electric Utility Industry," *Journal of Applied Psychology,* August 1992, pp 427–36.

[56] Based on discussion in R Ricklefs, "Whither the Payoff on Sales Commissions?" *The Wall Street Journal,* June 6, 1990, p B1.

[57] Another approach to getting employees to think and act like owners of the business, employee stock ownership plans, is given complete coverage in J R Blasi and D L Kruse, *The New Owners: The Mass Emergence of Employee Ownership in Public Companies and What It Means to American Business* (New York: HarperCollins, 1991). Also see N J Perry, "Talk about Pay for Performance," *Fortune,* May 4, 1992, p 77; and S Baker and K L Alexander, "The Owners vs the Boss at Weirton Steel," *Business Week,* November 15, 1993, p 38.

[58] J Labate, "Deal Those Workers In," *Fortune,* April 19, 1993, p 26.

[59] B Graham-Moore, "Review of the Literature," in *Gainsharing,* eds B Graham-Moore and T L Ross (Washington, DC: The Bureau of National Affairs, 1990), p 20 (emphasis added).

[60] Ibid., based largely on pp 3–4.

[61] Practical examples of gainsharing can be found in T Ehrenfeld, "Cashing In," *Inc.,* July 1993, pp 69–70; and T Ehrenfeld, "Gain-Sharing," *Inc.,* August 1993, pp 87–89.

[62] For details, see S E Markham, "Pay-for-Performance Dilemma Revisited: Empirical Example of the Importance of Group Effects," *Journal of Applied Psychology,* May 1988, pp 172–80.

[63] Data from K I Miller, "Cultural and Role-Based Predictors of Organizational Participation and Allocation Preferences," *Communication Research,* December 1988, pp 699–725; See also G W Florkowski, "Analyzing Group Incentive Plans," *HRMagazine,* January 1990, pp 36–38.

[64] For example, see H C Handlin, "The Company Built upon the Golden Rule: Lincoln Electric," *Journal of Organizational Behavior Management,* no. 1, 1992, pp 151–63.

[65] See P K Zingheim and J R Schuster, "Linking Quality and Pay," *HRMagazine,* December 1992, pp 55–59.

[66] This exercise is adapted from material in D M Herold and C K Parsons, "Assessing the Feedback Environment in Work Organizations: Development of the Job Feedback Survey," *Journal of Applied Psychology,* May 1985, pp 290–305.

LEADERSHIP

Learning OBJECTIVES

When you finish studying the material in this chapter, you should be able to:

1. Define the term *leadership* and explain the conceptual framework for understanding leadership.
2. Review trait theory research.
3. Explain results from the Ohio State studies and summarize derivative behavioral style theories.
4. Contrast the underlying philosophy of trait, behavioral, and situational theories of leadership.
5. Explain, according to Fiedler's contingency model, how leadership style interacts with situational control.
6. Discuss House's path–goal theory and review the theory's managerial implications.
7. Explain the role-making model (VDL) of leadership.
8. Define and differentiate transactional and charismatic leadership.
9. Explain how charismatic leadership transforms followers.
10. Summarize the managerial implications of charismatic leadership.

OPENING CASE

Microsoft's Bill Gates Is a Successful Transactional and Charismatic Leader

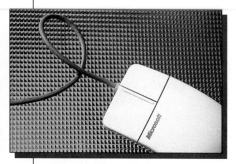

Sharon Hoogstraten

With resilience and tenacity, Gates succeeded in imposing his own long-term strategy on the rest of the industry. Windows flopped at its debut, and by 1986 Gates' advisers were pleading with him to abandon it. Every other major software company lined up behind IBM's OS/2 instead. But Gates persevered—and ultimately prevailed. When OS/2 appeared in 1988, it was sluggish and took up too much memory for most PCs. Microsoft dramatically improved Windows, and its fourth version, Windows 3.0, finally took off.

This October, Gates assembled his 7,200 Seattle-area staffers in the huge Kingdome arena, home of the Seahawks and Mariners, for the company's annual employee meeting. He called his speech "Microsoft's Vision." He talked about how the company's

current success sprang from the bets it made years ago and stuck with. And he outlined the bets Microsoft was making now that should pay off in the Nineties— multimedia, interactive TV, object-oriented programming, far-out projects like a wallet PC. His immodest aim: to transform not just Microsoft, or even the computer industry, but how people everywhere tap into information. . . .

Great empires, ancient (Rome) or modern (GM, IBM), tend to grow fat and complacent, forsaking austerity as they get sucked into believing in their own invincibility. Don't count on this fate befalling Microsoft, at least while Gates is in charge. The culture that got Microsoft where it is today remains remarkably strong, its values uncorrupted.

For one thing, Microsoft is frugal. At November's Comdex, two officers of the company shared a hotel room. While Gates can splurge with his own cash—the $380,000 Porsche 959, the $35 million house he's building—he remains unfailingly tight with the company's money. He even flies coach to Japan. . . .

Then there's the Microsoft work ethic. Rather than gloating over all they've accomplished, Gates and his followers remain as relentlessly indus-

trious as ever. Pete Higgins, 35, who's in charge of word processors and spreadsheets, steals time by shaving as he drives to the office. "Complaining about how hard you work at Microsoft," he says, "is like complaining about the weather in Seattle." . . .

Microsoft ranks No. 1 overall in software, but in most categories of applications it's No. 2, No. 3, or No. 4—and obsessively focused on the market leader. When Raikes was in charge of Microsoft's wordprocessing software, Gates challenged him to learn *everything* about Pete Peterson, who ran the top competitor, Word-Perfect. Raikes took Gates literally: He even memorized the names, ages, and birthdays of Peterson's six children.

To save money, ease communication, and preserve that underdog spirit, Microsoft intentionally understaffs its product teams. Gates *wants* to have fewer spreadsheet programmers than Lotus. Microsoft is organized into small bands of "people with a mission who can pound, pound, pound," says sales head Steve Ballmer, 36, striking his palm with his fist. A 50% increase in Microsoft's work force over just two years seems to violate the company's strategy of keeping head count low, but many of the new recruits are to work

Someone once observed that a leader is a person who finds out which way the parade is going, jumps in front of it, and yells "Follow me!" The plain fact is that this approach to leadership has little chance of working in today's rapidly changing world. Admired leaders, such as civil rights activist Martin Luther King, John Kennedy, and General Electric's CEO Jack Welch, led people in bold new directions. They envisioned how things could be improved, rallied followers, and refused to accept failure. In short, successful leaders are those individuals who can step into a difficult situation

OPENING CASE

(concluded)

either overseas or answering questions in an expanded customer support department.

For its crucial line positions—programmers and product managers—Microsoft can still pick with extreme selectivity from the graduates of elite universities and business schools. The chosen few get lots of responsibility right away. Gates earns high marks for pushing authority down through the ranks. He limits his own role largely to conceiving and spreading the vision, helping sell to key customers, and vetting R&D closely. . . .

Gates wears his success inconspicuously. Except for the Porsche and the house, nothing about him even whispers "America's richest man." In public he seems colorless, unprepossessing. Nor is he a stirring speaker, though he can mesmerize an audience when he holds forth on a technical subject he really cares about. He dresses casually at the office, like everyone else at Microsoft's college-like campus 15 miles from Seattle in Redmond, Washington. At a November press conference, the jacket of Gates' rumpled, off-the-rack suit was fastened by the bottom button, making it bulge awkwardly. "He'd rather talk about technology than himself," says Susan Hauser, a Microsoft sales repre-

sentative in New York City whom Gates has accompanied on visits to customers. "He's so down-to-earth that clients feel comfortable with him right away." . . .

A harder-edged persona emerges at headquarters than in public. Gates demands that his colleagues be remarkably well informed, logical, vocal, and thick-skinned. *Fortune* recently sat in on a so-called "Bill meeting" with the teams that develop and market programming languages. A product manager, just five years out of Princeton, opened with an energetic, rapid-fire, and confident analysis of the market. Gates interrupted often, questioning facts and assertions. Always calm and controlled, at times witty or profane, he shot criticisms and challenges at the youthful managers, who stood up to the chairman as if he were a classmate.

Gates still presides over the "spec review" for every new or revised key product, scrutinizing its features point by point with its programmers and managers. It would be hard to find a CEO in any industry with such in-depth knowledge of his company's products. Vice president Brad Silverberg says Gates recalls details from meetings six moths earlier—even if the product team doesn't. Gates

reads voraciously and devours detailed information. One frequently used term in the Microsoft lexicon is "granularity"—meaning fineness of detail. . . .

Gates' long-range vision will take at least a decade or two to realize. He calls it Information at Your Fingertips. "The idea here is very ambitious," says Gates. "Any piece of information you want should be available to you." No need to remember whether a particular piece of data is stored somewhere in a spreadsheet, a database, a slide presentation, or a long memo. Simply ask, in your own words, what you need to know. On-line data and electronic mail enriched with video and sound will make the PC more a communications tool than a computing devise. . . .

For Discussion

Would you like to work at Microsoft? Explain.

■ Additional discussion questions linking this case with the following material appear at the end of this chapter.

Source: Excerpted from A Deutschman, "Bill Gates' Next Challenge," *Fortune*, December 28, 1992, pp 30–41. © 1992 Time Inc. All Rights Reserved.

and make a noticeable difference. But how much of a difference can leaders make in modern organizations?

OB researchers have discovered that leaders can make a difference. One study, for example, tracked the relationship between net profit and leadership in 167 companies from 13 industries. It also covered a time span of 20 years. Higher net profits were earned by companies with effective leaders.[1] A more recent study examined the relationship between leadership and performance within major-league baseball teams. The sample consisted of all managers who directed a major-league baseball team during any season from 1945 to 1965. The researchers then tracked the performance of their teams up to the year the manager retired. Using a sophisticated measure of managerial effectiveness, results demonstrated that effective managers won more games with player performance held constant than did less effective managers.[2] Leadership makes a difference!

After formally defining the term leadership, this chapter focuses on the following areas: (1) trait and behavioral approaches to leadership, (2) alternative situational theories of leadership, and (3) charismatic leadership. Because there are many different leadership theories within each of these areas, it is impossible to discuss them all. This chapter is based on reviewing those theories with the most research support.

WHAT DOES LEADERSHIP INVOLVE?

leadership Influencing employees to voluntarily pursue organizational goals.

Because the topic of leadership has fascinated people for centuries, definitions abound. A common thread among these definitions is social influence. As the term is used in this chapter, **leadership** is defined as "a social influence process in which the leader seeks the voluntary participation of subordinates in an effort to reach organizational objectives."[3]

Tom Peters and Nancy Austin, authors of the best-seller, *A Passion for Excellence,* describe leadership in broader terms:

> Leadership means vision, cheerleading, enthusiasm, love, trust, verve, passion, obsession, consistency, the use of symbols, paying attention as illustrated by the content of one's calendar, out-and-out drama (and the management thereof), creating heroes at all levels, coaching, effectively wandering around, and numerous other things. Leadership must be present at all levels of the organization. It depends on a million little things done with obsession, consistency and care, but all of those million little things add up to nothing if the trust, vision, and basic belief are not there.[4]

As you can see from this definition, leadership clearly entails more than wielding power and exercising authority.

Figure 15–1 provides a conceptual framework for understanding leadership. It was created by integrating components of the different theories and models discussed in this chapter. Figure 15–1 indicates that certain leader characteristics/traits are the foundation of effective leadership. In turn, these characteristics affect an individual's ability to carry out various managerial behaviors/roles. Effective leadership also depends on various situational variables. These variables are important components of the contingency leadership theories discussed later in this chapter. Finally, leadership is results oriented. This conclusion is best summarized by Max DePree, chairman of Herman Miller, Inc. "Leaders are responsible for effectiveness. . . . Leaders can delegate efficiency, but they must deal personally with effectiveness."[5]

TRAIT AND BEHAVIORAL THEORIES OF LEADERSHIP

This section examines the two earliest approaches used to explain leadership. Trait theories, the old approach, focused on identifying the personal traits that differentiated leaders from followers. Behavioral theorists examined leadership from a different perspective. They tried to uncover the different kinds of leader behaviors that resulted in higher work group performance. Both approaches to leadership can teach present and future managers valuable lessons about leading.

• ⤳ FIGURE 15-1   A Conceptual Framework for Understanding Leadership

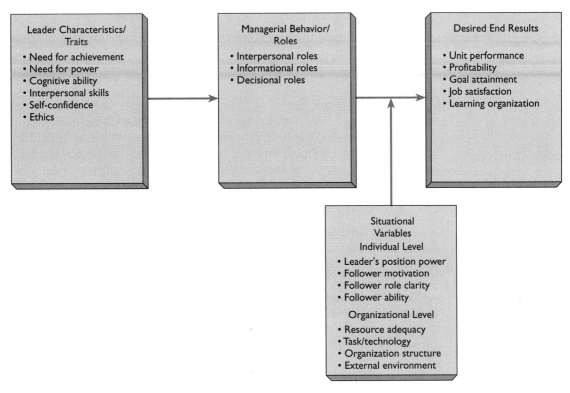

Source: Adopted in part from G Yukl, "Managerial Leadership: A Review of Theory and Research," *Journal of Management,* June 1989, p 274.

Trait Theory

At the turn of the 20th century, the prevailing belief was that leaders were born, not made. Selected people were thought to possess inborn traits that made them successful leaders. A **leader trait** is a physical or personality characteristic that can be used to differentiate leaders from followers.

leader trait   Personal characteristics that differentiate leaders from followers.

Before World War II, hundreds of studies were conducted to pinpoint the traits of successful leaders. Dozens of leadership traits were identified. During the postwar period, however, enthusiasm was replaced by widespread criticism. Studies conducted by Ralph Stogdill in 1948 and by Richard Mann in 1959, which sought to summarize the impact of traits on leadership, caused the trait approach to fall into disfavor.

Stogdill's and Mann's Findings   Based on his review, Stogdill concluded that five traits tended to differentiate leaders from average followers. They were (1) intelligence, (2) dominance, (3) self-confidence, (4) level of energy and activity, and (5) task-relevant knowledge.[6] However, these five traits did not accurately predict which individuals became leaders in organizations. People with these traits often remained followers.

Mann's review was similarly disappointing for the trait theorists. Among the seven categories of personality traits he examined, Mann found intelligence was the best predictor of leadership. However, Mann warned that all observed positive relationships between traits and leadership were weak (correlations averaged about 0.15).[7]

Together, Stogdill's and Mann's findings dealt a near deathblow to the trait approach. But now, decades later, leadership traits are once again receiving serious research attention.

Contemporary Trait Research   Two OB researchers concluded in 1983 that past trait data may have been incorrectly analyzed. By applying modern statistical techniques to an old database, they demonstrated that the majority of a leader's behavior could be attributed to stable underlying traits.[8] Unfortunately, their methodology did not single out specific traits.

A 1986 meta-analysis by Robert Lord and his associates remedied this shortcoming with the following insights: First, the Lord study criticized leadership researchers for misinterpreting Stogdill's and Mann's findings. Specifically, correlations between traits and *perceived leadership ability* were misinterpreted as linkages between traits and leader *effectiveness*. Second, a reanalysis of Mann's data and subsequent studies revealed that individuals tend to be perceived as leaders when they possess one or more of the following traits: intelligence, dominance, and masculinity. Thus, Lord and his colleagues concluded, ''Personality traits are associated with leadership perceptions to a higher degree and more consistently than the popular literature indicates.''[9] This conclusion was supported by results from several recent studies.[10]

Gender and Leadership   Three recent meta-analyses of more than 61 studies uncovered three key results. First, men and women differed in the type of leadership roles they assumed within work groups. Men were seen as displaying more overall leadership and task leadership. In contrast, women were perceived as displaying more social leadership.[11] Second, leadership styles varied by gender. Women used a more democratic or participative style than men. Men employed a more autocratic and directive style than women.[12] Third, female leaders were evaluated more negatively than equivalent male leaders. This bias was considerably stronger when women used an autocratic or directive leadership style. Women also were devalued relative to men when they occupied male dominated roles and when evaluators were male.[13]

Trait Theory in Perspective   We can no longer afford to ignore the implications of leadership traits. Traits play a central role in how we perceive leaders. Recalling the Chapter 5 discussion of social perception, it is important to determine the traits embodied in people's schemata (or mental pictures) for leaders. If those traits are inappropriate (i.e., foster discriminatory selection and invalid performance appraisals), they need to be corrected through training and development. Moreover, organizations may find it beneficial to consider selected leadership traits when choosing among candidates for leadership positions. Gender should not be used as one of these traits. In contrast, the International OB outlines the relevant leadership traits of Russian leaders from the 1400s to the present time. As you can see, Russian organizations need to nurture and develop a new set of leadership traits.

INTERNATIONAL OB

Russian Leadership Traits in Three Eras

Leadership Trait	Traditional Russian Society (1400s to 1917)	The Red Executive (1917 to 1991)	The Market-Oriented Manager (1991 to Present)
Leadership Motivation			
Power	Powerful autocrats	Centralized leadership stifled grass-roots democracy	Shared power and ownership
Responsibility	Centralization of responsibility	Micromanagers and macropuppets	Delegation and strategic decision making
Drive			
Achievement motivation	Don't rock the boat	Frustrated pawns	The sky's the limit
Ambition	Equal poverty for all	Service to party and collective good	Overcoming the sin of being a winner
Initiative	Look both ways	Meticulous rule following and behind-the-scenes finessing	Let's do business
Energy	Concentrated spasms of labor	"8-hour day," 8 to 8, firefighting	8-day week, chasing opportunities
Tenacity	Life is a struggle	Struggling to accomplish the routine	Struggling to accomplish the new
Honesty and Integrity			
Dual ethical standard	Deception in dealings, fealty in friendship	Two sets of books, personal integrity	Wild capitalism, personal trust
Using connections (*blat*)	Currying favor with landowners	Greasing the wheels of the state	Greasing palms, but learning to do business straight
Self-Confidence			
	From helplessness to bravado	From inferior quality to "big is beautiful"	From cynicism to over-promising

Source: S M Puffer, "Understanding the Bear: A Portrait of Russian Business Leaders," *Academy of Management Executive*, February 1994, p 42. Used with permission.

Behavioral Styles Theory

This phase of leadership research began during World War II as part of an effort to develop better military leaders. It was an outgrowth of two events: the seeming inability of trait theory to explain leadership effectiveness and the human relations movement, an outgrowth of the Hawthorne Studies. The thrust of early behavioral leadership theory was to focus on leader behavior, instead of on personality traits. It was believed that leader behavior directly affected work group effectiveness. This led researchers to identify patterns of behavior (called leadership styles) that enabled leaders to effectively influence others.

The Ohio State Studies   Researchers at Ohio State University began by generating a list of behaviors exhibited by leaders. At one point, the list contained 1,800 statements that described nine categories of leader behavior. Ultimately, the Ohio State researchers concluded there were only two independent dimensions of leader behavior: consideration and initiating structure. **Consideration** involves leader behavior associated with creating mutual respect or trust and focuses on a concern for group members' needs and desires. Researchers believe a lack of consideration does not foster job satisfaction and employee loyalty. Take the case of Ben Tisdale, CEO of Martech USA Inc., for example.

consideration   Creating mutual respect and trust with followers.

> Numerous former Martech employees say Mr. Tisdale is prone to profanity-laced tirades that have sometimes reduced workers to tears. A California state judge in January awarded a former Martech employee $160,000 in a sexual-discrimination case she brought against the company; the judge wrote in his final ruling that Mr. Tisdale had made "extremely inappropriate sexual advances on" at least three female Martech employees (charges Mr. Tisdale denies) and that Martech's Sacramento office had "a corporate milieu of sexual bias." . . . Several Martech executives say Mr. Tisdale openly talks about how stiffing subcontractors is just another corporate cost cutting tool. Subcontractors on numerous Martech jobs across the country tell of being strung along and stalled when they tried to collect payment.[14]

initiating structure   Organizing and defining what group members should be doing.

This example also reveals that a lack of consideration can negatively affect relationships between a company and its suppliers or vendors. **Initiating structure** is leader behavior that organizes and defines what group members should be doing to maximize output. These two dimensions of leader behavior were oriented at right angles to yield four behavioral styles of leadership (see Figure 15–2).

It initially was hypothesized that a high structure, high consideration style would be the one best style of leadership. Through the years, the effectiveness of the high-high style has been tested many times. Overall, results have been mixed. Researchers thus concluded that there is not one best style of leadership.[15] Rather, it is argued that effectiveness of a given leadership style depends on situational factors.

Derivatives of the Ohio State Studies   Behavioral styles theory spawned a lot of research and generated many prescriptive models. Perhaps the most widely

• FIGURE 15–2
Four Leadership Styles Derived from the Ohio State Studies

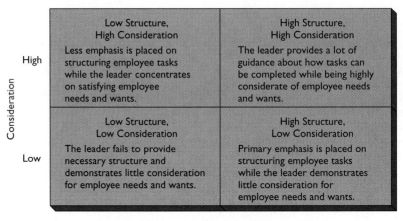

known behavioral styles model of leadership is the Managerial Grid® (renamed the Leadership Grid® in 1991).[16] This model is based on the premise that there is one best style of leadership. This model prescribes that leaders should demonstrate a high concern for people and a high concern for production. Situational leadership theory is another well-known prescriptive theory. According to the theory, appropriate leadership style is found by cross referencing an employee's readiness, which is defined as the extent to which an employee possesses the ability and willingness to complete a task, with one of four leadership styles.[17] Although both of these theories are extensively used in the training community, neither one is clearly supported by empirical research.

Behavioral Styles Theory in Perspective   By emphasizing leader *behavior,* something that is learned, the behavioral style approach makes it clear that leaders are made, not born. This is the opposite of the trait theorists' traditional assumption. Given what we know about behavior shaping and model-based training, leader *behaviors* can be systematically improved and developed. For example, a recent study demonstrated that employee creativity was increased when leaders were trained to (1) help employees identify problems and (2) enhance employees feelings of self-efficacy.[18]

Behavioral styles research also revealed that there is no one best style of leadership. The effectiveness of a particular leadership style depends on the situation at hand. For instance, employees prefer structure over consideration when faced with role ambiguity.[19] We now consider alternative situational theories of leadership.

SITUATIONAL THEORIES

Situational leadership theories grew out of an attempt to explain the inconsistent findings about traits and styles. **Situational theories** propose that the effectiveness of a particular style of leader behavior depends on the situation. As situations change, different styles become appropriate. This directly challenges the idea of one best style of leadership. Let us closely examine three alternative situational theories of leadership that reject the notion of one best leadership style (see International OB).

situational theories
Propose that leader styles should match the situation at hand.

Relationship-oriented leaders give individual employees one-on-one guidance in a supportive manner.

(*Jeff Greenberg/PhotoEdit*)

Fiedler's Contingency Model

Fred Fiedler, an OB scholar, developed a situational model of leadership. It is the oldest, most widely known, and most extensively researched situational model of leadership. Fiedler's basic premise is that leader effectiveness is *contingent* upon an appropriate match between the leader's style and the degree to which he or she controls the situation. Before we examine this matching process, we need to discuss Fiedler's ideas about leadership style and situational control. After linking these variables, we conclude this section with a discussion of relevant research and managerial implications.[20]

The Leader's Style: Task Oriented or Relationship Oriented? Fiedler developed the least preferred co-worker (LPC) scale to identify leadership styles. (You will be asked to complete the LPC scale when working on the exercise at the end of this chapter.) He contends that the LPC scale measures whether a leader has a **task-oriented style** or a **relationship-oriented style.** Although there has been much disagreement over the definition of these styles, they have been characterized as follows:

> Low-LPC persons, those describing their least preferred co-worker in quite negative terms, are thought to be primarily concerned with task success, i.e., they are "task-oriented." On the other hand, persons describing their least preferred co-worker in relatively positive terms (high-LPC persons) are thought to be "relationship-oriented," i.e., primarily concerned with attaining and maintaining successful interpersonal relationships.[21]

Consider the leadership styles of Lee Iacocca, former CEO of Chrysler, and Robert Eaton, his replacement.

> Far from being a good listener, Mr. Iacocca often couldn't stop talking. . . . The 53-year-old Mr. Eaton, on the other hand, is largely viewed by Chrysler insiders as a coach and a listener who eschews the trappings of power in favor of teamwork and consensus-building. . . . Mr. Iacocca liked summoning underlings to his office and reminding them that he took his management style from his mentor Henry Ford II, an old-style corporate autocrat who delighted in the arbitrary use of power. Few people ever got to talk to Mr.

task-oriented style Focuses on accomplishing tasks and goals.

relationship-oriented style Focuses on attaining and maintaining good interpersonal relationships.

FIGURE 15~3   Representation of Fiedler's Contingency Model

	High Control			Moderate Control			Low Control	
	I	II	III	IV	V	VI	VII	VIII
Situational Control	High Control			Moderate Control			Low Control	
Leader–Member Relations	Good	Good	Good	Good	Poor	Poor	Poor	Poor
Task Structure	Structured		Unstructured		Structured		Unstructured	
Position Power	Strong	Weak	Strong	Weak	Strong	Weak	Strong	Weak

Source: Adapted from F E Fiedler, "Situational Control and a Dynamic Theory of Leadership," in *Managerial Control and Organizational Democracy*, eds B King, S Streufert, and F E Fiedler (New York: John Wiley & Sons, 1978), p 114. Used with permission.

Iacocca without going through a secretary. . . . Mr. Eaton's style makes it clear that the 90s will be different. He is fond of dropping in, sans jacket, for informal chats with Chrysler subordinates. He often picks up the telephone himself.[22]

Situational Control   Situational control refers to the amount of control and influence the leader has in her or his immediate work environment. Situational control ranges from high to low. High control implies that the leader's decisions will produce predictable results because the leader has the ability to influence work outcomes. Low control implies that the leader's decisions may not influence work outcomes because the leader has very little influence. There are three dimensions of situational control: leader–member relations, task structure, and position power. These dimensions vary independently, forming eight combinations of situational control (see Figure 15–3).

The three dimensions of situational control are defined as follows:

- **Leader–member relations** reflect the extent to which the leader has the support, loyalty, and trust of the work group. This dimension is the most important component of situational control. Good leader–member relations suggest that the leader can depend on the group, thus ensuring that the work group will try to meet the leader's goals and objectives.

  leader-member relations Extent that leader has the support, loyalty, and trust of work group.

- **Task structure** is concerned with the amount of structure contained within tasks performed by the work group. For example, a managerial job contains less structure than that of a bank teller. Since structured tasks have guidelines for how the job should be completed, the leader has more control and influence over

  task structure   Amount of structure contained within work tasks.

employees performing such tasks. This dimension is the second most important component of situational control.

position power Degree to which leader has formal power.

■ **Position power** refers to the degree to which the leader has formal power to reward, punish, or otherwise obtain compliance from employees.[23]

Linking Leadership Style and Situational Control   Fiedler's complete contingency model is presented in Figure 15–3. The horizontal axis breaks out the eight control situations. Each situation represents a unique combination of leader–member relations, task structure, and position power. The vertical axis indicates the level of leader effectiveness. Plotted on the resulting quadrant are lines indicating those situations in which low-LPC (dotted line) and high-LPC (solid line) leaders are predicted to be effective.

For those situations in which the leader has high control (situations I, II, and III), task-oriented (low-LPC) leaders are hypothesized to be more effective than relationship-oriented (high-LPC) leaders. Under conditions of moderate control (situations IV, V, and VI), the interpersonal orientation of high-LPC leaders is predicted to be more effective. Finally, the task orientation of low-LPC leaders is hypothesized to be more effective under conditions of low control (situations VII and VIII). *In short, Fiedler contends that task-oriented leaders are more effective in extreme situations of either high or low control, but relationship-oriented leaders tend to be more effective in middle-of-the-road situations of moderate control.*

Research and Managerial Implications   The overall accuracy of Fiedler's contingency model was tested through a meta-analysis of 35 studies containing 137 leader style–performance relations. According to the researchers' findings: (1) the contingency theory was correctly induced from studies on which it was based; (2) for laboratory studies testing the model, the theory was supported for all leadership situations except situation II; and (3) for field studies testing the model, three of the eight situations (IV, V, and VII) produced completely supportive results, while partial support was obtained for situations I, II, III, VI, and VIII.[24] This last finding suggests that Fiedler's model may need theoretical refinement. Because the LPC scale has questionable validity, this refinement might entail a reconceptualization of the meaning of a least preferred co-worker.[25]

In conclusion, except for the validity of the LPC scale, Fiedler's contingency model has considerable support. This implies that organizational effectiveness can be enhanced by appropriately matching leaders with situations. Leaders with an inappropriate style need to change their degree of situational control by using one of the techniques listed in Table 15–1 or be moved to a situation in which they can be effective.

Path–Goal Theory

Path–goal theory is based on the expectancy theory of motivation discussed in Chapter 7. Expectancy theory proposes that motivation to exert effort increases as one's effort → performance → outcome expectations improve. Path–goal theory focuses on how leaders influence followers' expectations.

Robert House originated the path–goal theory of leadership. He proposed a model that describes how expectancy perceptions are influenced by the contingent relationships among four leadership styles and various employee attitudes and

• ↙ TABLE 15~1
Techniques to Modify
Situational Control

Modifying Leader–Member Relations

Spend more or less time with your subordinates.
Organize activities that take place outside of work (picnic, bowling, etc.).
Request trusted employees that you know to work for you.
Obtain positive outcomes for your employees (special bonus, time off, etc.).
Share information with your employees.

Modifying Task Structure

Break the job down into smaller subtasks.
Request additional training.
Develop procedures, guidelines, or diagrams related to completing tasks.
Seek advice from others.
Seek problems to solve.
Volunteer for new tasks or assignments.
Become more of a decision maker.

Modifying Position Power

Exercise the powers that are inherent in your position.
Become an expert on the tasks performed by your employees.
Control the type and amount of information that your employees receive.
Delegate authority.
Incorporate the work group into planning and decision-making activities.
Do not withhold information from employees.
Avoid any trappings of demonstrating power and rank.

Source: Adapted from F E Fiedler and M M Chemers, *Improving Leadership Effectiveness* (New York: John Wiley & Sons, 1984), pp 179–84. Used with permission.

• ↙ FIGURE 15~4
A General Representation of
House's Path–Goal Theory

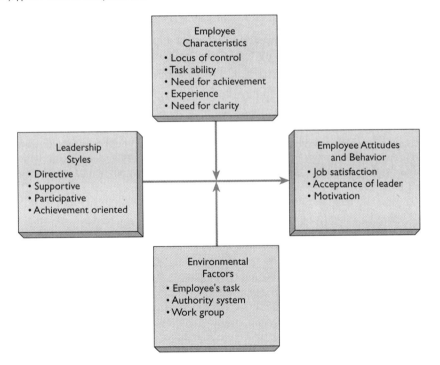

behaviors (see Figure 15–4).[26] According to the path–goal model, leader behavior is acceptable when employees view it as a source of satisfaction or as paving the way to future satisfaction. In addition, leader behavior is motivational to the extent it (1) reduces roadblocks that interfere with goal accomplishment, (2) provides the guidance and support needed by employees, and (3) ties meaningful rewards to goal accomplishment. Because the model deals with pathways to goals and rewards, it is called the path–goal theory of leadership. House sees the leader's main job as helping employees stay on the right paths to challenging goals and valued rewards.

Leadership Styles   House believes leaders can exhibit more than one leadership style. This contrasts with Fiedler, who proposes that leaders have one dominant style. The four leadership styles identified by House are as follows:

- *Directive leadership.*   Providing guidance to employees about what should be done and how to do it, scheduling work, and maintaining standards of performance.
- *Supportive leadership.*   Showing concern for the well-being and needs of employees, being friendly and approachable, and treating workers as equals.
- *Participative leadership.*   Consulting with employees and seriously considering their ideas when making decisions.
- *Achievement-oriented leadership.*   Encouraging employees to perform at their highest level by setting challenging goals, emphasizing excellence, and demonstrating confidence in employee abilities.[27]

Research evidence supports the idea that leaders exhibit more than one leadership style.[28] Descriptions of business leaders reinforce these findings. For example, Michael Walsh, prior to his recent untimely death from cancer, used multiple styles of leadership to engineer a turnaround at ailing Tenneco.

> Mr. Walsh has sought out inefficiencies, such as the 170-mile routes that some parts used to travel inside factories. Quality teams have reengineered some manufacturing processes to improve productivity and profit margins. . . . To increase management's effectiveness, Mr. Walsh decided on a simple strategy: Set higher targets on every measure of performance and make missing them unacceptable. At first, that sounded good to Tenneco executives. But those who fell short were stunned to find themselves called on the carpet, they hadn't thought Mr. Walsh really meant it. . . . Divisional vice-presidents, who previously had met one-on-one with the CEO to report results, got thrust into group confessionals. Now, they are encouraged to openly question and criticize one another's performances—a practice that several admit prompts them to work harder to meet objectives.[29]

Tenneco's value nearly doubled during Walsh's tenure.

contingency factors
Variables that influence the appropriateness of a leadership style.

Contingency Factors   **Contingency factors** are situational variables that cause one style of leadership to be more effective than another. In the present context, these variables affect expectancy or path–goal perceptions. This model has two groups of contingency variables (see Figure 15–4). They are employee characteristics and environmental factors. Five important employee characteristics are locus of control, task ability, need for achievement, experience, and need for clarity. Three relevant environmental factors are: (1) the employee's task, (2) the authority system, and (3) the work group. All these factors have the potential for hindering or motivating employees.

Research has focused on determining whether the various contingency factors influence the effectiveness of different leadership styles. The employee characteristics of need for achievement, experience, and need for clarity affected *employees' preferences for leadership.* Specifically, a study of 298 ROTC cadets revealed that individuals with high achievement needs preferred directive leadership. People with low achievement needs wanted supportive leadership. Experienced salespeople were more satisfied when leaders granted them more autonomy and less direction, whereas inexperienced salespeople desired directive leadership.[30] Finally, employees with a high need for clarity performed better and were more satisfied with directive leadership; the opposite was true of individuals with a low need for clarity.[31]

With respect to environmental contingency factors, supportive leader behavior promoted job satisfaction when individuals performed structured tasks.[32]

Managerial Implications   There are three important managerial implications. First, leaders possess and use more than one style of leadership. Managers thus should not be hesitant to try new behaviors when the situation calls for them. Second, managers should modify their leadership style to fit employee characteristics. Employees with high achievement needs, little experience, and high need for clarity generally should receive directive leadership to increase satisfaction and performance. Third, the degree of task structure is a relevant contingency factor. Managers should consider using supportive supervision when the task is structured. Supportive supervision is satisfying in this context because employees already know what they should be doing.

Graen's Role-Making (VDL) Model of Leadership

George Graen, an industrial psychologist, believes popular theories of leadership are based on an incorrect assumption. Theories such as the Leadership Grid® and Fiedler's contingency model assume that leader behavior is characterized by a stable or average leadership style. In other words, these models assume a leader treats all subordinates in about the same way. This traditional approach to leadership is shown in the left side of Figure 15–5. In this case, the leader (designated by the circled L) is thought to exhibit a similar pattern of behavior toward all employees (E_1 to E_5). In contrast, Graen contends that leaders develop unique one-to-one relationships with each of the people reporting to them. Behavioral scientists call this sort of relationship a *vertical dyad.* Hence, Graen's approach is labeled the *vertical dyad linkage (VDL) model* of leadership. The forming of vertical dyads is said to be a naturally occurring process, resulting from the leader's attempt to delegate and assign work roles. As a result of this process, Graen predicts that one of two distinct types of leader–member exchange relationships will evolve.[33]

One type of leader–member exchange is called the **in-group exchange.** In this relationship, leaders and followers develop a partnership characterized by reciprocal influence, mutual trust, respect and liking, and a sense of common fates. Figure 15–5 shows that E_1 and E_5 are members of the leader's in-group. In the second type of exchange, referred to as an **out-group exchange,** leaders are characterized as overseers who fail to create a sense of mutual trust, respect, or common fate.[34] E_2, E_3, and E_4 are members of the out-group on the right side of Figure 15–5.

in-group exchange   A partnership characterized by mutual trust, respect, and liking.

out-group exchange   A partnership characterized by a lack of mutual trust, respect, and liking.

Research Findings   This leadership model received more recent research focus than any of the other situational theories discussed thus far. If Graen's model is correct, there should be a significant relationship between the type of leader–member exchange and job-related outcomes. Research supports this prediction. For example, in-group members were found to have higher organizational

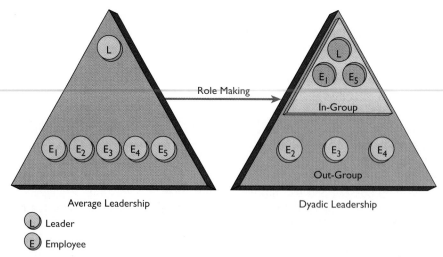

• FIGURE 15–5
A Role-Making (VDL) Model
of Leadership

Role Making

In-Group

Out-Group

Average Leadership   Dyadic Leadership

L Leader

E Employee

Source: Adapted from F Dansereau, Jr, G Graen, and W J Haga, "A Vertical Dyad Linkage Approach to Leadership within Formal Organizations," *Organizational Behavior and Human Performance*, February 1975, p 72.

commitment, job satisfaction, and job performance than did employees in the out-group.[35] In turn, this relationship was stronger when employees worked on complex tasks.[36] The type of leader–member exchange was found to predict not only turnover among nurses and computer analysts, but also career outcomes, such as promotability, salary level, and receipt of bonuses over a seven-year period.[37]

Managerial Implications   Graen's VDL model underscores the importance of training managers to improve leader–member relations. Ideally, this should enhance the job satisfaction and performance of employees and also reduce turnover. A large US government installation in the Midwest conducted such a training program. Results indicated a 19 percent increase on an objective measure of productivity. This improvement resulted in an estimated annual cost savings of more than $5 million.[38] In addition to training, VDL researcher Robert Vecchio offers the following tips to both followers and leaders for improving the quality of leader–member exchanges:

1. New employees should offer their loyalty, support, and cooperativeness to their manager.
2. If you are an out-group member, either accept the situation, try to become an in-group member by being cooperative and loyal, or quit.
3. Managers should consciously try to expand their in-groups.
4. Managers need to give employees ample opportunity to prove themselves.[39]

FROM TRANSACTIONAL TO CHARISMATIC LEADERSHIP

New perspectives of leadership theory have emerged in the past 15 years, variously referred to as "charismatic," "heroic," "transformational," or "visionary" leadership.[40] These competing but related perspectives have created confusion among researchers and practicing managers. Fortunately, Robert House and Boas Shamir have given us a practical, integrated theory. It is referred to as *charismatic leadership.*

This section begins by highlighting the differences between transactional and charismatic leadership. We then discuss a model of the charismatic leadership process and its research and management implications.

What Is the Difference between Transactional and Charismatic Leadership?

Most of the models and theories previously discussed in this chapter represent transactional leadership. **Transactional leadership** focuses on the interpersonal transactions between managers and employees. Leaders are seen as engaging in behaviors that maintain a quality interaction between themselves and followers. The two underlying characteristics of transactional leadership are that: (1) leaders use contingent rewards to motivate employees and (2) leaders exert corrective action only when subordinates fail to obtain performance goals.

In contrast, **charismatic leadership** emphasizes "symbolic leader behavior, visionary and inspirational messages, nonverbal communication, appeal to ideological values, intellectual stimulation of followers by the leader, display of confidence in self and followers, and leader expectations for follower self-sacrifice and for performance beyond the call of duty."[41] Charismatic leadership can produce significant organizational change and results because it "transforms" employees to pursue organizational goals in lieu of self-interests. Consider the leadership style of Anthony O'Reilly, CEO of H J Heinz Company. Since he took over as CEO in 1979, Heinz's market value increased from $900 million to $10 billion.

> Mr. O'Reilly clearly is a driven man—driven not just by a craving for success, but perfection. . . . And Mr. O'Reilly has always been an engaging presence—big, handsome, a marvelous storyteller. "He had a tremendous personality," says Fred Crabb, formerly Heinz's senior executive in Europe. "His ability to charm and entertain outside of business hours was a big plus." . . . Improved results at units he managed helped him climb the ladder to CEO in 1979. . . . Mr. O'Reilly accomplished this partly through vision: In 1978, he predicted a boom in health and fitness and bought Weight Watchers for just $71 million. For most of the 1980s, it powered the company's growth. He also did it partly through charm and contact. And he accomplished it by constantly squeezing more into the bottom line. . . . One way he did this was by getting people to work hard. Heinz executives are generally paid a lower salary than peers in the food business, but incentive bonuses tend to be higher, giving managers higher total compensation if they meet their short-term profit goals. In a good year, incentives might account for as much as 60% of top executives' compensation. As a result, 70-hour workweeks are not uncommon at Heinz—and the focus is largely on making the next quarter's projected results.[42]

Let us now examine how charismatic leadership transforms followers.

How Does Charismatic Leadership Transform Followers?

Charismatic leaders transform followers by creating changes in their goals, values, needs, beliefs, and aspirations. They accomplish this transformation by appealing to followers' self-concepts—namely, their values and personal identity. Figure 15–6 presents a model of how charismatic leadership accomplishes this transformation process.

Charismatic leaders first engage in three key sets of leader behavior. If done effectively, these behaviors positively affect followers' self-concepts. In turn, a positive self-concept propels employee motivation toward a host of personal

transactional leadership
Focuses on interpersonal interactions between managers and employees.

charismatic leadership
Transforms employees to pursue organizational goals over self-interests.

• FIGURE 15~6 A Charismatic Model of Leadership

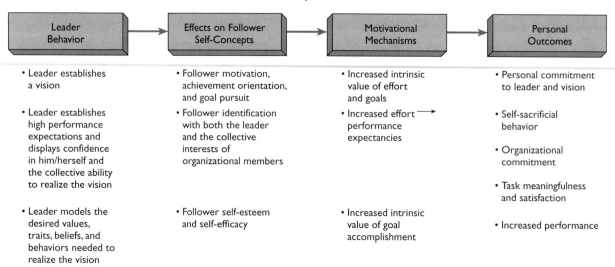

Leader Behavior	Effects on Follower Self-Concepts	Motivational Mechanisms	Personal Outcomes
• Leader establishes a vision	• Follower motivation, achievement orientation, and goal pursuit	• Increased intrinsic value of effort and goals	• Personal commitment to leader and vision
• Leader establishes high performance expectations and displays confidence in him/herself and the collective ability to realize the vision	• Follower identification with both the leader and the collective interests of organizational members	• Increased effort performance expectancies	• Self-sacrificial behavior • Organizational commitment • Task meaningfulness and satisfaction
• Leader models the desired values, traits, beliefs, and behaviors needed to realize the vision	• Follower self-esteem and self-efficacy	• Increased intrinsic value of goal accomplishment	• Increased performance

Based in part on B Shamir, R J House, and M B Arthur, "The Motivational Effects of Charismatic Leadership: A Self-Concept Based Theory," *Organization Science,* November 1993, pp 577–94; and R J House and B Shamir, "Toward the Integration of Transformation, Charismatic, and Visionary Theories," in *Leadership Theory and Research: Perspectives and Directions,* eds M M Chemers and R Ayman (New York: Academic Press, 1993), pp 81–107.

outcomes such as personal commitment to the leader and vision, self-sacrificial behavior, organizational commitment, task meaningfulness and satisfaction, intrinsic motivation, and increased performance.

Charismatic Leader Behavior The first set of charismatic leader behavior involves establishing a common vision of the future. A vision is "a realistic, credible, attractive future for your organization."[43] According to Burt Nanus, a leadership expert, the "right" vision unleashes human potential because it serves as a beacon of hope and common purpose. It does this by attracting commitment, energizing workers, creating meaning in employees' lives, establishing a standard of excellence, promoting high ideals, and bridging the gap between an organization's present problems and its future goals and aspirations.[44] In contrast, the "wrong" vision can be very damaging to an organization. Consider what happened to Borden as it pursued the vision of Romeo Ventres, Borden's former CEO.

> Sales and profits in every major division are declining. It has shed thousands of workers, slashed its dividend by 75% and, since 1989, has taken $1.5 billion in restructuring charges—a huge sum for a company with $7.14 billion in 1992 sales. In the third quarter [of 1993], the company posted its ninth consecutive quarterly decline in operating earnings. . . . He [Mr. Ventres] dreamed of transforming Borden from a sleepy conglomerate into a major food marketer. He pursued his vision relentlessly, spending nearly $2 billion on 91 acquisitions between 1986 and 1991 to accumulate such brands as Laura Scudder's potato chips, Steero bouillon, and Krazy Glue.[45]

As you can see, Borden's vision produced disastrous results. This highlights the fact that charismatic leaders do more than simply establish a vision. They also must gain input from others in developing an effective implementation plan. For example, Johnson & Johnson is planning to obtain input about its vision and implementation plan by surveying all of its 80,000 employees.[46]

Franklin Delano Roosevelt was clearly a charismatic leader. In his "stump" speeches as well as in his legendary "fireside chats," FDR set forth his vision for the future of America.

(*FPG International*)

The second set of leader behaviors involves two key components.

1. Charismatic leaders set high performance expectations and standards because they know challenging, attainable goals lead to greater productivity.
2. Charismatic leaders need to publicly express confidence in the followers' ability to meet high performance expectations. This is essential because employees are more likely to pursue difficult goals when they believe they can accomplish what is being asked of them.

The third and final set of leader behaviors involves being a role model. Through their actions, charismatic leaders model the desired values, traits, beliefs, and behaviors needed to realize the vision.

Effects on Follower Self-Concepts   Figure 15–6 also shows that charismatic leadership affects three aspects of a follower's self-concept.

1. It enhances follower motivation, achievement motivation, and goal pursuit.
2. It increases the extent to which followers identify with the leader's values, goals, and aspirations and with the collective interests of all employees.
3. Follower self-esteem and self-efficacy are heightened by charismatic leader behavior.

In contrast, followers' self-concepts are negatively affected by destructive charismatic leadership. Take Edwin Artzt, Chairman of Procter & Gamble Company, for example.

> Managers say meetings with their boss [Mr. Artzt] often turn into humiliating public hazings. At a meeting of beauty product managers about 18 months ago, Mr. Artzt berated the group for mishandling Noxema skin cream. With a severe tone of disgust, he said, "How could you people be so stupid to get into this mess?" says a former marketing manager. Mr. Artzt went on for half an hour, until someone reminded him that P&G had only recently acquired Noxema and they had been assigned the brand just six weeks before. No wonder more than a dozen senior executives have jumped the ship that

launched Ivory since Mr. Artzt took the helm in early 1990, taking with them years of advertising and product-development expertise. . . . Some managers, saying they are sick of being browbeaten or frightened of coming cutbacks, are updating their resumes.[47]

Motivational Mechanisms Charismatic leadership positively affects employee motivation (see Figure 15–6). One way in which this occurs is by increasing the intrinsic value of an employee's effort and goals. Leaders do this by emphasizing the symbolic value of effort; that is, charismatic leaders convey the message that effort reflects important organizational values and collective interests. Followers come to learn that their level of effort represents a moral statement. For example, high effort represents commitment to the organization's vision and values, whereas low effort reflects a lack of commitment.

Charismatic leadership also increases employees' effort → performance expectancies by positively contributing to followers' self-esteem and self-efficacy. Leaders also increase the intrinsic value of goal accomplishment by explaining the organization's vision and goals in terms of the personal values they represent. This helps employees to personally connect with the organization's vision. Charismatic leaders further increase the meaningfulness of actions aimed toward goal accomplishment by showing how goals move the organization toward its positive vision, which then gives followers a sense of "growth and development," both of which are important contributors to a positive self-concept.

Research and Managerial Implications

A recent review of research identified 35 empirical studies spanning a diversity of samples and organizations. Results indicated that charismatic leaders received higher performance ratings, were viewed as more effective leaders by both supervisors and followers, and had more satisfied and productive followers than noncharismatic leaders.[48] Charismatic leaders also had higher project quality and budget/schedule performance ratings and were identified as more effective role models.[49] Finally, a study of 31 presidents of the United States indicated that charisma significantly predicted presidential performance.[50]

These results underscore four important managerial implications. First, the best leaders are not just charismatic, they are both transactional and charismatic. Leaders should attempt these two types of leadership while avoiding a "laissez-faire" or "wait-and-see" style. Laissez-faire leadership is the most ineffective leadership style.[51]

Second, charismatic leadership is not applicable in all organizational situations. According to a team of experts, charismatic leadership is most likely to be effective when

1. The situation offers opportunities for "moral" involvement.
2. Performance goals cannot be easily established and measured.
3. Extrinsic rewards cannot be clearly linked to individual performance.
4. There are few situational cues or constraints to guide behavior.
5. Exceptional effort, behavior, sacrifices, and performance are required of both leaders and followers.[52]

Third, employees at any level in an organization can be trained to be more transactional and charismatic.[53] This reinforces the organizational value of developing and rolling out a combination of transactional and charismatic leadership training for all employees. Fourth, charismatic leaders can be ethical or unethical. Whereas ethical charismatic leaders enable employees to enhance their self-concepts, unethical ones select or produce obedient, dependent, and compliant followers.[54] Top management can create and maintain ethical charismatic leadership by

1. Creating and enforcing a clearly stated code of ethics.
2. Recruiting, selecting, and promoting people with high morals and standards.
3. Developing performance expectations around the treatment of employees—these expectations can then be assessed in the performance appraisal process.
4. Training employees to value diversity.
5. Identifying, rewarding, and publicly praising employees who exemplify high moral conduct.[55]

BACK TO THE OPENING CASE

Now that you have read Chapter 15, you should be able to answer the following questions about the Bill Gates case:

1. Citing examples, which different leadership traits and styles were exhibited by Bill Gates?
2. How did Bill Gates attempt to clarify path–goal relationships?
3. Is Bill Gates more of a transactional or charismatic leader? Explain.
4. Use Figure 15–6 to explain how Bill Gates relies on charismatic leadership to transform employees.

SUMMARY OF KEY CONCEPTS

1. *Define the term* leadership *and explain the conceptual framework for understanding leadership.* Leadership is defined as a social influence process in which the leader tries to obtain the voluntary participation of employees in an effort to reach organizational objectives. Leadership entails more than having authority and power. According to the conceptual framework for understanding leadership, certain leader characteristics/traits are the foundation of effective leadership. These characteristics affect an individual's ability to carry out various managerial behaviors/roles. In turn, effective leadership depends on a variety of situational variables.

2. *Review trait theory research.* Historical leadership research did not support the notion that effective leaders possessed unique traits from followers. However, teams of researchers reanalyzed this historical data with modern-day statistical

procedures. Results revealed that individuals tend to be perceived as leaders when they possess one or more of the following traits: intelligence, dominance, and masculinity. Recent research also examined the relationship between gender and leadership. Results demonstrated that (1) men and women differed in the type of leadership roles they assume, (2) leadership styles varied by gender, and (3) female leaders were evaluated more negatively than equivalent male leaders.

3. *Explain results from the Ohio State studies, and summarize derivative behavioral style theories.* The Ohio State studies revealed that there were two key, independent dimensions of leader behavior: consideration and initiating structure. Nonetheless, results did not support the premise that there is one best style of leadership. The Managerial Grid and Situational Leadership Theory are two derivatives

of the Ohio State studies. The Managerial Grid prescribes that leaders should demonstrate a high concern for both people and production. Situational Leadership Theory implies that effective leadership is based on cross referencing an employee's readiness with one of four leadership styles. Research has not supported these two derivative theories.

4. *Contrast the underlying philosophy of trait, behavioral, and situational theories of leadership.* Trait theories are based on the premise that leaders possess certain traits that uniquely differentiate them from followers. Behavioral styles theories are based on the premise that leader behaviors are the prime predictor of a leader's effectiveness. They led to the unsupported prediction that there is one best style of leadership. Situational theories propose that the effectiveness of a particular style of leadership depends on the situation.

5. *Explain, according to Fiedler's contingency model, how leadership style interacts with situational control.* Fiedler believes leader effectiveness depends on an appropriate match between leadership style, measured with the LPC scale, and situational control. Low-LPC leaders are task-oriented and high-LPC leaders are relationship oriented. Situational control is composed of leader–member relations, task structure, and position power. Low-LPC leaders are effective under situations of both high and low control. High-LPC leaders are more effective when they have moderate situational control.

6. *Discuss House's path–goal theory, and review the theory's managerial implications.* According to path–goal theory, leaders alternately can exhibit directive, supportive, participative, or achievement-oriented styles of leadership. The effectiveness of these styles depends on various employee characteristics and environmental factors. Path–goal theory has received limited support from research. There are three important managerial implications.

First, leaders possess and use more than one style of leadership. Second, managers should adopt their style to fit employee characteristics. Third, task structure is an important contingency factor.

7. *Explain the role-making model (VDL) of leadership.* The role-making approach assumes leaders develop unique vertical dyad linkages (VDL) with each employee. These leader–member exchanges qualify as either in-group or out-group relationships. Research supports this model of leadership.

8. *Define and differentiate transactional and charismatic leadership.* There is an important difference between transactional and charismatic leadership. Transactional leaders focus on the interpersonal transactions between managers and employees. Charismatic leaders motivate employees to pursue organizational goals above their own self-interests. Both forms of leadership are important for organizational success.

9. *Explain how charismatic leadership transforms followers.* Charismatic leaders transform followers by creating changes in their goals, values, needs, beliefs, and aspirations. Leaders accomplish this by first engaging in three key sets of leader behavior. These leader behaviors, in turn, positively affect followers' self-concepts. A positive self-concept then unleashes employee motivation toward achieving a host of preferred outcomes.

10. *Summarize the managerial implications of charismatic leadership.* There are four managerial implications: (1) The best leaders are both transactional and charismatic. (2) Charismatic leadership is not applicable in all organizational situations. (3) Employees at any level in an organization can be trained to be more transactional and charismatic. (4) Top management needs to promote and reinforce ethical charismatic leadership because charismatic leaders can be ethical or unethical.

Discussion Questions

1. Is everyone cut out to be a leader? Explain.
2. Has your college education helped you develop any of the traits that characterize leaders?
3. Should organizations change anything in response to research pertaining to gender and leadership? If yes, describe your recommendations.
4. What leadership traits and behavioral styles are possessed by the president of the United States?
5. Does it make more sense to change a person's leadership style or the situation? How would Fred Fiedler and Robert House answer this question?
6. Describe how a college professor might use House's

path–goal theory to clarify student's path–goal perceptions.

7. Have you ever been a member of an in-group or out-group? For either situation, describe the pattern of interaction between you and your manager.

8. Identify three charismatic leaders, and describe their leadership traits and behavioral styles.

9. Have you ever worked for a charismatic leader? Describe how he or she transformed followers.

10. In your view, which leadership theory has the greatest practical application? Why?

Exercise

Objectives

1. To promote understanding of Fiedler's contingency model.
2. To assess your leadership style and gain practice at applying the model.

Introduction

According to Fiedler, leader effectiveness is contingent upon an appropriate match between the leader's style and situational control. A leader's style is either task oriented or relationship oriented. Fiedler developed the least preferred co-worker (LPC) scale to measure these styles. You will complete the LPC scale as part of this exercise. You also will be given the opportunity to assess situational control and to consider which kind of leader is best suited for that situation.

Instructions

Complete the following LPC scale by following the directions at the top of the questionnaire. After completing your ratings, simply add the values associated with each of your 18 responses to calculate your LPC score. If your score is 73 or above, you are classified as a high-LPC person with a relationship-oriented style. A score below 64 identifies you as a low-LPC person, indicating that you have a task-oriented style. If your score is between 65 and 72, you are classified as a middle-LPC person. Middle-LPC leaders exhibit characteristics of both the high and low-LPC styles. Keep in mind that one style is not better than the other. Each is appropriate and necessary in certain situations. We next would like you to answer the questions for discussion listed directly after the LPC scale.

After answering these questions, read the leadership vignette shown after the LPC scale, and answer the questions for discussion.

Least Preferred Co-Worker (LPC) Scale

Throughout your life you have worked in many groups with a wide variety of different people—on your job, in social clubs, in church organizations, in volunteer groups, on athletic teams, and in many others. You probably found working with most of your co-workers quite easy, but working with others may have been very difficult or all but impossible.

Now, think of all the people with whom you have ever worked. Next, think of the one person in your life with whom you could work least well. This individual may or may not be the person you also disliked most. It must be the one person with whom you had the most difficulty getting a job done, the one single individual with whom you would least want to work—a boss, a subordinate, or a peer. This person is called your ''least preferred co-worker'' (LPC).

On the scale below, describe this person by placing an ''X'' in the appropriate space.

			Scoring
Pleasant	— — — — — — — —	Unpleasant	___
	8 7 6 5 4 3 2 1		
Friendly	— — — — — — — —	Unfriendly	___
	8 7 6 5 4 3 2 1		
Rejecting	— — — — — — — —	Accepting	___
	1 2 3 4 5 6 7 8		
Tense	— — — — — — — —	Relaxed	___
	1 2 3 4 5 6 7 8		
Distant	— — — — — — — —	Close	___
	1 2 3 4 5 6 7 8		
Cold	— — — — — — — —	Warm	___
	1 2 3 4 5 6 7 8		
Supportive	— — — — — — — —	Hostile	___
	8 7 6 5 4 3 2 1		
Boring	— — — — — — — —	Interesting	___
	1 2 3 4 5 6 7 8		
Quarrelsome	— — — — — — — —	Harmonious	___
	1 2 3 4 5 6 7 8		
Gloomy	— — — — — — — —	Cheerful	___
	1 2 3 4 5 6 7 8		
Open	— — — — — — — —	Guarded	___
	8 7 6 5 4 3 2 1		

Backbiting	—	—	—	—	—	—	—	—	Loyal	————
	1	2	3	4	5	6	7	8		
Untrustworthy	—	—	—	—	—	—	—	—	Trustworthy	————
	1	2	3	4	5	6	7	8		
Considerate	—	—	—	—	—	—	—	—	Inconsiderate	————
	8	7	6	5	4	3	2	1		
Rejecting Nasty	—	—	—	—	—	—	—	—	Nice	————
	1	2	3	4	5	6	7	8		
Agreeable	—	—	—	—	—	—	—	—	Disagreeable	————
	8	7	6	5	4	3	2	1		
Insincere	—	—	—	—	—	—	—	—	Sincere	————
	1	2	3	4	5	6	7	8		
Kind	—	—	—	—	—	—	—	—	Unkind	————
	8	7	6	5	4	3	2	1		
									Total	————

Source: F E Fiedler and M M Chemers, *Improving Leadership Effectiveness* (New York: John Wiley & Sons, 1984), pp 17–19. Used with permission.

Questions for Consideration/ Class Discussion

1. What is your leadership style?
2. Do you agree with this assessment? Explain.
3. Using Figure 15–3 as a frame of reference, what type of leadership situations are you best suited for?

Leadership Vignette

You are director of a large manufacturing firm. The manager in charge of the advertising department just had a serious accident and has to be replaced since it is doubtful that he will be able to return to work for quite some time. You need someone to fill in for him.

The situation is rather hard to define. The key people are temperamental and touchy, and there has been a great deal of infighting and conflict. The manager has had a difficult time holding the department together. Moreover, there has been a demand from other managers for more creative marketing campaigns. You need someone who can immediately take charge of this department and make it productive.[56]

Questions for Consideration/ Class Discussion

1. What is the situational control in the advertising department?
2. What type of leader is best suited for this situation?
3. What would you do if you were unable to find an optimum leadership match according to Fiedler's theory?

Notes

[1] See S Lieberson and J F O'Connor, "Leadership and Organizational Performance: A Study of Large Corporations," *American Sociological Review,* April 1972, pp 117–30.

[2] Results are presented in D Jacobs and L Singell, "Leadership and Organizational Performance: Isolating Links between Managers and Collective Success," *Social Science Research,* June 1993, pp 165–89.

[3] C A Schriesheim, J M Tolliver, and O C Behling, "Leadership Theory: Some Implications for Managers," *MSU Business Topics,* Summer 1978, p 35.

[4] T Peters and N Austin, *A Passion for Excellence* (New York: Random House, 1985), pp 5–6.

[5] M DePree, *Leadership Is an Art* (New York: Dell Publishing, 1989), p 19.

[6] For complete details, see R M Stogdill, "Personal Factors Associated with Leadership: A Survey of the Literature," *Journal of Psychology* 1948, pp 35–71; and R M Stogdill, *Handbook of Leadership* (New York: Free Press, 1974).

[7] See R D Mann, "A Review of the Relationships between Personality and Performance in Small Groups," *Psychological Bulletin,* July 1959, pp 241–70.

[8] See D A Kenny and S J Zaccaro, "An Estimate of Variance Due to Traits in Leadership," *Journal of Applied Psychology,* November 1983, pp 678–85. Results from a more recent verification can be found in S J Zaccaro, R J Foti, and D A Kenny, "Self-Monitoring and Trait-Based Variance in Leadership: An Investigation of Leader Flexibility across Multiple Group Situations," *Journal of Applied Psychology,* April 1991, pp 308–15.

[9] R G Lord, C L De Vader, and G M Alliger, "A Meta-Analysis of the Relation between Personality Traits and Leadership Perceptions: An Application of Validity Generalization Procedures," *Journal of Applied Psychology,* August 1986, p 407.

[10] Confirming evidence can be found in L E Atwater and F J Yammarino, "Personal Attributes as Predictors of Superiors' and Subordinates' Perceptions of Military Academy Leadership," *Human Relations,* May 1993, pp 645–68; R B Morgan, "Self- and Co-Worker Perceptions of Ethics and Their Relationships to Leadership and Salary," *Academy of Management Journal,* February 1993, pp 200–14; and T E Malloy and C L Janowski, "Perceptions and Metaperceptions of Leadership: Components, Accuracy, and Dispositional Correlates," *Personality and Social Psychology Bulletin,* December 1992, pp 700–8.

[11] Gender and the emergence of leaders was examined by

A H Eagly and S J Karau, "Gender and the Emergence of Leaders: A Meta-Analysis," *Journal of Personality and Social Psychology,* May 1991, pp 685–710.

[12] See A H Eagly, S J Karau, and B T Johnson, "Gender and Leadership Style among School Principals: A Meta-Analysis," *Educational Administration Quarterly,* February 1992, pp 76–102.

[13] Results can be found in A H Eagly, M G Makhijani, and B G Klonsky, "Gender and the Evaluation of Leaders: A Meta-Analysis," *Psychological Bulletin,* January 1992, pp 3–22.

[14] C McCoy, "Stained Image: Pollution Control Firm Cleans Up but Leaves a Trail of Allegations," *The Wall Street Journal,* November 2, 1993, p A1.

[15] This research is summarized and critiqued by B M Bass, *Bass & Stogdill's Handbook of Leadership: Theory, Research, and Managerial Applications* (New York: The Free Press, 1990), chap. 24.

[16] See R R Blake and A McCanse, *Leadership Dilemmas —Grid Solutions* (Houston: Gulf Publishing, 1990).

[17] A thorough discussion of this theory is provided by P Hersey and K H Blanchard, *Management of Organizational Behavior: Utilizing Human Resources,* 5th ed (Englewood Cliffs, NJ: Prentice-Hall, 1988).

[18] Results can be found in M R Redmond, M D Mumford, and R Teach, "Putting Creativity to Work: Effects of Leader Behavior on Subordinate Creativity," *Organizational Behavior and Human Decision Processes,* June 1993, pp 120–51.

[19] See Bass, *Bass & Stogdill's Handbook of Leadership: Theory, Research, and Managerial Applications,* chaps. 20–25.

[20] For more on this theory, see F E Fiedler, "A Contingency Model of Leadership Effectiveness," in *Advances in Experimental Social Psychology,* vol. 1, ed L Berkowitz (New York: Academic Press, 1964); F E Fiedler, *A Theory of Leadership Effectiveness* (New York: McGraw-Hill, 1967).

[21] R W Rice and F J Seaman, "Internal Analyses of the Least Preferred Co-Worker (LPC) Scale," *Educational and Psychological Measurement,* 1981, p 110.

[22] D Lavin, "Straight Shooter: Robert Eaton Thinks 'Vision' Is Overrated and He's Not Alone," *The Wall Street Journal,* October 4, 1993, p A1.

[23] Additional information on situational control is contained in F E Fiedler, "The Leadership Situation and the Black Box in Contingency Theories," in *Leadership Theory and Research: Perspectives and Directions,* eds M M Chemers and R Ayman (New York: Academic Press, 1993), pp 2–28.

[24] See L H Peters, D D Hartke, and J T Pohlmann, "Fiedler's Contingency Theory of Leadership: An Application of the Meta-Analyses Procedures of Schmidt and Hunter," *Psychological Bulletin,* March 1985, pp 274–85.

[25] Arguments about the validity of the LPC are contained in C A Schriesheim and N R Klich, "Fiedler's Least Preferred Coworker (LPC) Instrument: An Investigation of Its True Bipolarity," *Educational and Psychological Measurement,* Summer 1991, pp 305–315; and C A Schriesheim, B D Bannister, and W H Money, "Psychometric Properties of the LPC Scale: An Extension of Rice's Review," *Academy of Management Review,* April 1979, pp 287–90.

[26] For more detail on this theory, see R J House, "A Path–Goal Theory of Leader Effectiveness," *Administrative Science Quarterly,* September 1971, pp 321–38.

[27] Adapted from R J House and T R Mitchell, "Path–Goal Theory of Leadership," *Journal of Contemporary Business,* Autumn 1974, p 83.

[28] See House, "A Path–Goal Theory of Leader Effectiveness."

[29] R Johnson, "Tenneco Hired a CEO from Outside, and He Is Refocusing the Firm, *The Wall Street Journal,* March 29, 1993, pp A1, A11.

[30] The study of ROTC cadets was conducted by J E Mathieu, "A Test of Subordinates' Achievement and Affiliation Needs as Moderators of a Leader Path–Goal Relationships," *Basic and Applied Social Psychology,* June 1990, pp 179–89. The study of salespeople was conducted by A K Kohli, "Effects of Supervisory Behavior: The Role of Individual Differences among Salespeople," *Journal of Marketing,* October 1989, pp 40–50.

[31] See R T Keller, "A Test of the Path–Goal Theory of Leadership with Need for Clarity as a Moderator in Research and Development Organizations," *Journal of Applied Psychology,* April 1989, pp 208–12.

[32] For a discussion of related research, see R A Price, "An Investigation of Path–Goal Leadership Theory in Marketing Channels," *Journal of Retailing,* Fall 1991, pp 339–61: and C A Schriesheim and A S DeNisi, "Task Dimensions as Moderators of the Effects of Instrumental Leadership: A Two-Sample Replicated Test of Path–Goal Leadership Theory," *Journal of Applied Psychology,* October 1981, pp 589–97.

[33] See F Dansereau, Jr., G Graen, and W Haga, "A Vertical Dyad Linkage Approach to Leadership within Formal Organizations," *Organizational Behavior and Human Performance,* February 1975, pp 46–78; and R M Dienesch and R C Liden, "Leader–Member Exchange Model of Leadership: A Critique and Further Development," *Academy of Management Review,* July 1986, pp 618–34.

[34] These descriptions were taken from D Duchon, S G Green, and T D Taber, "Vertical Dyad Linkage: A Longitudinal Assessment of Antecedents, Measures, and Consequences," *Journal of Applied Psychology,* February 1986, pp 56–60.

[35] Supporting evidence can be found in A J Kinicki and R P Vecchio, "Influences on the Quality of Supervisor–Subordinate Relations: The Role of Time-Pressure, Organizational Commitment, and Locus of Control," *Journal of Organizational Behavior,* in press, 1994; and R C Liden, S J Wayne, and D Stilwell, "A Longitudinal Study on the Early Development of Leader–Member Exchanges," *Journal of Applied Psychology,* August 1993, pp 662–74.

[36] See K J Dunegan, D Duchon, and M Uhl-Bien, "Examining the Link between Leader–Member Exchange and Subordinate Performance: The Role of Task Analyzability and Variety as Moderators," *Journal of Management,* March 1992, pp 59–76.

[37] Turnover studies were conducted by G B Graen, R C Liden, and W Hoel, "Role of Leadership in the Employee Withdrawal Process," *Journal of Applied Psychology,* December 1982, pp 868–72; G R Ferris, "Role of Leadership in the Employee Withdrawal Process: A Constructive Replication," *Journal of Applied Psychology,* November 1985, pp 777–81. The career progress study was conducted by M Wakabayashi and G B Graen, "The Japanese Career Progress Study: A 7-Year Follow-Up," *Journal of Applied Psychology,* November 1984, pp 603–14.

[38] See T A Scandura and G B Graen, "Moderating Effects of Initial Leader–Member Exchange Status on the Effects of a Leadership Intervention," *Journal of Applied Psychology,* August 1984, pp 428–36.

[39] These recommendations are from R P Vecchio, "Are You In or Out with Your Boss?" *Business Horizons,* November–December 1986, pp 76–78.

[40] For details on these different theories, see J McGregor Burns, *Leadership* (New York: Harper & Row, 1978); N M Tichy and M A Devanna, *The Transformational Leader* (New York: John Wiley & Sons, 1986); J M Kouzes and B Z Posner, *The Leadership Challenge: How to Get Extraordinary Things Done in Organizations* (San Francisco: Jossey-Bass, 1990); B Bass and B J Avolio, "Transformational Leadership: A Response to Critiques," in *Leadership Theory and Research: Perspectives and Directions,* eds M M Chemers and R Ayman (New York: Academic Press, 1993), pp 49–80; B Nanus, *Visionary Leadership* (San Francisco: Jossey-Bass, 1992); and B Shamir, R J House, and M B Arthur, "The Motivational Effects of Charismatic Leadership: A Self-Concept Based Theory," *Organization Science,* November 1993, pp 577–94.

[41] Shamir, House, and Arthur, "The Motivational Effects of Charismatic Leadership: A Self-Concept Based Theory," p 578.

[42] T F O'Boyle, "Irish Charm: Inspired by His Roots, Heinz's Tony O'Reilly Demands More, Better," *The Wall Street Journal,* March 1, 1992, pp A1, A6.

[43] B Nanus, *Visionary Leadership* (San Francisco: Jossey-Bass, 1992), p 8.

[44] See Ibid.; and J Huey, "The New Post-Heroic Leadership," *Fortune,* February 21, 1994, pp 42–50.

[45] K Deveny and S L Hwang, "Elsie's Executives: Borden's Bottom Line has been Damaged by Conflicting Styles," *The Wall Street Journal,* January 18, 1994, p A1.

[46] See G Fuchsberg, " 'Visioning' Missions Becomes Its Own Mission," *The Wall Street Journal,* January 7, 1994, p B1.

[47] C Hymowitz and G Stern, "Taking Flak: At Procter & Gamble, Brands Face Pressure and So Do Executives," *The Wall Street Journal,* May 5, 1993, p A1.

[48] Results are summarized in R J House and B Shamir, "Toward the Integration of Transformational, Charismatic, and Visionary Theories," in *Leadership Theory and Research: Perspectives and Directions,* eds M M Chemers and R Ayman (New York: Academic Press, 1993), pp 81–107. Also see S L Hart and R E Quinn, "Roles Executives Play: CEO's, Behavioral Complexity, and Firm Performance," *Human Relations,* May 1993, pp 543–74.

[49] See M A Jolson, A J Dubinsky, F J Yammarino, and L B Comer, "Transforming the Salesforce with Leadership," *Sloan Management Review,* Spring 1993, pp 95–106; and R T Keller, "Transformation Leadership and the Performance of Research and Developmental Project Groups," *Journal of Management,* September 1992, pp 489–501.

[50] Results can be found in R J House, W D Spangler, and J Woycke, "Personality and Charisma in the US Presidency: A Psychological Theory of Leader Effectiveness," *Administrative Science Quarterly,* September 1991, pp 364–96.

[51] See Shamir, House, and Arthur, "The Motivational Effects of Charismatic Leadership: A Self-Concept Based Theory," pp 577–94.

[52] Ibid.

[53] Supporting research is summarized by Bass and Avolio, "Transformation Leadership: A Response to Critiques," pp 49–80. The effectiveness of leadership training is discussed by J Huey, "The Leadership Industry," *Fortune,* February 21, 1994, pp 54–56.

[54] The ethics of charismatic leadership is discussed by J M Howell and B J Avolio, "The Ethics of Charismatic Leadership: Submission or Liberation," *The Executive,* May 1992, pp 43–54.

[55] Ibid.

[56] This vignette is from F E Fiedler and M M Chemers, *Improving Leadership Effectiveness: The Leader Match Concept,* 2nd ed (New York: John Wiley & Sons, 1984), p 173.

MANAGING
OCCUPATIONAL STRESS

Learning OBJECTIVES

When you finish studying the material in this chapter, you should be able to:

1. Define the term *stress*.
2. Describe Matteson and Ivancevich's model of occupational stress.
3. Discuss four reasons why it is important for managers to understand the causes and consequences of stress.
4. Explain how stressful life events create stress.
5. Review the model of burnout and highlight the managerial solutions to reduce it.
6. Explain the mechanisms of social support.
7. Describe the coping process.
8. Discuss the personality characteristic of hardiness.
9. Discuss the Type A behavior pattern and its management implications.
10. Contrast the four dominant stress-reduction techniques.

Telephone Sales Reps Have a Stressful Job

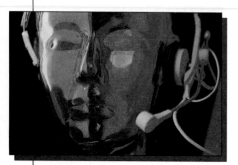

Sharon Hoogstraten

Bev DeMille is having a bad night.

The 51-year-old telemarketer is on her 14th phone call of the shift, but so far she has sold just one magazine renewal. "Come on computer, move it," she says, waiting for the next beep in her headset and the next name to flash on her screen. Around her, co-workers tethered to their desks by telephone cords gesture as they speak and signal supervisors to listen to the "confirmation" of a sale. A young supervisor half Ms. DeMille's age reprimands her: "You're low, girl—one in 14."

Ms. DeMille glares at her video screen. "I don't know where he gets off saying that," she says.

But Ms. DeMille knows that the pressure goes with the job. Working for nine other employers in her 10 years in telemarketing, she has seen co-workers take tranquilizers to relieve stress. She has seen people fired for missing sales targets. When confronted once on a previous job for leaving her desk to go to the ladies' room without permission, she retorted: "My bladder couldn't see you."

Says Ms. DeMille: "You don't get any credit. You feel like so many pounds of beef shuttling through the chute."

That strain is felt by many of the nation's estimated three million to four million telephone sales representatives, 70% of whom, according to Telemarketing Magazine, are women. One worker is likely to talk with hundreds of indifferent or outright hostile customers daily, while being monitored by supervisors who insist that sales reps remain cheerful and stick to their scripted patterns. Under the circumstances, workers burn out quickly and feel unappreciated. Management, powerless to relieve the monotony, must cope with disloyalty and high turnover. . . .

The new-collar workers spend their days not in factories but in air-conditioned offices. But unlike professionals and executives, who enjoy some variety in their work, they are stuck doing limited and repetitive tasks. They have little time for camaraderie and next to no chance for advancement. . . .

Next to the Goodyear dealership on Omaha's west side, the small brick office that houses a branch of Dial-America Marketing Inc. of Mahwah, N.J., gives little hint of the frenzy inside, where 325 telemarketers work in three shifts from 8 a.m. to noon, noon to 4 and 5 to 9:30 p.m. The evening shift—the company's busiest—is about to begin. As the sales reps arrive, supervisor's place magnetic name tags to direct workers to their assigned cubicles. "Let's do it," a supervisor says as the clock strikes 5:00 and the automatic dialing machine begins placing calls. Supervisors—one for every eight reps—pace about, eavesdropping on calls with cordless phones, logging sales on a big blackboard and coaching: "Toni is a goal buster. . . . Yippie! . . . Nice hour, Elmon. . . . Come on A-Team!"

Because DialAmerica bills clients by the sale, not by the hour, it looks for ways to boost productivity. Managers split the room into teams—the Killer B's, the Dream Team, the Terminators. Each rep has a bell to ring for each sale—a sign for the supervisor to listen to the confirmation and record the sale on the board.

As the shift drags on, the room heats up from all the bodies here—about 50 of them—some standing as they speak into their headsets. It sounds like a cocktail party, but without the laughter and clinking of glasses. On each screen, an electronic message reminds workers: "Our first job—happy customers."

Each rep will make at least 100 calls in a typical shift, pitching magazine subscription renewals or trying to get lapsed subscribers to re-up. The company does this work for a number of well-known publications. In a typical shift, a rep will speak to the person he or she is trying to reach about half the time and will "convert" about 15% of those who hear the "presentation."

Reps, who earn commissions based on the number of sales and on the presumed difficulty of selling a particular magazine, have no say in what they are pitching and to whom. The auto-

L ife in the 1990s can be hectic and stressful. As students you must cope with tests, projects, and increased competition in landing good jobs after graduation. Married couples must wrestle with the demands of managing careers and a family. Single parents encounter similar pressures. Occupational stress also is on the rise.

OPENING CASE

(concluded)

mated dialing system installed last year takes care of all that. Reps cheer for "hot titles" and "good codes." They groan when the code is for "dead expires" (people whose subscriptions lapsed long ago) or for "old leads"—names that have been picked over, called before or didn't answer last time. They also claim to have more luck with lists of Westerners than with Easterners, particularly New Yorkers. . . .

"You put the hook out and reel 'em in," says Ms. Jencks, casting an invisible line. She has logged eight sales in the first 35 minutes—twice anybody else's count.

But, just then, the supervisor announces that a different magazine is to be pitched by everybody in her group, and Ms. Jencks's luck changes. (The names of the magazines can't be mentioned here, a condition Dial-America insisted on in providing The Wall Street Journal the run of its sales floor.) An irate woman in Iowa demands to be taken off the calling list, which DialAmerica and other tele-marketers are obliged to do. Ms. Jencks wakes up one prospective customer, reaches another who doesn't speak English and a third who can no longer see well enough to read magazines. "I've had so many bills, and my car went bad, and when you're on Social Security, it just don't reach," another explains. Others don't bother with explanations: "I don't want it anymore." (Click.) "I'm not interested." (Click.)

One thing that keeps sales reps on their toes is the knowledge that super-

visors, company executives or clients, some of whom "seed" their lists to test DialAmerica's mettle, may well be listening in. . . .

A chart on the wall provides a constant measure of performance. It lists everybody's guaranteed pay for the previous week—currently $7.50 per hour—and their actual pay from commissions. The best anybody is doing is to make $13 an hour. Those whose work doesn't justify the guarantee are on "wage makeup"—the company's way of saying that they aren't pulling their weight. Too many weeks of that and they are out of a job.

Privately held DialAmerica is regarded by workers interviewed for this story as one of the best in the industry. . . .

Sitel Corp., by contrast, has factory-style time clocks. Employees must ask for bathroom breaks and can't bring food or drink into their cubicles. "Everything is a scheduled event," says Jim Lynch, Sitel's chief executive. . . .

Aggravating the tension is the tele-marketers' feeling that they can't fight back. "Before, if someone bothered me, I'd get in his face. Here, you've got to bite your tongue and be quiet," says Steve Mevert of DialAmerica, who became a telemarketer after losing his own business during a divorce. When one recent customer called Mr. Mevert a "son of a bitch," he clenched his teeth and replied: "Thank you very much, you have a nice day."

Three weeks into her job with Intellisel Corp., whose headquarters are also in Omaha, Annette Peterson

broke down in the middle of a call and began sobbing. An Arkansas man had called her a string of epithets. Before that, a woman advised her: "Why don't you get a real job and a real life?" Others just hung up. . . .

Turnover is almost inevitable. At Ms. Peterson's calling center in Stanton, Iowa, about an hour from here, more than 30 workers (of a total force of 42) quit in the first $3\frac{1}{2}$ months of the company's operations there. At Dial-America's Omaha facility, the average stay is 11 weeks, the company says, and more than three months is considered long-term employment. A poll at another telemarketing firm, which asked not to be identified, found that 88% of workers had held their jobs for a year or less. ITI says that for those who make it through training (and that is by no means everybody), annual turnover is 100%.

For Discussion

Would you like to work as a telephone sales rep? Explain.

- Additional questions linking this case with the following material appear at the end of this chapter.

Source: D Milbank, "New Collar Work: Telephone Sales Reps Do Unrewarding Jobs That Few Can Abide," *The Wall Street Journal*, September 9, 1993, pp A1, A8. Excerpted by permission of *The Wall Street Journal*, © 1993 Dow Jones & Company, Inc. All Rights Reserved Worldwide.

Due to increased competition, employees are being asked to deliver a better quality and a greater quantity of work in less time and with fewer resources. This is particularly true for survivors of layoffs. Approximately 75 percent of all *Fortune* 500 corporations have been affected by layoffs.[1] Consider the situation at American Telephone & Telegraph and Alliant Techsystems Inc.:

At American Telephone & Telegraph Co., for example, stress-related illnesses—from insomnia to high blood pressure—soared among middle managers after the company slashed large numbers of managerial jobs for the first time in 1986, a former official says. Of 250 middle managers studied by AT&T, nearly half had more marital strains after the cutbacks. A pending layoff is proving particularly painful for Alliant Techsystems Inc., an Edina, Minn., weapons maker that has shed nearly half of its workforce since 1990. Last January [1993], it announced that 1,700 more people will lose their jobs by next spring. Since then, Alliant says it has treated about 25 headquarters employees for disabling panic attacks. About 75% of the patients were people who would keep their jobs. Some became too fearful to leave home, and others were hospitalized for symptoms that mimicked heart attacks.[2]

Survivors, like those from AT&T and Alliant Techsystems, become stressed because they must cope with the loss of friends and co-workers and the fear of potentially being laid off themselves. In addition, survivors are asked to take on more responsibilities to cover the work that was previously done by the displaced workers.

All told, the incidence of stress is rising. This trend is supported by the dramatic growth in the number of published articles, magazines, and self-help books on the topic of stress. The amount of published material doubled between 1980 and 1990.[3] Although stress cannot be completely eliminated, it can be reduced and managed. With this end in mind, this chapter discusses the foundation of stress, examines stressors and burnout, highlights four moderators of occupational stress, and explores a variety of stress-reduction techniques.

FOUNDATIONS OF STRESS

fight-or-flight response   To either confront stressors or try to avoid them.

We all experience stress on a daily basis. Although stress is caused by many factors, researchers conclude that stress triggers one of two basic reactions: active fighting or passive flight (running away or acceptance), the so-called **fight-or-flight response.**[4] Physiologically, this stress response is a biochemical ''passing gear'' involving hormonal changes that mobilize the body for extraordinary demands. Imagine how our prehistoric ancestors responded to the stress associated with a charging saber-toothed tiger. To avoid being eaten, they could stand their ground and fight the beast or run away. In either case, their bodies would have been energized by an identical hormonal change, involving the release of adrenaline into the bloodstream.

In today's hectic urbanized and industrialized society, charging beasts have been replaced by problems such as deadlines, role conflict and ambiguity, financial responsibilities, traffic congestion, noise and air pollution, family problems, and work overload. As with our ancestors, our response to stress may or may not trigger negative side effects, including headaches, ulcers, insomnia, heart attacks, high blood pressure, and strokes. The same stress response that helped our prehistoric ancestors survive has too often become a factor that seriously impairs our daily lives. Consider the following three examples:

An advertising salesman treated by Bruce Yaffe, a New York internist, screamed so loudly when he argued with his boss that he punctured a lung. Another patient, an office receptionist, had such severe stress-induced vomiting that she eventually had to quit her job. And a third, a Wall Street broker treated by physician Larry Lerner for hypertension, was so certain his death was imminent that he refused to take his children to the park for fear they would be abandoned when he died.[5]

Since stress and its consequences are manageable, it is important for managers to learn as much as they can about occupational stress. This section provides a conceptual foundation by defining stress, presenting a model of occupational stress, and highlighting related organizational costs.

Defining Stress

To an orchestra violinist, stress may stem from giving a solo performance before a big audience. While heat, smoke, and flames may represent stress to a firefighter, delivering a speech or presenting a lecture may be stressful for those who are shy. In short, stress means different things to different people. Managers need a working definition.

Formally defined, **stress** is "an adaptive response, mediated by individual characteristics and/or psychological processes, that is a consequence of any external action, situation, or event that places special physical and/or psychological demands upon a person."[6] This definition is not as difficult as it seems when we reduce it to three interrelated dimensions of stress: (1) environmental demands, referred to as stressors, that produce (2) an adaptive response that is influenced by (3) individual differences.

Hans Selye, considered the father of the modern concept of stress, pioneered the distinction between stressors and the stress response. Moreover, Selye emphasized that both positive and negative events can trigger an identical stress response that can be beneficial or harmful. He also noted that

- Stress is not merely nervous tension.
- Stress can have positive consequences.
- Stress is not something to be avoided.
- The complete absence of stress is death.[7]

These points make it clear that stress is inevitable. Efforts need to be directed at managing stress, not at somehow escaping it altogether.

A Model of Occupational Stress

OB researchers Michael Matteson and John Ivancevich developed an instructive model of occupational stress. As illustrated in Figure 16–1, stressors lead to stress, which in turn produces a variety of outcomes. The model also specifies several individual differences that *moderate* the stressor-stress-outcome relationship. A moderator is a variable that causes the relationship between two variables—such as stress and outcomes—to be stronger for some people and weaker for others.

For example, a recent field study of 102 clinical staff in a hospital revealed that employees with high organizational commitment reported less stress and job displeasure than did people with low organizational commitment. Organizational commitment moderated the effects of stress.[8] Let us consider the major components of this stress model.

Stressors **Stressors** are environmental factors that produce stress. Stated differently, stressors are a prerequisite to experiencing the stress response. Figure 16–1 shows the four major types of stressors: individual, group, organizational, and extraorganizational. Individual-level stressors are those directly associated with a person's job duties. For example, emergency room nurses experience stress

stress Behavioral, physical, or psychological response to stressors.

stressors Environmental factors that produce stress.

● FIGURE 16~1   A Model of Occupational Stress

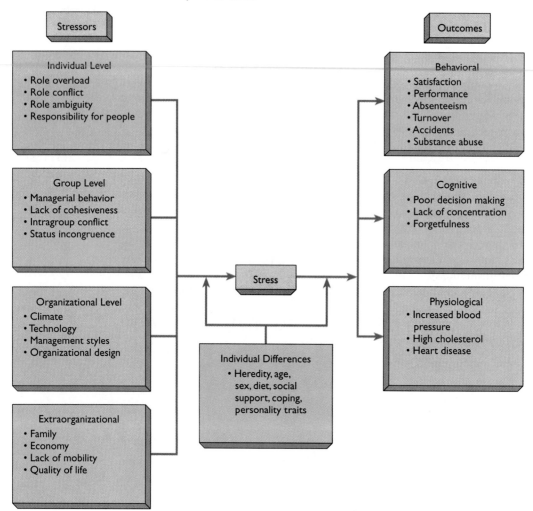

Source: Adapted from M T Matteson and J M Ivancevich, "Organizational Stressors and Heart Disease: A Research Model," *Academy of Management Review,* July 1979, p 350. Used with permission.

uniquely associated with treating patients who are high on drugs and alcohol. A recent study of 1,209 registered nurses showed that 64 percent were assaulted at least once in their careers.[9] The most common examples of stressors are role overload, role conflict, and role ambiguity. As discussed in Chapter 9, these role characteristics create stress because they make people feel both overworked and uncertain about what they should be doing.[10] Managers can reduce these stressors by providing direction and support for their employees.

Group-level stressors are caused by group dynamics (recall our discussion in Chapter 9) and managerial behavior. Managers create stress for employees by (1) exhibiting inconsistent behaviors, (2) failing to provide support, (3) showing lack of concern, (4) providing inadequate direction, (5) creating a high productivity environment, and (6) focusing on negatives while ignoring good performance.[11]

Organizational stressors affect large numbers of employees. Organizational climate or culture, which is discussed in Chapter 19, is a prime example. For

INTERNATIONAL OB

Saddam Hussein Shows the Wear-and-Tear of Stress

Javier Perez de Cuellar [the United Nations Secretary-General] said Saddam Hussein appeared totally detached from the crisis at hand, uninterested in anything his visitor had to say, and even unable to focus on issues he himself has previously stressed. Instead, he seemed preoccupied with plying Mr. Perez de Cuellar with tea and coffee—a strange departure for a man who earlier visitors report had little time for pleasantries. . . .

Veteran Saddam-watchers also notice odd changes in the Iraqi president's demeanor: His speech often seems slow, his face puffy and his eyes unfocused. It would be surprising if someone in his situation didn't exhibit signs of stress. Running what is essentially a one-man regime, he has had to be on round-the-clock alert since early summer, when his plans for invading Kuwait began to take shape.

Source: G Brooks and T Horwitz, "Saddam Watch: Embattled Iraqi Leader Grows More Isolated Amid Signs of Stress," *The Wall Street Journal*, January 16, 1991, p A1.

instance, a high-pressure environment that places chronic work demands on employees fuels the stress response.[12] In contrast, research provides preliminary support for the idea that participative management can reduce organizational stress.[13] Finally, the office design and general office environment are important organizational-level stressors. Research demonstrates that poor lighting, loud noise, improper placement of furniture, and a dirty or smelly environment create stress.[14] Managers are advised to monitor and eliminate these stressors.

Extraorganizational stressors are those caused by factors outside the organization. For instance, conflicts associated with balancing one's career and family life are stressful. So is an individual's socioeconomic status. Stress is higher for people with lower socioeconomic status, which represents a combination of (1) economic status, as measured by income, (2) social status, assessed by education level, and (3) work status, as indexed by occupation.[15] These stressors are likely to become more important in the future.

Outcomes   Theorists contend that stress has behavioral, cognitive, and physiological consequences, or outcomes. For example, the International OB describes the manifestation of these stress outcomes in Saddam Hussein, President of Iraq, just prior to the war with the United Nations coalition forces in 1991. A large body of research supports the conclusion that stress produces harmful physiological outcomes.[16] But researchers have only begun to examine the relationship between stress and work-related behavioral and cognitive outcomes. These studies indicate a negative relationship between stress and turnover, job satisfaction, and performance.[17]

Individual Differences   People do not experience the same level of stress or exhibit similar outcomes for a given type of stressor. As discussed later, stressors are less apt to produce stress for people with a strong social support network and those who employ a variety of coping strategies. *Perception* of a stressor is another important moderator. If a stressor is perceived as threatening, an individual tends to experience greater stress and more negative outcomes. A recent study of 90 married couples further showed that men and women experienced different levels of stress when they argued. Women had higher stress than men when the interaction was nasty.[18]

Finally, the personality trait of chronic hostility or cynicism also moderated stress. Research demonstrated that people who were chronically angry, suspicious, or mistrustful were twice as likely to have coronary artery blockages. We all can protect our hearts by learning to avoid these tendencies.[19] In summary, even though researchers have been able to identify several important moderators, a large gap still exists in identifying relevant individual differences.

Economic Costs and Legal Liabilities of Stress

Managers need to understand the causes and consequences of stress for at least four compelling reasons. First, from a quality-of-work life perspective, workers are more satisfied when they have a safe and comfortable work environment. Second, a moral imperative suggests that managers should reduce occupational stress because it leads to negative outcomes. For example, mental health experts estimate that 10 percent of the workforce suffers from depression or high levels of stress that may ultimately affect job performance.[20] A third reason centers on the staggering economic costs of stress. Experts estimate that stress-related illnesses cost American business approximately $68 billion a year.[21]

The fourth reason revolves around recent court cases where employees sued their employers for worker's compensation for stress-related problems. Consider the case of Dick Wilson:

> Dick Wilson spent a dozen years climbing the chain of command at a Houston Subsidiary of paper-products maker Alco Standard Corp. But when a new boss arrived in 1981, Wilson, by this time second in command, saw his star begin to fade. After refusing for months to heed hints to quit, he was transferred—at full salary—to a janitor's job, pushing a broom in the warehouse and mopping the employee cafeteria. Wilson soon suffered a nervous breakdown and left the company. . . . Eventually, he struck back. Wilson had no previous psychological problems, and he believed his boss's brutal management tactics led to his collapse. So did a jury. Last year [1991], Wilson won $3.5 million in damages, most of it for emotional abuse.[22]

In summary, managers cannot afford to ignore the many implications of occupational stress.

IMPORTANT STRESSORS AND STRESS OUTCOMES

As we have seen, stressors trigger stress, which in turn leads to a variety of outcomes. This section explores an important category of *extraorganizational* stressors: stressful life events. Burnout, another especially troublesome stress-related outcome, is also examined.

Stressful Life Events

Events such as experiencing the death of a family member, being assaulted, moving, ending an intimate relationship, being seriously ill, or taking a big test can create stress. These events are stressful because they involve significant changes that require adaptation and often social readjustment. Accordingly, **stressful life events** are defined as nonwork-related changes that disrupt an individual's lifestyle and social relationships. They have been the most extensively investigated extra-organizational stressors.

stressful life events Life events that disrupt daily routines and social relationships.

Thomas Holmes and Richard Rahe conducted pioneering research on the relationship between stressful life events and subsequent illness. During their research, they developed a widely used questionnaire to assess life stress.[23]

OB EXERCISE

The Holmes and Rahe Schedule of Recent Experiences Survey

Instructions:

Place a check mark next to each event you experienced within the past year. Then add the life change units associated with the various events to derive your total life stress score.

Life Event	Life Change Unit
_____ Death of spouse	100
_____ Divorce	73
_____ Marital separation from mate	65
_____ Detention in jail or other institution	63
_____ Death of a close family member	63
_____ Major personal injury or illness	53
_____ Marriage	50
_____ Being fired at work	47
_____ Marital reconciliation with mate	45
_____ Retirement from work	45
_____ Major change in the health or behavior of a famiy member	44
_____ Pregnancy	40
_____ Sexual difficulties	39
_____ Gaining a new family member (e.g., through birth, adoption, oldster moving in)	39
_____ Major business readjustment (e.g., merger, reorganization, bankruptcy)	39
_____ Major change in financial state (e.g., a lot worse off or a lot better off than usual)	38
_____ Death of a close friend	37
_____ Changing to a different line of work	36
_____ Major change in the number of arguments with spouse (e.g., either a lot more or a lot less than usual regarding childbearing, personal habits)	35
_____ Taking out a mortgage or loan for a major purchase (e.g., for a home, business)	31
_____ Foreclosure on a mortgage or loan	30
_____ Major change in responsibilities at work (e.g., promotion, demotion, lateral transfer)	29
_____ Son or daughter leaving home (e.g., marriage, attending college)	29
_____ Trouble with in-laws	29
_____ Outstanding personal achievement	28
_____ Wife beginning or ceasing work outside the home	26
_____ Beginning or ceasing formal schooling	26
_____ Major change in living conditions (e.g., building a new home, remodeling, deterioration of home or neighborhood)	25
_____ Revision of personal habits (dress, manners, association)	24
_____ Troubles with the boss	23
_____ Major change in working hours or conditions	20
_____ Change in residence	20
_____ Changing to a new school	20
_____ Major change in usual type and/or amount of recreation	19
_____ Major change in church activities (e.g., a lot more or a lot less than usual)	19
_____ Major change in social activities (e.g., clubs, dancing, movies, visiting)	18
_____ Taking out a mortgage or loan for a lesser purchase (e.g., for a car, TV, freezer)	17
_____ Major change in sleeping habits (a lot more or a lot less sleep, or change in part of day when asleep)	16
_____ Major change in number of family get-togethers (e.g., a lot more or a lot less than usual)	15
_____ Major change in eating habits (a lot more or a lot less food intake, or very different meal hours or surroundings)	15
_____ Vacation	13
_____ Christmas	12
_____ Minor violations of the law (e.g., traffic tickets, jaywalking, disturbing the peace	11

Total score =

Source: Adapted from T H Holmes and R H Rahe, "The Social Readjustment Rating Scale," *Journal of Psychosomatic Research,* August 1967, p 216. Used with permission. Copyright 1967, Pergamon Press.

Assessing Stressful Life Events   The *Schedule of Recent Experiences* (SRE), developed by Holmes and Rahe, is the dominant method for assessing an individual's cumulative stressful life events. As shown in the OB Exercise, the SRE consists of 43 life events. Each event has a corresponding value, called a life change unit, representing the degree of social readjustment necessary to cope with the event. The larger the value, the more stressful the event. These values were obtained from a convenience sample of 394 people who evaluated the stressfulness of each event. (Please take a moment to complete the SRE survey and calculate your total life stress score.)

Research revealed a positive relationship between the total score on the SRE and subsequent illness. For example, the odds are you will experience good health next year if you scored below 150. But there is a 50 percent chance of illness for those scoring between 150 and 300. Finally, a score above 300 suggests a 70 percent chance of illness.[24] A word of caution is in order, however. If you scored above 150, don't head for a sterile cocoon. High scores on the SRE do not guarantee you will become ill. Rather, a high score simply increases one's statistical risk of illness.

Research and Practical Implications   Numerous studies have examined the relationship between life stress and both illness and job performance. Subjects with higher SRE scores had significantly more problems with chronic headaches, sudden cardiac death, pregnancy and birth complications, tuberculosis, diabetes, anxiety, depression, and a host of minor physical ailments. Meanwhile, academic and work performance declined as SRE scores increased.[25] *Negative* (as opposed to positive) personal life changes were associated with greater susceptibility to colds and job stress and lower levels of job satisfaction and organizational commitment.[26] Finally, life events that were *uncontrollable* (e.g., death of spouse), rather than controllable (such as marriage), were more strongly associated with subsequent illness and depression.[27]

The key implication is that employee illness and job performance are affected by extraorganizational stressors, particularly those that are negative and uncontrollable. Because employees do not leave their personal problems at the office door or factory gate, management needs to be aware of external sources of employee stress. Once identified, training programs or counseling can be used to help employees cope with these stressors. This may not only reduce costs associated with illnesses and absenteeism, but may also lead to positive work attitudes and better job performance. In addition, by acknowledging that work outcomes are affected by extraorganizational stressors, managers may avoid the trap of automatically attributing poor performance to low motivation or lack of ability. Such awareness is likely to engender positive reactions from employees and lead to resolution of problems, not just symptoms. For individuals with a high score on the SRE, it would be best to defer controllable stressors, such as moving or buying a new car, until things settle down.

Burnout

Burnout is a stress-induced problem common among members of "helping" professions such as teaching, social work, employee relations, nursing, and law enforcement. It does not involve a specific feeling, attitude, or physiological

• ⟍ TABLE 16~1
Attitudinal Characteristics of Burnout

Attitude	Description
Fatalism	A feeling that you lack control over your work.
Boredom	A lack of interest in doing your job.
Discontent	A sense of being unhappy with your job.
Cynicism	A tendency to undervalue the content of your job and the rewards received.
Inadequacy	A feeling of not being able to meet your objectives.
Failure	A tendency to discredit your performance and conclude that you are ineffective.
Overwork	A feeling of having too much to do and not enough time to complete it.
Nastiness	A tendency to be rude or unpleasant to your co-workers.
Dissatisfaction	A feeling that you are not being justly rewarded for your efforts.
Escape	A desire to give up and get away from it all.

Source: Adapted from D P Rogers, "Helping Employees Cope with Burnout," *Business*, October–December 1984, p 4.

outcome anchored to a specific point in time. Rather, **burnout** is a condition that occurs over time and is characterized by emotional exhaustion and a combination of negative attitudes. Table 16–1 describes 10 attitudinal characteristics of burnout. Experts say a substantial number of people suffer from this problem. For example, a recent national study of 3,718 Americans indicated that 59 percent were burned out.[28] This result implies that burnout is not limited to people working in the helping professions. To promote better understanding of this important stress outcome, we turn our attention to a model of the burnout process and highlight relevant research and techniques for its prevention.

burnout   A condition of emotional exhaustion and negative attitudes.

A Model of Burnout   A model of burnout is presented in Figure 16–2. The fundamental premise underlying the model is that burnout develops in phases. The three key phases are emotional exhaustion, depersonalization, and feeling a lack of personal accomplishment.[29] As shown in Figure 16–2, emotional exhaustion is due to a combination of personal stressors and job and organizational stressors.[30] People who expect a lot from themselves and the organizations in which they work tend to create more internal stress, which in turn leads to emotional exhaustion. Similarly, emotional exhaustion is fueled by having too much work to do, by role conflict, and by the type of interpersonal interactions encountered at work. Frequent, intense face-to-face interactions that are emotionally charged are associated with higher levels of emotional exhaustion.

Over time, emotional exhaustion leads to depersonalization, which is a state of psychologically withdrawing from one's job. This ultimately results in a feeling of being unappreciated, ineffective, or inadequate. The additive effect of these three phases is a host of negative attitudinal and behavioral outcomes. Consider the case of Robert Belleville:

> At age 38, and just 11 years out of graduate school, he had broken enough technological ground to last a lifetime: computer-aided design work at the prestigious Stanford Research Institute; a stop at Xerox Corp.'s Palo Alto Research Center, where he helped bring to market the world's first office-automation system; and finally, an intoxicating assignment from Steve Jobs at Apple Computer Inc. as head engineer for the revolutionary Macintosh personal computer. . . . The 20-hour days, grueling deadline pressure and relentless obsession with the bottom line turned him, in his words, into a "sick" man. He

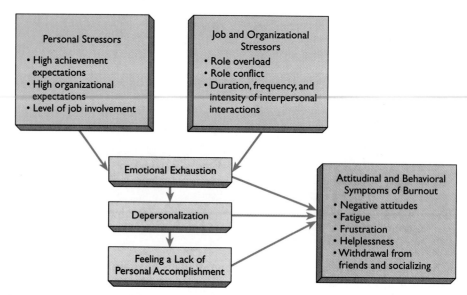

• FIGURE 16–2
A Model of Burnout

Source: Based in part on C L Cordes and T W Dougherty, "A Review and an Integration of Research on Job Burnout," *Academy of Management Review*, October 1993, p 641.

got even sicker in 1985, after Apple Chief Executive John Sculley fired him and just about everyone else connected with the Macintosh, as part of a palace coup against Mr. Jobs. He divorced his wife, entered psychotherapy, studied Hindu philosophy, and lived in isolation for six years, his career in tatters.[31]

buffers Resources or administrative changes that reduce burnout.

Research Findings and Prevention Burnout develops in phases.[32] It is also significantly associated with personal stressors, job and organizational stressors, a lack of feedback, low job satisfaction, turnover, absenteeism, impairment of interpersonal relationships with family and friends, insomnia, and quality and quantity of performance.[33] This research underscores the organizational need to reduce the stress-induced problem of burnout.

Removing personal stressors and job and organizational stressors is the most straightforward way to prevent burnout. Managers also can reduce burnout by buffering its effects. **Buffers** are resources or administrative changes that alleviate the symptoms of burnout. Potential buffers include extra staff or equipment at peak work periods, support from top management, increased freedom to make decisions, recognition for accomplishments, time off for personal development or rest, and equitable rewards. Decreasing the quantity and increasing the *quality* of communications is another possible buffer. Finally, managers can change the content of an individual's job by adding or eliminating responsibilities, increasing the amount of participation in decision making, altering the pattern of interpersonal contacts, or assigning the person to a new position.[34]

There also are two long-term strategies for reducing burnout that are increasingly being used by companies. Apple Computer, American Express, IBM, McDonald's Corporation, and Intel, for instance, use sabbaticals to replenish employees' energy and desire to work. These programs allow employees to take a designated amount of time off from work after being employed a certain number of years. McDonald's grants paid sabbaticals after 10 years of employment; for Intel, it is eight weeks off with pay after seven years for every full-time employee. An employee retreat is the second long-term strategy. Retreats entail sending

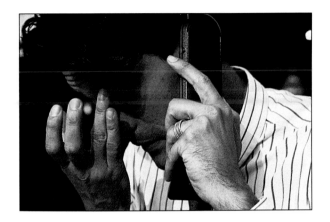

employees to an offsite location for 3 to 5 days. While there, everyone can relax, reflect, or engage in team and relationship building activities. Hallmark Cards uses retreats to help in the fight against burnout.[35]

MODERATORS OF OCCUPATIONAL STRESS

Moderators, once again, are variables that cause the relationships between stressors, stress, and outcomes to be weaker for some people and stronger for others. Managers with a working knowledge of important stress moderators can confront employee stress in the following ways:

1. Awareness of moderators helps identify those most likely to experience stress and its negative outcomes. Stress reduction programs then can be formulated for high-risk employees.
2. Moderators, in and of themselves, suggest possible solutions for reducing negative outcomes of occupational stress.

Keeping these objectives in mind, we will examine four important moderators: social support, coping, hardiness, and Type A behavior.

Social Support

Talking with a friend or taking part in a bull session can be comforting during times of fear, stress, or loneliness. For a variety of reasons, meaningful social relationships help people do a better job of handling stress. **Social support** is the amount of perceived helpfulness derived from social relationships. Importantly, social support is determined by both the quantity and quality of an individual's social relationships. Figure 16–3 illustrates the mechanisms of social support.

social support Amount of helpfulness derived from social relationships.

A Model of Social Support   As Figure 16–3 shows, one's support network must be perceived before it can be used. Support networks evolve from five sources: cultural norms, social institutions, companies, groups, or individuals. For example, there is more cultural emphasis on caring for the elderly in Japan than in America. Japanese culture is thus a strong source of social support for older Japanese people. Alternatively, individuals may fall back on social institutions such as Social

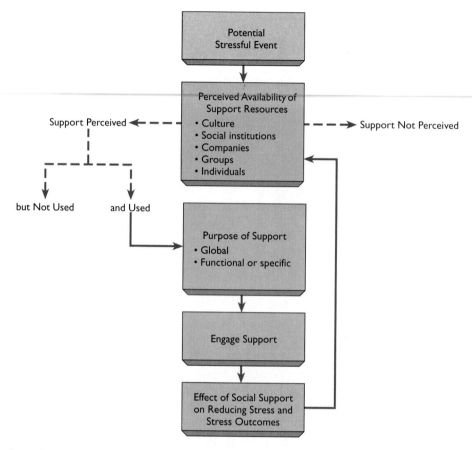

FIGURE 16~3

A Flow Model of the Mechanisms of Social Support

Source: Portions adapted from S Cohen and T A, Wills, "Stress, Social Support, and the Buffering Hypothesis," *Psychological Bulletin,* September 1985, pp 310–57; and J G Bruhn and B U Philips, "Measuring Social Support: A Synthesis of Current Approaches," *Journal of Behavioral Medicine,* June 1984, pp 151–69.

Security or the American Red Cross, religious groups, or family and friends for support. In turn, these various sources provide four types of support:

- *Esteem support.* Providing information that a person is accepted and respected despite any problems or inadequacies.
- *Informational support.* Providing help in defining, understanding, and coping with problems.
- *Social companionship.* Spending time with others in leisure and recreational activities.
- *Instrumental support.* Providing financial aid, material resources, or needed services.[36]

American companies are increasingly providing many different types of instrumental support following natural disasters. Take Monsanto, Kmart, and Anheuser-Busch, for instance:

Come the spring thaw, there is the possibility that another major flood may hit the Midwest, and Monsanto wants to be prepared. So, in addition to the more than $2 million the agricultural-products maker and its employees have already given to a $5 million American Red Cross rural-relief fund it spearheaded for flood victims, the Monsanto

Fund has set aside some $200,000 for potential use at two particularly susceptible river towns where it has plants. . . . After Hurricane Andrew, Kmart Corp. and others concluded that piling goods on a truck and racing to the disaster scene didn't work well. So, the morning after the L.A. quake, Kmart's disaster-relief committee sent a bulletin to all store managers not to accept any collections at the store. Instead, Kmart itself focused on gifts of cash and drinking water. . . . Anheuser-Busch Co., for instance, says it has given some $5 million in cash and over 17 million cans of drinking water since 1989. (The Red Cross figures that corporations have contributed about 25% of total disaster giving since 1989.)[37]

As you can see, corporations are a significant source of instrumental support to communities experiencing disasters.

If social support is perceived as available, an individual then decides whether or not to use it.[38] Generally, support is used for one or both of two purposes. The first purpose is very broad in scope. **Global social support,** encompassing the total amount of support available from the four sources, is applicable to any situation at any time. The narrower **functional social support** buffers the effects of stressors or stress in specific situations. When relied on in the wrong situation, functional social support is not very helpful. For example, if you lost your job, unemployment compensation (instrumental support) would be a better buffer than sympathy from a bartender. On the other hand, social companionship would be more helpful than instrumental support in coping with loneliness. After social support is engaged for one or both of these purposes, its effectiveness can be determined. If consolation or relief is not experienced, it may be that the type of support was inappropriate. The feedback loop in Figure 16–3, from effect of social support back to perceived availability, reflects the need to fall back on other sources of support when necessary.

global social support The total amount of social support available.

functional social support Support sources that buffer stress in specific situations.

Research Findings and Managerial Lessons   Research shows that global social support is negatively related to mortality. In other words, people with low social support tend to die earlier than those with strong social support networks. Further, global support protects against depression, mental illness, pregnancy complications, anxiety, high blood pressure, and a variety of other ailments. In contrast, negative social support, which amounts to someone undermining another person, negatively affects one's mental health.[39] We would all be well advised to avoid people who try to undermine us. Moreover, there is no clear pattern of results regarding the buffering effects of both global and functional social support. It appears that social support does buffer against stress, but we do not know precisely when or why.[40] Additional research is needed to figure out this inconsistency. Finally, as suggested in Figure 16–3, global social support is positively related to the availability of support resources; that is, people who interact with a greater number of friends, family, or co-workers have a wider base of social support to draw upon during stressful periods.[41]

One practical recommendation is to keep employees informed about external and internal social support systems. Internally, managers can use esteem and informational support while administering daily feedback and coaching.[42] Further, participative management programs and company-sponsored activities that make employees feel they are an important part of an ''extended family'' can be rich sources of social support. Employees need time and energy to adequately maintain their social relationships. If organizational demands are excessive, employees' social relationships and support networks will suffer, resulting in stress-related illness and decreased performance. Also, the positive effects of social support are enhanced when functional support is targeted precisely.

Coping

coping Process of managing stress.

Coping is "the process of managing demands (external or internal) that are appraised as taxing or exceeding the resources of the person."[43] Because effective coping helps reduce the impact of stressors and stress, your personal life and managerial skills can be enhanced by better understanding this process. Figure 16–4 depicts an instructive model of coping.

The coping process has three major components: (1) situational and personal factors, (2) cognitive appraisals of the stressor, and (3) coping strategies. As shown in Figure 16–4, both situational and personal factors influence appraisal of stressors. In turn, appraisal directly influences choice of coping strategy. Each of the major components of this model deserves a closer look.

Situational and Personal Factors   Situational factors are environmental characteristics that affect how people interpret (appraise) stressors. For example, the ambiguity of a situation—such as walking down a dark street at night in an unfamiliar area—makes it difficult to determine whether a potentially dangerous situation exists. Ambiguity creates differences in how people appraise and subsequently cope with stressors. Other situational factors are the frequency of exposure to a stressor and social support networks.

Personal factors are personality traits and personal resources that affect the appraisal of stressors. For instance, because being tired or sick can distort the interpretation of stressors, an extremely tired individual may appraise an innocent question as a threat or challenge. Traits such as locus of control, self-esteem, self-efficacy (recall our discussion in Chapter 4), and work experience also were found to affect the appraisal of stressors.[44]

Cognitive Appraisal of Stressors   Cognitive appraisal reflects an individual's overall evaluation of a situation or stressor. Appraisal is an important component within the stress process because people appraise the same stressors differently. For example, some individuals perceive unemployment as a positive, liberating experience, whereas others perceive it as a negative, debilitating one.[45]

⌐• FIGURE 16–4
A Model of the Coping Process

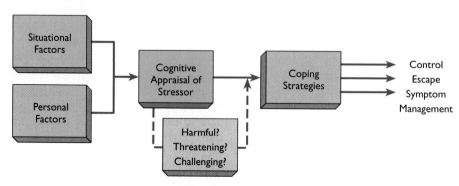

Source: Based in part on R S Lazarus and S Folkman, "Coping and Adaptation," in *Handbook of Behavioral Medicine,* ed W D Gentry (New York: The Guilford Press, 1984), pp 282–325.

Cognitive appraisal results in a categorization of the situation or stressor as either harmful, threatening, or challenging. It is important to understand the differences among these appraisals because they influence how people cope. " 'Harm' (including loss) represents damage already done; 'threat' involves the potential for harm; and 'challenge' means the potential for significant gain under difficult odds."[46] Coping with harm usually entails undoing or reinterpreting something that occurred in the past because the damage is already done. In contrast, threatening situations engage anticipatory coping. That is, people cope with threat by preparing for harm that may occur in the future. Challenge also activates anticipatory coping. In contrast with threat, an appraisal of challenge results in coping that focuses on what can be gained rather than what may be lost.[47]

Coping Strategies   Coping strategies are characterized by the specific behaviors and cognitions used to cope with a situation. People use a combination of three approaches to cope with stressors and stress (see Figure 16–4). The first, called a **control strategy,** consists of using behaviors and cognitions to directly anticipate or solve problems. A control strategy has a take-charge tone. Consider the control strategy used by President Clinton and his White House senior advisor George Stephanopoulos in October 1993, when Clinton was delivering a televised speech to the nation:

> Minutes before speech time, White House Senior Advisor George Stephanopoulos rushed in with the final version, but the aide running the TelePrompTer accidentally hit the wrong computer button, merging the new speech with the February economic address to Congress, still in the system. No one realized the mistake until Clinton himself reached the podium and saw the old speech on the TelePrompTer. With a stricken look, he turned to Al Gore and said, "We have to get this fixed." Gore alerted Stephanopoulos. . . . Stephanopoulos quickly found White House word whiz David Dreyer, who had a copy on a floppy disc in his laptop computer. When aides couldn't load it into the system, Steph says, he momentarily "went numb." It took a full seven minutes to get it straightened out. Reading from a written text, Clinton scarcely stumbled until the TelePrompTer caught up with him.[48]

In contrast to tackling the problem head-on, an **escape strategy,** amounts to running away. Behaviors and cognitions are used to avoid or escape situations. Individuals use this strategy when they passively accept stressful situations or avoid them by failing to confront the cause of stress (an obnoxious co-worker, for instance). Finally, a *symptom management strategy* consists of using methods such as relaxation, meditation, or medication to manage the symptoms of occupational stress.[49]

Research Findings and Managerial Recommendations   As suggested by the model in Figure 16–4, an individual's appraisal of a stressor correlates with the choice of a coping strategy.[50] In further support of the coping model, personal factors, appraisal, and coping all significantly predicted psychological symptoms of stress. Nonetheless, research has not clearly identified which type of coping strategy—control, escape, or symptom management—is most effective. It appears that the best coping strategy depends on the situation at hand.[51] Escaping stress—by going on vacation, for example—is sometimes better than confronting a stressor with a control-oriented coping strategy. Researchers are currently trying to determine these contingency relationships.

control strategy   Coping strategy that directly confronts or solves problems.

escape strategy   Coping strategy that avoids or ignores stressors and problems.

The preceding results suggest that employees should be taught a contingency approach to coping with organizational stressors. This might begin by helping employees identify those stressors that they perceive as harmful or threatening. Training or managerial support can then be used to help employees manage and possibly eliminate the most serious stressors. The final section of this chapter describes specific techniques for that purpose.

Hardiness

Suzanne Kobasa, a behavioral scientist, identified a collection of personality characteristics that neutralize occupational stress. This collection of characteristics, referred to as **hardiness,** involves the ability to perceptually or behaviorally transform negative stressors into positive challenges. Hardiness embraces the personality dimensions of commitment, locus of control, and challenge.[52]

Personality Characteristics of Hardiness   *Commitment* reflects the extent to which an individual is involved in whatever he or she is doing. Committed people have a sense of purpose and do not give up under pressure because they tend to invest themselves in the situation.

As discussed in Chapter 4, individuals with an *internal locus of control* believe they can influence the events that affect their lives. People possessing this trait are more likely to foresee stressful events, thereby reducing their exposure to anxiety-producing situations. Moreover, their perception of being in control leads "internals" to use proactive coping strategies.

Challenge is represented by the belief that change is a normal part of life. Hence, change is seen as an opportunity for growth and development rather than a threat to security.

Hardiness Research and Application   A five-year study of 259 managers from a public utility revealed that hardiness—commitment, locus of control, and challenge—reduced the probability of illness following exposure to stress.[53] Hardy undergraduate students were similarly found to display lower psychological distress and heart rate in response to a threatening task than their less hardy counterparts. Hardy students also were more likely to interpret stressors as positive and controllable, supporting the idea that hardy individuals perceive situations in less stressful ways. Finally, a study of 73 pregnant women further revealed that hardy women had fewer problems during labor and more positive perceptions about their infants than unhardy women.[54]

One practical offshoot of this research is organizational training and development programs that strengthen the characteristics of commitment, personal control, and challenge. Because of cost limitations, it is necessary to target key employees or those most susceptible to stress (e.g., air traffic controllers). The hardiness concept also meshes nicely with job design. Jobs can be redesigned to take fuller advantage of hardiness characteristics. A final application of the hardiness concept is as a diagnostic tool. Employees scoring low on hardiness would be good candidates for stress-reduction programs.

Type A Behavior Pattern

Cardiovascular disease is the leading cause of death among adults in Western industrialized countries. Because Type A behavior was linked to cardiovascular

hardiness   Personality characteristic that neutralizes stress.

disease, researchers devoted significant effort in identifying Type A characteristics and situations that elicit this behavior pattern.

Type A Behavior Defined According to Meyer Friedman and Ray Rosenman (the cardiologists who isolated the Type A syndrome in the 1950s):

> **Type A behavior pattern** is an action-emotion complex that can be observed in any person who is aggressively involved in a chronic, incessant struggle to achieve more and more in less and less time, and if required to do so, against the opposing efforts of other things or persons. It is not psychosis or a complex of worries or fears or phobias or obsessions, but a socially acceptable—indeed often praised—form of conflict. Persons possessing this pattern also are quite prone to exhibit a free-floating but extraordinarily well-rationalized hostility. As might be expected, there are degrees in the intensity of this behavior pattern.[55]

Type A behavior pattern
Aggressively involved in a chronic, determined struggle to accomplish more in less time.

Since Type A behavior is a matter of degree, it is measured on a continuum. This continuum has the hurried, competitive Type A behavior pattern at one end and the more relaxed Type B behavior pattern at the other. Take a moment to complete the Type A survey contained in the OB Exercise. This exercise will help you better understand the characteristics of the Type A behavior pattern. (Arbitrary norms for comparison purposes are: Type B = 9–22; Balanced Type A and Type B = 23–35; Type A = 36–45.)

OB Exercise

Where Are You on the Type A–B Behavior Continuum?

Instructions

For each question, indicate the extent to which each statement is true of you.

		Not At All True of Me		Neither Very True nor Very Untrue of Me		Very True of Me
1.	I hate giving up before I'm absolutely sure that I'm licked.	1	2	3	4	5
2.	Sometimes I feel that I shouldn't be working so hard, but something drives me on.	1	2	3	4	5
3.	I thrive on challenging situations. The more challenges I have, the better.	1	2	3	4	5
4.	In comparison to most people I know, I'm very involved in my work.	1	2	3	4	5
5.	It seems as if I need 30 hours a day to finish all the things I'm faced with.	1	2	3	4	5
6.	In general, I approach my work more seriously than most people I know.	1	2	3	4	5
7.	I guess there are some people who can be nonchalant about their work, but I'm not one of them.	1	2	3	4	5
8.	My achievements are considered to be significantly higher than those of most people I know.	1	2	3	4	5
9.	I've often been asked to be an officer of some group or groups.	1	2	3	4	5

Total score =

Source: Taken from R D Caplan, S Cobb, J R P French, Jr., R Van Harrison, and S R Pinneau, Jr., *Job Demands and Worker Health* (HEW Publication No. [NIOSH] 75–160), (Washington, DC: US Department of Health, Education, and Welfare, 1975), pp 253–54.

Type A Characteristics   While labeling Type A behavior as "hurry sickness," Friedman and Rosenmen noted that Type A individuals frequently tend to exhibit most of the behaviors listed in Table 16–2. In high-pressure, achievement-oriented schools and work environments, Type A behavior is unwittingly cultivated and even admired. Consider Arthur Marks, general partner in the venture-capital firm New Enterprise Associates of San Francisco:

> Mark estimates he is on the road four of every five days. Mark, who is based in Baltimore, travels armed with a laptop computer with a built-in fax-modem board, a cellular phone and a pager. . . . "The world isn't set up for people like us," he complains. "You find yourself increasingly intolerant of airline delays and slow hotel check-ins." . . . A typical week for Mark involves racing around the country visiting his companies. On planes, he writes or makes calls. In airports, he uses the fax machine in an airline club. He typically stays in a hotel that offers two telephone lines per room, so he can talk on one while using the other for his computer fax or modem. . . . "I also multiprocess," he says. "That is, if I'm in a meeting and it goes onto a topic that doesn't involve me, I'll send off faxes or e-mail while I wait."[56]

Type A Research and Management Implications   OB research has demonstrated that Type A employees tend to be more productive than their Type B co-workers. For instance, Type A behavior yielded a significant and positive correlation with 920 students' grade point average, the quantity and quality of 278 university professors' performance, and sales performance of 222 life insurance brokers.[57] On the other hand, Type A behavior is associated with some negative consequences.

A recent meta-analysis of 99 studies revealed that Type A individuals had higher heart rates, diastolic blood pressure, and systolic blood pressure than Type B people. Type A people also showed greater cardiovascular activity when they encountered the following situations:

ᐧ TABLE 16–2
Type A Characteristics

1. Hurried speech; explosive accentuation of key words.
2. Tendency to walk, move, and eat rapidly.
3. Constant impatience with the rate at which most events take place (e.g., irritation with slow-moving traffic and slow-talking and slow-to-act people).
4. Strong preference for thinking of or doing two or more things at once (e.g., reading this text and doing something else at the same time).
5. Tendency to turn conversations around to personally meaningful subjects or themes.
6. Tendency to interrupt while others are speaking to make your point or to complete their train of thought in your own words.
7. Guilt feelings during periods of relaxation or leisure time.
8. Tendency to be oblivious to surroundings during daily activities.
9. Greater concern for things worth *having* than with things worth *being.*
10. Tendency to schedule more and more in less and less time; a chronic sense of time urgency.
11. Feelings of competition rather than compassion when faced with another Type A person.
12. Development of nervous tics or characteristic gestures.
13. A firm belief that success is due to the ability to get things done faster than the other guy.
14. A tendency to view and evaluate personal activities and the activities of other people in terms of "numbers" (e.g., number of meetings attended, telephone calls made, visitors received).

Source: Adapted from M Friedman and R H Rosenman, *Type A Behavior and Your Heart* (Greenwich, CT: Fawcett Publications, 1974), pp 100–102.

1. Receipt of positive or negative feedback.
2. Receipt of verbal harassment or criticism.
3. Tasks requiring mental as opposed to physical work.[58]

Unfortunately for Type A individuals, these situations are frequently experienced at work. A second meta-analysis of 83 studies further demonstrated that the hard-driving and competitive aspects of Type A are related to coronary heart disease, but the speed and impatience and job involvement aspects are not. This meta-analysis also showed that feelings of anger, hostility, and aggression were more strongly related to heart disease than to Type A behavior.[59]

Do these results signal the need for Type A individuals to quit working so hard? Not necessarily. First off, the research indicated that feelings of anger, hostility, and aggression were more detrimental to our health than being Type A. We should all attempt to reduce these negative emotions. Second, researchers have developed stress reduction techniques to help Type A people pace themselves more realistically and achieve better balance in their lives; they are discussed in the next section of this chapter. Management can help Type A people, however, by not overloading them with work despite their apparent eagerness to take an ever-increasing work load. Managers need to actively help rather than unthinkingly exploit Type A individuals because the premature disability or death of valued employees erodes long-run organizational effectiveness.

STRESS-REDUCTION TECHNIQUES

A national survey conducted by Louis Harris Associates revealed that Americans are fatter, do less strenuous exercise, eat less healthful foods, experience more stress, and sleep less than they did in the 1980s. All told, the American Medical Association estimated that lifestyle and social problems contribute more than $171 billion annually to our nation's health care costs.[60] It is, therefore, not surprising that organizations are increasingly implementing a variety of stress-reduction programs to help employees cope with modern-day stress.

There are many different stress-reduction techniques available. The four most frequently used approaches are muscle relaxation, biofeedback, meditation, and cognitive restructuring. Each method involves somewhat different ways of coping with stress (see Table 16–3).

Muscle Relaxation

The common denominators of various muscle relaxation techniques are slow and deep breathing, a conscious effort to relieve muscle tension, and an altered state of consciousness. Among the variety of techniques available, progressive relaxation is probably most frequently used. It consists of repeatedly tensing and relaxing muscles beginning at the feet and progressing to the face. Relaxation is achieved by concentrating on the warmth and calmness associated with relaxed muscles. Take a few moments now to try this technique, as described here.

Sitting in a chair, start by taking slow, deep breaths. Inhale through your nose and exhale through your mouth. Continue until you feel calm. Begin progressive relaxation by pointing your toes toward the ceiling for 10 seconds. Concentrate on the tension within your calves and feet. Now return your toes to a normal position and focus on the relaxed state of your legs and feet. (Your goal is to experience this

TABLE 16~3
Stress-Reduction Techniques

Technique	Descriptions	Assessment
Muscle relaxation	Uses slow deep breathing, systematic muscle tension reduction, and an altered state of consciousness to reduce stress.	Inexpensive and easy to use; may require a trained professional to implement.
Biofeedback	A machine is used to train people to detect muscular tension; muscle relaxation is then used to alleviate this symptom of stress.	Expensive due to costs of equipment; however, equipment can be used to evaluate effectiveness of other stress-reduction programs.
Meditation	The relaxation response is activated by redirecting one's thoughts away from oneself; a four-step procedure is used.	Least expensive, simple to implement, and can be practiced almost anywhere.
Cognitive restructuring	Irrational or maladaptive thoughts are identified and replaced with those that are rational or logical.	Expensive because it requires a trained psychologist or counselor.
Holistic wellness	A broad, interdisciplinary approach that goes beyond stress reduction by advocating that people strive for personal wellness in all aspects of their lives.	Involves inexpensive but often behaviorally difficult lifestyle changes.

feeling all over your body.) Tense and relax your feet for 10 seconds one more time. Moving to your calves, and continuing all the way to the muscles in your face, tense one major muscle at a time for 10 seconds, and then let it relax. Do this twice for each muscle before moving to another one. You should feel totally relaxed upon completing this routine.

Biofeedback

A biofeedback machine is used to train people to detect and control stress-related symptoms such as tense muscles and elevated blood pressure. The machine translates unconscious bodily signs into a recognizable cue (flashing light or beeper). Muscle relaxation and meditative techniques are then used to alleviate the underlying stress. The person learns to recognize bodily tension without the aid of the machine. In turn, according to the advocates of biofeedback, this awareness helps the person proactively cope with stress.

Meditation

relaxation response State of peacefulness.

Meditation activates a relaxation response by redirecting one's thoughts away from oneself. The **relaxation response** is the physiological and psychological opposite of the fight-or-flight stress response. Importantly, however, the relaxation response must be learned and consciously activated, whereas the stress response is automatically engaged. Herbert Benson, a Harvard medical doctor, analyzed many meditation programs and derived a four-step relaxation response. The four steps are (1) find a *quiet environment,* (2) use a *mental device* such as a peaceful word or pleasant image to shift the mind from externally oriented thoughts, (3) disregard distracting thoughts by relying on a *passive attitude,* and (4) assume a *comfortable position*—preferably sitting erect—to avoid undue muscular tension or going to

"You are about to enter another dimension." Biofeedback is only one of the many stress-reduction techniques in which organizations are investing time and money.

(Charles Thatcher/Tony Stone Images)

sleep. Benson emphasizes that the most important factor is a passive attitude.[61] Maximum benefits supposedly are obtained by following this procedure once or twice a day for 10 to 20 minutes, preferably just before breakfast and dinner. People following this advice experienced favorable reductions in blood pressure and anxiety levels and slept better.[62]

Cognitive Restructuring

A two-step procedure is followed. First, irrational or maladaptive thought processes that create stress are identified. For example, Type A individuals may believe they must be successful at everything they do. The second step consists of replacing these irrational thoughts with more rational or reasonable ones. Perceived failure would create stress for the Type A person. Cognitive restructuring would alleviate stress by encouraging the person to adopt a more reasonable belief about the outcomes associated with failure. For instance, the person might be encouraged to adopt the belief that isolated failure does not mean he or she is a bad person or a loser.

Effectiveness of Stress-Reduction Techniques

Two teams of OB researchers reviewed the research on stress management interventions. Although much of the published research is methodologically weak, results offer preliminary support for the conclusion that muscle relaxation, biofeedback, meditation, and cognitive restructuring all help employees cope with occupational stress.[63]

Some researchers advise organizations not to implement these stress-reduction programs despite their positive outcomes. They rationalize that these techniques relieve *symptoms* of stress rather than eliminate stressors themselves.[64] Thus, they conclude that organizations are using a ''Band-Aid'' approach to stress reduction. A holistic approach has subsequently been offered as a more proactive and enduring solution.

A Holistic Wellness Model

A **holistic wellness approach** encompasses and goes beyond stress reduction by advocating that individuals strive for ''a harmonious and productive balance of physical, mental, and social well-being brought about by the acceptance of one's

holistic wellness approach
Advocates personal responsibility in reducing stressors and stress.

personal responsibility for developing and adhering to a health promotion program.''[65] Five dimensions of a holistic wellness approach are as follows:

1. *Self-responsibility.* Take personal responsibility for your wellness (e.g., quit smoking, moderate your intake of alcohol, wear your seat belt). A study of 4,400 people revealed that continuous smoking throughout one's life reduces life expectancy by 18 years.[66]

2. *Nutritional awareness.* Because we are what we eat, try to increase your consumption of foods high in fiber, vitamins, and nutrients—such as fresh fruits and vegetables, poultry, and fish—while decreasing those high in sugar and fat.

3. *Stress reduction and relaxation.* Use the techniques just discussed to relax and reduce the symptoms of stress.

4. *Physical fitness.* Exercise to maintain strength, flexibility, endurance, and a healthy body weight. More than 50,000 US companies have established fitness programs for employees. A recent review of employee fitness programs indicated that they were a cost-effective way to reduce medical costs, absenteeism, turnover, and occupational injuries. Fitness programs also were positively linked with job performance and job satisfaction.[67]

5. *Environmental sensitivity.* Be aware of your environment and try to identify the stressors that are causing your stress. A control coping strategy might be useful to eliminate stressors.

In conclusion, advocates say that both your personal and professional life can be enriched by adopting a holistic approach to wellness.

BACK TO THE OPENING CASE

Now that you have read Chapter 16, you should be able to answer the following questions about the telephone sales reps case.

1. What individual-level, group-level, and extraorganizational stressors are telephone sales reps exposed to?

2. Which types of stress outcomes do telephone sales reps experience?

3. Use the model of burnout (see Figure 16–2) to explain how and why telephone sales reps appear to burn out.

4. How might a telephone sales rep use a control coping strategy to reduce occupational stress?

5. How would the Type A person perform as a telephone sales rep? Based on Type A research, how would this job affect the behavioral, attitudinal, and physiological outcomes of Type A individuals?

SUMMARY OF KEY CONCEPTS

1. *Define the term* stress. Stress is an adaptive reaction to environmental demands or stressors that triggers a fight-or-flight response. This response creates hormonal changes that mobilize the body for extraordinary demands.

2. *Describe Matteson and Ivancevich's model of occupational stress.* Matteson and Ivancevich's model of occupational stress indicates that stress is caused by four sets of stressors: individual level, group level, organizational level, and extraorganizational. In turn, stress has behavioral, cognitive, and physiological outcomes. Several individual differences moderate relationships between stressors, stress, and outcomes.

3. *Discuss four reasons why it is important for managers to understand the causes and consequences of stress.* First, from a quality-of-work life perspective, workers are more satisfied when they are not under a lot of stress. Second, a moral imperative suggests that managers should reduce stress because it leads to negative outcomes. The third reason relates to the significant economic costs associated with stress. Fourth, because stress-related illnesses may be covered under worker's compensation laws, employers can be sued for exposing employees to undue stress.

4. *Explain how stressful life events create stress.* Stressful life events are changes that disrupt an individual's lifestyle and social relationships. Holmes and Rahe developed the Schedule of Recent Experiences (SRE) to assess an individual's cumulative stressful life events. A positive relationship exists between the SRE and illness. Uncontrollable events that are negative create the most stress.

5. *Review the model of burnout and highlight the managerial solutions to reduce it.* Burnout develops in phases. The three key phases are emotional exhaustion, depersonalization, and feeling a lack of personal accomplishment. Emotional exhaustion, the first phase, is due to a combination of personal stressors and job and organizational stressors. The additive effect of the burnout phases is a host of negative attitudinal and behavioral outcomes. Managers can reduce burnout by buffering its effects; potential buffers include extra staff or equipment, support from top management, increased freedom to make decisions, recognition for accomplishments, time off, equitable rewards, and increased communication from management.

Sabbaticals and employee retreats also are used to reduce burnout.

6. *Explain the mechanisms of social support.* Social support, an important moderator of relationships between stressors, stress, and outcomes, represents the amount of perceived helpfulness derived from social relationships. Cultural norms, social institutions, companies, groups, and individuals are sources of social support. These sources provide four types of support: esteem, informational, social companionship, and instrumental.

7. *Describe the coping process.* Coping is the management of stressors and stress. Coping is directly affected by the cognitive appraisal of stressors, which in turn is influenced by situational and personal factors. People cope by using control, escape, or symptom management strategies. Because research has not identified the most effective method of coping, a contingency approach to coping is recommended.

8. *Discuss the personality characteristic of hardiness.* Hardiness is a collection of personality characteristics that neutralizes stress. It includes the characteristics of commitment, locus of control, and challenge. Research has demonstrated that hardy individuals respond less negatively to stressors and stress than unhardy people. Unhardy employees would be good candidates for stress-reduction programs.

9. *Discuss the Type A behavior pattern and its management implications.* The Type A behavior pattern is characterized by someone who is aggressively involved in a chronic, determined struggle to accomplish more and more in less and less time. Type B is the opposite of Type A. Although there are several positive outcomes associated with being Type A, Type A behavior is positively correlated with coronary heart disease. Management can help Type A individuals by not overloading them with work despite their apparent eagerness to take on an ever-increasing work load.

10. *Constrast the four dominant stress-reduction techniques.* Muscle relaxation, biofeedback, meditation, and cognitive restructuring are predominant stress-reduction techniques. Slow and deep breathing, a conscious effort to relieve muscle tension, and altered consciousness are common denominators of muscle relaxation. Biofeedback relies on a machine to train people to detect bodily signs of stress. This awareness facilitates proactive

coping with stressors. Meditation activates the relaxation response by redirecting one's thoughts away from oneself. Cognitive restructuring entails identifying irrational or maladaptive thoughts and replacing them with rational or logical thoughts.

DISCUSSION QUESTIONS

1. What are the key stressors encountered by students? Which ones are under their control?
2. Describe the behavioral and physiological symptoms you have observed in others when they are under stress.
3. Why do uncontrollable events lead to more stress than controllable events? How can the SRE be used to identify uncontrollable stressors?
4. Why would people in the helping professions become burned out more readily than people in other occupations?
5. Do you think the president of the United States is likely to become burned out? Explain your rationale.
6. Which of the five sources of social support is most likely to provide individuals with social support? Explain.
7. Why would people have difficulty using a control coping strategy to cope with the aftermath of a natural disaster like an earthquake or flood?
8. How can someone increase their hardiness and reduce their Type A behavior?
9. Have you used any of the stress reduction techniques? Evaluate their effectiveness.
10. What is the most valuable lesson you learned from this chapter? Explain.

EXERCISE

Objectives

1. To determine the extent to which you are burned out.
2. To determine if your burnout scores are predictive of burnout outcomes.
3. To identify specific stressors that affect your level of burnout.

Introduction

An OB researcher named Christina Maslach developed a self-report scale measuring burnout. This scale assesses burnout in terms of three phases: depersonalization, personal accomplishment, and emotional exhaustion. To determine if you suffer from burnout in any of these phases, we would like you to complete an abbreviated version of this scale. Moreover, because burnout has been found to influence a variety of behavioral outcomes, we also want to determine how well burnout predicts three important outcomes.

Instructions

To assess your level of burnout, complete the following 18 statements developed by Maslach.[68] Each item probes how frequently you experience a particular feeling or attitude. If you are presently working, use your job as the frame of reference for responding to each statement. If you are a full-time student, use your role as a student as your frame of reference. After you have completed the 18 items, refer to the scoring key and follow its directions. Remember, there are no right or wrong answers. Indicate your answer for each statement by circling one number from the following scale:

1 = A few times a year
2 = Monthly
3 = A few times a month
4 = Every week
5 = A few times a week
6 = Every day

Burnout Inventory

1. I've become more callous toward people since I took this job.   1 2 3 4 5 6
2. I worry that this job is hardening me emotionally.   1 2 3 4 5 6
3. I don't really care what happens to some of the people who need my help.   1 2 3 4 5 6
4. I feel that people who need my help blame me for some of their problems.   1 2 3 4 5 6
5. I deal very effectively with the problems of those people who need my help.   1 2 3 4 5 6
6. I feel I'm positively influencing other people's lives through my work.   1 2 3 4 5 6

7. I feel very energetic.   1 2 3 4 5 6
8. I can easily create a relaxed atmosphere with those people who need my help.   1 2 3 4 5 6
9. I feel exhilarated after working closely with those who need my help.   1 2 3 4 5 6
10. I have accomplished many worthwhile things in this job.   1 2 3 4 5 6
11. In my work, I deal with emotional problems very calmly.   1 2 3 4 5 6
12. I feel emotionally drained from my work.   1 2 3 4 5 6
13. I feel used up at the end of the workday.   1 2 3 4 5 6
14. I feel fatigued when I get up in the morning.   1 2 3 4 5 6
15. I feel frustrated by my job.   1 2 3 4 5 6
16. I feel I'm working too hard on my job.   1 2 3 4 5 6
17. Working with people directly puts too much stress on me.   1 2 3 4 5 6
18. I feel like I'm at the end of my rope.   1 2 3 4 5 6

Scoring

Compute the average of those items measuring each phase of burnout.

Depersonalization (questions 1–4)   _____

Personal accomplishment (questions 5–11)   _____

Emotional exhaustion (questions 12–18)   _____

Assessing Burnout Outcomes

1. How many times were you absent from work over the last three months (indicate the number of absences from classes last semester if using the student role)?
   _____ absences

2. How satisfied are you with your job (or role as a student)? Circle one.

   Very
   dissatisfied   Dissatisfied   Neutral   Satisfied   Very satisfied

3. Do you have trouble sleeping? Circle one.
   Yes   No

Questions for Consideration/ Class Discussion

1. To what extent are you burned out in terms of depersonalization and emotional exhaustion?
   Low = 1–2.99   Moderate = 3–4.99   High = 5 or above

2. To what extent are you burned out in terms of personal accomplishment?
   Low = 5 or above   Moderate = 3–4.99   High = 1–2.99

3. How well do your burnout scores predict your burnout outcomes?

4. Do your burnout scores suggest that burnout follows a sequence going from depersonalization, to feeling a lack of personal accomplishment, to emotional exhaustion? Explain.

5. Which of the unique burnout stressors illustrated in Figure 16–2 are affecting your level of burnout?

NOTES

[1] Layoff statistics can be found in J S Lublin, "Walking Wounded: Survivors of Layoff Battle Angst, Anger, Hurting Productivity," *The Wall Street Journal*, December 6, 1993, pp A1, A6.

[2] Ibid., p A1.

[3] See S R Barley and D B Knight, "Toward a Cultural Theory of Stress Complaints," in *Research in Organizational Behavior*, eds B M Staw and L L Cummings (Greenwich, CT: JAI Press, 1992), pp 1–48.

[4] The stress response is thoroughly discussed by H Selye, *Stress without Distress* (New York: J. B. Lippincott, 1974).

[5] T F O'Boyle, "Fear and Stress in the Office Take Toll," *The Wall Street Journal*, November 6, 1990, p B1.

[6] J M Ivancevich and M T Matteson, *Stress and Work: A Managerial Perspective* (Glenview, IL: Scott, Foresman, 1980), pp 8–9.

[7] See Selye, *Stress without Distress*.

[8] Results can be found in T M Begley and J M Czajka, "Panel Analysis of the Moderating Effects of Commitment on Job Satisfaction, Intent to Quit, and Health Following Organizational Change," *Journal of Applied Psychology*, August 1993, pp 552–56.

[9] Results are discussed in "Labor Letter: A Special News Report on People and Their Jobs in Offices, Fields, and Factories," *The Wall Street Journal*, January 18, 1994, p A1.

[10] Supporting studies were conducted by J R Edwards and R Van Harrison, "Job Demands and Worker Health: Three-Dimensional Reexamination of the Relationship between Person-Environment Fit and Strain," *Journal of Applied Psychology*, August 1993, pp 628–48; C S Smith and J Tisak, "Discrepancy Measures of Role Stress Revisited: New Perspectives on Old Issues," *Organizational Behavior and Human Decision Processes*, November 1993, pp 285–307; and J Schaubroeck, D C Ganster, and M L Fox, "Dispositional Affect and Work-Related Stress," *Journal of Applied Psychology*, June 1992, pp 322–35.

[11] See M L Fox, D J Dwyer, and D G Ganster, "Effects of Stressful Job Demands and Control on Physiological and Attitudinal Outcomes in a Hospital Setting, *Academy of Management Journal,* April 1993, pp 289–318; and S Overman and L Thornburg, "Beating the Odds," *HRMagazine,* March 1992, pp 42–47.

[12] The relationship between chronic work demands and stress was investigated by J Schaubroeck and D C Ganster, "Chronic Demands and Responsivity to Challenge," *Journal of Applied Psychology,* February 1993, pp 73–85.

[13] See J M Ivancevich, M T Matteson, S M Freedman, and J S Phillips, "Worksite Stress Management Interventions" *American Psychologist,* February 1990, pp 252–61.

[14] See G Stern, "Take a Bite, Do Some Work, Take a Bite," *The Wall Street Journal,* January 17, 1994, pp B1, B2; R F Bettendorf, "Curing the New Ills of Technology: Proper Ergonomics Can Reduce Cumulative Trauma Disorders among Employees," *HRMagazine,* March 1990, pp 35–36, 80; and S Overman, "Prescriptions for a Healthier Office," *HRMagazine,* February 1990, pp 30–34.

[15] Supporting evidence is presented in F Jones and B C Fletcher, "An Empirical Study of Occupational Stress Transmission in Working Couples," *Human Relations,* July 1993, pp 881–903; N E Adler, T Boyce, M A Chesney, S Cohen, S Folkman, R L Kahn, and S L Syme, "Socioeconomic Status and Health: The Challenge of the Gradient," *American Psychologist,* January 1994, pp 15–24; and M Powers, "Stressed Out," *Human Ecology Forum,* Spring 1993, pp 7–9.

[16] A variety of evidence is presented in R M Kaplan, "Behavior as the Central Outcome in Health Care," *American Psychologist,* November 1990, pp 1211–20; and A O'Leary, "Stress, Emotion, and Human Immune Function," *Psychological Bulletin,* November 1990, pp 363–82.

[17] See Smith and Tisak, "Discrepancy Measures of Role Stress Revisited: New Perspectives on Old Issues, pp 285–307; Edwards and Van Harrison, "Job Demands and Worker Health: Three-Dimensional Reexamination of the Relationship Between Person-Environment Fit and Strain," pp 628–48; and M Jamal, "Job Stress and Job Performance Controversy: An Empirical Assessment," *Organizational Behavior and Human Performance,* February 1984, pp 1–21.

[18] The relationship between the perception of stressors and stress was examined by P J Decker and F H Borgen, "Dimensions of Work Appraisal: Stress, Strain, Coping, Job Satisfaction, and Negative Affectivity," *Journal of Counseling Psychology,* October 1993, pp 470–79. Gender and stress was discussed by T Adler, "Men and Women Affected by Stress, but Differently," *The American Psychological Association Monitor,* July 1993, pp 8–11.

[19] Research on chronic hostility is discussed by "Healthy Lives: A New View of Stress," *University of California, Berkeley Wellness Letter,* June 1990, pp 4–5.

[20] The link between stress and depression is discussed by P Freiberg, "Work and Well-Being: Experts Urge Changes in Work, Not the Work," *The APA Monitor,* January 1991, p 23.

[21] The economic cost of stress is discussed by V M Gibson, "Stress in the Workplace: A Hidden Cost Factor," *HR Focus,* January 1993, p 15.

[22] E Lesley, "Good-Bye, Mr. Dithers," *Business Week,* September 21, 1992, p 52.

[23] This landmark study was conducted by T H Holmes and R H Rahe, "The Social Readjustment Rating Scale," *Journal of Psychosomatic Research,* August 1967, pp 213–18.

[24] Normative predictions are discussed in O Behling and A L Darrow, "Managing Work-Related Stress," in *Modules in Management,* eds. J E Rosenzweig and F E Kast (Chicago: Science Research Associates, 1984).

[25] This research is discussed by G De Benedittis, A Lorenzetti, and A Pieri, "The Role of Stressful Life Events in the Onset of Chronic Primary Headache," *Pain,* January 1990, pp 65–75; and R S Bhagat, "Effects of Stressful Life Events on Individual Performance Effectiveness and Work Adjustment Processes within Organizational Settings: A Research Model," *Academy of Management Review,* October 1983, pp 660–71.

[26] See S Cohen, D A J Tyrrell, and A P Smith, "Negative Life Events, Perceived Stress, Negative Affect, and Susceptibility to the Common Cold," *Journal of Personality and Social Psychology,* January 1993, pp 131–40; and R S Bhagat, S J McQuaid, H Lindholm, and J Segovis, "Total Life Stress: A Multimethod Validation of the Construct and Its Effects on Organizationally Valued Outcomes and Withdrawal Behaviors," *Journal of Applied Psychology,* February 1985, pp 202–14.

[27] The influence of perceived control over stressors on stress outcomes is thoroughly discussed by S C Thompson, A Sobolew-Shubin, M E Galbraith, L Schwankovsky, and D Cruzen, "Maintaining Perceptions of Control: Finding Perceived Control in Low-Control Circumstances," *Journal of Personality and Social Psychology,* February 1993, pp 293–304; and P P Vitaliano, D J DeWolfe, R D Maiuro, J Russo, and W Katon, "Appraised Changeability of a Stressor as a Modifier of the Relationship between Coping and Depression: A Test of the Hypothesis of Fit," *Journal of Personality and Social Psychology,* September 1990, pp 582–92.

[28] Results are summarized in K H Hammonds, "Work: More Complex Than We Thought," *Business Week,* September 13, 1993, p 42.

[29] The phases are thoroughly discussed by C Maslach, *Burnout: The Cost of Caring* (Englewood Cliffs, NJ: Prentice-Hall, 1982).

[30] The discussion of the model is based on C L Cordes and T W Dougherty, "A Review and Integration of Research on Job Burnout," *Academy of Management Review,* October 1993, pp 621–56.

[31] M Allen, "Burnout! Too Few of the Best Ideas Come from the Over-30 Crowd. It Doesn't Have To Be That Way," *The Wall Street Journal,* May 24, 1993, p R10.

[32] Phases of burnout were examined by R T Lee and B E Ashforth, "A Longitudinal Study of Burnout among Supervisors and Managers: Comparisons between the Leiter and Maslach (1988) and Golembiewski et al. (1986) Models," *Organizational Behavior and Human Decision Processes,* April 1993, pp 369–98.

[33] See Cordes and Dougherty, "A Review and Integration of Research on Job Burnout," pp 621–56; and R J Burke and E Greenglass, "Work Stress, Role Conflict, Social Support, and Psychological Burnout among Teachers," *Psychological Reports,* October 1993, pp 371–81.

[34] Recommendations for reducing burnout are discussed by M Wylie, "Preventing Worker Burnout while Supporting the Users," *MacWeek,* October 4, 1993, pp 12–14; and "How To Avoid Burnout," *Training,* February 1993, pp 15, 16, 70.

[35] These examples and techniques are discussed by L Landon, "Pump Up Your Employees," *HRMagazine,* May 1990, pp 34–37.

[36] Types of support are discussed by S Cohen and T A Wills, "Stress, Social Support, and the Buffering Hypothesis," *Psychological Bulletin,* September 1985, pp 310–57.

[37] P Sebastian, "Firms Helping Disaster Areas Look to Future," *The Wall Street Journal,* February 1994, pp B1, B4.

[38] The perceived availability and helpfulness of support resources was examined by B R Sarason, G R Pierce, A Bannerman, and I G Sarason, "Investigating the Antecedents of Perceived Social Support: Parents' Views of and Behavior toward Their Children," *Journal of Personality and Social Psychology,* November 1993, pp 1071–85; and V S Helgeson, "Two Important Distinctions in Social Support: Kind of Support and Perceived versus Received," *Journal of Applied Social Psychology,* May 1993, pp 825–45.

[39] Supporting results can be found in A D Vinokur and M van Ryn, "Social Support and Undermining in Close Relationships: Their Independent Effects on the Mental Health of Unemployed Persons," *Journal of Personality and Social Psychology,* August 1993, pp 350–59; and N L Collins, C Dunkel-Schetter, M Lobel, and S C M Scrimshaw, "Social Support in Pregnancy: Psychosocial Correlates of Birth Outcomes and Postpartum Depression," *Journal of Personality and Social Psychology,* December 1993, pp 1243–58.

[40] See K R Parkes, C A Mendham, and C von Rabenau, "Social Support and the Demand-Discretion Model of Job Stress: Tests of Additive and Interactive Effects in Two Samples," *Journal of Vocational Behavior,* February 1994, pp 91–113; and J M George, T F Reed, K A Balard, J Colin, and J Fielding, "Contact with AIDS Patients as a Source of Work-Related Distress: Effects of Organizational and Social Support," *Academy of Management Journal,* February 1993, pp 157–71.

[41] For details, see B P Buunk, B J Doosje, L G J M Jans, and L E M Hopstaken, "Perceived Reciprocity, Social Support, and Stress at Work: The Role of Exchange and Communal Orientation," *Journal of Personality and Social Psychology,* October 1993, pp 801–11; and C E Cutrona, "Objective Determinants of Perceived Social Support," *Journal of Personality and Social Psychology,* February 1986, pp 349–55.

[42] The relationship between managerial behavior and organizational policies and the receipt of social support was investigated by I P Erera, "Social Support Under Conditions of Organizational Ambiguity," *Human Relations,* March 1992, pp 247–64.

[43] R S Lazarus and S Folkman, "Coping and Adaptation," in *Handbook of Behavioral Medicine,* ed W D Gentry (New York: The Guilford Press, 1984), p 283.

[44] See results and discussion in M Mikulincer, V Florian, and A Weller, "Attachment Styles, Coping Strategies, and Posttraumatic Psychological Distress: The Impact of the Gulf War in Israel," *Journal of Personality and Social Psychology,* May 1993, pp 817–26; and C Cozzarelli, "Personality and Self-Efficacy as Predictors of Coping with Abortion," *Journal of Personality and Social Psychology,* December 1993, pp 1224–36.

[45] For a thorough review of research on coping with unemployment, see J C Latack, A J Kinicki, and G E Prussia, "An Integrative, Process Model of Coping with Job Loss," *Academy of Management Review,* 1994, in press.

[46] Lazarus and Folkman, "Coping and Adaptation," p 289.

[47] The relationship between cognitive appraisal and the use of different coping strategies was tested by C S Carver and M F Scheier, "Situational Coping and Coping Dispositions in a Stressful Transaction," *Journal of Personality and Social Psychology,* January 1994, pp 184–95; and R F Scherer and P M Drumheller, Jr., "Consistency in Cognitive Appraisal of a Stressful Event Over Time," *Journal of Social Psychology,* August 1992, pp 553–55.

[48] "The President: Tale of the TelePrompTer," *Newsweek,* October 4, 1993, p 4.

[49] Descriptions of coping strategies are provided by D T Terry, "Determinants of Coping: The Role of Stable and Situational Factors," *Journal of Personality and Social Psychology,* May 1994, pp 895–910.

[50] Relevant studies can be found in T A Judge and E A Locke, "Effect of Dysfunctional Thought Processes on Subjective Well-Being and Job Satisfaction," *Journal of Applied Psychology,* June 1993, pp 475–90; and B C Kelley and D L Gill, "An Examination of Personal/Situational Variables, Stress Appraisal, and Burnout in Collegiate Teacher-Coaches," *Research Quarterly for Exercise and Sport,* March 1993, pp 94–102.

[51] See P J Dewe, "Applying the Concept of Appraisal to Work Stressors: Some Exploratory Analysis," *Human Relations,* February 1992, pp 143–64; and D L Nelson and C Sutton, "Chronic Work Stress and Coping: A Longitudinal Study and Suggested New Directions," *Academy of Management Journal,* December 1990, pp 859–969.

[52] This pioneering research is presented in S C Kobasa, "Stressful Life Events, Personality, and Health: An Inquiry into Hardiness," *Journal of Personality and Social Psychology,* January 1979, pp 1–11.

[53] See S C Kobasa, S R Maddi, and S Kahn, "Hardiness and Health: A Prospective Study," *Journal of Personality and Social Psychology,* January 1982, pp 168–77.

[54] Results can be found in D J Wiebe, "Hardiness and Stress Moderation: A Test of Proposed Mechanisms," *Journal of Personality and Social Psychology,* January 1991, pp 89–99; and B Priel, N Gonik, and B Rabinowitz, "Appraisals of Childbirth Experience and Newborn Characteristics: The Role of Hardiness and Affect," *Journal of Personality,* September 1993, pp 299–315. A review of research on hardiness is provided by J G Hull, R R Van Treuren, and S Virnelli, "Hardiness and Health: A Critique and Alternative Approach," *Journal of Personality and Social Psychology,* September 1987, pp 518–30.

[55] M Friedman and R H Rosenman, *Type A Behavior and Your Heart* (Greenwich, CT: Fawcett Publications, 1974), p 84. (Boldface added.)

[56] M S Malone, "Energized Execs: They Keep Going . . . and Going . . . and Going," *The Arizona Republic,* December 6, 1993, p E1.

[57] See J T Spence, R S Pred, and R L Helmreich, "Achievement Striving, Scholastic Aptitude, and Academic Performance: A Follow-Up to 'Impatience versus Achievement Striving in the Type A Pattern,'" *Journal of Applied Psychology,* February 1989, pp 176–78; S D Bluen, J Barling, and W Burns, "Predicting Sales Performance, Job Satisfaction, and Depression by Using the Achievement Strivings and Impatience-Irritability Dimensions of Type A Behavior," *Journal of Applied Psychology,* April 1990, pp 212–16; and M S Taylor, E A Locke, C Lee and M E Gist, "Type A Behavior and Faculty Research Productivity: What Are the Mechanisms?" *Organizational Behavior and Human Performance,* December 1984, pp 402–18.

[58] Results from the meta-analysis are contained in S A Lyness, "Predictors of Differences between Type A and B Individuals in Heart Rate and Blood Pressure Reactivity," *Psychological Bulletin,* September 1993, pp 266–95.

[59] See S Booth-Kewley and H S Friedman, "Psychological Predictors of Heart Disease: A Quantitative Review" *Psychological Bulletin,* May 1987, pp 343–62. More recent results can be found in J A Doster and J L Guynes, "Challenge and Type A Scorers: Implications of Situational Consistency and Control," *Perceptual and Motor Skills,* June 1993, pp 1267–73.

[60] Survey results are summarized in S Rich, "Are Healthy Lifestyles Just Another Hula Hoop?" *The Washington Post National Weekly Edition,* March 22–28, 1993, p 37.

[61] See H Benson, *The Relaxation Response* (New York: William Morrow and Co., 1975).

[62] Research pertaining to the relaxation response is discussed by D Sobel, "Outsmarting Stress," *Working Women,* May 1993, pp 83–84; and A Dunkin, "Meditation, The New Balm for Corporate Stress," *Business Week,* May 10, 1993, pp 86–87.

[63] See S Reynolds, E Taylor, and D A Shapiro, "Session Impact in Stress Management Training," *Journal of Occupational Psychology,* June 1993, pp 99–113; and J M Ivancevich, M T Matteson, S M Freedman, and J S Phillips, "Worksite Stress Management Interventions," *American Psychologist,* February 1990, pp 252–61.

[64] Criticisms of stress-reduction programs are summarized by D C Ganster, B T Mayes, W E Sime, and G D Tharp, "Managing Organizational Stress: A Field Experiment," *Journal of Applied Psychology,* October 1982, pp 533–42.

[65] R Kreitner, "Personal Wellness: It's Just Good Business," *Business Horizons,* May–June 1982, p 28.

[66] Results are presented in "The 18-Year Gap," *University of California, Berkeley Wellness Letter,* January 1991, p 2.

[67] A thorough review of this research is provided by D L Gebhardt and C E Crump, "Employee Fitness and Wellness Programs in the Workplace," *American Psychologist,* February 1990, pp 262–72. Also see F W Schott and S Wendel, "Wellness with a Track Record," *Personnel Journal,* April 1992, pp 98–104.

[68] Adapted from C Maslach and S E Jackson, "The Measurement of Experienced Burnout," *Journal of Occupational Behavior,* April 1981, pp 99–113.

THE EVOLVING ORGANIZATION

PART V

ORGANIZATIONS: STRUCTURE AND EFFECTIVENESS

Learning OBJECTIVES

When you finish studying the material in this chapter, you should be able to:

1. Describe the four characteristics common to all organizations.
2. Distinguish between line and staff positions.
3. Explain the difference between closed and open systems.
4. Contrast the following organizational metaphors: military/mechanical, biological, and cognitive systems.

5. Explain the term *reengineering*.
6. Identify Lawler's substitutes for hierarchy and explain their significance for managing today's flatter organizations.
7. Describe the four generic organizational effectiveness criteria.
8. Explain why a multidimensional approach to organizational effectiveness is recommended.

Carrier Thrives by Banning Bureaucracy

Sharon Hoogstraten

Arkadelphia, Ark.—On a pothole-filled road across from a big chicken processor in this remote town sits a Carrier Corp. plant that could be a blueprint for the future of U.S. manufacturing.

The plant looks more like an insurance office than a factory, with its sleek, one-story structure, pervasive automation and lean work force of only 150. On the factory floor, you could hear a whisper. And it's spotless—"probably cleaner than most of our houses," says Fred Cobb, a worker.

But just as Henry Ford changed the U.S. economy with mass production nearly a century ago, this plant and scores of small ones like it, many of them in isolated towns, are keeping U.S. manufacturing healthy. The Carrier plant, which produces compressors for air conditioners, operates in some unusual ways. For example, it maintains no finished-goods inventory because it makes the compressors

only to order. "This is rethinking the manufacturing process," says David Garvin, a Harvard Business School professor.

Worker Autonomy

What most distinguishes this plant, however, are its workers, a breed apart from yesterday's lunch-pail crowd. Hopeful job applicants must complete a grueling six-week course before being even considered for employment—a selection process that results in a job for only one of every 16 applicants and yields a top-quality work force. Once on the job, the workers have unusual authority. They can, for example, shut down production if they spot a problem, and, within limits, they can order their own supplies.

Workers, who are nonunion and earn $16,000 to $17,000 a year excluding fringe benefits, don't have to punch a time clock or prove illness. Shown a doctor's excuse for an absence, Tracy Bartels, a supervisor, said, "I don't need that." The surprised employee blurted out, "Really?" . . .

Carrier had no choice but to build a new factory: To be competitive, the United Technologies Corp. unit had to make its own compressors. But the big plants it built in the 1970s and 1980s, with their high fixed costs and inflexible production lines, proved to be money-losers, and the company began closing them.

So Thomas L. Kassouf, president of the compressor division, envisioned a streamlined plant that, even running at capacity, would employ no more than 400 workers. Carrier drew a circle around its Texas and Tennessee plants that would use the compressors and chose Arkadelphia as a possible site. The town, which has a population of 10,014, was eager; 1,700 people lost jobs there when three plants closed in 1986 and 1987. Unemployment soared to 15% of the work force from 5%. People were leaving. . . .

In early 1989, Carrier pledged $100 million to the project, and the plant opened [in October 1992].

It's like no other plant in Arkadelphia. Tiles that soak up sound and reflect light cover much of the ceiling. The gray floors gleam. In a dirty plant "you get a don't-give-a-darn attitude right away," says a worker, Chuck Pennington.

Women work beside men in every area and can handle every job. Carrier designed the plant so that no one has to lift anything heavier than 12 pounds repeatedly. "Why should there be any barriers in our plant?" Mr. Kassouf asks.

The plant is highly automated. In one work unit, a person places two pieces of metal in a cutting machine, shuts the glass doors and punches a button. Guided by a computer that keeps the cut from straying more than eight millionths of an inch, the machine slices steel like butter.

Virtually every aspect of life is affected at least indirectly by some type of organization.[1] We look to organizations to feed, clothe, house, educate, and employ us. Organizations attend to our needs for entertainment, police and fire protection, insurance, recreation, national security, transportation, news and information, legal assistance, and health care. Many of these organizations seek a profit, others do not. Some are extremely large, others are tiny ''mom-and-pop'' operations. Despite this

OPENING CASE

(concluded)

Carrier makes one part of the compressor—the part requiring the most complex machining—in just over a minute. As a result, the company expects to produce each compressor for $35 less than it now pays to buy them from suppliers, for a saving that could run $26.3 million a year when annual production hits 750,000.

Flexibility is crucial, both among workers and in the design of the plant. Carrier teaches workers several jobs, so that if one is sick, another can fill in quickly. In addition, "the whole plant could probably be reconfigured in several weeks' time," Mr. Kassouf says.

Suggestion Accepted

The first workers hired suggested that they themselves install the machines. Management agreed, and several workers jetted off to machine-tool plants—some flying for the first time—where they learned how to assemble the equipment. That experience instilled a sense of ownership; many talk about "my machine." It also saved $1 million of installation costs.

And because of their resulting familiarity with the equipment, employees don't have to wait for maintenance workers to fix a machine that breaks down.

When workers recently realized that their machines were arranged in a cumbersome way and that compressors were skipping a welding machine only to have to double back to it later, they pulled up seven machines and realigned them. They came up with the idea one morning and began implementing it that afternoon after clearing it only with their immediate supervisor. As a result, they completed the job in just four days. In a traditionally organized plant, by contrast, the need to consult an array of managers and wait for a maintenance crew to do the work would have dragged out the project for weeks.

Even during normal operations, says Mark Wells, an assembly-line employee, workers in teams quickly learn who has which skills and take directions from the most knowledgeable.

Getting a job at this Carrier plant is a bit like applying to college. It starts with a standard state test for job applicants, who must be high-school graduates or have a general education diploma. Only those scoring in the top third advance. Their references are checked closely, with Carrier managers zeroing in on how well applicants work with other people. The applicants are interviewed by managers and even assembly-line workers—and what the workers think strongly influences who gets hired. . . .

The workers clearly relish exercising their newfound authority. "We have the opportunity to prove that we can do it," says a beaming Mr. Pennington, who previously worked at an LTV Corp. missile plant that was struggling to push decision-making down into the ranks. "Every day, there are

100 problems that [managers] never know existed."

The plant's compressors are not only cheaper but also of high quality. Workers check the products constantly, rather than at prescribed intervals. All the finished compressors are cranked up, and at least one from every group is pulled off the line to test noise and energy levels.

That quality is critical to Carrier's success in the air-conditioning business, since compressors account for as much as 50% of an air conditioner's production costs. And faulty compressors can quickly increase the company's warranty costs. But Carrier executives believe the plant will not only serve as a model for future plants but keep it competitive. Says Mr. Kassouf: "My goal is to sell compressors from Arkansas to Japan."

For Discussion

What has Carrier done to create a *flexible* organization capable of competing in today's high-speed, global economy?

- Additional discussion questions linking this case with the following material appear at the end of this chapter.

Source: E Norton, "Small, Flexible Plants May Play Crucial Role in US Manufacturing," *The Wall Street Journal,* January 13, 1993, pp A1, A8. Excerpted by permission of *The Wall Street Journal,* © 1993 Dow Jones & Company, Inc. All Rights Reserved Worldwide.

mind-boggling diversity, modern organizations have one basic thing in common. They are the primary context for *organizational* behavior. In a manner of speaking, organizations are the chessboard upon which the game of organizational behavior is played. Therefore, present and future managers need a working knowledge of modern organizations to improve their chances of making the right moves when managing people at work.

This chapter explores the structure and effectiveness of modern organizations.

We begin by defining the term *organization,* discussing important dimensions of organization charts, and analyzing fundamental models of organization. Next, a way of dealing with the recent wave of corporate reorganizations is examined. We conclude this chapter with criteria for assessing the effectiveness of organizations.

DEFINING AND CHARTING ORGANIZATIONS

As a necessary springboard for this chapter, we need to formally define the term *organization* and clarify the meaning of organization charts.

What Is an Organization?

organization System of consciously coordinated activities of two or more people.

According to Chester I. Barnard's classic definition, an **organization** is "a system of consciously coordinated activities or forces of two or more persons."[2] Embodied in the *conscious coordination* aspect of this definition are four common denominators of all organizations: coordination of effort, a common goal, division of labor, and a hierarchy of authority[3] (see Figure 17–1). Organization theorists refer to these factors as the organization's *structure.*[4]

Coordination of effort is achieved through formulation and enforcement of policies, rules, and regulations. Division of labor occurs when the common goal is pursued by individuals performing separate but related tasks. The hierarchy of authority, also called the chain of command, is a control mechanism dedicated to making sure the right people do the right things at the right time. Historically, managers have maintained the integrity of the hierarchy of authority by adhering to the unity of command principle. The **unity of command principle** specifies that each employee should report to only one manager. Otherwise, the argument goes, inefficiency would prevail because of conflicting orders and lack of personal accountability. Managers in the hierarchy of authority also administer rewards and punishments. When the four factors in Figure 17–1 operate in concert, the dynamic entity called an organization exists.

unity of command principle Each employee should report to a single manager.

Organization Charts

organization chart Boxes-and-lines illustration showing chain of formal authority and division of labor.

An **organization chart** is a graphic representation of formal authority and division of labor relationships. To the casual observer, the term *organization chart* means the family tree-like pattern of boxes and lines posted on workplace walls. Within

FIGURE 17–1

Four Characteristics Common to All Organizations

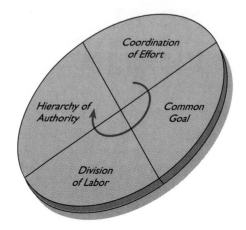

each box one usually finds the names and titles of current position holders. To organization theorists, however, organization charts reveal much more. The partial organization chart in Figure 17–2 reveals four basic dimensions of organizational structure: (1) hierarchy of authority (who reports to whom), (2) division of labor, (3) spans of control, and (4) line and staff positions.

Hierarchy of Authority As Figure 17–2 illustrates, there is an unmistakable hierarchy of authority.[5] Working from bottom to top, the 10 directors report to the 2 executive directors who report to the president who reports to the chief executive officer. Ultimately, the chief executive officer answers to the hospital's board of directors. The chart in Figure 17–2 shows strict unity of command up and down the line. A formal hierarchy of authority also delineates the official communication network.

Division of Labor In addition to showing the chain of command, the sample organization chart indicates extensive division of labor. Immediately below the

• ◢ FIGURE 17–2   Sample Organization Chart for a Hospital (executive and director levels only)

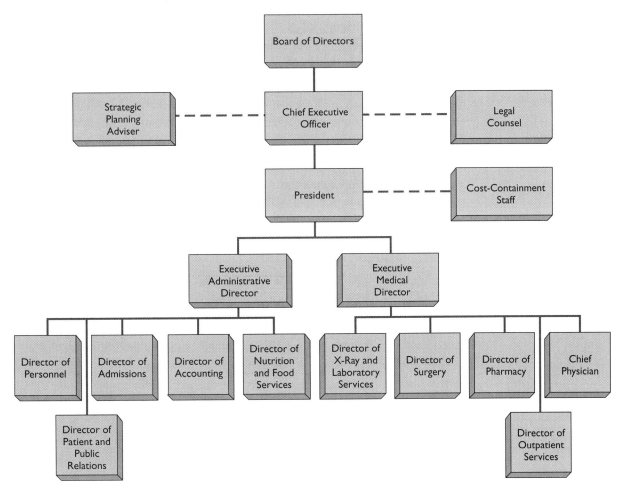

hospital's president, one executive director is responsible for general administration while another is responsible for medical affairs. Each of these two specialties is further subdivided as indicated by the next layer of positions. At each successively lower level in the organization, jobs become more specialized.

span of control   The number of people reporting directly to a given manager.

Spans of Control   The **span of control** refers to the number of people reporting directly to a given manager.[6] Spans of control can range from narrow to wide. For example, the president in Figure 17–2 has a narrow span of control of two. (Staff assistants usually are not included in a manager's span of control.) The executive administrative director in Figure 17–2 has a wider span of control of five. Spans of control exceeding 30 can be found in assembly-line operations where machine-paced and repetitive work substitutes for close supervision. Historically, spans of five to six were considered best. Despite years of debate, organization theorists have not arrived at a consensus regarding the ideal span of control.

Generally, the narrower the span of control, the closer the supervision and the higher the administrative costs due to a higher manager-to-worker ratio. Recent emphasis on leanness and administrative efficiency dictates spans of control as wide as possible but guarding against inadequate supervision and lack of coordination. Wider spans also complement the trend toward greater worker autonomy.

staff personnel   Provide research, advice, and recommendations to line managers.

line managers   Have authority to make organizational decisions.

Line and Staff Positions   The organization chart in Figure 17–2 also distinguishes between line and staff positions. Line managers such as the president, the two executive directors, and the various directors occupy formal decision-making positions within the chain of command. Line positions generally are connected by solid lines on organization charts. Dotted lines indicate staff relationships. **Staff personnel** do background research and provide technical advice and recommendations to their **line managers** who have the authority to make decisions. For example, the cost-containment specialists in the sample organization chart merely advise the president on relevant matters. Apart from supervising the work of their own staff assistants, they have no line authority over other organizational members.

According to a study of 207 police officers in Israel, line personnel exhibited greater job commitment than did their staff counterparts.[7] This result was anticipated because the line managers' decision-making authority empowered them and gave them comparatively more control over their work situations.

THE EVOLUTION OF ORGANIZATIONAL METAPHORS

The complexity of modern organizations makes them somewhat difficult to describe. Consequently, organization theorists have resorted to the use of metaphors.[8] A *metaphor* is a figure of speech that characterizes one object in terms of another object. Good metaphors help us comprehend complicated things by describing them in everyday terms. For example, consider the following metaphor that envisions the modern organization as an orchestra:

> The system can be thought of as a large modern orchestra with a number of professionals playing quite different instruments and performing separate—and often very difficult—tasks. Each instrumentalist, like so many in large organizations, is indeed a specialist in a particular field whose work must be integrated with the work of others to make up the whole.
>
> The manager's job is more than what the concert-goer sees. It includes planning the performance, helping to select those numbers that the orchestra can best perform,

presiding at rehearsals, and doing many of the things that are required to make the final concert notable. The manager's contribution is much more than being the one with the baton, and what the audience sees should be understood in that context.[9]

OB scholar Kim Cameron sums up the value of organizational metaphors as follows: "Each time a new metaphor is used, certain aspects of organizational phenomena are uncovered that were not evident with other metaphors. In fact, the usefulness of metaphors lies in their possession of some degree of falsehood so that new images and associations emerge."[10] With the orchestra metaphor, for instance, one could come away with an exaggerated picture of harmony in large and complex organizations. On the other hand, it realistically encourages us to view managers as facilitators rather than absolute dictators.

Three organizational metaphors that have evolved over the years characterize organizations alternatively as military/mechanical systems, biological systems, and cognitive systems. These three metaphors can be plotted on a continuum ranging from simple closed systems to complex open systems (see Figure 17–3). We need to clarify the important distinction between closed and open systems before exploring the metaphors.

Closed versus Open Systems

A **closed system** is said to be a self-sufficient entity. It is "closed" to the surrounding environment. In contrast, an **open system** depends on constant interaction with the environment for survival. The distinction between closed and open systems is a matter of degree. Since every worldly system is partly closed and partly open, the key question is: How great a role does the environment play in the functioning of the system? For instance, a battery-powered clock is a relatively closed system. Once the battery is inserted, the clock performs its time-keeping function hour after hour until the battery goes dead. The human body, on the other hand, is a highly open system because it requires a constant supply of life-sustaining oxygen from the environment. Nutrients also are imported from the environment. Open systems are capable of self-correction, adaptation, and growth thanks to characteristics such as homeostasis and feedback control.

The traditional military/mechanical metaphor is a closed system model because it largely ignores environmental influences. It gives the impression that organizations are self-sufficient entities. Conversely, the biological and cognitive metaphors

closed system A relatively self-sufficient entity.

open system Organism that must constantly interact with its environment to survive.

• ➚ FIGURE 17~3   Three Contrasting Organizational Metaphors

	Closed Systems	Open Systems	
	Military/Mechanical Model (bureaucracy)	**Biological Model (resource transformation system)**	**Cognitive Model (interpretation and meaning system)**
Metaphorical comparison	Precision military unit/well-oiled machine	Human body	Human mind
Assumption about organization's environment	Predictable (controllable impacts)	Uncertain (filled with surprises)	Uncertain and ambiguous
Organization's primary goal	Maximum economic efficiency through rigorous planning and control	Survival through adaptation to environmental constraints and opportunities	Growth and survival through environmental scanning, interpretation, and learning

emphasize interaction between organizations and their environments. These newer models are based on open-system assumptions. A closer look at the three organizational metaphors reveals instructive insights about organizations and how they work. Each perspective offers something useful.

Organizations as Military/Mechanical Bureaucracies

A major by-product of the Industrial Revolution was the factory system of production. People left their farms and cottage industries to operate steam-powered machines in centralized factories. The social unit of production evolved from the family to formally managed organizations encompassing hundreds or even thousands of people. Managers sought to maximize the economic efficiency of large factories and offices by structuring them according to military principles. At the turn of the century, German sociologist, Max Weber, formulated what he termed the most rationally efficient form of organization. He patterned his ideal organization after the vaunted Prussian army and called it **bureaucracy.**

bureaucracy   Max Weber's idea of the most rationally efficient form of organization.

Weber's Bureaucracy   According to Weber's theory, the following four factors should make bureaucracies the epitome of efficiency:

1. Division of labor (people become proficient when they perform standardized tasks over and over again).
2. A hierarchy of authority (a formal chain of command ensures coordination and accountability).
3. A framework of rules (carefully formulated and strictly enforced rules ensure predictable behavior).
4. Administrative impersonality (personnel decisions such as hiring and promoting should be based on competence, not favoritism).[11]

How the Term *Bureaucracy* Became a Synonym for Inefficiency   All organizations possess varying degrees of these characteristics. Thus, every organization is a bureaucracy to some extent. In terms of the ideal metaphor, a bureaucracy should run like a well-oiled machine, and its members should perform with the precision of a polished military unit. But practical and ethical problems arise when bureaucratic characteristics become extreme or dysfunctional. For example, extreme expressions of specialization, rule following, and impersonality can cause a bureaucrat to treat a client as a number rather than as a person.[12]

Weber probably would be surprised and dismayed that his model of rational efficiency has become a synonym for inefficiency. Today, bureaucracy stands for being put on hold, waiting in long lines, and getting shuffled from one office to the next. (See the International OB.) This irony can be explained largely by the fact that organizations with excessive or dysfunctional bureaucratic tendencies become rigid, inflexible, and resistant to environmental demands and influences.[13]

Organizations as Biological Systems

Drawing upon the field of general systems theory that emerged during the 1950s,[14] organization theorists suggested a more dynamic model for modern organizations. As noted in Figure 17–3, this metaphor likens organizations to the human body. Hence, it has been labeled the *biological model.* In his often-cited organization

INTERNATIONAL OB

The *Mugama:* Egypt's Bureaucratic Legacy

Cairo—In Egypt, the bureaucracy is not just an engine of policy, or even a state of mind. It is a semicircular concrete behemoth in the center of this city's central square.

In this towering edifice—the Mugama ("Uniting") Central Government Complex—office opens onto office, crumbling stairway onto stairway, and the circular corridors that wheel 14 stories high around a dusky inner courtyard seem to have no end. . . .

The Mugama holds 20,000 public employees in 1,400 rooms. It is headquarters to 14 government departments. So deep is its reach into the everyday life of Cairenes that most adult city dwellers will find themselves forced to visit it several times a year. Upward of 45,000 people pass through its portals each day.

Perhaps unrivaled anywhere in the world as a symbol of government dithering and public despair, it is at once the most feared and hated structure in Egypt and the evolutionary product of millennia of bureaucracy on the shores of the Nile.

Twelve hapless clients of the Mugama have hurled themselves from its broken windows or from the soaring circular balconies that ring the central lobby up to the 13th-floor dome. A generation of Arab social engineers, who threw off a monarchy and seized Egypt in the name of its poor and unrepresented, planted their dreams in the Mugama's corridors and largely watched them die there. . . .

"The Mugama is to Egypt generally a symbol of 4,000 years of bureaucracy, and for the average Egyptian, it means all that is negative about bureaucracy: routine, slow paperwork, complicated paperwork, a lot of signatures, impersonality. It is a Kafka building," said political sociologist Saad Eddin Ibrahim.

"You enter there, you can get the job done—the same job—in five minutes, in five days, in five months or five years," Ibrahim said. "You can never predict what might happen to you in that building. Anybody who has dealt with that building for whatever reason knows the uncertainty of his affairs there."

In Egypt, the legacy of bureaucracy dates back to the time of the pharaohs. Temple walls and statues depict countless scribes, papyrus and pen in hand, taking down for the files of posterity everything from the deeds of the Pharaoh to the tax man's inventory. Subsequent French, Turkish and British occupiers refined Egyptian red tape to a fine art.

Today, it takes 11 different permits for a foreign resident to buy an apartment in downtown Cairo. A bride wishing to join her husband working abroad in the Persian Gulf region must get stamps and signatures from the Foreign Ministry, the Ministry of Justice, the prosecutor general, the local court in her district and the regional court, a process that one Cairo newspaper referred to as "legalized torture."

One young physician recently left the Mugama in tears after three days of trying to resign from her government job.

"They told me finally it would be easier if I just took a long sick leave," she said with a sigh. "But I'm leaving the country for a year!"

Source: Excerpted from K Murphy, "Woe Awaits in Tower of Babble," *Los Angeles Times,* May 24, 1993, pp A1, A10–A11. Copyright, 1993, *Los Angeles Times.* Reprinted by permission.

theory text, *Organizations in Action,* James D Thompson explained the biological model of organizations in the following terms:

> Approached as a natural system, the complex organization is a set of interdependent parts which together make up a whole because each contributes something and receives something from the whole, which in turn is interdependent with some larger environment. Survival of the system is taken to be the goal, and the parts and their relationships presumably are determined through evolutionary processes. . . .
>
> Central to the natural-system approach is the concept of homeostasis, or self-stabilization, which spontaneously, or naturally, governs the necessary relationships among parts and activities and thereby keeps the system viable in the face of disturbances stemming from the environment.[15]

Unlike the traditional military/mechanical theorists who downplayed the environment, advocates of the biological model stress organization–environment

● FIGURE 17~4   The Organization as an Open System: The Biological Model

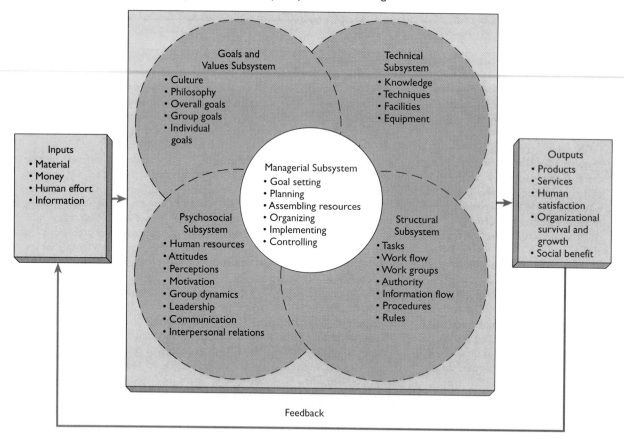

Source: This model is a combination of Figures 5–2 and 5–3 in F E Kast and J E Rosenzweig, *Organization and Management: A Systems and Contingency Approach,* 4th ed (New York: McGraw-Hill, 1986), pp 112, 114. Used with permission.

interaction. As Figure 17–4 illustrates, the biological model characterizes the organization as an open system that transforms inputs into various outputs. The outer boundary of the organization is permeable. People, information, capital, and goods and services move back and forth across this boundary. Moreover, each of the five organizational subsystems—goals and values, technical, psychosocial, structural, and managerial—is dependent on the others. Feedback about such things as sales and customer satisfaction or dissatisfaction enables the organization to self-adjust and survive despite uncertainty and change.[16] In effect, the organization is alive.

Organizations as Cognitive Systems

A more recent metaphor characterizes organizations in terms of mental functions. According to respected organization theorists Richard Daft and Karl Weick:

> This perspective represents a move away from mechanical and biological metaphors of organizations. Organizations are more than transformation processes or control systems. To survive, organizations must have mechanisms to interpret ambiguous events and to provide meaning and direction for participants. Organizations are meaning systems, and this distinguishes them from lower-level systems. . . .

This Motorola work team is determined to stay ahead of the pack by delivering higher quality at a faster pace and lower cost.

(Brian Smith)

> Almost all outcomes in terms of organization structure and design, whether caused by the environment, technology, or size, depend on the interpretation of problems or opportunities by key decision makers. Once interpretation occurs, the organization can formulate a response.[17]

This interpretation process, carried out at the top-management or strategic level, leads to organizational *learning* and adaptation.

In fact, the concept of the *learning organization,*[18] discussed in detail in Chapter 20, is very popular in management circles these days. Motorola Inc. is an excellent case in point. The giant maker of electronics equipment and communications gear has a strong reputation for product quality that its executives fear will not be enough to compete globally during the next decade. While working hard to maintain its lead in quality, Motorola now seeks to become a learning organization that is creative, adaptive, and responsive to change:

> To develop those attributes, Motorola is gearing up a new campaign built around lifelong learning. Under a program conceived by Robert W Galvin, the 71-year-old former chairman, . . . Motorola will dramatically increase training of all employees, from the factory floor to the corner office. The goal is a workforce that is disciplined yet free-thinking. The initiative will aim to inculcate them with company procedures so they're a well-oiled machine but also to develop the knowledge and independent-mindedness that Motorola will need to conquer rapidly changing technologies and markets.[19]

Organizational Metaphors in Perspective

In newly industrialized nations with poorly educated workers, like the United States in the early 1900s, the military/mechanical approach was widely applicable. Narrowly defined jobs, military-like discipline, and strict chains of command enabled factory and office managers to control their employees and meet production quotas. As things grew more complex, however, the military/mechanical model was found lacking. Thanks to modern open-system thinking, we now see organizations as more than internally focused control mechanisms.

A useful model of modern organizations emerges when we integrate the biological and cognitive metaphors. Conceptually, the organization's *body* and *head* need to be connected. One cannot function without the other. Managers of today's productive organizations are responsible for transforming factors of production into needed goods and services (the body). Yet they can remain competitive only if they wisely *interpret* environmental opportunities and obstacles (the head). By combining the biological and cognitive models, we gain a realistic organizational context for theory and practice.

THE ROLE OF HIERARCHY IN TODAY'S DOWNSIZED, REENGINEERED ORGANIZATIONS

reengineering Radical redesign of entire organization for dramatic improvement.

As we documented and discussed in Chapter 1, the downsizing of corporate America during the 1980s and 1990s yielded stunning layoff statistics but disappointing productivity improvement. Millions of employees were laid off as big companies attempted to become leaner and more responsive global competitors.[20] In recent years, the ranks of middle managers have been particularly hard hit by so-called delayering. Copper smelter Asarco, for instance, went from 13 layers of management in 1985 to 5 layers in 1992.[21] And just when the downsizing/delayering era seemed to be nearing an end, the idea of reengineering caught the fancy of large company executives. **Reengineering** involves the radical redesign of the entire organization to achieve dramatically improved results. ''Reengineers start from the future and work backwards, as if unconstrained by existing methods, people, or departments. In effect they ask, 'If we were a new company, how would we run this place?' ''[22]

While we await credible research evidence that reengineering works as promised, ethics specialists worry that countless careers could be ruined by ill-prepared reengineering zealots. Putting things in perspective, this reorganization revolution of downsizing, delayering, and reengineering is nothing less than a frontal assault on the once-unquestioned notion of hierarchy. The chain of command concept, discussed earlier as an element common to all organizations, will never be the same.

How Necessary Is Hierarchy?

According to the traditional chain-of-command concept, adapted from the military, supervisors are needed to assign, monitor, motivate, and control the work of subordinates. But workers and workplaces have changed. Knowledge workers in our service-oriented economy are better educated and hungry for responsibility. Tasks are more complex. And the trend toward fewer organizational layers is gaining momentum. Consequently, management's traditional heavy reliance on hierarchical control is subject to debate (see Table 17–1). According to Lawler's side of the argument, less emphasis on hierarchy is better. In other words, the best management may be self-management. Lawler's contingency model deserves careful consideration because it is a necessary tool for getting the most out of today's organizations that have fewer layers of management.

Substitutes for Hierarchy: A Contingency Approach

substitutes for hierarchy Organizational factors such as computer networks and self-management training that reduce the need for direct supervision.

Lawler's contingency model of substitutes for hierarchy is portrayed in Table 17–2. He believes the 12 supervisory functions in the left-hand column are vital and need to be performed. However, thanks to various combinations of the eight **substitutes for hierarchy** (work design, information systems technology, and so on), the need for direct supervisory control can be reduced or perhaps eliminated. For instance, the X in the upper-left corner indicates the motivational power of work that provides variety and challenge to the jobholder. Notice that there is *no perfect substitute for hierarchy* capable of handling all 12 supervisory functions (work

Pro	Con
Elliot Jacques: Bureaucracy is a dirty word even among bureaucrats, and in business there is a widespread view that managerial hierarchy kills initiative, crushes creativity, and has therefore seen its day. Yet 35 years of research have convinced me that managerial hierarchy is the most efficient, the hardiest, and in fact the most natural structure ever devised for large organizations. Properly structured, hierarchy can release energy and creativity, rationalize productivity, and actually improve morale. Moreover, I think most managers know this intuitively and have only lacked a workable structure and a decent intellectual justification for what they have always known could work and work well. . . . The hierarchical kind of organization we call bureaucracy did not emerge accidentally. It is the only form of organization that can enable a company to employ large numbers of people and yet preserve unambiguous accountability for the work they do. And that is why, despite its problems, it has so doggedly persisted.	Edward E Lawler III: More and more organizations are concluding that they simply cannot afford the salary and other costs of maintaining an extensive hierarchy. . . . In a real sense, all members of the organizational hierarchy above the people who produce the organization's products or services produce nothing of value. Their only purpose is facilitating the performance of those involved in making the organization's products or delivering the organization's services. Thus they constitute an overhead expense whether they are in line or staff positions. They are worth having only if they add significant value to what is done by the people who actually produce the organization's products or services. . . . Without a thorough redesign of the organization, however, it is unlikely that a significant part of the hierarchy can be made unnecessary. Hierarchies perform some very important organizational functions that must be done in some way if coordinated, organized behavior is to take place. On the other hand, if an organization design is adopted that includes work teams, new reward systems, extensive training, and . . . various other practices . . . , organizations can operate effectively with substantially less hierarchy.

• ➤ **TABLE 17–1**
Organizational Hierarchies:
Pro and Con

Sources: Excerpted from E Jacques, "In Praise of Hierarchy," *Harvard Business Review*, January–February 1990, p 127; and E E Lawler III, "Substitutes for Hierarchy," *Organizational Dynamics*, Summer 1988, pp 5–6, 15. Reprinted by permission of publisher from *Organizational Dynamics*, Summer 1988 © 1988. American Management Association, New York. All rights reserved.

• ➤ TABLE 17–2   Substitutes for Hierarchy: Lawler's Contingency Model

Supervisory Functions	Work Design	Information Systems Technology	Financial Data	Reward System Practices	Supplier/ Customer Contact	Training	Vision/ Values	Emergent Leadership
Motivating	X		X	X	X	X	X	
Recordkeeping	X	X						
Coordinating	X	X	X	X	X	X	X	X
Assigning work	X							X
Making personnel decisions	X						X	X
Providing expertise		X				X		X
Setting goals	X	X	X	X	X	X	X	
Planning	X	X	X					
Linking communications	X	X	X	X			X	
Training/Coaching	X	X		X				X
Leading	X							X
Controlling		X	X	X				X

Source: E E Lawler III, "Substitutes for Hierarchy," *Organizational Dynamics*, Summer 1988, p 12.

design comes the closest). Brief descriptions of each substitute for hierarchy follow (with relevant chapter cross-references):

- *Work design.*   Jobs are enriched to include greater variety, challenge, autonomy, and personal responsibility for results (Chapter 6).
- *Information systems technology.*   This includes networked personal computers. Free access to vital information empowers employees (Chapters 10 and 13).
- *Financial data.*   Cost, sales, and profitability data are shared with all employees as a form of feedback (Chapter 14).
- *Reward system practices.*   Skill-based pay, gainsharing, and profit sharing are powerful motivational tools (Chapter 14).
- *Supplier/customer contact.*   Direct contact with internal and external customers provides valuable feedback on performance (Chapter 14).
- *Training.*   Employees can learn how to handle supervisory functions (Chapters 8 and 12).
- *Vision/values.*   Central values in the organizational culture need to emphasize personal responsibility for results (Chapters 15 and 19).
- *Emergent leadership.*   Leadership potential among nonmanagerial employees can be identified and cultivated (Chapters 8 and 15).

Lawler emphasizes the need to rely on the substitutes for hierarchy in a situationally appropriate manner. He notes: ''Technology, work interdependence, work complexity, and required knowledge clearly influence the opportunities for adopting an organizational approach that is based on minimal hierarchy and high involvement.''[23] But employees must want to take greater control of their organizational lives. If they do, and the effectiveness criteria discussed next are met, today's compressed hierarchies can be both productive and satisfying.

ORGANIZATIONAL EFFECTIVENESS

How effective are you? If someone asked you this apparently simple question, you would likely ask for clarification before answering. For instance, you might want to know if they were referring to your grade point average, annual income, actual accomplishments, ability to get along with others, public service, or perhaps something else entirely. So it is with modern organizations. Effectiveness criteria abound. For example, in its annual Most Admired Corporations survey, *Fortune* magazine applies the following eight effectiveness criteria:

- Quality of management.
- Quality of products/services.
- Innovativeness.
- Long-term investment value.
- Financial soundness.
- Ability to attract, develop, and keep talented people.
- Responsibility to the community and the environment.
- Wise use of corporate assets.[24]

In 1993, Rubbermaid broke Merck's seven-year reign as America's Most Admired Corporation. The maker of over 5,000 products ranging from dustpans to playground equipment earned the top spot by ranking number one on four of *Fortune*'s eight effectiveness criteria.[25] But perceived organizational effectiveness can be a fleeting thing in an era of rapid-fire change. For example, Exxon plunged from the number 6 spot on *Fortune*'s Most Admired list in 1989 to number 110 in 1990 after the *Exxon Valdez* oil tanker spill in Alaska.[26]

Assessing organizational effectiveness is an important topic for an array of people, including managers, stockholders, government agencies, and OB specialists. The purpose of this final section is to introduce a widely applicable and useful model of organizational effectiveness.

Generic Organizational-Effectiveness Criteria

A good way to better understand this complex subject is to consider four generic approaches to assessing an organization's effectiveness (see Figure 17–5). These effectiveness criteria apply equally well to large or small and profit or not-for-profit organizations. Moreover, as denoted by the overlapping circles in Figure 17–5, the four effectiveness criteria can be used in various combinations. The key thing to remember is "no single approach to the evaluation of effectiveness is appropriate in all circumstances or for all organization types."[27] What do Rubbermaid and Exxon, for example, have in common, other than being large profit-seeking

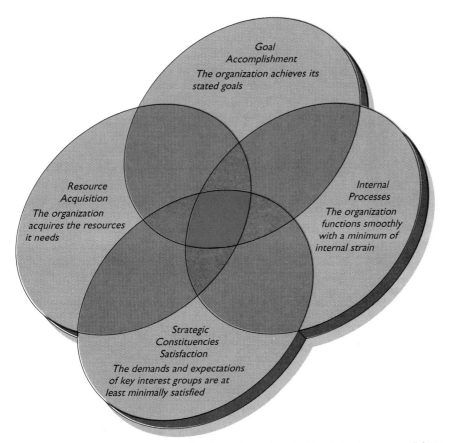

● ➤ FIGURE 17–5
Four Ways to Assess Organizational Effectiveness

Goal Accomplishment
The organization achieves its stated goals

Internal Processes
The organization functions smoothly with a minimum of internal strain

Resource Acquisition
The organization acquires the resources it needs

Strategic Constituencies Satisfaction
The demands and expectations of key interest groups are at least minimally satisfied

Source: Adapted from discussion in K Cameron, "Critical Questions in Assessing Organizational Effectiveness," *Organizational Dynamics,* Autumn 1980, pp 66–80; and K S Cameron, "Effectiveness as Paradox: Consensus and Conflict in Conceptions of Organizational Effectiveness," *Management Science,* May 1986, pp 539–53.

These Pacific Gas and Electric workers gave around-the-clock dedication to the goal of repairing the California earthquake damage in record time.

(Courtesy Pacific Gas & Electric Photo Department, Photography by Judson Allen)

corporations? Because a multidimensional approach is required, we need to look more closely at each of the four generic effectiveness criteria.

Goal Accomplishment   Goal accomplishment is the most widely used effectiveness criterion for organizations. Key organizational results or outputs are compared with previously stated goals or objectives. Deviations, either plus or minus, require corrective action. This is simply an organizational variation of the personal goal-setting process discussed in Chapter 7. Effectiveness, relative to the criterion of goal accomplishment, is gauged by how well the organization meets or exceeds its goals.

Productivity improvement, involving the relationship between inputs and outputs, is a common organization-level goal.[28] Goals also may be set for organizational efforts such as minority recruiting, pollution prevention, and quality improvement. Given today's competitive pressures, *innovation* and *speed* are very important organizational goals worthy of measurement and monitoring. Small companies, such as Ultra Pac Inc., often have a service quality edge in this regard:

> In the production of recyclable plastic food containers, . . . Ultra Pac Inc. has grown in six years to $27 million in sales and a work force of 300 while competing against Mobil Corp. and Tenneco Inc. Using specialized equipment, the Rogers, Minn., company can turn out 400 to 500 different kinds of packaging, often customized, and normally ship them within three days of an order. Ultra Pac claims that is about one-third of the time it usually takes its larger competitors to deliver off-the-shelf containers. "We saw that if we reacted and made decisions faster, we could get a nice chunk of the market," says Calvin Krupa, Ultra Pac's founder, chairman and chief executive.[29]

Resource Acquisition   This second criterion relates to inputs rather than outputs. An organization is deemed effective in this regard if it acquires necessary factors of production such as raw materials, labor, capital, and managerial and technical expertise. Charitable organizations such as the Salvation Army judge

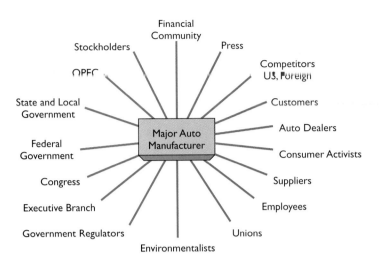

Source: N C Roberts and P J King, "The Stakeholder Audit Goes Public," *Organizational Dynamics,* Winter 1989, p 66. Reprinted, by permission of publisher, from *Organizational Dynamics,* Winter 1989 © 1989. American Management Association, New York. All rights reserved.

FIGURE 17-6
A Sample Stakeholder Audit Identifying Strategic Constituencies

their effectiveness in terms of how much money they raise from private and corporate donations.

Internal Processes Some refer to this third effectiveness criterion as the "healthy systems" approach. An organization is said to be a healthy system if information flows smoothly and if employee loyalty, commitment, job satisfaction, and trust prevail. Goals may be set for any of these internal processes. Healthy systems, from a behavioral standpoint, tend to have a minimum of dysfunctional conflict and destructive political maneuvering.

Strategic Constituencies Satisfaction Organizations both depend on people and affect the lives of people. Consequently, many consider the satisfaction of key interested parties to be an important criterion of organizational effectiveness.

A **strategic constituency** is any group of individuals who have some stake in the organization—for example, resource providers, users of the organization's products or services, producers of the organization's output, groups whose cooperation is essential for the organization's survival, or those whose lives are significantly affected by the organization.[30]

strategic constituency Any group of people with a stake in the organization's operation or success.

Strategic constituencies (or *stakeholders*) generally have competing or conflicting interests. For instance, stock investors who want higher dividends and consumers who seek low prices would likely disagree with a union's demand for a wage increase. Strategic constituents or stakeholders can be identified systematically through a stakeholder's audit.[31] A **stakeholder audit** enables management to identify all parties significantly impacted by the organization's performance (see Figure 17–6). Conflicting interests and relative satisfaction among the listed stakeholders can then be dealt with.

stakeholder audit
Systematic identification of all parties likely to be affected by the organization.

A never-ending challenge for management is to strike a workable balance among strategic constituencies so as to achieve at least minimal satisfaction on all fronts. McDonald's is an interesting and compelling case in point. After the smoke had cleared from the riots in south central Los Angeles in April 1992, observers were amazed to find *every* McDonald's restaurant in the area untouched by arsonists. But that outcome was not surprising to McDonald's:

For Edward H Rensi, president and CEO of McDonald's U.S.A., the explanation of what happened, or didn't happen, in South Central L.A. was simple: "Our businesses there are owned by African-American entrepreneurs who hired African-American managers who hired African-American employees who served everybody in the community, whether they be Korean, African American, or Caucasian."[32]

Multiple Effectiveness Criteria: Some Practical Guidelines

Experts on the subject recommend a multidimensional approach to assessing the effectiveness of modern organizations. This means no single criterion is appropriate for all stages of the organization's life cycle (the organizational life cycle concept is covered in Chapter 18). Nor will a single criterion satisfy competing stakeholders. Well-managed organizations mix and match effectiveness criteria to fit the unique requirements of the situation.[33] Managers need to identify and seek input from strategic constituencies. This information, when merged with the organization's stated mission and philosophy, enables management to derive an appropriate *combination* of effectiveness criteria. The following guidelines are helpful in this regard:

- *The goal accomplishment approach* is appropriate when "goals are clear, consensual, time-bounded, measurable."[34]
- *The resource acquisition approach* is appropriate when inputs have a traceable impact on results or output. For example, the amount of money the American Red Cross receives through donations dictates the level of services provided.
- *The internal processes approach* is appropriate when organizational performance is strongly influenced by specific processes (e.g., cross-functional teamwork).
- *The strategic constituencies approach* is appropriate when powerful stakeholders can significantly benefit or harm the organization.[35]

Keeping these basic concepts of organizational structure and effectiveness in mind, we turn our attention in Chapter 18 to the building of effective organizations.

BACK TO THE OPENING CASE

Now that you have read Chapter 17, you should be able to answer the following questions about the Carrier case:

1. Which metaphor—military/mechanical, biological, or cognitive—best describes the organization in this case? Explain your choice. *Hint:* Use Figure 17–3 as a guide.

2. Using Table 17–2 as a reference, which substitutes for hierarchy are evident in this case? Which supervisory functions evidently have been taken over by Carrier's nonmanagerial employees?

3. Which of the four generic effectiveness criteria in Figure 17–5 would be appropriate (in rank order) for assessing the effectiveness of Carrier's Arkadelphia factory? Explain your reasoning.

4. What strategic constituencies would probably show up on a stakeholder audit for Carrier's Arkadelphia plant?

SUMMARY OF KEY CONCEPTS

1. *Describe the four characteristics common to all organizations.* They are coordination of effort (achieved through policies and rules), a common goal (a collective purpose), division of labor (people performing separate but related tasks), and a hierarchy of authority (the chain of command).

2. *Distinguish between line and staff positions.* Line managers have decision-making authority. Staff personnel support line managers by doing background research, providing technical advice, and making recommendations.

3. *Explain the difference between closed and open systems.* These are relative terms. Closed systems, such as a battery-powered clock, are relatively self-sufficient. Open systems, such as the human body, are highly dependent on the environment for survival. Organizations are said to be open systems.

4. *Contrast the following organizational metaphors: military/mechanical, biological, and cognitive systems.* According to the military/mechanical model, a relatively closed system perspective, the organization seeks to maximize economic efficiency in a predictable environment. The biological metaphor views the organization as a living organism striving to survive in an uncertain environment. In terms of the cognitive metaphor, an organization is like the human mind, capable of interpreting and learning from uncertain and ambiguous situations.

5. *Explain the term* reengineering. Reengineering is a blank-sheet-of-paper approach to radically redesigning the entire organization for dramatically improved performance. Ill-conceived or haphazard reengineering programs are an ethical issue.

6. *Identify Lawler's substitutes for hierarchy and explain their significance for managing today's flatter organizations.* Lawler's eight substitutes for hierarchy reduce or even eliminate the need for direct supervision. They are (1) work design (enriched jobs), (2) information systems technology (computer networks), (3) financial data (direct performance feedback), (4) reward systems practices (e.g., gainsharing), (5) supplier/customer contact (direct feedback from customers), (6) training (e.g., self-management skills), (7) vision/values (value-driven personal responsibility), and (8) emergent leadership (e.g., informal leaders and self-managed teams).

7. *Describe the four generic organizational effectiveness criteria.* They are goal accomplishment (satisfying stated objectives), resource acquisition (gathering the necessary productive inputs), internal processes (building and maintaining healthy organizational systems), and strategic constituencies satisfaction (achieving at least minimal satisfaction for all key stakeholders).

8. *Explain why a multidimensional approach to organizational effectiveness is recommended.* Because no two industries or organizations are exactly alike, managers need to mix and match effectiveness criteria in a manner appropriate to the situation. Moreover, different effectiveness criteria become important as the organization moves through its life cycle.

DISCUSSION QUESTIONS

1. How many organizations directly affect your life today? List as many as you can.

2. What would an organization chart of your present (or last) place of employment look like? Does the chart you have drawn reveal the hierarchy (chain of command), division of labor, span of control, and line–staff distinctions? Does it reveal anything else? Explain.

3. Why is it appropriate to view modern organizations as open systems?

4. How would you respond to a person who said, ''All bureaucracies are useless?''

5. Why is it instructive to characterize today's complex organizations as cognitive (learning) systems?

6. How important is hierarchy in today's typical organization?

7. Which of Lawler's eight substitutes for hierarchy do you think has the greatest promise? Why?

8. How would you respond to a manager who claimed the only way to measure a business's effectiveness is in terms of how much profit it makes?

9. What role can stakeholder audits play in assessing organizational effectiveness?

10. Why do you suppose goal accomplishment is the most widely used effectiveness criterion?

EXERCISE

Objectives

1. To focus your attention on the organizational level of analysis.
2. To get hands-on experience with specifying organizational effectiveness criteria.
3. To conduct a stakeholder audit and thus more fully appreciate the competing demands placed upon today's managers.

Introduction

This exercise introduces you to an organization in transition. Put yourself in the place of the head of the US Army Corps of Engineers as you carry out the following instructions.

Instructions

Read the following case about the US Army Corps of Engineers' changing mission and then carry out the subsequent tasks.

Case: An About-Face for the US Army Corps of Engineers[36]

There is an old movie, now hidden away in the archives of the US Army Corps of Engineers, that the Corps used in years past to explain its mission. In it, the Army Engineers point with pride to the bridges and other engineering achievements they built overseas to aid fighting men in all of the nation's wars.

As the film switches to scenes of flooded rivers and the music swells, the announcer explains the Corps' domestic role. "At home," he says, "the enemy is nature." To combat the enemy, the 1936 Flood Control Act gave the Corps responsibility for federal flood protection and immediately authorized some 250 projects.

Now, as the Corps begins to restyle itself as a protector of the environment, nature is no longer seen as a foe but as an opportunity for the engineers to expand their mission. Chief of Engineers General Henry Hatch has made the rounds of the Army Corps' 36 districts promoting an ambitious environmental agenda.

"Embracing and promoting our environmental ethic will change the way we do our traditional business," he says, as the agency strives to become "the environmental engineers of the future."

Dan Mauldin, who is the Army Corps of Engineers' chief of planning and director of civil works, says, "We see this as a big shift in how engineers will be used. There are a lot of environmental problems and not any of them are going to be solved without an engineer. So it is a big push on our part." In southern Florida the Corps has embraced plans to restore natural water flows to Everglades National Park, to fill in canals, and tear down levees. It is the first time that the Army Engineers have undertaken an environmental restoration project of this magnitude and the first time they have ever acknowledged that at least some of what they built caused more harm than good.

"We have messed up nature, it's no doubt," says Richard Bonner, the deputy district engineer in Jacksonville. "Now we've got to use all of our skills to put things right. Our natural environment is diminishing, and we've got to protect it."

The drainage system built by the Corps—some 1,500 miles of canals and levees—made it possible to farm what was once Everglades swamp. And the system opened the way for urban development.

But it also left Florida with a legacy of polluted and declining water supplies and a dying ecosystem in Everglades National Park. Now, having spent hundreds of millions to drain the Everglades, the Corps has enthusiastically agreed to spend hundreds of millions more to undo some of the damage. "What's good for the environment is good for us," Mauldin says.

Tasks

1. Assume you are General Henry Hatch, Chief of Engineers, and explain in detail how you will assess the Corps' organizational effectiveness during the next three to five years.
2. Making reasonable assumptions about the circumstances of this case, conduct a stakeholder audit for the Florida Everglades project. Which strategic constituents, if any, should be given a higher priority?[37]

Questions for Consideration/ Class Discussion

1. How do your effectiveness criteria measure up to those suggested by your classmates? Did you overlook any important factors? Explain.
2. Did your stakeholder audit broaden your awareness of outside interests? Explain.
3. Which strategic constituents could prove most troublesome relative to pursuing the Corps' new mission? Why? Which most helpful?

NOTES

[1] See P F Drucker, "The New Society of Organizations," *Harvard Business Review,* September–October 1992, pp 95–104.

[2] C I Barnard, *The Functions of the Executive* (Cambridge, MA: Harvard University Press, 1938), p 73.

[3] Drawn from E H Schein, *Organizational Psychology,* 3rd ed (Englewood Cliffs, NJ: Prentice-Hall, 1980), pp 12–15.

[4] For interesting and instructive insights about organization structure, see G Morgan, *Images of Organization* (Newbury Park, CA: Sage, 1986); and G Morgan, *Creative Organization Theory: A Resource Book* (Newbury Park, CA: Sage, 1989).

[5] For an interesting historical perspective of hierarchy, see P Miller and T O'Leary, "Hierarchies and American Ideals, 1900–1940," *Academy of Management Review,* April 1989, pp 250–65.

[6] For an excellent overview of the span of control concept, see D D Van Fleet and A G Bedeian, "A History of the Span of Management," *Academy of Management Review,* July 1977, pp 356–72. Also see E E Lawler III and J R Galbraith, "New Roles for the Staff: Strategic Support and Service," in *Organizing for the Future: The New Logic for Managing Complex Organizations,* eds J R Galbraith, E E Lawler III, and Associates, (San Francisco: Jossey-Bass, 1993), pp 65–83.

[7] M Koslowsky, "Staff/Line Distinctions in Job and Organizational Commitment," *Journal of Occupational Psychology,* June 1990, pp 167–73.

[8] See, for example, R J Marshak, "Managing the Metaphors of Change," *Organizational Dynamics,* Summer 1993, pp 44–56.

[9] D S Brown, "Managers' New Job Is Concert Building," *HRMagazine,* September 1990, p 42.

[10] K S Cameron, "Effectiveness as Paradox: Consensus and Conflict in Conceptions of Organizational Effectiveness," *Management Science,* May 1986, pp 540–41. Also see S Sackmann, "The Role of Metaphors in Organization Transformation," *Human Relations,* June 1989, pp 463–84; and H Tsoukas, "The Missing Link: A Transformational View of Metaphors in Organizational Science," *Academy of Management Review,* July 1991, pp 566–85.

[11] Based on M Weber, *The Theory of Social and Economic Organization,* translated by A M Henderson and T Parsons (New York: Oxford University Press, 1947). An instructive analysis of the mistranslation of Weber's work may be found in R M Weiss, "Weber on Bureaucracy: Management Consultant or Political Theorist?" *Academy of Management Review,* April 1983, pp 242–48.

[12] For a critical appraisal of bureaucracy, see R P Hummel, *The Bureaucratic Experience,* 3rd ed (New York: St. Martin's Press, 1987). The positive side of bureaucracy is presented in C T Goodsell, *The Case for Bureaucracy: A Public Administration Polemic* (Chatham, NJ: Chatham House Publishers, 1983).

[13] For examples of what managers are doing to counteract bureaucratic tendencies, see B Dumaine, "The Bureaucracy Busters," *Fortune,* June 17, 1991, pp 36–50.

[14] A management-oriented discussion of general systems theory—an interdisciplinary attempt to integrate the various fragmented sciences—may be found in K E Boulding, "General Systems Theory—The Skeleton of Science," *Management Science,* April 1956, pp 197–208.

[15] J D Thompson, *Organizations in Action* (New York: McGraw-Hill, 1967), pp 6–7. Also see A C Bluedorn, "The Thompson Interdependence Demonstration," *Journal of Management Education,* November 1993, pp 505–09.

[16] For more on this subject, see V-W Mitchell, "Organizational Homoeostasis: A Role for Internal Marketing," *Management Decision,* no. 2, 1992, pp 3–7.

[17] R L Daft and K E Weick, "Toward a Model of Organizations as Interpretation Systems," *Academy of Management Review,* April 1984, p 293.

[18] For background reading, see M E McGill, J W Slocum, Jr., and D Lei, "Management Practices in Learning Organizations," *Organizational Dynamics,* Summer 1992, pp 5–17; D A Garvin, "Building a Learning Organization," *Harvard Business Review,* July–August 1993, pp 78–91; and F Kofman and P M Senge, "Communities of Commitment: The Heart of Learning Organizations," *Organizational Dynamics,* Autumn 1993, pp 5–23. The entire Autumn 1993 issue of *Organizational Dynamics* is devoted to organizational learning.

[19] K Kelly, "Motorola: Training for the Millennium," *Business Week,* March 28, 1994, p 158.

[20] For 1993 layoff data, see J Schmit, "AMR Quarterly Loss Totals $253 Million," *USA Today,* January 20, 1994,

p 2B. Also see K Maney, ''High Price of Layoffs,'' *USA Today,* March 24, 1994, p 6B; and J A Byrne, ''The Pain of Downsizing,'' *Business Week,* May 9, 1994, pp 60–68.

[21] Data from R Sookdeo, ''Why to Buy Big in Bad Times,'' *Fortune,* July 27, 1992, p 96.

[22] T A Stewart, ''Reengineering: The Hot New Managing Tool,'' *Fortune,* August 23, 1993, p 41. Also see S Pearlstein, ''Down with the Organizational Chart,'' *The Washington Post National Weekly Edition,* August 2–8, 1993, pp 21–22; J Hillkirk, ''Challenging Status Quo Now in Vogue,'' *USA Today,* November 9, 1993, pp 1B–2B; and S Baker, ''How One Medical Center Is Healing Itself,'' *Business Week,* February 21, 1994, p 106.

[23] E E Lawler III, ''Substitutes for Hierarchy,'' *Organizational Dynamics,* Summer 1988, p 13.

[24] Excerpted and adapted from T Welsh, ''Best and Worst Corporate Reputations,'' *Fortune,* February 7, 1994, pp 58–66.

[25] Data from A Farnham, ''America's Most Admired Company,'' *Fortune,* February 7, 1994, pp 50–54.

[26] Data from S Smith, ''America's Most Admired Corporations,'' *Fortune,* January 29, 1990, p 58.

[27] K Cameron, ''Critical Questions in Assessing Organizational Effectiveness,'' *Organizational Dynamics,* Autumn 1980, p 70.

[28] See, for example, R O Brinkerhoff and D E Dressler, *Productivity Measurement: A Guide for Managers and Evaluators* (Newbury Park, CA: Sage Publications, 1990).

[29] M Selz, ''Small Manufacturers Display the Nimbleness the Times Require,'' *The Wall Street Journal,* December 29, 1993, p A1.

[30] Cameron, ''Critical Questions in Assessing Organizational Effectiveness,'' p. 67.

[31] See N C Roberts and P J King, ''The Stakeholder Audit Goes Public,'' *Organizational Dynamics,* Winter 1989, pp 63–79.

[32] E M Reingold, ''America's Hamburger Helper,'' *Time,* June 29, 1992, p 66.

[33] See C Ostroff and N Schmitt, ''Configurations of Organizational Effectiveness and Efficiency,'' *Academy of Management Journal,* December 1993, pp 1345–61.

[34] K S Cameron, ''Effectiveness as Paradox: Consensus and Conflict in Conceptions of Organizational Effectiveness,'' *Management Science,* May 1986, p 542.

[35] Alternative effectiveness criteria are discussed in Ibid.; A G Bedeian, ''Organization Theory: Current Controversies, Issues, and Directions,'' in *International Review of Industrial and Organizational Psychology,* eds C L Cooper and I T Robertson (New York: John Wiley & Sons, 1987), pp 1–33; and M Keeley, ''Impartiality and Participant-Interest Theories of Organizational Effectiveness,'' *Administrative Science Quarterly,* March 1984, pp 1–25.

[36] V Monks, ''Engineering the Everglades,'' *National Parks,* September/October 1990, pp 32, 34. Excerpted by permission of *National Parks Magazine,* copyright © 1990 by National Parks and Conservation Association.

[37] For an instructive update on the Florida Everglades Project, see D Sharp, ''River of Discontent Swirls Around 'River of Grass,' '' *USA Today,* May 4, 1994, p 8A.

ORGANIZATIONAL LIFE CYCLES AND DESIGN

Learning OBJECTIVES

When you finish studying the material in this chapter, you should be able to:

1. Identify and briefly explain the three stages of the organizational life cycle.

2. Discuss organizational decline relative to the organizational life cycle.

3. Explain what the contingency approach to organization design involves.

4. Describe the relationship between differentiation and integration in effective organizations.

5. Discuss Burns and Stalker's findings regarding mechanistic and organic organizations.

6. Define and briefly explain the practical significance of centralization and decentralization.

7. Discuss the effective management of organizational size.

8. Distinguish among hourglass, cluster, and network organizations.

Why Hewlett-Packard Didn't Follow IBM and DEC into Decline

Sharon Hoogstraten

"If we didn't fix things, we'd be in the same shape as IBM is today," says Silicon Valley Legend David Packard. "I was sure of that."

If less than three years ago Packard hadn't stepped in to fix what was beginning to go wrong at Hewlett-Packard Co., it's quite possible that it would have turned into another IBM or Digital Equipment Corp.: a technologic powerhouse that couldn't make money. In 1990, when Packard and William Hewlett were nearing 80 and long since retired from full-time positions at the company, they reasserted themselves. . . .

Even excluding special charges, both IBM and DEC were in the red [in 1992]. HP faced many of the same problems DEC and IBM did: decades of heady growth, followed by bloat and sluggish markets. Yet, excluding a charge for an accounting change for retiree pensions, HP posted earnings of $881 million, or $3.49 per share, on revenues of $16.4 billion for the fiscal year ended in October 1992.

Unlike Thomas Watson Jr., the retired chairman of IBM, Hewlett and Packard had the power to effect change: Between them they had picked most of the board members and owned a fourth of the stock. As engineers, they also commanded the respect, even reverence, of employees in an engineers' company.

Other than that, HP was a lot like IBM and DEC, its two largest competitors. All three electronic companies had grown at least tenfold over the previous quarter century; all were, for most of that time, prosperous, complacent and paternalistic, with firm no-layoff policies. All have since undergone convulsive change.

Why, alone of the big three, has Hewlett-Packard emerged as healthy as ever, while the other two are still stumbling from writeoff to writeoff? Some outsiders are saying that IBM's new chairman, Louis Gerstner Jr., will have to dump another third of IBM's employees.

Bypassing their headquarters staff in Palo Alto, the two founders of HP visited with small groups of low-level employees in the field, and concluded from these meetings that the company had grown too centralized and bureaucratic. So they moved people, and power, away from headquarters.

The shift meant, for example, that Lewis Platt, then head of HP's computer systems group, had to transfer from Palo Alto to an office 20 miles away in Cupertino. This was more than a symbolic move. Platt, now 52, tested his freedom with a program to build a workstation, on a demanding one-year schedule that Platt chose on his own without having to consult HP Chief Executive John Young.

Finally, Hewlett and Packard engineered a smooth transition last year of the chief executive's job from Young, who reached the usual retirement age for officers of 60, to Platt. Unlike the recent boardroom coups at IBM and DEC, the HP management changeover was orderly; Young joined the selection committee that chose Platt.

Revitalized and refreshed, HP [in 1992] managed the considerable task of ousting DEC from second place in workstations; today HP is second there only to Sun Microsystems. HP strengthened its dominance in laser printers over Apple Computer and a half-dozen Japanese outfits. . . .

While other corporate managements talked decentralization, Hewlet and Packard saw to it that their company practiced decentralization. IBM, under John Akers, was talking about breaking itself into 13 independent companies; DEC's new chief executive, Robert Palmer, is reorganizing DEC into nine business units, which just may turn out to be leaner and more agile than the company that founder Kenneth Olsen left behind.

But dispersing power is old hat at HP. From the earliest days, Hewlett and Packard made a fetish of splitting any division that accumulated more than 1,500 workers. Each division has its own engineering, marketing, manufacturing and personnel staffs. . . .

"Packard never wanted [divisions] to get so large that the people in them would lose pride in the work their division was doing," says David Kirby, a retired HP manager now helping Packard write a book on management. . . .

"HP started as groups of obstreperous, entrepreneurial, arrogant engi-

OPENING CASE

(concluded)

neers running their own shows," says management consultant and author Tom Peters. In contrast, he says, "DEC was always one man, one product"—founder Kenneth Olsen and his seamlessly integrated VAX computer line.

IBM had a different sort of institutional impediment to independents within its midst. At IBM, the organization took precedence over the individual. The organization man was a well-rounded executive who had served in different divisions, and so IBM moved those on the management fast track every two years or so. The problem was that one of these executives could barely settle into a new job before it was time to start angling for the next rung on the corporate ladder. The joke was that IBM stood for "I've been moved." This is no joke: A 70-person group within IBM did nothing but handle the paperwork for international transfers.

Doesn't HP transfer managers? Yes, but it's usually at their own request. They learn of a job opening elsewhere within the company, and compete with outside candidates for the slot.

Here's another sharp difference between Hewlett-Packard and IBM. Usually four layers of management separate HP Chairman Packard from an assembly line worker. IBM, even though it is only four times HP's size, and thus seemingly in need of only one more tier on the pyramid, has more like eight layers in the middle.

Can't too much divisional independence create conflicts or duplication in the product lines? It can, and it did at

Hewlett-Packard. . . .

Young tried to orchestrate the computer business from headquarters. A central R&D organization designed all HP computer products. . . . Conflicts between divisions were settled by committees who made "least common denominator decisions or none at all," says Willem Roelandts, an HP vice president. Robert Frankenberg, another vice president, remembers seeking 19 signatures to institute a one-time pricing program for a PC software package. Launching a new version of one networking product required approval from 38 committees.

In short, HP was starting to get more like IBM and DEC. . . .

Bright ideas began to get squelched if they sounded unorthodox. Someone suggested that PCs be sold—à la Dell—through the same (800) lines that sold HP supplies like cables and power supplies. Not HP, was headquarters' response. Price changes had to be submitted 45 days in advance to the right committees, a disastrous delay in a business where mail-order PC firms can knock down their prices by 30% in a week.

Even HP's medical products group, tucked away in Andover, Mass., wasn't spared the drift toward centralization. Financial experts back in Palo Alto had decided that all HP customers were to pay up within 45 days. "Hospitals are typically slow to pay, but they always do—slow, but sure," says medical general manager Ben L. Holmes. When Palo Alto clerks leaned on hospitals used to paying in 70 days, Holmes got a lot of angry phone calls.

It was then that Hewlett and Packard pulled their company back from the brink. "I'm a strong believer in finding out what the troops think," Hewlett says. This is what they told him. "We had too damn many committees," he says. "Decisions weren't being made. Overhead is something that creeps in. It's not something that overtakes you overnight."

The shakeup engineered by the founders erased a lot of committees, let the medical division choose its own payment policies, and freed Platt to undertake the crash program to build a low-cost engineering workstation. Platt's project resulted in a winner, an $11,000 machine that debuted, on time, in the spring of 1991. . . .

For octogenarians, David Packard and Bill Hewlett are still alert and vigorous, but they can't go on forever. At 52, Lewis Platt is steeped in the tradition of decentralization and knows from personal experience that executives function best when freed from micromanagement by book and by committee.

For Discussion

What does this case teach us about the balance between freedom and managerial control?

- Additional discussion questions linking this case with the following material appears at the end of this chapter.

Source: Excerpted from J Pitta, "It Had To Be Done and We Did It," *Forbes,* April 26, 1993, pp 148–52.

rganizations are much more than the familiar pattern of boxes and lines we see on organization charts. Charts may be a necessary starting point, but we need to know more if we are to adequately understand and manage organizations. Organization design scholar and consultant Robert W Keidel put it this way:

> Our historical preoccupation with organization *charts*—hierarchical displays of reporting relationships—is counterproductive. Organizational design is far more a matter of *charting direction* and navigating among autonomy, control, and cooperation than of moving boxes around. The process is never-ending.[1]

Indeed, organizations take on a life of their own. As has been said many times, organizations are more than the sum of their parts. This chapter explores important dynamics of organizations including the life-cycle perspective, with special emphasis on decline, and the contingency approach to organization design. Our underlying challenge is to learn how to build organizations capable of thriving in an environment characterized by rapid change and rugged global competition.[2]

ORGANIZATIONAL LIFE CYCLES

Like the people who make up organizations, organizations themselves go through life cycles. Organizations are born and, barring early decline, eventually grow and mature. If decline is not reversed, the organization dies. Just as you will face new problems and challenges during different phases of your lifetime, so do organizations. Thus, managers need a working knowledge of organizational life cycles and the closely related topic of organizational decline. According to a pair of experts on the subject: ''A consistent pattern of development seems to occur in organizations over time, and organizational activities and structures in one stage are not the same as the activities and structures present at another stage. This implies that the criteria used to evaluate an organization's success in one stage of development also may be different from criteria used to evaluate success at another stage of development.''[3] This section examines stages of the organizational life-cycle concept and discusses the threat of organizational decline.

Organizational Life-Cycle Stages

Although the organizational life-cycle concept has been around for a long time, it has enjoyed renewed interest among respected researchers in recent years. Many life-cycle models have been proposed.[4] One point of agreement among the competing models is that organizations evolve in a predictable sequence of identifiable stages. Table 18–1 presents a basic organizational life-cycle model. Stages 1 through 3 of the model are inception, high-growth, and maturity. Changes during these three stages can be summed up in the following rule: *As organizations mature, they tend to become larger, more formalized, and more differentiated (fragmented).* Differentiation increases because of added levels in the hierarchy, further division of labor, and formation of political coalitions.

Life-Cycle Timing and Type of Change   Two key features of this life-cycle model address the timing and type of changes experienced by the organization. Relative to timing, the duration of each phase is highly variable, depending on a host of organizational and environmental factors. This explains why there is no

● ▰ TABLE 18~1   Stages of the Organizational Life Cycle

Characteristics	Stage 1: Inception	Stage 2: High-growth	Stage 3: Maturity ----------- Decline	
Type of organizational structure	No formal structure	Centralized Formal	Decentralized Formal	Rigid, top-heavy, overly complex
Communication process and planning	Informal Face-to-face Little planning	Moderately formal Budgets	Very formal Five-year plans Rules and regulations	Communication breakdown Blind adherence to "success formula"
Method of decision making	Individual judgment Entreprenurial	Professional management Analytical tools	Professional management Bargaining	Emphasis on form rather than substance Self-serving politics
Organizational growth rate	Inconsistent but improving	Rapid positive growth	Growth slowing or declining	Declining
Organizational age and size	Young and small	Larger and older	Largest or once large and oldest	Variable age and shrinking

Source: Characteristics and first three stages excerpted from K G Smith, T R Mitchell, and C E Summer, "Top Level Management Priorities in Different Stages of the Organizational Life Cycle," *Academy of Management Journal*, December 1985, p 802. Organizational decline portion adapted from discussion in P Lorange and R T Nelson, "How to Recognize—and Avoid—Organizational Decline," *Sloan Management Review*, Spring 1987, pp 41–48.

time frame in Table 18–1. Some organizations have short life-cycles, with abbreviated or missing stages. For example, toy-maker Worlds of Wonder Inc., "with such hits as Teddy Ruxpin, reached $327 million in revenues its second year, then lost $187 million in a single quarter and plunged into bankruptcy before its third birthday."[5] The Roman Catholic Church, on the other hand, has been around for nearly two millenia.

Regarding the type of change that organizations undergo from one stage to the next, Indiana University researchers noted, "The very nature of the firm changes as a business grows in size and matures. These are not changes in degree; rather, they are fundamental changes in kind."[6] This sort of *qualitative* change helps explain the unexpected departure of founder Mitchell D Kapor from Lotus Development Corporation, maker of the highly successful 1–2–3® computer spreadsheet program. When asked by *Inc.* magazine why he walked away from it all, Kapor replied:

> If you look at Lotus as it started and as it is today, I think you'll see more differences than similarities. In the beginning, it was classically entrepreneurial; a small group of people trying to break into a market with a new product around which they hoped to build a company and achieve market share for the company and financial success for themselves and their investors. Today, Lotus is a company of 1,350 people with diversified, worldwide operations, with the organizational structure and challenges of a $275 million company. And so the nature of the challenges facing the company, and facing the people in it—and, to your question, facing me—is radically different.[7]

Entrepreneurs, such as Kapor, tend to miss the inception-stage excitement and risk as their organizations move into the high-growth and maturity stages.[8] Some entrepreneurs become liabilities because they fail to grow with their organizations. Others, Kapor included, wisely turn the reins over to professional managers who possess the ability and desire to manage large and complex organizations. Managerial skills needed during one stage of the organization's life-cycle may be inappropriate or inadequate during a later stage.

The Ever-Present Threat of Decline   While decline is included in the model, it is not a distinct stage with predictable sequencing (hence the broken line between maturity and decline in Table 18–1). Organizational decline is a *potential,* rather than automatic, outcome that can occur any time during the life-cycle. Stage 1 and stage 2 organizations are as readily victimized by the forces of decline as mature stage 3 organizations. According to a recent study of more than 800,000 US businesses, 18 percent failed within their first eight years of operation.[9] (Thus, the often-heard statistic that four out of five new businesses fail during the first five years turns out to be a myth.) Most of the failed businesses experience decline after an extended inception stage or an abbreviated high-growth stage. While noting ''decline is almost unavoidable unless deliberate steps are taken to prevent it,''[10] specialists on the subject have alerted managers to 14 early-warning signs of organizational decline:

1. Excess personnel.
2. Tolerance of incompetence.
3. Cumbersome administrative procedures.
4. Disproportionate staff power (e.g., technical staff specialists politically overpower line managers whom they view as unsophisticated and too conventional).
5. Replacement of substance with form (e.g., the planning process becomes more important than the results achieved).
6. Scarcity of clear goals and decision benchmarks.
7. Fear of embarrassment and conflict (e.g., formerly successful executives may resist new ideas for fear of revealing past mistakes).
8. Loss of effective communication.
9. Outdated organizational structure.[11]

Toyota is known for its emphasis on *kaizen,* Japanese for "continuous improvement."

(Courtesy Toyota Motor Sales USA, Inc.)

10. Increased scapegoating by leaders.
11. Resistance to change.
12. Low morale.
13. Special interest groups are more vocal.
14. Decreased innovation.[12]

Managers who monitor these early warning signs of organizational decline are better able to reorganize in a timely and effective manner.[13]

Preventing Organizational Decline   The time to start doing something about organizational decline is when everything is going *right*. For it is during periods of high success that the seeds of decline are sown.[14] *Complacency* is the number one threat because it breeds overconfidence and inattentiveness.[15]

> GM [General Motors] is an example of a firm that grew so rich and powerful that it became oblivious to the signals of changing times. Despite the oil crises of the 1970s and the Japanese challenge of the '80s, GM never put its heart into developing smaller, high-quality cars. It took a new division, Saturn, to develop GM's first winning US small car. "When you're on top of the heap, there's a disdain for change, a disdain for new ideas," says Lawrence Hrebiniak, a professor at the Wharton School. "It just goes with the territory, because you are No. 1."[16]

Toyota's quest for continuous improvement is an inspiring example of how to avoid organizational decline by not becoming complacent (see the International OB).

Organizational Life-Cycle Research and Practical Implications   The best available evidence in this area comes from the combination of a field study and a laboratory simulation. Both studies led researchers to the same conclusions. In the field study, 38 top-level electronics industry managers from 27 randomly selected

---

INTERNATIONAL OB

Kaizen Helps Toyota Prevent Organizational Decline

Of all the slogans kicked around Toyota City, the key one is *kaizen,* which means "continuous improvement" in Japanese. While many other companies strive for dramatic breakthroughs, Toyota keeps doing lots of little things better and better. . . .

One consultant calls Toyota's strategy "rapid inch-up": Take enough tiny steps and pretty soon you outdistance the competition. . . .

The company simply is tops in quality, productivity, and efficiency. From its factories pour a wide range of cars, built with unequaled precision.

Toyota turns out luxury sedans with Mercedes-like quality using *one-sixth* the labor Mercedes does. The company originated just-in-time mass production and remains its leading practitioner.

In short, Toyota is the best carmaker in the world. And it keeps getting better. Says Iwao Isomura, chief of personnel: "Our current success is the best reason to change things." Extensive interviews with Toyota executives in the US and Japan demonstrate the company's total dedication to continuous improvement. What is often mis-

taken for excessive modesty is, in fact, an expression of permanent dissatisfaction—even with exemplary performance. So the company is simultaneously restructuring its manufacturing processes, planning its global strategy for the 21st century, tinkering with its corporate culture, and even becoming a fashion leader.

Source: Excerpted from A Taylor III, "Why Toyota Keeps Getting Better and Better and Better," *Fortune,* November 19, 1990, pp 66–67. © 1990 The Time Inc. Magazine Company. All rights reserved.

companies were presented with a decision-making scenario. They then were asked to complete a questionnaire about priorities. It was found that priorities shifted across the three life-cycle stages introduced in Table 18–1. As the organization matured from stage 1 to stages 2 and 3, top management's priorities shifted as follows:

- A strong emphasis on technical efficiency grew even stronger.
- The desire for personal power and commitment from subordinates increased significantly.
- The desire for organizational integration (coordination and cooperation) decreased significantly.[17]

In a separate but related study, researchers examined the relationship between life-cycle stages and effectiveness criteria. This five-year case study of a New York State mental health agency revealed that top management's effectiveness criteria changed during the organization's life cycle. Early emphasis on flexibility, resource acquisition, and employee development/satisfaction gave way to formalization as the agency matured. Formalization criteria encompassed increased attention to factors such as goal setting, information management, communication, control, productivity, and efficiency.[18]

This research reveals that different stages of the organizational life cycle are associated with distinctly different managerial responses. It must be noted, however, that management's priorities and effectiveness criteria in the foregoing studies were not necessarily the *right* ones. Much research remains to be done to identify specific contingencies. Still, the point remains that managers need to be flexible and adaptive as their organizations evolve through the various life-cycle stages.[19] As learned the hard way by General Motors, IBM, and Sears, yesterday's formula for success can be today's formula for noncompetitiveness and decline.[20]

THE CONTINGENCY APPROACH TO ORGANIZATION DESIGN

contingency approach to organization design
Creating an effective organization-environment fit.

According to the **contingency approach to organization design,** organizations tend to be more effective when they are structured to fit the demands of the situation.[21] A contingency approach can be put into practice by first assessing the degree of environmental uncertainty.[22] Next, the contingency model calls for using various organization design configurations to achieve an effective organization-environment fit. This section presents an environmental uncertainty model along with two classic contingency design studies.

Assessing Environmental Uncertainty

Robert Duncan proposed a two-dimensional model for classifying environmental demands on the organization (see Figure 18–1). On the horizontal axis is the simple → complex dimension. This dimension "focuses on whether the factors in the environment considered for decision making are few in number and similar or many in number and different."[23] On the vertical axis of Duncan's model is the static → dynamic dimension. "The static-dynamic dimension of the environment is concerned with whether the factors of the environment remain the same over time or change."[24] When combined, these two dimensions characterize four situations that represent increasing uncertainty for organizations. According to Duncan, the complex-dynamic situation of highest uncertainty is the most common organizational environment today.

• ◢ FIGURE 18~1   A Four-Way Classification of Organizational Environments

	Simple	Complex
Static	**Low Perceived Uncertainty** • Small number of factors and components in the environment • Factors and components are somewhat similar to one another • Factors and components remain basically the same and are not changing • Example: Soft drink industry	**Moderately low perceived uncertainty** • Large number of factors and components in the environment • Factors and components are not similar to one another • Factors and components remain basically the same • Example: Food products
Dynamic	**Moderately High Perceived Uncertainty** • Small number of factors and components in the environment • Factors and components are somewhat similar to one another • Factors and components of the environment are in continual process of change • Example: Fast-food industry	**High Perceived Uncertainty** • Large number of factors and components in the environment • Factors and components are not similar to one another • Factors and components of environment are in a continual process of change • Examples: Commercial airline industry Telephone communications (AT&T)

Source: Reprinted, by permission of the publisher, from "What Is the Right Organization Structure?" by R Duncan, *Organizational Dynamics,* Winter 1979, p 63. © 1979 American Management Association, New York. All rights reserved.

Amid these fast-paced times, nothing stands still. Not even in the simple–static quadrant. For example, during the first 94 years of Coca-Cola's history (through 1980), only one soft drink bore the company's name. Just six years later, Coke had its famous name on seven soft drinks, including Coca-Cola Classic, Coke, and Cherry Coke. Despite operating in an environment characterized as simple and static, Coca-Cola has had to become a more risk-taking, entrepreneurial company.[25] This means organizations facing moderate to high uncertainty (quadrants 3 and 4 in Figure 18–1) have to be highly flexible, responsive, and adaptive today. Contingency organization design is more important than ever because it helps managers structure their organizations to fit the key situational factors discussed next.

Differentiation and Integration: The Lawrence and Lorsch Study

In their classic text, *Organization and Environment,* Harvard researchers Paul Lawrence and Jay Lorsch explained how two structural forces simultaneously fragment the organization and bind it together. They cautioned that an imbalance between these two forces—labeled *differentiation* and *integration*—could hinder organizational effectiveness.

Differentiation Splits the Organization Apart   **Differentiation** occurs through division of labor and technical specialization. A behavioral outcome of differentiation is that technical specialists such as computer programmers tend to think and act differently than specialists in, say, accounting or marketing. Excessive differentiation can cause the organization to bog down in miscommunication, conflict, and

differentiation Division of labor and specialization that causes people to think and act differently.

◣ • FIGURE 18~2
Differentiation and
Integration Are Opposing
Structural Forces

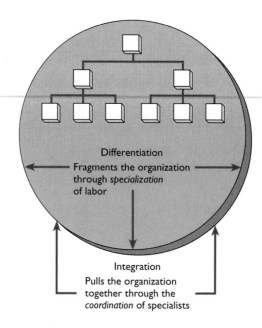

politics. Thus, differentiation needs to be offset by an opposing structural force to ensure needed *coordination*. This is where integration enters the picture (see Figure 18–2).

integration   Cooperation among specialists to achieve common goal.

Integration Binds the Organization Together   Integration occurs when specialists cooperate to achieve a common goal. According to the Lawrence and Lorsch model, integration can be achieved through various combinations of the following six mechanisms: (1) a formal hierarchy; (2) standardized policies, rules, and procedures; (3) departmentalization; (4) committees and cross-functional teams; (5) human relations training, and (6) individuals and groups acting as liaisons between specialists.

Achieving the Proper Balance   When Lawrence and Lorsch studied successful and unsuccessful companies in three industries, they concluded the following: *As environmental complexity increased, successful organizations exhibited higher degrees of both differentiation and integration.* In other words, an effective balance was achieved. Unsuccessful organizations, in contrast, tended to suffer from an imbalance of too much differentiation and not enough offsetting integration. This outcome was confirmed by the life-cycle research discussed earlier. As the organization matured, management's desire for integration became a significantly less important priority. Managers need to fight this tendency if their growing and increasingly differentiated organizations are to be coordinated.

Lawrence and Lorsch also discovered that "the more differentiated an organization, the more difficult it is to achieve integration."[26] Managers of today's complex organizations need to strive constantly and creatively to achieve greater integration.[27] For example, how does 3M Company, with its dozens of autonomous divisions and over 60,000 products, successfully maintain its competitive edge in technology? Among other things, 3M makes sure its technical specialists frequently interact with one another so cross-fertilization of ideas takes place. Art Fry, credited with inventing the now ubiquitous Post-It Notes, actually owes much of

The success of 3M's Post-It Notes is due in part to the importance the company places on cross-fertilization. Two technical specialists shared ideas that resulted in the ubiquitous stick-on notes.

(Courtesy 3M)

his success to colleague Spencer Silver, an engineer down the hall who created an apparently useless semi-adhesive. If Fry and Silver had worked in a company without a strong commitment to integration, we probably would not have Post-It Notes. 3M does not leave this sort of cross-fertilization to chance. It organizes for integration with such things as a Technology Council that regularly convenes researchers from various divisions and an annual science fair at which 3M scientists enthusiastically hawk their new ideas, not to customers, but to each other![28]

Mechanistic versus Organic Organizations

A second landmark contingency design study was reported by a pair of British behavioral scientists, Tom Burns and G M Stalker. In the course of their research, they drew a very instructive distinction between what they called mechanistic and organic organizations. **Mechanistic organizations** are rigid bureaucracies with strict rules, narrowly defined tasks, and top-down communication. For example, when *Business Week* correspondent Kathleen Deveny spent a day working in a McDonald's restaurant, she found a very mechanistic organization:

mechanistic organizations Rigid, command-and-control bureaucracies.

> Here every job is broken down into the smallest of steps, and the whole process is automated. . . .
>
> Anyone could do this, I think. But McDonald's restaurants operate like Swiss watches, and the minute I step behind the counter I am a loose part in the works. . . .
>
> I bag French fries for a few minutes, but I'm much too slow. Worse, I can't seem to keep my station clean enough. Failing at French fries is a fluke, I tell myself. . . .
>
> I try to move faster, but my co-workers are playing at 45 rpm, and I'm stuck at 33⅓.[29]

This sort of mechanistic structure is necessary at McDonald's because of the competitive need for uniform product quality, speedy service, and cleanliness. Oppositely, **organic organizations** are flexible networks of multitalented individuals who perform a variety of tasks. W L Gore & Associates, The Newark, Delaware, maker of waterproof Gore-Tex fabric, is a highly organic organization because it lacks job descriptions and a formalized hierarchy and de-emphasizes titles and status.[30]

organic organizations
Fluid and flexible network of multitalented people.

A Matter of Degree Importantly, as illustrated in Figure 18–3, each of the mechanistic-organic characteristics is a matter of degree. Organizations tend to be *relatively* mechanistic or *relatively* organic. Pure types are rare because divisions, departments, or units in the same organization may be more or less mechanistic or organic. From an employee's standpoint, which organization structure would you prefer?

Different Approaches to Decision Making Decision making tends to be centralized in mechanistic organizations and decentralized in organic organizations. **Centralized decision making** occurs when key decisions are made by top management. **Decentralized decision making** occurs when important decisions are made by middle- and lower-level managers. Generally, centralized organizations are more tightly controlled while decentralized organizations are more adaptive to changing situations.[31] Each has its appropriate use. For example, both Delta Air Lines and General Electric are very respected and successful companies, yet the former prefers centralization while the latter pushes decentralization.

centralized decision making
Top managers make all key decisions.

decentralized decision making Lower-level managers are empowered to make important decisions.

Experts on the subject warn against extremes of centralization or decentralization. The challenge is to achieve a workable balance between the two extremes. A management consultant recently put it this way:

> The modern organization in transition will recognize the pull of two polarities: a need for greater centralization to create low-cost shared resources; and, a need to improve market responsiveness with greater decentralization. Today's winning organizations are the ones that can handle the paradox and tensions of both pulls. These are the firms that analyze the optimum organizational solution in each particular circumstance, without prejudice

• **FIGURE 18–3** Characteristics of Mechanistic and Organic Organizations

Characteristic	Mechanistic Organization		Organic Organization
1. Task definition and knowledge required	Narrow; technical	⟶	Broad; general
2. Linkage between individual's contribution and organization's purpose	Vague or indirect	⟶	Clear or direct
3. Task flexibility	Rigid; routine	⟶	Flexible; varied
4. Specification of techniques, obligations, and rights	Specific	⟶	General
5. Degree of hierarchical control	High	⟶	Low (self-control emphasized)
6. Primary communication pattern	Top-down	⟶	Lateral (between peers)
7. Primary decision-making style	Authoritarian	⟶	Democratic; participative
8. Emphasis on obedience and loyalty	High	⟶	Low

Source: Adapted from discussion in T Burns and G M Stalker, *The Management of Innovation* (London: Tavistock, 1961), pp 119–25.

for one type of organization over another. The result is, almost invariably, a messy mixture of decentralized units sharing cost-effective centralized resources.[32]

Relevant Research Findings   When they classified a sample of actual companies as either mechanistic or organic, Burns and Stalker discovered one type was not superior to the other. Each type had its appropriate place, depending on the environment. When the environment was relatively *stable and certain,* the successful organizations tended to be *mechanistic. Organic* organizations tended to be the successful ones when the environment was *unstable and uncertain.*[33]

In a more recent study of 103 department managers from eight manufacturing firms and two aerospace organizations, managerial skill was found to have a greater impact on a global measure of department effectiveness in organic departments than in mechanistic departments. This led the researchers to recommend the following contingencies for management staffing and training:

> If we have two units, one organic and one mechanistic, and two potential applicants differing in overall managerial ability, we might want to assign the more competent to the organic unit since in that situation there are few structural aids available to the manager in performing required responsibilities. It is also possible that managerial training is especially needed by managers being groomed to take over units that are more organic in structure.[34]

Another interesting finding comes from a study of 42 voluntary church organizations. As the organizations became more mechanistic (more bureaucratic) the intrinsic motivation of their members decreased. Mechanistic organizations apparently undermined the volunteers' sense of freedom and self-determination. Additionally, the researchers believe their findings help explain why bureaucracy tends to feed on itself: "A mechanistic organizational structure may breed the need for a more extremely mechanistic system because of the reduction in intrinsically motivated behavior."[35] Thus, bureaucracy begets greater bureaucracy.

Most recently, field research in two factories, one mechanistic and the other organic, found expected communication patterns. Command-and-control (downward) communication characterized the mechanistic factory. Consultative or participative (two-way) communication prevailed in the organic factory.[36]

Both Mechanistic and Organic Structures Are Needed   Although achievement-oriented students of OB typically express a distaste for mechanistic organizations, not all organizations or subunits can or should be organic. For example, as mentioned earlier, McDonald's could not achieve its admired quality and service standards without extremely mechanistic restaurant operations. Imagine the food and service you would get if McDonald's employees used their own favorite ways of doing things and worked at their own pace! On the other hand, mechanistic structure alienates some employees because it erodes their sense of self-control.

Both contingency theories just discussed have one important thing in common. Each is based on an "environmental imperative," meaning the environment is said to be the primary determinant of effective organizational structure. Other organization theorists disagree. They contend that factors such as the organization's core technology, size, and corporate strategy hold the key to organizational structure. This section examines the significance of these three additional contingency variables.

THREE IMPORTANT CONTINGENCY VARIABLES: TECHNOLOGY, SIZE, AND STRATEGIC CHOICE

The Impact of Technology on Structure

Joan Woodward proposed a *technological imperative* in 1965 after studying 100 small manufacturing firms in southern England. She found distinctly different structural patterns for effective and ineffective companies based on technologies of low, medium, or high *complexity.* Effective organizations with either low- or high-complexity technology tended to have an organic structure. Effective organizations based on a technology of medium complexity tended to have a mechanistic structure. Woodward concluded that technology was the overriding determinant of organizational structure.[37]

Since Woodward's landmark work, many studies of the relationship between technology and structure have been conducted. Unfortunately, disagreement and confusion have prevailed. For example, a comprehensive review of 50 studies conducted between 1965 and 1980 found six technology concepts and 140 technology-structure relationships.[38] A statistical analysis of those studies prompted the following conclusions:

■ The more the technology requires *interdependence* between individuals and/or groups, the greater the need for integration (coordination).

■ "As technology moves from routine to nonroutine, subunits adopt less formalized and [less] centralized structures."[39]

Additional insights can be expected in this area as researchers coordinate their definitions of technology and refine their methodologies.[40]

Organizational Size and Performance

Size is an important structural variable subject to two schools of thought. According to the first school, economists have long extolled the virtues of economies of scale. This approach, often called the "bigger is better" model, assumes the per-unit cost of production decreases as the organization grows. In effect, bigger is said to be more efficient. For example, on an annual basis, General Motors supposedly can produce its 100,000th car less expensively than its 10th car.

The second school of thought pivots on the law of diminishing returns. Called the "small is beautiful" model,[41] this approach contends that oversized organizations and subunits tend to be plagued by costly behavioral problems. Large and impersonal organizations are said to breed apathy and alienation, with resulting problems such as turnover and absenteeism. Two strong advocates of this second approach are the authors of the best-selling *In Search of Excellence:*

> In the excellent companies, small *in almost every case* is beautiful. The small facility turns out to be the most efficient; its turned-on, motivated, highly productive worker, in communication (and competition) with his peers, outproduces the worker in the big facilities time and again. It holds for plants, for project teams, for divisions—for the entire company.[42]

Recent research suggests that when designing their organizations, managers should follow a middle ground between "bigger is better" and "small is beautiful" because both models have been oversold. Indeed, a newer perspective says *complexity,* not size, is the central issue.[43]

Research Insights   Researchers measure the size of organizations and organizational subunits in different ways. Some focus on financial indicators such as total sales or total asset value. Others look at the number of employees, transactions (such as the number of students in a school district), or capacity (such as the number of beds in a hospital). A meta-analysis[44] of 31 studies conducted between 1931 and 1985 that related organizational size to performance found:

- Larger organizations (in terms of assets) tended to be more productive (in terms of sales and profits).
- There were ''no positive relationships between organizational size and efficiency, suggesting the absence of net economy of scale effects.''[45]
- There were zero to slightly negative relationships between *subunit* size and productivity and efficiency.
- A more recent study examined the relationship between organizational size and employee turnover over a period of 65 months. Turnover was unrelated to organizational size.[46]

Striving for Small Units in Big Organizations   In summary, bigger is not necessarily better and small is not necessarily beautiful.[47] Hard-and-fast numbers regarding exactly how big is too big or how small is too small are difficult to come by. Management consultants offer some rough estimates (see Table 18–2). Until better evidence is available, the best that managers can do is monitor the productivity, quality, and efficiency of divisions, departments, and profit centers. Unwieldy and overly complex units need to be promptly broken into ones of more manageable size. The trick is to *create smallness within bigness*.[48] For example, Parker Hannifin, the Cleveland industrial valve and automobile parts maker, has developed this workable formula:

> [Parker Hannifin] is broken down into nearly 80 autonomous divisions, and although the company has 159 plants worldwide, most divisions operate only a few plants each. Small plants keep the company nonunion and allow managers to stay close to their customers, says [Chairman Patrick] Parker. ''Whenever we get more than 200 people in a plant, we like to move 50 miles down the road and start another,'' he says.[49]

Strategic Choice and Organizational Structure

In 1972, British sociologist John Child rejected the environmental imperative approach to organizational structure. He proposed a *strategic choice* model based on behavioral rather than rational economic principles.[50] Child believed structure

---

● ⟋ TABLE 18–2

Organizational Size: Management Consultants Address the Question of "How Big Is Too Big?"

Peter F Drucker, well-known management consultant:

> The real growth and innovation in this country has been in medium-size companies that employ between 200 and 4,000 workers. If you are in a small company, you are running all out. You have neither the time nor the energy to devote to anything but yesterday's crisis.
>
> A medium-sized company has the resources to devote to new products and markets, and it's still small enough to be flexible and move fast. And these companies now have what they once lacked—they've learned how to manage.

Thomas J Peters and Robert H Waterman, Jr., best-selling authors and management consultants:

> A rule of thumb starts to emerge. We find that the lion's share of the top performers keep their division size between $50 and $100 million, with a maximum of 1,000 or so employees each. Moreover, they grant their divisions extraordinary independence—and give them the functions and resources to exploit.

Source: Excerpted from J A Byrne, "Advice from the Dr. Spock of Business," *Business Week*, September 28, 1987, p 61; and T J Peters and R H Waterman, Jr., *In Search of Excellence* (New York: Harper & Row, 1982), pp 272–73.

resulted from a political process involving organizational power holders. According to the strategic choice model that has evolved from Child's work,[51] an organization's structure is determined largely by a dominant coalition of top-management strategists.[52]

A Strategic Choice Model   As Figure 18–4 illustrates, specific strategic choices or decisions reflect how the dominant coalition perceives environmental constraints and the organization's objectives. These strategic choices are tempered by the decision makers' personal beliefs, attitudes, values, and ethics.[53] For example, consider this unusual relationship between top management's ethics and corporate strategy, as recently reported by *Business Ethics* magazine:

> As a manufacturer and retailer of outdoor clothing and equipment, it's natural for Patagonia to be concerned about the environment. But as a for-profit business, it's also natural for the company to feel a need to look at its bottom line.
>
> Patagonia has found a way to do both, and to turn upside down traditional concepts of how companies grow in the bargain.
>
> The company first warned its customers of the impending change in its fall/winter catalog last year [1992]. "We are limiting Patagonia's growth in the United States with the eventual goal of halting growth altogether. We dropped 30 percent of our clothing line. . . .
>
> "What does this mean to you? Well, last fall you had a choice of five ski pants; now you may choose between two. This is, of course, unAmerican, but two styles of ski pants are all anyone needs."
>
> And this fall's [1993] catalog featured the following message: "At Patagonia, as a company, and as individuals, we sometimes find the array of choices dizzying. But the choices must be faced, resolved soberly, and judicious action taken. To fully include environmental concerns in our ordinary work is to give something back to the planet that

FIGURE 18~4   The Relationship between Strategic Choice and Organizational Structure

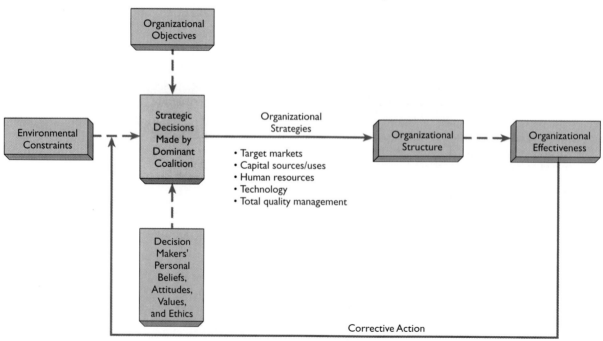

sustains us, and that we have taxed so heavily. It's a complex process, but the simplest of gifts.''

To that end, say Patagonia spokespeople Lu Setnicksa and Mike Harrelson, the company has embarked on an aggressive effort to examine everything from the materials it uses to produce its products, to which products it actually makes, to what kind of paper it uses in its copying machines.[54]

So far, a more efficient Patagonia has enjoyed increased profits, despite a decrease in sales revenue. Directing our attention once again to Figure 18–4, the organization is structured to accommodate its mix of strategies. Ultimately, corrective action is taken if organizational effectiveness criteria are not met.

Research and Practical Lessons   In a study of 97 small and mid-size companies in Quebec, Canada, strategy and organizational structure were found to be highly interdependent. Strategy influenced structure and structure influenced strategy. This was particularly true for larger, more innovative, and more successful firms.[55]

Strategic choice theory and research teaches managers at least two practical lessons. First, the environment is just one of many codeterminants of structure. Second, like any other administrative process, organization design is subject to the byplays of interpersonal power and politics.

**THE SHAPE OF
TOMORROW'S
ORGANIZATIONS**

Organizations are basically tools invented to get things done through collective action. As any carpenter or plumber knows, different jobs require different tools. So it is with organizations. When the situation changes significantly, according to contingency thinking, a different type of organization may be appropriate. The need for new organizations is greater than ever today because managers face revolutionary changes. *Fortune* magazine recently offered this perspective:

> We all sense that the changes surrounding us are not mere trends but the workings of large, unruly forces; the globalization of markets; the spread of information technology and computer networks; the dismantling of hierarchy, the structure that has essentially organized work since the mid-19th century. Growing up around these is a new, information-age economy, whose fundamental sources of wealth are knowledge and communication rather than natural resources and physical labor.[56]

What sorts of organizations will prosper in the information-age economy? Will they be adaptations of the traditional pyramid-shaped organization? Or will they be radically different? Let us put our imaginations to work by envisioning the shape of tomorrow's organizations.

New-Style versus Old-Style Organizations

Organization theorists Jay R Galbraith and Edward E Lawler III have called for a ''new logic of organizing.''[57] They recommend a whole new set of adjectives to describe organizations (see Table 18–3). Traditional pyramid-shaped organizations, conforming to the old-style pattern, tend to be too slow and inflexible today. Leaner, more organic organizations are needed to accommodate today's strategic balancing act between cost, quality, and speed.[58] These new-style organizations will embrace the total quality management (TQM) principles discussed in Chapter 1. This means they will be customer focused, dedicated to continuous improvement

● TABLE 18~3
Profiles of the New-Style
and Old-Style Organizations

New	Old
Dynamic, learning	Stable
Information rich	Information is scarce
Global	Local
Small and large	Large
Product/customer oriented	Functional
Skills oriented	Job oriented
Team oriented	Individual oriented
Involvement oriented	Command/control oriented
Lateral/networked	Hierarchical
Customer oriented	Job requirements oriented

Source: J R Galbraith and E E Lawler III, "Effective Organizations: Using the New Logic of Organizing," in *Organizing for the Future: The New Logic for Managing Complex Organizations,* eds J R Galbraith, E E Lawler III, and Associates (San Francisco; Jossey-Bass, 1993), p 298.

and learning, and structured around teams. These qualities, along with computerized information technology, hopefully will enable big organizations to mimic the speed and flexibility of small organizations.[59]

Three New Organizational Patterns

Figure 18–5 illustrates three radical departures from the traditional pyramid-shaped organization. Each is the logical result of various trends that are evident today. In other words, we have exaggerated these new organizations for instructional purposes. You will likely encounter various combinations of these pure types in the years ahead. Let us imagine life in the organizations of tomorrow.[60] (Importantly, these characterizations are not intended to be final answers. We simply seek to stimulate thoughtful debate.)

Hourglass Organizations   This pattern gets its name from the organization's pinched middle. Thanks to modern information technology, a relatively small executive group will be able to coordinate the efforts of numerous operating personnel who make goods or render services.[61] Multiple and broad layers of middle managers who served as conduits for information in old-style organizations will be unnecessary in hourglass organizations. Competition for promotions among operating personnel will be intense because of the restricted hierarchy. Lateral transfers will be more common. Management will compensate for the lack of promotion opportunities with job rotation, skill training, and pay-for-performance. What few middle managers there are will be cross-functional problem solvers who also possess a number of technical skills. The potential for alienation between the executive elite and those at the base of the hourglass will be great, thus giving labor unions an excellent growth opportunity.

Cluster Organizations   Teams will be the primary structural unit here. In addition to a strategic executive team, there will be overlapping teams of technical and operating personnel. Reengineering will give the cluster organization a distinctive horizontal rather than vertical orientation.[62] In other words, old-style functional departments such as manufacturing and sales will give way to cross-functional

The Hourglass Organization   **The Cluster Organization**   **The Network Organization**

• ➤ FIGURE 18-5
The Shape of Tomorrow's
Organizations

teams that translate customer needs into promptly delivered products and/or services. Training in both technical and teamwork skills will be a top priority. Multiskilled employees at all levels will find themselves working on different teams and various projects during the year. Constant change will take its toll in terms of interpersonal conflict and personal stress. Skill-based pay will supplement pay-for-performance.

Network Organizations   Actually, this configuration will be a fluid family of several interdependent organizations. Tasks commonly performed by employees in old-style organizations—including, but not limited to, product design, manufacturing, human resource management, training, accounting, data processing, packaging, warehousing, and delivery—will be contracted out to other companies. At the center of the network will be an entrepreneurial individual or team and a small, comparatively low-paid clerical staff. Conflict between these ''haves'' and ''have nots'' will be constant, thus leading to high turnover among the clerical staff. Telephones, fax machines, computer networks, overnight delivery services, and contract lawyers will be crucial linking resources in these so-called ''virtual corporations.''[63] Independent contractors will belong to many different network organizations. The length of their membership in a given network will be determined by their performance. Working conditions at some of the small contractors will make them little more than information-age sweatshops. Companies living from one contract to another will offer little in the way of job security. Network companies will employ a wide variety of compensation plans, ranging from very generous to very unfair. Opportunities to start new businesses will be numerous.[64]

BACK TO THE OPENING CASE

Now that you have read Chapter 18, you should be able to answer the following questions about the Hewlett-Packard case:

1. What did this case teach you about organizational life cycles and decline? Explain.

2. Why do you suppose HP became a centralized and bureaucratic company before the founders stepped in to correct things?

3. Did William Hewlett and David Packard make HP a more organic or more mechanistic company? Explain, using Figure 18-3 as a guide.

4. Could HP's renewed emphasis on decentralization be carried too far? Explain.

Summary of Key Concepts

1. *Identify and briefly explain the three stages of the organizational life cycle.* They are inception (small, informal, entrepreneurial), high-growth (centralized, formal, and large and growing), and maturity (decentralized, formal, slowing growth).

2. *Discuss organizational decline relative to the organizational life cycle.* Decline is an ever-present threat during the organizational life cycle, with complacency during periods of success particularly troublesome. A culture of continuous improvement can avoid organizational decline.

3. *Explain what the contingency approach to organization design involves.* The contingency approach to organization design calls for fitting the organization to the demands of the situation. Environmental uncertainty can be assessed in terms of various combinations of two dimensions: (1) simple or complex and (2) static or dynamic.

4. *Describe the relationship between differentiation and integration in effective organizations.* Harvard researchers Lawrence and Lorsch found that successful organizations achieved a proper balance between the two opposing structural forces of differentiation and integration. Differentiation forces the organization apart. Through a variety of mechanisms—including hierarchy, rules, teams, and liaisons—integration draws the organization together.

5. *Discuss Burns and Stalker's findings regarding mechanistic and organic organizations.* British researchers Burns and Stalker found that mechanistic (bureaucratic, centralized) organizations tended to be effective in stable situations. In unstable situations, organic (flexible, decentralized) organizations were more effective. These findings underscored the need for a contingency approach to organization design.

6. *Define and briefly explain the practical significance of centralization and decentralization.* Because key decisions are made at the top of centralized organizations, they tend to be tightly controlled. In decentralized organizations, employees at lower levels are empowered to make important decisions. Contingency design calls for a proper balance.

7. *Discuss the effective management of organizational size.* Regarding the optimum size for organizations, the challenge for today's managers is to achieve smallness within bigness by keeping subunits at a manageable size.

8. *Distinguish among hourglass, cluster, and network organizations.* Hourglass organizations have a small executive level, a short and narrow middle-management level (because information technology links the top and bottom levels), and a broad base of operating personnel. The primary productive units in cluster organizations are overlapping teams. Network organizations actually are families of interdependent companies. They are contractual and fluid in nature.

Discussion Questions

1. Why is it instructive to view organizations from a life-cycle perspective?

2. Which phase of the organizational life-cycle—inception, high-growth, maturity—do you think would be the most difficult for management?

3. How does decline relate to organizational life cycles?

4. Why is it important to focus on the role of complacency in organizational decline?

5. In a nutshell, what does contingency organization design entail?

6. What evidence of integration can you find in your present (or last) place of employment?

7. What is wrong with an organization having too much differentiation and too little integration?

8. If organic organizations are popular with most employees, why can't all organizations be structured in an organic fashion?

9. How can you tell if an organization (or subunit) is too big?

10. Which of the three new organizational configurations probably will be most prevalent 10 to 15 years from now? Why?

EXERCISE

Objectives

1. To get out into the field and talk to a practicing manager about organizational structure.
2. To increase your understanding of the important distinction between mechanistic and organic organizations.
3. To broaden your knowledge of contingency design, in terms of organization-environment fit.

Introduction

A good way to test the validity of what you have just read about organizational design is to interview a practicing manager. (Note: If you are a manager, simply complete the questionnaire yourself.)

Instructions

Your objective is to interview a manager about aspects of organizational structure, environmental uncertainty, and organizational effectiveness. A *manager* is defined as anyone who supervises other people in an organizational set-ting. The organization may be small or large and for-profit or not-for-profit. Higher-level managers are preferred, but middle managers and first-line supervisors are acceptable. If you interview a lower-level manager, be sure to remind him or her that you want a description of the overall organization, not just an isolated subunit. Your interview will center on the adaptation of Figure 18–3, as discussed below.

When conducting your interview, be sure to explain to the manager what you are trying to accomplish. But assure the manager that his or her name will not be mentioned in class discussion or any written projects. Try to keep side notes during the interview for later reference.

Questionnaire

The following questionnaire, adapted from Figure 18–3, will help you determine if the manager's organization is relatively mechanistic or relatively organic in structure. Note: For items 1 and 2 on the following questionnaire, have the manager respond in terms of the average non-managerial employee. (Circle one number for each item.)

Characteristic

1.	Task definition and knowledge required	Narrow; technical	1—2—3—4—5—6—7	Broad; general
2.	Linkage between individual's contribution and organization's purpose	Vague or indirect	1—2—3—4—5—6—7	Clear or direct
3.	Task flexibility	Rigid; routine	1—2—3—4—5—6—7	Flexible; varied
4.	Specification of techniques, obligations, and rights	Specific	1—2—3—4—5—6—7	General
5.	Degree of hierarchical control	High	1—2—3—4—5—6—7	Low (self-control emphasized)
6.	Primary communication pattern	Top-down	1—2—3—4—5—6—7	Lateral (between peers)
7.	Primary decision-making style	Authoritarian	1—2—3—4—5—6—7	Democratic; participative
8.	Emphasis on obedience and loyalty	High	1—2—3—4—5—6—7	Low

Total score=

Additional question about the organization's environment:

This organization faces an environment that is (circle one number):

Stable and certain 1—2—3—4—5—6—7—8—9—10 Unstable and uncertain

Additional questions about the organization's effectiveness:

a. Profitability (if a profit-seeking business):
Low 1—2—3—4—5—6—7—8—9—10 High

b. Degree of organizational goal accomplishment:
   Low   1—2—3—4—5—6—7—8—9—10   High
c. Customer or client satisfaction:
   Low   1—2—3—4—5—6—7—8—9—10   High
d. Employee satisfaction:
   Low   1—2—3—4—5—6—7—8—9—10   High

Total effectiveness score =
(Add responses from above)

Questions for Consideration/ Class Discussion

1. Using the following norms, was the manager's organization relatively mechanistic or organic?

8–24 = Relatively mechanistic
25–39 = Mixed
40–56 = Relatively organic

2. In terms of Burns and Stalker's contingency theory, does the manager's organization seem to fit its environment? Explain.

3. Does the organization's degree of effectiveness reflect how well it fits its environment? Explain.

NOTES

[1] R W Keidel, "Triangular Design: A New Organizational Geometry," *Academy of Management Executive,* November 1990, p 35.

[2] For instructive background and examples, see T A Stewart, "Welcome to the Revolution," *Fortune,* December 13, 1993, pp 66–77.

[3] R E Quinn and K Cameron, "Organizational Life Cycles and Shifting Criteria of Effectiveness: Some Preliminary Evidence," *Management Science,* January 1983, p 40.

[4] Ten organizational life-cycle models are reviewed in Ibid., pp 34–41. Also see R K Kazanjian and R Drazin, "A Stage-Contingent Model of Design and Growth for Technology-Based New Ventures," *Journal of Business Venturing,* 1990, pp 137–50; R Drazin and R K Kazanjian, "A Reanalysis of Miller and Friesen's Life Cycle Data," *Strategic Management Journal,* May–June 1990, pp 319–25; and A C Bluedorn, "Pilgrim's Progress: Trends and Convergence in Research on Organizational Size and Environments," *Journal of Management,* Summer 1993, pp 163–91.

[5] R Brandt, "Don Kingsborough's Latest World of Wonder," *Business Week,* June 11, 1990, p 23.

[6] R A Cosier and D R Dalton, "Search for Excellence, Learn from Japan—Are These Panaceas or Problems?" *Business Horizons,* November–December 1986, p 67.

[7] R A Mamis and S Pearlstein, " '1-2-3' Creator Mitch Kapor," *Inc.,* January 1987, p 31. (Kapor retained a seat on Lotus's board of directors and 1.6 million shares of the firm's stock.)

[8] A good collection of entrepreneur profiles can be found in C Burck, "The Real World of the Entrepreneur," *Fortune,* April 5, 1993, pp 62–81.

[9] Data from J Aley, "Debunking the Failure Fallacy," *Fortune,* September 6, 1993, p 21.

[10] P Lorange and R T Nelson, "How to Recognize—and Avoid—Organizational Decline," *Sloan Management Review,* Spring 1987, p 47.

[11] Excerpted from Ibid., pp 43–45.

[12] For details, see K S Cameron, M U Kim, and D A Whetten, "Organizational Effects of Decline and Turbulence," *Administrative Science Quarterly,* June 1987, pp 222–40.

[13] Twelve dysfunctional consequences of decline are discussed and empirically tested in K S Cameron, D A Whetten, and M U Kim, "Organizational Dysfunctions of Decline," *Academy of Management Journal,* March 1987, pp 126–38.

[14] Additional scholarly treatment of organizational decline can be found in R I Sutton and T D'Aunno, "Decreasing Organizational Size: Untangling the Effects of Money and People," *Academy of Management Review,* April 1989, pp 194–212; and R I Sutton, "Organizational Decline Processes: A Social Psychological Perspective," in *Research in Organizational Behavior,* vol. 12, eds B M Staw and L L Cummings (Greenwich, CT: JAI Press, 1990), pp 205–54.

[15] A culture of "entitlement" also hastens organizational decline. See J M Bardwick, *Danger in the Comfort Zone: From Boardroom to Mailroom—How to Break the Entitlement Habit That's Killing American Business* (New York: AMACOM, 1991).

[16] J Greenwald, "Are America's Corporate Giants a Dying Breed?" *Time,* December 28, 1992, p 28. Procter & Gamble's fight against decline is discussed in B Saporito, "Behind the Tumult at P&G," *Fortune,* March 7, 1994, pp 74–82.

[17] Based on K G Smith, T R Mitchell, and C E Summer, "Top Level Management Priorities in Different Stages of

the Organizational Life Cycle," *Academy of Management Journal,* December 1985, pp 799–820.

[18] Additional details may be found in Quinn and Cameron, "Organizational Life Cycles and Shifting Criteria of Effectiveness: Some Preliminary Evidence," pp 33–51.

[19] For an instructive conceptual model of the relationship between organizational politics, strategy, and organizational life cycles, see B Gray and S S Ariss, "Politics and Strategic Change across Organizational Life Cycles," *Academy of Management Review,* October 1985, pp 707–23. Practical advice regarding the organizational life cycle can be found in J Mayers, "How to Withstand a Merger," *Management Review,* October 1986, pp 39–42; and B G Posner and B Burlingham, "Getting to Prime," *Inc.,* January 1991, pp 27–33.

[20] See K Kerwin, "Can Jack Smith Fix GM?" *Business Week,* November 1, 1993, pp 126–31; R Henkoff, "Getting Beyond Downsizing," *Fortune,* January 10, 1994, pp 58–64; M Magnet, "Let's Go for Growth," *Fortune,* March 7, 1994, pp 60–72; and I Sager, "Lou Gerstner Unveils His Battle Plan," *Business Week,* April 4, 1994, pp 96–98.

[21] For updates, see J M Pennings, "Structural Contingency Theory: A Reappraisal," *Research in Organizational Behavior* (Greenwich, CT: JAI Press, 1992), vol. 14, pp 267–309; A D Meyer, A S Tsui, and C R Hinings, "Configurational Approaches to Organizational Analysis," *Academy of Management Journal,* December 1993, pp 1175–95; and D H Doty, W H Glick, and G P Huber, "Fit, Equifinality, and Organizational Effectiveness: A Test of Two Configurational Theories," *Academy of Management Journal,* December 1993, pp 1196–1250.

[22] An interesting distinction between three types of environmental uncertainty can be found in F J Milliken, "Three Types of Perceived Uncertainty about the Environment: State, Effect, and Response Uncertainty," *Academy of Management Review,* January 1987, pp 133–43.

[23] R Duncan, "What Is the Right Organization Structure?" *Organizational Dynamics,* Winter 1979, p 63.

[24] Ibid.

[25] See J Huey, "The World's Best Brand," *Fortune,* May 31, 1993, pp 44–54; and M T Moore, "Coke Spins Bottle for Classic Look," *USA Today,* March 28, 1994, pp 1B–2B.

[26] P R Lawrence and J W Lorsch, *Organization and Environment* (Homewood, IL: Richard D. Irwin, 1967), p 157.

[27] Pooled, sequential, and reciprocal integration are discussed in J W Lorsch, "Organization Design: A Situational Perspective," *Organizational Dynamics,* Autumn 1977, pp 2–14. Also see J E Ettlie and E M Reza, "Organizational Integration and Process Innovation," *Academy of Management Journal,* October 1992, pp 795–827.

[28] See R Mitchell, "Masters of Innovation," *Business Week,* April 10, 1989, pp 58–63; and B Dumaine, "Ability to Innovate," *Fortune,* January 29, 1990, pp 43, 46.

[29] K Deveny, "Bag Those Fries, Squirt That Ketchup, Fry That Fish," *Business Week,* October 13, 1986, p 86.

[30] See J Huey, "The New Post-Heroic Leadership," *Fortune,* February 21, 1994, pp 42–50; and F Shipper and C C Manz, "Employee Self-Management without Formally Designated Teams: An Alternative Road to Empowerment," *Organizational Dynamics,* Winter 1992, pp 48–61.

[31] See G P Huber, C C Miller, and W H Glick, "Developing More Encompassing Theories about Organizations: The Centralization-Effectiveness Relationship as an Example," *Organization Science,* no. 1, 1990, pp 11–40; and C Handy, "Balancing Corporate Power: A New Federalist Paper," *Harvard Business Review,* November–December 1992, pp 59–72.

[32] P Kaestle, "A New Rationale for Organizational Structure," *Planning Review,* July–August 1990, p 22.

[33] Details of this study can be found in T Burns and G M Stalker, *The Management of Innovation* (London: Tavistock, 1961).

[34] D J Gillen and S J Carroll, "Relationship of Managerial Ability to Unit Effectiveness in More Organic versus More Mechanistic Departments," *Journal of Management Studies,* November 1985, pp 674–75.

[35] J D Sherman and H L Smith, "The Influence of Organizational Structure on Intrinsic versus Extrinsic Motivation," *Academy of Management Journal,* December 1984, p 883.

[36] See J A Courtright, G T Fairhurst, and L E Rogers, "Interaction Patterns in Organic and Mechanistic Systems," *Academy of Management Journal,* December 1989, pp 773–802.

[37] See J Woodward, *Industrial Organization: Theory and Practice* (London: Oxford University Press, 1965); and P D Collins and F Hull, "Technology and Span of Control: Woodward Revisited," *Journal of Management Studies,* March 1986, pp 143–64.

[38] See L W Fry, "Technology-Structure Research: Three Critical Issues," *Academy of Management Journal,* September 1982, pp 532–52.

[39] Ibid., p 548.

[40] For example, see J W Alexander and B Mark, "Technology and Structure of Nursing Organizations," *Nursing & Health Care,* April 1990, pp 194–99; and C C Miller, W H Glick, Y-D Wang, and G P Huber, "Understanding Technology-Structure Relationships: Theory Development and Meta-Analytic Theory Testing," *Academy of Management Journal,* June 1991, pp 370–99.

[41] The phrase "small is beautiful" was coined by the late

British economist E F Schumacher. See E F Schumacher, *Small Is Beautiful: Economics as If People Mattered* (New York: Harper & Row, 1973).

[42] T J Peters and R H Waterman, Jr., *In Search of Excellence* (New York: Harper & Row, 1982), p 321. Also see T Peters, "Rethinking Scale," *California Management Review,* Fall 1992, pp 7–29.

[43] See, for example, J A Byrne, "Is Your Company Too Big?" *Business Week,* March 27, 1989, pp 84–94; and W McKinley, "Decreasing Organizational Size: To Untangle or Not to Untangle?" *Academy of Management Review,* January 1992, pp 112–23.

[44] R Z Gooding and J A Wagner III, "A Meta-Analytic Review of the Relationship between Size and Performance: The Productivity and Efficiency of Organizations and Their Subunits," *Administrative Science Quarterly,* December 1985, pp 462–81.

[45] Ibid., p 477.

[46] Results are presented in P G Benson, T L Dickinson, and C O Neidt, "The Relationship between Organizational Size and Turnover: A Longitudinal Investigation," *Human Relations,* January 1987, pp 15–30. Also see M Yasai-Ardekani, "Effects of Environmental Scarcity and Munificence on the Relationship of Context to Organizational Structure," *Academy of Management Journal,* March 1989, pp 131–56.

[47] The comparative advantages of large and small companies are presented in J O'Toole and W Bennis, "Our Federalist Future: The Leadership Imperative," *California Management Review,* Summer 1992, pp 73–90.

[48] See V Sathe, "Fostering Entrepreneurship in the Large, Diversified Firm," *Organizational Dynamics,* Summer 1989, pp 20–32; J R Galbraith and E E Lawler III, "Effective Organizations: Using the New Logic of Organizing," in *Organizing for the Future: The New Logic for Managing Complex Organizations,* eds J R Galbraith, E E Lawler III, and Associates (San Francisco: Jossey-Bass, 1993), pp 290–92; and J Kim, "Welch Thinks Small, Acts Big," *USA Today,* February 26, 1993, p 2B.

[49] C Palmeri, "A Process That Never Ends," *Forbes,* December 21, 1992, p 55.

[50] See J Child, "Organizational Structure, Environment and Performance: The Role of Strategic Choice," *Sociology,* January 1972, pp 1–22.

[51] See J Galbraith, *Organization Design* (Reading, MA: Addison-Wesley Publishing, 1977); J R Montanari, "Managerial Discretion: An Expanded Model of Organization Choice," *Academy of Management Review,* April 1978, pp 231–41; and H R Bobbitt, Jr., and J D Ford, "Decision-Maker Choice as a Determinant of Organizational Structure," *Academy of Management Review,* January 1980, pp 13–23.

[52] For an alternative model of strategy making, see S L Hart, "An Integrative Framework for Strategy-Making Processes," *Academy of Management Review,* April 1992, pp 327–51. Also see F E Harrison and M A Pelletier, "A Typology of Strategic Choice," *Technological Forecasting and Social Change,* November 1993, pp 245–63; and H Mintzberg, "The Rise and Fall of Strategic Planning," *Harvard Business Review,* January–February 1994, pp 107–14.

[53] See A Bhide, "How Entrepreneurs Craft Strategies That Work," *Harvard Business Review,* March–April 1994, pp 150–61.

[54] S Perlstein, "Less Is More," *Business Ethics,* September–October 1993, p 15. Excerpted with permission from *Business Ethics* Magazine, Minneapolis, MN.

[55] Details may be found in D Miller, "Strategy Making and Structure: Analysis and Implications for Performance," *Academy of Management Journal,* March 1987, pp 7–32. Also see J B Thomas and R R McDaniel, Jr., "Interpreting Strategic Issues: Effects of Strategy and the Information-Processing Structure of Top Management Teams," *Academy of Management Journal,* June 1990, pp 286–306. Contrary evidence is presented in M I A At-Twaijri and J R Montanari, "The Impact of Context and Choice on the Boundary-Spanning Process: An Empirical Extension," *Human Relations,* December 1987, pp 783–98. A related study is reported in W Q Judge, Jr., and C P Zeithaml, "Institutional and Strategic Choice Perspectives on Board Involvement in the Strategic Decision Process," *Academy of Management Journal,* October 1992, pp 766–94.

[56] T A Stewart, "Welcome to the Revolution," *Fortune,* December 13, 1993, p 66.

[57] See Galbraith and Lawler, "Effective Organizations: Using the New Logic of Organizing," pp 285–99.

[58] See J P Womack and D T Jones, "From Lean Production to the Lean Enterprise," *Harvard Business Review,* March–April 1994, pp 93–103.

[59] See H Bahrami, "The Emerging Flexible Organization: Perspectives from Silicon Valley," *California Management Review,* Summer 1992, pp 33–52.

[60] For a parallel discussion, see W Kiechel III, "How We Will Work in the Year 2000," *Fortune,* May 17, 1993, pp 38–52.

[61] For related discussion, see B Filipczak, "The Ripple Effect of Computer Networking," *Training,* March 1994, pp 40–47.

62 Based on discussion in T A Stewart, "The Search for the Organization of Tomorrow," *Fortune,* May 18, 1992, pp 92–98; T A Stewart, "Reengineering: The Hot New Managing Tool," *Fortune,* August 23, 1993, pp 40–48; and G Hall, J Rosenthal, and J Wade, "How to Make Reengineering *Really* Work," *Harvard Business Review,* November–December 1993, pp 119–31.

63 See J A Byrne, "The Virtual Corporation," *Business Week,* February 8, 1993, pp 98–102.

64 For more on network organizations, see C C Snow, R E Miles, and H J Coleman, Jr., "Managing 21st Century Network Organizations," *Organizational Dynamics,* Winter 1992, pp 5–20; and P Smith Ring and A H Van De Ven, "Developmental Processes of Cooperative Interorganizational Relationships, *Academy of Management Review,* January 1994, pp 90–118.

ORGANIZATIONAL CULTURE

Learning OBJECTIVES

When you finish studying the material in this chapter, you should be able to:

1. Define the term *organizational culture*.
2. Describe the manifestation of an organization's culture and the four functions of organizational culture.
3. Summarize research on organizational culture.
4. Highlight the three perspectives that explain the type of cultures that enhance an organization's long-term financial performance.
5. Discuss the process of developing an adaptive culture.
6. Describe the HOME model for developing an organization's culture.
7. Describe the three phases in Feldman's model of organizational socialization.
8. Discuss the two basic functions of mentoring.
9. Summarize the phases of mentoring.

OPENING CASE

Levi Strauss Is Developing a High Performance Culture

Sharon Hoogstraten

Before you learn anything about Levi Strauss, however, you have to learn about its new vision. In 1987, the senior management team at the company designed a new pattern of values for the company in the form of a *new mission statement.*

The senior group didn't leave it at that. It also designed a set of ideals by which the management team and employees could weave that mission into the organization—in the form of an aspiration statement. (See "Aspiration Statement," shown at the end of this case.)

These two guiding principles have

become more than just words on paper. They are the ideals by which every operation, department and employee is measured. They also are the way in which the company has made everyone in the organization a partner in its success. . . .

That focus is apparent when you look closely at the kinds of programs that have come out of the HR [human resources] department at Levi's recently, namely, such programs as domestic partner benefits, a flexible work-hours program for all employees (including production-line workers— something virtually unheard-of in the apparel industry) and a child care voucher program. Individually, each of these innovations is worthy of special notice, but to HR leaders at Levi's, they're just by-products of a larger corporate strategy: Levi's aspiration statement.

Although Goya [Donna Goya is senior vice-president of HR] provides focus for her team, she gives each department the freedom to scrutinize their own areas to ensure that they're in alignment with the aspirations statement. Many changes now are made

using employee input through task forces. Each task force has a sponsor from senior management to ensure employee interaction and to support its work. Task forces usually are broad-based in terms of functions, grade levels and locations. The company pays for employees from field locations to fly to the home office to participate in the meetings. . . .

For example, a new compensation plan for salaried employees called *Partners in Performance,* (formerly called *Remuneration 2000* or *Rem 2000*) has been developed to evaluate and reward individuals for performance that reflects *aspirational* behavior and supports the aspirational performance of others.

"The Partners in Performance task force was brought together in response to employees' concerns," says Cathy Unruh, director of compensation, who has been at Levi's for nine years. "The employees raised their concerns and issues about the management pay and performance program during the leadership week. They said that it didn't align well with the aspiration statement and the direction of the

Much has been written and said about organizational or corporate cultures in recent years. The results of this activity can be arranged on a continuum of academic rigor. At the low end of the continuum are simplistic typologies and exaggerated claims about the benefits of imitating Japanese-style corporate cultures. Here the term *corporate culture* is little more than a pop psychology buzzword. At the other end of the continuum is a growing body of theory and research with valuable insights but plagued by definitional and measurement inconsistencies.[1] By systematically sifting this diverse collection of material, we find that an understanding of organizational culture is central to learning how to manage people at work in both domestic and international operations.

This chapter will help you better understand how managers can use organizational culture as a competitive advantage. We discuss (1) the foundation of organizational culture, (2) the development of a high-performance culture, (3) the organization socialization process, and (4) the role of mentoring in socialization.

(continued)

company." It was clear from those encounters that employees saw the previous compensation plan as traditional and focusing on a hierarchical boss-subordinate structure, rather than on that of an empowered work force.

A task force of approximately 100 employees from all functional areas met in 1990 to discuss the issue. The group's recommendations were approved by the board of directors in November 1991. Unruh's department is in the process of training employees to use the new system, which she's hoping to roll out to the work force in a year or two. . . .

The program is designed to open the lines of communication between bosses and employees, and bases pay on how well those goals and other job objectives are met. "It isn't just paying for coming to work anymore," says Unruh. "You have to be a contributor; you have to make a difference and be accountable, and in a way that models the company's aspirations. It isn't just

what you get done, it's also how you do it. The Partners in Performance plan will make that a reality." . . .

The new philosophical direction of the organization is communicated to every employee through an ongoing series of classes called *core curriculum.*

The training began in 1989. "We're still at it," says Goya, "and will be for a long time to come."

Every employee participates in these classes, usually on-site at the facility in which they work. Senior managers from Levi's many facilities come to a retreat center in the local Santa Cruz Mountains near San Francisco for a week of training that centers on the aspiration statement.

Such subjects as valuing diversity, leadership and ethics are the topics of discussion. Also up for discussion for participants is determining what the barriers are that prevent Levi Strauss from achieving real diversity and having everybody take leadership roles, or from being an ethical company.

After the senior managers return to their business units, Levi's provides consulting assistance to help them train their local work forces. This training helps these employees think about what they can bring to the organization as leaders. "They talk about not waiting for people at the top to come up with the answers," says Goya.

"First of all, the people at the top don't have the answers—that's a good reason not to sit around and wait for the tablets and answers to come from on high. Individuals can start with themselves in trying to make a difference. They need to decide what that difference is, what they can do in their own work environments and how they can take a greater role in leadership," Goya says. "We used to have management making these dictates and then sitting back and wondering why nothing changed—It was because we didn't give people a reason to want to make the changes," she adds. . . .

Aspiration Statement

We all want a Company that our people are proud of and committed to, where all employees have an opportunity to contribute, learn, grow and advance based on merit, not politics or background. We want our

---

FOUNDATION OF ORGANIZATIONAL CULTURE

organizational culture
Social glue that binds organizational members together.

Organizational culture is the social glue that binds members of the organization together. Organizational culture operates on two levels, which vary in terms of outward visibility and resistance to change.[2] At the less visible level, culture reflects the values shared among organizational members. These values tend to persist over time and are more resistant to change. Consider the values George Fisher, the new CEO at Eastman Kodak Company, is up against as he tries to change Kodak's culture:

> Kodak is far too inbred in its Rochester (N.Y.) base. Most high-level executives are lifers. . . . Kodak's organization lacks clear lines of authority. It's rife with petty fiefdoms, and rarely is anyone held responsible when things go wrong.[3]

OPENING CASE

(concluded)

people to feel respected, treated fairly, listened to and involved. Above all, we want satisfaction from accomplishments and friendships, balanced personal and professional lives, and to have fun in our endeavors.

When we describe the kind of LS&CO. we want in the future, what we are talking about is building on the foundation we have inherited: affirming the best of our Company's traditions, closing gaps that may exist between principles and practices, and updating some of our values to reflect contemporary circumstances.

What Type of Leadership Is Necessary To Make Our Aspirations a Reality?

New Behaviors: Leadership that exemplifies directness, openness to influence, commitment to the success of others, willingness to acknowledge our own contributions to problems, personal accountability, teamwork and trust. Not only must we model these behaviors, but we must coach others to adopt them.

Diversity: Leadership that values a diverse work force (age, sex, ethnic group, etc.) at all levels of the organization, diversity in experience, and a diversity in perspectives. We have committed to taking full advantage of the rich backgrounds and abilities of all our people and to promote a greater diversity in positions of influence. Differing points of view will be sought; diversity will be valued and honesty rewarded, not suppressed.

Recognition: Leadership that provides greater recognition—both financial and psychic—for individuals and teams that contribute to our success. Recognition must be given to all who contribute; those who create and innovate and also those who continually support the day-to-day business requirements.

Ethical Management Practices: Leadership that epitomizes the stated standards of ethical behavior. We must provide clarity about our expectations and must enforce these standards through the corporation.

Communications: Leadership that is clear about Company, unit, and individual goals and performance. People must know what is expected of them and receive timely, honest feedback on their performance and career aspirations.

Empowerment: Leadership that increases the authority and responsibility of those closest to our products and customers. By actively pushing responsibility, trust and recognition into the organization, we can harness and release the capabilities of all our people.

For Discussion

Would you like to work at Levi Strauss? Explain.

■ Additional discussion questions linking this case with the following material appear at the end of this chapter.

Source: Excerpted with permission from J J Laabs, "HR's Vital Role at Levi Strauss," *Personnel Journal*, December 1992, pp 34–46.

Fisher will surely encounter resistance as he tries to hold operating managers more accountable for their performance. At the more visible level, culture represents the normative behavior patterns accepted by organizational members. These patterns are passed on to others through the socialization process. Culture is more susceptible to change at this level.

Each level of culture influences the other. For example, if a company truly values providing high-quality service, employees are more likely to adopt the behavior of responding faster to customer complaints. Similarly, causality can flow in the other direction. Employees can come to value high-quality service based on their experiences as they interact with customers.

To gain a better understanding of how organizational culture is formed and used by employees, this section reviews the manifestations of organizational culture, the four functions of organizational culture, and research on organizational cultures.

Manifestations of Organizational Culture

When is an organization's culture most apparent? According to one observer, cultural assumptions assert themselves through socialization of new employees, subculture clashes, and top management behavior.[4] Consider these three situations, for example: A newcomer who shows up late for an important meeting is told a story about someone who was fired for repeated tardiness. Conflict between product design engineers who emphasize a product's function and marketing specialists who demand a more stylish product reveals an underlying clash of subculture values. Top managers, through the behavior they model and the administrative and reward systems they create, prompt a significant improvement in the quality of a company's products.

A Model for Interpreting Organizational Culture A useful model for observing and interpreting organizational culture was developed by a Harvard researcher (see Figure 19–1). Four general manifestations or evidence of organizational culture in his model are shared things (objects), shared sayings (talk), shared doings (behavior), and shared feelings (emotion). One can begin collecting cultural information within the organization by asking, observing, reading, and feeling. However, a more detailed analysis is required to capture the essence of an organization's culture. We need to supplement the foregoing model with a more extensive list of cultural manifestations.

A Closer Look Organizational culture expresses itself in a rich variety of ways. For example, a comprehensive list of cultural manifestations and definitions is presented in Table 19–1. We now see why culture expert Edgar Schein has called organizational culture ''a deep phenomenon.''[5] Missing from the list in Table 19–1 are values and organizational heroes, both worthy of mention. The instrumental and terminal values discussed in Chapter 4 become culturally embedded through group or organizational consensus. American Express, for example, published a list of six American Express corporate values. This list, which is imparted during the socialization process for all new employees and is widely reinforced throughout the organization, includes the following corporate values:

1. Placing the interests of clients and customers first.
2. A continuous quest for quality in everything we do.
3. Treating our people with respect and dignity.
4. Conduct that reflects the highest standards of integrity.
5. Teamwork—from the smallest unit to the enterprise as a whole.
6. Being good citizens in the communities in which we live and work.

Johnson & Johnson also has formally documented its cherished corporate values and ideals, as conceived over four decades ago by the founder's son. The resulting Credo has helped J&J become a role model for corporate ethics.

> The Credo stresses honesty, integrity, and putting people before profits—phrases common to most such documents. What's unusual is the amount of energy J&J's high executives devote to ensuring that employees live by those words. Every few years, in a

• ⟍⟶ FIGURE 19~1 A Model for Observing and Interpreting General Manifestations of Organizational Culture

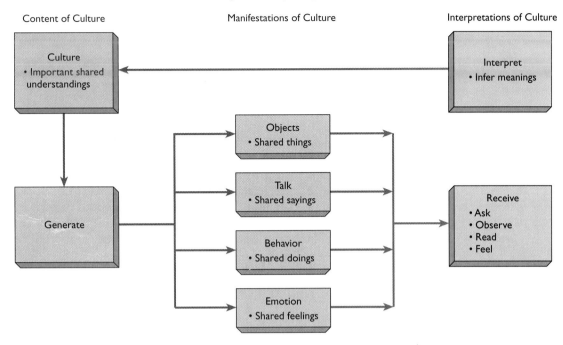

Source: Excerpted, by permission of the publisher, from "Implications of Corporate Culture: A Manager's Guide to Action," by V Sathe, from *Organizational Dynamics*, Autumn 1983, © 1983 American Management Association, New York. All rights reserved.

Rite	A relatively elaborate, dramatic planned set of activities that combines various forms of cultural expressions and that often has both practical and expressive consequences.
Ritual	A standardized, detailed set of techniques and behaviors that manages anxieties but seldom produces intended, practical consequences of any importance.
Myth	A dramatic narrative of imagined events, usually used to explain origins or transformations of something; also, an unquestioned belief about the practical benefits of certain techniques and behaviors that is not supported by demonstrated facts.
Saga	A historical narrative of some wonderful event that has a historical basis but has been embellished with fictional details.
Folktale	A completely fictional narrative.
Symbol	Any object, act, event, quality, or relation that serves as a vehicle for conveying meaning, usually by representing another thing.
Language	A particular manner in which members of a group use vocal sounds and written signs to convey meanings to each other.
Gesture	Movements of parts of the body used to express meanings.
Physical setting	Those things that physically surround people and provide them with immediate sensory stimuli as they carry out culturally expressive activities.
Artifact	Material objects manufactured by people to facilitate culturally expressive activities.

• ⟍⟶ TABLE 19~1

Specific Manifestations of Organizational Culture

Source: Excerpted, by permission of the publisher, from "How an Organization's Rites Reveal Its Culture," by J M Beyer and H M Trice, from *Organizational Dynamics*, Spring 1987, © 1987 American Management Association, New York. All rights reserved.

kind of conference of bishops, the company gathers senior managers to debate the Credo's contents, a process meant to keep its ideals fresh. On his globe-trotting tours [CEO Ralph] Larsen never fails to mention the document. ''I tell employees that they have to be prepared to take the short hit,'' he says. ''In the end, they'll prosper.'' As an example, Larsen cites the tragic Tylenol case in which eight people died from swallowing poisoned capsules. Although J&J believed someone altered the pill in the stores, not the factory, it recalled all its product and quickly lost $240 million in earnings. That swift action persuaded consumers to stay loyal, and today Tylenol remains the nation's leading brand of painkiller.[6]

organizational heroes
People who personify an organization's highest ideals.

Organizational Heroes   Those individuals who personify the organization's highest ideals are known as **organizational heroes,** and they play a big role in reinforcing and perpetuating an organization's culture. A person becomes an organizational hero by exhibiting some type of extraordinary behavior or performance. Over time, employees reinforce the behavior and associated corporate values displayed by the hero by telling stories about him or her. Consider the story of Chuck Abbadessa, a firefighter paramedic in Tempe, Arizona, and his captain, James Bailey:

Their fire station received a call to respond to a situation in which a car hit a power line pole. The pole had snapped in half and the gas tank ruptured. The car was engulfed in flames and smoke. Meanwhile, the downed power lines started arcing or jumping all around the burning car. If one survived the fire and smoke, direct contact with one of the power lines would mean certain death. Although one woman was ejected from the vehicle, the firefighters knew that a second person was hanging out of one of the windows. Without considering the danger to his own person, Chuck Abbadessa went in. After disappearing into smoke, flames, and jumping power lines, James Bailey thought Chuck was dead. To James's surprise, Chuck emerged a few seconds later dragging a body across the ground. Unfortunately, Chuck knew that there was a third person in the vehicle. After telling James about this situation, they both rushed back into this deadly situation to try and save the third person trapped in the car. Their quest was successful.

Chuck and James ultimately received the medal of valor from the fire department: It is the highest honor one can receive.[7] When management makes heroes of outstanding employees, like Chuck Abbadessa and James Bailey, the message is clear: ''Look at these people. Be like them. It pays.'' Often-repeated stories and legends of company heroes deepen the culture.

Heroes personify an organization's highest ideals. These firefighter paramedics risked their lives to save the people in a burning car. They were rewarded with the highest honor one can receive: the fire department's medal of valor.

(Frederick McKinney/FPG International)

Four Functions of Organizational Culture

As illustrated in Figure 19–2, an organization's culture fulfills four functions.[8] To help bring these four functions to life, let us consider how each of them has taken shape at United Parcel Service (UPS), the company with the familiar brown delivery vans. UPS is a particularly instructive example because it is the most profitable company in its industry and has a very strong and distinctive culture.

1. *Gives members an organizational identity:* According to *Fortune* magazine, ''What makes UPS stand out is its ability to attract, develop, and keep talented people. Top managers, most of whom have come up through the ranks, instill a spirit of winning so pervasive that people who fail are ranked as least best, not losers. Workers, in turn, have almost a Japanese-like identification with the company.''[9]

2. *Facilitates collective commitment:* UPS managers own almost all of the firm's stock. Many managers who began their careers with UPS as drivers and clerks have retired as multimillionaires. Compensation throughout the company is high by industry standards, with delivery truck drivers averaging $16 per hour. Middle managers receive generous stock bonuses and dividend checks.

3. *Promotes social system stability:* UPS is known for its strict standards and tight controls. For instance, employees must meet grooming standards and task performance is specified down to the finest detail. ''Longtime UPSers—most of the workforce due to a 4 percent turnover rate—talk about their company's 'mystique,' an aura that generates an unusual mixture of pas-

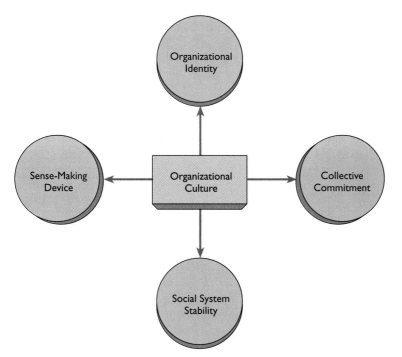

● ⟍ FIGURE 19~2

Four Functions of Organizational Culture

Source: Adapted from discussion in L Smircich, "Concepts of Culture and Organizational Analysis," *Administrative Science Quarterly,* September 1983, pp 339–58.

sionate commitment to hard work and a strong identification with the company.''[10]

4. *Shapes behavior by helping members make sense of their surroundings:* UPS recruits primarily from its 40,000-person part-time workforce of college students. Only the most promising are offered full-time positions. Even those with college degrees start at bottom-rung jobs to learn the basics of the business.

This example shows why the term *social glue* is indeed appropriate in reference to organizational culture.

Research on Organizational Cultures

Because the concept of organizational culture is a relatively recent addition to OB, the research base is incomplete. Studies to date are characterized by inconsistent definitions and varied methodologies. Quantitative treatments are rare since there is no agreement on how to measure cultural variables. Anecdotal accounts, in the form of practical examples drawn from interviews, are the norm. As a matter of convenience, we will review two streams of organizational culture research in this section. One stream has been reported in best-selling books and the other in research journal articles.[11]

Anecdotal Evidence from Best-Selling Books about Organizational Culture

Initial widespread interest in organizational cultures was stirred by William Ouchi's 1981 best-seller, *Theory Z: How American Business Can Meet the Japanese Challenge.* Interviews with representatives from 20 large American corporations doing business in both the United States and Japan led Ouchi to formulate his Theory Z model. Ouchi applied the Theory Z label to a few highly successful American organizations—including IBM, Eli Lilly, Intel, Eastman Kodak, and Hewlett-Packard—that exhibited Japanese-like qualities. Primary among those qualities was a participative, consensual decision-making style (see Figure 19–3). Ouchi found the internal cultures of these hybrid companies so consistent that he called them *clans.*

Ouchi noted, however, that clannish Theory Z organizations can become socially inbred to the point of rejecting unfamiliar ideas and people. Theory Z characteristics, when taken to extreme, can stifle creativity and foster unintentional sexism and racism. For instance, Ouchi described top management in one Theory Z company as ''wholesome, disciplined, hard-working, and honest, but unremittingly white, male, and middle class.''[12] From a research standpoint, Ouchi's two main contributions were (1) focusing attention on internal culture as a key determinant of organizational effectiveness and (2) developing an instructive typology of organizations based in part on cultural variables.

Close on the heels of Ouchi's book came two 1982 best-sellers: Deal and Kennedy's *Corporate Cultures: The Rites and Rituals of Corporate Life*[13] and Peters and Waterman's *In Search of Excellence.*[14] Both books drew upon interviews and the authors' consulting experience. Each team of authors relied on abundant anecdotal evidence to make the point that successful companies tend to have strong cultures. For example, Peters and Waterman observed:

> Without exception, the dominance and coherence of culture proved to be an essential quality of the excellent companies. Moreover, the stronger the culture and the more it was directed toward the marketplace, the less need was there for policy manuals,

FIGURE 19-3   Ouchi's Theory Z Model of Organization

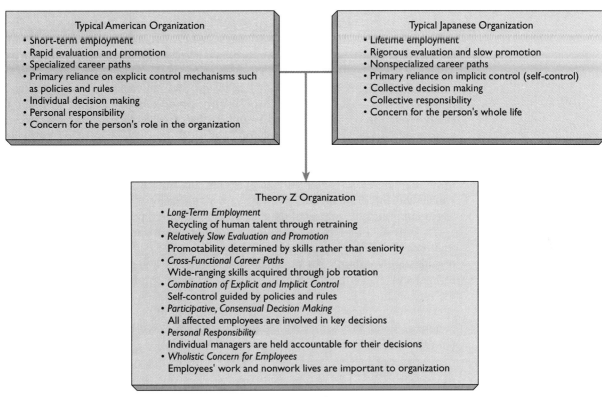

Typical American Organization
• Short-term employment
• Rapid evaluation and promotion
• Specialized career paths
• Primary reliance on explicit control mechanisms such as policies and rules
• Individual decision making
• Personal responsibility
• Concern for the person's role in the organization

Typical Japanese Organization
• Lifetime employment
• Rigorous evaluation and slow promotion
• Nonspecialized career paths
• Primary reliance on implicit control (self-control)
• Collective decision making
• Collective responsibility
• Concern for the person's whole life

Theory Z Organization
• *Long-Term Employment*
  Recycling of human talent through retraining
• *Relatively Slow Evaluation and Promotion*
  Promotability determined by skills rather than seniority
• *Cross-Functional Career Paths*
  Wide-ranging skills acquired through job rotation
• *Combination of Explicit and Implicit Control*
  Self-control guided by policies and rules
• *Participative, Consensual Decision Making*
  All affected employees are involved in key decisions
• *Personal Responsibility*
  Individual managers are held accountable for their decisions
• *Wholistic Concern for Employees*
  Employees' work and nonwork lives are important to organization

Source: Adapted from discussion in W G Ouchi, *Theory Z: How American Business Can Meet the Japanese Challenge* (Reading, MA: Addison-Wesley Publishing, 1981).

organization charts, or detailed procedures and rules. In these companies, people way down the line know what they are supposed to do in most situations because the handful of guiding values is crystal clear.[15]

These best-sellers generated excitement about cultural factors such as heroes and stories. They also created the impression that organizations have one distinct culture and that management can shape and mold it. Few people accept this generic conclusion. Rather, organizational researchers now accept the belief that organizations have multiple subcultures in addition to a potentially distinctive, organization-wide culture.[16] For example, organizations can have functional subcultures determined by one's job function or department, operating unit subcultures, hierarchical subcultures based on one's level in the organization, and social subcultures derived from social activities like a bowling or golf league and a reading club.[17] Finally, these best-sellers failed to break any new ground in the measurement and evaluation of organizational cultures.

Evidence from Research Articles and Management Implications   As previously mentioned, very little empirical research exists. This is partly due to problems associated with measuring organizational culture. It is a very complex phenomena to evaluate. Although there is not a uniformly agreed-upon method to assess culture, there are several cultural surveys and interviewing protocols that have been recommended.[18] So, what have we learned to date?

First, John Kotter and James Heskett tried to determine if organizational culture was related to a firm's long-term financial performance. They studied 207 companies from 22 industries for the period 1977 to 1988. After correlating results from a cultural survey and three different measures of economic performance, results uncovered a significant relationship between culture and financial performance.[19] A similar finding was obtained on a sample of 11 US insurance companies from the period 1981 to 1987.[20] Second, studies of mergers indicated that they frequently failed due to incompatible cultures.[21] Third, organizational culture was significantly related to performance and voluntary turnover for a sample of 904 accountants employed in six public accounting firms. A second sample of 80 Australian manufacturing employees from two companies revealed that culture was also significantly related to employees' organization commitment.[22] Finally, results from several studies demonstrated that the congruence between an individual's values and the organization's values was significantly correlated with organizational commitment, job satisfaction, intention to quit, and turnover.[23]

These results underscore the significance of organizational culture. They also reinforce the need to learn more about the process of cultivating and changing an organization's culture. An organization's culture is not determined by fate. It is formed and shaped by the combination and integration of everyone who works in the organization. As exemplified in the opening case on Levi Strauss, both managers and employees can take an active role in helping to change the organization culture in which they work. Although this is no easy task, the next section provides a preliminary overview of how this might be done.

DEVELOPING HIGH-PERFORMANCE CULTURES

An organization's culture may be strong or weak, depending on variables such as cohesiveness, value consensus, and individual commitment to collective goals. Contrary to what one might suspect, a strong culture is not necessarily a good thing.[24] The nature of the culture's central values is more important than its strength. For example, a strong but change-resistant culture may be worse, from the standpoint of profitability and competitiveness, than a weak but innovative culture. IBM is a prime example: its strong culture, coupled with a dogged determination to continually pursue a strategic plan that was out of step with the market, surely contributed to its $5 billion loss in 1992.[25] When trying to develop a high-performance culture, we need to consider the strategic appropriateness of its central values as well as its strength. Let us consider the central value within Prudential Insurance Company's group department.

Employees within the department conducted a cultural assessment and identified the following current norms: lack of teamwork across functions, divisions, and regions; lack of decision-making autonomy; competitiveness among functions, divisions, and regions; reluctance to delegate; atmosphere of risk avoidance and conformity; lack of emphasis on employee-career development; lack of compensation and rewards tied to performance; and lack of vertical and horizontal communication. Prudential's management is currently turning the department around as part of its organization-wide culture-change initiative.[26] But what could you, as a manager in the department, have done to change the organizational culture? This section suggests some workable answers by discussing the type of cultures that enhance an organization's financial performance and by introducing a practical model for developing a high-performance culture.

What Type of Cultures Enhance an Organization's Financial Performance?

Three perspectives have been proposed to explain the type of cultures that enhance an organization's economic performance. They are referred to as the strength, fit, and adaptive perspectives, respectively.

1. The **strength perspective** predicts a significant relationship between strength of corporate culture and long-term financial performance. The idea is that strong cultures create goal alignment, employee motivation, and needed structure and controls to improve organizational performance.[27]

2. The **fit perspective** is based on the premise that an organization's culture must align with its business or strategic context. Accordingly, there is no one best culture. A culture is predicted to facilitate economic performance only if it "fits" its context.[28]

3. The **adaptive perspective** assumes that good cultures help organizations anticipate and adapt to environmental changes. This proactive adaptability is expected to enhance long-term financial performance.[29]

strength perspective Assumes that the strength of corporate culture is related to a firm's financial performance.

fit perspective Assumes that culture must align with its business or strategic context.

adaptive perspective Assumes that adaptive cultures enhance a firm's financial performance.

A Test of the Three Perspectives   John Kotter and James Heskett tested the three perspectives on a sample of 207 companies from 22 industries for the period 1977 to 1988. Although their results partially supported the strength and fit perspectives, findings were completely consistent with the adaptive culture perspective. Long-term financial performance was highest for organizations with an adaptive culture.[30]

Developing an Adaptive Culture   Figure 19–4 illustrates the process of developing and preserving an adaptive culture. The process begins with charismatic leadership; that is, leaders must create and implement a business vision and associated strategies that fit the organizational context. Over time, adaptiveness is developed by a combination of organizational success and a specific leadership focus. Leaders must get employees to buy into a timeless philosophy or set of values that emphasizes service to the organization's key constituents—customers, stockholders, and employees—and also emphasizes the improvement of leadership. An infrastructure must then be created to preserve the organization's adaptiveness. Management does this by consistently reinforcing and supporting the organization's core philosophy or values of satisfying constituency needs and improving leadership. A practical model for creating this infrastructure is discussed in the next section.

A Practical Model for Developing a Cultural Infrastructure

Judging from the foregoing discussion, imitation of another organization's culture is unsatisfactory. (Careful study of successful organizations' cultures and skillful *adaptation,* on the other hand, is a good idea.) This is true not only from a competitive standpoint but also because management has imperfect control over culture. According to Edgar Schein, every culture is unique because:

FIGURE 19–4

Developing and Preserving an Adaptive Culture

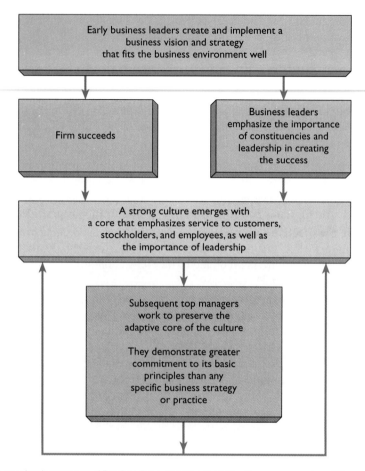

Source: Reprinted with permission of The Free Press, Macmillan Publishing Company, a member of Paramount Publishing from *Corporate Culture and Performance* by J F Kotter and J L Heskett. Copyright © 1992 by Kotter Associates, Inc. and James L. Heskett.

> The culture that eventually evolves in a particular organization is . . . a complex outcome of external pressures, internal potentials, responses to critical events, and, probably, to some unknown degree, chance factors that could not be predicted from a knowledge of either the environment or the members.[31]

The best alternative for management is to influence and develop the organization's unique culture as it evolves naturally. The model in Figure 19–5 is a practical road map for this endeavor.

Because the authors of this model view an adaptive and cohesive organizational culture as being analogous to a well-functioning family, the word HOME is a particularly appropriate acronym.[32] H stands for *history,* O stands for *oneness,* M stands for *membership,* and E stands for *exchange.* Each of these intervening conditions can foster the desired outcome, a cohesive organizational culture, if management makes a concerted and coordinated effort to implement the methods listed in Figure 19–5. Also, as discussed in Chapter 14, reward systems (in the M portion of the model) are a potent cultural force subject to managerial control.

• ➤ FIGURE 19–5   How to Develop an Organization's Culture

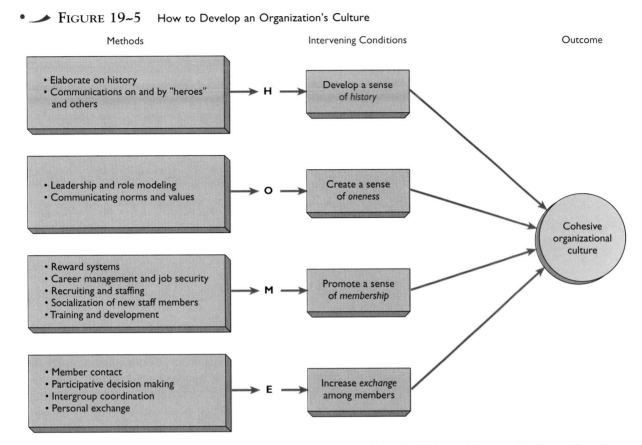

| Methods | Intervening Conditions | Outcome |

- Elaborate on history
- Communications on and by "heroes" and others

H → Develop a sense of *history*

- Leadership and role modeling
- Communicating norms and values

O → Create a sense of *oneness*

- Reward systems
- Career management and job security
- Recruiting and staffing
- Socialization of new staff members
- Training and development

M → Promote a sense of *membership*

- Member contact
- Participative decision making
- Intergroup coordination
- Personal exchange

E → Increase *exchange* among members

→ Cohesive organizational culture

Source: Excerpted, by permission of the publisher, from "How to Grow an Organizational Culture," by W Gross and S Shichman, from *Personnel*, September 1987, © 1987 American Management Association, New York. All rights reserved.

THE ORGANIZATIONAL SOCIALIZATION PROCESS

Joining the military, going to college, pledging a sorority or fraternity, taking a full-time job, and getting transferred have more in common than initially meets the eye. In each case, the individual experiences the shaping process called "organizational socialization." As shown in Figure 19–6, this process involves many sources of influence, some of which are beyond management's direct control. One authority on the subject refers to **organizational socialization** as "people processing" and defines it as "the process by which a person learns the values, norms, and required behaviors which permit him to participate as a member of the organization."[33] In short, organizational socialization turns outsiders into fully functioning insiders. Consider the socialization process at General Electric:

organizational socialization
Process by which employees learn an organization's values, norms, and required behaviors.

> GE's socialization process demands that individuals continually hone their skills. . . . At GE, job security is only maintained as long as an individual remains the best person for his/her job. If the company acquires another business, or closes down a business, that has personnel who can perform the person's job better, s/he is replaced. Education is constant; managers continually experience state-of-the-art leadership development train-

FIGURE 19–6

Newcomers Receive
Information from a Variety
of Sources during the
Socialization Process

Information Sources
Organizationally Controlled Influences

| The employment interview (2) | The formal orientation (3) | Job training (4) | Organizational supervision (6) |

The employee going through the socialization process

| (1) Initial observations by the prospect | (5) Perceptions of the behavior of others | (7) Personal needs fulfillment |

Factors Influenced but Not Controlled by the Organization

Source: Reprinted, by permission of the publisher, from "First Impressions: How They Affect Long-Term Performance,"
R T George, *Supervisory Management*, March 1986, p 6, © (1986) American Management Association, New York. All
rights reserved.

ing. As a result of the socialization, GE's employees are strongly rooted in the corporate value system of competitiveness and self-reliance.[34]

GE's socialization process can certainly be anxiety producing; newcomers—called recruits, new hires, rookies, pledges, trainees, or apprentices—must adapt or fall by the wayside. This section introduces a three-phase model of organizational socialization and examines the practical application of socialization research.

Present and future managers need to have a working knowledge of organizational socialization for at least four reasons.

1. Such understanding can enhance one's chances of successfully clearing the career hurdles into and through the organized world of work.

2. Human resource management specialists report there is a turnover epidemic among recent college graduates. Moreover, management experts estimate that this problem will become more severe in response to organizational restructuring.[35] Organizations can counter this costly trend by skillfully managing the socialization process.

3. Because socialization helps people's transition into productive employees, effective socialization can increase both job satisfaction and productivity.

4. More effective socialization programs help enhance an organization's continuity and chances of survival in an increasingly competitive world.

A Three-Phase Model of Organizational Socialization

One's first year in a complex organization can be confusing. There is a constant swirl of new faces, strange jargon, conflicting expectations, and apparently unrelated events. Some organizations treat new members in a rather haphazard, sink-or-swim manner. More typically, though, the socialization process is characterized by a sequence of identifiable steps.[36]

Organizational behavior researcher Daniel Feldman has proposed a three-phase model of organizational socialization that promotes deeper understanding of this important process. As illustrated in Figure 19–7, the three phases are (1) anticipatory socialization, (2) encounter, and (3) change and acquisition. Each phase has its associated perceptual and social processes. Feldman's model also specifies behav-

FIGURE 19–7   A Model of Organizational Socialization

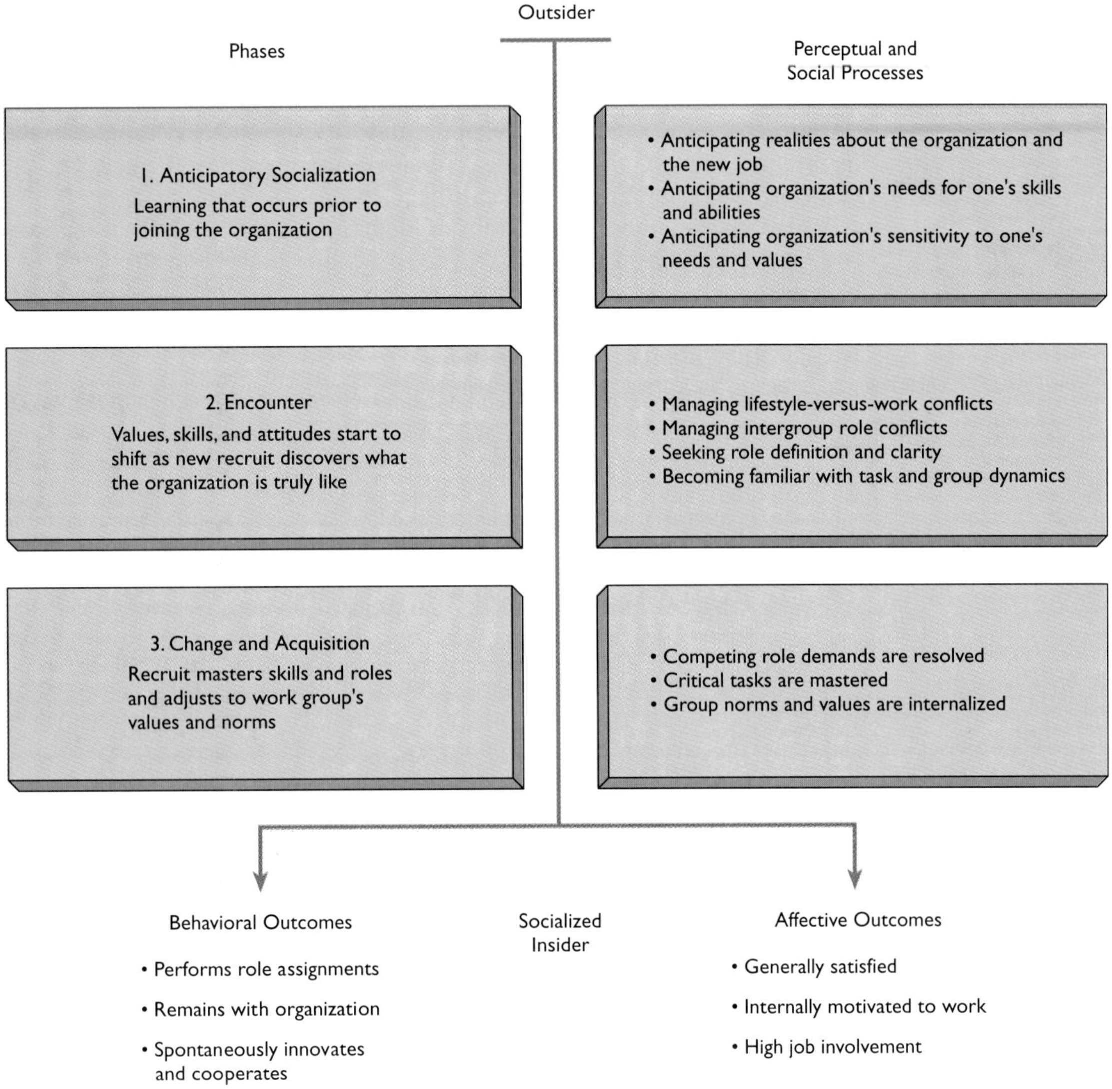

Source: Adapted from material in D C Feldman, "The Multiple Socialization of Organization Members," *Academy of Management Review*, April 1981, pp 309–18.

ioral and affective outcomes that can be used to judge how well the individual has been socialized. The entire three-phase sequence may take from a few weeks to a year to complete, depending on individual differences and the complexity of the situation.

Phase 1: Anticipatory Socialization

Organizational socialization begins *before* the individual actually joins the organization. Anticipatory socialization information comes from many sources. US Marine recruiting ads, for example, prepare future recruits for a rough-and-tumble experience. Widely circulated stories about IBM being the ''white shirt'' company probably deter those who would prefer working in jeans from applying.

All of this information—whether formal or informal, accurate or inaccurate—helps the individual anticipate organizational realities. Unrealistic expectations about the nature of the work, pay, and promotions are often formulated during phase I. Because employees with unrealistic expectations are more likely to quit their jobs in the future, management should use realistic job previews.[37] A **realistic job preview** (RJP) involves giving recruits a realistic idea of what lies ahead by presenting both positive and negative aspects of the job. RJPs may be verbal, in booklet form, audiovisual, or hands-on.

realistic job preview
Presents both positive and negative aspects of a job.

What are the ethical implications of providing potential applicants an unrealistic job preview? Consider what happened to John Sculley, former CEO of Apple Computer when he was recruited by Spectrum Information Technologies Inc. Although Sculley dropped the suit he filed against Peter Caserta, Spectrum's president, he ultimately quit the job.

He [Sculley] has been forced to admit that he accepted a multimillion-dollar pay package without knowing the company was under federal investigation. . . . And his shining reputation as a high-tech visionary has dimmed. In Mr. Sculley's wake, Spectrum was forced to restate financial results yesterday, turning slender profits into losses. . . . The suit charges Spectrum President Peter Caserta with ''fraudulent misrepresentations'' and alleges what amounts to a plot to reap profits on insider stock sales after Mr. Sculley's hiring sent Spectrum shares soaring. . . . Only two weeks ago, Mr. Sculley denied news reports that Spectrum was being investigated by the Securities and Exchange Commission—which turned out to be true—and that he planned to resign. Spectrum later confirmed that an SEC probe had been going on since May, leading some industry

US Coast Guard recruiting ads are a form of anticipatory socialization. They prepare recruits for the organizational realities of dealing with some of society's toughest jobs.

(Courtesy U.S. Coast Guard)

executives to wonder whether Mr. Sculley had been mislead or—perhaps worse—duped.[38]

As you can see, Sculley's suit is the result of inaccurate expectations formed during the recruiting process.

Phase 2: Encounter   This second phase begins when the employment contract has been signed. It is a time for surprise and making sense as the newcomer enters unfamiliar territory. Behavioral scientists warn that **reality shock** can occur during the encounter phase.

> Becoming a member of an organization will upset the everyday order of even the most well-informed newcomer. Matters concerning such aspects as friendships, time, purpose, demeanor, competence, and the expectations the person holds of the immediate and distant future are suddenly made problematic. The newcomer's most pressing task is to build a set of guidelines and interpretations to explain and make meaningful the myriad of activities observed as going on in the organization.[39]

As an example, the International OB describes the reality shock experienced by Mr. Akiro Kusumoto following his transfer from Japan to one of its American subsidiaries.

During the encounter phase, the individual is challenged to resolve any conflicts between the job and outside interests. If the hours prove too long, for example, family duties may require the individual to quit and find a more suitable work schedule. Also, as indicated in Figure 19–7, role conflict stemming from competing demands of different groups needs to be confronted and resolved.

Phase 3: Change and Acquisition   Mastery of important tasks and resolution of role conflict signals the beginning of this final phase of the socialization process. Those who do not make the transition to phase 3 leave voluntarily or involuntarily or become network isolates.

reality shock   A newcomer's feeling of surprise after experiencing unexpected situations or events.

INTERNATIONAL OB

Japanese Manager Transferred to the United States Encounters Reality Shock

Around a conference table in a large U.S. office tower, three American executives sat with their new boss, Mr. Akiro Kusumoto, the newly appointed head of a Japanese firm's American subsidiary, and two of his Japanese lieutenants. The meeting was called to discuss ideas for reducing operating costs. Mr. Kusumoto began by outlining his company's aspiration for its long-term U.S. presence. He then turned to the current budgetary matter. One Japanese manager politely offered one suggestion, and an American then proposed another. After gingerly discussing the alternatives for quite some time, the then exasperated American blurted out: "Look, *that* idea is just not going to have much impact. Look at the numbers! We should cut *this* program, and I think we should do it as soon as possible!" In the face of such bluntness, uncommon and unacceptable in Japan, Mr. Kusumoto fell silent. He leaned back, drew air between his teeth, and felt a deep longing to "return East." He realized his life in this country would be filled with many such jarring encounters and lamented his posting to a land of such rudeness.

Source: R G Linowes, "The Japanese Manager's Traumatic Entry into the United States: Understanding the American–Japanese Cultural Divide," *The Academy of Management Executive*, November 1993, p 21. Used with permission.

Practical Application of Socialization Research

Although credible research results in this area have begun to appear only recently, findings suggest four practical guidelines for managing organizational socialization.

1. Managers should avoid a haphazard, sink-or-swim approach to organization socialization because it is a key aspect of creating an adaptive organizational culture.[40] Socialization needs to be managed systematically so that newcomers get a clear idea of what is expected of them.

2. Organizations should pay more attention to the anticipatory socialization phase. Two recent studies demonstrated that company policies and procedures affect this phase of socialization. A survey of 352 US banks revealed that pay level and the level of flexibility in benefit packages significantly influenced the number of applicants attracted to teller jobs and the length of time it took banks to fill open teller positions.[41] A second experimental study with 284 undergraduate students also revealed that students were differentially attracted to various companies. Students with low self-esteem were more attracted to decentralized and larger firms than those with high self-esteem. Students with a high need for achievement also preferred working for companies that rewarded performance rather than seniority.[42]

3. The encounter phase of socialization is particularly important. Studies of newly hired accountants demonstrated that the frequency and type of information obtained during their first six months of employment significantly affected their job performance, their role clarity, their understanding of the organizational culture, and the extent to which they were socially integrated.[43] Managers play a key role during the encounter phase. A recent study of 151 new employees revealed that newcomers relied primarily on observation of others, followed by supervisors and co-workers, to obtain task and role information.[44] In summary, managers need to ensure that new employees have access to the type of information they need to successfully integrate within the organizational culture.

4. Support for stage models is mixed. Although there are different stages of socialization, they are not identical in order, length, or content for all people or jobs.[45] Managers are advised to use a contingency approach toward organizational socialization. In other words, different techniques are appropriate for different people at different times.

SOCIALIZATION THROUGH MENTORING

mentoring   Process of forming and maintaining developmental relationships between a mentor and a junior person.

Mentoring is defined as the process of forming and maintaining an intensive and lasting developmental relationship between a senior person (the mentor) and a junior person (the protégé, if male; or protégée, if female). The modern word *mentor* derives from Mentor, the name of a wise and trusted counselor in Greek mythology. Terms typically used in connection with mentoring are *teacher, coach, godfather,* and *sponsor.*

Mentoring is an important part of developing a high-performance culture. Let us reconsider Figure 19–5 to explain why this is the case. First off, mentoring contributes to creating a sense of oneness by promoting the acceptance of the organization's core values throughout the organization. The socialization aspect of mentoring also promotes a sense of membership. Finally, mentoring increases interpersonal exchanges among organizational members.

Functions of Mentoring

Kathy Kram, a Boston University researcher, conducted in-depth interviews with both members of 18 pairs of senior and junior managers. Each pair exhibited a significant developmental relationship. All the subjects worked for a large public utility in the northeastern United States. While there were seven female protégées, only one of the mentors was a woman.[46] As a by-product of this study, Kram identified two general functions—career and psychosocial—of the mentoring process (see Figure 19–8). Five *career functions* that enhanced career development were sponsorship, exposure-and-visibility, coaching, protection, and challenging assignments. Four *psychosocial functions* were role modeling, acceptance-and-confirmation, counseling, and friendship. The psychosocial functions clarified the participants' identities and enhanced their feelings of competence.

Both members of the mentoring relationship can benefit from these career and psychosocial functions. Mentoring is not strictly a top-down proposition, as many mistakenly believe. According to a team of mentoring experts:

> The mentor is also doing something for himself. The mentor is making productive use of his own knowledge and skill . . . and is learning in ways that would otherwise not be possible for him. Thus the mentoring relationship is one of mutual benefit.[47]

Phases of Mentoring

In addition to identifying the functions of mentoring, Kram's research revealed four phases of the mentoring process: (1) initiation, (2) cultivation, (3) separation, and (4) redefinition. As indicated in Table 19–2, the phases involve *variable* rather than fixed time periods. Telltale turning points signal the evolution from one phase to the next. For example, when a junior manager begins to resist guidance and strives to work more autonomously, the separation phase begins. The mentoring relationships in Kram's sample lasted an average of five years.

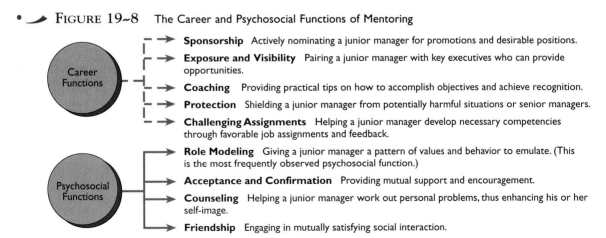

• ↗ FIGURE 19~8   The Career and Psychosocial Functions of Mentoring

Career Functions

Sponsorship   Actively nominating a junior manager for promotions and desirable positions.

Exposure and Visibility   Pairing a junior manager with key executives who can provide opportunities.

Coaching   Providing practical tips on how to accomplish objectives and achieve recognition.

Protection   Shielding a junior manager from potentially harmful situations or senior managers.

Challenging Assignments   Helping a junior manager develop necessary competencies through favorable job assignments and feedback.

Psychosocial Functions

Role Modeling   Giving a junior manager a pattern of values and behavior to emulate. (This is the most frequently observed psychosocial function.)

Acceptance and Confirmation   Providing mutual support and encouragement.

Counseling   Helping a junior manager work out personal problems, thus enhancing his or her self-image.

Friendship   Engaging in mutually satisfying social interaction.

Source: Adapted from discussion in K E Kram, *Mentoring of Work: Developmental Relationships in Organizational Life* (Glenview, IL: Scott, Foresman, 1985), pp 22–39.

TABLE 19~2

Phases of the Mentor Relationship

Phase	Definition	Turning Points*
Initiation	A period of six months to a year during which time the relationship gets started and begins to have importance for both managers.	Fantasies become concrete expectations. Expectations are met; senior manager provides coaching, challenging work, visibility; junior manager provides technical assistance, respect, and desire to be coached. There are opportunities for interaction around work tasks.
Cultivation	A period of two to five years during which time the range of career and psychosocial functions provided expand to a maximum.	Both individuals continue to benefit from the relationship. Opportunities for meaningful and more frequent interaction increase. Emotional bond deepens and intimacy increases.
Separation	A period of six months to two years after a significant change in the structural role relationship and/or in the emotional experience of the relationship.	Junior manager no longer wants guidance but rather the opportunity to work more autonomously. Senior manager faces midlife crisis and is less available to provide mentoring functions. Job rotation or promotion limits opportunities for continued interaction; career and psychosocial functions can no longer be provided. Blocked opportunity creates resentment and hostility that disrupts positive interaction.
Redefinition	An indefinite period after the separation phase, during which time the relationship is ended or takes on significantly different characteristics, making it a more peerlike friendship.	Stresses of separation diminish, and new relationships are formed. The mentor relationship is no longer needed in its previous form. Resentment and anger diminish; gratitude and appreciation increase. Peer status is achieved.

*Examples of the most frequently observed psychological and organizational factors that cause movement into the current relationship phase.

Source: K E Kram, "Phases of the Mentor Relationship," *Academy of Management Journal,* December 1983, p 622. Used with permission.

Consider how Ed Fu, CEO of Fu Associates, an Arlington, Virginia, computer consulting firm with approximately 100 employees and $7.8 million in revenue, conducts the initiation and cultivation phases:

> At Fu Associates, Ltd., all new hires go through a formal but somewhat unstructured mentoring program. Each newcomer starts out working directly with a midlevel employee. After a couple of months, Fu begins choosing from among the new employees for designers to serve on projects for which he is senior systems analyst. He describes this exercise as "looking for talent," which he can then nurture and mold into a top programmer or systems analyst at his firm. . . . "The best way for me to mentor people is to work really closely with them," says Fu, who is directly involved in about 65 different consulting projects annually at his nine-year old company. "Then I can bring them along," he adds, "and show them how I think they should be structuring their work."[48]

Research Evidence on Mentoring

Research findings uncovered both individual and organizational benefits of mentoring programs. Individual benefits include career mobility and increased performance, job satisfaction, and pay. For example, a recent study of 265 and 284 mentored and nonmentored employees, respectively, examined the effects of career-related mentoring and psychosocial mentoring. Results demonstrated that career-related mentoring was significantly related to performance proficiency, job satisfaction, and salary. In contrast, psychosocial mentoring was significantly correlated only with job satisfaction. Findings also revealed that informal mentoring was more effective than formal mentorships.[49] A second study of 147 women and 173 men reinforced these findings. In this case, individuals who were extensively mentored received more promotions, had higher incomes, and were more satisfied with their jobs than individuals who experienced little mentoring.[50]

Research also investigated the dynamics associated with the establishment of mentoring relationships. Two key findings were uncovered. First, mentoring relationships were more likely to form when the mentor and protégé/protégée possessed similar attitudes, philosophies, personalities, interests, background, and education.[51] Second, the most common cross-gender mentor relationship involved a male mentor and female protégée. This trend occurred for two reasons: (1) There is an underrepresentation of women in executive-level positions; and (2) there are a number of individual, group, and organizational factors that inhibit mentoring relationships between women.[52] Cross-gender relationships involving a male mentor and female protégée have long been considered problematic due to the potential for romantic involvement. Results of 32 mentor–protégée pairings (14 male–female; 18 female–female) suggest that male–female mentor relationships are more beneficial than harmful. According to the researcher:

> It would appear that the most productive mentoring functions occur *after* the initial attraction of identification has mellowed. From a practical perspective, it may be that we should stop advising young women to avoid or maintain their distance with male mentors despite the acknowledged possibility that sexual entanglements can emerge. If, as was found in this sample, male mentors are at least as likely (if not more so) to provide psychosocial functions for female protégées, young women may find cross-sex mentoring uniquely valuable.[53]

Research also supports the organizational benefits of mentoring. In addition to the obvious benefit of employee development, mentoring enhances the effectiveness of organizational communication. Specifically, mentoring increases the amount of vertical communication both up and down an organization, and it provides a mechanism for modifying or reinforcing organizational culture.[54]

Getting the Most Out of Mentoring

Mentoring can be an informal, spontaneous process or a formally structured one. For example, NCR, a large computer company located in Dayton, Ohio, uses a loosely administered program that does not formally match protégés with mentors. According to Bill Holloway, NCR's vice president of personnel and education, "We encourage the use of the program and provide guidelines for the program, but we don't force it. You can lay it out there, you can encourage it, but if you try to force it you've got a problem."[55]

Regardless of the approach taken, it is important to realize that mentoring has been zealously oversold in recent years. Some managers do not want to be a mentor or a protégé/protégée. If managers are forced into such roles by a formal mentoring program, resistance and resentment could damage relationships and careers.

A workable alternative involves establishing a career development program that fosters the performance of mentoring functions and behaviors without forcing artificial relationships. This organizational climate encourages emergence of informal and trusting relationships that are essential to successful mentoring.

BACK TO THE OPENING CASE

Now that you have read Chapter 19, you should be able to answer the following questions about the Levi Strauss case:

1. What are the shared things, sayings, doings, and feelings at Levi Strauss? Explain.
2. Using Figure 19–4, how is Levi Strauss trying to develop an adaptive culture?
3. How is Levi Strauss using the HOME model to develop its culture?
4. How does Levi Strauss practice socialization? Explain.
5. What are Levi Strauss's core corporate values?

SUMMARY OF KEY CONCEPTS

1. *Define the term* organizational culture. Organizational culture is the social glue that binds organizational members together through shared values, symbolic devices, and social ideals. Most of the assumptions underlying an organization's culture are taken for granted. A culture's central values are more important than its strength.

2. *Describe the manifestations of an organization's culture and the four functions of organizational culture.* General manifestations of an organization's culture are shared objects, talk, behavior, and emotion. Specific manifestations of culture include rituals, legends, stories, values, and heroes. Four functions of organization culture are organizational identity, collective commitment, social system stability, and sense-making device.

3. *Summarize research on organizational culture.* Best-selling books generated interest in organizational culture. Unfortunately, they created the false impression that organizations have one distinct culture, and they failed to break any new ground in the measurement and evaluation of organizational culture. Empirical research has uncovered four key findings. (1) There is a significant relationship between organization culture

and a firm's long-term financial performance. (2) Mergers frequently failed due to incompatible cultures. (3) Organizational culture is significantly related to employee performance, voluntary turnover, and organizational commitment. (4) The congruence between an individual's values and the organization's values was significantly correlated with organizational commitment, job satisfaction, intention to quit, and turnover.

4. *Highlight the three perspectives that explain the type of cultures that enhance an organization's long-term financial performance.* The three perspectives are referred to as strength, fit, and adaptive. The strength perspective predicts a significant relationship between the strength of corporate culture and long-term economic performance. The fit perspective is based on the premise that an organization's culture must align with its business or strategic context. A culture is expected to facilitate economic performance only if it "fits" its context. The adaptive perspective assumes that good cultures help organizations anticipate and adapt to environmental changes.

5. *Discuss the process of developing an adaptive culture.* The process begins with charismatic

leadership that creates a business vision and strategy. Over time, adaptiveness is created by a combination of organizational success and leaders' ability to get employees to buy into a philosophy or set of values of satisfying constituency needs and improving leadership. Finally, an infrastructure is created to preserve the organization's adaptiveness.

6. *Describe the* HOME *model for developing an organization's culture.* The HOME model prescribes that organizational culture is developed by (1) developing a sense of history, (2) creating a sense of oneness, (3) promoting a sense of members, and (4) increasing the amount of interpersonal exchange among organizational members. Leaders can use a variety of methods to influence organizational culture.

7. *Describe the three phases in Feldman's model of organizational culture.* The three phases of Feldman's model are anticipatory socialization, encounter, and change and acquisition. Anticipatory socialization begins before an individual actually joins the organization. The encounter phase begins when the employment contract has been signed. Phase 3 involves the period in which employees master important tasks and resolve any role conflicts.

8. *Discuss the two basic functions of mentoring.* Mentors help protégés in two basic functions: career and psychosocial functions. For career functions, mentors provide advice and support in regard to sponsorship, exposure and visibility, coaching, protection, and challenging assignments. Psychosocial functions entail role modeling, acceptance and confirmation, counseling, and friendship.

9. *Summarize the phases of mentoring.* There are four phases of the mentoring process: (1) initiation, (2) cultivation, (3) separation, and (4) redefinition. Each phase involves variable rather than fixed periods of time, and there are key activities that occur during each phase.

DISCUSSION QUESTIONS

1. How would you respond to someone who made the following statement? "Organizational cultures are not important as far as managers are concerned."

2. What taken-for-granted assumptions do you have about the organization where you presently work or go to school? How did you learn those assumptions?

3. Can you think of any organizational heroes who have influenced your work behavior? Describe them, and explain how they affected your behavior.

4. Do you know of any successful companies that do not have a positive adaptive culture? Why do you think they are successful?

5. Think of a company you worked for that did not have a positive culture. Use the HOME model to generate a list of recommendations about how top management from this company could change its organizational culture.

6. Why is it inappropriate for a manager to read a book like Peters and Waterman's best-seller, *In Search of Excellence,* and attempt to imitate the culture of an excellent company such as IBM?

7. Why is socialization essential to organizational success?

8. What sort of anticipatory socialization did you undergo at your present school or job?

9. Have you ever had a mentor? Explain how things turned out.

10. What are the individual, group, and organizational factors that inhibit mentoring relationships between women?

EXERCISE

Objectives

1. To promote deeper understanding of organizational socialization processes.

2. To provide you with a useful tool for analyzing and comparing organizations.

Introduction

Employees are socialized in many different ways in today's organizations. Some organizations, such as IBM, have made an exact science out of organizational socialization. Others leave things to chance in hopes that collective goals will somehow be achieved. The questionnaire[56] in this exercise is designed to help you gauge how widespread and systematic the socialization process is in a particular organization.

Instructions

If you are presently employed and have a good working knowledge of your organization, you can complete this questionnaire yourself. If not, identify a manager or professional (e.g., corporate lawyer, engineer, nurse), and have that individual complete the questionnaire for his or her organization.

Respond to the items below as they apply to the handling of professional employees (including managers). Upon completion, compute the total score by adding up your responses. For comparison, scores for a number of strong, intermediate, and weak culture firms are provided.

	Not True of This Company				Very True of This Company
1. Recruiters receive at least one week of intensive training.	1	2	3	4	5
2. Recruitment forms identify several key traits deemed crucial to the firm's success; traits are defined in concrete terms, and interviewer records specific evidence of each trait.	1	2	3	4	5
3. Recruits are subjected to at least four in-depth interviews.	1	2	3	4	5
4. Company actively facilitates de-selection during the recruiting process by revealing minuses as well as pluses.	1	2	3	4	5
5. New hires work long hours, are exposed to intensive training of considerable difficulty, and/or perform relatively menial tasks in the first months.	1	2	3	4	5
6. The intensity of entry-level experience builds cohesiveness among peers in each entering class.	1	2	3	4	5
7. All professional employees in a particular discipline begin in entry-level positions regardless of experience or advanced degrees.	1	2	3	4	5
8. Reward systems and promotion criteria require mastery of a core discipline as a precondition of advancement.	1	2	3	4	5
9. The career path for professional employees is relatively consistent over the first 6 to 10 years with the company.	1	2	3	4	5
10. Reward systems, performance incentives, promotion criteria and					

other primary measures of success reflect a high degree of congruence.	1	2	3	4	5
11. Virtually all professional employees can identify and articulate the firm's shared values (i.e., the purpose or mission that ties the firm to society, the customer, or its employees).	1	2	3	4	5
12. There are very few instances when actions of management appear to violate the firm's espoused values.	1	2	3	4	5
13. Employees frequently make personal sacrifices for the firm out of commitment to the firm's shared values.	1	2	3	4	5
14. When confronted with trade-offs between systems measuring short-term results and doing what's best for the company in the long term, the firm usually decides in favor of the long term.	1	2	3	4	5
15. This organization fosters mentor-protégé relationships.	1	2	3	4	5
16. There is considerable similarity among high potential candidates in each particular discipline.	1	2	3	4	5

Total score = _____

For comparative purposes:

	Scores	
Strongly socialized firms	65–80	IBM, P&G, Morgan Guaranty
	55–64	AT&T, Morgan Stanley, Delta Airlines
	45–54	United Airlines, Coca-Cola
	35–44	General Foods, PepsiCo
	25–34	United Technologies, ITT
Weakly socialized firms	Below 25	Atari

Questions for Consideration/Class Discussion

1. How strongly socialized is the organization in question? What implications does this degree of socialization have for satisfaction, commitment, and turnover?

2. In examining the 16 items in the preceding questionnaire, what evidence of realistic job previews and behavior modeling can you find? Explain.

3. What does this questionnaire say about how organizational norms are established and enforced? Frame your answer in terms of specific items in the questionnaire.

4. Using this questionnaire as a gauge, would you rather work for a strongly, moderately, or weakly socialized organization?

NOTES

[1] For a comprehensive review of recent research, see M J Hatch, "The Dynamics of Organizational Culture," *Academy of Management Review,* October 1993, pp 657–93.

[2] This discussion is based on material presented in J P Kotter and J L Heskett, *Corporate Culture and Performance* (New York: The Free Press, 1992), and E H Schein, *Organizational Culture and Leadership* (San Francisco: Jossey-Bass, 1985).

[3] M Maremont and L Therrien, "To: George Fisher, Re: How to Fix Kodak," *Business Week,* November 8, 1993, p 37.

[4] Based on E H Schein, "Legitimating Clinical Research in the Study of Organizational Culture," *Journal of Counseling and Development,* July/August 1993, pp 703–8.

[5] E H Schein, "What You Need to Know about Organizational Culture," *Training and Development Journal,* January 1986, p 30.

[6] B Dumaine, "Corporate Citizenship," *Fortune,* January 29, 1990, pp 50, 54.

[7] This story was relayed by R Matthews, a firefighter paramedic in Tempe, Arizona, 1994.

[8] Adapted from L Smircich, "Concepts of Culture and Organizational Analysis," *Administrative Science Quarterly,* September 1983, pp 339–58.

[9] K Labich, "Big Changes at Big Brown," *Fortune,* January 18, 1988, p 56.

[10] Ibid., p 58. Also see T Vogel, "Hello, I Must Be Going: On the Road with UPS," *Business Week,* June 4, 1990, p 82.

[11] An historical overview of research on organizational culture is provided by H M Trice and J M Beyer, *The Cultures of Work Organizations* (Englewood Cliffs, NJ: Prentice-Hall, 1993).

[12] W G Ouchi, *Theory Z: How American Business Can Meet the Japanese Challenge* (Reading, MA: Addison-Wesley Publishing, 1981), p 91.

[13] See T E Deal and A A Kennedy, *Corporate Cultures: The Rites and Rituals of Corporate Life* (Reading, MA: Addison-Wesley Publishing, 1982).

[14] See T J Peters and R H Waterman, Jr., *In Search of Excellence* (New York: Harper & Row, 1982).

[15] Ibid., pp 75–76.

[16] See Trice and Beyer, *The Cultures of Work Organizations.*

[17] Types of subcultures are discussed by S Caudron, "Subculture Strife Hinders Productivity," *Personnel Journal,* December 1992, pp 60–64.

[18] See C A O'Reilly III, J Chatman, and D F Caldwell, "People and Organizational Culture: A Profile Comparison Approach to Assessing Person-Organization Fit," *Academy of Management Journal,* September 1991, pp 487–516; Caudron, "Subculture Strife Hinders Productivity;" and Schein, "Legitimating Clinical Research in the Study of Organizational Culture."

[19] Details of this study and results are presented in Kotter and Heskett, *Corporate Culture and Performance.*

[20] Results can be found in G G Gordon and N DiTomaso, "Predicting Corporate Performance from Organizational Culture," *Journal of Management Studies,* November 1992, pp 783–98.

[21] See S Cartwright and C L Cooper, "If Cultures Don't Fit, Mergers May Fail," *The New York Times,* August 29, 1993, p 142; and J Marren, *Mergers & Acquisitions: A Valuation Handbook* (Homewood, IL: Business One Irwin, 1993).

[22] See J E Sheridan, "Organizational Culture and Employee Retention," *Academy of Management Journal,* December 1992, pp 1036–56; and C Orpen, "The Effect of Organizational Cultural Norms on the Relationship between Personnel Practices and Employee Commitment," *The Journal of Psychology,* September 1993, pp 577–89.

[23] Supportive findings can be found in B Z Posner and W H Schmidt, "Values Congruence and Differences between the Interplay of Personal and Organizational Value Systems," *Journal of Business Ethics,* May 1993, pp 341–47; O'Reilly III, Chatman, and Caldwell, "People and Organizational Culture: A Profile Comparison Approach to Assessing Person-Organization Fit;" and J A Chatman, "Matching People and Organizations: Selection and Socialization in Public Accounting Firms," *Administrative Science Quarterly,* September 1991, pp 459–84.

[24] See G S Saffold III, "Culture Traits, Strength, and Organizational Performance: Moving beyond 'Strong' Culture," *Academy of Management Review,* October 1988, pp 546–58.

[25] The culture at IBM is discussed in S Losee and J Reese, "Can This Man Save IBM?" *Fortune,* April 19, 1993, pp 63–67.

[26] Results from the cultural audit at Prudential are presented in E Randall Moore, "Prudential Reinforces Its Business Values," *Personnel Journal,* January 1993, pp 84–89.

[27] This perspective was promoted by Deal and Kennedy,

Corporate Cultures: The Rites and Rituals of Corporate Life.

[28] See the discussion in Kotter and Heskett, *Corporate Culture and Performance;* and M J Morgan, "How Corporate Culture Drives Strategy," *Long Range Planning,* April 1993, pp 110–18.

[29] See the discussion in Kotter and Heskett, *Corporate Culture and Performance.*

[30] Ibid.

[31] Schein, *Organizational Culture and Leadership,* pp 83–84.

[32] See W Gross and S Schichman, "How to Grow an Organizational Culture," *Personnel,* September 1987, pp 52–56. Alternative approaches are presented in R Hooijberg and F Petrock, "On Cultural Change: Using the Competing Values Framework to Help Leaders Execute a Transformational Strategy," *Human Resource Management,* Spring 1993, pp 29–50; and W Wilhelm, "Changing Corporate Culture or Corporate Behavior? How to Change Your Company," *Academy of Management Executive,* November 1992, pp 72–77.

[33] J Van Maanen, "Breaking In: Socialization to Work," in *Handbook of Work, Organization, and Society,* ed R Dubin (Chicago: Rand-McNally, 1976), p 67.

[34] A M Nicotera and D P Cushman, "Organizational Ethics: A Within-Organization View," *Journal of Applied Communication,* November 1992, p 447.

[35] See R Goffee and R Scase, "Organizational Change and the Corporate Career: The Restructuring of Managers' Job Aspirations," *Human Relations,* April 1992, pp 363–86.

[36] For an instructive capsule summary of the five different organizational socialization models, see J P Wanous, A E Reichers, and S D Malik, "Organizational Socialization and Group Development: Toward an Integrative Perspective," *Academy of Management Review,* October 1984, pp 670–83, table 1. Also see D C Feldman, *Managing Careers in Organizations* (Glenview, IL: Scott, Foresman, 1988), chap. 5.

[37] Supportive results can be found in A M Saks, W H Weisner, and R J Summers, "Effects of Job Previews on Self-Selection and Job Choice," *Journal of Vocational Behavior,* June 1994, pp 297–316; and B M Meglino, A S DeNisi, and E C Ravlin, "Effects of Previous Job Exposure and Subsequent Job Status on the Functioning of a Realistic Job Preview," *Personnel Psychology,* Winter 1993, pp 803–22.

[38] J J Keller, "Ups and Downs: Sculley Suddenly Quits New Job and Accuses a Top Officer of a Plot," *The Wall Street Journal,* February 8, 1994, p A1.

[39] J Van Maanen, "People Processing: Strategies of Organizational Socialization," *Organizational Dynamics,* Summer 1978, p 21.

[40] This issue is discussed by Kotter and Heskett, *Corporate Culture and Performance;* and Trice and Beyer, *The Cultures of Work Organizations.*

[41] Results can be found in M L Williams and G F Dreher, "Compensation System Attributes and Applicant Pool Characteristics," *Academy of Management Journal,* August 1992, pp 571–95.

[42] See D B Turban and T L Keon, "Organizational Attractiveness: An Interactionist Perspective," *Journal of Applied Psychology,* April 1993, pp 184–93.

[43] Results from two separate studies can be found in E W Morrison, "Longitudinal Study of the Effects of Information Seeking," *Journal of Applied Psychology,* April 1993, pp 173–83; and E W Morrison, "Newcomer Information Seeking: Exploring Types, Modes, Sources, and Outcomes," *Academy of Management Journal,* June 1993, pp 557–89.

[44] For details, see C Ostroff and S W J Kozlowski, "Organizational Socialization as a Learning Process: The Role of Information Acquisition," *Personnel Psychology,* Winter 1992, pp 849–74.

[45] A summary of socialization research is provided by J P Wanous and A Colella, "Organizational Entry Research: Current Status and Future Directions," in *Research in Personnel and Human Resources Management,* eds G R Ferris and K M Rowland (Greenwich, CT: JAI Press, 1989), pp 59–120; and C D Fisher, "Organizational Socialization: An Integrative Review," in *Research in Personnel and Human Resources Management,* eds K M Rowland and G R Ferris (Greenwich, CT: JAI Press, 1986), pp 101–45.

[46] See K E Kram, "Phases of the Mentor Relationship," *Academy of Management Journal,* December 1983, pp 608–25.

[47] R J Burke and C A McKeen, "Mentoring in Organizations: Implications for Women," *Journal of Business Ethics,* April/May 1990, p 322.

[48] H Rothman, "The Boss as Mentor," *Nation's Business,* April 1993, p 66.

[49] Results from this study can be found in G T Chao, P M Walz, and P D Gardner, "Formal and Informal Mentorships: A Comparison on Mentoring Functions and Contrast with Nonmentored Counterparts," *Personnel Psychology,* Autumn 1992, pp 619–36.

[50] Results can be found in G F Dreher and R A Ash, "A Comparative Study of Mentoring among Men and Women in Managerial, Professional, and Technical Positions," *Journal of Applied Psychology,* October 1990, pp 539–46.

[51] See E Kaplan, "Confronting the Issue of Race in Developmental Relationships: Does Open Discussion Enhance or Suppress the Mentor-Protégé Bond?" *Academy of Management Executive,* May 1994, pp 79–80; and R J Burke, C A McKeen, and C McKenna, "Correlates of

Mentoring in Organizations: The Mentor's Perspective,'' *Psychological Reports,* 1993, pp 883–96.

[52] For a thorough discussion of the inhibitors of women mentoring women, see V A Parker and K E Kram, ''Women Mentoring Women: Creating Conditions for Connection,'' *Business Horizons,* March–April 1993, pp 42–51.

[53] D D Bowen, ''The Role of Identification in Mentoring Female Protégées,'' *Group & Organization Studies,* March–June 1986, p 72. Also see J G Clawson and K E Kram, ''Managing Cross-Gender Mentoring,'' *Business Horizons,* May–June 1984, pp 22–32; and S Feinstein, ''Women and Minority Workers in Business Find a Mentor Can Be a Rare Commodity,'' *The Wall Street Journal,* November 11, 1987, p 37.

[54] The organizational benefits of mentoring are thoroughly discussed by J A Wilson and N S Elman, ''Organizational Benefits of Mentoring,'' *Academy of Management Executive,* November 1990, pp 88–94.

[55] B Rogers, ''Mentoring Takes a New Twist,'' *HRMagazine,* August 1992, p 48.

[56] This exercise was adapted from Richard Pascale, ''The Paradox of 'Corporate Culture': Reconciling Ourselves to Socialization,'' pp 26–41. © 1985 by the Regents of the University of California. Reprinted/condensed from the *California Management Review,* 27, no. 2, by permission of The Regents.

MANAGING CHANGE IN LEARNING ORGANIZATIONS

Learning OBJECTIVES

When you finish studying the material in this chapter, you should be able to:

1. Discuss the external and internal forces that create the need for organizational change.
2. Explain Lewin's change model.
3. Describe the systems model of change.
4. Demonstrate your familiarity with the four identifying characteristics of organization development (OD).
5. Discuss the 10 reasons employees resist change.
6. Identify alternative strategies for overcoming resistance to change.
7. Define a learning organization.
8. Describe the three types of learning.
9. Review the reasons organizations naturally resist learning.
10. Discuss the role of leadership in creating a learning organization.

OPENING CASE

Organizational Change Meant Life or Death to Will-Burt Co.

Sharon Hoogstraten

It's no fun being up against the wall, which is where Harry Featherstone found himself in the autumn of 1985. He had recently taken command of The Will-Burt Co., a troubled manufacturing outfit in Orrville, Ohio. The company's troubles began with a product liability lawsuit.

The lawsuit centered on a scaffold that collapsed in Miami in 1980, killing one person and crippling another. The scaffold maker declared bankruptcy. But Will-Burt, which had produced one of the parts, was sued under the principle of joint and several liability. Its insurer settled out of court in 1984, paying $6.2 million. A year later it canceled the company's coverage.

Amid the legal proceedings, Will-Burt's chief executive dropped dead of a heart attack. And with other lawsuits pending, the family that owned the company, fearful of losing everything, decided to sell or liquidate Will-Burt.

"We could have liquidated, but I didn't want to tell 350 people and their families that the business was closing," he recalls. "We thought of merging, but who wants a company burdened with all that litigation?" . . .

Finally Featherstone's lawyer proposed that he do a leveraged buyout and place Will-Burt into an employee stock ownership plan [ESOP]. This made sense in a rather elegant way. "My attorney told me that if we got ourselves highly leveraged, we wouldn't make much money, but neither would we be a deep-pocket target for some liability lawyer," Featherstone says. "Lawyers love rich companies, and we wouldn't be one." And so on December 30, 1985—the deadline set by the owners to avoid liquidation—Featherstone completed a frantic two-month negotiation with an Ohio bank. He borrowed $3.2 million to buy 97 percent of Will-Burt stock, all he could get hold of. . . .

The company was in dismal shape. It had $20 million in sales, but profitability ranged from 1 percent to 5 percent over the past few years. Product quality was such that workers spent nearly 25,000 hours a year redoing faulty parts. Its wage rate was $2 below the area's average, and turnover often topped 30 percent. The pension plan was so bad that a 35-year veteran could expect to retire with $80 to $120 a month. . . .

And now, on top of everything else, Will-Burt had the ESOP . . . loan to repay—at a first-year cost of a cool $1 million and a second-year tab of almost $900,000. That weighed heavily on Featherstone. "This company had never even made $1 million a year," he says. "So I had quite a task." . . .

Featherstone's first steps, imperative though they were, won him few friends. He stopped making parts for ladders, scaffolds, and aircraft—anything that could create liability problems—and shut down some plants in the process. That forced him to let go of 80 people, factory and office workers alike. If morale was low before, this stomped it to the ground. . . .

But making money would be even harder now. The plant closings backed sales down from $20 million to $15 million and eliminated some high-margin items. To curb costs, Featherstone brought in "the toughest controller I could find, somebody who would say no even to me." He slashed capital outlays, cutting machinery purchases from $1 million a year to $50,000. . . .

But the controversy attending those early moves was nothing compared with the conflicts that erupted over the ESOP itself. Companies converting to ESOPs often spend months preparing employees for the change. But in Featherstone's scramble to do the leveraged buyout, he had told the employees very little about what was going on. "We all heard the word ESOP, but nobody knew what it was all

arry Featherstone's experience at Will-Burt is not the exception. Increased international competition is forcing companies to shape up or ship out. Customers are demanding greater value and lower prices. Jack Welch, CEO of General Electric, is well aware of this value proposition. He concluded that ''Only the most productive

OPENING CASE

(continued)

about," Cecil Martin recalls. "We all said, ESOP? What's an ESOP? They got some pamphlets out to us and said we'd all own a piece of the place. But a lot of people had trouble grasping the concept." . . .

The rumor mill kicked into overdrive. Will-Burt had never been unionized, but that didn't matter. There was labor–management animosity, and the workers harbored suspicions about Featherstone's motives. "There were lots of misconceptions," recalls welder Russ White. "Some guys said it was Harry's way to get control of the company for his own private gain." Others thought it was some kind of trick, a ruse, so that if the company fell apart, then they, the new owners, could be blamed.

But gradually the fog cleared. "As we had more meetings and got information, we learned that the ESOP was under strict government guidelines," says Martin. "We learned it wasn't just for Harry but all of us. That made everybody feel a little better. We also liked the fact that it might stave off some lawsuits." . . .

That wasn't all. In late 1986, after countless meetings, the workers began to understand that they did, in fact, own the company. And as owners, they wanted benefits—namely, some fat raises. . . . But money wasn't all they wanted. "When people hear employee-owned, they think, hey, I'm a boss now," says Larry Murgatroyd, a gear machinist. "That means control."

They wanted to elect the board of directors and the president and call the shots on all major decisions.

This wasn't everyone, but enough to make life miserable for the beleaguered Featherstone. "I tried to explain that this was a business, not Athenian democracy," he recalls. "You can't have 300 people making decisions—it would be anarchy. . . ."

Will-Burt needed some edge, Featherstone knew, something to set it apart.

He decided to shoot for perfect quality and perfect on-time delivery. Perfect quality meant manufacturing parts exactly to blueprint—zero defects. That sounded good. But pulling it off, Featherstone knew, would require the dedication and participation of each and every worker. Ownership alone would not generate the kind of commitment he needed. No, the employees would have to be given a more sharply defined role in the running of the business—more power to make their own decisions. They'd have to work harder and smarter.

His work force, though, was hardly eager to pioneer new-fangled techniques. Its overall education level was somewhere around the 10th grade. There were fourth-generation welders. Many workers were high-school dropouts, and more than a few were illiterate. "I think we had four degrees in the company at that time," Featherstone recalls, "and I had two of them." If Featherstone needed a work

force that would move mountains— and he did now—he was starting with little muscle.

"I had been a troubleshooter all my life," he says. "I had spent a lot of time in Japan with Ford and was really interested in how the Japanese did things. I studied them and decided that their success hinged on education, training, and their emphasis on business. . . ."

For openers, Featherstone focused on math. "Our people work from blueprints, and to make sense of them you have to know some math," he says. "I started out on a voluntary basis, on company time, and it just didn't work. You take someone who's been out of school for 20 years and put him back in a classroom atmosphere, and he hates it. Here's a teacher saying, 'Go home tonight and figure out the cosine of this tangent,' and the guy says, 'You've got to be out of your mind! I volunteered for this?' We started out with 25 people and ended up with 3. It was bad."

So Featherstone made the training mandatory, still on company time. He began with basic blueprint reading for all production workers—it remained voluntary for office workers—taught by a local high-school teacher for an hour or two a week. There were tests and homework. From there he moved into advanced blueprint reading, and for this he enlisted the continuing education staff of the University of Akron. . . .

Featherstone himself caught some

companies are going to win. If you can't sell a top-quality product at the world's lowest price, you're going to be out of the game. In that environment, 6% annual improvement in productivity may not be good enough anymore; you may need 8% or 9%."[1]

Companies no longer have a choice, they must change to survive. Unfortunately, people tend to resist change. It is not easy to change an organization, let alone an

OPENING CASE

(concluded)

flak. "When I made it mandatory, some people got mad at me, called me dictatorial," he says. "I even got hate mail." But the price was worth paying. Almost immediately, product quality picked up and the number of rejects dropped. "Now I knew why we were getting hammered," he says. "It turned out we had guys running machines who couldn't read a scale, let alone a blueprint. And they worked with blueprints all day long." . . .

Something had to change. In 1987 Featherstone decided to put the floor workers on salary. He totaled up each one's base compensation and overtime pay and divided that by 40, effectively raising wages by up to $3.50 an hour for a standard week, which didn't include overtime. That made Will-Burt competitive. Turnover dropped to single-digit numbers. Featherstone cashed in some insurance policies, enabling him to increase pensions nearly tenfold. He started a 401(k) retirement plan and installed a disability program that provided full pay for up to six months. A new policy awarding two extra floating holidays for perfect attendance over a year cut daily absenteeism from 8 percent to 2 percent.

And Featherstone pressed on with education, relying heavily on a University of Akron industrial training specialist named Hank Jeanneret. He sent his floor workers through a rigorous course on geometric tolerancing, a three-dimensional view of blueprints.

Then came basic high-school mathematics—fractions, decimals, a touch of algebra. . . .

Finally, Featherstone introduced statistical process control, which entails measuring and tracking parts through a manufacturing process. By examining random parts, for instance, one can spot deviations and trends that might signal problems with machinery or tooling. "I said we had to do this or we wouldn't have a company," he recalls. "The people we sell to were preaching quality and beating on us to provide better products."

But Will-Burt was looking better all the time. In December 1987 . . . [another] product liability suit was dismissed. By 1988 the company once again could obtain full-coverage liability insurance. Banks suddenly agreed to lend the company money. . . .

On-time delivery was running at 98 percent for months on end. Product quality was surging dramatically. In 1986, for example, the part rejection rate stood at 35 percent. By late 1988 it fell below 10 percent. Time spent reworking faulty parts dropped from 2,000 hours a month to 400, even though Will-Burt was doing far more high-precision work than ever. That slashed annual reject reworking costs from $800,000 to less than $180,000. . . .

To get the employees even more involved in decision making, this year [1990] Featherstone launched a two-year cross-training program he calls

the "Mini M.B.A." The University of Akron's Jeanneret is leading the instruction, which embraces everything from accounting to inventory control. . . .

What astounded Featherstone was the turnout. He expected 15 people. Instead, 54 signed up. They are welders, machinists, metal punchers. By and large, they are the younger workers, the ones betting their future on Will-Burt. "It's remarkable," he says. "Four years ago I couldn't get 10 people to stick with basic blueprint reading on a voluntary basis, and they see blueprints every day. Now, I've got 25 percent of the factory guys taking these classes on their own time. And they're pretty much the same people. It's a long process to teach people what ownership is all about, but education is really working."

For Discussion

What was the most important contribution to successful change at Will-Burt?

- Additional discussion questions linking this case with the following material appear at the end of this chapter.

Source: Excerpted from J Finegan, "The Education of Harry Featherstone," *Inc.,* July 1990, pp 57–66. Reprinted with permission, *Inc.* Magazine. Copyright © 1990 by Goldhirsh Group, Inc. 38 Commercial Wharf, Boston, MA 02110.

individual. This puts increased pressure on management to learn the subtleties of change. This final chapter was written to help managers navigate the journey of change.

Specifically, we discuss the forces that create the need for organization change, models of planned change, resistance to change, and creating a learning organization.

FIGURE 20~1
The External and Internal
Forces for Change

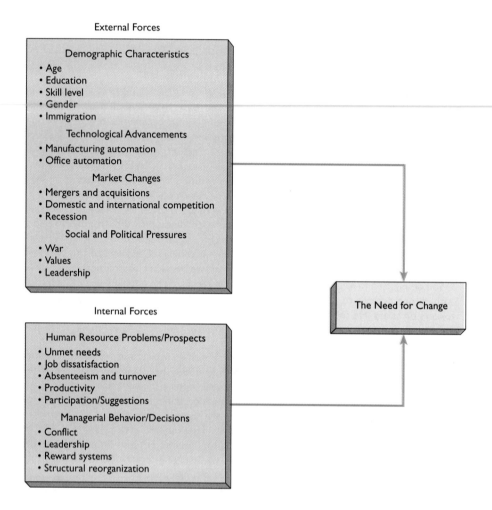

External Forces

Demographic Characteristics
- Age
- Education
- Skill level
- Gender
- Immigration

Technological Advancements
- Manufacturing automation
- Office automation

Market Changes
- Mergers and acquisitions
- Domestic and international competition
- Recession

Social and Political Pressures
- War
- Values
- Leadership

Internal Forces

Human Resource Problems/Prospects
- Unmet needs
- Job dissatisfaction
- Absenteeism and turnover
- Productivity
- Participation/Suggestions

Managerial Behavior/Decisions
- Conflict
- Leadership
- Reward systems
- Structural reorganization

The Need for Change

FORCES OF CHANGE

How do organizations know when they should change? What cues should an organization look for? Although there are no clear-cut answers to these questions, the "cues" that signal the need for change are found by monitoring the forces for change.

Organizations encounter many different forces for change. These forces come from external sources outside the organization and from internal sources. This section examines the forces that create the need for change. Awareness of these forces can help managers determine when they should consider implementing an organizational change. The external and internal forces for change are presented in Figure 20–1.

External Forces

external forces for change
Originate outside the organization.

External forces for change originate outside the organization. Because these forces have global effects, they may cause an organization to question the essence of what business it is in and the process by which products and services are produced. There are four key external forces for change: demographic characteristics, technological advancements, market changes, and social and political pressures. Each is now discussed.

Demographic Characteristics   Chapter 3 provided a detailed discussion of the demographic changes occurring in the US workforce. Two key trends identified in this discussion were that (1) the workforce is more diverse and (2) there is a business imperative to effectively manage diversity. Organizations need to effectively manage diversity if they are to receive maximum contribution and commitment from employees.

Technological Advancements   Both manufacturing and service organizations are increasingly using technology as a means to improve productivity and market competitiveness. Manufacturing companies, for instance, have automated their operations with robotics, computerized numerical control (CNC), which is used for metal cutting operations, and computer-aided design (CAD). CAD is a computerized process of drafting and designing engineering drawings of products. Companies have just begun to work on computer-integrated manufacturing (CIM). This highly technical process attempts to integrate product design with product planning, control, and operations.[2] In contrast to these manufacturing technologies, the service sector of the US economy is using office automation. **Office automation** consists of a host of computerized technologies that are used to obtain, store, analyze, retrieve, and communicate information.[3]

office automation
Computerized technologies used to obtain, store, analyze, and retrieve information.

Market Changes   The emergence of a global economy is forcing US companies to change the way they do business. Companies are having to forge new partnerships with their suppliers in order to deliver higher quality products at lower prices. Consider how Thomas Stalkamp, Chrysler Corporation's vice president of purchasing, uses a win-win approach to lower suppliers' costs:

> Chrysler has abandoned unilateral price cuts. It has abandoned competitive bidding. It has stopped writing detailed specifications for many parts. Instead, it relies on suppliers to design and build the right parts and to find ways to lower prices. Chrysler and the supplier split the savings, and the supplier gets a long-term relationship.[4]

Moreover, organizations and unions are also beginning to pursue collaborative, win-win relationships rather than adversarial ones. As found by Xerox, this change can significantly reduce costs and increase quality:

> In the early 1980s, Xerox was losing market share to the Japanese and closing plants. Fearing the worst, union leaders offered to explore ways to improve quality and efficiency. When they sat down with management, they busted a bunch of old shop taboos. To avoid the periodic layoffs and rehiring that follow manufacturing cycles, they agreed to let Xerox hire temporary workers for specified tasks, as long as their number did not exceed 10% of the workforce and they worked for no more than six months. In exchange, management granted union members job security for the duration of their contract. The union also agreed to something called ''no-fault termination'': If a worker is absent on four occasions for two or more hours per year, he or she may be terminated. . . . Our absenteeism has fallen from 8.5% to 2.5%. Union members threw themselves into the task of making Xerox a world-beating competitor.[5]

Social and Political Pressures   These forces are created by social and political events. Personal values, which were discussed in Chapter 4, affect employees'

The fall of Soviet Communism, as symbolized by the toppling of Lenin's statue, created many new business opportunities both inside and outside the former USSR.

(Reuters/Bettmann)

needs, priorities, and motivation. Managers thus may need to adjust their managerial style or approach to fit changing employee values. Political events can create substantial change. For example, the collapse of both the Berlin Wall and communism in Russia created many new business opportunities. Although it is difficult for organizations to predict changes in political forces, many organizations hire lobbyists and consultants to help them detect and respond to social and political changes.

Internal Forces

internal forces for change Originate inside the organization.

Internal forces for change come from inside the organization. These forces may be subtle, such as low morale, or can manifest in outward signs, such as low productivity and conflict. Internal forces for change come from both human resource problems and managerial behavior/decisions.

Human Resource Problems/Prospects These problems stem from employee perceptions about how they are treated at work and the match between individual and organization needs and desires. Chapter 6 highlighted the relationship between an employee's unmet needs and job dissatisfaction. Dissatisfaction is a symptom of an underlying employee problem that should be addressed. Unusual or high levels of absenteeism and turnover also represent forces for change. Organizations might respond to these problems by using the various approaches to job design discussed in Chapter 6, by implementing realistic job previews, which were discussed in Chapter 19, by reducing employees' role conflict, overload, and ambiguity (recall our discussion in Chapter 9), and by removing the different stressors discussed in Chapter 16. Prospects for positive change stem from employee participation and suggestions.

Managerial Behavior/Decisions Excessive interpersonal conflict between managers and their subordinates is a sign that change is needed. Both the manager and the employee may need interpersonal skills training, or the two individuals may simply need to be separated. For example, one of the parties might be transferred to a new department. Inappropriate leader behaviors such as inadequate direction or

FIGURE 20–2

A Generic Typology of Organizational Change

support may result in human resource problems requiring change. As discussed in Chapter 15, leadership training is one potential solution for this problem. Inequitable reward systems—recall our discussion in Chapters 7 and 14—and the type of structural reorganizations discussed in Chapter 17 are additional forces for change.

American managers are criticized for emphasizing short-term, quick-fix solutions to organizational problems. When applied to organizational change, this approach is doomed from the start. Quick-fix solutions do not really solve underlying problems, and they have little staying power.[6] Researchers and managers alike have thus tried to identify effective ways to manage the change process. This section sheds light on their insights. After discussing different types of organizational changes, we review Lewin's change model, a systems model of change, and organization development.

MODELS AND DYNAMICS OF PLANNED CHANGE

Types of Change

A useful three-way typology of change is displayed in Figure 20–2.[7] This typology is generic because it relates to all sorts of change, including both administrative and technological changes. Adaptive change is lowest in complexity, cost, and uncertainty.[8] It involves reimplementation of a change in the same organizational unit at a later time or imitation of a similar change by a different unit. For example, an adaptive change for a department store would be to rely on 12-hour days during the annual inventory week. The store's accounting department could imitate the same change in work hours during tax preparation time. Adaptive changes are not particularly threatening to employees because they are familiar.

Innovative changes fall midway on the continuum of complexity, cost, and uncertainty. An experiment with flexible work schedules by a farm supply warehouse company qualifies as an innovative change if it entails modifying the way other firms in the industry already use it. Unfamiliarity, and hence greater uncertainty, make fear of change a problem with innovative changes.

At the high end of the continuum of complexity, cost, and uncertainty are radically innovative changes. Changes of this sort are the most difficult to implement and tend to be the most threatening to managerial confidence and employee job security.[9] They can tear the fabric of an organization's culture. Resistance to change tends to increase as changes go from adaptive, to innovative, to radically innovative.

Lewin's Change Model

Most theories of organizational change originated from the landmark work of social psychologist Kurt Lewin. Lewin developed a three-stage model of planned change which explained how to initiate, manage, and stabilize the change process.[10] The three stages are unfreezing, changing, and refreezing. Before reviewing each stage, it is important to highlight the assumptions that underlie this model:[11]

1. The change process involves learning something new, as well as discontinuing current attitudes, behaviors, or organizational practices.
2. Change will not occur unless there is motivation to change. This is often the most difficult part of the change process.
3. People are the hub of all organizational changes. Any change, whether in terms of structure, group process, reward systems, or job design, requires individuals to change.
4. Resistance to change is found even when the goals of change are highly desirable.
5. Effective change requires reinforcing new behaviors, attitudes, and organizational practices.

Let us now consider the three stages of change.

Unfreezing   The focus of this stage is to create the motivation to change. In so doing, individuals are encouraged to replace old behaviors and attitudes with those desired by management. Managers can begin the unfreezing process by disconfirming the usefulness or appropriateness of employees' present behaviors or attitudes. In other words, employees need to become dissatisfied with the old way of doing things. Consider how Lawrence Bossidy, CEO of AlliedSignal, unfroze the organization:

> To inaugurate large-scale change, you may have to create the burning platform. You have to give people a reason to do something differently. Examples from the real world can get them motivated. Chrysler is now bringing products to market in three to 3½ years—a major competitive advantage. So even if your company's financials are terrific, you might want to focus on the Chrysler case to build support for improving your own performance before you're attacked. Scaring people isn't the answer. You try to appeal to them. The more they understand why you want to change, the easier it is to commit to it. And they must believe they can win. You have to define a goal line, so if they're successful, they have a chance to stop and say, "Hey this is a victory." Celebration is crucial.[12]

Managers also need to devise ways to reduce the barriers to change during this stage.

Changing   Because change involves learning, this stage entails providing employees with new information, new behavioral models, or new ways of looking at things. The purpose is to help employees learn new concepts or points of view. Role models, mentors, experts, benchmarking the company against world-class organizations, and training are useful mechanisms to facilitate change.[13] For example, Dennis Longstreet, president of Ortho Biotech, used a combination of role modeling and personal change in his leadership to create the organizational changes needed to increase teamwork, commitment, and flexibility:

Longstreet, for example, meets regularly with a number of so-called affinity groups—African American men; gay, lesbian, and bisexual men and women; white men; secretaries, single people. "This isn't about designing a customized approach for every group and every issue. It's about listening to people—their problems and their aspirations. It's amazing how unaware you can be of the impact you have on people different from you. It's very easy for people to start feeling excluded because of artificial barriers." Once he committed to listening, of course, Longstreet realized he had to change everything about the way he managed. . . . "I was used to standing up on a stage behind a podium with slides and rehearsed scripts and saying, 'This is our policy. Thank you. Goodbye.' Now everything is done in a town-meeting fashion, with them doing most of the talking and me doing the listening."[14]

Refreezing   Change is stabilized during refreezing by helping employees integrate the changed behavior or attitude into their normal way of doing things. This is accomplished by first giving employees the chance to exhibit the new behaviors or attitudes. Once exhibited, positive reinforcement is used to reinforce the desired change (recall our discussion in Chapter 8). Additional coaching and modeling also are used at this point to reinforce the stability of the change.[15]

A Systems Model of Change

A systems approach takes a "big picture" perspective of organizational change. It is based on the notion that any change, no matter how large or small, has a cascading impact throughout an organization. For example, promoting an individual to a new work group affects the group dynamics in both the old and new groups. Similarly, creating project or work teams may necessitate the need to revamp compensation practices. These examples illustrate that change creates additional change. Today's solutions are tomorrow's problems. A systems model of change offers managers a framework to understand the broad complexities of organizational change.[16] The three main components of a systems model are inputs, target elements of change, and outputs (see Figure 20–3).

Inputs   All organizational changes should be consistent with an organization's strategic mission and resulting strategic plan. A **strategic mission statement** describes an organization's ultimate purpose. It broadly establishes what an organization intends to do, for whom, and under what philosophical premises.

A **strategic plan** outlines an organization's long-term direction and actions necessary to achieve planned results.[17] Strategic plans are based on considering an organization's strengths and weaknesses relative to its environmental opportunities and threats. This comparison results in developing an organizational strategy to attain desired outputs such as profits, customer satisfaction, quality, adequate return on investment, and acceptable levels of turnover and employee commitment (see Figure 20–3). In summary, organizations tend to commit resources to counterproductive or conflicting activities when organizational changes are not consistent with its strategic plan.

Target Elements of Change   **Target elements of change** represent the components of an organization that may be changed. As shown in Figure 20–3, change can be directed at realigning organizing arrangements, social factors, methods, goals, and people.[18] The choice is based on the strategy being pursued or the

strategic mission statement
Describes an organization's ultimate purpose.

strategic plan   A long-term plan outlining actions needed to achieve planned results.

target elements of change
Components of an organization that may be changed.

◝ • FIGURE 20~3 A Systems Model of Change

Target Elements of Change

Inputs

Internal
• Strengths
• Weaknesses

External
• Opportunities
• Threats

→ Strategy →

Organizing Arrangements
• Policies
• Procedures
• Roles
• Structure
• Rewards
• Physical setting

Goals
• Desired end results
• Priorities
• Standards
• Resources
• Linkage throughout organization

People
• Knowledge
• Ability
• Attitudes
• Motivation
• Behavior

Social Factors
• Organization culture
• Group processes
• Interpersonal interactions
• Communication
• Leadership

Methods
• Processes
• Work flow
• Job design
• Technology

Outputs

• Organizational level
• Department/ Group level
• Individual level

Sources: Adapted from D R Fuqua and D J Kurpius, "Conceptual Models in Organizational Consultation," *Journal of Counseling & Development,* July/August 1993, pp 602–18; and D A Nadler and M L Tushman, "Organizational Frame Bending: Principles for Managing Reorientation," *Academy of Management Executive,* August 1989, pp 194–203.

organizational problem at hand. For example, if lack of cooperation or teamwork is causing low productivity, change might be geared toward people or tasks. Moreover, the double-headed arrows among the target elements of change indicate that a change in one organizational component affects the others.

Consider how multiple target elements of change were affected by a reorganization at Chesapeake Packaging Company's Baltimore cardboard-box plant. The plant manager reorganized the plant into eight separate companies to achieve the strategy of getting employees to think more like owners:

> The companies correspond to the departments of any similar plant. Unlike departments, those companies choose their own leaders, do their own hiring, and determine their own work processes. They take responsibility for budgets, production, and quality levels. They deal with their own customers, internal and external.[19]

This example illustrates that change begets change. Specifically, a change in organizing arrangements led to additional changes in social factors, methods, goals, and people. Finally, Figure 20–3 underscores the assumption that people are the hub of all change. Change will not succeed unless individuals embrace it in one way or another. As you will see in the next section on outputs, the employees at Chesapeake Packaging Company bought in to and supported the new organizational structure.

Outputs   Output represents the desired end results of a change. Once again, these end results should be consistent with an organization's strategic plan. Figure 20–3 indicates that change may be directed at the organizational level, department/group level, or individual level. Let us return to the reorganization example of Chesapeake Packaging Company's cardboard-box plant and consider the effect on outputs. "The Baltimore plant was losing money when Argabright [the plant manager] took it over, in 1988. It turned a small profit in 1989, doubled that profit in 1990 and again in 1991, and saw profits rise 60% last year [1992], all while sales remained flat."[20] The change appears to have positively affected the organizational level output of profit.

Change efforts are more complicated and difficult to manage when they are targeted at the organizational level. This occurs because organizational-level changes are more likely to affect multiple target elements of change shown in the model.

Organization Development

Organization development (OD) is an applied field of study and practice. A pair of OD experts defined **organization development** as follows:

> Organization development is concerned with helping managers plan change in organizing and managing people that will develop requisite commitment, coordination, and competence. Its purpose is to enhance both the effectiveness of organizations and the well-being of their members through planned interventions in the organization's human processes, structures, and systems, using knowledge of behavioral science and its intervention methods.[21]

organization development
A set of tools to manage organizational change.

As you can see from this definition, OD provides managers with the tools needed to manage organizational change.[22]

In this section, we briefly review the four identifying characteristics of OD and its research and practical implications.

OD Involves Profound Change   Change agents using OD generally desire deep and long-lasting improvement. OD consultant Warner Burke, for example, who strives for fundamental *cultural* change, wrote: "By fundamental change, as opposed to fixing a problem or improving a procedure, I mean that some significant aspect of an organization's culture will never be the same."[23]

OD is Value-Loaded   Owing to the fact that OD is rooted partially in humanistic psychology, many OD consultants carry certain values or biases into the client organization. They prefer cooperation over conflict, self-control over institutional control, and democratic and participative management over autocratic management.[24]

OD Is a Diagnosis/Prescription Cycle   OD theorists and practitioners have long adhered to a medical model of organization. Like medical doctors, internal and external OD consultants approach the "sick" organization, "diagnose" its ills, "prescribe" and implement an intervention, and "monitor" progress.

OD Is Process-Oriented   Ideally, OD consultants focus on the form and not the content of behavioral and administrative dealings. For example, product design engineers and market researchers might be coached on how to communicate more effectively with one another without the consultant knowing the technical details of their conversations. In addition to communication, OD specialists focus on other processes, including problem solving, decision making, conflict handling, trust, power sharing, and career development.

OD Research and Practical Implications   OD-related interventions produced the following insights:

- A recent meta-analysis of 18 studies indicated that employee satisfaction with change was higher when top management was highly committed to the change effort.[25]
- A recent meta-analysis of 52 studies provided support for the systems model of organizational change. Specifically, varying one target element of change created changes in other target elements. Also, there was a positive relationship between individual behavior change and organizational-level change.[26]
- A meta-analysis of 126 studies demonstrated that multifaceted interventions using more than one OD technique were more effective in changing job attitudes and work attitudes than interventions that relied on only one human-process or technostructural approach.[27]

There are two practical implications derived from this research. First, planned organization change works. However, management and change agents are advised to rely on multifaceted interventions. As indicated elsewhere in this book, goal setting, feedback, recognition and rewards, training, participation, and challenging job design have good track records relative to improving performance and satisfaction. Second, change programs are more successful when they are geared toward meeting both short-term and long-term results. Managers should not engage in organizational change for the sake of change. Change efforts should produce positive results.[28]

UNDERSTANDING AND MANAGING RESISTANCE TO CHANGE

We are all creatures of habit. It generally is difficult for people to try new ways of doing things. It is precisely because of this basic human characteristic that most employees do not have enthusiasm for change in the workplace. Rare is the manager who does not have several stories about carefully cultivated changes that died on the vine because of resistance to change. It is important for managers to learn to manage resistance because failed change efforts are costly. Costs include decreased employee loyalty, lowered probability of achieving corporate goals, a waste of money and resources, and difficulty in fixing the failed change effort.[29] This section examines employee resistance to change, relevant research, and practical ways of dealing with the problem.

Why People Resist Change in the Workplace

No matter how technically or administratively perfect a proposed change may be, people make or break it. Individual and group behavior following an organizational change can take many forms (see Figure 20–4). The extremes range from acceptance to active resistance. **Resistance to change** is an emotional/behavioral response to real or imagined threats to an established work routine.

Figure 20–4 shows that resistance can be as subtle as passive resignation and as overt as deliberate sabotage. Managers need to learn to recognize the manifestations of resistance both in themselves and in others if they want to be more

resistance to change
Emotional/behavioral response to real or imagined work changes.

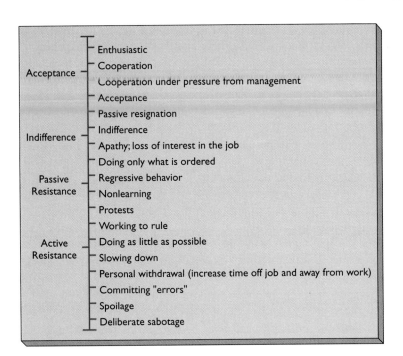

Source: A S Judson, *Changing Behavior in Organizations: Minimizing Resistance to Change* (Cambridge, MA: Basil Blackwell, Inc., 1991), p 48. Used with permission.

effective in creating and supporting change. For example, managers can use the list in Figure 20–4 to prepare answers and tactics to combat the various forms of resistance.

Now that we have examined the manifestations of resistance to change, let us consider the reasons employees resist change in the first place. Ten of the leading reasons are listed here:[30]

1. *An individual's predisposition toward change.* This predisposition is highly personal and deeply ingrained. It is an outgrowth of how one learns to handle change and ambiguity as a child. Consider the hypothetical examples of Mary and Jim. Mary's parents were patient, flexible, and understanding. From the time Mary was weaned from a bottle, she was taught that there were positive compensations for the loss of immediate gratification. She learned that love and approval were associated with making changes. In contrast, Jim's parents were unreasonable, unyielding, and forced him to comply with their wishes. They forced him to take piano lessons even though he hated them. Changes were demands for compliance. This taught Jim to be distrustful and suspicious of change. These learned predispositions ultimately affect how Mary and Jim handle change as adults.[31]

2. *Surprise and fear of the unknown.* When innovative or radically different changes are introduced without warning, affected employees become fearful of the implications. Grapevine rumors fill the void created by a lack of official announcements. Harvard's Rosabeth Moss Kanter recommends appointing a transition manager charged with keeping all relevant parties adequately informed.[32]

3. *Climate of mistrust.* Trust, as discussed in Chapter 12, involves reciprocal faith in others' intentions and behavior. Mutual mistrust can doom to failure an otherwise well-conceived change. Mistrust encourages secrecy, which begets deeper mistrust. Managers who trust their employees make the change process an open, honest, and participative affair. Employees who in turn trust management are more willing to expend extra effort and take chances with something different.

4. *Fear of failure.* Intimidating changes on the job can cause employees to doubt their capabilities. Self-doubt erodes self-confidence and cripples personal growth and development.

5. *Loss of status and/or job security.* Administrative and technological changes that threaten to alter power bases or eliminate jobs generally trigger strong resistance. For example, most corporate restructuring involves the elimination of managerial jobs.[33] One should not be surprised when middle managers resist restructuring and participative management programs that reduce their authority and status.

6. *Peer pressure.* Someone who is not directly affected by a change may actively resist it to protect the interest of his or her friends and co-workers.

7. *Disruption of cultural traditions and/or group relationships.* Whenever individuals are transferred, promoted, or reassigned, cultural and group dynamics are thrown into disequilibrium.

8. *Personality conflicts.* Just as a friend can get away with telling us something we would resent hearing from an adversary, the personalities of change agents can breed resistance.

9. *Lack of tact and/or poor timing.* Undue resistance can occur because changes are introduced in an insensitive manner or at an awkward time.

10. *Nonreinforcing reward systems.* Individuals resist when they do not foresee positive rewards for changing. For example, an employee is unlikely to support a change effort that is perceived as requiring him or her to work longer with more pressure.[34]

Research on Resistance to Change

The classic study of resistance to change was reported in 1948 by Lester Coch and John R P French. They observed the introduction of a new work procedure in a garment factory. The change was introduced in three different ways to separate groups of workers. In the ''no participation'' group, the garment makers were simply told about the new procedure. Members of a second group, called the ''representative'' group, were introduced to the change by a trained co-worker. Employees in the ''total participation'' group learned of the new work procedure through a graphic presentation of its cost-saving potential. Mixed results were recorded for the representative group. The no participation and total participation groups, meanwhile, went in opposite directions. Output dropped sharply for the no participation group, while grievances and turnover climbed. After a small dip in performance, the total participation group achieved record-high output levels while experiencing no turnover.[35] Since the Coch and French study, participation has been the recommended approach for overcoming resistance to change.[36]

Empirical research uncovered three additional personal characteristics related to resistance to change. A study of 284 nonmanagerial office personnel (43 percent male) showed that hands-on experience with computers, whether through training

---

OB EXERCISE

Assessing an Organization's Readiness for Change

Instructions: Circle the number that best represents your opinions about the company being evaluated.

	Yes	Somewhat	No
1. Is the change effort being sponsored by a senior-level executive (CEO, COO)?	3	2	1
2. Are all levels of management committed to the change?	3	2	1
3. Does the organization culture encourage risk taking?	3	2	1
4. Does the organization culture encourage and reward continuous improvement?	3	2	1
5. Has senior management clearly articulated the need for change?	3	2	1
6. Has senior management presented a clear vision of a positive future?	3	2	1
7. Does the organization use specific measures to assess business performance?	3	2	1
8. Does the change effort support other major activities going on in the organization?	3	2	1
9. Has the organization benchmarked itself against world-class companies?	3	2	1
10. Do all employees understand the customers' needs?	3	2	1
11. Does the organization reward individuals and/or teams for being innovative and for looking for root causes of organizational problems?	3	2	1
12. Is the organization flexible and cooperative?	3	2	1
13. Does management effectively communicate with all levels of the organization.	3	2	1
14. Has the organization successfully implemented other change programs?	3	2	1
15. Do employees take personal responsibility for their behavior?	3	2	1
16. Does the organization make decisions quickly?	3	2	1
Total Score: _____			

Source: Based on the discussion contained in T A Stewart, "Rate Your Readiness to Change," *Fortune,* February 7, 1994, pp 106–10.

---

or on-the-job practice, fostered more positive attitudes toward working with computers.[37] Finally, high self-efficacy and an internal locus of control were negatively associated with resistance to change.[38]

Alternative Strategies for Overcoming Resistance to Change

Before recommending specific approaches to overcome resistance, there are three key conclusions that should be kept in mind. First, an organization must be ready for change. Just as a table must be set before you can eat, so must an organization be ready for change before it can be effective.[39] The OB exercise contains a survey that assesses an organization's readiness for change. Use the survey to evaluate a company that you worked for or are familiar with that undertook a change effort.

(Arbitrary norms are as follows: 48–40 = High readiness for change; 39–24 = Moderate readiness for change; and 23–16 = Low readiness for change.) What was the company's readiness for change, and how did this evaluation relate to the success of the change effort?

Second, organizational change is less successful when top management fails to keep employees informed about the process of change. Third, employees' perceptions or interpretations of a change significantly affect resistance. Employees are less likely to resist when they perceive that the benefits of a change overshadow the personal costs. At a minimum then, managers are advised to (1) provide as much information as possible to employees about the change, (2) inform employees about the reasons/rationale for the change, (3) conduct meetings to address employees' questions regarding the change, and (4) provide employees the opportunity to discuss how the proposed change might affect them.[40] These recommendations underscore the importance of communicating with employees throughout the process of change.

In addition to communication, employee participation in the change process is another generic approach for reducing resistance. Organizational change experts have nonetheless criticized the tendency to treat participation as a cure-all for resistance to change. They prefer a contingency approach because resistance can take many forms and, furthermore, because situational factors vary (see Table 20–1). As seen in Table 20–1, Participation + Involvement does have its place, but it takes time that is not always available. Also as indicated in Table 20–1, each of

TABLE 20–1   Six Strategies for Overcoming Resistance to Change

Approach	Commonly Used in Situations	Advantages	Drawbacks
Education + Communication	Where there is a lack of information or inaccurate information and analysis.	Once persuaded, people will often help with the implementation of the change.	Can be very time consuming if lots of people are involved.
Participation + Involvement	Where the initiators do not have all the information they need to design the change and where others have considerable power to resist.	People who participate will be committed to implementing change, and any relevant information they have will be integrated into the change plan.	Can be very time consuming if participators design an inappropriate change.
Facilitation + Support	Where people are resisting because of adjustment problems.	No other approach works as well with adjustment problems.	Can be time consuming, expensive, and still fail.
Negotiation + Agreement	Where someone or some group will clearly lose out in a change and where that group has considerable power to resist.	Sometimes it is a relatively easy way to avoid major resistance.	Can be too expensive in many cases if it alerts others to negotiate for compliance.
Manipulation + Co-optation	Where other tactics will not work or are too expensive.	It can be a relatively quick and inexpensive solution to resistance problems.	Can lead to future problems if people feel manipulated.
Explicit + Implicit coercion	Where speed is essential and where the change initiators possess considerable power.	It is speedy and can overcome any kind of resistance.	Can be risky if it leaves people mad at the initiators.

Source: Reprinted by permission of the *Harvard Business Review*. An exhibit from "Choosing Strategies for Change" by J P Kotter and L A Schlesinger (March/April 1979). Copyright © 1979 by the President and Fellows of Harvard College; all rights reserved.

the other five methods has its situational niche, advantages, and drawbacks. In short, there is no universal strategy for overcoming resistance to change. Managers need a complete repertoire of change strategies.[41]

Organizations are finding that yesterday's competitive advantage is becoming the minimum entrance requirement for staying in business.[42] This puts tremendous pressure on organizations to learn how best to improve and stay ahead of competitors. This new business reality is nicely summarized by Japanese management professor Ikusiro Nonara:

> In an economy where the only certainty is uncertainty, the one sure source of lasting competitive advantage is knowledge. When markets shift, technologies proliferate, competitors multiply, and products become obsolete virtually overnight, successful companies are those that consistently create new knowledge, disseminate it widely throughout the organization, and quickly embody it in new technologies and products. These activities define the knowledge-creating company, whose sole business is continuous innovation.[43]

Consider Rubbermaid, for example. In 1993, it was ranked as the most admired company among 404 companies in 42 industries in *Fortune*'s annual Corporate Reputations Survey.

Rubbermaid enters a new product category every 12 to 18 months, and it achieved 33 percent of sales in 1993 from products introduced in the last five years. The company introduced new products (not just improved ones) at the rate of one per day in 1993. More importantly, Rubbermaid's CEO, Wolfgang Schmitt, indicated that 9 out of 10 new products hit their commercial targets. How does the company innovate so successfully?[44]

> Most ideas for products flow from a single source: teams. Twenty teams, each made up of five to seven people (one each from marketing, manufacturing, R&D, finance, and other departments), focus on specific product lines, such as bathroom accessories. . . . Even Rubbermaid top management has acquired the habit of seeing new product ideas everywhere. When Schmitt and Gates [Rubbermaid's head of business development] visited London recently, they found themselves forced to disagree with Fred Astaire: The British Museum had not lost its charm. From an exhibit of Egyptian antiquities they came away with 11 product ideas.[45]

So how do organizations like Rubbermaid create a learning organization? It is not easy! To help clarify what this process entails, this section begins by defining a learning organization and identifies three kinds of organizational learning. We conclude by discussing new roles and skills required of leaders to create learning organizations and several management practices that must be unlearned.

CREATING A LEARNING ORGANIZATION

Defining a Learning Organization

Peter Senge, a professor at the Massachusetts Institute of Technology, popularized the term *learning organization* in his best-selling book entitled *The Fifth Discipline.* He described learning organizations as places ''where people continually expand their capacity to create the results they truly desire, where new and expansive patterns of thinking are nurtured, where collective aspiration is set free, and where people are continually learning how to learn together.''[46] A practical

learning organization
Proactively creates, acquires, and transfers knowledge throughout the organization.

interpretation of these ideas results in the following definition. A **learning organization** is one that proactively creates, acquires, and transfers knowledge and that changes its behavior on the basis of new knowledge and insights.[47]

By breaking this definition into its three component parts, we can clearly see the characteristics of a learning organization. First, new ideas are a prerequisite for learning. Learning organizations actively try to infuse their organizations with new ideas and information. They do this by constantly scanning their external environments, hiring new talent and expertise when needed, and by devoting significant resources to train and develop their employees. Second, new knowledge must be transferred throughout the organization. Learning organizations strive to reduce structural, process, and interpersonal barriers to the sharing of information, ideas, and knowledge among organizational members. Finally, behavior must change as a result of new knowledge. Learning organizations are results oriented. They foster an environment in which employees are encouraged to use new behaviors and operational processes to achieve corporate goals.

Types of Learning

There are three distinct types of learning that apply at various stages of an organization change process: (1) knowledge acquisition and insight, (2) habit and skill learning, and (3) emotional conditioning and learned anxiety. Awareness of each type will help you understand how they are used to create a learning organization.[48]

Knowledge Acquisition and Insight   This is the most common view of learning. It involves cognitive learning through reading, observing, listening, and memorizing. This type of learning is the fundamental first step in creating new levels of understanding and insight.

Habit and Skill Learning   This learning involves acquiring new behaviors or skills. It is best achieved by relying on the carrot instead of the stick; that is, employees need to be positively rewarded for exhibiting the desired or correct behaviors. Errors and incorrect behaviors should be pointed out but not punished. This reinforcement strategy encourages learning because it enables the learner to stay focused on developing and improving the desired or correct behavior without feeling anxious about failing.

Habit and skill learning is slow because it takes practice and the willingness to make mistakes and fail. It also requires people to overcome bad habits and cultural rules. For example, although problem solving is more effective when people are open and honest with each other, group members frequently hide their true feelings and opinions because of cultural rules about saving face and protecting themselves.[49]

Emotional Conditioning and Learned Anxiety   This type of learning is very powerful and is associated with learning in response to being punished. It is the anxiety associated with punishment that causes learning. For example, punishing people for making mistakes and errors powerfully motivates them to be risk averse, to hide mistakes, and to set lower goals. Managers should not emphasize the stick over the carrot during an organizational change effort if they want people to learn new information, behaviors, or skills.

Organizations Naturally Resist Learning

You may be wondering why any rational person or organization would resist learning. It just does not make sense. Well, organizations do not consciously resist learning. They do it because of three fundamental problems that plague society at large: focusing on fragmentation rather than systems, emphasizing competition over collaboration, and a tendency to be reactive rather than proactive.[50] Overcoming these problems requires a fundamental shift in how we view the world.

Focusing on Fragmentation Rather than Systems   Fragmentation involves the tendency to break down a problem, project, or process into smaller pieces. For example, as students you are taught to memorize isolated facts, study abstract theories, and learn ideas and concepts that bear no resemblance to your personal life experiences. This reinforces the use of an analytic strategy that entails solving complex problems by studying subcomponents rather than wholes. Unfortunately, modern-day problems such as the United States' runaway health care costs or national debt cannot be solved with piecemeal linear approaches.

In organizations, fragmentation creates functional ''walls'' or ''silos'' that separate people into independent groups. In turn, this results in creating specialists who work within specific functional areas. It also generates internal fiefdoms that battle over power, resources, and control. Learning, sharing, cooperation, and collaboration are ultimately lost on the battlefield.

Emphasizing Competition over Collaboration   Competition is a dominant societal and management paradigm: A **paradigm** represents a generally accepted way of viewing the world. Although nothing is intrinsically wrong with competition, this paradigm results in employees competing with the very people with whom they need to collaborate for success. Moreover, it creates an overemphasis on looking good rather than being good, which prohibits learning because people become reluctant to admit when they do not know something. This is especially true of leaders. In turn, employees hesitate to accept tasks or assignments that they are not good at. Finally, competition produces a fixation on short-term measurable results rather than on long-term solutions to root causes of problems.

paradigm   A generally accepted way of viewing the world.

Fragmentation in organizations creates "walls" such as those pictured here, which result in tunnel vision and prevent big-picture learning from taking place.

(Michael Rochipp/The Image Bank)

Being Reactive Rather than Creative and Proactive   People are accustomed to changing only when they need to because life is less stressful and frustrating when we stay within our comfort zones. This contrasts with the fundamental catalyst of real learning. The drive to learn is fueled by personal interest, curiosity, aspiration, imagination, experimentation, and risk taking. The problem is that all of us have been conditioned to respond and react to others' directions and approval. This undermines the intrinsic drive to learn. When this tendency is coupled with management by fear, intimidation, and crisis, people not only resist learning, they become paralyzed by the fear of taking risks.

Effective Leadership Is the Solution

There is hope! Effective leadership chisels away at these natural tendencies and paves the way for organizational learning. Leaders can create an organizational culture that promotes systems thinking over fragmentation, collaboration and cooperation over competition, and innovation and proaction over reactivity. Leaders must, however, adopt new roles and associated activities to create a learning organization.

Specifically, leaders perform three key functions in building a learning organization: (1) building a commitment to learning, (2) working to generate ideas with impact, and (3) working to generalize ideas with impact.[51] Table 20–2 contains a list of leadership activities needed to support each role.

◣ • TABLE 20–2   Leadership Roles and Activities for Building a Learning Organization

Leadership Activities	Role 1: Build a Commitment to Learning	Role 2: Work to Generate Ideas with Impact	Role 3: Work to Generalize Ideas with Impact
Make learning a component of the vision and strategic objectives	X		
Invest in learning	X		
Publicly promote the value of learning	X		
Measure, benchmark, and track learning	X		
Create rewards and symbols of learning	X		
Implement continuous improvement programs		X	
Increase employee competence through training, or buy talent from outside the organization		X	
Experiment with new ideas, processes, and structural arrangements		X	
Go outside the organization to identify world-class ideas and processes		X	
Identify mental models of organizational processes		X	
Instill systems thinking throughout the organization.		X	
Create an infrastructure that moves ideas across organizational boundaries			X
Rotate employees across functional and divisional boundaries			X

Source: Based in part on D Ulrich, T Jick, and M Von Glinow, "High-Impact Learning: Building and Diffusing Learning Capability," *Organizational Dynamics*, Autumn 1993, pp 52–66.

Building a Commitment to Learning   Leaders need to instill an intellectual and emotional commitment to learning by using the ideas shown in Table 20–2. For example, Harley Davidson has identified "intellectual curiosity" as one of its core corporate values. Leaders can promote the value of learning by modeling the desired attitudes and behaviors. They can attend seminars as presenters or participants, share effective managerial practices with peers, and disseminate readings, videos, and other educational materials. Steve Miller, the CEO of SAWTEK Inc., a high-tech firm located in central Florida, encourages learning by providing employees with an incentive to obtain patents. Consider how Home Depot promotes learning:

> But the focus on learning at Home Depot is not geared just toward the customer. Before Home Depot opens a new store, employees receive nearly four weeks of training. The retailer also holds quarterly Sunday-morning meetings for its 23,000 employees, using satellite TV hook-ups in each store. Known as "Breakfast with Bernie and Arthur" (the company's founders), these meetings inform employees about the past quarter's performance and the company's growth plans and allow employees to phone the company's top executives to ask questions. The company's in-house TV station also produces programs designed to instill the Home Depot "service spirit" in new stores and their employees.[52]

Working to Generate Ideas with Impact   Ideas with impact are those that add value to one or more of an organization's three key stakeholders: employees, customers, and shareholders. The leadership activities shown in Table 20–2 reveal six ways to generate ideas with impact.

Working to Generalize Ideas with Impact   Leaders must make a concerted effort to reduce interpersonal, group, and organizational barriers to learning. This can be done by creating a learning infrastructure. This is a large-scale effort that includes the following activities:

- Measuring and rewarding learning.
- Increasing open and honest dialogue among organizational members.
- Reducing conflict.
- Increasing horizontal and vertical communication.
- Promoting teamwork.
- Rewarding risk taking and innovation.
- Reducing the fear of failure.
- Increasing the sharing of successes, failures, and best practices across organizational members.
- Reducing stressors and frustration.
- Reducing internal competition.
- Increasing cooperation and collaboration.
- Creating a psychologically safe and comforting environment.[53]

Unlearning the Organization

In addition to implementing the ideas listed in Table 20–2, organizations must concurrently unlearn organizational practices and paradigms that made them successful. Quite simply, traditional organizations and the associated organizational behaviors they created have outlived their usefulness. Management must seriously question and challenge the ways of thinking that worked in the past if they want to create a learning organization. For example, the old management paradigm of planning, organizing, and control might be replaced with one of vision, values, and empowerment. The time has come for management and employees to think as owners, not as "us" and "them" adversaries.

Let us close our study of organizational behavior by considering a mission statement that promotes this new managerial paradigm:

> This is a company of owners, of partners, of businesspeople. We are in business together. Our economic figures—which is to say, our jobs and our financial security—depend not on management's generosity ("them") or on the strength of a union ("us") but on our collective success in the marketplace. We will share in the rewards just as—by definition—we share in the risks.
>
> No one in this company is just an employee. People have different jobs, make different salaries, have different levels of authority. But all workers will see the same basic information and will have a voice in matters affecting them. And it will be everyone's responsibility to understand how the business operates, to keep track of its results, and to make decisions that contribute to its success in the marketplace.[54]

BACK TO THE OPENING CASE

Now that you have read Chapter 20, you should be able to answer the following questions about the Will-Burt case:

1. What were the external and internal forces for change?
2. Explain how Harry Featherstone used components of both Lewin's change model and the systems model of change.
3. Which of the 10 reasons for resistance to change affected Harry Featherstone's attempt to radically change Will-Burt?
4. Did Featherstone try to create a learning organization at Will-Burt? Use Table 20–2 to explain your answer.
5. What were the two best and two worst things that Mr. Featherstone did during the change process? Discuss your rationale.

SUMMARY OF KEY CONCEPTS

1. *Discuss the external and internal forces that create the need for organizational change.* Organizations encounter both external and internal forces for change. There are four key external forces for change: demographic characteristics, technological advancements, market changes, and social and political pressures. Internal forces for change come from both human resource problems and managerial behavior/decisions.

2. *Explain Lewin's change model.* Lewin developed a three-stage model of planned change that explained how to initiate, manage, and stabilize the change process. The three states were *unfreezing,* which entails creating the motivation to change, *changing,* and stabilizing change through *refreezing.*

3. *Describe the systems model of change.* A systems model of change takes a big picture perspective of change. It focuses on the interaction among the key

components of change. The three main components of change are inputs, target elements of change, and outputs. The target elements of change represent the components of an organization that may be changed. They include organizing arrangements, social factors, methods, goals, and people.

4. *Demonstrate your familiarity with the four identifying characteristics of organization development (OD).* The identifying characteristics of OD are that it (1) involves profound change, (2) is value loaded, (3) is a diagnosis/prescription cycle, and (4) is process oriented.

5. *Discuss the 10 reasons employees resist change.* Resistance to change is an emotional/behavioral response to real or imagined threats to an established work routine. Ten reasons employees resist change are (1) an individual's predisposition toward change, (2) surprise and fear of the unknown, (3) climate of mistrust, (4) fear of failure, (5) loss of status and/or job security, (6) peer pressure, (7) disruption of cultural traditions and/or group relationships, (8) personality conflicts, (9) lack of tact and/or poor timing, and (10) nonreinforcing reward systems.

6. *Identify alternative strategies for overcoming resistance to change.* Organizations must be ready for change. Assuming an organization is ready for change, the alternative strategies for overcoming resistance to change are education + communication, participation + involvement, facilitation + support, negotiation + agreement, manipulation + co-optation, and explicit + implicit coercion. Each has its situational appropriateness and advantages and drawbacks.

7. *Define a learning organization.* A learning organization is one that proactively creates, acquires, and transfers knowledge and changes its behavior on the basis of new knowledge and insights.

8. *Describe the three types of learning.* The three types are knowledge acquisition and insight, habit and skill learning, and emotional conditioning and learned anxiety. Knowledge acquisition and insight involves cognitive learning through reading, observing, listening, and memorizing. Habit and skill learning involves acquiring new behaviors and skills. Emotional conditioning and learned anxiety is associated with learning in response to being punished. The anxiety associated with punishment causes learning.

9. *Review the reasons organizations naturally resist learning.* There are three underlying reasons. The first involves the tendency to focus on fragmentation rather than systems. Fragmentation involves the tendency to break down a problem, project, or process into smaller pieces. It reinforces a linear analytic strategy that examines subcomponents rather than wholes. A dominant management paradigm that emphasizes competition over collaboration is the second reason. The third reason organizations naturally resist learning is that people have a tendency to be reactive rather than creative and proactive. This tendency stems from the fact that all of us have been conditioned to respond and react to others' directions and approval.

10. *Discuss the role of leadership in creating a learning organization.* Leaders perform three key functions in building a learning organization: (1) building a commitment to learning, (2) working to generate ideas with impact, and (3) working to generalize ideas with impact. There are 13 different leadership activities needed to support each role (see Table 20–2).

DISCUSSION QUESTIONS

1. Which of the external forces for change do you believe will prompt the greatest change during the 1990s?

2. Have you worked in an organization where internal forces created change? Describe the situation and the resulting change.

3. How would you respond to a manager who made the following statement: "Unfreezing is not important, employees will follow my directives"?

4. What are some useful methods that can be used to refreeze an organizational change?

5. Have you ever observed the systems model of change in action? Explain what occurred.

6. Have you ever resisted a change at work? Explain the circumstances and your thinking at the time.

7. Which source of resistance to change do you think is the most common? Which is the most difficult for management to deal with?

8. Does the company you work for act like a learning organization? Explain your rationale.

9. Which of the three reasons for organizations' natural resistance to learning is the most powerful? Explain.

10. Using Table 20–2 as a frame of reference, evaluate the extent to which the president of the United States engages in the leadership activities needed to create a learning organization. Is the US government a learning organization?

EXERCISE

Objectives

1. To help you understand the diagnosis step of planned organization change.
2. To give you a practical diagnostic tool to assess which target elements of change in Figure 20–3 should be changed during a change process.

Introduction

Diagnosis is the first step in planned organizational change. It is used to identify past or current organizational problems that inhibit organizational effectiveness. As indicated in Figure 20–3, there are five organizational areas in which to look for problems: organizing arrangements, social factors, methods, goals, and people. In this exercise, you will be asked to complete a brief survey assessing these five areas of an organization.

Instructions

If you currently have a full-time or part-time job, think of your organization and describe it by circling an appropriate response for each of the following 18 statements. If you are not currently employed, describe the last organization you worked for. If you have never worked, use your current university or school as your frame of reference. Compute a total score for each diagnostic area.

After completing the survey, think of an "ideal" organization: an organization that you believe would be most effective. How do you believe this organization would stand in terms of the six diagnostic areas? We would like you to assess this organization with the same diagnostic survey. You may want to use a different color pen to highlight the difference between your two sets of evaluations.

Organizational Diagnostic Survey

	Strongly Disagree	Disagree	Neutral	Agree	Strongly Agree
Organizing Arrangements					
1. The company has the right recognition and rewards in place to support its vision and strategies.	1	2	3	4	5
2. The organizational structure facilitates goal accomplishment.	1	2	3	4	5
3. Organizational policies and procedures are administered fairly.	1	2	3	4	5
Total Organizing Arrangements score = _____					
Social Factors					
4. The culture promotes adaptability and flexibility.	1	2	3	4	5
5. Interpersonal and group conflict are handled in a positive manner.	1	2	3	4	5
6. Horizontal and vertical communication is effective.	1	2	3	4	5
7. Leaders are good role models and decision makers.	1	2	3	4	5
Total Social Factors score = _____					
Methods					
8. The work flow promotes higher quality and quantity of performance.	1	2	3	4	5
9. Technology is effectively utilized.	1	2	3	4	5
10. People focus on solving root cause problems rather than symptoms.	1	2	3	4	5
Total Methods score = _____					

Goals

11. I am aware of the organization's vision and strategic goals.	1	2	3	4	5
12. I have all the tools and resources I need to do my job.	1	2	3	4	5
13. Corporate goals are cascaded down the organization.	1	2	3	4	5
14. I am evaluated against specific standards of performance.	1	2	3	4	5

Total Goals score = _____

People

15. This organization inspires the very best in me in the way of job performance.	1	2	3	4	5
16. I understand my job duties and responsibilities.	1	2	3	4	5
17. I like working in this company.	1	2	3	4	5
18. People are motivated to do the best job they can.	1	2	3	4	5

Total People score = _____

Questions for Consideration/ Class Discussion

1. Based on your evaluation of your current organization, which diagnostic area(s) is most in need of change?

2. Based on a comparison of your current and ideal organizations, which diagnostic area(s) is most in need of change? If your answer is different from the first question, explain the difference.

3. What sort of intervention would be appropriate for your work group or organization? Give details.

NOTES

[1] "Jack's Welch's Lessons for Success," *Fortune,* January 25, 1993, p 86.

[2] An international study of technological advancement was conducted by A Mody, R Suri, and J Sanders, "Keeping Pace with Change: Organizational and Technological Imperatives," *World Development,* December 1992, pp 1797–1816.

[3] For a thorough discussion of technological advancements in office automation, see the special insert "Telecommunications," *The Wall Street Journal Reports,* February 11, 1994, pp R1–28.

[4] D Lavin, "Chrysler's Man of Many Parts Cuts Costs," *The Wall Street Journal,* May 14, 1993, p B1.

[5] P Nulty, "Look What the Unions Want Now," *Fortune,* February 8, 1993, p 132.

[6] See D Dunphy and D Stace, "The Strategic Management of Corporate Change," *Human Relations,* August 1993, pp 905–20; and R H Kilman, *Managing Beyond the Quick Fix* (San Francisco, CA: Jossey-Bass, 1989).

[7] This three-way typology of change is adapted from discussion in P C Nutt, "Tactics of Implementation," *Academy of Management Journal,* June 1986, pp 230–61.

[8] These variables come from M London and J P Mac-Duffe, "Technological Innovations: Case Examples and Guidelines," *Personnel,* November 1987, pp 26–38.

[9] Radical organizational change is discussed by N M Tichy, "Revolutionize Your Company," *Fortune,* December 13, 1993, pp 114–18.

[10] For a thorough discussion of the model, see K Lewin, *Field Theory in Social Science* (New York: Harper & Row, 1951).

[11] These assumptions are discussed in E H Schein, *Organizational Psychology,* 3rd ed (Englewood Cliffs, NJ: Prentice-Hall, 1980).

[12] J E Davis, "A Master Class in Radical Change," *Fortune,* December 13, 1993, p 84.

[13] Benchmarking is discussed by C B Adair, *Breakthrough Process Redesign: New Pathways to Customer Value* (New York: AMACOM, American Management Association, 1994); G H Watson, *Strategic Benchmarking: How to Rate Your Company's Performance Against the World's Best* (New York: John Wiley & Sons, 1993); and S Sherman, "Are You as Good as the Best in the World?" *Fortune,* December 13, 1993, pp 95–96.

[14] J Huey, "The Post-Heroic Leadership," *Fortune,* February 21, 1994, p 50.

[15] Top management's role in implementing change according to Lewin's model is discussed by E H Schein, "The Role of the CEO in the Management of Change: The Case of Information Technology," in *Transforming*

Organizations, eds T A Kochan and M Useem (New York: Oxford University Press, 1992), pp 80–95.

[16] Systems models of change are discussed by D R Fuqua and D J Kurpius, "Conceptual Models in Organizational Consultation," *Journal of Counseling & Development,* July/August 1993, pp 607–18; and D A Nadler and M L Tushman, "Organizational Frame Bending: Principles for Managing Reorientation," *Academy of Management Executive,* August 1989, pp 194–204.

[17] The process of strategic planning is discussed by M J Kiernan, "The New Strategic Architecture: Learning to Compete in the Twenty-First Century," *Academy of Management Executive,* February 1993, pp 7–21.

[18] A thorough discussion of the target elements of change can be found in M Beer and B Spector, "Organizational Diagnosis: Its Role in Organizational Learning," *Journal of Counseling & Development,* July/August 1993, pp 642–50; and P Dainty, "Organizational Change: A Strategy for Successful Implementation," *Journal of Business and Psychology,* Summer 1990, pp 463–81.

[19] J Case, "A Company of Businesspeople," *Inc.,* April 1993, p 86.

[20] Ibid.

[21] M Beer and E Walton, "Developing the Competitive Organization: Interventions and Strategies," *American Psychologist,* February 1990, p 154.

[22] An historical overview of the field of OD can be found in J Sanzgiri and J Z Gottlieb, "Philosophic and Pragmatic Influences on the Practice of Organization Development, 1950–2000," *Organizational Dynamics,* Autumn 1992, pp 57–69.

[23] W W Burke, *Organization Development: A Normative View* (Reading, MA: Addison-Wesley Publishing, 1987), p 9.

[24] The role of values and ethics in OD is discussed by M McKendall, "The Tyranny of Change: Organizational Development Revisited," *Journal of Business Ethics,* February 1993, pp 93–104.

[25] See R Rodgers, J E Hunter, and D L Rogers, "Influence of Top Management Commitment on Management Program Success," *Journal of Applied Psychology,* February 1993, pp 151–55.

[26] Results can be found in P J Robertson, D R Roberts, and J I Porras, "Dynamics of Planned Organizational Change: Assessing Empirical Support for a Theoretical Model," *Academy of Management Journal,* June 1993, pp 619–34.

[27] Results from the meta-analysis can be found in G A Neuman, J E Edwards, and N S Raju, "Organizational Development Interventions: A Meta-Analysis of Their Effects on Satisfaction and Other Attitudes," *Personnel Psychology,* Autumn 1989, pp 461–90.

[28] The importance of results-oriented change efforts is discussed by R J Schaffer and H A Thomson, "Successful Change Programs Begin with Results," *Harvard Business Review,* January–February 1992, pp 80–89.

[29] Costs of failed change efforts are discussed by J Iacovini, "The Human Side of Organization Change," *Training & Development,* January 1993, pp 65–68.

[30] Adapted in part from A S Judson, *Changing Behavior in Organizations: Minimizing Resistance to Change* (Cambridge, MA: Blackwell, Inc., 1991); and J Stanislao and B C Stanislao, "Dealing with Resistance to Change," *Business Horizons,* July–August 1983, pp 74–78.

[31] See R Sandroff, "The Psychology of Change," *Working Woman,* July 1993, pp 52–56.

[32] See R Moss Kanter, "Managing Traumatic Change: Avoiding the 'Unlucky 13,' " *Management Review,* May 1987, pp 23–24.

[33] The effects of corporate restructuring on managerial careers is discussed by R Goffee and R Scase, "Organizational Change and the Corporate Career: The Restructuring of Managers' Job Aspirations," *Human Relations,* April 1992, pp 363–85.

[34] The role of rewards and resistance to change is discussed by S Demiski, "Resistance to Change: Why Your TQM Efforts May Fail," *Journal of Management in Engineering,* October 1993, pp 426–32.

[35] See L Coch and J R P French, Jr., "Overcoming Resistance to Change," *Human Relations,* 1948, pp 512–32.

[36] For a thorough review of the role of participation in organizational change, see W A Pasmore and M R Fagans, "Participation, Individual Development, and Organizational Change: A Review and Synthesis," *Journal of Management,* June 1992, pp 375–97.

[37] Complete details may be found in A Rafaeli, "Employee Attitudes toward Working with Computers," *Journal of Occupational Behavior,* April 1986, pp 89–106.

[38] L Morris, "Research Capsules," *Training & Development,* April 1992, pp 74–76; and T Hill, N D Smith, and M F Mann, "Role of Efficacy Expectations in Predicting the Decision to Use Advanced Technologies: The Case of Computers," *Journal of Applied Psychology,* May 1987, pp 307–14.

[39] Readiness for change is discussed by T A Steward, "Rate Your Readiness to Change," *Fortune,* February 7, 1994, pp 106–10.

[40] See D Rosenberg, "Eliminating Resistance to

Change," *Security Management,* January 1993, pp 20–21; and J M Jellison, "We've Always Done It That Way: 14 Ways Employees Resist Change and How to Turn Them Around," *Executive Female,* July/August 1993, pp 38–42, 74.

41 Excellent advice on how to reduce the resistance to change can be found in J Lawrie, "The ABCs of Change Management," *Training and Developmental Journal,* March 1990, pp 87–89; and R McKnight and M Thompson, "Navigating Organizational Change," *Training and Development Journal,* December 1990, pp 46–49.

42 See M J Kiernan, "The New Strategic Architecture: Learning to Compete in the Twenty-First Century," *Academy of Management Executive,* February 1993, pp 7–21.

43 I Nonara, "The Knowledge-Creating Company," *Harvard Business Review,* November/December 1991, pp 96–104.

44 See A Farnham, "America's Most Admired Company," *Fortune,* February 7, 1994, pp 50–54.

45 Ibid., p 52.

46 P M Senge, *The Fifth Discipline* (New York: Doubleday, 1990), p 1.

47 This definition was based on D A Garvin, "Building a Learning Organization," *Harvard Business Review,* July/August 1993, pp 78–91.

48 This discussion is based on material presented in E H Schein, "How Can Organizations Learn Faster? The Challenge of Entering the Green Room," *Sloan Management Review,* Winter 1993, pp 84–92.

49 See C Argyris, *Overcoming Organizational Defenses: Facilitating Organizational Learning* (Boston: Allyn and Bacon, 1990).

50 This discussion is based on material presented in F Kofman and P M Senge, "Communities of Commitment: The Heart of Learning Organizations," *Organizational Dynamics,* Autumn 1993, pp 5–23.

51 The role of leadership in building a learning organization is discussed by D Ulrich, T Jick, and M Von Glinow, "High-Impact Learning: Building and Diffusing Learning Capability," *Organizational Dynamics,* Autumn 1993, pp 52–66; P A Galagan, "The Learning Organization Made Plain," *Training & Development,* October 1991, pp 37–44; and P M Senge, "The Leader's New Work: Building Learning Organizations," *Sloan Management Review,* Fall 1990, pp 1–17.

52 M E McGill and J W Slocum, Jr., "Unlearning the Organization," *Organizational Dynamics,* Autumn 1993, p 73.

53 See Ulrich, Jick, and Von Glinow, "High-Impact Learning: Building and Diffusing Learning Capability," pp 52–66; Garvin, "Building a Learning Organization," pp 78–91; E H Schein, "On Dialogue, Culture, and Organizational Learning," *Organizational Dynamics,* Autumn 1993, pp 40–51; and J Gordon, "Performance Technology: Blueprint for the Learning Organization," *Training,* May 1992, pp 27–36.

54 Case, "A Company of Businesspeople," p 86.

Advanced Learning Module

Research Methods in Organizational Behavior

As a future manager, you probably will be involved in developing and/or implementing programs for solving managerial problems. You may also be asked to assess recommendations derived from in-house research reports or judge the usefulness of management consulting proposals. These tasks might entail reading and evaluating research findings presented both in scientific and professional journal articles. Thus, it is important for managers to have a basic working knowledge of the research process. Moreover, such knowledge can help you critically evaluate research information encountered daily in newspaper, magazine, and television reports. Problems receiving recent research attention in the popular media include the dangers of passive smoke, cancer-causing chemicals, and the value of routine mammograms.[1] As a specific case in point, let us consider the issue of whether to wear rear-seat lap belts while riding in an automobile.

A study conducted by the National Transportation Safety Board (NTSB) concluded, "Instead of protecting people, rear-seat lap belts can cause serious or fatal internal injuries in the event of a head-on crash."[2] Despite previous recommendations to wear seat belts, do you now believe rear-seat lap belts are dangerous? To answer this question adequately, one needs to know more about how the NTSB's study was conducted and what has been found in related studies. Before providing you with this information, however, this advanced learning module presents a foundation for understanding the research process. Our purpose is not to make you a research scientist. The purpose is to make you a better consumer of research information, such as that provided by the NTSB.

THE RESEARCH PROCESS

Research on organizational behavior is based on the scientific method. The *scientific method* is a formal process of using systematically gathered data to test hypotheses or to explain natural phenomena. To gain a better understanding of how to evaluate this process, we discuss a model of how research is conducted, explore how researchers measure organizationally relevant variables, highlight three ways to evaluate research methods, and provide a framework for evaluating research conclusions. We also discuss how to read a research article. Finally, we return to the NTSB study and evaluate its conclusions on the basis of lessons from this advanced learning module.

A Model of the Research Process

A flowchart of the research process is presented in Figure A–1. Organizational research is conducted to solve problems. The problem may be one of current interest to an organization, such as absenteeism or low motivation, or may be derived from published research studies. In either case, properly identifying and attempting to solve the problem necessitates a familiarity with previous research on the topic. This familiarity contributes background knowledge and insights for formulating a hypothesis to solve the problem. Students who have written formal library-research papers are well-acquainted with this type of *secondary* research.

◄ • FIGURE A-1
Model of the
Research Process

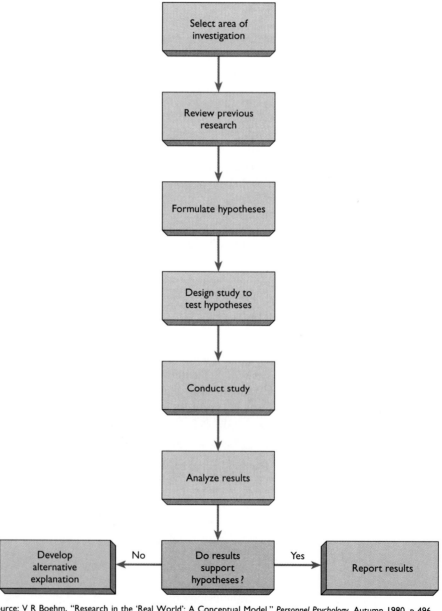

Source: V R Boehm, "Research in the 'Real World': A Conceptual Model," *Personnel Psychology,* Autumn 1980, p 496. Used with permission.

According to a respected researcher: "A *hypothesis* is a conjectural statement of the relation between two or more variables. Hypotheses are always in declarative form, and they relate, either generally or specifically, variables to variables."[3] Regarding the problem of absenteeism, for instance, a manager might want to test the following hypothesis: "Hourly employees who are dissatisfied with their pay are absent more often than those who are satisfied." Hypothesis in hand, a researcher is prepared to design a study to test it.

There are two important, interrelated components to designing a study. The first consists of deciding how to measure independent and dependent variables. An *independent variable* is a variable that is hypothesized to affect or cause a certain state of events. For example, a recent study demonstrated that losing one's job led to lower self-esteem and greater depression.[4] In this case, losing one's job, the independent variable, produced lower levels of self-esteem and higher levels of depression. A *dependent variable* is the variable being explained or predicted.[5] Returning to the example, self-esteem and depression were the dependent variables (the variables being explained). In an everyday example, those who eat less (independent variable) are likely to lose weight (dependent variable). The second component of designing a study is to determine which research method to use (recall the discussion in Chapter 1). Criteria for evaluating the appropriateness of different research methods are discussed in a later section.

After a study is designed and completed, data are analyzed to determine whether the hypothesis is supported. Researchers look for alternative explanations of results when a hypothesis is not supported.[6]

Measurement and Data Collection

"In its broadest sense, measurement is the assignment of numerals to objects or events according to rules."[7] Organizational researchers measure variables. Job satisfaction, turnover, performance, and perceived stress are variables typically measured in OB research. Valid measurement is one of the most critical components of any research study because research findings are open to conflicting interpretations when variables are poorly measured.[8] Poor measurement reduces the confidence one has in applying research findings. Four techniques are frequently used to collect data: (1) direct observation, (2) questionnaires, (3) interviews, and (4) indirect methods.

Observation   This technique consists of recording the number of times a prespecified behavior is exhibited. For example, psychologist Judith Komaki developed and validated an observational categorization of supervisory behavior. She then used the instrument to identify behavior differences between effective and ineffective managers from a large medical insurance firm. Managerial effectiveness was based on superior ratings. Results indicated that effective managers spent more time monitoring their employees' performance than did ineffective managers. Komaki recently applied the same instrument to examine the performance of sailboat captains competing in a race. Similar to the managerial study, skippers finished higher in the overall race standings when they monitored and rewarded their crews.[9] There are few "valid" observational schemes for use in OB research outside of Komaki's taxonomy.

Questionnaires   Questionnaires ask respondents for their opinions or feelings about work-related issues. They generally contain previously developed and validated instruments and are self-administered. Given their impersonal nature, poorly designed questionnaires are susceptible to rater bias. Nevertheless, a well-developed survey can be an accurate and economical way to collect large quantities of data.

Interviews   Interviews rely on either face-to-face or telephone interactions to ask respondents questions of interest. In a *structured* interview, interviewees are asked the same questions in the same order. *Unstructured* interviews do not require interviewers to use the same questions or format. Unstructured interviews are more spontaneous. Structured interviews are the better of the two because they permit consistent comparisons among people.[10] Accordingly, human resource management experts strongly recommend structured interviews during the hiring process to permit candidate-to-candidate comparisons.

Indirect Methods   These techniques obtain data without any direct contact with respondents. This approach may entail observing someone without his or her knowledge. Other examples include searching existing records, such as personnel files, for data on variables such as absenteeism, turnover, and output. This method reduces rater error and generally is used in combination with one of the previously discussed techniques.

Evaluating Research Methods

All research methods can be evaluated from three perspectives: (1) generalizability, (2) precision in control and measurement, and (3) realism of the context.[11] *Generalizability,* which also is referred to as external validity, reflects the extent to which results from one study are generalizable to other individuals, groups, or situations. *Precision in control and measurement* pertains to the level of accuracy in manipulating or measuring variables. A *realistic context* is one that naturally exists for the individuals participating in the research study. In other words, realism implies that the context is not an artificial situation contrived for purposes of conducting the study. Table A–1 presents an evaluation of the five most frequently used research methods, in terms of these three perspectives.

In summary, there is no one best research method. Choosing a method depends on the purpose of the specific study.[12] For example, if high control is necessary, as in testing for potential radiation leaks in pipes that will be used at a nuclear power

◣ • TABLE A-1
Assessment of
Frequently Used
Research Methods

Method	Generalizability	Precision in Control and Measurement	Realistic Context
Case study	Low	Low	High
Sample survey	High	Low	Low
Field study	Moderate	Moderate	High
Laboratory experiment	Low	High	Low
Field experiment	Moderate	Moderate	Moderate

Source: Adapted in part from J E McGrath, J Martin, and R A Kulka, *Judgment Calls in Research* (Beverly Hills, CA: Sage Publications, 1982).

plant, a laboratory experiment is appropriate (see Table A–1). In contrast, sample surveys would be useful if a company wanted to know the generalizable impact of a television commercial for light beer.

Evaluating Research Conclusions

There are several issues to consider when evaluating the quality of a research study. The first is whether results from the specific study are consistent with those from past research. If not, it is helpful to determine why discrepancies exist. For instance, it is insightful to compare the samples, research methods, measurement of variables, statistical analyses, and general research procedures across the discrepant studies. Extreme differences suggest that future research may be needed to reconcile the inconsistent results. In the meantime, however, we need to be cautious in applying research findings from one study that are inconsistent with those from a larger number of studies.

The type of research method used is the second consideration. Does the method have generalizability (see Table A–1)? If not, check the characteristics of the sample. If the sample's characteristics are different from the characteristics of your work group, conclusions may not be relevant for your organization. Sample characteristics are very important in evaluating results from both field studies and experiments.

The level of precision in control and measurement is the third factor to consider. It is important to determine whether valid measures were used in the study. This can be done by reading the original study and examining descriptions of how variables were measured. Variables have questionable validity when they are measured with one-item scales or ''ad-hoc'' instruments developed by the authors. In contrast, standardized scales tend to be more valid because they are typically developed and validated in previous research studies. We have more confidence in results when they are based on analyses using standardized scales. As a general rule, validity in measurement begets confidence in applying research findings.

Finally, it is helpful to brainstorm alternative explanations for the research results. This helps to identify potential problems within research procedures.

READING A SCIENTIFIC JOURNAL ARTICLE

Research is published in scientific journals and professional magazines. *Journal of Applied Psychology* and *Academy of Management Journal* are examples of scientific journals reporting OB research. *Management Review* and *HRMagazine* are professional magazines that sometimes report research findings in general terms. Table A–2 contains a list of 50 highly regarded management journals and magazines. You may find this list to be a useful source of information when writing term papers.

Scientific journal articles report results from empirical research studies, overall reviews of research on a specific topic, and theoretical articles. To help you obtain relevant information from scientific articles, let us consider the content and structure of these three types of articles.[13]

Empirical Research Studies

Reports of these studies contain summaries of original research. They typically comprise four distinct sections consistent with the logical steps of the research process model shown in Figure A–1. These sections are as follows:

TABLE A-2

A List of Highly Regarded Management Journals and Magazines

1. Administrative Science Quarterly	26. Journal of Occupational Behavior
2. Journal of Applied Psychology	27. Public Administration Quarterly
3. Organizational Behavior and Human Decision Processes	28. Journal of Organizational Behavior Management
4. Academy of Management Journal	29. Organizational Dynamics
5. Psychological Bulletin	30. Monthly Labor Review
6. Industrial and Labor Relations Review	31. Columbia Journal of World Business
7. Journal of Personality and Social Psychology	32. Journal of Business Research
8. Academy of Management Review	33. Group and Organizational Studies
9. Industrial Relations	34. Human Resource Planning
10. Journal of Labor Economics	35. Journal of Management Studies
11. Personnel Psychology	36. Administration and Society
12. American Psychologist	37. Negotiation Journal
13. Journal of Labor Research	38. Arbitration Journal
14. Journal of Vocational Labor	39. Compensation and Benefits Review
15. Journal of Applied Behavioral Science	40. Journal of Collective Negotiations in the Public Sector
16. Occupational Psychology	41. Public Personnel Management
17. Sloan Management Review	42. Journal of Management Education*
18. Journal of Conflict Resolution	43. Review of Business and Economic Research
19. Human Relations	44. Personnel Journal
20. Journal of Human Resources	45. Journal of Small Business Management
21. Labor Law Journal	46. SAM Advanced Management Journal
22. Harvard Business Review	47. Business Horizons
23. Social Forces	48. Business and Public Affairs
24. Journal of Management	49. HRMagazine**
25. California Management Review	50. Training and Development Journal

* Formerly *Organizational Behavior Teaching Review*
** Formerly *Personnel Administrator*
Source: Adapted by permission from M M Extejt and J E Smith, "The Behavioral Sciences and Management: An Evaluation of Relevant Journals," *Journal of Management*, September 1990, p 545.

- *Introduction.* This section identifies the problem being investigated and the purpose of the study. Previous research pertaining to the problem is reviewed and sometimes critiqued.
- *Method.* This section discusses the method used to conduct the study. Characteristics of the sample or subjects, procedures followed, materials used, measurement of variables, and analytic procedures typically are discussed.
- *Results.* A detailed description of the documented results is presented.
- *Discussion.* This section provides an interpretation, discussion, and implications of results.

Review Articles

These articles "are critical evaluations of material that has already been published. By organizing, integrating, and evaluating previously published material, the author of a review article considers the progress of current research toward clarifying a problem."[14] Although the structure of these articles is not as clear-cut as reports of empirical studies, the general format is as follows:

- A statement of the problem.

- A summary or review of previous research that attempts to provide the reader with the state of current knowledge about the problem (meta-analysis frequently is used to summarize past research).
- Identification of shortcomings, limitations, and inconsistencies in past research.
- Recommendations for future research to solve the problem.

Theoretical Articles

These articles draw on past research to propose revisions to existing theoretical models or to develop new theories and models. The structure is similar to that of review articles.

This module was introduced with a National Transportation Safety Board study that suggested it is not safe to wear rear-seat lap belts while riding in an automobile. Given what we have just discussed, take a few minutes now to jot down any potential explanations for why the NTSB findings conflict with past research supporting the positive benefits of rear-seat lap belts. Now compare your thoughts with an evaluation presented in the *University of California, Berkeley Wellness Letter:*

BACK TO THE NTSB STUDY

> Critics claim that the NTSB study paints a misleadingly scary picture by focusing on 26 unrepresentative accidents, all unusually serious and all but one frontal. The National Highway Traffic Safety Administration has strongly disputed the board's findings, citing five earlier studies of thousands of crashes showing that safety belts—including lap belts—are instrumental in preventing death and injury. And a new study of 37,000 crashes in North Carolina shows that rear-seat lap belts reduce the incidence of serious injury and death by about 40 percent. . . .
>
> In the meantime, most evidence indicates that you should continue to use rear-seat lap belts. You can minimize the risk of injury by wearing them as low across the hips as possible and keeping them tight.[15]

The NTSB findings were based on a set of unrepresentative serious frontal accidents. In other words, the NTSB's sample was not reflective of the typical automobile accident. Thus, the generalizability of the NTSB results is very limited. Buckle up!

NOTES

[1] See J E Bishop, "Statisticians Occupy Front Lines in Battle over Passive Smoking," *The Wall Street Journal,* July 28, 1993, pp B1, B4; H Kurtz, "Everything You Do Causes Cancer," *The Washington Post National Weekly Edition,* August 2–8, 1993, p 37; E Tanouye, "Mammograms: Should She or Shouldn't She?" *The Wall Street Journal,* February 22, 1994, pp B1, B7; and B Ziegler, "The Cellular Cancer Risk: How Real Is It?" *Business Week,* February 8, 1993, pp 94–95.

[2] "Buckle Up in the Rear Seat?" *University of California, Berkeley Wellness Letter,* August 1987, p 1.

[3] F N Kerlinger, *Foundations of Behavioral Research* (New York: Holt, Rinehart & Winston, 1973), p 18. (Emphasis added.)

[4] See A H Winefield and M Tiggemann, "Employment Status and Psychological Well-Being: A Longitudinal Study," *Journal of Applied Psychology,* August 1990, pp 455–59.

[5] See J Pfeffer, "Barriers to the Advance of Organizational Science: Paradigm Development as a Dependent Variable," *Academy of Management Review,* October 1993, pp 599–620.

[6] See P J Frost and R E Stablein, eds, *Doing Exemplary Research* (Newbury Park, CA: Sage: 1992); and S Begley, "The Meaning of Junk," *Newsweek,* March 22, 1993, pp 62–64.

[7] S S Stevens, "Mathematics, Measurement, and Psychophysics," in *Handbook of Experimental Psychology,* ed S S Stevens (New York: John Wiley & Sons, 1951), p 1.

[8] A thorough discussion of the importance of measurement is provided by D P Schwab, "Construct Validity in Organizational Behavior," in *Research in Organizational Behavior,* eds B M Staw and L L Cummings (Greenwich, CT: JAI Press, 1980), pp 3–43.

[9] See J L Komaki, "Toward Effective Supervision: An Operant Analysis and Comparison of Managers at Work," *Journal of Applied Psychology,* May 1986, pp 270–79. Results from the sailing study can be found in J L Komaki, M L Desselles, and E D Bowman, "Definitely Not a Breeze: Extending an Operant Model of Effective Supervision to Teams," *Journal of Applied Psychology,* June 1989, pp 522–29.

[10] Advantages and disadvantages of different interviews are discussed by R D Arvey and R H Faley, *Fairness in Selecting Employees,* 2nd ed (Reading, MA: Addison-Wesley Publishing, 1988).

[11] A complete discussion of research methods is provided by T D Cook and D T Campbell, *Quasi-Experimentation: Design & Analysis Issues for Field Settings* (Chicago: Rand McNally, 1979).

[12] Ibid.

[13] This discussion is based on material presented in the *Publication Manual of the American Psychological Association,* 3rd ed (Washington, DC: American Psychological Association, 1983).

[14] Ibid., p 21.

[15] "Buckle Up in the Rear Seat?"

Name Index

A

Abbadessa, Chuck, 536
Ackman, Fred, 284
Adams, J. Stacy, 172
Adler, Nancy, 39
Akers, John, 506
Allaire, Paul, 340
Amin, Idi, 29
Anderson, George, 202
Arbona, Marisa, 140
Artzt, Edwin, 443
Asch, Solomon, 254
Austin, Nancy, 428
Azzaretti, Angela, 156

B

Bagwell, Kris, 367
Bailey, James, 536
Ball, George, 310
Ballmer, Steve, 426
Bandura, Albert, 87, 220, 222
Barker, Larry, 379
Barnard, Chester I., 486
Bartels, Tracy, 484
Baughman, James, 335
Beach, Lee Roy, 307
Beckhard, Richard, 355
Begala, Paul, 80
Bell, Chip, 407
Belleville, Robert, 461
Benchimol, Claude, 32
Benson, Herbert, 472–73
Bernstein, Leonard, 86
Blake, Robert, 254
Blanchard, Kenneth, 434
Boddie, Will, 298–99
Bontempo, Robert, 28

Borowski, John, 150
Bossidy, Lawrence, 566
Bottger, Preston, 247
Bradford, David L., 269
Bradshaw, Charles J., 278
Briggs, Katherine C., 95
Brodie, John, 348
Brug, L.J.P., 356
Buffett, Warren, 267
Burke, Warner, 569
Burns, Tom, 515, 517

C

Caldwell, Edward, 91
Calvo, Karen Monte, 321
Cameron, Kim, 489
Carroll, Lewis, 183
Caserta, Peter, 546
Chan, Charlie, 111
Chiang, Kai-shek, 111
Chiat, Jay, 387
Child, John, 519, 520
Clay, Marc, 57
Clinton, Bill, 80, 467
Cobb, Fred, 484
Coch, Lester, 572
Cohen, Allan R., 269
Coletti, 298
Confucius, 40, 111
Covey, Stephen R., 221
Cox, Craig, 4
Cuellar, Javier Perez de, 457

D

Daft, Richard, 371, 492
Davis, Keith, 385

Davis, Phyllis B, 250
DeMille, Bev, 452
Deming, W. Edwards, 16
DePree, Max, 428
Deveny, Kathleen, 515
Dewey, Patricia, 65
Dreyer, David, 467
Drucker, Peter, 335
Drucker, Peter F., 519
Duncan, Robert, 512
Dusenberg, Doug, 268

E

Eaton, Robert, 414, 434–35
Eden, Dov, 252
Einstein, Albert, 323

F

Featherstone, Harry, 559–61
Feldman, Daniel, 544
Festinger, Leon, 171
Fiedler, Fred, 434, 436, 438, 439
Fisher, George, 532–33
Follett, Mary Parker, 14
Ford, Henry, 334, 484
Ford, Henry II, 434
Franceschi, Dave, 397–99
Frees, Bob, 188
French, John, 272, 572
Friberg, Hans Olav, 356
Friedman, Meyer, 469–70
Fry, Art, 514
Fryer, Bruce, 64
Fu, Ed, 550
Funabiki, Jon, 110

Company Index

Subject Index